Personal Finance

Version 3.0

Rachel S. Siegel

978-1-4533-9200-3

Personal Finance
Version 3.0

Rachel S. Siegel

Published by:

FlatWorld
175 Portland Street
Boston, MA 02114

Brief Contents

Contents

About the Author

Rachel S. Siegel, CFA

Photograph courtesy of the author.

Rachel S. Siegel, CFA, was a professor of finance, economics, and accounting at Northern Vermont University from 1990-2016. She has also taught as an adjunct faculty member at Trinity College (Vermont), Granite State College (New Hampshire), Springfield College (Massachusetts), the University of Vermont, and in Tel Aviv, Israel, for Champlain College.

Siegel earned the Chartered Financial Analyst designation in 2003. She has been a consultant to the CFA Institute on exam development, data forensics, and curricula, and has consulted on various exam prep courses in finance.

Siegel has also developed a freelance career as a financial editor and writer, for both investments firms and academics. Her column "Follow the Money" has been a regular feature of the Northstar Monthly since 2001.

Originally from Providence, Rhode Island, Siegel earned a BA in English literature (1980) and an MBA (1989) from Yale University. She lives in Barnet, Vermont.

Acknowledgments

I am very grateful to Sean Wakely, Nechama Ross, and Vicki Brentnall at FlatWorld for helping to launch Version 3.0 of this text. Jeff Shelstad nurtured the project at inception and introduced me to Carol Yacht, who has been a generous mentor. Irwin Gelber has been and continues to be more than patient throughout; his faith has been unfailing and his support has been vital. I am thankful for the inspiration of several great teachers and colleagues, both in finance and in pedagogy. Most of all, I have been fortunate to have been taught by hundreds of students, of all ages and stages, from whom I have learned so much.

Dedications

This text is dedicated to my parents, Jason and Tovia Siegel.

Preface

This text has a goal: in addition to providing sources of practical information, it should introduce you to a way of thinking about your personal financial decisions. This should lead you to thinking harder and further about the larger and longer consequences of your decisions. Many of the more practical aspects of personal finance will change over time, as practices, technologies, intermediaries, customs, and laws change, but a fundamental awareness of ways to think well about solving financial questions can always be useful. Some of the more practical ideas may be obviously and immediately relevant—and some not—but decision-making and research skills are lasting.

You may be enrolled in a traditional two- or four-year degree program or may just be taking the course for personal growth. You may be of any age and may have already done more or less academic and experiential learning. You may be a business major, with some prerequisite knowledge of economics or level of accounting or math skills, or you may be filling in an elective and have no such skills. In fact, although they enhance personal finance decisions, such skills are not necessary. Software, downloadable applications, and calculators perform ever more sophisticated functions with ever more approachable interfaces. The emphasis in this text is on understanding the fundamental relationships behind the math and being able to use that understanding to make better decisions about your personal finances.

Entire tomes, both academic texts and trade books, have been and will be written about any of the subjects featured in each chapter of this text. The idea here is to introduce you to the practical and conceptual framework for making personal financial decisions in the larger context of your life, and in the even larger context of your individual life as part of a greater economy of financial participants.

Structure

The text may be divided into five sections:

1. Learning Basic Skills, Knowledge, and Context (Chapter 1–Chapter 6)
2. Getting What You Want (Chapter 7–Chapter 9)
3. Protecting What You've Got (Chapter 10–Chapter 11)
4. Building Wealth (Chapter 12–Chapter 17)
5. Getting Started (Chapter 18)

This structure is based on the typical life cycle of personal financial decisions, which in turn is based on the premise that in a market economy, an individual participates by trading something of value: labor or capital. Most of us start with nothing to trade but labor. We hope to sustain our desired lifestyle on the earnings from labor and to gradually (or quickly) amass capital that will then provide additional earnings.

Learning Basic Skills, Knowledge, and Context (Chapter 1–Chapter 6)

Chapter 1 introduces four of its major themes:

- Financial decisions are individual decisions (Chapter 1 Section 2).
- Financial decisions are economic decisions (Chapter 1 Section 3).
- Financial decision making is a continuous process (Chapter 1 Section 4).
- Professional advisors work for financial decision makers (Chapter 1 Section 5).

These themes emphasize the idiosyncratic, systemic, and continuous nature of personal finance, putting decisions within the larger contexts of an entire lifetime and an economy.

Chapter 2 introduces the basic financial and accounting categories of revenues, expenses, assets, liabilities, and net worth as tools to understand the relationships between them as a way, in turn, of organizing financial thinking. It also introduces the concepts of opportunity costs and sunk costs as implicit but critical considerations in financial thinking.

Chapter 3 continues with the discussion of organizing financial data to help in decision making and introduces basic analytical tools that can be used to clarify the situation portrayed in financial statements.

Chapter 4 introduces the critical relationships of time and risk to value. It demonstrates the math but focuses on the role that those relationships play in financial thinking, especially in comparing and evaluating choices in making financial decisions.

Chapter 5 demonstrates how organized financial data can be used to create a plan, monitor progress, and adjust goals.

Chapter 6 discusses the role of taxation in personal finance and its effects on earnings and on accumulating wealth. The chapter emphasizes the types, purposes, and impacts of taxes; the organization of resources for information; and the areas of controversy that lead to changes in the tax rules.

Getting What You Want (Chapter 7–Chapter 9)

Chapter 7 focuses on financing consumption using current earnings and/or credit, and financing longer-term assets with debt.

Chapter 8 discusses purchasing decisions, starting with recurring consumption, and then goes into detail on the purchase of a car, a more significant and longer-term purchase in terms of both its use and financing.

Chapter 9 applies the ideas developed in the previous chapter to what, for most people, will be the major purchase: a home. The chapter discusses its role both as a living expense and an investment, as well as the financing and financial consequences of the purchase.

Protecting What You've Got (Chapter 10–Chapter 11)

Chapter 10 introduces the idea of incorporating risk management into financial planning. An awareness of the need for risk management often comes with age and experience. This chapter focuses on planning for the unexpected. It progresses from the more obvious risks to property to the less obvious risks, such as the possible inability to earn due to temporary ill health, permanent disability, or death.

Chapter 11 focuses on planning for the expected: retirement, loss of income from wages, and the subsequent distribution of assets after death. Retirement planning discusses ways to develop alternative sources of income from capital that can eventually substitute for wages. Estate planning also touches on the considerations and mechanics of distributing accumulated wealth.

Building Wealth (Chapter 12–Chapter 17)

Chapter 12 presents basic information about investment instruments and markets and explains the classic relationships of risk and return developed in modern portfolio theory.

Chapter 13 then digresses from classical theory to take a look at how both personal and market behavior can deviate from the classic risk-return relationships and the consequences for personal financial planning and thinking.

Chapter 14 looks at the mechanics of the investment process, discussing issues of technology, the investor-broker relationship, ethics and regulation, and the differences between domestic and international investing.

Chapter 15, Chapter 16, and Chapter 17 look at investments commonly made by individual investors and their use in and risks for building wealth as part of a diverse investment strategy.

How to Get Started (Chapter 18)

Chapter 18 brings the planning process full circle with a discussion on how to think about getting started, that is, deciding how to approach the process of selling your labor. The chapter introduces the idea of selling labor as a consumable commodity to employers in the labor market and explores how to search and apply for a job in light of its strategic as well as immediate potential.

What's New in Version 3.0?

Version 3.0 of *Personal Finance* features a number of exciting updates. The content covered in the text has been updated to remain relevant to students' everyday lives. Figures, statistics, references, and links throughout the text have all been updated, and most photos and artwork have been refreshed or replaced as well. Other specific revisions to Version 3.0 include:

1. Chapter 4 includes expanded explanation of math steps and calculations.
2. Chapter 6 reflects changes created by the Tax Cuts and Jobs Act, passed in December 2017.

3. Chapter 17 includes a more in-depth discussion of exchange traded funds (ETFs).
4. Chapter 18 presents more web-based platforms.

Ancillary materials for the text have also been updated; all have been revised to reflect content changes. In addition, test bank items have been reviewed and revised to reflect assessment best practices; quizzes and homework items have been refreshed; and instructor's manuals and PowerPoint lecture slides have been updated and reformatted.

CHAPTER 1

Personal Financial Planning

1.1 Introduction

Bryon and Tomika are just one semester shy of graduating from a state college. Bryon is getting a degree in protective services and is thinking of going for certification as a fire protection engineer, which would cost an additional $4,500. With his protective services degree many other fields will be open to him as well—from first responder to game warden or correctional officer. Bryon will have to specialize immediately and wants a job in his state that comes with some occupational safety and a lot of job security.

Tomika is getting a Bachelor of Science degree in medical technology and hopes to parlay that into a job as a lab technician. She has interviews lined up at a nearby regional hospital and a local pharmaceutical firm. She hopes she gets the hospital job because it pays a little better and offers additional training on site. Both Bryon and Tomika will need additional training to have the jobs they want, and they are already in debt for their educations.

Tomika qualified for a Stafford loan, and the federal government subsidizes her loan by paying the interest on it until six months after she graduates. She will owe about $40,000 of principal plus interest at a fixed annual rate of 6.8%. Tomika plans to start working immediately on graduation and to take classes on the job or at night for as long as it takes to get the extra certification she needs. Unsubsidized, the extra training would cost about $3,500. She presently earns about $5,000 a year working weekends as a home health aide and could easily double that after she graduates. Tomika also qualified for a Pell grant of around $5,000 each year she was a full-time student, which has paid for her rooms in an off-campus student co-op housing unit. Bryon also lives there, and that's how they met.

Bryon would like to get to a point in his life where he can propose marriage to Tomika and looks forward to being a family man one day. He was awarded a service scholarship from his hometown and received windfall money from his grandmother's estate after she died in his sophomore year. He also borrowed $30,000 for five years at only 2.25% interest from his local bank through a family circle savings plan. He has been attending classes part-time year-round so he can work to earn money for college and living expenses. He earns about $19,000 a year working for catering services. Bryon feels very strongly about repaying his relatives who have helped finance his education and also is willing to help Tomika pay off her Stafford loan after they marry.

Tomika has $3,000 in U.S. Treasury Series EE savings bonds, which mature in two years, and has managed to put aside $600 in a savings account earmarked for clothes and gifts. Bryon has sunk all his savings into tuition and books, and his only other asset is his old pickup truck, which has no liens and a trade-in value of $3,900. For both Tomika and Bryon, having reliable transportation to their jobs is a concern. Tomika hopes to continue using public transportation to get to a new job after graduation. Both Bryon and Tomika are smart enough about money to have avoided getting into credit card debt. Each keeps only one major credit card and a debit card and with rare exceptions pays statements in full each month.

Bryon and Tomika will have to find new housing after they graduate. They could look for another cooperative housing opportunity or rent apartments, or they could get married now instead of waiting. Bryon also has a rent-free option of moving in temporarily with his brother. Tomika feels very strongly about saving money to buy a home and wants to wait until her career is well established before having a child. Tomika is concerned about getting good job benefits, especially medical insurance and family leave. Although still young, Bryon is concerned about being able to retire, the sooner the better, but he has no idea how that would be possible. He thinks he would enjoy running his own catering firm as a retirement business someday.

Tomika's starting salary as a lab technician will be about $30,000, and as a fire protection engineer, Bryon would have a starting salary of about $38,000. Both have the potential to double their salaries after fifteen years on the job, but they are worried about the economy. Their graduations are coinciding with a downturn. Aside from Tomika's savings bonds, she and Bryon are not in the investment market, although, as soon as he can, Bryon wants to invest in a diversified portfolio of money market funds that include corporate stocks and municipal bonds. Nevertheless, the state of the economy affects their situation. Money is tight and loans are hard to get, jobs are scarce and highly competitive, purchasing power and interest rates are rising, and pension plans and retirement funds are at risk of losing value. It's uncertain how long it will be before the trend reverses, so for the short term, they need to play it safe. What if they can't land the jobs they're preparing for?

Tomika and Bryon certainly have a lot of decisions to make, and some of those decisions have high-stakes consequences for their lives. In making those decisions, they will have to answer some questions, such as the following:

1. What individual or personal factors will affect Tomika's and Bryon's financial thinking and decision making?
2. What are Bryon's best options for job specializations in protective services? What are Tomika's best options for job placement in the field of medical technology?
3. When should Bryon and Tomika invest in the additional job training each will need, and how can they finance that training?
4. How will Tomika pay off her college loan, and how much will it cost? How soon can she get out of debt?
5. How will Bryon repay his loan reflecting his family's investment in his education?
6. What are Tomika's short-term and long-term goals? What are Bryon's? If they marry, how well will their goals mesh or need to adjust?
7. What should they do about medical insurance and retirement needs?
8. What should they do about saving and investing?
9. What should they do about getting married and starting a family?
10. What should they do about buying a home and a car?
11. What is Bryon's present and projected income from all sources? What is Tomika's?
12. What is the tax liability on their present incomes as singles? What would their tax liability be on their future incomes if they filed jointly as a married couple?
13. What budget categories would you create for Tomika's and Bryon's expenses and expenditures over time?
14. How could Tomika and Bryon adjust their budgets to meet their short-term and long-term goals?
15. On the basis of your analysis and investigations, what five-year financial plan would you develop for Tomika and Bryon?
16. How will larger economic factors affect the decisions Bryon and Tomika make and the outcomes of those decisions?

You will make financial decisions all your life. Sometimes you can see those decisions coming and plan deliberately; sometimes, well, stuff happens, and you are faced with a more sudden decision. Personal financial planning is about making deliberate decisions that allow you to get closer to your goals or sudden decisions that allow you to stay on track, even when things take an unexpected turn.

The idea of personal financial planning is really no different from the idea of planning most anything: you figure out where you'd like to be, where you are, and how to go from here to there. The process is complicated by the number of factors to consider, by their complex relationships to each other, and by the profound nature of these decisions because how you finance your life will, to a large extent, determine the life that you live. The process is also, often enormously, complicated by risk: you are making decisions with plenty of information, but little certainty or even predictability.

Personal financial planning is a lifelong process. Your time horizon is as long as can be—until the very end of your life—and during that time your circumstances will change in predictable and unpredictable ways. A financial plan has to be re-evaluated, adjusted, and re-adjusted. It has to be flexible enough to be responsive to unanticipated needs and desires, robust enough to advance toward goals, and all the while be able to protect from unimagined risks.

One of the most critical resources in the planning process is information. We live in a world awash in information—and no shortage of advice—but to use that information well, you have to understand what it is telling you, why it matters, where it comes from, and how to use it in the planning process. You need to be able to put that information in context before you can use it wisely. That context includes factors in your individual situation that affect your financial thinking and factors in the wider economy that affect your financial decision making.

1.2 Individual or "Micro" Factors That Affect Financial Thinking

Learning Objectives

1. List individual factors that strongly influence financial thinking.
2. Discuss how income, income needs, risk tolerance, and wealth are affected by individual factors.
3. Explain how life stages affect financial decision making.
4. Summarize the basis of sound financial planning.

The circumstances or characteristics of your life influence your financial concerns and plans. What you want and need—and how and to what extent you want to protect the satisfaction of your wants and needs—all depend on how you live and how you'd like to live in the future. While everyone is different, there are common circumstances of life that affect personal financial concerns and thus affect everyone's financial planning. Factors that affect personal financial concerns are family structure, health, career choices, and age.

Family Structure

Marital status and dependents, such as children, parents, or siblings, determine whether you are planning only for yourself or for others as well. If you have a spouse or dependents, you have a financial responsibility to someone else, and that includes a responsibility to include them in your financial thinking. You may expect the dependence of a family member to end at some point, as with children or elderly parents, or you may have lifelong responsibilities to and for another person.

Partners and dependents affect your financial planning as you seek to provide for them, such as paying for children's education. Parents typically want to protect or improve the quality of life for their children and may choose to limit their own fulfillment to achieve that end.

Providing for others increases income needs. Being responsible for others also affects your attitudes toward and tolerance of risk. Typically, both the willingness and ability to assume risk diminishes with dependents, and a desire for more financial protection grows. People often seek protection for their income or assets even past their own lifetimes to ensure the continued well-being of partners and dependents. An example is a life insurance policy naming a spouse or dependents as beneficiaries.

Health

Your health is another defining circumstance that will affect your expected income needs and risk tolerance and thus your personal financial planning. Personal financial planning should include some protection against the risk of chronic illness, accident, or long-term disability and some provision for short-term events, such as pregnancy and birth. If your health limits your earnings or ability to work or adds significantly to your expenditures, your income needs may increase. The need to protect yourself against further limitations or increased costs may also increase. At the same time, your tolerance for risk may decrease, further affecting your financial decisions.

Career Choice

Your career choices affect your financial planning, especially through educational requirements, income potential, and characteristics of the occupation or profession you choose. Careers have different hours, pay, benefits, risk factors, and patterns of advancement over time. Thus, your financial planning will reflect the realities of being a postal worker, professional athlete, commissioned sales representative, corporate lawyer, freelance photographer, librarian, building contractor, tax preparer, professor, website designer, and so on. For example, the careers of most athletes end before middle age, have higher risk of injury, and command steady higher-than-average incomes, while the careers of most sales representatives last longer with greater risk of unpredictable income fluctuations. Table 1.1 compares median salaries of certain careers.

TABLE 1.1 Mean Annual Salary Comparisons by Profession

Profession	Mean Annual Salary ($)
Accountant	77,920
Attorney	141,890
Cafeteria cook	27,450
Commercial pilot	89,350
Dentist	174,110
Elementary school teacher	60,830
Fire fighter	51,930
Health technician	53,230
News reporter	51,550
Personal financial advisor	124,140
Pharmacist	121,710

Profession	Mean Annual Salary ($)
Professional athlete	88,300
Retail salesperson	27,460
Software developer, applications	106,710

Based on data from the Bureau of Labor Statistics, U.S. Department of Labor, http://www.bls.gov (accessed May 8, 2018).

Most people begin their independent financial lives by selling their labor to create an income by working. Over time they may choose to change careers, develop additional sources of concurrent income, move between employment and self-employment, or become unemployed or re-employed. Along with career choices, all these changes affect personal financial management and planning.

Age

Needs, desires, values, and priorities all change over a lifetime, and financial concerns change accordingly. Ideally, personal finance is a process of management and planning that anticipates or keeps abreast with changes. Although everyone is different, some financial concerns are common to or typical of the different stages of adult life. Analysis of **life stages** is part of financial planning.

At the beginning of your adult life, you are more likely to have no dependents, little if any accumulated wealth, and few **assets**. (Assets are resources that can be used to create income, decrease expenses, or store wealth as an investment.) As a young adult you also are likely to have comparatively small income needs, especially if you are providing only for yourself. Your employment income is probably your primary or sole source of income. Having no one and almost nothing to protect, your willingness to assume risk is usually high. At this point in your life, you are focused on developing your career and increasing your earned income. Any investments you may have are geared toward growth.

life stages

Periods of a person's life based on age and personal circumstances that reflect different needs, goals, and financial capabilities.

assets

Resources that can be used to create future economic benefit, such as increasing income, decreasing expenses, or storing wealth as an investment.

FIGURE 1.1

As your career progresses, income increases but so does spending. Lifestyle expectations increase. If you now have a spouse and dependents and elderly parents to look after, you have additional needs to manage. In middle adulthood you may also be acquiring more assets, such as a house, a retirement account, or an inheritance.

As income, spending, and asset base grow, ability to assume risk grows, but willingness to do so typically decreases. Now you have things that need protection: dependents and assets. As you age, you realize that *you* require more protection. You may want to stop working one day, or you may suffer a decline in health. As an older adult you may want to create alternative sources of income, perhaps a retirement fund, as insurance against a loss of employment or income. Table 1.2 suggests the effects of life stages on financial decision making.

TABLE 1.2 Financial Decisions Related to Life Stages

	Young Adulthood	Middle Adulthood	Older Adulthood	Retirement
Source of Income	Wages	Wages/Investment	Wages/Investment	Investment
Asset Base	None	Accumulating	Growing	Using up
Expenses	Low	Higher	Higher	Lower
Risk: Ability	Low	Higher	Higher	High
Risk: Willingness	High	Lower	Lower	Low

Early and middle adulthoods are periods of building up: building a family, building a career, increasing earned income, and accumulating assets. Spending needs increase, but so do investments and alternative sources of income.

Later adulthood is a period of spending down. There is less reliance on earned income and more on the accumulated wealth of assets and investments. You are likely to be without dependents, as your children have grown up or your parents passed on, and without the responsibility of providing for them, your expenses are lower. You are likely to have more leisure time, especially after retirement.

Without dependents, spending needs decrease. On the other hand, you may feel free to finally indulge in those things that you've "always wanted." There are no longer dependents to protect, but assets demand even more protection as, without employment, they are your only source of income. Typically, your ability to assume risk is high because of your accumulated assets, but your willingness to assume risk is low, as you are now dependent on those assets for income. As a result, risk tolerance decreases: you are less concerned with increasing wealth than you are with protecting it.

Effective financial planning depends largely on an awareness of how your current and future stages in life may influence your financial decisions.

Key Takeaways

- Personal circumstances that influence financial thinking include family structure, health, career choice, and age.
- Family structure and health affect income needs and risk tolerance.
- Career choice affects income and wealth or asset accumulation.
- Age and stage of life affect sources of income, asset accumulation, spending needs, and risk tolerance.
- Sound personal financial planning is based on a thorough understanding of your personal circumstances and goals.

Exercises

1. Use FlatWorld's My Notes feature to start keeping a written record of observations and insights about your financial thinking and behavior. You may be surprised at what you discover. In the process, consider how information in this text specifically relates to your observations and insights. Reading this chapter, for example, identify and describe your current life stage. How does your current age or life stage affect your financial thinking and behavior? To what extent and in what ways does your financial thinking anticipate your next stage of life? What financial goals are you aware of that you have set? How are your current experiences informing your financial planning for the future?
2. Continue your personal financial journal by describing how other micro factors, such as your present family structure, health, career choices, and other individual factors, are affecting your financial planning. The My Notes feature allows you to share given entries or to keep them private. You can save your notes. You also can highlight and right click on your notes to copy and paste them into a word document on your computer.
3. Find the age range for your stage of life and read the advice at "Your Financial Checklist for Every Stage of Life" (https://www.forbes.com/sites/laurashin/2014/04/30/your-financial-checklist-for-every-stage-of-life/#27f3b0e02b2f). According to this article, what should be your top priorities in financial planning right now? Read the articles on the next life stage. How are your financial planning priorities likely to change?

1.3 Systemic or "Macro" Factors That Affect Financial Thinking

Learning Objectives

1. Identify the systemic or macro factors that affect personal financial planning.
2. Describe the impact of inflation or deflation on disposable income.
3. Describe the effect of rising unemployment on disposable income.
4. Explain how economic indicators can have an impact on personal finances.

labor market

Where labor is traded through hiring or employment and price is determined by the interaction of employers and employees.

capital market

A market where long-term liquidity is traded.

credit market

A part of the capital market where capital is lent and borrowed through the trading of debt securities such as bonds.

Financial planning has to take into account conditions in the wider economy and in the markets that make up the economy. The **labor market**, for example, is where labor is traded through hiring or employment. Workers compete for jobs and employers compete for workers. In the **capital market**, capital (cash or assets) is traded, most commonly in the form of stocks and bonds (along with other ways to package capital). In the **credit market**, a part of the capital market, capital is loaned and borrowed rather than bought and sold. These and other markets exist in a dynamic economic environment, and those environmental realities are part of sound financial planning.

In the long term, history has proven that an economy can grow over time, that investments can earn returns, and that the value of currency can remain relatively stable. In the short term, however, that is not continuously true. Contrary or unsettled periods can upset financial plans, especially if they last long enough or happen at just the wrong time in your life. Understanding large-scale economic patterns and factors that indicate the health of an economy can help you make better financial decisions. These systemic factors include business cycles and employment rates.

Business Cycles

An economy tends to be productive enough to provide for the wants of its members. Normally, economic output increases as population increases or as people's expectations grow. An economy's output or productivity is measured by its **gross domestic product**, or GDP: the value of what is produced in a period. When the GDP is increasing, the economy is in an expansion; when it is decreasing, the economy is in a contraction. An economy that contracts for half a year is said to be in **recession**; a prolonged recession is a **depression**. The GDP is a closely watched barometer of the economy (see Figure 1.2).

gross domestic product (GDP)

The total value of all final goods and services produced in a year in a nation's economy. It is used as a fundamental measure of an economy's growth based on its ability to use resources productively and provide for its members.

recession

A period of economic contraction lasting at least six consecutive months or two consecutive quarters.

depression

A prolonged and severe recession.

FIGURE 1.2 U.S. Real GDP Percent Change Year-over-Year, Seasonally Adjusted

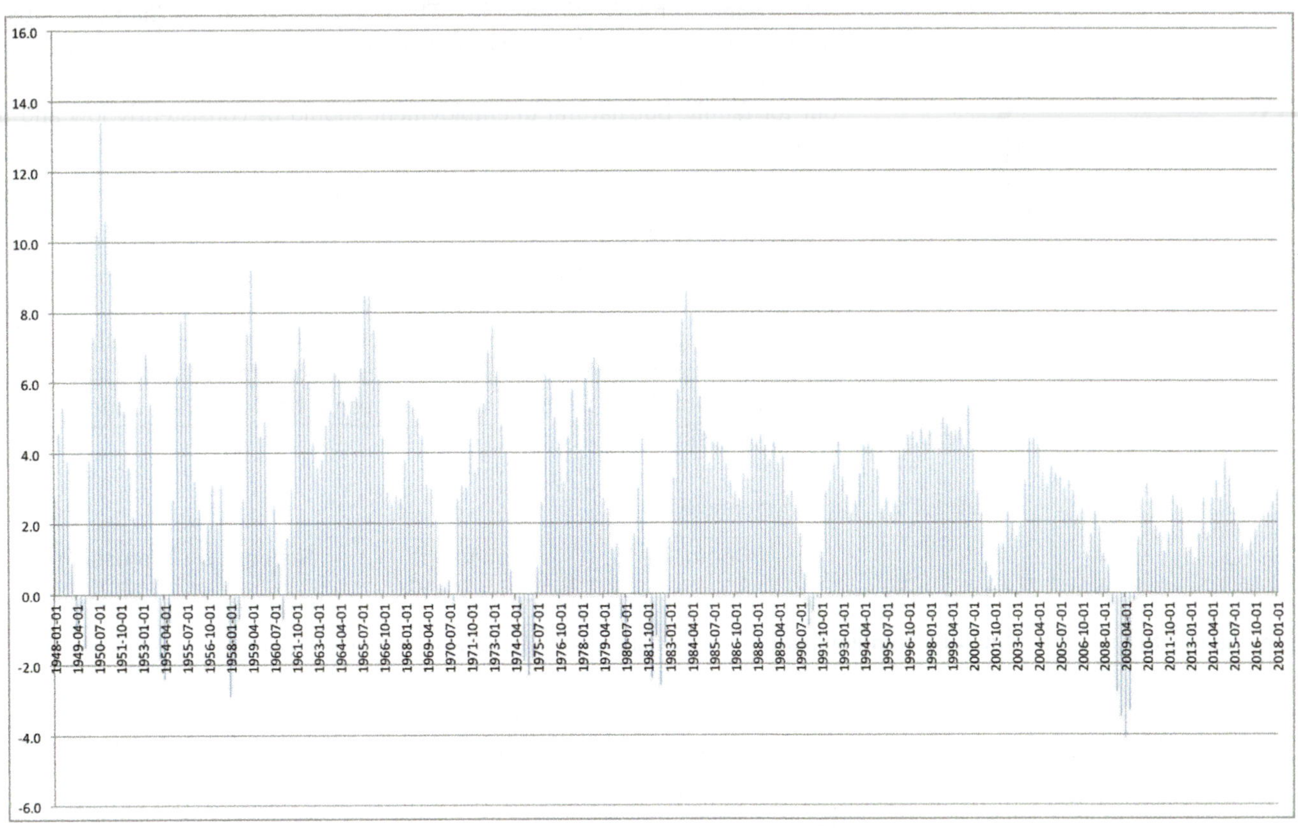

Based on data from the Bureau of Economic Analysis, U.S. Department of Commerce, "National Economic Accounts," http://www.bea.gov/national/ (accessed May 8, 2018).

Over time, the economy tends to be cyclical, usually expanding but sometimes contracting. This is called the **business cycle**. Periods of contraction are generally seen as market corrections, or the market regaining its equilibrium, after periods of growth. Growth is never perfectly smooth, so sometimes certain markets become unbalanced and need to correct themselves. Over time, the periods of contraction seem to have become less frequent, as you can see in Figure 1.2. The business cycles still occur nevertheless.

business cycles

Recurring periods of economy-wide expansion, when the economy is growing, and contraction, when the economy is shrinking. Cycles are often measured by the increase or decrease in the GDP.

There are many metaphors to describe the cyclical nature of market economies: "peaks and troughs," "boom and bust," "growth and contraction," "expansion and correction," and so on. While each cycle is born in a unique combination of circumstances, cycles occur because things change and upset economic equilibrium. That is, events change the balance between supply and demand in the economy overall. Sometimes demand grows too fast and supply can't keep up, and sometimes supply grows too fast for demand. There are many reasons that this could happen, but whatever the reasons, buyers and sellers react to this imbalance, which then creates a change.

Employment Rate

An economy doesn't just produce goods and services to satisfy its members. It also creates jobs because most people participate in the market economy by selling their labor for wages, and most rely on wages as their primary source of income. The economy therefore must provide the opportunity to earn wages so more people can participate in the economy through the market. Otherwise, more people must be provided for in some other way, such as a private or public subsidy such as charity or welfare.

FIGURE 1.3

unemployment rate

A measure of the percentage of people in the labor force who are unemployed, that is, those who would like to be working but cannot find a suitable job.

employment rate

A measure of the rate of labor force participation, or the percentage of the labor force that is employed, that is, people who want to work and are working.

The **unemployment rate** is a measure of an economy's shortcomings. It shows the proportion of people who want to work but don't because the economy cannot provide them jobs. There is always some "natural" rate of unemployment as people move in and out of the workforce as the circumstances of their lives change—for example, as they retrain for a new career or take time out for family. But natural unemployment should be consistently low and not affect the productivity of the economy.

Unemployment also shows that the economy is not efficient because it is not able to put all its productive human resources to work.

The **employment rate**, or the participation rate of the labor force, shows how successful an economy is at creating opportunities to sell labor and efficiently using its human resources. A healthy market economy uses its labor productively, is productive, and provides employment opportunities as well as consumer satisfaction through its markets. Table 1.3 shows the relationship between GDP and unemployment and each stage of the business cycle.

TABLE 1.3 Cyclical Economic Effects

	Boom	Expansion	Recession	Depression
Rate of GDP Change	Unsustainably high	Positive	Negative	Unsustainably low
Rate of Unemployment	Unsustainably low	"Natural" or minimal	Higher	Unsustainably high

At either end of this scale of growth, the economy is in an unsustainable position: either growing too fast, with too much demand for labor, or shrinking, with too little demand for labor.

If there is too much demand for labor—more jobs than workers to fill them—then wages will rise, pushing up the cost of everything and causing prices to rise. Prices usually rise faster than wages, for many reasons, which would discourage consumption that would eventually discourage production and cause the economy to slow down from its "boom" condition into a more manageable rate of growth.

If there is too little demand for labor—more workers than jobs—then wages will fall or, more typically, there will be people without jobs, or unemployment. If wages become low enough, employers theoretically will be encouraged to hire more labor, which would bring employment levels back up. However, it doesn't always work that way because people have job mobility—they are willing and able to move between economies to seek employment.

If unemployment is high and prolonged, then too many people are without wages for too long, and they are not able to participate in the economy because they have no income. In that case, the market economy is just not working for too many people, and they will eventually demand a change (which is how most revolutions have started).

Other Indicators of Economic Health

Other economic indicators give us clues as to how "successful" our economy is, how well it is growing, or how well positioned it is for future growth. These indicators include statistics such as the number of houses being built or existing home sales, orders for durable goods (e.g., appliances and automobiles), consumer confidence, producer prices, and so on. However, GDP growth and unemployment are the two most closely watched indicators because they get at the heart of what our economy is supposed to accomplish: to provide diverse opportunities for the most people to participate in the economy, to create jobs, and to satisfy the consumption needs of the most people by enabling them to get what they want.

An expanding and healthy economy will offer more choices to participants: more choices for trading labor and for trading capital. It offers more opportunities to earn a return or an income and therefore also offers more diversification and less risk.

Naturally, everyone would rather operate in a healthier economy at all times, but this is not always possible. Financial planning must include planning for the risk that economic factors will affect financial realities. A recession may increase unemployment, lowering the return on labor—wages—or making it harder to anticipate an increase in income. Wage income could be lost altogether. Such temporary involuntary loss of wage income probably will happen to you during your lifetime, as you inevitably will endure economic cycles.

A hedge against lost wages is investment to create other forms of income. In a period of economic contraction, however, the usefulness of capital, and thus its value, may decline as well. Some businesses and industries are considered immune to economic cycles (e.g., public education and health care), but overall, investment returns may suffer. Thus, during your lifetime business cycles will likely affect your participation in the capital markets as well.

Currency Value

Stable currency value is another important indicator of a healthy economy and a critical element in financial planning. Like anything else, the value of a currency is based on its usefulness. We use currency as a medium of exchange, so the value of a currency is based on how it can be used in trade, which in turn is based on what is produced in the economy. If an economy produces little that anyone wants, then its currency has little value relative to other currencies because there is little use for it in trade. In that sense, a currency's value is an indicator of how productive an economy is.

A currency's usefulness is based on what it can buy, or its **purchasing power**. The more a currency can buy, the more useful and valuable it is. When prices rise or when things cost more, purchasing power decreases; the currency buys less and its value decreases.

When the value of a currency decreases, an economy has **inflation**. Its currency has less value because it is less useful; that is, less can be bought with it. Prices are rising. It takes more units of currency to buy the same amount of goods. When the value of a currency increases, on the other hand, an economy has **deflation**. Prices are falling; the currency is worth more and buys more.

purchasing power

A currency's usefulness and thus its value as measured by how much it can buy, that is, the quantity of goods and services that can be purchased with one unit of currency.

inflation

Period characterized by rising prices, declining purchasing power, and lower currency values (one unit of currency is worth less because it buys a smaller quantity of goods and services).

deflation

Period characterized by falling prices, increasing purchasing power, and higher currency values (one unit of currency is worth more because it buys a greater quantity of goods and services).

FIGURE 1.4

Bliss Hunter Images / Shutterstock.com

For example, say you can buy five video games for $20. Each game is worth $4, or each dollar buys ¼ of a game. Then we have inflation, and prices—including the price of video games—rise. A year later you want to buy games, but now your $20 only buys two games. Each one costs $10, or each dollar only buys one-tenth of a game. Rising prices have eroded the purchasing power of your dollars.

If there is deflation, prices fall, so maybe a year later you could buy ten video games with your same $20. Now each game costs only $2, and each dollar buys half a game. The same amount of currency buys more games: its purchasing power has increased, as has its usefulness and its value (Table 1.4).

TABLE 1.4 Dynamics of Currency Value

	Inflation	Deflation
Prices	Rise	Fall
Purchasing Power	Decreases	Increases
Currency Value	Falls	Rises

consumer price index (CPI)

A measure of inflation or deflation based on a national average of prices for a "basket" of common goods and services purchased by the average consumer.

Inflation is most commonly measured by the **consumer price index** (CPI), an index created and tracked by the federal government. It measures the average nationwide price of a "basket" of goods and services purchased by the average consumer. It is an accepted way of tracking rising or falling price levels, indicative of inflation or deflation. Figure 1.5 shows the percent change in the consumer price index as a measure of inflation from 1958-2017.

FIGURE 1.5 U.S. Inflation, 1958–2017

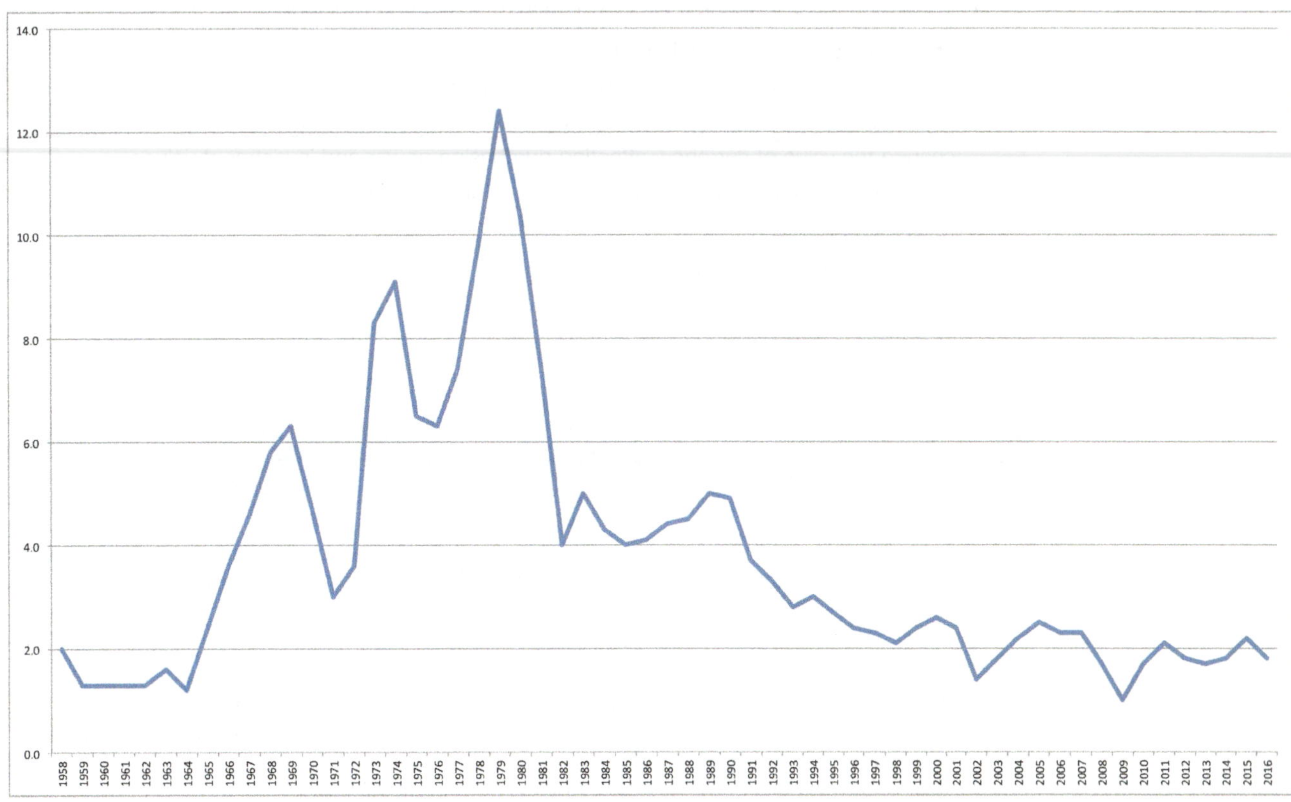

Based on data from the Bureau of Labor Statistics, U.S. Department of Labor, http://www.bls.gov (accessed May 8, 2018).

Currency instabilities can also affect investment values because the dollars that investments return don't have the same value as the dollars that the investment was expected to return. Say you lend $100 to your sister, who is supposed to pay you back one year from now. There is inflation, so over the next year, the value of the dollar decreases (it buys less as prices rise). Your sister does indeed pay you back on time, but now the $100 that she gives back to you is worth less (because it buys less) than the $100 you gave her. Your investment, although nominally returned, has lost value: you have your $100 back, but you can't do as much with it; it is less useful.

If the value of currency—the units in which wealth is measured and stored—is unstable, then investment returns are harder to predict. In those circumstances, investment involves more risk. Both inflation and deflation are currency instabilities that are troublesome for an economy and also for the financial planning process. An unstable currency affects the value or purchasing power of income. Price changes affect consumption decisions, and changes in currency value affect investing decisions.

It is human nature to assume that things will stay the same, but financial planning must include the assumption that over a lifetime you will encounter and endure economic cycles. You should try to anticipate the risks of an economic downturn and the possible loss of wage income and/or investment income. At the same time, you should not assume or rely on the windfalls of an economic expansion.

Key Takeaways

- Business cycles include periods of expansion and contraction (including recessions), as measured by the economy's productivity (gross domestic product).
- An economy is in an unsustainable situation when it grows too fast or too slowly, as each situation causes too much stress in the economy's markets.

- In addition to GDP, measures of the health of an economy include
  - the rates of employment and unemployment,
  - the value of currency (the consumer price index).
- Financial planning should take into account the fact that periods of inflation or deflation change the value of currency, affecting purchasing power and investment values.
- Thus, personal financial planning should take into account
  - business cycles,
  - changes in the economy's productivity,
  - changes in the currency value,
  - changes in other economic indicators.

Exercises

1. Go to http://www.nber.org/cycles.html to see a chart published by the National Bureau of Economic Research. The chart shows business cycles in the United States and their durations between 1854 and 2009. What patterns and trends do you see in these historical data? Which years saw the longest recessions? How can you tell that the U.S. economy has tended to become more stable over the decades?
2. Record in your personal financial journal or in My Notes the macroeconomic factors that are influencing your financial thinking and behavior today. What are some specific examples? How have large-scale economic changes or cycles, such as the economic recession of 2008–2009, affected your financial planning and decision making?
3. How does the health of the economy affect your financial health? How healthy is the U.S. economy right now? On what measures do you base your judgments? How will your appreciation of the big picture help you in planning for your future?
4. How do business cycles and the health of the economy affect the value of your labor? In terms of supply and demand, what are the optimal conditions in which to sell your labor? How might further education increase your mobility in the labor market (the value of your labor)?
5. Brainstorm with others taking this course on effective personal financial strategies for
   a. protecting against recession,
   b. hedging against inflation,
   c. mitigating the effects of deflation,
   d. taking realistic advantage of periods of expansion.

1.4 The Planning Process

Learning Objectives

1. Trace the steps of the financial planning process and explain why that process needs to be repeated over time.
2. Characterize effective goals and differentiate goals in terms of timing.
3. Explain and illustrate the relationships among costs, benefits, and risks.
4. Analyze cases of financial decision making by applying the planning process.

A **financial planning process** involves figuring out where you'd like to be, where you are, and how to go from here to there. More formally, a financial planning process means the following:

- Defining goals
- Assessing the current situation
- Identifying choices
- Evaluating choices
- Choosing
- Assessing the resulting situation
- Redefining goals
- Identifying new choices
- Evaluating new choices
- Choosing
- Assessing the resulting situation...over and over again

financial planning process

A recursive process of defining goals, assessing situations, identifying and evaluating choices, making choices and assessing the results, redefining goals, and so on.

Personal circumstances change, and the economy changes, so your plans must be flexible enough to adapt to those changes, yet be steady enough to eventually achieve long-term goals. You must be constantly alert to those changes but "have a strong foundation when the winds of changes shift."[1]

Defining Goals

Figuring out where you want to go is a process of defining goals. You have shorter-term (1–2 years), intermediate (2–10 years), and longer-term goals that are quite realistic and goals that are more wishful. Setting goals is a skill that usually improves with experience. According to a popular model, to be truly useful goals must be Specific, Measurable, Attainable, Realistic, and Timely (S.M.A.R.T.). Goals change over time, and certainly over a lifetime. Whatever your goals, however, life is complicated and risky, and having a plan and a method to reach your goals increases the odds of doing so.

For example, after graduating from college, Alice has an immediate focus on earning income to provide for living expenses and debt (student loan) obligations. Within the next decade, she foresees having a family; if so, she will want to purchase a house and perhaps start saving for her children's educations. Her income will have to provide for her increased expenses and also generate a surplus that can be saved to accumulate these assets.

In the long term, she will want to be able to retire and derive all her income from her accumulated assets, and perhaps travel around the world in a sailboat. She will have to have accumulated enough assets to provide for her retirement income and for the travel. Table 1.5 shows the relationship between timing, goals, and sources of income.

TABLE 1.5 Timing, Goals, and Income

Timing	Goals	Income Source
Short-Term	Reduce debt	Wages/Salary
Intermediate	Accumulate assets	Wages/Salary
Long-Term	Create retirement income	Investment returns

Alice's income will be used to meet her goals, so it's important for her to understand where her income will be coming from and how it will help in achieving her goals. She needs to assess her current situation.

Assessing the Current Situation

Figuring out where you are or assessing the current situation involves understanding what your present situation is and the choices that it creates. There may be many choices, but you want to identify those that will be most useful in reaching your goals.

Assessing the current situation is a matter of organizing personal financial information into summaries that can clearly show different and important aspects of financial life—your assets, debts, incomes, and expenses. These numbers are expressed in financial statements—in an income statement, balance sheet, and cash flow statement (topics discussed in Chapter 3). Businesses also use these three types of statements in their financial planning.

For now, we can assess Alice's simple situation by identifying her assets and debts and by listing her annual incomes and expenses. That will show if she can expect a budget surplus or deficit, but more important, it will show how possible her goals are and whether she is making progress toward them. Even a ballpark assessment of the current situation can be illuminating.

Alice's assets may be a car worth about $5,000 and a savings account with a balance of $250. Debts include a student loan with a balance of $53,000 and a car loan with a balance of $2,700; these are shown in Table 1.6.

TABLE 1.6 Alice's Financial Situation

Assets		Debts	
Car	5,000	Car Loan	2,700
Savings	250	Student Loan	53,000
Total	5,250	Total	55,700

Her annual disposable income (after-tax income or take-home pay) may be $35,720, and annual expenses are expected to be $10,800 for rent and $14,400 for living expenses—food, gas, entertainment, clothing, and so on. Her annual loan payments are $2,400 for the car loan and $7,720 for the student loan, as shown in Table 1.7.

TABLE 1.7 Alice's Income and Expenses

After tax income	35,720
Rent	10,800
Living expenses	14,400
Remaining for debt reduction and savings	10,520
Student loan payments	7,720
Car loan payments	2,400
Remaining for savings	400

Alice will have an annual budget surplus of just $400 (income = $35,720 - $35,320 [total expenses + loan repayments]). She will be achieving her short-term goal of reducing debt, but with a small annual budget surplus, it will be difficult for her to begin to achieve her goal of accumulating assets.

To reach that intermediate goal, she will have to increase income or decrease expenses to create more of an annual surplus. When her car loan is paid off next year, she hopes to buy another car, but she will have at most only $650 (250 + 400) in savings for a down payment for the car, and that assumes she can save all her surplus. When her student loans are paid off in about five years, she will no longer have student loan payments, and that will increase her surplus significantly (by $7,720 per year) and allow her to put that money toward asset accumulation.

Alice's long-term goals also depend on her ability to accumulate productive assets, as she wants to be able to quit working and live on the income from her assets in retirement. Alice is making progress toward meeting her short-term goals of reducing debt, which she must do before being able to work toward her intermediate and long-term goals. Until she reduces her debt, which would reduce her expenses and increase her income, she will not make progress toward her intermediate and long-term goals.

Assessing her current situation allows Alice to see that she has to delay accumulating assets until she can reduce expenses by reducing debt (and thus her student loan payments). She is now reducing debt, and as she continues to do so, her financial situation will begin to look different, and new choices will be available to her.

Alice learned about her current situation from two simple lists: one of her assets and debts and the other of her income and expenses. Even in this simple example it is clear that the process of articulating the current situation can put information into a very useful context. It can reveal the critical paths to achieving goals.

Evaluating Alternatives and Making Choices

Figuring out how to go from here to there is a process of identifying immediate choices and longer-term strategies or series of choices. To do this, you have to be realistic and yet imaginative about your current situation to see the choices it presents and the future choices that current choices may create. The characteristics of your living situation—family structure, age, career choice, health—and the larger context of the economic environment will affect or define the relative value of your choices.

After you have identified alternatives, you evaluate each one. The obvious things to look for and assess are its costs and benefits, but you also want to think about its risks, where it will leave you, and how well positioned it will leave you to make the next decision. You want to have as many choices as you can at any point in the process, and you want your choices to be well diversified. That way, you can choose with an understanding of how this choice will affect the next choices and the next. The further along in the process you can think, the better you can plan.

FIGURE 1.6

© 2010 Jupiterimages Corporation

In her current situation, Alice is reducing debt, so one choice would be to continue. She could begin to accumulate assets sooner, and thus perhaps more of them, if she could reduce expenses to create more of a budget surplus. Alice looks over her expenses and decides she really can't cut them back much. She decides that the alternative of reducing expenses is not feasible. She could increase income, however. She has two choices: work a second job or go to Las Vegas to play poker.

Alice could work a second, part-time job that would increase her after-tax income but leave her more tired and with less time for other interests. The economy is in a bit of a slump too—unemployment is up a bit—so her second job probably wouldn't pay much. She could go to Vegas and win big, with the cost of the trip as her only expense. To evaluate her alternatives, Alice needs to calculate the benefits and costs of each (Table 1.8).

TABLE 1.8 Alice's Choices: Benefits and Costs

Choices	Benefit	Explicit Cost	Implicit Cost
Continue	Reduce debt	None	None
Second Job	Reduce debt and increase surplus a little (more income)	None	Give up leisure pursuits
Vegas	Eliminate debt and increase surplus a lot (no debt payments)	Airfare and hotel in Vegas	Risk of increased deficit and debt

Laying out Alice's choices in this way shows their consequences more clearly. The alternative with the biggest benefit is the trip to Vegas, but that also has the biggest cost because it has the biggest risk: if she loses, she could have even more debt. That would put her further from her goal of beginning to accumulate assets, which would have to be postponed until she could eliminate that new debt as well as her existing debt.

Thus, she would have to increase her income and decrease her expenses. Simply continuing as she does now would no longer be an option because the new debt increases her expenses and creates a budget deficit. Her only remaining alternative to increase income would be to take the second job that she had initially rejected because of its implicit cost. She would probably have to reduce expenses as well, an idea she initially rejected as not even being a reasonable choice. Thus, the risk of the Vegas option is that it could force her to "choose" alternatives that she had initially rejected as too costly.

FIGURE 1.7 Considering Risk in Alice's Choice

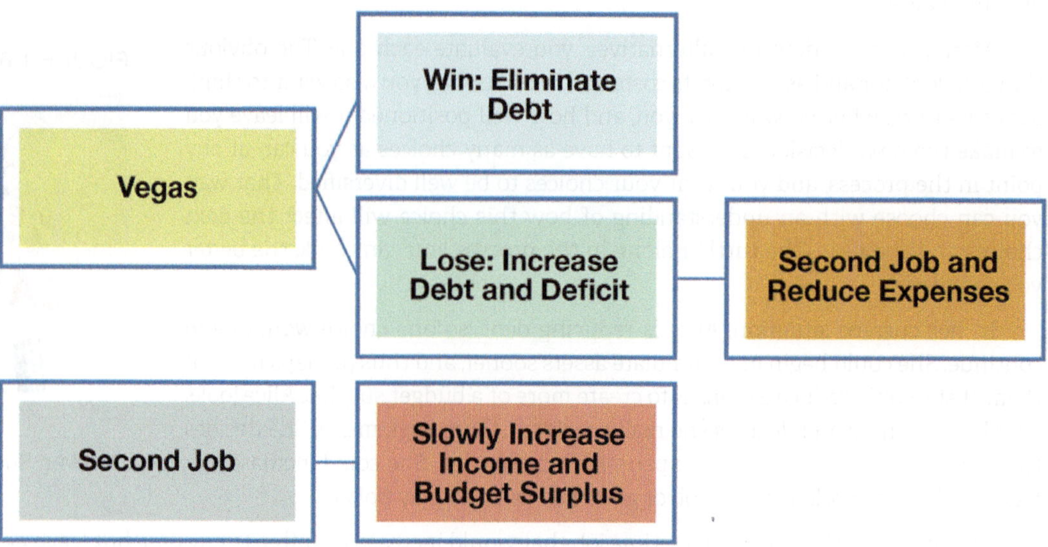

The Vegas option becomes least desirable when its risk is included in the calculations of its costs, especially as they compare with its benefits.

The obvious risk is that Alice will lose wealth, but an even costlier risk is that it will limit her future choices. Without including risk as a cost, the Vegas option looks attractive, which is, of course, why Vegas exists. But when risk is included, and when the decision involves thinking strategically not only about immediate consequences but also about the choices it will preserve or eliminate, that option can be seen in a very different light (Table 1.9).

TABLE 1.9 Alice's Choices: Benefits and More Costs

Choices	Benefit	Explicit Cost	Implicit Cost	Strategic Cost
Continue	Reduce debt	None	None	Preserves alternatives
Second Job	Reduce debt and increase surplus a little (more income)	None	Give up leisure pursuits	Preserves alternatives
Vegas	Eliminate debt and increase surplus a lot (no debt payments)	Airfare and hotel in Vegas	Risk of increased deficit and debt	Eliminates alternatives

You may sometimes choose an alternative with less apparent benefit than another but also with less risk. You may sometimes choose an alternative that provides less immediate benefit but more choices later. Risk itself is a cost, and choice a benefit, and they should be included in your assessment.

Key Takeaways

- Financial planning is a recursive process that involves
  - defining goals,
  - assessing the current situation,
  - identifying choices,
  - evaluating choices,
  - choosing.
- Choosing further involves assessing the resulting situation, redefining goals, identifying new choices, evaluating new choices, and so on.
- Goals are shaped by current and expected circumstances, family structure, career, health, and larger economic forces.
- Depending on the factors shaping them, goals are short-term, intermediate, and long-term.
- Choices will allow faster or slower progress toward goals and may digress or regress from goals; goals can be eliminated.
- You should evaluate your feasible choices by calculating the benefits, explicit costs, implicit costs, and the strategic costs of each one.

Exercises

1. Assess and summarize your current financial situation. What measures are you using to describe where you are? Your assessment should include an appreciation of your financial assets, debts, incomes, and expenses.
2. Use the S.M.A.R.T. planning model and information in this section to evaluate Alice's goals. Write your answers in your financial planning journal or My Notes and discuss your evaluations with classmates.
   a. Pay off student loan
   b. Buy a house and save for children's education
   c. Accumulate assets

d. Retire
e. Travel around the world in a sailboat

3. Identify and prioritize your immediate, short-term, and long-term goals at this time in your life. Why will you need different strategies to achieve these goals? For each goal identify a range of alternatives for achieving it. How will you evaluate each alternative before making a decision?
4. In your personal financial journal or My Notes record specific examples of your use of the following kinds of strategies in making financial decisions:

   a. Weigh costs and benefits
   b. Respond to incentives
   c. Learn from experience
   d. Avoid a feared consequence or loss
   e. Avoid risk
   f. Throw caution to the wind

   On average, would you rate yourself as more of a rational than nonrational financial decision maker?

1.5 Financial Planning Professionals

Learning Objectives

1. Identify the professions of financial advisors.
2. Discuss how training and compensation may affect your choice of advisor.
3. Describe the differences between objective and subjective advice and how that may affect your choice of advisor.
4. Discuss how the kind of advice you need may affect your choice of advisor.

Even after reading this book, or perhaps especially after reading this book, you may want some help from a professional who specializes in financial planning. As with any professional that you go to for advice, you want expertise to help make your decisions, but in the end, you are the one who will certainly have to live with the consequences of your decisions, and you should make your own decisions.

financial advisors

Professionals with various backgrounds and training who give financial advice and assist with personal and business financial planning, including tax, estate, and investment planning.

There are a multitude of **financial advisors** to help with financial planning, such as accountants, investment advisors, tax advisors, estate planners, or insurance agents. They have different kinds of training and qualifications, different educations and backgrounds, and different approaches to financial planning. To have a set of initials after their name, all have met educational and professional experience requirements and have passed exams administered by professional organizations, testing their knowledge in the field. Table 1.10 provides a perspective on the industry classifications of financial planning professionals.

TABLE 1.10 Professional Classifications

CPA	Certified Public Accountant	• Qualified to audit publicly traded corporations • Often does accounting for individuals, especially tax accounting • Often helps with financial planning and advising, especially tax planning	• Certified by the American Institute of Certified Public Accountants (AICPA)
CA (Canada)	Chartered Accountant	• Canadian equivalent of a U.S. CPA	• Certified by the Canadian Institute of Chartered Accountants (CICA)
CCA (UK, recognized globally)	Chartered Certified Accountant	• UK equivalent of U.S. CPA	• Certified by the Association of Chartered Certified Accountants (ACCA)
CFA (recognized globally)	Chartered Financial Analyst	• Works in the investment professions or banking • Focuses on financial analysis • Often advises on personal strategies for building and managing wealth through an investment portfolio	• Chartered by the Chartered Financial Analyst Institute
CFP (recognized globally)	Certified Financial Planner	• Trained to assist with all aspects of the financial planning process	• Certified by the Certified Financial Planner Board of Standards, Inc.
ChFC	Chartered Financial Consultant	• Trained to assist with aspects of the personal financial planning process relating to life insurance	• Chartered by The American College
CLU	Chartered Life Underwriter	• Trained to structure and sell life insurance	• Chartered by The American College
AFC	Accredited Financial Counselor	• Assists with financial planning	• Certified by the Association for Financial Counseling and Planning Education (AFCPE)
AEC	Accredited Estate Counselor	• Specializes in the disposal of assets and wealth after someone's death	• Certified by the National Association of Estate Planners and Councils
RIA	Registered Investment Adviser	• Advises on investment management	• Registered with the Securities and Exchange Commission (U.S. government agency)
EA	Enrolled Agent	• Advises on tax issues	• Certified by the Internal Revenue Service (of the U.S.)

Certifications are useful because they indicate training and experience in a particular aspect of financial planning. When looking for advice, however, it is important to understand where the advisor's interests lie (as well as your own). It is always important to know where your information and advice come from and what that means for the quality of that information and advice. Specifically, how is the advisor compensated?

Some advisors just give, and get paid for, advice; some are selling a product, such as a particular investment or mutual fund or life insurance policy, and get paid when it gets sold. Others are selling a service, such as brokerage or mortgage servicing, and get paid when the service is used. All may be highly ethical and well intentioned, but when choosing a financial planning advisor, it is important to be able to distinguish among them.

FIGURE 1.8

© Shutterstock, Inc.

Sometimes a friend or family member who knows you well and has your personal interests in mind may be a great resource for information and advice, but perhaps not as objective or knowledgeable as a disinterested professional. It is good to diversify your sources of information and advice, using professional and "amateur," subjective and objective advisors. As always, diversification decreases risk.

Now you know a bit about the planning process, the personal factors that affect it, the larger economic contexts, and the business of financial advising. The next steps in financial planning get down to details, especially how to organize your financial information to see your current situation and how to begin to evaluate your alternatives.

References to Professional Organizations

The references that follow provide information for further research on the professionals and professional organizations mentioned in the chapter.

- American Institute of Certified Public Accountants (AICPA): http://www.aicpa.org.
- Canadian Institute of Chartered Accountants (CICA): http://www.cica.ca.

- Association of Chartered Certified Accountants (ACCA): http://www.accaglobal.com.
- Chartered Financial Analyst Institute: http://www.cfainstitute.org.
- Certified Financial Planner Board of Standards: http://www.cfp.net.
- Financial Planners Standards Council of Canada: http://www.fpsccanada.org.
- The American College: http://www.theamericancollege.edu.
- The Association for Financial Counseling and Planning Education: http://www.afcpe.org.
- The National Association of Estate Planners and Councils: http://www.naepc.org.
- U.S. Securities and Exchange Commission: http://www.sec.gov.
- Internal Revenue Service, U.S. Treasury Department: http://www.irs.gov.

Key Takeaways

- Financial advisors may be working as accountants, investment advisors, tax advisors, estate planners, or insurance agents.
- You should always understand how your advisor is trained and how that may be related to the kind of advice that you receive.
- You should always understand how your advisor is compensated and how that may be related to the kind of advice that you receive.
- You should diversify your sources of information and advice by using subjective advisors—friends and family—as well as objective, professional advisors. Diversification, as always, reduces risk.

Exercises

1. Where do you get your financial advice? Identify all the sources. In what circumstances might you seek a professional financial advisor?
2. Read the article "How to Choose a Financial Planner" (http://guides.wsj.com/personal-finance/managing-your-money/how-to-choose-a-financial-planner/). Which advice about getting financial advice do you find most valuable? Share your views with classmates. Also read "What is a Financial Adviser" (https://www.nerdwallet.com/blog/investing/what-is-a-financial-advisor/). According to this article, is financial planning advice for everyone? How do you know when you need a financial planner?
3. Explore the following links for more information on financial advisors:
   a. National Association of Personal Financial Advisors (http://www.napfa.org)
   b. U.S. Department of Labor Bureau of Labor Statistics on the job descriptions, training requirements, and earnings of financial analysts (http://www.bls.gov/ooh/business-and-financial/financial-analysts.htm) and personal financial advisors (http://www.bls.gov/ooh/business-and-financial/personal-financial-advisors.htm)
   c. The Motley Fool's guidelines (https://www.fool.com/investing/general/2015/03/20/how-to-choose-a-financial-advisor.aspx) for choosing a financial advisor.

Endnotes

1. "Forever Young," music and lyrics by Bob Dylan.

CHAPTER 2
Basic Ideas of Finance

2.1 Introduction

> *"Money, says the proverb, makes money. When you have got a little, it is often easy to get more. The great difficulty is to get that little."*
> — Adam Smith, *The Wealth of Nations*

Personal finance addresses the "great difficulty" of getting a little money. It is about learning to manage income and wealth to satisfy desires in life or to create more income and more wealth. It is about creating productive **assets** and about protecting existing and expected value in those assets. In other words, personal finance is about learning how to get what you want and how to protect what you've got.

assets
Resources that can be used to create future economic benefit, such as increasing income, decreasing expenses, or storing wealth, as an investment.

There is no trick to managing personal finances. Making good financial decisions is largely a matter of understanding how the economy works, how money flows through it, and how people make financial decisions. The better your understanding, the better your ability to plan, take advantage of opportunities, and avoid disappointments. Life can never be planned entirely, of course, and the best-laid plans do go awry, but anticipating risks and protecting against them can minimize exposure to the inevitable mistakes and "the hazards and vicissitudes"[1] of life.

2.2 Income and Expenses

Learning Objectives

1. Identify and compare the sources and uses of income.
2. Define and illustrate the budget balances that result from the uses of income.
3. Outline the remedies for budget deficits and surpluses.
4. Define opportunity and sunk costs and discuss their effects on financial decision making.

Personal finance is the process of paying for or financing a life and a way of living. Just as a business must be financed—its buildings, equipment, use of labor and materials, and operating costs must be paid for—so must a person's possessions and living expenses. Just as a business relies on its revenues from selling goods or services to finance its costs, so a person relies on income earned from selling labor or capital to finance costs. You need to understand this financing process and the terms used to describe it. In the next chapter, you'll look at how to account for it.

Where Does Income Come From?

income

Earnings of a given period. In the case of an individual or household, this is generally cash from wages, interest, dividends, or assets (such as rental income from real estate) that can be used for consumption or saved.

Income is what is earned or received in a given period. There are various terms for income because there are various ways of earning income. Income from employment or self-employment is wages or salary. Deposit accounts, like savings accounts, earn interest, which could also come from lending. Owning stock entitles the shareholder to a dividend, if there is one. Owning a piece of a partnership or a privately held corporation entitles one to a draw.

The two fundamental ways of earning income in a market-based economy are by selling labor or selling capital. Selling labor means working, either for someone else or for yourself. Income comes in the form of a paycheck. Total compensation may include other benefits, such as retirement contributions, health insurance, or life insurance. Labor is sold in the labor market.

FIGURE 2.1

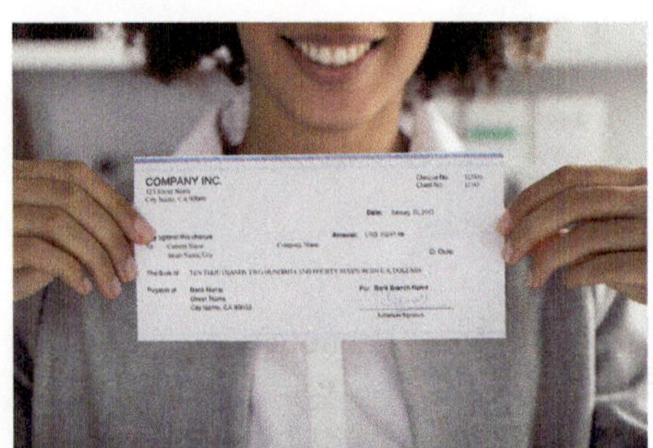

© Shutterstock, Inc.

Selling capital means investing: taking excess cash and selling it or renting it to someone who needs **liquidity** (access to cash). Lending is renting out capital; the interest is the rent. You can lend privately by direct arrangement with a borrower, or you can lend through a public debt exchange by buying corporate, government, or government agency bonds. Investing in or buying corporate stock is an example of selling capital in exchange for a share of the company's future value.

liquidity

Nearness to cash, or how easily and cheaply—with low transaction costs—an asset can be turned into cash.

You can invest in many other kinds of assets, such as antiques, art, coins, land; or commodities, such as soybeans, live cattle, platinum, or light crude oil. The principle is the same: investing is renting capital or selling it for an asset that can be resold later, or that can create future income, or both. Capital is sold in the capital market and lent in the credit market—a specific part of the capital market (just like the dairy section is a specific part of the supermarket). Table 2.1 shows the sources of income.

TABLE 2.1 Sources of Income

	Work	Invest	Lend
Trade	Sell labor	Sell capital	Rent capital
Return/Income	Wages or salary	Profit or dividend, capital gain (loss)	Interest
Market	Labor market	Capital market	Credit market

In the labor market, the price of labor is the wage that an employer (buyer of labor) is willing to pay to the employee (seller of labor). For any given job, that price is determined by many factors. The nature of the work defines the education and skills required, and the price may reflect other factors as well, such as the status or desirability of the job.

In turn, the skills needed and the attractiveness of the work determine the supply of labor for that particular job—the number of people who could and would want to do the job. If the supply of labor is greater than the demand, if there are more people to work at a job than are needed, then employers will have more hiring choices. That labor market is a buyers' market, and the buyers can hire labor at lower prices. If there are fewer people willing and able to do a job than there are jobs, then that labor market is a sellers' market, and workers can sell their labor at higher prices.

Similarly, the fewer skills required for the job, the more people there will be who are able to do it, creating a buyers' market. The more skills required for a job, the fewer people there will be to do it, and the more leverage or advantage the seller has in negotiating a price. People pursue education to make themselves more highly skilled and therefore able to compete in a sellers' labor market.

When you are starting your career, you are usually in a buyers' market (unless you have some unusual gift or talent), if only because of your lack of experience. As your career progresses, you have more, and perhaps more varied, experience and presumably more skills, and so can sell your labor in more of a sellers' market. You may change careers or jobs more than once, but you would hope to be doing so to your advantage, that is, always to be gaining bargaining power in the labor market.

Many people love their work for many reasons other than the pay, however, and choose it for those rewards. Labor is more than a source of income; it is also a source of many intellectual, social, and other personal gratifications. Nevertheless, your labor is a tradable commodity and has a market value. The personal rewards of your work may ultimately determine your choices, but you should be aware of the market value of those choices as you make them.

Your ability to sell labor and earn income reflects your situation in your labor market. Earlier in your career, you can expect to earn less than you will as your career progresses. Most people would like to reach a point where they don't have to sell labor at all. They hope to retire someday and pursue other hobbies or interests. They can retire if they have alternative sources of income—if they can earn income from savings and from selling capital.

Capital markets exist so that buyers can buy capital. Businesses always need capital and have limited ways of raising it. Sellers and lenders (investors), on the other hand, have many more choices of how to invest their excess cash in the capital and credit markets, so those markets are much more like sellers' markets. The following are examples of ways to invest in the capital and credit markets:

- Buying stocks
- Buying government or corporate bonds
- Lending

The market for any particular investment or asset may be a sellers' or buyers' market at any particular time, depending on economic conditions. For example, the market for real estate, modern art, sports memorabilia, or vintage cars can be a buyers' market if there are more sellers than buyers. Typically, however, there is as much or more demand for capital as there is supply. The more capital you have to sell, the more ways you can sell it to more kinds of buyers, and the more those buyers may be willing to pay. At first, however, for most people, selling labor is their only practical source of income.

Where Does Income Go?

Expenses are costs for items or resources that are used up or consumed in the course of daily living. Expenses recur (i.e., they happen over and over again) because food, housing, clothing, energy, and so on are used up on a daily basis.

expenses

The costs of consumption or daily living.

When income is less than expenses, you have a **budget deficit**—too little cash to provide for your wants or needs. A budget deficit is not sustainable; it is not financially viable. The only choices are to eliminate the deficit by (1) increasing income, (2) reducing expenses, or (3) borrowing to make up the difference. Borrowing may seem like the easiest and quickest solution, but borrowing also increases expenses because it creates an additional expense: interest. Unless income can also be increased, borrowing to cover a deficit will only increase it.

budget deficit

A shortfall of available funds created when income is less than the expenses.

Better, although usually harder, choices are to increase income or decrease expenses. Table 2.2 shows the choices created by a budget deficit.

TABLE 2.2 Choices created by a Budget Deficit

Choice	Action	Result
Decrease Expenses	Consume less	Decrease deficit
Increase Income	Sell more labor or capital	Decrease deficit
Borrow	Rent money	Increase deficit

FIGURE 2.2

© Shutterstock, Inc.

budget surplus

An excess of available funds created when income is greater than the expenses.

When income for a period is greater than expenses, there is a **budget surplus**. That situation is sustainable and remains financially viable. You could choose to decrease income by, say, working less. More likely, you would use the surplus in one of two ways: consume more or save it. If consumed, the income is gone, although presumably you enjoyed it.

If saved, however, the income can be stored, perhaps in a piggy bank or cookie jar, and used later. A more profitable way to save is to invest it in some way—deposit in a bank account, lend it with interest, or trade it for an asset, such as a stock or a bond or real estate. Those ways of saving are ways of selling your excess capital in the capital markets to increase your wealth. The following are examples of savings:

1. Depositing into a statement savings account at a bank
2. Contributing to a retirement account
3. Purchasing a certificate of deposit (CD)
4. Purchasing a government savings bond
5. Depositing into a money market account

Table 2.3 shows the choices created by a budget surplus.

TABLE 2.3 Choices created by a Budget Surplus

Choice	Action	Result
Increase Expenses	Consume more	Decrease surplus
Decrease Income	Sell less labor or capital	Decrease surplus
Save and Invest	Sell or rent money	Increase surplus

Opportunity Costs and Sunk Costs

opportunity cost

The cost of sacrificing the next best choice because of the choice made; the value of the next best choice, which is forgone once a choice is made.

There are two other important kinds of costs aside from expenses that affect your financial life. Suppose you can afford a new jacket or new boots, but not both, because your resources—the income you can use to buy clothing—are limited. If you buy the jacket, you cannot also buy the boots. Not getting the boots is an **opportunity cost** of buying the jacket; it is cost of sacrificing your next best choice.

In personal finance, there is always an opportunity cost. You always want to make a choice that will create more value than cost, and so you always want the opportunity cost to be less than the benefit from trade. You bought the jacket instead of the boots because you decided that having the jacket would bring more benefit than the cost of not having the boots. You believed your benefit would be greater than your opportunity cost.

In personal finance, opportunity costs affect not only consumption decisions but also financing decisions, such as whether to borrow or to pay cash. Borrowing has obvious costs, whereas paying with your own cash or savings seems costless. Using your cash does have an opportunity cost, however. You lose whatever interest you may have had on your savings, and you lose liquidity—that is, if you need cash for something else, like a better choice or an emergency, you no longer have it and may even have to borrow it at a higher cost.

When buyers and sellers make choices, they weigh opportunity costs, and sometimes regret them, especially when the benefits from trade are disappointing. Regret can color future choices. Sometimes regret can keep us from recognizing **sunk costs**.

sunk costs

Costs that have been incurred in past transactions and cannot be recovered.

Sunk costs are costs that have already been spent; that is, whatever resources you traded are gone, and there is no way to recover them. Decisions, by definition, can be made only about the future, not about the past. A trade, when it's over, is over and done, so recognizing that sunk costs are truly sunk can help you make better decisions.

For example, the money you spent on your jacket is a sunk cost. If it snows next week and you decide you really do need boots, too, that money is gone, and you cannot use it to buy boots. If you really want the boots, you will have to find another way to pay for them.

Unlike a price tag, opportunity cost is not obvious. You tend to focus on what you are getting in the trade, not on what you are *not* getting. This tendency is a cheerful aspect of human nature, but it can be a weakness in the kind of strategic decision making that is so essential in financial planning. Human nature also may make you focus too much on sunk costs, but all the relish or regret in the world cannot change past decisions. Learning to recognize sunk costs is important in making good financial decisions.

Key Takeaways

- It is important to understand the sources (incomes) and uses (expenses) of funds, and the budget deficit or budget surplus that may result.
- Wages or salary is income from employment or self-employment; interest is earned by lending; a dividend is the income from owning corporate stock; and a draw is income from a partnership.
- Deficits or surpluses need to be addressed, and that means making decisions about what to do with them.
- Increasing income, reducing expenses, and borrowing are three ways to deal with budget deficits.
- Spending more, saving, and investing are three ways to deal with budget surpluses.
- Opportunity costs and sunk costs are hidden expenses that affect financial decision making.

Exercises

1. Where does your income come from and where does it go? Analyze your inflows of income and outflows from expenditures in a month, quarter, or year. After analyzing your numbers and converting them to percentages, show your results in two figures, using proportions of a dollar bill to show where your income comes from and proportions of another dollar bill to show how you spend your income. How would you like your income to change? How would you like your distribution of expenses to change? Use your investigation to develop a rough personal budget.
2. Examine your budget and distinguish between wants and needs. How do you define a financial need? What are your fixed expenses, or costs you must pay regularly each week, month, or year? Which of your budget categories must you provide for first before satisfying others? To what extent is each of your expenses discretionary—under your control in terms of spending more or less for that item or resource? Which of your expenses could you reduce if you had to or wanted to for any reason?

3. If you had a budget deficit, what could you do about it? What would be the best solution for the long term? If you had a budget surplus, what could you do about it? What would be your best choice, and why?
4. You need a jacket, boots, and gloves, but the jacket you want will use up all the money you have available for outerwear. What is your opportunity cost if you buy the jacket? What is your sunk cost if you buy the jacket? How could you modify your consumption to reduce opportunity cost? If you buy the jacket but find that you need the boots and gloves, how could you modify your budget to compensate for your sunk cost?

2.3 Assets

Learning Objectives

1. Identify the purposes and uses of assets.
2. Identify the types of assets.
3. Explain the role of assets in personal finance.
4. Explain how a capital gain or loss is created.

As defined earlier in this chapter, an asset is any item with economic value that can be converted to cash. Assets are resources that can be used to create income or reduce expenses and to store value. The following are examples of tangible (material) assets:

- Car
- Savings account
- Wind-up toy collection
- Money market account
- Shares of stock
- Forty acres of farmland
- House

When you sell excess capital in the capital markets in exchange for an asset, it is a way of storing wealth, and hopefully of generating income as well. The asset is your investment—a use of your liquidity. Some assets are more liquid than others. For example, you can probably sell your car more quickly than you can sell your house. As an investor, you assume that when you want your liquidity back, you can sell the asset. This assumes that it has some liquidity and market value (some use and value to someone else) and that it trades in a reasonably efficient market. Otherwise, the asset is not an investment, but merely a possession, which may bring great happiness but will not serve as a store of wealth.

Assets may be used to store wealth, create income, and reduce future expenses.

Assets Store Wealth

If the asset is worth more when it is resold than it was when it was bought, then you have earned a **capital gain**. The investment has not only stored wealth but also increased it. Of course, things can go the other way too: the investment can decrease in value while owned and be worth less when resold than it was when bought. In that case, you have a **capital loss**. The investment not only did not store wealth; it lost some. Table 2.4 shows how capital gains and losses are created.

capital gain

Wealth created when an asset is sold for more than the original investment.

capital loss

Wealth lost when an asset is sold for less than the original investment.

TABLE 2.4 Gains and Losses

	Actions
Capital GAIN	Buy at a lower price, then sell for a higher price
Capital LOSS	Buy at a higher price, then sell for a lower price

The better investment asset is the one that increases in value—creates a capital gain—during the time you are storing it.

FIGURE 2.3

Assets Create Income

Some assets not only store wealth but also create income. An investment in an apartment house stores wealth and creates rental income, for example. An investment in a share of stock stores wealth and also perhaps creates dividend income. A deposit in a savings account stores wealth and creates interest income.

Some investors care more about increasing asset value than about income. For example, an investment in a share of corporate stock may produce a dividend, which is a share of the corporation's profit, or the company may keep all its profit rather than pay dividends to shareholders. Reinvesting that profit in the company may help the company to increase in value. If the company increases in value, the stock increases in value, increasing investors' wealth. Further, increases in wealth through capital gains are taxed differently than income, making capital gains more valuable than an increase in income for some investors.

On the other hand, other investors care more about receiving income from their investments. For example, retirees who no longer have employment income may be relying on investments to provide income for living expenses. Being older and having a shorter horizon, retirees may be less concerned with growing wealth than with creating income.

Assets Reduce Expenses

Some assets are used to reduce living expenses. Purchasing an asset and using it may be cheaper than arranging for an alternative. For example, buying a car to drive to work may be cheaper, in the long run, than renting one or using public transportation. The car typically will not increase in value, so it cannot be expected to be a store of wealth; its only role is to reduce future expenses.

Sometimes an asset may be expected to both store wealth and reduce future expenses. For example, buying a house to live in may be cheaper, in the long run, than renting one. In addition, real estate may appreciate in value, allowing you to realize a gain when you sell the asset. In this case, the house has effectively stored wealth. Appreciation in value depends on the real estate market and demand for housing when the asset is sold, however, so you cannot count on it. Still, a house usually can reduce living expenses and be a potential store of wealth.

Table 2.5 shows the roles of assets in reducing expenses, increasing income, and storing wealth.

TABLE 2.5 Assets and the Roles of Assets

Asset	Reduce Expenses	Increase Income	Store Wealth
Car	Yes	No	No
Savings Account	No	Yes	Yes
Money Market Account	No	Yes	Yes
Home	Yes	No	Yes
Rental Property	No	Yes	Yes
Investment in Bonds	No	Yes	Yes
Investment in Stocks	No	Yes	Yes

The choice of investment asset, then, depends on your belief in its ability to store and increase wealth, create income, or reduce expenses. Ideally, your assets will store and increase wealth while increasing income or reducing expenses. Otherwise, acquiring the asset will not be a productive use of liquidity. Also, in that case the opportunity cost will be greater than the benefit from the investment, since there are many assets to choose from.

Key Takeaways

- Assets are items with economic value that can be converted to cash. You use excess liquidity or surplus cash to buy an asset and store wealth until you resell the asset.

- An asset can create income, reduce expenses, and store wealth.
- To have value as an investment, an asset must either store wealth or create income (reduce expenses); ideally, an asset can do both.
- Whatever the type of asset you choose, investing in assets or selling capital can be more profitable than selling labor.
- Selling an asset can result in a capital gain or capital loss.
- Selling capital means trading in the capital markets, which is a sellers' market. You can do this only if you have a budget surplus, or an excess of income over expenses.

Exercises

1. Record your answers to the following questions in your personal finance journal or My Notes. What are your assets? How do your assets store your wealth? How do your assets make income for you? How do your assets help you reduce your expenses?
2. List your assets in the order of their cash or market value (most valuable to least valuable). Then list them in terms of their degree of liquidity. Which assets do you think you might sell in the next ten years? Why? What new assets do you think you would like to acquire and why? How could you reorganize your budget to make it possible to invest in new assets?

2.4 Debt and Equity

Learning Objectives

1. Define equity and debt.
2. Compare and contrast the benefits and costs of debt and equity.
3. Illustrate the uses of debt and equity.
4. Analyze the costs of debt and of equity.

Buying capital, usually by selling another asset in exchange, enables you to invest with your own capital. In essence, it enables you to get one asset by exchanging it for another.

Borrowing capital, using other people's money to finance the investment, allows you to use an asset before actually owning it, assuming you can repay the debt out of future earnings.

Borrowing capital has costs, however, so the asset will have to increase wealth, increase earnings, or decrease expenses enough to compensate for its costs. In other words, the asset will have to be more productive to earn enough to cover its financing costs—the cost of borrowing capital to buy the asset.

Buying capital creates equity (i.e., ownership of new asset) and borrowing capital gives you debt; both kinds of financing have costs and benefits. When you buy or borrow liquidity or cash, you become a buyer in the capital market.

The Costs of Debt and Equity

equity

An ownership share in an asset, entitling the holder to a share of the future gain (or loss) in asset value and of any future income (or loss) created.

cost of equity

The cost of having to share the benefits—capital gains or income (dividends)—from the investment.

risk

In finance, the probability that the value of an asset, income, or investment may decline in the future.

Corporations can buy capital from other investors in exchange for an ownership share or **equity**, which represents your claim on any future gains or future income. If the asset is productive in storing wealth, generating income, or reducing expenses, the equity holder, also called the shareholder or owner, enjoys that benefit in proportion to the share of the asset owned. If the asset actually loses value, the owner bears a portion of the loss in proportion to the share of the asset owned. The **cost of equity** is in having to share the benefits from the investment.

For example, in 2004, Google, a company that produced a very successful Internet search engine, decided to buy capital by selling shares of the company (shares of stock or equity securities) in exchange for cash. Google sold over 19 million shares for a total of $1.67 billion. Those who bought the shares were then owners or shareholders of Google, Inc. Each shareholder has equity in Google, and as long as they own the shares, they will share in the profits and value of Google, Inc. The original founders and owners of Google, Larry Page and Sergey Brin, have since had to share their company's gains (or income) or losses with all those shareholders. In this case, the cost of equity is the minimum rate of return Google must offer its shareholders to compensate them for waiting for their returns and for bearing some **risk** that the company might not do as well in the future.

It is more difficult for an individual to sell shares in his future income (although some rock musicians and athletes have tried it), so it is not really a practical way of financing for most personal finance decisions. However, it is useful to understand the idea and costs of equity, especially as it contrasts with debt.

debt

Borrowed capital, a liability, a loan that must be repaid.

interest

The cost of debt expressed as an annual percentage of the principal.

cost of debt

The cost of borrowing capital because of having to pay interest on the principal.

principal

The original amount of borrowed capital (a loan).

Borrowing is renting someone else's money for a period of time, and the result is **debt**. During that period of time, rent or **interest** must be paid, which is a **cost of debt**. When that period of time expires, all the capital (the **principal** amount borrowed) must be given back. The investment's earnings must be enough to cover the interest, and its growth in value must be enough to return the principal. Thus, debt is a liability, an obligation for which the borrower is liable.

In contrast, the cost of equity may need to be paid only if there is an increase in income or wealth, and even then can be deferred. So, from the buyer's point of view, purchasing liquidity by borrowing (debt) has a more immediate effect on income and expenses. Interest must be added as an expense, and repayment must be anticipated.

Table 2.6 shows the implications of equity and debt as the sources of capital.

TABLE 2.6 Sources of Capital

	Equity	Debt
Trade	Buy capital	Borrow capital
Cost/Expense	Share profits and gains	Pay interest
Market	Capital market	Credit market

The Uses of Debt and Equity

FIGURE 2.4

© Shutterstock, Inc.

Debt is a way to make an investment that could not otherwise be made, to buy an asset (e.g., house, car, corporate stock) that you couldn't buy without borrowing. If that asset is expected to provide enough benefit (i.e., increase value or create income or reduce expense) to compensate for its additional costs, then the debt is worth it. However, if debt creates additional expense without enough additional benefit, then it is not worth it. The trouble is, while the costs are usually known up front, the benefits are not. That adds a dimension of risk to debt, which is another factor in assessing whether it's desirable.

For example, after the housing boom began to go bust in 2008, homeowners began losing value in their homes as housing prices dropped. Some homeowners were in the unfortunate position of owing more on their mortgage than their house was worth. The costs of their debt were knowable up front, but the consequences—the house losing value and becoming worth less than the debt—were not.

Debt may also be used to cover a budget deficit, or the excess of expenses over income. As mentioned previously, however, in the long run the cost of the debt will increase expenses that are already too big, which is what created the deficit in the first place. Unless income can also be increased, debt can only aggravate a deficit.

The Value of Debt

The value of debt includes the benefits of having the asset sooner rather than later, something that debt financing enables. For example, many people want to buy a house when they have children, perhaps because they want bedrooms and bathrooms and maybe a yard for their children. Not far into adulthood, would-be homebuyers may not have had enough time to save enough to buy the house outright, so they borrow to make up the difference. Over the length of their mortgage (real estate loan), they pay the interest.

The alternative would be to rent a living space. If the rent on a comparable home were more than the mortgage interest (which it often is, because a landlord usually wants the rent to cover her mortgage *and* create a profit), it would make more sense, if possible, to borrow and buy a home and be able to live in it. And extra bedrooms and bathrooms and a yard are valuable while children are young and live at home. If you wait until you have saved enough to buy a home, you may be much older, and your children may be off on their own.

Another example of the value of debt is using debt to finance an education. Education is valuable because it has many benefits that can be enjoyed over a lifetime. One benefit is an increase in potential earnings in wages and salaries. Demand for the educated or more skilled employee is generally greater than for the uneducated or less-skilled employee. So education creates a more valuable and thus higher-priced employee.

It makes sense to be able to maximize value by becoming educated as soon as possible so that you have as long as possible to benefit from increased income. It even makes sense to invest in an education before you sell your labor because your opportunity cost of going to school—in this case, the "lost" wages of not working—is lowest. Without income or savings (or very little) to finance your education, typically, you borrow. Debt enables you to use the value of the education to enhance your income, out of which you can pay back the debt.

The alternative would be to work and save and then get an education, but you would be earning income less efficiently until you completed your education, and then you would have less time to earn your return. Waiting decreases the value of your education, that is, its usefulness, over your lifetime.

TABLE 2.7 Debt: Uses, Value, and Cost

Debt	Debt Used to Finance	Value	Cost Paid from
Credit Cards	Living expense	Convenience	Income
Auto Loan	Car	Reduce expenses	Income
Mortgage	Home	Reduce expenses	Income
College Loan	Education	Increase (future) income	Future income

In these examples (Table 2.7), debt creates a cost, but it reduces expenses or increases income to offset that cost. Debt allows this to happen sooner than it otherwise would, which allows you to realize the maximum benefit for the investment. In such cases, debt is "worth" it.

Key Takeaways

- Financing assets through equity means sharing ownership and whatever gains or losses that brings.
- Financing assets through borrowing and creating debt means taking on a financial obligation that must be repaid.
- Both equity and debt have costs and value.
- Both equity and debt enable you to use an asset sooner than you otherwise would and therefore to reap more of its rewards.

Exercises

1. Research the founding of Apple, Inc. Start by reading this article at https://www.entrepreneur.com/article/197538. How did the young entrepreneurs Steve Jobs and Steve Wozniak use equity and debt to make their business successful and increase his personal wealth? Discuss your findings with classmates.
2. Record your answers to the following questions in your personal finance journal or My Notes. What equity do you own? What debt do you owe? In each case, what do your equity and debt finance? What do they cost you? How do they benefit you?
3. Read the article "How to Pay Off Student Loans": http://www.realsimple.com/work-life/money/how-to-pay-off-student-loans-00100000077561. Students fear going into debt for their education or later have difficulty paying off student loans. This article presents personal financial planning strategies for addressing this issue.
    - What are some practical financial planning tips to take advantage of debt financing for your education?
    - Pick one of the tips mentioned in the article and explain why it may be impractical for you.

2.5 Income and Risk

Learning Objectives

1. Describe how sources of income may be diversified.
2. Describe how investments in assets may be diversified.
3. Explain the use of diversification as a risk management strategy.

Personal finance is not just about getting what you want; it is also about protecting what you have. Since the way to accumulate assets is to create surplus capital by having an income larger than expenses, and since you rely on income to provide for living expenses, you also need to think about protecting your income. One way to do so is through **diversification**, or spreading the risk.

diversification

The strategy of reducing risk by spreading income and investments among a number of different kinds, sources, and locations.

You already know not to put all your eggs in one basket, because if something happens to that basket, all the eggs are gone. If the eggs are in many baskets, on the other hand, the loss of any one basket would mean the loss of just a fraction of the eggs. The more baskets, the smaller your proportional loss would be. Then if you put many different baskets in many different places, your eggs are diversified even more effectively, because all the baskets aren't exposed to the same environmental or systematic risks.

Diversification is more often discussed in terms of investment decisions, but diversification of sources of income works the same way and makes the same kind of sense for the same reasons. If sources of income are diverse—in number and kind—and one source of income ceases to be productive, then you still have others to rely on.

If you sell your labor to only one buyer, then you are exposed to more risk than if you can generate income by selling your labor to more than one buyer. You have only so much time you can devote to working, however. Having more than one employer could be exhausting and perhaps impossible. Selling your labor to more than one buyer also means that you are still dependent on the labor market, which could suffer from an economic cycle such as a recession affecting many buyers (employers).

Mark, for example, works as a school counselor, tutors on the side, paints houses in the summers, and buys and sells sports memorabilia on the Internet. If he got laid off from his counseling job, he would lose his paycheck but still be able to create income by tutoring, painting, and trading memorabilia.

Similarly, if you sell your capital to only one buyer—invest in only one asset—then you are exposed to more risk than if you generate income by investing in a variety of assets. Diversifying investments means you are dependent on trade in the capital markets, however, which likewise could suffer from unfavorable economic conditions.

Mark has a checking account, an online money market account, and a balanced portfolio of stocks. If his stock portfolio lost value, he would still have the value in his money market account.

A better way to diversify sources of income is to sell both labor *and* capital. Then you are trading in different markets and are not totally exposed to risks in either one. In Mark's case, if all his incomes dried up, he would still have his investments, and if all his investments lost value, he would still have his paycheck and other incomes. To diversify to that extent, you need surplus capital to trade. This brings us full circle to Adam Smith, quoted at the beginning of this chapter, who said, essentially, "It takes money to make money."

Key Takeaway

- Diversifying sources of income in both the labor market and the capital markets is the best hedge against risks in any one market.

Exercise

1. Record your answers to the following questions in your personal finance journal or My Notes. How can you diversify your sources of income to spread the risk of losing income? How can you diversify your investments to spread the risk of losing return on investment?

Endnotes

1. Franklin D. Roosevelt, "Remarks when Signing the Social Security Act, August 14, 1935." Social Security Administration archives, "Presidential Statement Signing the Social Security Act. August 14, 1935," http://www.socialsecurity.gov/history/fdrstmts.html#signing (accessed November 23, 2009).

CHAPTER 3

Financial Statements

3.1 Introduction

> *"Man is the measure of all things; of that which is, that it is; of that which is not, that it is not."*
>
> — Protagoras (ca. 490-421 BC), in Plato's *Protagoras*

Man is also the measurer of all things. Measuring by counting, by adding it all up, and by taking stock is probably as old as any human activity. In recorded history, there are "accounts" on clay tablets from ancient Sumeria dating from ca. 3,700 BC. Since the first shepherd counted his sheep, there has been accounting.

FIGURE 3.1

In financial planning, assessing the current situation, or figuring out where you are at present, is crucial to determining any sort of financial plan. This assessment becomes the point of departure for any strategy. It becomes the mark from which any progress is measured, the principal from which any return is calculated. It can determine the practical or realistic goals to have and the strategies to achieve them. Eventually, the current situation becomes a time forgotten with the pride of success, or remembered with the regret of failure.

Understanding the current situation is not just a matter of measuring it, but also of putting it in perspective and in context, relative to your own past performance and future goals, and relative to the realities in the economic world around you. Tools for understanding your current situation are your accounting and financial statements.

3.2 Accounting and Financial Statements

Learning Objectives

1. Distinguish accrual and cash accounting.
2. Compare and contrast the three common financial statements.
3. Identify the results shown on the income statement, balance sheet, and cash flow statement.
4. Explain the calculation and meaning of net worth.
5. Trace how a bankruptcy can occur.

accrual accounting

A method of accounting in which economic consequences rather than cash flow consequences define transactions.

cash accounting

A method of accounting in which cash flow consequences rather than economic consequences define transactions. Events are defined as cash transactions and recorded only when cash changes hands.

Clay tablets interested Sumerian traders because the records gave them a way to see their financial situation and to use that insight to measure progress and plan for the future. The method of accounting universally used in business today is known as **accrual accounting**, in which events are accounted for even if cash does not change hands. That is, transactions are recorded at the time they occur rather than when payment is actually made or received. Anticipated or preceding payments and receipts (cash flows) are recorded as accrued or deferred. Accrual accounting is the opposite of **cash accounting**, in which transactions are recognized only when cash is exchanged.

Accrual accounting defines earning as an economic event signified by an exchange of goods rather than by an exchange of cash. In this way, accrual accounting allows for the separation in time of the exchange of goods and the exchange of cash. A transaction can be completed over time and distance, which allows for extended—and extensive—trade. Another advantage of accrual accounting is that it gives a business a more accurate picture of its present situation in reality.

Modern accounting techniques developed during the European Age of Discovery, which was motivated by ever-expanding trade. Both the principles and the methods of modern accrual accounting were first published in a text by Luca Pacioli in 1494.[1] These methods of "keeping the books" can be applied to personal finance today as they were to trading in the age of long voyages for pepper and cloves, and with equally valuable results.

Nevertheless, in personal finance it almost always makes more sense to use cash accounting, to define and account for events when the cash changes hands. So in personal finance, incomes and expenses are noted when the cash is received or paid, or when the cash flows.

The Accounting Process

Financial decisions result in transactions, actual trades that buy or sell, invest or borrow. In the market economy, something is given up in order to get something, so each trade involves at least one thing given up and one thing gotten—two things flowing in at least two directions. The process of accounting records these transactions and records what has been gotten and what has been given up to get it, what flows in and what flows out.

In business, accounting journals and ledgers are set up to record transactions as they happen. In personal finance, a checkbook records most transactions, with statements from banks or investment accounts providing records of the rest. Periodically, the transaction information is summarized in financial statements so it can be read most efficiently.

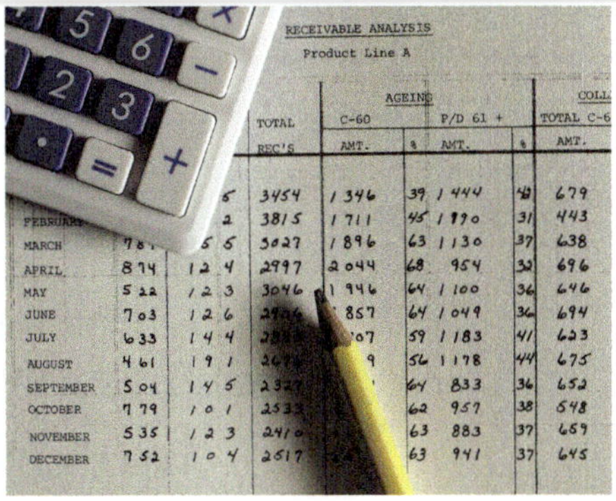

FIGURE 3.2

© Shutterstock, Inc.

Bookkeeping—the process of recording what and how and by how much a transaction affects the financial situation—is how events are recorded. Since the advent of accounting software, knowledge of bookkeeping, like knowledge of long division and spelling, has become somewhat obsolete, although human judgment is still required. What is more interesting and useful are the summary reports that can be produced once all this information is recorded: the income statement, cash flow statement, and balance sheet.

Income Statement

The **income statement** summarizes incomes and expenses for a period of time. In business, income is the value of whatever is sold, expenses are the costs of sustaining the business while it earns that income, and the difference is profit. In personal finance, income is what is earned as wages or salary and as interest or dividends, and expenses are the costs of things consumed in the course of daily living: the costs of sustaining *you* while you earn income. Thus, the income statement is a measure of what you have earned and what your cost of living was while earning it. The difference is personal profit, which, if accumulated as investment, becomes your wealth.

income statement

A summary statement of income and expenses for a period; an income statement shows the difference between them or the net profit (net loss) for the period.

The income statement clearly shows the relative size of your income and expenses. If income is greater than expenses, there is a surplus, and that surplus can be used to save or to spend more (and create more expenses). If income is less than expenses, then there is a deficit that must be addressed. If the deficit continues, it creates debts—unpaid bills—that must eventually be paid. Over the long term, a deficit is not a viable scenario.

The income statement can be useful for its level of detail too. You can see which of your expenses consumes the greatest portion of your income or which expense has the greatest or least effect on your bottom line. If you want to reduce expenses, you can see which would have the greatest impact or which would free up more income if you reduced it. If you want to increase income, you can see how much more that would buy you in terms of your expenses (Table 3.1). For example, consider Alice's situation per year.

TABLE 3.1 Alice's Situation (Per Year in Dollars)

Gross wages	44,650
Income taxes and deductions	8,930
Rent expense	10,800
Living expenses	14,400

She also had car payments of $2,400 and student loan payments of $7,720. Each loan payment actually covers the interest expense and partial repayment of the loan. The interest is an expense representing the cost of borrowing, and thus of having, the car and the education. The repayment of the loan is not an expense, however, but is just giving back something that was borrowed. In this case, the loan payments break down as follows (Table 3.2).

TABLE 3.2 Alice's Loan Payments (Annually)

	Interest	Debt Repayment
Car Loan	240	2,160
Student Loan	4,240	3,480

Breaking down Alice's living expenses in more detail and adding in her interest expenses, Alice's income statement would look like this (Table 3.3).

TABLE 3.3 Alice's Income Statement for Year 1

Gross wages		44,650
Income taxes and deductions	8,930	
Disposable income		35,720
Rent expense	10,800	
Food	3,900	
Car expenses	3,600	
Clothing	1,800	
Cell phone	1,200	
Internet and cable TV	1,200	
Entertainment, travel, etc.	2,700	
Total living expenses		25,200
Car loan interest	240	
Student loan interest	4,240	
Total interest expenses		4,480
Net income		6,040

disposable income

Income available for expenses after tax expense has been deducted; gross income less income tax.

Alice's **disposable income**, or income to meet expenses after taxes have been accounted for, is $35,720. Alice's net income, or net earnings or personal profit, is the remaining income after all other expenses have been deducted: in this case, $6,040.

Now Alice has a much clearer view of what's going on in her financial life. She can see, for example, that living expenses take the biggest bite out of her income and that rent is the biggest single expense. If she wanted to decrease expenses, finding a place to live with a cheaper rent will make the most impact on her bottom line. Or perhaps it would make more sense to make many small changes rather than one large change, to cut back on several other expenses. She could begin by cutting back on the expense items that she feels are least necessary or that she could most easily live without. Perhaps she could do with less entertainment or clothing or travel, for example. Whatever choices she subsequently made would be reflected in her income statement. The value of the income statement is in presenting income and expenses in detail for a particular period of time.

Cash Flow Statement

The **cash flow statement** shows how much cash came in and where it came from, and how much cash went out and where it went over a period of time. This differs from the income statement because it may include cash flows that are not from income and expenses. Examples of such cash flows would be receiving repayment of money that you loaned, repaying money that you borrowed, or using money in exchanges such as buying or selling an asset.

cash flow statement

A summary of actual cash flows for a period, detailing the sources and uses of cash and classifying them as from operating, investing, or financing activities.

The cash flow statement is important because it can show how well you do at creating liquidity, as well as your net income. Liquidity is nearness to cash, and liquidity has value. An excess of liquidity can be sold or lent, creating additional income. A lack of liquidity must be addressed by buying or borrowing it, creating additional expense.

Looking at Alice's situation, she has two loan repayments that are not expenses and so are not included on her income statement. These payments reduce her liquidity, however, making it harder for her to create excess cash. Her cash flow statement looks like this (Table 3.4). *Note: On a cash flow statement, negative and positive numbers indicate direction of flow. A negative number is cash flowing out, and a positive number is cash flowing in.*

TABLE 3.4 Alice's Cash Flow Statement for Year 1

Cash from gross wages	**44,650**
Cash paid for:	
Income taxes and deductions	-8,930
Rent expense	-10,800
Food	-3,900
Car expenses	-3,600
Clothing	-1,800
Cell phone	-1,200
Internet and cable TV	-1,200
Entertainment, travel, etc.	-2,700
Car loan interest	-240
Student loan interest	-4,240
Cash for repayment of car loan	-2,160
Cash for repayment of student loan	-3,480
Net cash flow	400

operating cash flows

Recurring cash flows that result from income and expense events.

cash flows from financing

Nonrecurring cash flows that result from the borrowing or repayment of debt, or from the issue or repurchase of equity.

cash flows from investing

Nonrecurring cash flows that result from buying or selling assets.

free cash flow

Income remaining after the deduction of living expenses and debt obligations that is available for capital expenditures or investment.

As with the income statement, the cash flow statement is more useful if there are subtotals for the different kinds of cash flows, as defined by their sources and uses. The cash flows from income and expenses are **operating cash flows**, or cash flows that are a consequence of earning income or paying for the costs of earning income. The loan repayments are **cash flows from financing** assets or investments that will increase income. In this case, cash flows from financing include repayments on the car and the education. Although Alice doesn't have any in this example, there could also be **cash flows from investing**, from buying or selling assets. **Free cash flow** is the cash available to make investments or financing decisions after taking care of operations and debt obligations. It is calculated as cash flow from operations less debt repayments.

The most significant difference among the three categories of cash flows—operating, investing, or financing—is whether the cash flows may be expected to recur regularly. Operating cash flows recur regularly; they are the cash flows that result from income and expenses or consumption and therefore can be expected to occur in every year. Operating cash flows may be different amounts in different periods, but they will happen in every period. Investing and financing cash flows, on the other hand, may or may not recur and often are unusual events. Typically, for example, you would not borrow, lend, buy, or sell assets in every year. Here is how Alice's cash flows would be classified (Table 3.5).

TABLE 3.5 Alice's Cash Flow Statement for Year 1

Cash from gross wages	**44,650**	
Cash paid for:		
Income taxes and deductions	-8,930	
Rent expense	-10,800	
Food	-3,900	
Car expenses	-3,600	
Clothing	-1,800	
Cell phone	-1,200	
Internet and cable TV	-1,200	
Entertainment, travel, etc.	-2,700	
Car loan interest	-240	
Student loan interest	-4,240	
Operating cash flows		6,040
Cash for repayment of car loan	-2,160	
Cash for repayment of student loan	-3,480	
Financing cash flows		-5,640
Net cash flow		400

This cash flow statement more clearly shows how liquidity is created and where liquidity could be increased. If Alice wanted to create more liquidity, it is obvious that eliminating those loan payments would be a big help: without them, her net cash flow would increase by more than 3,900%.

Balance Sheet

In business or in personal finance, a critical piece in assessing the current situation is the balance sheet. Often referred to as the "statement of financial condition," the **balance sheet** is a snapshot of what you have and what you owe at a given point in time. Unlike the income or cash flow statements, it is not a record of performance over a period of time, but simply a statement of where things stand at a certain moment.

balance sheet

A list of all assets, liabilities, and equity or net worth, at a given point in time, providing a concise picture of financial condition at that time.

The balance sheet is a list of assets, debts or liabilities, and equity or net worth, with their values. In business, assets are resources that can be used to create income, while debt and equity are the capital that financed those assets. Thus, the value of the assets must equal the value of the debt and the equity. In other words, the value of the business's resources must equal the value of the capital it borrowed or bought in order to get those resources.

$$\text{Assets} = \text{Liabilities} + \text{Equity}$$

In business, the **accounting equation** is as absolute as the law of gravity. It simply must always be true, because if there are assets, they must have been financed somehow—through either debt or equity. The value of that debt and equity financing must equal or balance the value of the assets it bought. Thus, it is called the "balance" sheet because it *always* balances the debt and equity with the value of the assets.

accounting equation

Assets = liabilities + equity, or the value of assets must be equal to the value of the debt and equity that financed them. In personal finance, assets = debts + net worth, or net worth = assets – debts.

In personal finance, assets are also things that can be sold to create liquidity. Liquidity is needed to satisfy or repay debts. Because your assets are what you use to satisfy your debts when they become due, the assets' value should be greater than the value of your debts. That is, you should have more to work with to meet your obligations than you owe.

The difference between what you have and what you owe is your **net worth**. Literally, net worth is the share that you own of everything that you have. It is the value of what you have *net of* (less) what you owe to others. Whatever asset value is left over after you meet your debt obligations is your own worth. It is the value of what you have that you can claim free and clear.

net worth

The value of assets owned after creditors' claims (debts) are accounted for, or literally, assets – debts.

$$\text{Assets - Debt} = \text{Net Worth}$$

Your net worth is really your equity or financial ownership in your own life. Here, too, the personal balance sheet must balance, because if

$$\text{Assets - Debt} = \text{Net Worth}$$

then it should also be that

$$\text{Assets} = \text{Debt} + \text{Net Worth}$$

Alice could write a simple balance sheet to see her current financial condition. She has two assets (her car and her savings account), and she has two debts (her car and student loans (Table 3.6).

TABLE 3.6 Alice's Balance Sheet, December 31, Year 1

Assets		Liabilities	
Car	5,000	Car Loan	2,700
Savings	250	Student Loan	53,000
Total	5,250	Total	55,700
		Net Worth	-50,450

negative net worth

The mathematical result of liabilities being greater than the value of assets, or debts being larger than the value that can be used to meet them.

Alice's balance sheet presents her with a much clearer picture of her financial situation, but also with a dismaying prospect: she seems to have negative net worth. **Negative net worth** results whenever the value of debts or liabilities is actually greater than the assets' value.

Position	Result	Net Worth	
Liabilities < Assets	Assets – Liabilities > 0	Net Worth > 0	Positive
Liabilities > Assets	Assets – Liabilities < 0	Net Worth < 0	Negative

Negative net worth implies that the assets don't have enough value to satisfy the debts. Since debts are obligations, this would cause concern.

Net Worth and Bankruptcy

creditors

Lenders; anyone to whom debt is owed.

bankruptcy

An economic situation when the value of debts is greater than the value of the assets that can be used to satisfy them. Formal bankruptcy is also a legal process aiming to compensate creditors, governed by the laws of the nation or state in which it occurs.

In business, when liabilities are greater than the assets to meet them, the business has negative equity and is literally bankrupt. In that case, it may go out of business, selling all its assets and giving whatever it can to its **creditors** or lenders, who will have to settle for less than what they are owed. More usually, the business continues to operate in bankruptcy, if possible, and must still repay its creditors, although perhaps under somewhat easier terms. Creditors (and the laws) allow these terms because creditors would rather get paid in full later than get paid less now or not at all.

In personal finance, personal **bankruptcy** may occur when debts are greater than the value of assets. But because creditors would rather be paid eventually than never, the bankrupt is usually allowed to continue to earn income in the hopes of repaying the debt later or with easier terms. Often, the bankrupt is forced to liquidate (sell) some or all of its assets.

Because debt is a legal as well as an economic obligation, there are laws governing bankruptcies that differ from state to state in the United States and from country to country. Although debt forgiveness was discussed in the Old Testament, throughout history it was not uncommon for bankrupt people in many cultures to be put to death, maimed, enslaved, or imprisoned.[2] The use of another's property or wealth is a serious responsibility, so debt is a serious obligation.

FIGURE 3.3

© Shutterstock, Inc.

However, Alice's case is actually not as dismal as it looks, because Alice has an "asset" that is not listed on her balance sheet, that is, her education. It is not listed on her balance sheet because the value of her education, like the value of any asset, comes from how useful it is, and its usefulness has not happened yet, but will happen over her lifetime. It will happen in her future, based on how she chooses to use her education to increase her income and wealth. It is difficult to assign a monetary value to her education now. Alice knows what she paid for her education, but, sensibly, its real value is not its cost but its potential return, or what it can earn for her as she puts it to use in the future.

Current studies show that a college education has economic value because a college graduate earns more over a lifetime than a high school graduate. Recent estimates put that difference at about $1,000,000.[3] So, if Alice assumes that her education will be worth $1,000,000 in extra income over her lifetime, and she includes that asset value on her balance sheet, then it would look more like this (Table 3.7):

TABLE 3.7 Alice's Balance Sheet (Revised), December 31, Year 1

Assets		Liabilities	
Car	5,000	Car Loan	2,700
Savings	250	Student Loan	53,000
Education	1,000,000	Total	55,700
Total	1,005,250	Net Worth	949,550

This looks much better, but it's not sound accounting practice to include an asset—and its value—on the balance sheet before it really exists. After all, education generally pays off, but until it does, it hasn't yet and there is a chance, however slim, that it won't for Alice. A balance sheet is a snapshot of one's financial situation at one particular time. At this particular time, Alice's education has value, but its amount is unknown.

It is easy to see, however, that the only thing that creates negative net worth for Alice is her student loan. The student loan causes her liabilities to be greater than her assets—and if that were paid off, her net worth would be positive. Given that Alice is just starting her adult earning years, her situation seems quite reasonable.

Key Takeaways

- Three commonly used financial statements are the income statement, the cash flow statement, and the balance sheet.
- Results for a period are shown on the income statement and the cash flow statement. Current conditions are shown on the balance sheet.
- The income statement lists income and expenses.
- The cash flow statement lists three kinds of cash flows: operating (recurring), financing (nonrecurring), and investing (nonrecurring).
- The balance sheet lists assets, liabilities (debts), and net worth.
- Net worth = assets – debts.
- Bankruptcy occurs when there is negative net worth, or when debts are greater than assets.

Exercises

1. Prepare a personal income statement for the past year, using the same format as Alice's income statement in this chapter. Include all relevant categories of income and expenses. What does your income statement tell you about your current financial situation? For example, where does your income come from, and where does it go? Do you have a surplus of income over expenses? If so, what are you doing with the surplus? Do you have a deficit? What can you do about that? Which of your expenses has the greatest effect on your bottom line? What is the biggest expense? Which expenses would be easiest to reduce or eliminate? How else could you reduce expenses? Realistically, how could you increase your income? How would you like your income statement for the next year to look?
2. Using the format for Alice's cash flow statement, prepare your cash flow statement for the same one-year period. Include your cash flows from all sources in addition to your operating cash flows—the income and expenses that appear on your income statement. What, if any, were the cash flows from financing and the cash flows from investing? Which of your cash flows are recurring, and which are nonrecurring? What does your cash flow statement tell you about your current financial situation? If you wanted to increase your liquidity, what would you try to change about your cash flows?
3. Now prepare a balance sheet, again based on Alice's form. List all your assets, liabilities and debts, and your equity from all sources. What does the balance sheet show about your

financial situation at this moment in time? What is your net worth? Do you have positive or negative net worth at this time, and what does that mean? To increase your liquidity, how would your balance sheet need to change? What would be the relationship between your cash flow statement and your budget?

4. Read the CNNMoney.com article "How Much Are You Worth" (http://money.cnn.com/2003/09/30/pf/millionaire/networth/), and use the data and calculator to determine your net worth. How does your net worth compare to that of other Americans in your age and income brackets?

3.3 Comparing and Analyzing Financial Statements

Learning Objectives

1. Explain the use of common-size statements in financial analysis.
2. Discuss the design of each common-size statement.
3. Demonstrate how changes in the balance sheet may be explained by changes on the income and cash flow statements.
4. Identify the purposes and uses of ratio analysis.
5. Describe the uses of comparing financial statements over time.

Financial statements are valuable summaries of financial activities because they can organize information and make it easier and clearer to see and therefore to understand. Each one—the income statement, cash flow statement, and balance sheet—conveys a different aspect of the financial picture; put together, the picture is pretty complete. The three provide a summary of earnings and expenses, of cash flows, and of assets and debts.

Since the three statements offer three different kinds of information, sometimes it is useful to look at each in the context of the others, and to look at specific items in the larger context. This is the purpose of financial statement analysis: creating comparisons and contexts to gain a better understanding of the financial picture.

Common-Size Statements

common-size statements

Financial statements where each item's value is listed as a percentage of or in relation to another value.

On **common-size statements**, each item's value is listed as a percentage of another. This compares items, showing their relative size and their relative significance (see Table 3.8). On the income statement, each income and expense may be listed as a percentage of the total income. This shows the contribution of each kind of income to the total, and thus the diversification of income. It shows the burden of each expense on total income or how much of the income is needed to support each expense.

On the cash flow statement, each cash flow can be listed as a percentage of total positive cash flows, again showing the relative significance and diversification of the sources of cash, and the relative size of the burden of each use of cash.

On the balance sheet, each item is listed as a percentage of total assets, showing the relative significance and diversification of assets, and highlighting the use of debt as financing for the assets.

TABLE 3.8 Common-Size Statements

	Income Statement	Cash Flow Statement	Balance Sheet
Item as a % of	Total income	Total positive cash flows	Total assets

Common-Size Income Statement

Alice can look at a **common-size income statement** by looking at her expenses as a percentage of her income and comparing the size of each expense to a common denominator: her income. This shows her how much of her income, proportionately, is used up for each expense (Table 3.9).

common-size income statement

An income statement that lists each kind of revenue and each expense as a percentage of total revenues.

TABLE 3.9 Alice's Common-Size Income Statement for Year 1

Gross wages		**44,650**		**100.00%**
Income taxes and deductions	8,930		20.00%	
Disposable income		35,720		80.00%
Rent expense	10,800		24.19%	
Food	3,900		8.73%	
Car expenses	3,600		8.06%	
Clothing	1,800		4.03%	
Cell phone	1,200		2.69%	
Internet and cable TV	1,200		2.69%	
Entertainment, travel, etc.	2,700		6.05%	
Total living expenses		25,200		56.44%
Car loan interest	240		0.54%	
Student loan interest	4,240		9.50%	
Total interest expense		4,480		10.03%
Net income		6,040		13.53%

Seeing the common-size statement as a pie chart makes the relative size of the slices even clearer (Figure 3.4).

FIGURE 3.4 Pie Chart of Alice's Expenses as a Percentage of Income for the Year 1

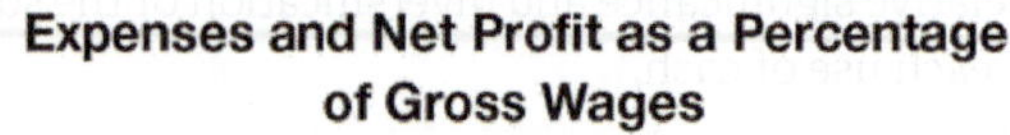

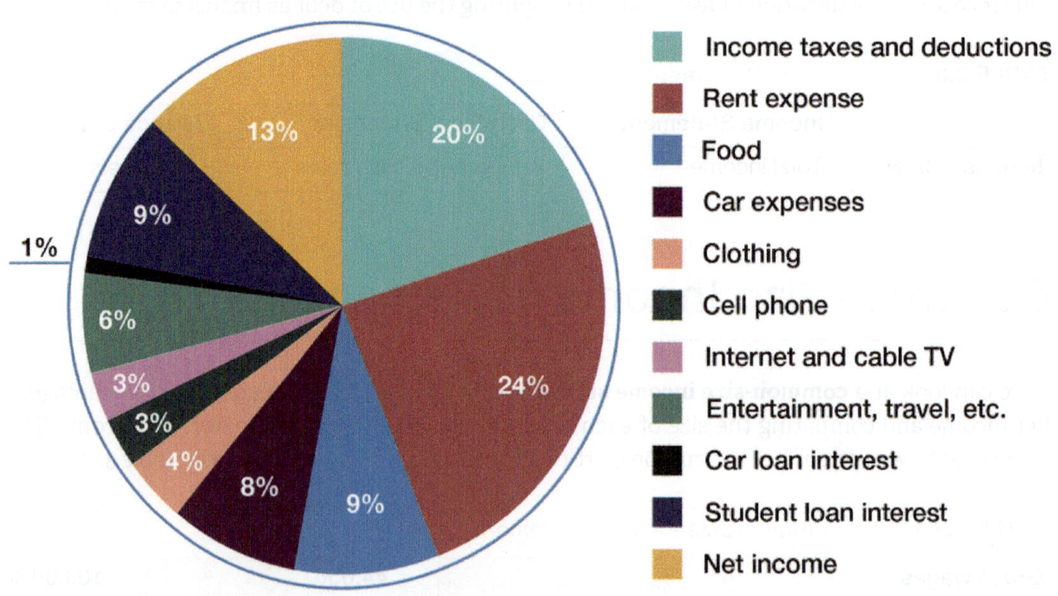

The biggest discretionary use of Alice's wages is her rent expense, followed by food, car expenses, and entertainment. Her income tax expense is a big use of her wages, but it is unavoidable or nondiscretionary. As Supreme Court Justice Oliver Wendell Holmes, Jr., said, "Taxes are what we pay for a civilized society."[4] Ranking expenses by size offers interesting insight into lifestyle choices. It is also valuable in framing financial decisions, pointing out which expenses have the largest impact on income and thus on the resources for making financial decisions. If Alice wanted more discretionary income to make more or different choices, she can easily see that reducing rent expense would have the most impact on freeing up some of her wages for another use.

Common-Size Cash Flow Statement

common-size cash flows

A cash flow statement that lists each cash flow as a percentage of total positive cash flows.

Looking at Alice's negative cash flows as percentages of her positive cash flow (on the cash flow statement), or the uses of cash as percentages of the sources of cash, creates the **common-size cash flows**. As with the income statement, this gives Alice a clearer and more immediate view of the largest uses of her cash (Table 3.10 and Figure 3.5).

TABLE 3.10 Alice's Common-Size Cash Flow Statement for Year 1

Cash from gross wages	**44,650**		**100.00%**
Cash paid for:			
Income taxes and deductions	-8,930		-20.00%
Rent expense	-10,800		-24.19%
Food	-3,900		-8.73%
Car expenses	-3,600		-8.06%
Clothing	-1,800		-4.03%
Cell phone	-1,200		-2.69%

Cash from gross wages	44,650		100.00%
Internet and cable TV	-1,200		-2.69%
Entertainment, travel, etc.	-2,700		-6.05%
Car loan interest	-240		-0.54%
Student loan interest	-4,240		-9.50%
Operating cash flows		6,040	13.53%
Cash for repayment of car loan	-2,160		-4.84%
Cash for repayment of student loan	-3,480		-7.79%
Financing cash flows		-5,640	-12.63%
Net cash flow		400	0.00%

FIGURE 3.5 Pie Chart of Alice's Common-Size Cash Flow Statement

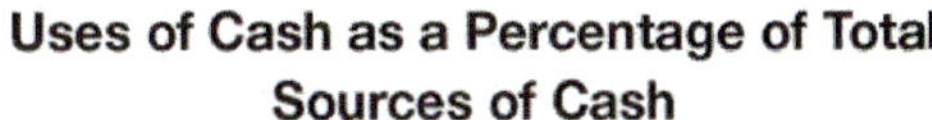

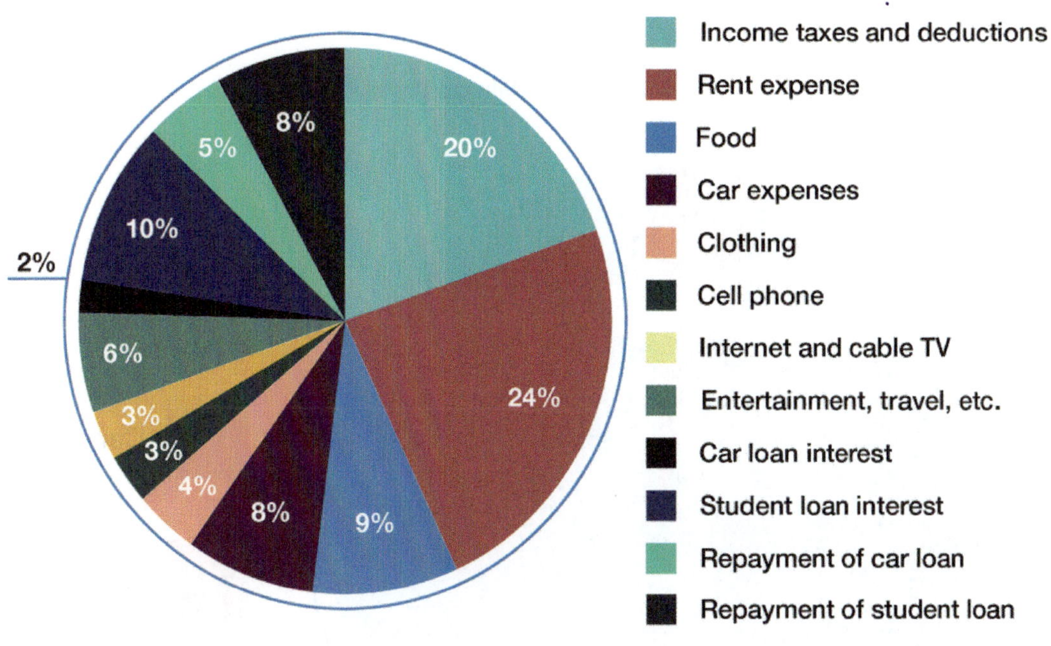

Again, rent is the biggest discretionary use of cash for living expenses, but debts demand the most significant portion of cash flows. Repayments and interest together are 30% of Alice's cash—as much as she pays for rent and food. Eliminating those debt payments would create substantial liquidity for Alice.

Common-Size Balance Sheet

On the balance sheet, looking at each item as a percentage of total assets allows for measuring how much of the assets' value is obligated to cover each debt, or how much of the assets' value is claimed by each debt (Table 3.11).

TABLE 3.11 Alice's Common-Size Balance Sheet, December 31, Year 1

Assets			Liabilities		
Car	5,000	95%	Car Loan	2,700	51%
Savings	250	5%	Student Loan	53,000	1010%
Total	5,250	100%	Total	55,700	1061%
			Net Worth	-50,450	-961%

common-size balance sheet

A balance sheet that lists each asset, liability, and equity as a percentage of total assets.

This **common-size balance sheet** allows "over-sized" items to be more obvious. For example, it is immediately obvious that Alice's student loan dwarfs her assets' value and creates her negative net worth.

Common-size statements allow you to look at the size of each item relative to a common denominator: total income on the income statement, total positive cash flow on the cash flow statement, or total assets on the balance sheet. The relative size of the items helps you spot anything that seems disproportionately large or small. The common-size analysis is also useful for comparing the diversification of items on the financial statement—the diversification of incomes on the income statement, cash flows on the cash flow statement, and assets and liabilities on the balance sheet. Diversification reduces risk, so you want to diversify the sources of income and assets you can use to create value (Figure 3.6).

FIGURE 3.6 Pie Chart of Alice's Common-Size Balance Sheet: The Assets

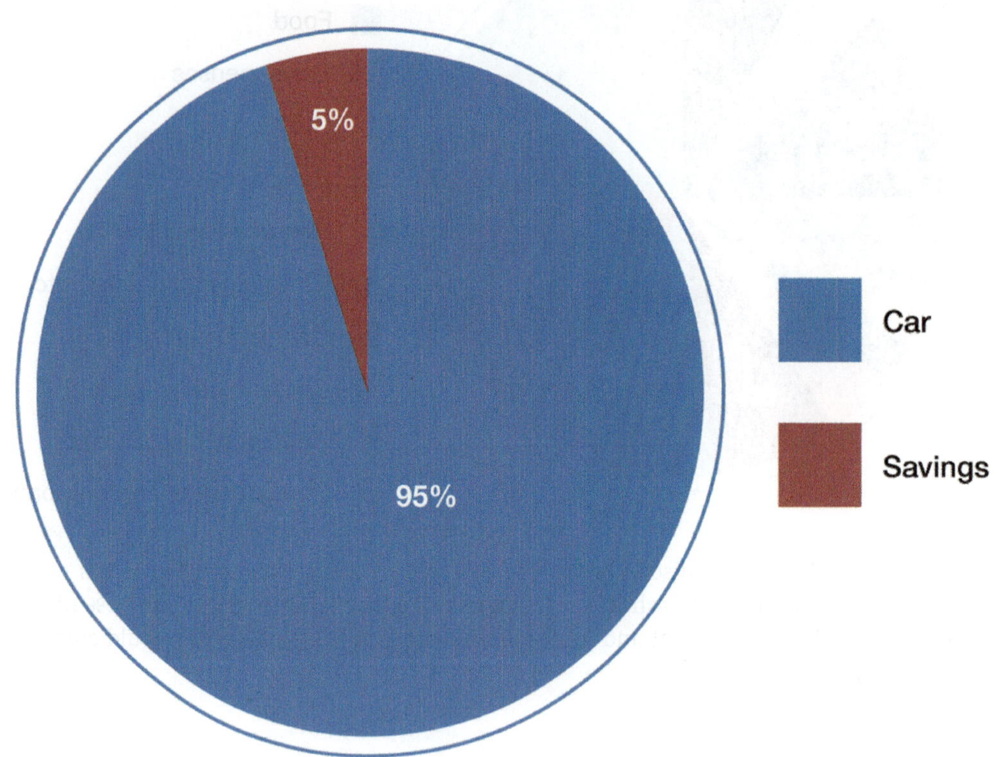

For example, Alice has only two assets, and one—her car—provides 95% of her assets' value. If something happened to her car, her assets would lose 95% of their value. Her asset value would be less exposed to risk if she had asset value from other assets to diversify the value invested in her car.

Likewise, both her income and her positive cash flows come from only one source, her paycheck. Because her positive net earnings and positive net cash flows depend on this one source, she is exposed to risk, which she could decrease by diversifying her sources of income. She could diversify by adding earned income—taking on a second job, for example—or by creating investment income. In order to create investment income, however, she needs to have a surplus of liquidity, or cash, to invest. Alice has run head first into Adam Smith's "great difficulty"[5] (that it takes some money to make money; see Chapter 2).

Relating the Financial Statements

Common-size statements put the details of the financial statements in clear relief relative to a common factor for each statement, but each financial statement is also related to the others. Each is a piece of a larger picture, and as important as it is to see each piece, it is also important to see that larger picture. To make sound financial decisions, you need to be able to foresee the consequences of a decision, to understand how a decision may affect the different aspects of the bigger picture.

For example, what happens in the income statement and cash flow statements is reflected on the balance sheet because the earnings and expenses and the other cash flows affect the asset values, and the values of debts, and thus the net worth. Cash may be used to purchase assets, so a negative cash flow may increase assets. Cash may be used to pay off debt, so a negative cash flow may decrease liabilities. Cash may be received when an asset is sold, so a decrease to assets may create positive cash flow. Cash may be received when money is borrowed, so an increase in liabilities may create a positive cash flow.

There are many other possible scenarios and transactions, but you can begin to see that the balance sheet at the end of a period is changed from what it was at the beginning of the period by what happens during the period, and what happens during the period is shown on the income statement and the cash flow statement. So, as shown in the figure, the income statement and cash flow information, related to each other, also relate the balance sheet at the end of the period to the balance sheet at the beginning of the period (Figure 3.7).

FIGURE 3.7 Relationships Among Financial Statements

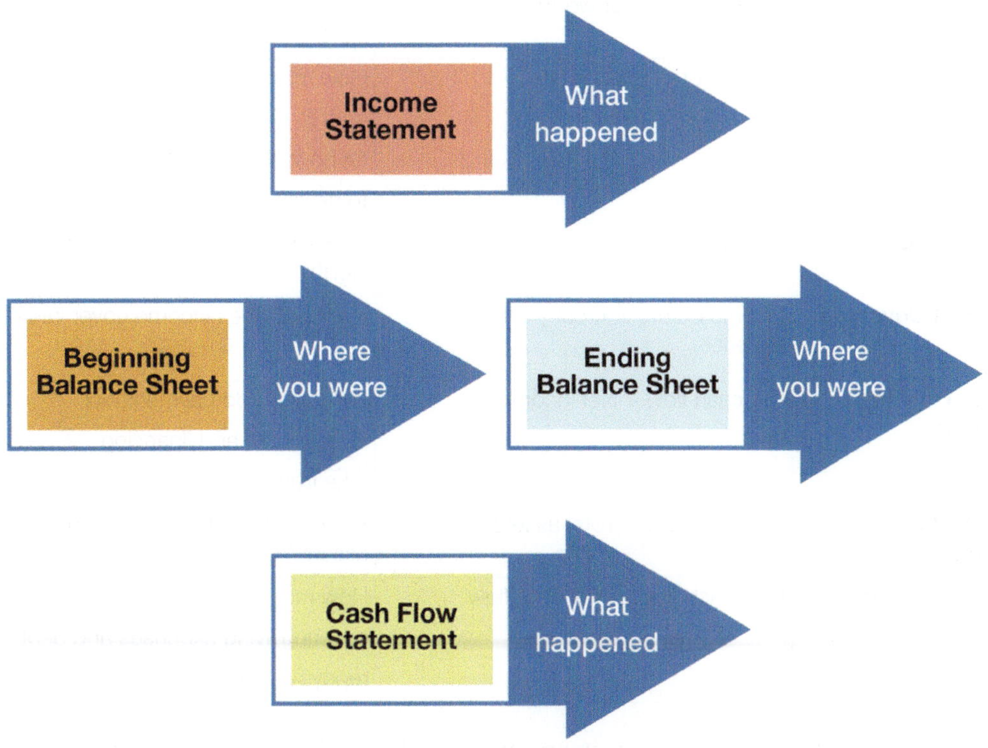

The significance of these relationships becomes even more important when evaluating alternatives for financial decisions. When you understand how the statements are related, you can use that understanding to project the effects of your choices on different aspects of your financial reality and see the consequences of your decisions.

Ratio Analysis

ratio analysis

A way of comparing amounts by creating ratios or fractions that compare the amount in the numerator to the amount in the denominator.

financial ratios

Ratios used to understand financial statement amounts relative to each other.

Creating ratios is another way to see the numbers in relation to each other. Any ratio shows the relative size of the two items compared, just as a fraction compares the numerator to the denominator or a percentage compares a part to the whole. The percentages on the common-size statements are ratios, although they only compare items within a financial statement. Ratio analysis is used to make comparisons across statements. For example, you can see how much debt you have just by looking at your total liabilities, but how can you tell if you can afford the debt you have? That depends on the income you have to meet your interest and repayment obligations, or the assets you could use (sell) to meet those obligations. **Ratio analysis** can give you the answer.

The **financial ratios** you use depend on the perspective you need or the question(s) you need answered. Some of the more common ratios (and questions) are presented in the following chart (Table 3.12).

TABLE 3.12 Common Personal Financial Ratios

Ratio	Calculation	Question it helps to answer
Net Income Margin	Net income ÷ Total income	How much income is not used up by expenses?
Return on Assets	Net income ÷ Total assets	How big is the income supporting the assets?
Return on Net Worth	Net income ÷ Net worth	How big is income relative to net worth?
Debt to Assets	Total debt ÷ Total assets	How much asset value is financed by debt? Or how much asset value is there to satisfy debt?
Total Debt	Total debt ÷ Net worth	How large is debt relative to net worth?
Interest Coverage	Income before interest ÷ Interest expense	How well does income cover interest expenses?
Cash Flow to Income	Net cash flow ÷ Net income	How much do payments for investments and financing take from income?
Cash Flow to Assets	Net cash flow ÷ Total assets	How much cash flow supports assets?
Free Cash Flow	Free cash flow ÷ Net cash flow	How much cash is left to invest after covering living expenses and debt repayments?

These ratios all get "better" or show improvement as they get bigger, with two exceptions: debt to assets and total debt. Those two ratios measure levels of debt, and the smaller the ratio, the less the debt. Ideally, the two debt ratios would be less than one. If your debt-to-assets ratio is greater than one, then debt is greater than assets, and you are bankrupt. If the total debt ratio is greater than one, then debt is greater than net worth, and you "own" less of your assets' value than your creditors do.

Some ratios will naturally be less than one, but the bigger they are, the better. For example, net income margin will always be less than one because net income will always be less than total income (net income = total income - expenses). The larger that ratio is and the fewer expenses that are taken away from the total income, the better.

Some ratios should be greater than one, and the bigger they are, the better. For example, the interest coverage ratio should be greater than one, because you should have more income to cover interest expenses than you have interest expenses, and the more you have, the better. Table 3.13 suggests what to look for in the results of your ratio analyses.

TABLE 3.13 Interpreting the Results of Ratio Analysis

Ratio	Calculation	Question it helps to answer	Better as it gets...
Net Income Margin	Net income ÷ Total income	How much income is not used up by expenses?	Bigger Will be <1
Return on Assets	Net income ÷ Total assets	How big is the income supporting the assets?	Bigger
Return on Net Worth	Net income ÷ Net worth	How big is income relative to net worth?	Bigger
Debt to Assets	Total debt ÷ Total assets	How much asset value is financed by debt? Or how much asset value is there to satisfy debt?	Smaller Should be <1
Total Debt	Total debt ÷ Net worth	How large is debt relative to net worth?	Smaller Should be <1
Interest Coverage	Income before interest ÷ Interest expense	How well does income cover interest expenses?	Bigger Should be >1
Cash Flow to Income	Net cash flow ÷ Net income	How much do payments for investments and financing take from income?	Bigger
Cash Flow to Assets	Net cash flow ÷ Total assets	How much cash flow supports assets?	Bigger
Free Cash Flow	Free cash flow ÷ Net cash flow	How much cash is left to invest after covering living expenses and debt repayments?	Bigger

While you may have a pretty good "feel" for your situation just by paying the bills and living your life, it often helps to have the numbers in front of you. Here is Alice's ratio analysis for Year 1 (Table 3.14).

TABLE 3.14 Alice's Ratio Analysis, Year 1

Ratio	Calculation	Result
Net Income Margin	Net income ÷ Total income	0.1353
Return on Assets	Net income ÷ Total assets	1.1505
Return on Net Worth	Net income ÷ Net worth	-0.1197
Debt to Assets	Total debt ÷ Total assets	10.6095
Interest Coverage	Income before interest ÷ Interest expense	2.3482
Cash Flow to Income	Net cash flow ÷ Net income	0.0662
Cash Flow to Assets	Net cash flow ÷ Total assets	0.0762
Free Cash Flow	Free cash flow ÷ Net cash flow	1.0000

The ratios that involve net worth—return-on-net-worth and total debt—are negative for Alice, because she has negative net worth, as her debts are larger than her assets. She can see how much larger her debt is than her assets by looking at her debt-to-assets ratio. Although she has a lot of debt (relative to assets and to net worth), she can earn enough income to cover its cost or interest expense, as shown by the interest coverage ratio.

Alice is earning well. Her income is larger than her assets. She is able to live efficiently. Her net income is a healthy 13.53% of her total income (net income margin), which means that her expenses are only 86.47% of it, but her cash flows are much less (cash flow to income), meaning that a significant portion of earnings is used up in making investments or, in Alice's case, debt repayments. In fact, her debt repayments don't leave her with much free cash flow; that is, cash flow not used up on living expenses or debts.

Looking at the ratios, it is even more apparent how much—and how subtle—a burden Alice's debt is. In addition to giving her negative net worth, it keeps her from increasing her assets and creating positive net worth—and potentially more income—by obligating her to use up her cash flows. Debt repayment keeps her from being able to invest.

Currently, Alice can afford the interest and the repayments. Her debt does not keep her from living her life, but it does limit her choices, which in turn restricts her decisions and future possibilities.

Comparisons over Time

Another useful way to compare financial statements is to look at how the situation has changed over time. Comparisons over time provide insights into the effects of past financial decisions and changes in circumstance. That insight can guide you in making future financial decisions, particularly in foreseeing the potential costs or benefits of a choice. Looking backward can be very helpful in looking forward.

Fast-forward ten years: Alice is now in her early thirties. Her career has progressed, and her income has grown. She has paid off her student loan and has begun to save for retirement and perhaps a down payment on a house.

A comparison of Alice's financial statements shows the change over the decade, both in absolute dollar amounts and as a percentage (see Table 3.15, Table 3.16, and Table 3.17). For the sake of simplicity, this example assumes that neither inflation nor deflation have significantly affected currency values during this period.

TABLE 3.15 Alice's Income Statements: Comparison over Time

For the Year Ending	Year 1	Year 11	Change	% Change
Gross wages	44,650	74,000	29,350	65.73%
Income taxes and deductions	8,930	18,500	9,570	107.17%
Disposable income	35,720	55,500	19,780	55.38%
Rent expense	10,800	18,000	7,200	66.67%
Food	3,900	3,900	0	0.00%
Car expenses	3,600	3,600	0	0.00%
Clothing	1,800	1,800	0	0.00%
Cell phone	1,200	1,200	0	0.00%
Internet and cable TV	1,200	1,200	0	0.00%
Entertainment, travel, etc.	2,700	5,200	2,500	92.59%
Total living expenses	25,200	34,900	9,700	38.49%
Car loan interest	240	757	517	215.42%
Student loan interest	4,240	0	-4,240	-100.00%
Total interest expense	4,480	757	-3,723	-83.10%
Net Income	6,040	19,843	13,803	228.53%

TABLE 3.16 Alice's Cash Flow Statements: Comparison over Time

For the Year Ending	Year 1	Year 11	Change	% Change
Cash from gross wages	44,650	74,000	29,350	65.73%
Cash paid for:				
Income taxes and deductions	-8,930	-18,500	-9,570	107.17%
Rent expense	-10,800	-18,000	-7,200	66.67%
Food	-3,900	-3,900	0	0.00%
Car expenses	-3,600	-3,600	0	0.00%
Clothing	-1,800	-1,800	0	0.00%
Cell phone	-1,200	-1,200	0	0.00%
Internet and cable TV	-1,200	-1,200	0	0.00%
Entertainment, travel, etc.	-2,700	-5,200	-2,500	92.59%
Car loan interest	-240	-757	-517	215.42%
Student loan interest	-4,240	0	4,240	-100.00%
Operating Cash Flows	6,040	19,843	13,803	228.53%
Cash invested in 401k	0	-3,000	-3,000	100.00%
Cash invested in car	0	-6,300	-6,300	100.00%
Investing Cash Flows	0	-9,300	-9,300	100.00%
Repayment of car loan	-2,160	-4,610	-2,450	113.43%
Repayment of student loan	-3,480	0	3,480	-100.00%
Financing Cash Flows	-5,640	-4,610	1,030	-18.26%
Net Cash Flow	400	5,933	5,533	1383.25%

TABLE 3.17 Alice's Balance Sheets: Comparison over Time

For the Year Ending	Year 1	Year 11	Change	% Change
Assets				
Cash/checking	0	5,000	5,000	100.00%
Savings	250	250	0	0.00%
Money Market	0	2,600	2,600	100.00%
Retirement 401k	0	13,000	13,000	100.00%
Retirement IRA	0	7,400	7,400	100.00%
Car	5,000	15,000	10,000	200.00%
Total Assets	5,250	43,250	38,000	723.81%
Liabilities				
Car loan	2,700	4,610	1,910	70.74%
Student loan	53,000	0	-53,000	-100.00%
Total Liabilities	55,700	4,610	-51,090	-91.72%
Net Worth	-50,450	38,640	89,090	176.59%

Starting with the income statement, Alice's income has increased. Her income tax withholding and deductions have also increased, but she still has higher disposable income (take-home pay). Many of her living expenses have remained consistent; rent and entertainment have increased. Interest expense on her car loan has increased, but since she has paid off her student loan, that interest expense has been eliminated, so her total interest expense has decreased. Overall, her net income, or personal profit, what she clears after covering her living expenses, has almost doubled.

Her cash flows have also improved. Operating cash flows, like net income, have almost doubled—due primarily to eliminating the student loan interest payment. The improved cash flow allowed her to make a down payment on a new car, invest in her 401(k), make the payments on her car loan, and still increase her net cash flow by a factor of ten.

Alice's balance sheet is most telling about the changes in her life, especially her now positive net worth. She has more assets. She has begun saving for retirement and has more liquidity, distributed in her checking, savings, and money market accounts. Since she has less debt, having paid off her student loan, she now has positive net worth.

Comparing the relative results of the common-size statements provides an even deeper view of the relative changes in Alice's situation (Table 3.18, Table 3.19, and Table 3.20).

TABLE 3.18 Comparing Alice's Common-Size Statements: Income Statements

For the Year Ending	Year 1	Year 11
Gross wages	100.00%	100.00%
Income taxes and deductions	20.00%	25.00%
Disposable income	80.00%	75.00%
Rent expense	24.19%	24.32%
Food	8.73%	5.27%
Car expenses	8.06%	4.86%
Clothing	4.03%	2.43%
Cell phone	2.69%	1.62%
Internet and cable TV	2.69%	1.62%
Entertainment, travel, etc.	6.05%	7.03%
Total living expenses	56.44%	47.16%
Car loan interest	0.54%	1.02%
Student loan interest	9.50%	0.00%
Total interest expense	10.03%	1.02%
Net Income	13.53%	26.81%

TABLE 3.19 Comparing Alice's Common-Size Statements: Cash Flow Statements

For the Year Ending	Year 1	Year 11
Cash from gross wages	100.00%	100.00%
Cash paid for:		
Income taxes and deductions	-20.00%	-25.00%
Rent expense	-24.19%	-24.32%
Food	-8.73%	-5.27%
Car expenses	-8.06%	-4.86%
Clothing	-4.03%	-2.43%
Cell phone	-2.69%	-1.62%
Internet and cable TV	-2.69%	-1.62%
Entertainment, travel, etc.	-6.05%	-7.03%
Car loan interest	-0.54%	-1.02%
Student loan interest	-9.50%	0.00%
Operating Cash Flows	13.53%	26.81%
Cash invested in 401k	0.00%	-4.05%
Cash invested in car	0.00%	-8.51%
Investing Cash Flows	0.00%	-12.57%
Repayment of car loan	-4.84%	-6.23%
Repayment of student loan	-7.79%	0.00%
Financing Cash Flows	-12.63%	-6.23%
Net Cash Flow	0.90%	8.02%

TABLE 3.20 Comparing Alice's Common-Size Statements: Balance Sheets

For the Year Ending	Year 1	Year 11
Assets		
Cash/checking	0.00%	11.56%
Savings	4.76%	0.58%
Money Market	0.00%	6.01%
Retirement 401k	0.00%	30.06%
Retirement IRA	0.00%	17.11%
Car	95.24%	34.68%
Total Assets	100.00%	100.00%
Liabilities	0.00%	0.00%
Car loan	51.43%	10.66%
Student loan	1009.52%	0.00%
Total Liabilities	1060.95%	10.66%
Net Worth	-960.95%	89.34%

Although income taxes and rent have increased as a percentage of income, living expenses have declined, showing real progress for Alice in raising her standard of living: it now costs her less of her income to sustain herself. Interest expense has decreased substantially as a portion of income, resulting in a net income or personal profit that is not only larger, but is larger relative to income. More of her income is profit, left for other discretionary uses.

The change in operating cash flows confirms this. Although her investing activities now represent a significant use of cash, her need to use cash in financing activities—debt repayment—is so much less that her net cash flow has increased substantially. The cash that used to have to go toward supporting debt obligations now goes toward building an asset base, some of which (the 401(k)) may provide income in the future.

Changes in the balance sheet show a much more diversified and therefore much less risky asset base. Although almost half of Alice's assets are restricted for specific purposes, such as her 401(k) account and individual retirement account (IRA), she still has significantly more liquidity and more liquid assets. Debt has fallen from 10 times the assets' value to one-tenth of it, creating some ownership for Alice.

Finally, Alice can compare her ratios over time (Table 3.21).

TABLE 3.21 Ratio Analysis Comparison

Ratio Analysis	Year 1	Year 11
Net Income Margin	0.1353	0.2681
Return on Assets	1.1505	0.4588
Return on Net Worth	-0.1197	0.5135
Debt-to-Assets	10.6095	0.1066
Interest Coverage	1.3482	26.2127
Cash Flow to Income	0.0662	0.2990
Cash Flow to Assets	0.0762	0.1372
Free Cash Flow	1.0000	2.5675

Most immediately, her net worth is now positive, and so are the return-on-net-worth and the total debt ratios. As her debt has become less significant, her ability to afford it has improved (to pay for its interest and repayment). Both her interest coverage and free cash flow ratios show large increases. Since her net income margin (and income) has grown, the only reason her return-on-asset ratio has decreased is because her assets have grown even faster than her income.

By analyzing over time, you can spot trends that may be happening too slowly or too subtly for you to notice in daily living, but which may become significant over time. You would want to keep a closer eye on your finances than Alice does, however, and review your situation at least every year.

Key Takeaways

- Each financial statement shows a piece of the larger picture. Financial statement analysis puts the financial statement information in context and so in sharper focus.
- Common-size statements show the size of each item relative to a common denominator.
- On the income statement, each income and expense is shown as a percentage of total income.
- On the cash flow statement, each cash flow is shown as a percentage of total positive cash flow.
- On the balance sheet, each asset, liability, and net worth is shown as a percentage of total assets.
- The income and cash flow statements explain the changes in the balance sheet over time.
- Ratio analysis is a way of creating a context by comparing items from different statements.
- Comparisons made over time can demonstrate the effects of past decisions to better understand the significance of future decisions.
- Financial statements should be compared at least annually.

Exercises

1. Prepare common-size statements for your income statement, cash flow statement, and balance sheet. What do your common-size statements reveal about your financial situation? How will your common-size statements influence your personal financial planning?
2. Calculate your debt-to-income ratio and other ratios using the financial tools described in the article "Are You In Over Your Head" (https://money.usnews.com/money/personal-finance/articles/2012/03/29/are-you-in-over-your-head). According to the calculation, are you carrying a healthy debt load? Why, or why not? If not, what can you do to improve your situation?
3. Read this article (https://www.moneycontrol.com/news/business/personal-finance/-1895677.html) about using personal financial ratios. The article stresses using ratios that describe liquidity and savings. Calculate your own savings ratio. According to this calculation, are you saving enough? What does your liquidity ratio tell you about how much you can save?
4. If you increased your income and assets and reduced your expenses and debt, your personal wealth and liquidity would grow. In My Notes or in your personal financial journal, outline a general plan for how you would use or allocate your growing wealth to further reduce your expenses and debt, to acquire more assets or improve your standard of living, and to further increase your real or potential income.

3.4 Accounting Software: An Overview

Learning Objectives

1. Identify the uses of personal finance software.
2. List the common features of personal financial software.
3. Demonstrate how actual financial calculations may be accomplished using personal financial software.
4. Discuss how personal financial software can assist in your personal financial decisions.

Many software products are available to help you organize your financial information to be more useful in making financial decisions. They are designed to make the record-keeping aspects of personal finance—the collection, classification, and sorting of financial data—as easy as possible. The programs also are designed to produce summary reports such as income statements, cash flow statements, and balance sheets, as well as many calculations that may be useful for various aspects of financial planning. For example, financial planning software exists for managing education and retirement savings, debt and mortgage repayment, and income and expense budgeting.

Collecting the Data

Most programs have designed their data input to look like a checkbook, which is what most people use to keep personal financial records. This type of user interface is intended to be recognizable and familiar, similar to the manual record keeping that you already do.

FIGURE 3.8

© Shutterstock, Inc.

When you input your checkbook data into the program, the software does the bookkeeping—creating the journals, ledgers, adjustments, and trial balances that generations of people have done, albeit more tediously, with parchment and quill or with ledger paper and pencil. Most personal financial transactions happen as cash flows through a checking account, so the checkbook becomes the primary source of data.

More and more, personal transactions are done by electronic transfer; that is, no paper changes hands, but cash still flows to and from an account, usually a checking account.

Data for other transactions, such as income from investments or changes in investment value, are usually received from periodic statements issued by investment managers, such as banks where you have savings accounts; brokers or mutual fund companies that manage investments; or employers' retirement account statements.

Most versions of personal financial software allow you to download account information directly from the source—your bank, broker, or employer—which saves you from manually entering the data into the program. Aside from providing convenience, downloading directly should eliminate human error in transferring the data.

Reporting Results and Planning Ahead

All personal financial software produces the essential summary reports—the income statement, cash flow statement, and balance sheet—that show the results of financial activity for the period. Most will also report more specific aspects of activities, such as listing all transactions for a particular income or expense.

Most will provide separate reports on activities that have some tax consequence, since users always need to be aware of tax obligations and the tax consequences of financial decisions. Some programs, especially those produced by companies that also sell tax software, allow you to export data from your financial software to your tax program, which makes tax preparation—or at least tax record keeping—easier. In some programs, you need to know which activities are taxable and flag them as such. Some programs recognize that information already, while others may still prompt you for tax information.

All programs allow you to play "what if": a marvelous feature of computing power and the virtual world in general and certainly helpful when it comes to making financial decisions. All programs include a budgeting feature that allows you to foresee or project possible scenarios and gauge your ability to live with them. This feature is particularly useful when budgeting for income and living expenses. (Budgeting is discussed more thoroughly in Chapter 5.) Most programs have features that allow you to project the results of savings plans for education or retirement. None can dictate the future, or allow you to, but they can certainly help you to have a better view.

Security, Benefits, and Costs

All programs are designed to be installed on a personal computer or a handheld device such as a smartphone or tablet, but some can also be run from a website or a cloud and so do not require a download.

As with all Internet transactions, you should be aware that the more your data is transferred, downloaded, or exported over the Internet, the more exposed it is to theft. Personal financial data theft is a serious and growing problem worldwide, and security systems are hard pressed to keep up with the ingenuity of hackers. The convenience gained by having your bank, brokerage, tax preparer, and so on accessible to you (and your data accessible to them) or your data accessible to you wherever you are must be weighed against the increased exposure to data theft. As always, the potential benefit should be considered against the costs.

Keeping digital records of your finances may be more secure than keeping them scattered in shoeboxes or files, exposed to risks such as fire, flood, and theft. Digital records are often easily retrievable because the software organizes them systematically for you. Space is not a practical issue with digital storage, so records may be kept longer. As with anything digital, however, you must be diligent about backing up your data, although many programs will do that automatically or regularly prompt you to do so. Hard copy records must be disposed of periodically, and judging how long to keep them is always difficult. Throwing them in the trash may be risky because of "dumpster diving," a well-known method of identity theft, so documents with financial information should always be shredded before disposal.

Personal financial software is usually quite reasonably priced, with many programs selling for less than $50, and most for less than $100. Many programs now are cloud-based, with monthly or annual subscription payments. Buying the software usually costs less than buying an hour of accounting expertise from an accountant or financial planner. While software cannot replace financial planning professionals who provide valuable judgment, it can allow you to hire them only for their judgment and not have to pay them to collect, classify, sort, and report your financial data.

A great way to research different software options is to read reviews online. There are many websites—from *The Wall Street Journal* (http://guides.wsj.com/personal-finance/managing-your-money/how-to-choose-and-use-financial-software/) to *Consumer Reports* (https://www.consumerreports.org/cro/2014/03/simplify-your-financial-life/index.htm)—that will give you a quick comparison of costs and features as well as more in-depth and user reviews.

Software will not improve your financial situation, but it can improve the organization of your financial data monthly and yearly, allowing you a much clearer view and almost certainly a much better understanding of your situation.

Key Takeaways

- Personal finance software provides convenience and skill for collecting, classifying, sorting, reporting, and securing financial data to better assess you current situation.
- To help you better evaluate your choices, personal finance software provides calculations for projecting information such as the following:
  - Education savings
  - Retirement savings
  - Debt repayment
  - Mortgage repayment
  - Income and expense budgeting

Exercises

1. Explore free online resources for developing and comparing baseline personal financial statements. One good resource is a blog from Money Musings called "It's Your Money" (http://www.mdmproofing.com/iym/networth.shtml). This site also explains how and where to find the figures you need for accurate and complete income statements and balance sheets.
2. Compare and contrast the features of popular personal financial planning software at the following websites: Mint.com (http://www.mint.com), Quicken.intuit.com (http://www.quicken.intuit.com), and Moneydance.com (http://www.moneydance.com). In My Notes or your personal finance journal, record your findings. Which software, if any, would be your first choice, and why? Share your experience and views with others taking this course.
3. View these videos online and discuss with classmates your answers to the questions that follow.
   a. "Three Principles of Personal Finance" by the founder of Mint: http://www.youtube.com/watch?v=IRVzqROJmR4. What are the three principles of personal finance described in this video? How is each principle relevant to you and your personal financial situation? What will be the outcome of observing the three principles?
   b. A financial planner explains what goes into a financial plan in "How to Create a Financial Plan": http://www.youtube.com/watch?v=Wmhif6hmPTQ. According to this video, what goes into a financial plan? What aspects of financial planning do you already have in place? What aspects of financial planning should you consider next?
   c. Certified Financial Planner (CFP) Board's Financial Planning Clinic, Washington, DC, October 2008: http://www.youtube.com/watch?v=eJS5FMF_CFA. Each year the Certified Financial Planner Board conducts a clinic in which people can get free advice about all areas of financial planning. This video is about the 2008 Financial Planning Clinic in Washington, DC. What reasons or benefits did people express about attending this event?

Endnotes

1. Luca Pacioli, *Summa de arithmetica, geometria, proportioni et proportionalita* (Venice: Luca Pacioli, 1494). For more information on Pacioli, see Wikipedia, "Luca Pacioli," http://en.wikipedia.org/wiki/Luca_Pacioli (accessed May 3, 2014).
2. BankruptcyData.com, "A Brief History of Bankruptcy," http://www.bankruptcydata.com/Ch11History.htm (accessed May 3, 2014).
3. Sandy Baum, Jennifer Ma, and Kathleen Payea, *Education Pays: The Benefits of Higher Education for Individuals and Society* (Princeton, NJ: The College Board, 2013).
4. U.S. Department of the Treasury, "Taxes and Society," Resource Center, http://www.treasury.gov/resource-center/faqs/Taxes/Pages/taxes-society.aspx (accessed August 6, 2014).
5. Adam Smith, *The Wealth of Nations* (New York: The Modern Library, 2000), Book I, Chapter ix.

CHAPTER 4

Evaluating Choices: Time, Risk, and Value

4.1 Introduction

> *"The land may vary more/ But wherever the truth may be/ The water comes ashore/ And the people look at the sea."*
>
> — Robert Frost, from "Neither Out Far Nor In Deep"

FIGURE 4.1

Financial decisions can only be made about the future. As much as analysis may tell us about the outcomes of past decisions, the past is "sunk": it can be known but not decided upon. Decisions are made about the future, which cannot be known with certainty, so evaluating alternatives for financial decisions always involves speculation on both the kind of result and the value of the result that will occur. It also involves understanding and measuring the risks or uncertainties that time presents and the opportunities—and opportunity costs—that time creates.

4.2 The Time Value of Money

Learning Objectives

1. Explain the value of liquidity.
2. Demonstrate how time creates distance, risk, and opportunity cost.
3. Demonstrate how time affects liquidity.
4. Analyze how time affects value.

Part of the planning process is evaluating the possible future results of a decision. Since those results will occur some time from now, it is critical to understand how time passing may affect those benefits and costs—not only the probability of their occurrence, but also their value when they do. Time affects value because time affects liquidity.

Liquidity is valuable, and the liquidity of an asset affects its value: all things being equal, the more liquid an asset is, the better. This relationship—how the passage of time affects the liquidity of money and thus its value—is commonly referred to as the **time value of money**, which can actually be calculated concretely as well as understood abstractly.

FIGURE 4.2

© Shutterstock, Inc.

time value of money

The impact of the passing of time on the value of money, based on the premise that being separated from liquidity creates opportunity cost.

transaction cost

The costs of achieving a trade or "doing a deal" that do not contribute to the value of the thing being traded; a cost created by making an economic transaction.

Suppose you go to Mexico, where the currency is the peso. Coming from the United States, you have a fistful of dollars. When you get there, you are hungry. You see and smell a taco stand and decide to have a taco. Before you can buy the taco, however, you have to get some pesos so that you can pay for it because the right currency is needed to trade in that market. You have wealth (your fistful of dollars), but you don't have wealth that is liquid. In order to change your dollars into pesos and acquire liquidity, you need to exchange currency. There is a fee to exchange your currency: a **transaction cost**, which is the cost of simply making the trade. It also takes a bit of time, and you could be doing other things, so it creates an opportunity cost (see Chapter 2). There is also the chance that you won't be able to make the exchange for some reason, or that it will cost more than you thought, so there is a bit of risk involved. Obtaining liquidity for your wealth creates transaction costs, opportunity costs, and risk.

In general, transforming not-so-liquid wealth into liquid wealth creates transaction costs, opportunity costs, and risk, all of which take away from the value of wealth. Liquidity has value because it can be used without any additional costs.

One dimension of difference between not-so-liquid wealth and liquidity is time. Cash flows (CF) in the past are sunk, cash flows in the present are liquid, and cash flows in the future are not yet liquid. You can only choose to use liquid wealth, not with cash that you don't have yet or that has already been spent. Separated from your liquidity and your choices by time, there is an opportunity cost: if you had liquidity now, you could use it for consumption or investment and benefit from it now. There is also risk, as there is always some uncertainty about the future: whether or not you will actually get your cash flows and just how much they'll be worth when you do.

The further in the future cash flows are, the further away you are from your liquidity, the more opportunity cost and risk you have, and the more that takes away from the present value (PV) of your wealth, which is not yet liquid. In other words, time puts distance between you and your liquidity, and that creates costs that take away from value. The more time there is, the larger its effect on the value of wealth.

Financial plans are expected to happen in the future, so financial decisions are based on values some distance away in time. You could be trying to project an amount at some point in the future—perhaps an investment payout or college tuition payment. Or perhaps you are thinking about a series of cash flows that happen over time—for example, annual deposits into and then withdrawals from a retirement account. To really understand the time value of those cash flows, or to compare them in any reasonable way, you have to understand the relationships between the nominal or face values in the future and their equivalent, present values, or what their values would be if they were liquid today. The equivalent present values today will be less than the nominal or face values in the future because that distance over time, that separation from liquidity, costs us by discounting those values.

Key Takeaways

- Liquidity has value because it enables choice.
- Time creates distance or delay from liquidity.
- Distance or delay creates risk and opportunity costs.
- Time affects value by creating distance, risk, and opportunity costs.
- Time discounts value.

Exercises

1. How does the expression "a bird in the hand is worth two in the bush" relate to the concept of the time value of money?
2. In what four ways can "delay to liquidity" affect the value of your wealth?

4.3 Calculating the Relationship of Time and Value

Learning Objectives

1. Identify the factors you need to know to relate a present value to a future value.
2. Write the algebraic expression for the relationship between present and future value.
3. Discuss the use of the algebraic expression in evaluating the relationship between present and future values.
4. Explain the importance of understanding the relationships among the factors that affect future value.

Financial calculation is not often a necessary skill, since it is easier to use calculators, spreadsheets, and software. However, understanding the calculations is important in understanding what they represent: the relationships among time, risk, opportunity cost, and value.

To do the math, you need to know

- what the future cash flows (CF) will be,
- when the future cash flows will be,
- the rate at which time affects value (e.g., the costs per time period, or the magnitude [the size or amount] of the effect of time on value).

discount rate

The effect of time on value or the rate at which time affects value; used when calculating the equivalent present value of a nominal future value.

It is usually not difficult to forecast the timing and amounts of future cash flows. Although there may be some uncertainty about them, gauging the rate at which time affects money can require some judgment. That rate, commonly called the **discount rate** because time discounts value, is the opportunity cost of not having liquidity. Opportunity cost derives from forgone choices or sacrificed alternatives, and sometimes it is not clear what those might have been (see Chapter 2). It is an important judgment call to make, though, because the rate will directly affect the valuation process.

FIGURE 4.3

© Shutterstock, Inc.

At times, the alternatives are clear: you could be putting the liquidity in an account earning 3%, so that's your opportunity cost of not having it. Or you are paying 6.5% on a loan, which you wouldn't be paying if you had enough liquidity to avoid having to borrow, so that's your opportunity cost. Sometimes, however, your opportunity cost is not so clear.

Say today is your 20th birthday. Your grandparents have promised to give you $1,000 for your 21st birthday, one year from today. If you had the money today, what would it be worth? That is, how much would $1,000 worth of liquidity one year from now be worth today?

That depends on the cost of its not being liquid today, or on the opportunity costs and risks created by not having liquidity today. If you had $1,000 today, you could buy things and enjoy them, or you could deposit it in an interest-bearing account. If you save the money, you would have more than $1,000 on your 21st birthday. You would have the $1,000 plus whatever interest it had earned. If your bank pays 4% per year (interest rates are always stated as annual rates) on your account, then you would earn $40 of interest in the next year, or $1,000 × 0.04. So, on your 21st birthday, you would have $1,040.

$$1,000 + (1,000 \times 0.04) = 1,000 \times (1 + 0.04) = 1,040$$

Today	Interest Rate	Time (years)	One Year from Now
$1,000$	0.04	1	$1,040 = 1,000 \times (1 + 0.04)$

If you left that amount in the bank until your 22nd birthday, you would have

$$\begin{aligned} &1,040 + (1,040 \times 0.04) \\ &= 1,040 \times (1 + 0.04) \\ &= [1,000 \times (1 + 0.04)] \times (1 + 0.04) \\ &= 1,040 \times (1 + 0.04)^2 \\ &= 1,081.60 \end{aligned}$$

present value

Liquid value in the present, or the discounted value of a nominal amount of future liquidity, taking into account the effect of time on value.

future value

The value of a present liquidity or projected series of cash flows in the future, accounting for the effects of time on value.

To generalize the computation, if your **present value**, or PV, is your value today, *r* is the rate at which time affects value or discount rate (in this case, your interest rate), and if *t* is the number of time periods between you and your liquidity, then the **future value**, or FV, of your wealth would be

Today	Interest Rate	Time (years)	One Year from Now
$1,000$	0.04	1	$1,040 = 1,000 \times (1 + 0.04)^1$
$1,000$	0.04	2	$1,081.60 = 1,000 \times (1 + 0.04)^2$
PV	r	t	$FV = PV \times (1 + r)^t$

$$PV \times (1 + r)^t = FV$$

In this case,

$$1,000 \times (1 + 0.04)^1 = 1,040$$

and

$$1,000 \times (1 + 0.04)^2 = 1,081.60$$

Assuming there is little chance that your grandparents will not be able to give this gift, there is negligible risk. Your only cost of not having liquidity now is the opportunity cost of having to delay consumption or not earning the interest you could have earned.

The cost of delayed consumption is largely derived from a subjective valuation of whatever is consumed, or its **utility** or satisfaction. The more value you place on having something, the more it "costs" you not to have it, and the more the time that you are without it affects its value.

utility

Value, including subjective or nonmarket value as well as objective or market value.

Assuming that if you had the money today you would save it (as it's much harder to quantify your joy from consumption), by having to wait to get it until your 21st birthday—and *not* having it today—you miss out on $40 it could have earned.

So, what would that nominal $1,000 (that future value that you get one year from now) actually be worth today? The rate at which time affects your value is 4% because that's what having a choice (spend it or invest it) could earn for you if only you had received the $1,000. That's your opportunity cost. That's what it costs you to not have liquidity. Since

$$PV \times (1 + r)^t = FV$$

then

$$PV = \frac{FV}{(1 + r)^t}$$

so

$$PV = \frac{1,000}{(1 + 0.04)^1} = 961.5385$$

Your gift is worth $961.5385 today (its present value). If your grandparents offered to give you your 21st birthday gift on your 20th birthday, they could give you $961.5385 today, which would be the equivalent value to you of getting $1,000 one year from now.

It is important to understand the relationships between time, risk, opportunity cost, and value. This equation describes that relationship:

$$PV \times (1 + r)^t = FV$$

The "r" is more formally called the "discount rate" because it is the rate at which your liquidity is discounted by time, and it includes not only opportunity costs but also risk. (On some financial calculators, "r" is displayed as "I" or "i.")

The "t" is how far away you are from your liquidity over time.

Studying this equation yields valuable insights into the relationship it describes. Looking at the equation, you can observe the following relationships.

The more time (t) separating you from your liquidity, the more time affects value. The less time separating you from your liquidity, the less time affects value .

As *t* increases	the PV of your FV liquidity decreases
As *t* decreases	the PV of your FV liquidity increases

The greater the rate at which time affects value (r), or the greater the opportunity cost and risk, the more time affects value. The less your opportunity cost or risk, the less your value is affected.

As *r* increases	the PV of your FV liquidity decreases
As *r* decreases	the PV of your FV liquidity increases

Table 4.1 presents examples of these relationships.

TABLE 4.1 Present Values, Interest Rates, Time, and Future Values

	Today	Interest Rate	Time (years)	Future Value
Example A	1,000	0.04	1	1,040 = PV × 1.04
Greater effect r increases	1,000	0.10	1	1,100 = PV × 1.10
More time t increases	1,000	0.04	3	1,124.86 = PV × 1.04^3
Less effect r decreases	1,000	0.01	1	1,010 = PV × 1.01
Less time t decreases	1,000	0.04	0.5	1,019.80 = PV × $1.04^{0.5}$
Example B	961.54 = FV ÷ 1.04	0.04	1	1,000
Greater effect r increases	909.09 = FV ÷ 1.10	0.10	1	1,000
More time t increases	889.00 = FV ÷ 1.04^3	0.04	3	1,000
Less effect r decreases	990.10 = FV ÷ 1.01	0.01	1	1,000
Less time t decreases	980.58 = FV ÷ $1.04^{0.5}$	0.04	0.5	1,000

The strategy implications of this understanding are simple, yet critical. All things being equal, it is more valuable to have liquidity (get paid, or have positive cash flow) *sooner* rather than later and give up liquidity (pay out, or have negative cash flow) *later* rather than sooner.

If possible, accelerate incoming cash flows and decelerate outgoing cash flows: get paid sooner, but pay out later. Or, as Popeye's pal Wimpy used to say, "I'll give you 50 cents tomorrow for a hamburger today."

Key Takeaways

- To relate a present (liquid) value to a future value, you need to know
  - what the present value is or the future value will be,

- when the future value will be,
- the rate at which time affects value: the costs per time period, or the magnitude of the effect of time on value.
- The relationship of
  - present value (PV),
  - future value (FV),
  - risk and opportunity cost (the discount rate, r), and
  - time (t), may be expressed as
  - $PV \times (1 + r)^t = FV$.
- The above equation yields valuable insights into these relationships:
  - The more time (t) creates distance from liquidity, the more time affects value.
  - The greater the rate at which time affects value (r), or the greater the opportunity cost and risk, the more time affects value.
  - The closer the liquidity, the less time affects value.
  - The less the opportunity cost or risk, the less value is affected.
- To maximize value, get paid sooner and pay later.

Exercises

1. In My Notes or your financial planning journal, identify a future cash flow. Calculate its present value and then calculate its future value based on the discount rate and time to liquidity. Repeat the process for other future cash flows you identify. What pattern of relationships do you observe between time and value?
2. Try the Time Value of Money calculator at http://www.money-zine.com/Calculators/Investment-Calculators/Time-Value-of-Money-Calculator/. How do the results compare with your calculations in Exercise 1?
3. View the animated audio slide show "The Time Value of Money" at https://www.khanacademy.org/economics-finance-domain/core-finance/interest-tutorial/present-value/v/time-value-of-money. This slide show will walk you through an example of how to calculate the present and future values of money.
4. To have more liquidity, when should you increase positive cash flows and decrease negative cash flows, and why?

4.4 Valuing a Series of Cash Flows

Learning Objectives

1. Discuss the importance of the idea of the time value of money in financial decisions.
2. Define the present value of a series of cash flows.
3. Define an annuity.
4. Identify the factors you need to know to calculate the value of an annuity.
5. Discuss the relationships of those factors to the annuity's value.
6. Define a perpetuity.

It is quite common in finance to have to value a series of future cash flows (CF), perhaps a series of withdrawals from a retirement account, interest payments from a bond, or deposits for a savings account. The present value (PV) of the series of cash flows is equal to the sum of the present value of each cash flow, so valuation is straightforward: find the present value of each cash flow and then add them up.

FIGURE 4.4

annuity

A series of cash flows in which equal amounts happen at regular, periodic intervals.

Often, the series of cash flows is such that each cash flow has the same future value. When there are regular payments at regular intervals and each payment is the same amount, that series of cash flows is an **annuity**. Most consumer loan repayments are annuities, as are, typically, installment purchases, mortgages, retirement investments, savings plans, and retirement plan payouts. Fixed-rate bond interest payments are an annuity, as are stable stock dividends over long periods of time. You could think of your paycheck as an annuity, as are many living expenses, such as groceries and utilities, for which you pay roughly the same amount regularly.

To calculate the present value of an annuity, you need to know

- the amount of the future cash flows (the same for each),
- the frequency of the cash flows,
- the number of cash flows (t),
- the rate at which time affects value (r).

Almost any calculator and the many readily available software applications can do the math for you, but it is important for you to understand the relationships between time, risk, opportunity cost, and value.

Here is how those relationships look mathematically.

$$PV_{Annuity} = CF\left[\frac{1-\frac{1}{(1+r)^t}}{r}\right]$$

To find the present value (PV) of an annuity, you need to know the amount of each equal cash flow (CF), the number of cash flows (t), and the rate at which time affects value or the discount rate (r).

The future value of an annuity (FV) is, like any FV,

$$FV_{Annuity} = PV_{Annuity}(1+r)^t$$

$$FV_{Annuity} = CF\left[\frac{1-\frac{1}{(1+r)^t}}{r}\right](1+r)^t$$

which simplifies to

$$FV_{Annuity} = CF\left[\frac{(1+r)^t-1}{r}\right]$$

To find the future value (FV) of an annuity, you need to know the amount of each equal cash flow (CF), the number of cash flows (t), and the rate at which time affects value or the discount rate (r).

If you win the lottery, for example, you are typically offered a choice of payouts for your winnings: a lump sum or an annual payment over 20 years.

The lottery agency would prefer that you took the annual payment because it would not have to give up as much liquidity all at once; it could hold on to its liquidity longer. To make the annual payment more attractive for you—it isn't, because you would want to have more liquidity sooner—the lump-sum option is discounted to reflect the present value of the payment annuity. The discount rate, which determines that present value, is chosen at the discretion of the lottery agency.

Say you win $10 million. The lottery agency offers you a choice: take $500,000 per year over 20 years or take a one-time lump-sum payout of $6,700,000. You would choose the alternative with the greatest value. The present value of the lump-sum payout is $6,700,000. The value of the annuity is not simply $10 million, or $500,000 × 20, because those $500,000 payments are received over time and time affects liquidity and thus value. So the question is, What is the annuity worth to you?

Your discount rate or opportunity cost will determine the annuity's value to you, as Table 4.2 shows.

TABLE 4.2 Lottery Present Value with Different Discount Rates

CF	Rate (*r*) in Percent	Time (*t*) in Years	PV
500,000	0.0200	20	8,175,717
500,000	0.0400	20	6,795,163
500,000	0.0600	20	5,734,961
500,000	0.0800	20	4,909,074
500,000	0.1000	20	4,256,782
500,000	0.1200	20	3,734,722
500,000	0.1400	20	3,311,565
500,000	0.0416	20	6,700,000

As expected, the present value of the annuity is less if your discount rate—or opportunity cost or next best choice—is more. The annuity would be worth the same to you as the lump-sum payout if your discount rate were 4.16%.

In other words, if your discount rate is about 4% or less—if you don't have more lucrative choices than earning 4% with that liquidity—then the annuity is worth more to you than the immediate payout. You can afford to wait for that liquidity and collect it over 20 years because you have no better choice. On the other hand, if your discount rate is higher than 4%, or if you feel that your use of that liquidity would earn you more than 4%, then you have more lucrative things to do with that money and you want it now: the annuity is worth less to you than the payout.

For an annuity, as when relating one cash flow's present and future value, the greater the rate at which time affects value, the greater the effect on the present value. When opportunity cost or risk is low, waiting for liquidity doesn't matter as much as when opportunity costs or risks are higher. When opportunity costs are low, you have nothing better to do with your liquidity, but when opportunity costs are higher, you may sacrifice more by having no liquidity. Liquidity is valuable because it allows you to make choices. After all, if there are no more valuable choices to make, you lose little by giving up liquidity. The higher the rate at which time affects value, the more it costs to wait for liquidity, and the more choices pass you by while you wait for liquidity.

When risk is low, it is not really important to have your liquidity firmly in hand any sooner because you'll have it sooner or later anyhow. But when risk is high, getting liquidity sooner becomes more important because it lessens the chance of not getting it at all. The higher the rate at which time affects value, the more risk there is in waiting for liquidity and the more chance that you won't get it at all.

As *r* increases	the PV of the annuity decreases
As *r* decreases	the PV of the annuity increases

You can also look at the relationship of time and cash flow to annuity value. Suppose your payout was more (or less) each year, or suppose your payout happened over more (or fewer) years (Table 4.3).

TABLE 4.3 Lottery Payout Present Values

CF	Rate	Time	PV
500,000	0.0400	20	6,795,163
500,000	0.0200	20	8,175,717
500,000	0.0600	20	5,734,961
750,000	0.0400	20	10,192,745
250,000	0.0400	20	3,397,582
500,000	0.0400	30	8,646,017
500,000	0.0400	10	4,055,448

As seen in Table 4.3, the amount of each payment, or cash flow, affects the value of the annuity because more cash means more liquidity and greater value.

As CF increases	the PV of the annuity increases
As CF decreases	the PV of the annuity decreases

Although time increases the distance from liquidity, with an annuity, it also increases the number of payments because payments occur periodically. The more periods in the annuity, the more cash flows and the more liquidity there are, thus increasing the value of the annuity.

As *t* increases	the PV of the annuity increases
As *t* decreases	the PV of the annuity decreases

It is common in financial planning to calculate the FV of a series of cash flows. This calculation is useful when saving for a goal where a specific amount will be required at a specific point in the future (e.g., saving for college, a wedding, or retirement).

It turns out that the relationships between time, risk, opportunity cost, and value are predictable going forward as well. Say you decide to take the $500,000 annual lottery payout for 20 years. If you deposit that payout in a bank account earning 4%, how much would you have in 20 years? What if the account earned more interest? Less interest? What if you won more (or less) so the payout was more (or less) each year?

What if you won $15 million and the payout was $500,000 per year for 30 years, how much would you have then? Or if you won $5 million and the payout was only for 10 years? Table 4.4 shows how future values would change.

TABLE 4.4 Lottery Payout Future Values

CF	Rate	Time	PV	FV
500,000	0.0400	20	6,795,163	14,889,039
500,000	0.0200	20	8,175,717	12,148,685
500,000	0.0600	20	5,734,961	18,392,796
750,000	0.0400	20	10,192,745	22,333,559
250,000	0.0400	20	3,397,582	7,444,520
500,000	0.0400	30	8,646,017	28,042,469
500,000	0.0400	10	4,055,448	6,003,054

Going forward, the rate at which time affects value (r) is the rate at which value grows, or the rate at which your value compounds. It is also called the **rate of compounding**. The bigger the effect of time on value, the more value you will end up with because more time has affected the value of your money while it was growing as it waited for you. So, looking forward at the future value of an annuity:

rate of compounding

The effect of time on value or the rate at which time affects value; used when calculating the equivalent future value of a present amount of liquidity.

As *r* increases	the FV of the annuity increases
As *r* decreases	the FV of the annuity decreases

The amount of each payment or cash flow affects the value of the annuity because more cash means more liquidity and greater value. If you were getting more cash each year and depositing it into your account, you'd end up with more value.

As CF increases	the FV of the annuity increases
As CF decreases	the FV of the annuity decreases

The more time there is, the more time can affect value. As payments occur periodically, the more cash flows there are, the more liquidity there is. The more periods in the annuity, the more cash flows, and the greater the effect of time, thus increasing the future value of the annuity.

As *t* increases	the FV of the annuity increases
As *t* decreases	the FV of the annuity decreases

There is also a special kind of annuity called a **perpetuity**, which is an annuity that goes on forever (i.e., a series of cash flows of equal amounts occurring at regular intervals that never ends). It is hard to imagine a stream of cash flows that never ends, but it is actually not so rare as it sounds. The dividends from a share of corporate stock are a perpetuity, because in theory, a corporation has an infinite life (as a separate legal entity from its shareholders or owners) and because, for many reasons, corporations like to maintain a steady dividend for their shareholders.

perpetuity

An infinite annuity; a stream of periodic cash flows that continues indefinitely.

The perpetuity represents the maximum value of the annuity, or the value of the annuity with the most cash flows and therefore the most liquidity and therefore the most value.

Life Is a Series of Cash Flows

Once you understand the idea of the time value of money, and of its use for valuing a series of cash flows and of annuities in particular, you can't believe how you ever got through life without it.

These are the fundamental relationships that structure so many financial decisions, most of which involve a series of cash inflows or outflows. Understanding these relationships can be a tool to help you answer some of the most common financial questions about buying and selling liquidity, because loans and investments are so often structured as annuities and certainly take place over time.

Loans are usually designed as annuities, with regular periodic payments that include interest expense and principal repayment. Using these relationships, you can see the effect of a different amount borrowed ($PV_{annuity}$), interest rate (r), or term of the loan (t) on the periodic payment (CF).

For example, if you get a $250,000 (PV), 30-year (t), 6.5% (r) mortgage, the monthly payment will be $1,577 (CF). If the same mortgage had an interest rate of only 5.5% (r), your monthly payment would decrease to $1,423 (CF). If it were a 15-year (t) mortgage, still at 6.5% (r), the monthly payment would be $2,175 (CF). If you can make a larger down payment and borrow less, say $200,000 (PV), then with a 30-year (t), 6.5% (r) mortgage you monthly payment would be only $1,262 (CF) (Table 4.5).

TABLE 4.5 Mortgage Calculations

CF	Rate (*r*)	Time (*t*)	PV
1,577	0.0054	360	250,000
1,423	0.0046	360	250,000
2,175	0.0054	180	250,000
1,262	0.0054	360	200,000

Note that in Table 4.5 the mortgage rate is the monthly rate, that is, the annual rate divided by 12 (months in the year) or $r \div 12$, and that t is stated as the number of months, or the number of years × 12 (months in the year). That is because the mortgage requires monthly payments, so all the variables must be expressed in units of months. In general, the periodic unit used is defined by the frequency of the cash flows and must agree for all variables. In this example, because you have monthly cash flows, you must calculate using the monthly discount rate (r) and the number of months (t).

Saving to reach a goal—to provide a down payment on a house, a child's education, or retirement income—is often accomplished by a plan of regular deposits to an account for that purpose. The savings plan is an annuity, so these relationships can be used to calculate how much would have to be saved each period (CF) to reach the goal, or given how much can be saved each period, how long it will take to reach the goal (t), or how a better investment return (r) would affect the periodic savings, or the time needed (t), or the goal (FV).

For example, if you want to have $1 million (FV) in the bank when you retire, and your bank pays 3% (r) interest per year, and you can save $10,000 per year (CF) toward retirement, can you afford to retire at age 65? You could if you start saving at age 18, because with that annual saving at that rate of return, it will take 47 years (t) to have $1 million (FV). If you could save $20,000 per year (CF), it would only take 31 years (t) to save $1 million (FV). If you are already 40 years old, you could do it if you save $27,428 per year (CF) or if you can earn a return of at least 5.34% (r) (Table 4.6).

TABLE 4.6 Retirement Savings Calculations

CF	Rate (*r*)	Time (*t*)	PV	FV
10,000	0.0300	47	250,000	1,000,000
20,000	0.0300	31	400,000	1,000,000
27,428	0.0300	25	477,606	1,000,000
20,000	0.0534	25	272,621	1,000,000

As you can see, the relationships between time, risk, opportunity cost, and value are some of the most important relationships you will ever encounter in life, and understanding them is critical to making sound financial decisions.

Financial Calculations

Modern tools make it much easier to do the math. Calculators, spreadsheets, and software have been developed to be very user friendly and widely available.

Financial calculators are designed for financial calculations and have the equations relating the present and future values, cash flows, the discount rate, and time embedded, for single amounts or for a series of cash flows, so that you can calculate any one of those variables if you know all the others.

Personal finance software packages usually come with a planning calculator, which is nothing more than a formula with these equations embedded, so that you can find any variable if you know the others. These tools are usually presented as a "mortgage calculator," a "loan calculator," or a "retirement planner" and are set up to answer common planning questions, such as "How much do I have to save every year for retirement?" or "What will my monthly loan payment be?"

FIGURE 4.5

Spreadsheets also have the equations already designed and readily accessible as functions or as macros. There are also stand-alone software applications that may be downloaded to a mobile device, such as a smartphone or tablet. They are useful in answering planning questions but may lack the ability to store and track your situation in the way that a more complete software package can.

The calculations are discussed here not so that you can perform them, as you have many tools to choose from that can do that more efficiently, but so that you can understand them, and most importantly, so that you can understand the relationships that they describe.

Key Takeaways

- The idea of the time value of money is fundamental to financial decisions.
- The present value of the series of cash flows is equal to the sum of the present value of each cash flow.
- A series of cash flows is an annuity when there are regular payments at regular intervals and each payment is the same amount.
- To calculate the present value of an annuity, you need to know
  - the amount of the identical cash flows (CF),
  - the frequency of the cash flows,
  - the number of cash flows (t),
  - the discount rate (r) or the rate at which time affects value.
- The calculation for the present value of an annuity yields valuable insights.
  - The more time (t), the more periods and the more periodic payments—that is, the more cash flows, and so the more liquidity and the more value.
  - The greater the cash flows, the more liquidity and the more value.
  - The greater the rate at which time affects value (r) or the greater the opportunity cost and risk or the greater the rate of discounting, the more time affects value.
- The calculation for the future value of an annuity yields valuable insights.
  - The more time (t), the more periods and the more periodic payments—that is, the more cash flows, and so the more liquidity and the more value.
  - The greater the cash flows, the more liquidity and the more value.
  - The greater the rate at which time affects value (r) or the greater the rate of compounding, the more time affects value.
- A perpetuity is an infinite annuity.

Exercises

1. In My Notes or in your financial planning journal, identify and record all your cash flows. Which cash flows function as annuities or perpetuities? Calculate the present value of each. Then calculate the future value. Which cash flows give you the greatest liquidity or value?
2. How can you determine if a lump-sum payment or an annuity will have greater value for you?
3. Survey and sample financial calculators listed at http://www.dinkytown.net/ and http://www.financialcalculators.com. Which ones might prove especially useful to you? What do you identify as the chief strengths and weaknesses of using financial calculators?

4.5 Using Financial Statements to Evaluate Financial Choices

Learning Objectives

1. Define pro forma financial statements.
2. Explain how pro forma financial statements can be used to project future scenarios for the planning process.

Now that you understand the relationship of time and value, especially looking forward, you can begin to think about how your ideas and plans will look as they happen. More specifically, you can begin to see how your future will look in the mirror of your financial statements. Projected or **pro forma financial statements** can show the consequences of choices. To project future financial statements, you need to be able to envision the expected results of all the items on them. This can be difficult, for there can be many variables that may affect your income and expenses or cash flows (CF), and some of them may be unpredictable. Predictions always contain uncertainty, so projections are always, at best, educated guesses. Still, they can be useful in helping you to see how the future may look.

pro forma financial statements (pro formas)

Projected results for financial statements in the future, given assumptions about what will happen in the meantime.

We can glimpse Alice's projected cash flow statements and balance sheets for each of her choices, for example, and their possible outcomes. Alice can actually project how her financial statements will look after each choice is followed.

When making financial decisions, it is helpful to be able to think in terms of their consequences on the financial statements, which provide an order to our summary of financial results. For example, in previous chapters, Alice was deciding how to decrease her debt. Her choices were to continue to pay it down gradually as she does now; to get a second job to pay it off faster; or to go to Vegas, hit it big (or lose big), and eliminate her debt altogether (or wind up with even more). Alice can look at the effects of each choice on her financial statements (Table 4.7).

TABLE 4.7 Potential Effects on Alice's Financial Statements

Choices	Income Statement	Cash Flow Statement	Balance Sheet
Continue	No new effects	No new effects	↓Debt ↑Net Worth
Second Job	↑Income	No net effect (increased cash flow from wages is used to pay debt)	↓Debt faster ↑Net worth faster
Vegas: Win	↑Expenses (for the trip)	No net effect (increased cash flow from winnings is used to pay debt)	Eliminate debt ↑Net worth
Vegas: Lose	↑Expenses (for the trip)	↓Net cash flow	↑Debt ↓Net worth

Looking more closely at the actual numbers on each statement gives a much clearer look at Alice's situation. Beginning with the income statement, income will increase if she works a second job or goes to Las Vegas and wins, while expenses will increase (travel expense) if she goes to Vegas at all. Assume that her second job would bring in an extra $20,000 income and that she could win or lose $100,000 in Vegas. Any change in gross wages or winnings (losses) would have a tax consequence: if she loses in Vegas, she will still have income taxes on her salary. Table 4.8 begins with Alice's pro forma income statements.

TABLE 4.8 Alice's Pro Forma Income Statements

Income Statement	Continue	2nd Job	Vegas: Win	Vegas: Lose
Gross wages	44,650	64,650	144,650	(55,350)
Income taxes and deductions	8,930	12,930	28,930	0
Disposable income	35,720	51,720	115,720	(55,350)
Rent expense	10,800	10,800	10,800	10,800
Food	3,900	3,900	3,900	3,900
Car expenses	3,600	3,600	3,600	3,600
Clothing	1,800	1,800	1,800	1,800
Cell phone	1,200	1,200	1,200	1,200
Internet and cable TV	1,200	1,200	1,200	1,200
Entertainment, travel, etc.	2,700	2,700	3,700	3,700
Total living expenses	25,200	25,200	26,200	26,200
Car loan interest	240	240	240	240
Student loan interest	4,240	4,240	4,240	4,240
Total interest expenses	4,480	4,480	4,480	4,480
Net income	6,040	22,040	85,040	(86,030)

While Vegas yields the largest increase in net income or personal profit if she wins, it creates the largest decrease if she loses. It is clearly the riskiest option. The pro forma cash flow statements (Table 4.9) reinforce this observation.

TABLE 4.9 Alice's Pro Forma Cash Flow Statements

Cash Flow Statement	Continue	2nd Job	Vegas: Win	Vegas: Lose
Cash from gross wages	44,650	64,650	44,650	44,650
Cash paid for:				
Income taxes and deductions	(8,930)	(12,930)	(8,930)	(8,930)
Rent expense	(10,800)	(10,800)	(10,800)	(10,800)
Food	(3,900)	(3,900)	(3,900)	(3,900)
Car expenses	(3,600)	(3,600)	(3,600)	(3,600)
Clothing	(1,800)	(1,800)	(1,800)	(1,800)
Cell phone	(1,200)	(1,200)	(1,200)	(1,200)
Internet and cable TV	(1,200)	(1,200)	(1,200)	(1,200)
Entertainment, travel, etc.	(2,700)	(2,700)	(3,700)	(3,700)
Car loan interest	(240)	(240)	(240)	(240)
Student loan interest	(4,240)	(4,240)	(4,240)	(4,240)
Operating Cash Flows	6,040	22,040	5,040	5,040
Cash from gambling	-	-	100,000	(100,000)
Cash for repayment of car loan	(2,160)	(2,160)	(2,700)	(2,160)
Cash for repayment of student loan	(3,480)	(19,000)	(53,000)	(7,760)
Proceeds from new loan	-	-	-	100,000

Cash Flow Statement	Continue	2nd Job	Vegas: Win	Vegas: Lose
Financing Cash Flows	(5,640)	(21,160)	44,300	(9,920)
Net Cash Flow	400	880	49,340	(4,880)

If Alice has a second job, she will use the extra cash flow, after taxes, to pay down her student loan, leaving her with a bit more free cash flow than she would have had without the second job. If she wins in Vegas, she can pay off both her car loan and her student loan and still have an increased free cash flow. However, if she loses in Vegas, she will have to secure more debt to cover her losses. Assuming she borrows as much as she loses, she will have a small negative net cash flow and no free cash flow, and her other assets will have to make up for this loss of cash value.

So, how will Alice's financial condition look in one year? That depends on how she proceeds, but the pro forma balance sheets (Table 4.10) can give a glimpse.

TABLE 4.10 Alice's Pro Forma Balance Sheets

Balance Sheet	Continue	2nd Job	Vegas: Win	Vegas: Lose
Assets				
Car	5,000	5,000	5,000	5,000
Savings	650	1,130	49,590	0
Total assets	5,650	6,130	54,590	5,000
Liabilities				
Car loan	540	540	-	540
Student loan	45,240	34,000	-	45,240
New loan	3,880	-	-	104,880
Total liabilities	49,660	34,540	0	150,660
Net Worth	(44,010)	(28,410)	54,590	(145,660)

If Alice has a second job, her net worth increases but is still negative, as she has paid down more of her student loan than she otherwise would have, but it is still larger than her asset value. If she wins in Vegas, her net worth can be positive; with her loan paid off entirely, her asset value will equal her net worth. However, if she loses in Vegas, she will have to borrow more, her new debt quadrupling her liabilities and decreasing her net worth by that much more.

A summary of the critical "bottom lines" from each pro forma statement (Table 4.11) most clearly shows Alice's complete picture for each alternative.

TABLE 4.11 Alice's Pro Forma Bottom Lines

Alice's Choices	Continue	2nd Job	Vegas: Win	Vegas: Lose
Net income	6,040	22,040	85,040	(86,030)
Net cash flow	400	880	49,340	(4,880)
Net worth	(44,010)	(28,410)	54,590	(145,660)

Going to Vegas creates the best and the worst scenarios for Alice, depending on whether she wins or loses. While the outcomes for continuing or getting a second job are fairly certain, the outcome in Vegas is not; there are two possible outcomes in Vegas. The Vegas choice has the most risk or the least certainty.

The Vegas alternative also has strategic costs: if she loses, her increased debt and its obligations—more interest and principal payments on more debt—will further delay her goal of building an asset base from which to generate new sources of income. In the near future, or until her new debt is repaid, she will have even fewer financial choices.

The strategic benefit of the Vegas alternative is that if she wins, she can eliminate debt, begin to build her asset base, and have even more choices (by eliminating debt and freeing cash flow).

The next step for Alice would be to try to assess the probabilities of winning or of losing in Vegas. Once she has determined the risk involved—given the consequences now illuminated on the pro forma financial statements—she would have to decide if she can tolerate that risk, or if she should reject that alternative because of its risk.

Key Takeaway

- Pro forma financial statements show the consequences of financial choices in the context of the financial statements.

Exercises

1. What do pro forma financial statements show?
2. What are pro forma financial statements based on?
3. What are the strategic benefits of making financial projections on pro forma statements?

4.6 Evaluating Risk

Learning Objectives

1. Explain the basic dynamics of probabilities.
2. Discuss how probabilities can be used to measure expected value.
3. Describe how probabilities can be used in financial projections.
4. Analyze expected outcomes of financial choices.

Risk affects financial decision making in mysterious ways, many of which are the subject of an entire area of scholarship now known as behavioral finance. The study of risk and the interpretation of probabilities are complex. In making financial decisions, a grasp of their basic dynamics is useful. One of the most important to understand is the idea of independence.

independent event

An event made neither more nor less probable by the occurrence of another event.

An **independent event** is one that happens by chance. It cannot be willed or decided upon. The probability or likelihood of an independent event can be measured, based on its frequency in the past, and that probability can be used to predict whether it will recur. Independent events can be the result of complex situations. They can be studied to see which confluence of circumstances or conditions make them more or less likely or affect their probability. But an independent event is, in the end, no matter how skillfully analyzed, a matter of some chance or uncertainty or risk; it cannot be determined or chosen.

FIGURE 4.6

Alice can choose whether or not to go to Vegas, but she cannot choose whether or not to win. Winning—or losing—is an independent event. She can predict her chances, the probability, that she'll win based on her past experiences, her apparent skill and knowledge, and the known odds of casino gambling (about which many studies have been done and there is much knowledge available). But she cannot choose to win; there is always some uncertainty or risk that she will not.

The probability of any one outcome for an event is always stated as a percentage of the total outcomes possible. An independent or risky event has at least two possible outcomes: it happens or it does not happen. There may be more outcomes possible, but there are at least two; if there were only one outcome possible, there would be no uncertainty or risk about the outcome.

For example, you have a "50-50 chance" of "heads" when you flip a coin, or a 50% probability of that outcome. That probability is based on historical frequency: on average "heads" comes up half the time. "On average" means that for all the times that coins have been flipped, half the time "heads" is the result. There are only two possible outcomes when you flip a coin, and based on historical outcomes, there is a 50% chance of each. The probabilities of each possible outcome add up to 100% because there is 100% probability that something will happen. In this case, half the time it is one result, and half the time it is the other. In general, the probabilities of each possible outcome—and there may be many—add to 100%.

Probabilities can be used in financial decisions to measure the expected result of an independent event. That expectation is based on the probabilities of each outcome and its result if it does occur. Suppose you have a little wager going on the coin flip. You will win $1.00 if it comes up "heads," and you will lose $1.00 if it does not ("tails"). You have a 50% chance of $1.00 and a 50% chance of -$1.00. Half the time you can expect to gain one dollar, and half the time you can expect to lose one dollar. Your expectation of the average result, based on the historic frequency or probability of each outcome and its actual result, is:

$$(0.50 \times 1.00) + (0.50 \times -1.00) = 0.50 + -0.50 = 0$$

$$(\text{probability}_{\text{heads}} \times \text{result}_{\text{heads}}) + (\text{probability}_{\text{tails}} \times \text{result}_{\text{tails}})$$

expected value

The weighted average result for an event, or the value expected, on average, given the probabilities of each of its possible outcomes.

Note that the $probability_{heads}$ + the $probability_{tails}$ = 1 or 100%, because those are all the possible outcomes. The expected result for each outcome is its probability or likelihood multiplied by its result. The expected result or **expected value** for the action, for flipping a coin, is its weighted average outcome, with the "weights" being the probabilities of each of its outcomes.

If you get $1.00 every time the coin flips "heads," and it does so half the time, then half the time you get $1.00, or you can expect overall to realize half a dollar or $0.50 from flipping "heads." The other half of the time, you can expect to lose a dollar, so your expectation has to include the possibility of flipping "tails" with an overall or average result of losing $0.50 or -$0.50. So you can expect 0.50 from one outcome and -$0.50 from the other: altogether, you can expect $0.50 + -$0.50 = 0 (which is why "flipping coins" is not a popular casino game).

The expected value (E(V)) of an event is the sum of each possible outcome's probability multiplied by its result, or:

$$E(V) = \sum p_n \times r_n$$

where Σ means summation, *p* is the probability of an outcome, *r* is its result, and *n* is the number of outcomes possible.

When faced with the uncertainty of an alternative that involves an independent event, it is often quite helpful to be able to at least calculate its expected value. Then, when making a decision, that expectation can be weighed against or compared to those of other choices.

FIGURE 4.7

© Shutterstock, Inc.

For example, Alice has projected four possible outcomes for her finances depending on whether she continues, gets a second job, wins in Vegas, or loses in Vegas, but there are really only three choices: continue, second job, or go to Vegas—since winning or losing are outcomes of the one decision to go to Vegas. She knows, with little or no uncertainty, how her financial situation will look if she continues or gets a second job. To compare the Vegas choice with the other two, she needs to predict what she can expect from going to Vegas, given that she may win or lose once there.

Alice can calculate the expected result of going to Vegas if she knows the probabilities of its two outcomes, winning and losing. Alice does a bit of research and has a friend show her a few tricks and decides that, for her, the probability of winning is 30%, which makes the probability of losing 70%. (As there are only two possible outcomes in this case, and their probabilities must add to 100%.) Her expected result in Vegas, then, is:

$$(0.30 \times 100,000) + (0.70 \times -100,000) = 30,000 + -70,000 = -40,000$$

Using the same calculations, she can project the expected result of going to Vegas on her pro forma financial statements (Table 4.12). Look at the effect on her bottom lines:

TABLE 4.12 Alice's Expected Outcomes, with a 30% Chance of Winning in Vegas

Alice's Choices	Continue	2nd Job	Go to Vegas P_{win} = 30%
Net income	6,040	22,040	(34,709)
Net cash flow	400	880	11,386
Net worth	(44,010)	(28,410)	(100,632)

If she only has a 30% chance of winning in Vegas, then going there at all is the worst choice for her in terms of her net income and net worth. Her net cash flow (CF) actually seems best with the Vegas option, but that assumes she can borrow to pay her gambling losses, so her losses don't create net negative cash flow. She does, however, create debt.

Alice can also calculate what the probability of winning would have to be to make it a worthwhile choice at all, that is, to give her at least as good a result as either of her other choices (Table 4.13).

TABLE 4.13 Alice's Expected Outcomes to Make Vegas a Competitive Choice

Alice's Choices	Continue	2nd Job	Go to Vegas P_{win} = 78%
Net income	6,040	22,040	47,404
Net cash flow	400	880	37,412
Net worth	(44,010)	(28,130)	(28,130)

To be the best choice in terms of all three bottom lines, Alice would have to have a 78% chance of winning at Vegas.

Her net worth would still be negative, but all three bottom lines would be at least as good or better than they would be with her other two choices. If Alice thought she had at least a 78% chance of winning and could tolerate the risk that she might not, Vegas would be a viable choice for her.

Those are two very big "ifs," but by being able to project an expected value or result for each of her choices, using the probabilities of each outcome for the choice with uncertainty, Alice can at least measure and compare the choices.

Using probabilities to derive the expected value of a choice provides a way to evaluate an alternative with uncertainty. It requires projecting the probabilities and results of each possible outcome or independent event. It cannot remove the uncertainty or the risk that independence presents, but it can at least provide a way to measure and then compare with other measurable, certain or uncertain, choices.

Key Takeaways

- Probabilities can be used in financial decisions to measure the expected result of an independent event.
- The expected value for a choice may be figured as $E(V) = \Sigma\ (p_n \times r_n)$.
- Expected value can be weighed against or compared to the values of other choices.

Exercises

1. How are probabilities used in financial decisions?
2. How can you calculate the expected values of financial alternatives?
3. Compared to her other two choices and her financial goals, should Alice go to Vegas? Why, or why not?
4. Read the explanation of expected value and its application to poker playing at CardsChat: The Worldwide Poker Community (http://www.cardschat.com/poker-odds-expected-value.php). Alice might have used similar information to calculate her chances of winning at Vegas.

CHAPTER 5
Financial Plans: Budgets

5.1 Introduction

Seeing the value of reaching a goal can be much easier than seeing a way to reach that goal. People often resolve to somehow improve themselves or their lives. But while they are not lacking sincerity, determination, or effort, they nevertheless fall short for want of a plan, a map, a picture of why and how to get from here to there.

Pro forma financial statements provide a look at the potential results of financial decisions. They can also be used as a tool to plan for certain results. When projected in the form of a **budget**, figures become not only an estimated result but also an actual strategy or plan, a map illustrating a path to achieve a goal. Later, when you compare actual results to the original plan, you can see how shortfalls or successes can point to future strategies.

FIGURE 5.1

Budgets are usually created with a specific goal in mind: to cut living expenses, to increase savings, or to save for a specific purpose such as education or retirement. While the need to do such things may be brought into sharper focus by the financial statements, the budget provides an actual plan for doing so. It is more a document of action than of reflection.

As an action statement, a budget is meant to be dynamic: a reconciliation of "facts on the ground" and "castles in the air." While financial statements are summaries of historic reality—that is, of all that has already happened and is "sunk"—budgets reflect the current realities that define the next choices. A budget should never be merely followed but should constantly be revised to reflect new information.

budget

A projection of the financial requirements and consequences of a plan.

5.2 The Budget Process

Learning Objectives

1. Trace the budget process.
2. Discuss the relationships of goals and behaviors.
3. Demonstrate the importance of conservatism in the budget process.
4. Show the importance of timing in the budget process.

The budget process is an infinite loop similar to the larger financial planning process. It involves:

- defining goals and gathering data;
- forming expectations and reconciling goals and data;
- creating the budget;
- monitoring actual outcomes and analyzing variances;
- adjusting budget, expectations, or goals;
- redefining goals.

FIGURE 5.2 The Budget Process

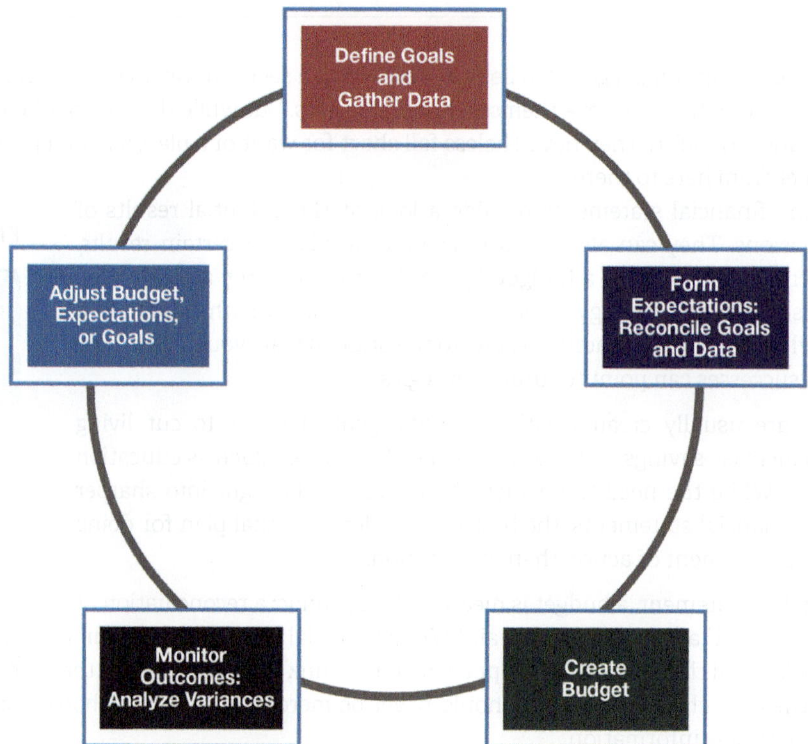

A review of your financial statements or your current financial condition—as well as your own ideas about how you are and could be living—should indicate immediate and longer-term goals. It may also point out new choices. For example, an immediate goal may be to lower housing expense. In the short-term you could look for an apartment with lower rent, but in the long run, it may be more advantageous to own a home. This long-term goal may indicate a need to start a savings plan for a down payment.

The process of creating a budget can be instructive. Creating a budget involves projecting realistic behavior. Your assumptions may come from your actual past behavior based on accurate records that you have gathered. If you have been using personal finance software, it has been keeping those records for you; if not, a thorough review of your checkbook and investment statements will reveal that information. Financial statements are useful summaries of the information you need to create a budget.

After formulating realistic expectations based on past behavior and current circumstances, you still must reconcile your future behavior with your original expectations. For example, you may recognize that greater sacrifices need to be made, or that you must change your behavior, or even that your goals are unattainable and should be more realistic—perhaps based on less desirable choices. On the other hand, this can be a process of happy discovery: goals may be closer or require less sacrifice than you may have thought.

FIGURE 5.3

Whether it results in sobering dismay or ambitious joy, the budget process is one of reconciling your financial realities to your financial dreams. How you finance your life determines how you can live your life, so budgeting is really a process of mapping out a life strategy. You may find it difficult to separate the emotional and financial aspects of your goals, but the more successfully you can do so, the more successfully you will reach your goals.

A budget is a projection of how things should work out, but there is always some uncertainty. If the actual results are better than expected, if incomes are more or expenses less, expectations can be adjusted upward as a welcome accommodation to good fortune. On the other hand, if actual results are worse than expected, if incomes are less or expenses more, not only the next budget but also current living choices may have to be adjusted to accommodate that situation. Those new choices are less than preferred or you would have chosen them in your original plan.

To avoid unwelcome adjustments, you should be **conservative** in your expectations so as to maximize the probability that your actual results will be better than expected. Thus, when estimating, you would always underestimate the income items and potential gains and overestimate the expense items and potential losses.

conservative (conservatism)

In finance, an approach preferred in all financial planning: overestimate expenses, losses, and the value of liabilities and underestimate incomes, gains, and the value of assets. This is based on the idea that any surprises should be advantageous. The use of this word in finance and accounting has absolutely no relation to any political associations that the word may have gained in common usage.

You will also need to determine a time period and frequency for your budget process: annually, monthly, or weekly. The timing will depend on how much financial activity you have and how much discipline or guidance you want your budget to provide. You should assess your progress at least annually. In general, you want to keep a manageable amount of data for any one period, so the more financial activity you have, the shorter your budget period should be. Since your budget needs to be monitored consistently, you don't want to be flooded with so much data that monitoring becomes too daunting a task. On the other hand, you want to choose an ample period or time frame to show meaningful results. Choose a time period that makes sense for your quantity of data or level of financial activity.

Key Takeaways

- A budget is a process that mirrors the financial planning process.
- The process of creating a budget can suggest goals, behaviors, and limitations.
- For the budget to succeed, goals and behaviors must be reconciled.
- Budgets should be prepared conservatively:
  - Overestimate costs.
  - Underestimate earnings.
- The appropriate time period is one that is:
  - short enough to limit the amount of data,
  - long enough to capture meaningful data.

Exercises

1. View the video "7 Steps on How to Create a Budget" (https://www.youtube.com/watch?v=K5UlgTkadV0). How do the steps described fit into the budget process discussed in this chapter? What is the 50-30-20 Rule? Discuss with your classmates how reasonable you think it is.
2. What is the "envelope system"? Discuss with your classmates whether the envelope system is practical in our increasingly cashless society.

5.3 Creating the Comprehensive Budget

Learning Objectives

1. Describe the components of the comprehensive budget and their purposes.
2. Describe the components of an operating budget.
3. Discuss the sources of recurring income and expenses.
4. Identify the factors in the operating budgeting process.
5. Identify the factors in the capital budgeting process.

comprehensive budget

A budget that includes the operating budget and the capital budget, that is, it is designed to show all aspects of financial activities.

Gathering data and creating a budget—with some goals already in mind—are the initial steps in the process. Understanding the format or shape of the budget will help guide you to the kind of information you need. A **comprehensive budget**—that is, a budget covering all aspects of financial life—will include a projection of recurring incomes and expenses and of nonrecurring expenditures. (Nonrecurring income or "windfalls" should not be counted on or "budgeted for," conservatively.) Recurring incomes would be earnings from wages, interest, or dividends. Recurring expenditures may include living expenses, loan repayments, and regular savings or investment deposits. Nonrecurring expenditures may be for capital improvements such as a new roof for your house or for purchases of durable items such as a refrigerator or a car. These are purchases that would not be made each period. A comprehensive budget diagram is shown in Figure 5.4.

FIGURE 5.4 Comprehensive Budget Diagram

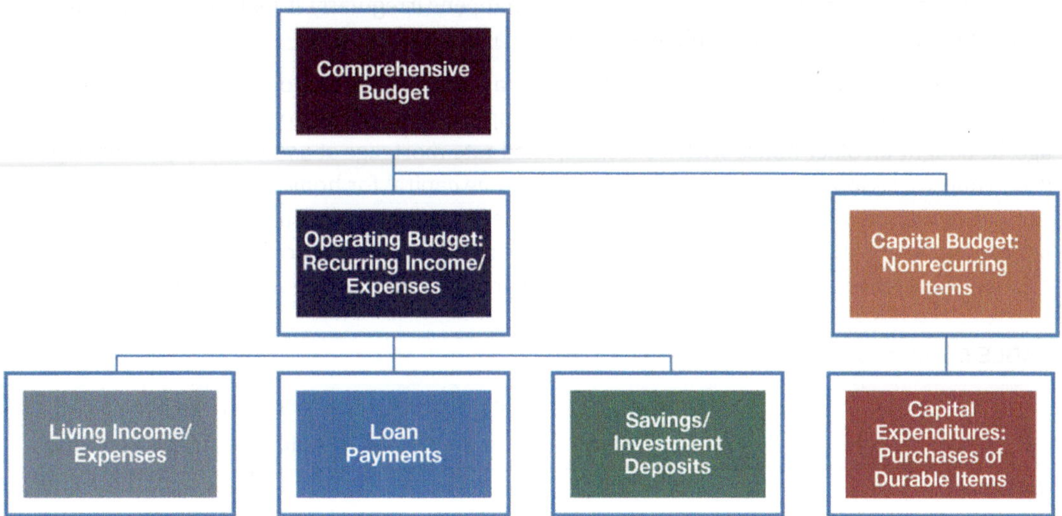

Another distinction in recognizing recurring and nonrecurring items is the time frame for each. Recurring items need to be taken care of repeatedly and are therefore considered in the short term, while the items on the capital budget may allow for long-term planning because they happen less frequently. The different time horizons for planning for recurring and nonrecurring items may allow for different strategies to reach those different goals.

A comprehensive budget is a compilation of an **operating budget** for short-term goals involving recurring items and a **capital budget** for long-term goals involving nonrecurring items.

operating budget

The budget that shows recurring income and expenses, usually living expenses and incomes from wages, interest, and dividends, usually related to short-term financial goals.

capital budget

The budget that shows nonrecurring events that are usually associated with long-term financial goals.

Operating Budget: Recurring Incomes and Expenditures

Using Financial History

Recurring incomes and expenditures are usually the easiest to determine and project, as they happen consistently and have an immediate effect on your everyday living. An income statement shows incomes and expenses; cash flow statements show actual cash expenditures. Recurring incomes and expenditures are planned in the context of short-term lifestyle goals or preferences.

Look at a time period large enough to capture relevant data. Some incomes and expenditures recur reliably but only periodically or seasonally. For example, you may pay the premium on your auto insurance policy twice per year. It is a recurring expense, but it happens in only two months of the year, so you would have to look at expenditures over enough months to see it. Or your heating or cooling expenses may change seasonally, affecting your utility expenses in some months more than in others.

The time period you choose for a budget should be long enough to show intermittent items as recurring and nonrecurring items as unusual, yet short enough to follow and to manage choices within the period. For personal budgets, a month is the most common budget period to use, since most living expenses are paid at least monthly. However, it is best to use at least one full year's worth of data to get a reasonable monthly average and to see seasonal and periodic items as they occur.

Some items may recur, but not reliably: either their frequency or their amount is uncertain. Taking a conservative approach, you should include the maximum possible amount of uncertain expenses in your budget. If income occurs regularly but the amount is uncertain, conservatively include the minimum amount. If income actually happens irregularly, it may be better just to leave it out of your budget—and your plans—since you can't "count" on it.

Consider the following example: Mark works as a school counselor, tutors on the side, does house painting in the summer, and buys and sells sports memorabilia on the Internet. Four years ago, he bought an older house with a $200,000, fixed-rate mortgage at 5.75%. Every year, he deposits $1,000 into his retirement account (IRA) and uses some capital for home improvements. He used a car loan to buy his car. Whatever cash is left over after he has paid his bills is saved in a money market account that earns 3% interest. At the end of Year 4, Mark is trying to draw up a budget for Year 5. Since he bought the house, he has been keeping pretty good financial records, shown in Table 5.1.

TABLE 5.1 Mark's Financial Data, Years 1-4

	Time 0	Year 1 Actual	Year 2 Actual	Year 3 Actual	Year 4 Actual
Incomes					
Wages		32,000	33,500	35,000	36,500
Tutoring		3,000	4,000	5,000	500
Memorabilia sales		2,500	950	2,650	5,300
House painting		10,000	11,000	4,500	10,250
Interest income		180	187	162	129
Total income		47,680	49,637	47,312	52,679
Payroll/income taxes		8,000	8,375	8,750	9,125
Disposable income		39,680	41,262	38,562	43,554
Living expenses					
Groceries		3,120	3,120	3,120	3,120
Car - fuel		1,688	1,875	2,813	1,500
Car - service, etc.		350	350	350	350
Car - insurance		800	800	800	800
Electricity		780	780	780	780
Phone/cable/internet		1,500	1,188	1,188	1,068
Heat		1,240	1,200	1,990	1,125
Health insurance		320	335	350	365
Medical		50	50	1,200	50
Dental		200	200	200	200
Travel/entertainment		3,000	3,000	3,000	3,000
Car loan payment		3,600	5,400	5,400	5,400
Mortgage interest		11,433	11,281	11,120	10,950
Property tax		3,450	3,450	3,450	4,350
Total living expenses		31,531	33,029	35,761	33,058
Income after living expenses		8,149	8,233	2,801	10,496
Interest expense					
Capital expenditures/investment					
Mortgage principal		2,573	2,725	2,886	3,056

	Time 0	Year 1 Actual	Year 2 Actual	Year 3 Actual	Year 4 Actual
Free cash flow		5,576	5,508	(85)	7,440
Retirement account deposit		1,000	1,000	1,000	1,000
Home improvement		4,356	5,327	0	4,146
Money market deposit (withdrawal)		220	(819)	(1,085)	2,294
Draw on (pay off) line of credit					
Net cash flow		0	0	0	0
Line of credit					
Money market account balance	6,000	6,220	5,401	4,316	6,610

Mark has five sources of income—some more constant, some more reliable, and some more seasonal. His counseling job provides a steady, year-round paycheck. House painting is a seasonal although fairly reliable source of income; in Year 3 it was less because Mark fell from a ladder and was unable to paint for two months. Tutoring is a seasonal source of income, and since the school hired an additional counselor in Year 3, it has decreased. Memorabilia trading is a year-round but unpredictable source of income. In Year 3 he made some very lucrative trades, but in Year 2 almost none. Interest income depends on the balance in the money market account. He would include his counseling, painting, and interest incomes in his budget, but he should be conservative about including his tutoring or trading incomes.

Mark's expenses are reliable and easily predictable, with a few exceptions. His accident in Year 3 increased his medical expenses for that year. Both gas for the car and heating expenses vary with the weather and the highly volatile price of oil. In Year 3, those expenses were unusually high. Property tax increased in Year 4 but is unlikely to do so again for several years.

Using New Information and "Micro" Factors

Along with your known financial history, you would want to include any new information that may change your expectations. As with any forecast, the more information you can include in your projections, the more accurate it is likely to be.

Mark knows that the hiring of a new counselor has significantly cut into his tutoring income and will likely continue to do so. He will get a modest raise in his wages but has been notified that the co-pays and deductibles on his medical and dental insurance will increase in Year 5. He has just traded in his car and gotten a new loan for a "new" used car.

The personal or micro characteristics of your situation influence your expectations, especially if they are expected to change. Personal factors such as family structure, health, career choice, and age have significant influence on financial choices and goals. If any of those factors is expected to change, your financial situation should be expected to change as well, and that expectation should be included in your budget projections.

For example, if you are expecting to increase or decrease the size of your family or household, that would affect your consumption of goods and services. If you anticipate a change of job or of career, that will affect your income from wages. A change in health may result in working more or less and thus changing income from wages. There are many ways that personal circumstances can change, and they can change your financial expectations, choices, and goals. All these projected changes need to be included in the budget process.

FIGURE 5.5

Using Economics and "Macro" Factors

Macro factors affecting your budget come from the context of the wider economy, so understanding how incomes and expenses are created is useful in forming estimates. Incomes are created when labor or capital (liquidity or assets) are sold. The amount of income created depends on the quantity sold and on the price.

The price of labor depends on the relative supply and demand for labor reflected in unemployment rates. The price of liquidity depends on the relative supply and demand for capital reflected in interest rates. Unemployment rates and interest rates, in turn, depend on the complex, dynamic economy.

The economy tends to behave cyclically. If the economy is in a period of contraction or recession, demand for labor is lower, competition among workers is higher, and wages cannot be expected to rise. As unemployment rises, especially if you are working in an industry that is cyclically contracting with the economy, wages may become unreliable or increasingly risky if there is risk of losing your job. Interest rates are, as a rule, more volatile and thus more difficult to predict, but generally tend to fall during a period of contraction and rise in a period of expansion. A budget period is usually short so that economic factors will not vary widely enough to affect projections over that brief period. Still, those economic factors should inform your estimates of potential income.

Expenses are created when a quantity of goods or services is consumed for a price. That price depends on the relative supply of and demand for those goods and services. It also depends on the larger context of price levels in the economy. If inflation or deflation is decreasing or increasing the value of our currency, then its purchasing power is changing and so is the real cost of expenses. Again, as a rule, the budget period should be short enough so that changes in purchasing power won't affect the budget too much; still, these changes should not be ignored. Price levels are much quicker to change than wage levels, so it is quite possible to have a rise in prices before a rise in wages, which decreases the real purchasing power of your paycheck.

If you have a variable rate loan—that is, a loan for which the interest rate may be adjusted periodically—you are susceptible to interest rate changes or volatility. You should be aware of that particular macro factor when creating your budget.

Macroeconomic factors are difficult to predict, as they reflect complex scenarios, but news about current and expected economic conditions is easily available in the media every day. A good financial planner will also keep a sharp eye on economic indicators and forecasts. You will have a pretty concrete idea of where the economy is in its cycles, and how that affects you just by seeing how your paycheck meets your living expenses (e.g., filling up your car with gas or shopping for groceries). Figure 5.6 suggests how personal history, microeconomic factors, and macroeconomic factors can be used to make projections about items in your budget.

FIGURE 5.6 Factors for Determining a Projected Operating Budget Item

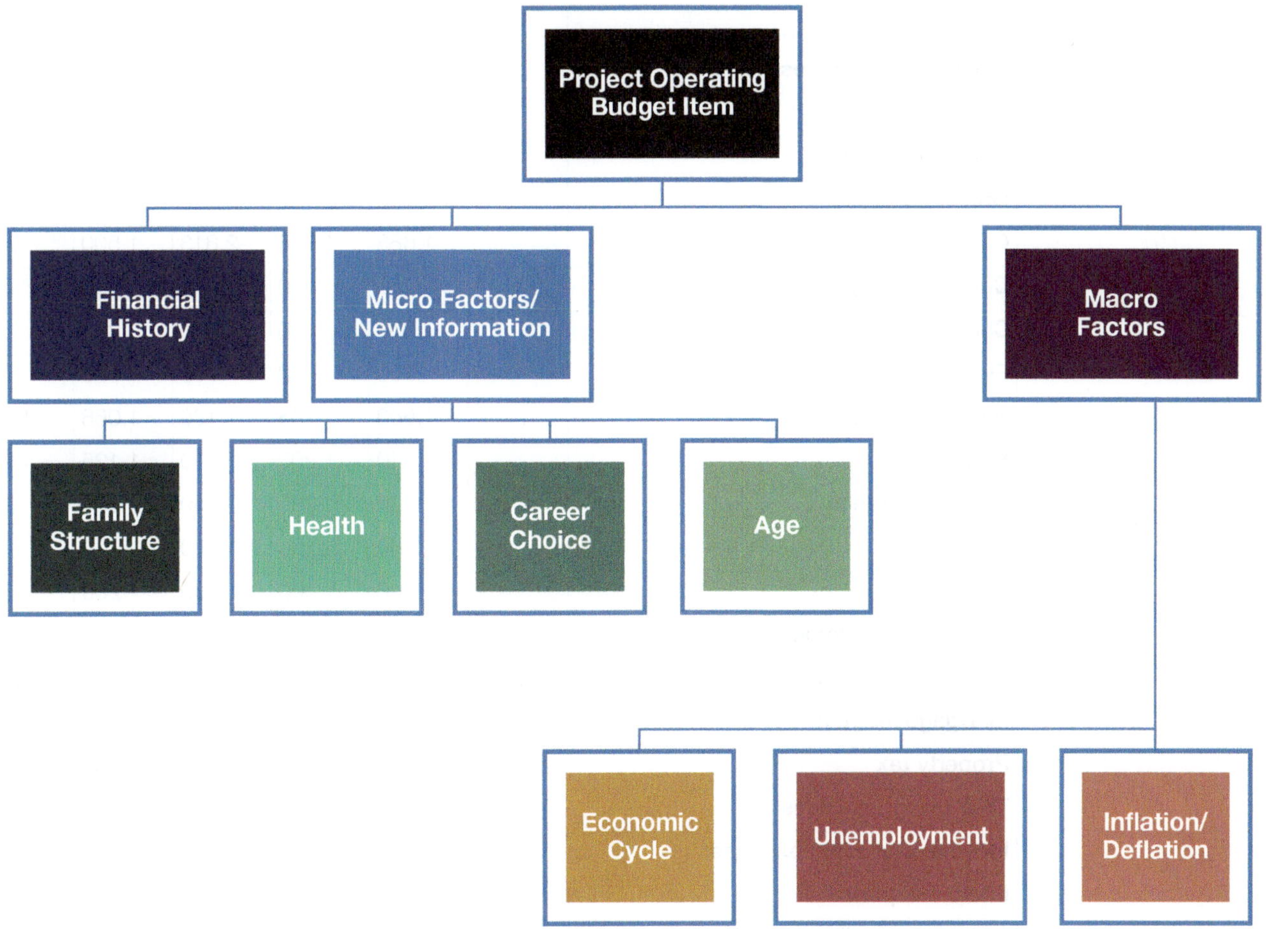

Using his past history, current information, and understanding of current and expected macroeconomic factors, Mark has put together the budget shown in Table 5.2.

TABLE 5.2 Mark's Year 5 Budget

	Time 0	Year 1 Actual	Year 2 Actual	Year 3 Actual	Year 4 Actual	Year 5 Budget
Incomes						
Wages		32,000	33,500	35,000	36,500	38,000
Tutoring		3,000	4,000	5,000	500	0
Memorabilia sales		2,500	950	2,650	5,300	950
House painting		10,000	11,000	4,500	10,250	10,417
Interest income		180	187	162	129	198
Total income		47,680	49,637	47,312	52,679	49,565
Payroll/income taxes		8,000	8,375	8,750	9,125	9,500
Disposable income		39,680	41,262	38,562	43,554	40,065
Living expenses						
Groceries		3,120	3,120	3,120	3,120	3,120
Car - fuel		1,688	1,875	2,813	1,500	1,875
Car - services, etc.		350	350	350	350	350
Car - insurance		800	800	800	800	800
Electricity		780	780	780	780	780
Phone/cable/internet		1,500	1,188	1,188	1,068	1,068
Heat		1,240	1,200	1,990	1,125	1,200
Health insurance		320	335	350	365	760
Medical		50	50	1,200	50	50
Dental		200	200	200	200	500
Travel/entertainment		3,000	3,000	3,000	3,000	3,000
Car loan payment		3,600	5,400	5,400	5,400	5,988
Mortgage interest		11,433	11,281	11,120	10,950	10,769
Property tax		3,450	3,450	3,450	4,350	4,350
Total living expenses		31,531	33,029	35,761	33,058	34,610
Income after living expenses		8,149	8,233	2,801	10,496	5,455
Interest expense						
Capital expenditures/investment						
Mortgage principal		2,573	2,725	2,886	3,056	3,236
Free cash flow		5,576	5,508	(85)	7,440	2,219
Retirement account deposit		1,000	1,000	1,000	1,000	1,000
Home improvement		4,356	5,327	0	4,146	15,000
Money market deposit (withdrawal)		220	(819)	(1,085)	2,294	(6,610)
Draw on (pay off) line of credit						
Net cash flow		0	0	0	0	(7,171)
Line of credit						
Money market account balance	6,000	6,220	5,401	4,316	6,610	0

To project incomes, Mark relied on his newest information to estimate his wages and tutoring income. He used the minimum income from the past four years for memorabilia sales, which is conservative and reasonable given its volatility. His painting income is less volatile, so his estimate is an average, excluding the unusual year of his accident. Interest income is based on his current money market account balance, which is adjusted for an expected drop in interest rates.

Mark expects his expenses to be what they were in Year 4, since his costs and consumption are not expected to change. However, he has adjusted his medical and dental insurance and his car lease payments on the basis of his new knowledge.

The price of gas and heating oil has been extraordinarily volatile during this period (Years 1-4), affecting Mark's gas and heating expenses, so he bases his estimates on what he knows about his expected consumption and the price. He knows he drives an average of about 15,000 miles per year and that his car gets about 20 miles per gallon. He estimates his gas expense for Year 5 by guessing that since oil price levels are about where they were in Year 3, gas will cost, on average, what it did then, which was $2.50 per gallon. He will buy, on average, 750 gallons per year (15,000 miles ÷ 20 mpg), so his total expense will be $1,875. Mark also knows that he uses 500 gallons of heating oil each year. Estimating heating oil prices at Year 3 levels, his cost will be about the same as it was then, or $1,200.

Mark knows that the more knowledge and information he can bring to bear, the more accurate and useful his estimates are likely to be.

Capital Budget: Capital Expenditures and Investments

Income remaining after the deduction of living expenses and debt obligations, or **free cash flow**, is cash available for capital expenditures or investment. Capital expenditures are usually part of a long-term plan of building an asset base. Investment may also be part of a longer-term plan to build an asset base or to achieve a specific goal such as financing education or retirement.

free cash flow
Income remaining after the deduction of living expenses and debt obligations that is available for capital expenditures or investment.

Long-term strategies are based on expected changes to the micro factors that shape goals. For example, you want to save for retirement because you anticipate aging and not being as willing or able to sell labor. Expanding or shrinking the family structure may create new savings goals or a change in housing needs that will indicate a change in asset base (e.g., buying or selling a house).

Some changes will eliminate a specific goal. A child finishing college, for example, ends the need for education savings. Some changes will emphasize the necessity of a goal, such as a decline in health underscoring the need to save for retirement. As personal factors change, you should reassess your longer-term goals and the capital expenditure toward those goals because long-term goals and thus capital expenditures may change with them.

While many personal factors are relatively predictable over the long-term (e.g., you will get older, not younger), the macroeconomic factors that will occur simultaneously are much harder to predict. Will the economy be expanding or contracting when you retire? Will there be inflation or deflation? The further (in time) you are from your goals, the harder it is to predict those factors and the less relevant they are to your budgeting concerns. As you get closer to your goals, macro factors become more influential in the assessment of your goals and your progress toward them.

FIGURE 5.7

© Shutterstock, Inc.

Since long-term strategies happen over time, you should use the relationships between time and value to calculate capital expenditures and progress toward long-term goals. Long-term goals are often best reached by a progression of steady and even steps; for example, a saving goal is often reached by a series of regular and steady deposits. Those regular deposits form an annuity. Knowing how much time there is and how much compounding there can be to turn your account balance (the present value of this annuity) into your savings goal (its future value), you can calculate the amount of the deposits into the account. This can then be compared to your projected free cash flow to see if such a deposit is possible. You can also see if your goal is too modest or too ambitious and should be adjusted in terms of the time to reach a goal or the rate at which you do.

Capital expenditures may be a one-time investment, like a new roof. A capital expenditure may also be a step toward a long-term goal, like an annual savings deposit. That goal should be assessed with each budget, and that "step" or capital expenditure should be reviewed. Figure 5.8 shows the relationship of factors used to determine the capital budget.

FIGURE 5.8 Factors for Determining the Projected Capital Budget Item

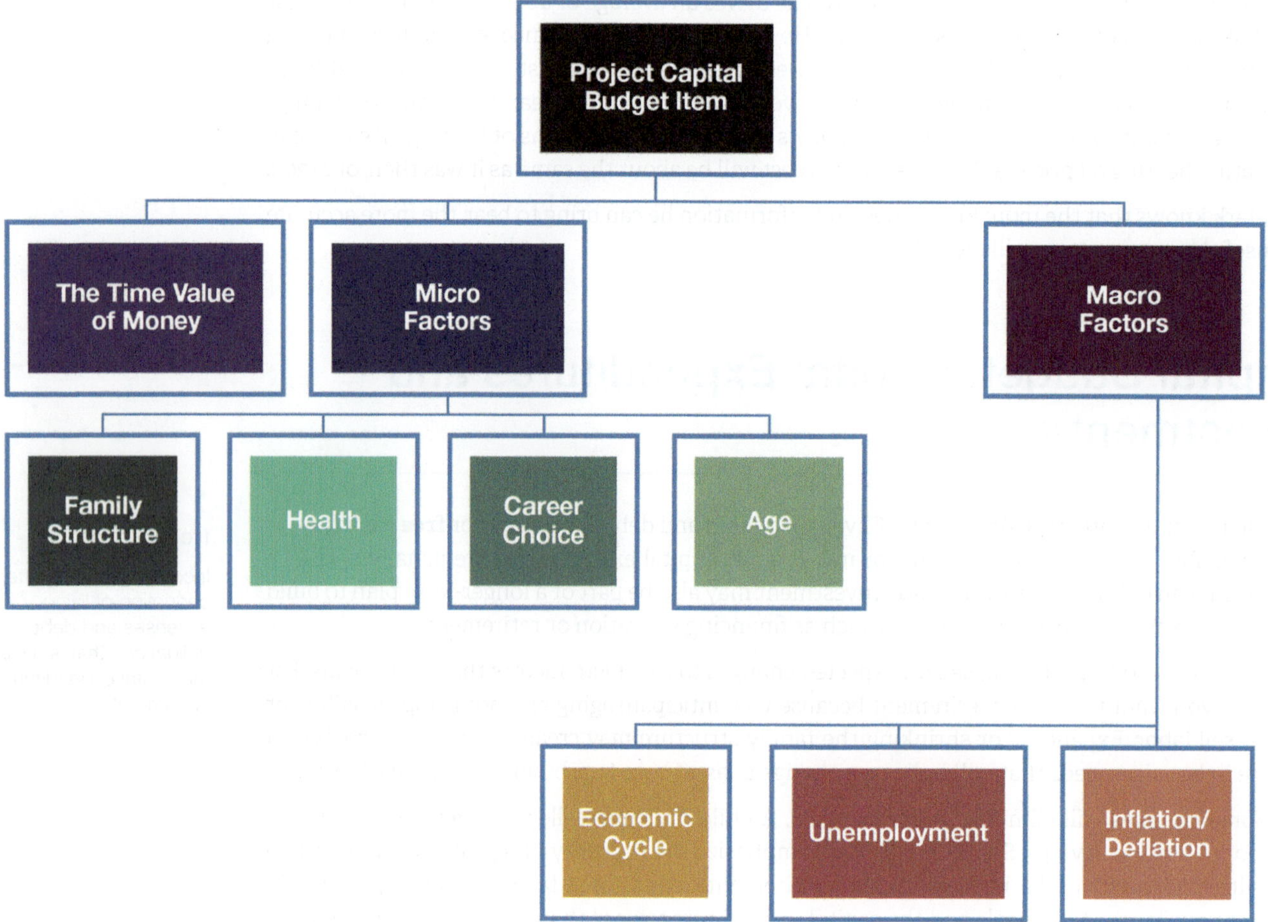

Mark's Year 5 budget (shown in Table 5.2) projects a drop in income and disposable income and a rise in living expenses, leaving him with less free cash flow for capital expenditures or investments. He knows that his house needs a new roof (estimated cost = $15,000) and was hoping to have that done in Year 5. However, that capital expenditure would create negative net cash flow, even if he also uses the savings from his money market account. Mark's budget shows that both his short-term lifestyle preferences (projected income and expenses) and progress toward his longer-term goals (property improvement and savings) cannot be achieved without some changes and choices. What should those changes and choices be?

Key Takeaways

- A comprehensive budget consists of an operating budget and a capital budget.
- The operating budget accounts for recurring incomes and expenses.
- Recurring incomes result from selling labor and/or liquidity.
- Recurring expenses result from consumption of goods and/or services.
- Recurring incomes and expenses:
  - satisfy short-term, lifestyle goals,
  - create free cash flow for capital expenditures.
- The capital budget accounts for capital expenditures or nonrecurring items.
- Capital expenditures are usually part of a longer-term plan or goal.
- Projecting recurring incomes and expenses involves using:
  - financial history,
  - new information and microeconomic factors,
  - macroeconomic factors.
- Different methods may be used to project different incomes and expenses depending on the probability, volatility, and predictability of quantity and price.
- Projecting capital expenditures involves using the following:
  - New information and microeconomic factors,
  - Macroeconomic factors, although these are harder to predict for a longer period, and therefore are less relevant,
  - The relationships described by the time value of money.

Exercises

1. Using Mark's budget sheet as a guide, adapt the budget categories and amounts to reflect your personal financial realities and projections. Develop an operating budget and a capital budget, distinguishing recurring incomes and expenses from nonrecurring capital expenditures. On what bases will you make projections about your future incomes and expenses?
2. How does your budget sheet relate to your income statement, your cash flow statement, and your balance sheet? How will you use this past history to develop a budget to reach your short-term and long-term goals?

5.4 The Details of Budgeting and Specialized Budgets

Learning Objectives

1. Discuss the use of a cash budget as a cash management tool.
2. Explain the cash budget's value in clarifying risks and opportunities.

3. Explain the purpose of a specialized budget, including a tax budget.
4. Demonstrate the importance of including specialized budgets in the comprehensive budget.

The Cash Budget

A cash budget is a way to identify the sources and uses of cash expected within a period. For a business using accrual accounting, there are often differences between income earned and cash inflows, and between expenses incurred and cash outflows. In personal finance, there are fewer differences, but there are some worth noting.

One issue can be the timing of income and expenditures. Cash flows may not be periodic, for example, when they are affected by seasonality or occur with a different frequency than the budgetary period, so a closer look at cash flow management can be helpful. Cash flows from income may be less frequent than cash flows for expenses, for example, or may be seasonal while expenses are more regular. Most expenses must be paid on a monthly basis, and if some income cash flows occur less frequently or only seasonally, there is a risk of running out of cash in a specific month. For cash flows, timing is everything.

A helpful management tool can be the cash budget, which is a rearrangement of budget items to show cash flows as they occur. This means having more and shorter periods within the budget. Irregular cash flows can be placed in the specific periods when they will occur, allowing you to see the effects of cash flow timing more clearly.

line of credit

A loan structured such that money can be borrowed as needed, up to a limit, and paid down as desired, and interest is paid regularly but only on the outstanding balance.

Mark's original annual budget (Table 5.2) shows that although his income is enough to cover his living expenses, it does not produce enough cash to support his capital expenditures: specifically, to fix the roof. In fact, his cash flow would fall short by roughly $7,000, even after he uses the cash from his money market account. If he must make the capital expenditure this year, he can finance it with a **line of credit**: a loan where money can be borrowed as needed, up to a limit, and paid down as desired, and interest is paid only on the outstanding balance.

Mark's monthly cash budget (Table 5.3) shows a more detailed and slightly different story (differences in the totals for each line item are due to rounding errors, the effect of rounding the amounts to whole dollars). Mark's wages are steady and year round, but his painting income is seasonal and his income from memorabilia sales is "lumpy," that is, irregular. Because of the seasonality of some of Mark's income, if he has the roof fixed in May, he will need to draw down his money market account and also borrow in May. As he earns income from painting over the summer, he can pay that balance down until September, when his seasonal extra income from painting disappears. Then in October, he will need to extend the loan again to pay his property tax, since he used up his money market balance for the roof. He then has one year to pay down the loan and build up the money market account to pay his property taxes the next October.

TABLE 5.3 Mark's Monthly Cash Budget for Year 5
(Part 1)

Year 5	Jan	Feb	Mar	Apr	May	June	July	Aug	Sept	Oct	Nov	Dec	Total
Incomes													
Wages	3,167	3,167	3,167	3,167	3,167	3,167	3,167	3,167	3,167	3,167	3,167	3,167	38,004
Tutoring	0	0	0	0	0	0	0	0	0	0	0	0	0
Memorabilia sales	0	250	0	0	0	0	0	0	0	200	0	500	950
House painting						3,472	3,472	3,473					10,417
Interest income	17	16	14	11	10	0	0	0	0	0	0	0	68
Total income	3,184	3,433	3,181	3,178	3,177	6,639	6,639	6,640	3,167	3,367	3,167	3,667	49,439
Payroll/income taxes	792	792	792	792	792	792	792	792	792	792	792	792	9,501
Disposable income	2,392	2,641	2,390	2,386	2,386	5,847	5,847	5,848	2,375	2,575	2,375	2,875	39,938
Living expenses													
Groceries	260	260	260	260	260	260	260	260	260	260	260	260	3,120
Car - fuel	156	156	156	156	156	156	156	156	156	156	156	156	1,875
Car - service, etc.	29	29	29	29	29	29	29	29	29	29	29	29	350
Car - insurance		400						400					800
Electricity	65	65	65	65	65	65	65	65	65	65	65	65	780
Phone/cable/internet	89	89	89	89	89	89	89	89	89	89	89	89	1,068
Heat	100	100	100	100	100	100	100	100	100	100	100	100	1,200
Health insurance	63	63	63	63	63	63	63	63	63	63	63	63	760
Medical	4	4	4	4	4	4	4	4	4	4	4	4	50

(Part 2)

Year 5	Jan	Feb	Mar	Apr	May	June	July	Aug	Sept	Oct	Nov	Dec	Total
Dental	42	42	42	42	42	42	42	42	42	42	42	42	500
Travel/entertainment	250	250	250	250	250	250	250	250	250	250	250	250	3,000
Car loan payment	499	499	499	499	499	499	499	499	499	499	499	499	5,988
Mortgage interest	897	897	897	897	897	897	897	897	897	897	897	897	10,769
Property tax										4,350			4,350
Total living expenses	2,455	2,855	2,455	2,455	2,455	2,455	2,455	2,855	2,455	6,805	2,455	2,455	34,610
Income after living expenses	(63)	(214)	(65)	(69)	(69)	3,392	3,392	2,993	(80)	(4,230)	(80)	420	5,328
Interest expense						56	41	25	12	14	36	38	222
Capital expenditures/investment													
Mortgage principal	270	270	270	270	270	270	270	270	270	270	270	270	3,240
Free cash flow	(333)	(484)	(335)	(339)	(339)	3,066	3,081	2,698	(362)	(4,513)	(386)	112	1,866
Retirement account deposit			1,000										1,000
Home improvement					15,000								15,000
Money market deposit (withdrawal)	(333)	(484)	(1,335)	(339)	(4,119)	0	0	0	0	0	0	50	(6,560)
Draw on (pay off) line of credit					11,221	(3,066)	(3,081)	(2,698)	362	4,513	386	(62)	7,575
Net cash flow	0	0	0	0	0	0	0	0	0	0	0	0	0
Line of credit balance					(11,221)	(8,155)	(5,073)	(2,375)	(2,737)	(7,251)	(7,637)	(7,575)	
Money market account balance	6,277	5,793	4,457	4,119	0	0	0	0	0	0	0	50	

By the end of the year, his outstanding debt will be a bit more than originally shown, with an ending balance of around $7,500. The difference is the interest expense on the loan, and the loss of interest earned from his money market account.

The cash (monthly) budget shows a different story than the annual budget because of the seasonal nature of Mark's incomes. Since he is planning the capital expenditures before he begins to earn income from painting, he actually has to borrow more—and assume more risk—than originally indicated.

The cash budget may show risks but also remedies that otherwise may not be apparent. In Mark's case, it is clear that the capital expenditure cannot be financed without some external source of capital, in this case the line of credit. He would have to pay interest on that loan, creating an additional expense. That expense would be in proportion to the amount borrowed and the time it is borrowed for. In his original plan, the capital expenditure occurred in May, and Mark would have had to borrow about $11,200, paying interest (on varying amounts) for the next seven months of the year.

Delaying the capital expenditure until October, however, would cost him less because he could use his painting income to build up his savings, then use the savings and borrow less (about $7,000) and pay interest in fewer months. An alternative cash budget illustrating this scenario is shown in Table 5.4.

TABLE 5.4 Mark's Alternate Monthly Cash Budget for Year 5
(Part 1)

Year 5	Jan	Feb	Mar	Apr	May	June	July	Aug	Sept	Oct	Nov	Dec	Total
Incomes													
Wages	3,167	3,167	3,167	3,167	3,167	3,167	3,167	3,167	3,167	3,167	3,167	3,167	38,004
Tutoring	0	0	0	0	0	0	0	0	0	0	0	0	0
Memorabilia sales	0	250	0	0	0	0	0	0	0	200	0	500	950
House painting						3,472	3,472	3,473					10,417
Interest income	17	16	14	11	10	9	17	25	32	31	0	0	183
Total income	3,184	3,433	3,181	3,178	3,177	6,648	6,656	6,665	3,199	3,398	3,167	3,667	49,554
Payroll/ income taxes	792	792	792	792	792	792	792	792	792	792	792	792	9,501
Disposable income	2,392	2,641	2,390	2,386	2,386	5,857	5,865	5,873	2,407	2,606	2,375	2,875	40,053
Living expenses													
Groceries	260	260	260	260	260	260	260	260	260	260	260	260	3,120
Car - fuel	156	156	156	156	156	156	156	156	156	156	156	156	1,875
Car - service, etc.	29	29	29	29	29	29	29	29	29	29	29	29	350
Car - insurance		400						400					800
Electricity	65	65	65	65	65	65	65	65	65	65	65	65	780
Phone/cable/ internet	89	89	89	89	89	89	89	89	89	89	89	89	1,068
Heat	100	100	100	100	100	100	100	100	100	100	100	100	1,200
Health insurance	63	63	63	63	63	63	63	63	63	63	63	63	760
Medical	4	4	4	4	4	4	4	4	4	4	4	4	50

(Part 2)

Year 5	Jan	Feb	Mar	Apr	May	June	July	Aug	Sept	Oct	Nov	Dec	Total
Dental	42	42	42	42	42	42	42	42	42	42	42	42	500
Travel/ entertainment	250	250	250	250	250	250	250	250	250	250	250	250	3,000
Car loan payment	499	499	499	499	499	499	499	499	499	499	499	499	5,988
Mortgage interest	897	897	897	897	897	897	897	897	897	897	897	897	10,769
Property tax										4,350			4,350
Total living expenses	2,455	2,855	2,455	2,455	2,455	2,455	2,455	2,855	2,455	6,805	2,455	2,455	34,610
Income after living expenses	(63)	(214)	(65)	(69)	(69)	3,402	3,410	3,018	(48)	(4,199)	(80)	420	5,443
Interest expense						0	0	0	0	0	35	37	72
Capital expenditures/investment													
Mortgage principal	270	270	270	270	270	270	270	270	270	270	270	270	3,240
Free cash flow	(333)	(484)	(335)	(339)	(339)	3,132	3,140	2,748	(318)	(4,469)	(386)	112	2,130
Retirement account deposit			1,000										1,000
Home improvement										15,000			15,000
Money market deposit (withdrawal)	(333)	(484)	(1,335)	(339)	(339)	3,132	3,140	2,748	(318)	(12,450)	0	50	(6,528)
Draw on (pay off) line of credit					0	0	0	0	0	7,019	386	(62)	7,343
Net cash flow	0	0	0	0	0	0	0	0	0	0	0	0	0
Line of credit balance					0	0	0	0	0	(7,019)	(7,405)	(7,343)	
Money market account balance	6,277	5,793	4,457	4,119	3,780	6,912	10,052	12,800	12,482	32	32	82	

Delaying the capital expenditure until October would also allow the money market account to build value—Mark's seasonal income would be deposited during the summer—which would finance more of the capital expenditure. In either case, he leaves a small balance in his money market account. In the alternative budget, he would end the year with a slightly smaller loan balance (about $7,300) and his interest expense would also be much less because he has borrowed less initially and because he can wait until October to borrow, thus paying interest for only three months of the year.

Timing matters for cash flows because you need to get cash before you spend it, but also because time affects value. It is always better to have liquidity sooner and hang onto it longer. A cash budget provides a much more detailed look at these timing issues, and the risks—and opportunities—of cash management that you may otherwise have missed.

Other Specialized Budgets

specialized budget

A budget that focuses on one particular financial asset, activity, or goal.

A cash flow budget is a budget that projects one specific aspect of your finances, that is, the cash flows. Other kinds of **specialized budgets** focus on one particular financial aspect or goal. A specialized budget is ultimately included in the comprehensive budget, as it is a part of total financial activity. It usually reflects one particular activity in more detail, such as the effect of owning and maintaining a particular asset or of pursuing a particular activity. You create a budget for that asset or that activity by segregating its incomes and expenses from your comprehensive budget. It is possible to create such a focused budget only if you can identify and separate its financial activity from the rest of your financial life. If so, you may want to track an activity separately that is directly related to a specific goal.

FIGURE 5.9

© Shutterstock, Inc.

For example, suppose you decide to take up weekend backpacking as a recreational activity. You are going to try it for two years, and then decide if you want to continue. Aside from assessing the enjoyment that it gives you, you want to be able to assess its impact on your finances. Typically, weekend backpacking requires specialized equipment and clothing, travel to a hiking trail access or campground, and perhaps lodging and meals. There is capital investment (in the equipment) and then recurring expenses. You may want to create a separate budget for your backpacking investment and expenses in order to assess the value of this new recreational activity.

tax budget

A budget that focuses on the tax consequences of projected financial activities.

One common type of specialized budget is a **tax budget**, including activities—incomes, expenses, gains, and losses—that have direct tax consequences. A tax budget can be useful in planning for or anticipating an event that will have significant tax consequences—for example, income from self-employment; the sale of a long-term asset such as a stock portfolio, business, or real estate; or a gift of significant wealth or the settling of an estate.

While it can be valuable to isolate and identify the effects of a specific activity or the progress toward a specific goal, that activity or goal is ultimately part of your larger financial picture. Specialized budgets need to remain a part of your comprehensive financial planning.

Key Takeaways

- The cash flow budget is an alternative format used as a cash management tool that provides:
  - more detailed information about the timing and amounts of cash flows,
  - a clearer view of risks and opportunities.
- Specialized budgets focus on a specific asset or activity.

- A tax budget is commonly used to track taxable activities.
- Eventually, specialized budgets need to be included in the comprehensive budget to have a complete perspective.

Exercises

1. When is a cash flow budget a useful alternative to a comprehensive budget?
2. Create a specialized budget and a tax budget from your comprehensive budget.

5.5 Budget Variances

Learning Objectives

1. Define and discuss the uses of budget variances.
2. Identify the importance of budget-monitoring activities.
3. Analyze budget variances to understand their causes, including possible changes in micro or macro factors.
4. Analyze budget variances to see potential remedies and to gauge their feasibility.

A **budget variance** occurs when the actual results of your financial activity differ from your budgeted projections. Since your expectations were based on knowledge from your financial history, micro- and macroeconomic factors, and new information, if there is a variance, it is because your estimate was inaccurate or because one or more of those factors changed unexpectedly. If your estimate was inaccurate—perhaps you had overlooked or ignored a factor—knowing that can help you improve. If one or more of those factors has changed unexpectedly, then identifying the cause of the variance creates new information with which to better assess your situation. At the very least, variances will alert you to the need for adjustments to your budget and to the appropriate choices.

budget variance

A difference between the actual results of your financial activity and your expected, budgeted results.

Once you have created a budget, your financial life continues. As actual data replace projections, you must monitor the budget compared to your actual activities so that you will notice any serious variances or deviations from the expected outcomes detailed in the budget. Your analysis and understanding of variances constitute new information for adjusting your current behavior, preparing the next budget, or perhaps realistically reassessing your behavior or original goals.

The sooner you notice a budget variance, the sooner you can analyze it and, if necessary, adjust for it. The sooner you correct the variance, the less it costs. For example, perhaps you have had a little trouble living within your means, so you have created a budget to help you do so. You have worked out a plan so that total expenses are just as much as total income. In your original budget you expected to have a certain expense for putting gas in your car, which you figured by knowing the mileage that you usually drive and the current price of gas. You are following your budget and going along just fine. Suddenly, the price of gas goes way up. So does your monthly expense. That means you'll have to:

FIGURE 5.10

© Shutterstock, Inc.

- spend less for other expenses in order to keep your total expenses within your budget,
- lower your gas expense by driving less, and/or
- increase your income to accommodate this larger expense.

In the short term, monitoring your gas expense alerts you to a need to change your financial behavior by driving less, spending less on other things, or earning more. In the long run, if you find this increased expense intolerable, you will make additional choices to avoid it. Perhaps you would buy a more fuel-efficient car, for example, or change your lifestyle to necessitate less driving. The number and feasibility of your choices will depend on your elasticity of demand for that particular budget item. But if you hadn't been paying attention, if you had not been monitoring your budget against the real outcomes as they were happening, you would not have been aware that any change was needed, and you would have found yourself with a surprising budget deficit.

It bears repeating that once you have discovered a significant budget variance, you need to analyze what caused it so that you can address it properly.

Income results from the sale of labor (wages) or liquidity (interest or dividends). If income deviates from its projection, it is because:

- a different quantity of labor or liquidity was sold at the expected price, e.g., Mark may have had fewer house painting contracts than usual but kept his rates the same;
- the expected quantity of labor or liquidity was sold at a different price, e.g., Mark may have had the usual number of contracts but earned less from them; or
- a different quantity of labor or liquidity was sold at a different price, e.g., Mark may have had fewer contracts and charged less to be more competitive.

Expenses result from consuming goods or services at a price. If an expense deviates from its projected outcome, it is because:

- a different quantity was consumed at the expected price, e.g., you did not use as much gas;
- the expected quantity was consumed at a different price, e.g., you used as much gas but the price of gas fell; or
- a different quantity was consumed at a different price, e.g., you used less gas and bought it for less.

Isolating the cause of a variance is useful because different causes will dictate different remedies or opportunities. For example, if your gas expense has increased, is it because you are driving more miles or because the price of gas has gone up? You can't control the price of gas, but you can control the miles you drive. Isolating the cause allows you to identify realistic choices. In this case, if the variance is too costly, you will need to address it by somehow driving fewer miles.

If your income falls, is it because your hourly wage has fallen or because you are working fewer hours? If your wage has fallen, you need to try to increase it either by negotiating with your employer or by seeking a new job at a higher wage. Your success will depend on demand in the labor market and on your usefulness as a supplier of labor.

If you are working fewer hours, it may be because your employer is offering you less work or because you choose to work less. If the problem is with your employer, you may need to renegotiate your position or find a new one. However, if your employer is buying less labor because of decreased demand in the labor market, that may be due to an industry or economic cycle, which may affect your success in making that change.

If it is your choice of hours that has caused the variance, perhaps that is due to personal factors—you are aging or your dependents require more care and attention—that need to be resolved to allow you to work more. Or perhaps you could simply choose to work more.

Identifying why you are going astray from your budget is critical in identifying remedies and choices. Putting those causes in the context of the micro- and macroeconomic factors that affect your situation will make your feasible choices clearer. Figure 5.11 shows how these factors can combine to cause a variance.

FIGURE 5.11 The Causes of a Budget Variance

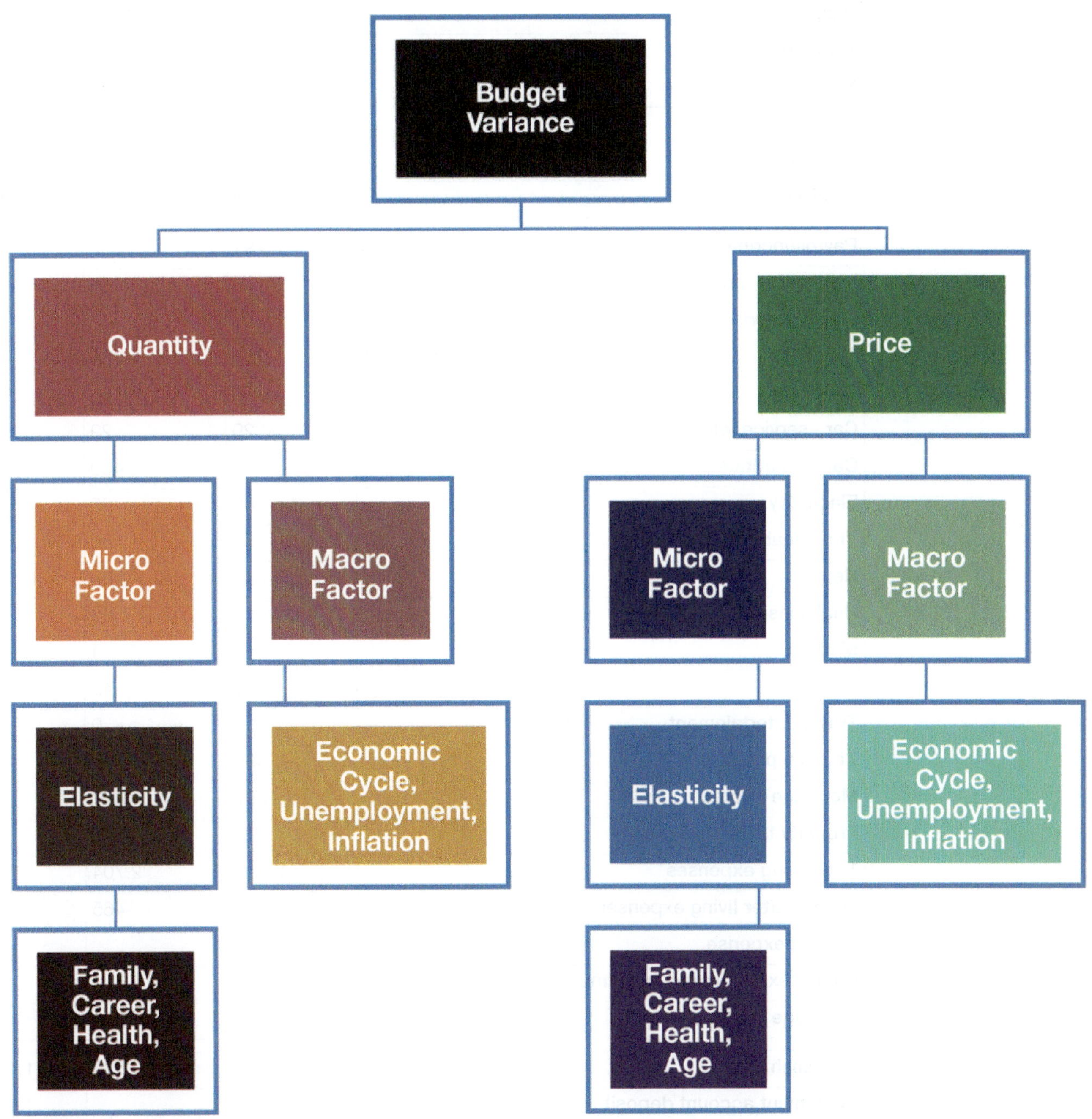

After three months, Mark decides to look at his budget variances to make sure he's on track. His actual results for January–March, Year 5 are detailed in Table 5.5.

TABLE 5.5 Mark's Actual Income and Expenditures, January-March, Year 5

Year 5	January	February	March
	Actual	**Actual**	**Actual**
Incomes			
Wages	3,167	3,167	3,167
Tutoring	400	400	400
Memorabilia sales	450	360	1,200
House painting			
Interest income	31	34	34
Total income	4,048	3,961	4,801
Payroll/income taxes	792	792	792
Disposable income	3,256	3,169	4,009
Living expenses			
Groceries	260	260	260
Car - fuel	156	156	156
Car - service, etc.	29	29	29
Car - insurance		400	
Electricity	65	65	65
Phone/cable/internet	89	89	89
Heat	200	200	200
Health insurance	63	63	63
Medical	4	4	4
Dental	42	42	42
Travel/entertainment	0	0	0
Car loan payment	499	499	499
Mortgage interest	897	897	897
Property tax			
Total living expenses	2,304	2,704	2,304
Income after living expenses	952	465	1,705
Interest expense			
Capital expenditures/investment			
Mortgage principal	270	270	270
Free cash flow	682	195	1,435
Retirement account deposit			1,000
Home improvement			
Money market deposit (withdrawal)	682	195	435
Draw on (pay off) line of credit			
Net cash flow	0	0	0
Line of credit			
Money market account balance	7,292	7,488	7,923

How will Mark analyze the budget variances he finds? In Mark's case, the income variances are positive. He has picked up a couple of tutoring clients who have committed to lessons through the end of the school year in June; this new information can be used to adjust income. His memorabilia business has done well; the volume of sales has not increased, but the memorabilia market seems to be up and prices are better than expected. The memorabilia business is cyclical; economic expansion and increases in disposable incomes enhance that market. Given the volatility of prices in that market, however, and the fact that there has been no increase in the volume of sales—Mark is not doing more business, just more lucrative business—Mark will not make any adjustments going forward. Interest rates have risen; Mark can use that macroeconomic news to adjust his expected interest income.

His expenses are as expected. The only variance is the result of Mark's decision to cut his travel and entertainment budget for this year (i.e., giving up his vacation) to offset the costs of the roof. He is planning that capital expenditure for October, which will actually make it cheaper because his roofer will not be as busy and will give Mark a discount of $1,000. His adjusted cash budget is shown in Table 5.6. (Any small discrepancies in the totals for line items are due to rounding errors—that is, rounding to whole dollars.)

TABLE 5.6 Mark's Adjusted Cash Budget for Year 5
(Part 1)

Year 5	Jan	Feb	March	April	May	June	July	Aug	Sept	Oct	Nov	Dec	Total
	Actual	**Actual**	**Actual**										
Incomes													
Wages	3,167	3,167	3,167	3,167	3,167	3,167	3,167	3,167	3,167	3,167	3,167	3,167	38,000
Tutoring	400	400	400	400	400	400	33	33	33	33	33	33	2,600
Memorabilia sales	450	360	1,200	0	0	0	0	0	0	200	0	500	2,710
House painting						3,472	3,472	3,472					10,417
Interest income	19	23	24	25	26	27	38	48	57	56	2	2	349
Total income	4,047	3,960	4,801	3,660	3,661	7,134	6,741	6,747	3,280	3,246	3,248	3,248	54,076
Payroll/income taxes	792	792	792	792	792	792	792	792	792	792	792	792	9,500
Disposable income	3,255	3,168	4,009	2,868	2,869	6,342	5,949	5,955	2,488	2,454	2,456	2,456	44,273
Living expenses													
Groceries	260	260	260	260	260	260	260	260	260	260	260	260	3,120
Car - fuel	156	156	156	156	156	156	156	156	156	156	156	156	1,872
Car - service, etc.	29	29	29	29	29	29	29	29	29	29	29	29	348
Car - insurance		400						400					800
Electricity	65	65	65	65	65	65	65	65	65	65	65	65	780
Phone/cable/internet	89	89	89	89	89	89	89	89	89	89	89	89	1,068
Heat	200	200	200	200	200	200	200	200	200	200	200	200	2,400
Health insurance	63	63	63	63	63	63	63	63	63	63	63	63	756
Medical	4	4	4	4	4	4	4	4	4	4	4	4	48

(Part 2)

Year 5	Jan	Feb	March	April	May	June	July	Aug	Sept	Oct	Nov	Dec	Total
	Actual	Actual	Actual										
Dental	42	42	42	42	42	42	42	42	42	42	42	42	504
Travel/entertainment	0	0	0	0	0	0	0	0	0	0	0	0	0
Car loan payment	499	499	499	499	499	499	499	499	499	499	499	499	5,988
Mortgage interest	897	897	897	897	897	897	897	897	897	897	897	897	10,764
Property tax										4,350			4,350
Total living expenses	2,340	2,704	2,304	2,304	2,304	2,304	2,304	2,704	2,304	6,654	2,304	2,304	32,798
Income after living expenses	951	464	1,705	564	565	4,038	3,645	3,251	184	(4,200)	152	152	11,475
Interest expense	0	0	0	0	0	0	0	0	0	0	0	0	0
Capital/expenditures/ investment													
Mortgage principal	270	270	270	270	270	270	270	270	270	270	270	270	3,240
Free cash flow	681	194	1,435	294	295	3,768	3,375	2,981	(86)	(4,470)	(118)	(118)	8,235
Retirement account deposit			1,000										1,000
Home improvement										14,000			14,000
Money market deposit (withdrawal)	681	194	435	294	295	3,768	3,375	2,981	(86)	(18,470)	(118)	(118)	(6,766)
Draw on (pay off) line of credit										0			
Net cash flow	0	0	0	0	0	0	0	0	0	0	0	0	0
Line of credit				0	0	0	0	0	0	0	0	0	
Money market account balance	8,047	8,241	8,677	8,971	9,266	13,035	16,410	19,391	19,306	836	718	600	

With these adjustments, it turns out that Mark can avoid new debt and still support the capital expenditure of the new roof. The increased income that Mark can expect and his decreased expenses (if he can maintain his resolve) can finance the project and still leave him with a bit of savings in his money market account.

This situation bears continued monitoring, however. Some improvements are attributable to Mark's efforts (cutting back on entertainment expenses, giving up his vacation, cultivating new tutoring clients). But Mark has also benefited from macroeconomic factors that have changed to his advantage (rising interest rates, rising memorabilia prices), and those factors could change again to his disadvantage. He has tried to be conservative about making adjustments going forward, but he should continue to keep a close eye on the situation, especially as he gets closer to making the relatively large capital expenditure in October.

Sometimes a variance cannot be "corrected" or is due to a micro- or macroeconomic factor beyond your control. In that case, you must adjust your expectations to reality. You may need to adjust expected outcomes or even your ultimate goals.

Variances are also measures of the accuracy of your projections; what you learn from them can improve your estimates and your budgeting ability. The unexpected can always occur, but the better you can anticipate what to expect, the more accurate—and useful—your budget process can be.

Key Takeaways

- Recognizing and analyzing variances between actual results and budget expectations:
  - identifies potential problems,
  - identifies potential remedies.
- The more frequently the budget is monitored, generally:
  - the sooner adjustments may be made,
  - the less costly adjustments are to make.
- Budget variances for incomes and expenses should be analyzed to see if they are caused by a difference in:
  - actual quantity,
  - actual price,
  - both actual quantity and actual price.
- Variances also need to be analyzed in the context of micro and macro factors that may change.

Exercise

1. You are working fewer hours, which is reducing your income from employment and causing a budget variance. If the choice to work fewer hours is yours, what are some microeconomic factors that could be causing this outcome? If the choice is your employer's, what are some macroeconomic factors that could be sources of the variance? What are your choices for increasing income? Alternatively, what might you change in your financial behavior, budget, or goals to your improve outcomes?

5.6 Budgets, Financial Statements, and Financial Decisions

Learning Objectives

1. Describe the budget process as a financial planning tool.
2. Discuss the relationships between financial statements and budgets.
3. Demonstrate the use of budgets in assessing choices.
4. Identify factors that affect the value of choices.

Whatever type of budget you create, the budget process is one aspect of personal financial planning, a tool to make better financial decisions. Other tools include financial statements, assessments of risk and of the time value of money, macroeconomic indicators, and microeconomic or personal factors. The usefulness of these tools is that they provide a clearer view of "what is" and "what is possible." It puts your current situation and your choices into a larger context, giving you a better way to think about where you are, where you'd like to be, and how to go from here to there.

Mark has to decide whether to go ahead with the new roof. Because the house needs a new roof, his decision is really only about his choice of financing. An analysis of Mark's budget variances has shown that he can actually pay for the roof with the savings in his money market account. This means his goal is more attainable (and less costly) than in his original budget. This favorable outcome is due to his efforts to increase income and reduce expenses and to macroeconomic changes that have been to his advantage. So, Mark can make progress toward his long-term goals of building his asset base. He can continue saving for retirement with deposits to his retirement account and can continue improving and protecting his property with a new roof on his house.

Because Mark is financing the roof with the savings from his money market account, he can avoid new debt and thus additional interest expense. He will lose the interest income from his money market account but the increases from his tutoring and sales income will offset the loss. Mark's income statement will be virtually unaffected by the roof. His cash flow statement will show unchanged operating cash flow, a large capital expenditure, and use of savings.

FIGURE 5.12

© Shutterstock, Inc.

Mark can finance this increase of asset value (his new roof) with another asset, his money market account. His balance sheet will not change substantially—value will just shift from one asset to another—but the money market account earns income, while the house does not, although there may be a gain in value when the house is sold in the future.

Right now that interest income is insignificant, but since it seems to be a period of rising interest rates, the opportunity cost of forgone interest income could be significant in the future if that account balance were allowed to grow.

Moreover, Mark will be moving value from a very liquid money market account to a not-so-liquid house, decreasing his overall liquidity. Looking ahead, this loss of liquidity could create another opportunity cost: it could narrow his options. Mark's liquidity will be pretty much depleted by the roof, so future capital expenditures may have to be financed with debt or wait until he can rebuild his savings. If interest rates continue to rise, that will make financing future capital expenditures more expensive and perhaps will cause Mark to delay those expenditures or even cancel them.

However, Mark also has a very reliable source of liquidity in his earnings—his paycheck, which can offset this loss. If he can continue to generate free cash flow to add to his savings, he can restore his money market account and his liquidity. Having no dependents makes Mark more able to assume the risk of depleting his liquidity now and relying on his income to restore it later.

spread

A difference between two interest rates, quoted in basis points. The most commonly noted spreads are those between Treasury and corporate securities of the same maturity.

The opportunity cost of losing liquidity and interest income will be less than the cost of new debt and new interest expense. That is because interest rates on loans are always higher than interest rates on savings. Banks always charge more than they pay for liquidity. That **spread**, or difference between those two rates, is the bank's profit, so the bank's cost of buying money will always be less than the price it sells for. The added risk and obligation of new debt could also create opportunity cost and make it more difficult to finance future capital expenditures. So financing the capital expenditure with an asset rather than with a liability is less costly both immediately and in the future because it creates fewer obligations and more opportunities, less opportunity cost, and less risk.

The budget and the financial statements allow Mark to project the effects of this financial decision in the larger context of his current financial situation and ultimate financial goals. His understanding of opportunity costs, liquidity, the time value of money, and of personal and macroeconomic factors also helps him evaluate his choices and their consequences. Mark can use this decision and its results to inform his next decisions and his ultimate horizons.

Financial planning is a continuous process of making financial decisions. Financial statements and budgets are ways of summarizing the current situation and projecting the outcomes of choices. Financial statement analysis and budget variance analysis are ways of assessing the effects of choices. Personal factors, economic factors, and the relationships of time, risk, and value affect choices as their dynamics—how they work and bear on decisions—affect outcomes.

Key Takeaways

- Financial planning is a continuous process of making financial decisions.
- Financial statements are ways of summarizing the current situation.
- Budgets are ways of projecting the outcomes of choices.
- Financial statement analysis and budget variance analysis are ways of assessing the effects of choices.
- Personal factors, economic factors, and the relationships of time, risk, and value affect choices, as their dynamics affect outcomes.

Exercise

1. Analyze Mark's budget as a financial planning tool for making decisions in the following situations. In each case, how will other financial planning tools affect Mark's decisions? For each case, create a new budget showing the projected effects of Mark's decisions.
   a. Mark injures himself on the cross-trainer, and the doctor recommends a course of physical therapy.
   b. A neighbor and coworker suggest that he and Mark commute to work together.
   c. The roofers inform Mark that his chimney needs to be repointed and relined.
   d. Mark wants to give up tutoring and put more time into his memorabilia business.
   e. Mark wants to marry and start a family and needs to know when would be a good time.

CHAPTER 6

Taxes and Tax Planning

6.1 Introduction

All developed and most less-developed economies have a tax system that finances their governments, at least in part. The design of that tax system reflects the society's view of the responsibilities of government and of its citizens for their government.

In the United States there has always been disagreement about the role of government as a producer for and a protector of the economy and its citizens. Even before the United States was a nation, "taxation without representation" was a rallying cry for rebellion against the British colonial authority, and the colonists protested taxes on everything from stamps to tea. The American Revolution was as much about economic democracy—the fundamental right of every individual to participate in the economy and to own the fruits of labor—as it was about political democracy.

It is perhaps no coincidence that Adam Smith's *Wealth of Nations* was published in 1776, the same year that independence was declared in the 13 colonies. Smith recognized a role for government in a market-based economy, but societies have argued about what that role should be and how it should be paid for ever since. The U.S. tax code is based on the idea that everyone should help finance the government according to one's ability to pay. Changes in how "everyone" is defined and how "ability to pay" is measured have led to tax law changes that keep the system evolving.

In the United States, tax laws are written by Congress and, therefore, through compromise. As views on government financing have changed, tax laws have been amended and refined, enacted and repealed. The result is a tax code that can seem overly complex and even unreasonable or illogical. However, each element of the tax system has a reason and a purpose. The better you understand the elements of the tax system, the better you will understand how to live with it—and plan for it—to your best advantage.

6.2 Sources of Taxation and Kinds of Taxes

Learning Objectives

1. Identify the levels of government that impose taxes.
2. Define the different kinds of incomes, assets, and transactions that may be taxed.
3. Compare and contrast progressive and regressive taxes.

Any government that needs to raise revenue and has the legal authority to do so may tax. Tax jurisdictions reflect government authorities. In the United States, federal, state, and municipal governments impose taxes. Similarly, in many countries there are national, provincial or state, county, and municipal taxes. Regional economic alliances, such as the European Union, may also levy taxes.

FIGURE 6.1

© Shutterstock, Inc.

Jurisdictions may overlap. For example, in the United States, federal, state, and local governments may tax income, which becomes complicated for those earning income in more than one state, or living in one state and working in another. Governments tax income because it is a way to tax broadly based on the ability to pay. Most adults have an income from some source, even if it is a government distribution. Those with higher incomes should be able to pay more taxes, and in theory should be willing to do so, for they have been more successful in or have benefited more from the economy that the government protects.

progressive taxation

A tax rate that increases as the amount to be taxed increases, a common design of an income tax.

tax bracket

A range of income that defines an income tax rate.

Income tax is usually a **progressive tax**: the higher the income or the more to be taxed, the greater the tax rate. The percentage of income that is paid in tax increases as income rises. Those income categories are called **tax brackets**. Most developed economies have a progressive income tax system; the table shows the progressive income tax rates for the United States in 2018.[1]

TABLE 6.1 U.S. Income Tax Brackets in 2018 (Single Filing Status)

If your taxable income is greater than	and less than	Your tax rate is
0	9,525	10%
9,526	38,700	12%
38,701	82,500	22%
82,501	157,500	24%
157,500	200,000	32%
200,001	500,000	35%
500,001		37%

Based on information from "2018 Tax Brackets (Updated)," *Fiscal Facts*, No. 567, January 2018. https://files.taxfoundation.org/20180207142513/TaxFoundation-FF567-Updated.pdf(accessed July 3, 2018)

Tax is levied on income from many sources:

- Wages (selling labor)
- Interest, dividends, and gains from investment (selling capital)
- Self-employment (operating a business or selling a good or service)
- Property rental
- Royalties (rental of intellectual property)
- "Other" income such as alimony, gambling winnings, or prizes

A **sales tax** or **consumption tax** taxes the consumption financed by income. In the United States, sales taxes are imposed by state or local governments; as yet, there is no national sales tax. Sales taxes are said to be more efficient and fair in that consumption reflects income as income determines ability to consume and therefore level of consumption. Consumption is also hard to hide, making sales tax a good way to collect taxes based on the ability to pay. Consumption taxes typically tax all consumption, including nondiscretionary items such as food, clothing, and housing. Opponents of sales tax argue that it is a **regressive tax**, because those with smaller incomes must use a greater percentage of their incomes on nondiscretionary purchases than those with greater incomes.

consumption tax

A sales or excise tax that taxes the consumption of discretionary and nondiscretionary goods and services.

regressive taxation

A tax rate that decreases as the amount to be taxed increases.

The **value-added tax** (VAT) or goods and services tax (GST) is widely used outside the United States. It is a consumption tax, but it differs from the sales tax, which is paid only by the consumer as an end user. With a VAT or GST, the value added to the product is taxed at each stage of production. Governments use a VAT or GST instead of a sales tax to spread the tax burden among producers and consumers and thus reduce the incentive to evade the tax. A consumption tax, like the sales tax, it is a regressive tax. When traveling abroad, you should be aware that a VAT may add substantially to the cost of a purchase (such as meals, accommodations, events, and transportation).

value-added tax

A consumption tax that spreads the tax burden among producers and consumers by taxing the value added to goods at each stage of production and consumption.

Excise taxes are taxes on specific consumption items such as alcohol, cigarettes, motor vehicles, fuel, or highway use. Excise taxes are justified by the discretionary nature of the purchases, however, they may be criticized as exercises in social engineering, i.e., using the tax code to encourage or discourage certain social or personal behaviors. Excise taxes tend to be levied on items that people will buy even if a tax increases the price. For example, people who enjoy nicotine or alcohol tend to purchase cigarettes or liquor even if an excise tax increases their cost—and are therefore a reliable source of tax revenue.

excise taxes

A tax on a specific item produced within a country.

Property taxes are used by more local—state, municipal, provincial, and county—governments, and are most commonly imposed on real property (land and buildings) but also on personal assets such as vehicles and boats. Property values theoretically reflect wealth (accrued income) and thus ability to pay taxes. Property values are also a matter of public record (real property is deeded, boats or automobiles are licensed, etc.), which allows more efficient tax collection.

Estate taxes are taxes on the transfer of wealth from the deceased to the living. Estate taxes are usually imposed on the very wealthiest based on their unusual ability to pay. Because death and the subsequent dispersal of property is legally a matter of public record, estate taxes are generally easy to collect. Estate taxes are controversial because they can be seen as a tax on the very idea of ownership and on incomes that have already been taxed and saved or stored as wealth and properties. Still, estate taxes are a substantial source of revenue for the governments that use them, and so they remain.

estate tax

A tax on the intergenerational transfer of wealth after death.

A summary of the kinds of taxes used by the three different jurisdictions is shown in Table 6.2.

TABLE 6.2 Taxes and Jurisdictions

Type of Tax	National or Federal	Provincial or State	County or Municipal
Income	√	√	√
Sales		√	√
VAT or GST	√	√	
Excise	√	√	√
Property		√	√
Estate	√	√	

Key Takeaways

- Governments at all levels use taxes as a source of financing.
- Taxes may be imposed on the following:
  - Incomes from
    - wages,
    - interest, dividends, and gains (losses),
    - rental of real or intellectual property.
  - Consumption of discretionary and nondiscretionary goods and services.
  - Wealth from
    - asset ownership,
    - asset transfer after death.
- Taxes may be:
  - progressive, such as the income tax, in which you pay proportionally more taxes the more income you have;
  - regressive, such as a sales tax, in which you pay proportionally more taxes the less income you have.

Exercises

1. Examine the state, federal, and other tax returns that you filed last year. Alternatively, estimate based on your present financial situation. On what incomes were you (or would you be) taxed? What tax bracket were you (or would you be) in? How did (or would) your state, federal, and other tax liabilities differ? What other types of taxes did you (or would you) pay and to which government jurisdictions?
2. In My Notes or your financial planning journal, record all the types of taxes you will be paying next year and to whom. How will you plan for paying these taxes? How will your tax liabilities affect your budget?
3. Is there any kind of income that is not taxed? Read the article, "What qualifies as nontaxable income" (Kay Bell, https://www.nerdwallet.com/blog/taxes/nontaxable-income/, March 2, 2017). Discuss with your classmates whether it is practical to avoid taxes by using these types of income.
4. Can student income can be taxed? Read the article, "Student Tax Myths and How to File Tips" (https://www.efile.com/student-tax-aid-money-savings-tips-benefits/). How do you think this will affect your next tax return?

6.3 The U.S. Federal Income Tax Process

Learning Objectives

1. Identify the taxes most relevant for personal financial planning.
2. Identify taxable incomes and the schedules used to report them.
3. Identify deductions, exemptions, and credits.
4. Compare methods of tax payment.

The U.S. government relies most on an income tax. The income tax is the most relevant for personal financial planning, as everyone has some sort of income over a lifetime. Most states model their tax systems on the federal model or base their tax rates on federally defined income. While the estate tax may become more of a concern as you age, the federal income tax system will affect you and your financial decisions throughout your life.

Taxable Entities

There are four taxable entities in the federal system: the individual or family unit, the corporation, the nonprofit corporation, and the trust. Personal financial planning focuses on your decisions as an individual or family unit, but other tax entities can affect individual income. Corporate profit may be distributed to individuals as a **dividend**, for example, which then becomes the individual's taxable income. Likewise, funds established for a specific purpose may distribute money to an individual that is taxable as individual income. A **trust**, for example, is a legal arrangement whereby control over property is transferred to a person or organization (the trustee) for the benefit of someone else (the beneficiary). If you were a beneficiary and received a distribution, that money would be taxable as individual income.

dividend

A share of corporate profit distributed to shareholders, usually as cash or corporate stock.

trust

A legal entity created to own and manage assets for the benefit of beneficiaries.

The definition of the taxable individual or family unit is further classified by filing status:

- Single, never married, widowed, or divorced
- Married, in which case two adults file as one taxable "unit," combining all taxable activities and incomes, deductions, exemptions, and credits
- Married filing separately, in which case two married adults file as two separate taxable individuals, individually declaring and defining incomes, deductions, exemptions, and credits
- Head-of-household, for a family of one adult with dependents

Some taxes are levied differently depending on filing status, following the assumption that family structure affects ability to pay taxes.

FIGURE 6.2

© Shutterstock, Inc.

All taxable entities have to file a declaration of incomes and pay any tax obligations annually. Not everyone who files a return actually pays taxes, however. Individuals with low incomes and tax exempt, nonprofit corporations typically do not. All potential taxpayers nevertheless must declare income and show their obligations to the government. For the individual filing in the United States, that declaration is filed on Form 1040. Although it has been revised and alternative versions (1040A, 1040EZ) have been created over the years, the Form 1040 has been in use since income tax was initiated in the United States in 1913.

Income

For individuals, the first step in the process is to calculate total income. Income may come from many sources, and each income must be calculated and declared. The most common source of income is wages or salaries from an employer. Other types of income may require a separate form or schedule to show their more detailed calculations. The following are common kinds of income, besides wages or salaries, by source.

Interest and Dividend Income

Interest income is income from selling liquidity. For example, the interest that your savings account, certificates of deposit, and bonds earn in a year is income. You are earning interest from lending cash to a bank, a money market mutual fund, a government, or a corporation (though not all your interest income may be taxable). Dividend income, on the other hand, is income from investing in corporate ownership. Dividends are your share of corporate profits as a shareholder, distributed in proportion to the number of shares of corporate stock you own.

Business Income

Business income is income from self-employment or entrepreneurial ventures or business enterprises. For sole proprietors and partners in a partnership, business income may be the primary source of income. Many other individuals rely on wages, but have a small business on the side for extra income. Business expenses can be deducted from business income, including, for example, business use of your car and home. If expenses are greater than income, the business is operating at a loss. Business losses can be deducted from total income, just as business income adds to total income.

The tax laws distinguish between a business and a hobby that earns or loses money. You are considered to have a business for tax purposes if you earned a profit in three of the past five years including the current year or if you are operating as a registered business with the intention of making a profit. If you are operating your own business, you also must also pay self-employment tax on business income. In addition, the self-employed must pay estimated income taxes in quarterly installments based on expected income.

Tariq is thinking about turning his hobby into a business. He has been successful buying and selling South Asian folk art online. He thinks he has found a large enough market to support a business enterprise. As a business, he would be able to deduct the costs of website promotion, his annual art buying trip, his home office, and shipping, which would reduce the taxes he would have to pay on his business income. Tariq decides to enroll in online courses on how to become an entrepreneur, how to write a business plan, and how to find capital for a new venture.

FIGURE 6.3

Self-Employment Tax

Self-employment tax is an additional tax on income from self-employment or business income earned by a sole proprietor. It represents the employer's contribution to Social Security and to

Medicare, which are both mandatory programs of the federal government. Both employers and employees are required to contribute to the employee's Social Security account. When you are both the employee and the employer, as in self-employment, you must contribute both shares of the contribution.

Capital Gains (or Losses)

Gains or losses from investments derive from changes in asset value during ownership from the asset's original cost to its market value at the time of sale. If you sell an asset for more than you paid for it, you have a gain. If you sell an asset for less than you paid for it, you have a loss. You may have frequent gains or losses from trading investments in financial instruments such as stocks, bonds, or mutual funds. One-time gains or losses, such as the sale of a home, are also reported.

The tax code distinguishes between assets held for a short time, less than one year, and assets held for a long time, one year or more. Short-term capital gains or losses are taxed at a different rate than long-term capital gains or losses. Short-term capital gains are taxed as regular income (refer to the tax brackets in Section 6.2). Long-term capital gains are taxed at 0%, 15% or 20%, depending on the investor's income tax bracket, and thus long-term capital gains are taxed at lower rates than short-term capital gains or regular income.

cost basis

The original cost of an asset that is used to calculate a gain (loss) upon sale of the asset.

When you invest in financial assets, such as stocks, bonds, and mutual funds, or property or equipment, be sure to keep good records by noting the date when you bought them and the original price. These records establish the **cost basis** of your investments, which is used to calculate your gain or loss when you sell them.

Rental and Royalty Income; Income from Partnerships, S Corporations, and Trusts

Rental or royalty income is income earned from renting an asset, either real property or a creative work such as a book or a song. This can be a primary source of income, although many individuals rely on wages and have some rental or royalty income on the side. Home ownership may be made more affordable, for example, if the second half of a duplex can be rented for extra income. Rental expenses can also be deducted from rental income, which can create a loss from rental activity rather than a gain. Unlike a business, which must become profitable to remain a business for tax purposes, rental activities may generate losses year after year. Such losses are a tax advantage, as they reduce total income.

Partnerships and S corporations are alternative business structures for a business with more than one owner. For example, partnerships and S corporations are commonly used by professional practices, such as accounting firms, law firms, medical practices, and the like, as well as by family businesses.

The partnership or S corporation is not a taxable entity, but the share of its profits distributed to each owner is taxable income for the owner and must be declared.

Farm Income

Farm income is income from growing food, livestock, or livestock products, such as wool, to sell. Farmers have a special status in the tax code, stemming from the original agricultural basis of the U.S. economy and the strategic importance of self-sufficiency in food production. Thus, the tax code applies exemptions specifically to farmers.

Other Taxable and Nontaxable Income

Other taxable income includes alimony, state or local tax refunds, retirement fund distributions from individual retirement accounts (IRAs) and/or pensions, unemployment compensation, and a portion of Social Security benefits.

Your total income is then adjusted for items that the government feels should not be taxed under certain circumstances, such as savings in health savings or retirement accounts; a portion of self-employment taxes; student loan interest; tuition and educational fees; and alimony paid. A portion of income from qualified business, partnerships, and S corporations, may also be deducted. Income that is not taxed by the U.S. government and does not have to be reported as income includes the following:

- Welfare benefits
- Interest from *most* municipal bonds
- *Most* gifts
- *Most* inheritance and bequests
- Workers compensation
- Veteran's benefits
- Federal tax refunds
- *Some* scholarships and fellowships

FIGURE 6.4

© Shutterstock, Inc.

It's important to read tax filing instructions carefully, however, because not everything you'd think would qualify actually does. The government allows adjustments to be reported (or not reported) as income only under certain circumstances or up to certain income limits, and some adjustments require special forms.

The result of deducting adjustments from your total income is a calculation of your adjusted gross income (AGI). Your AGI is then further adjusted by amounts that may be deducted or exempted from your taxable income and by amounts already credited to your tax obligations.

Deductions, Exemptions, and Credits

Deductions and exemptions reduce taxable income, while credits reduce taxes. Deductions are tax breaks for incurring certain expenditures or for living in certain circumstances that the government thinks you should not have to include in your taxable income. There are deductions for age and for blindness. For other deductions, there is a standard, lump-sum deduction that you can take, or you may choose to itemize your deductions, that is, detail each one separately and then calculate the total. If your itemized deductions are more than your standard deduction, it makes sense to itemize.

Other deductions involve financial choices that the government encourages by rewarding with an extra incentive in the form of a tax break. For example, charitable donations are deductible to encourage charitable giving.

Deductions are also created for expenditures that may be considered nondiscretionary, such as medical and dental expenses or state and local income and property taxes. As with income adjustments, you have to read the instructions carefully, however, to know what expenditures qualify as deductions. Some deductions only qualify if they amount to more than a certain percentage of income and some deductions are capped at a maximum amount, while others may be deducted regardless. Some deductions require an additional form to calculate specifics, such as charitable gifts not given in cash, investment interest, and some mortgage interest.

There are exemptions based on the number of your dependents, who are usually children, but may be elderly parents or disabled siblings, that is, relatives who generally cannot care for themselves financially. Exemptions are made for dependents as nondiscretionary expenditures, but the government also encourages individuals to care for their financially dependent children, parents, and siblings because without such care they might become dependents of a government safety net or a charity.

FIGURE 6.5

After deductions and exemptions are subtracted from adjusted gross income, the remainder is your taxable income. Your tax is based on your taxable income, on a progressive scale. You may have additional taxes, such as self-employment tax, and you may be able to apply credits against your taxes, such as the earned income credit for lower-income taxpayers with children.

Deductions, exemptions, and credits are some of the more disputed areas of the tax code. Because of the depth of dispute about them, they tend to change more frequently than other areas of the tax code. For example, in 2009, a credit was added to encourage first-time homebuyers to purchase a home in the hopes of stimulating the residential real estate market. Most recently, the 2017 Tax Cuts and Jobs Act resulted in the elimination of some long-standing deductions and exemptions and in significant changes to the limits or qualifications for others. As a taxpayer, you want to stay alert to changes that may be to your advantage or disadvantage. Usually, but not always, such changes are phased in and out gradually so you can include them in your financial planning process.

Payments and Refunds

Once you have calculated your tax obligation for the year, you can compare that to any taxes you have paid during the year and calculate the amount still owed or the amount to be refunded to you.

You pay taxes during the tax year by having them withheld from your paycheck if you earn income through wages, or by making quarterly estimated tax payments if you have other kinds of income. When you begin employment, you fill out a form (Form W-4) that determines the taxes to be withheld from your regular pay. You may adjust this amount, within limits, at any time. If you have both wages and other incomes, but your wage income is your primary source of income, you may be able to increase the taxes withheld from your wages to cover the taxes on your other income, and thus avoid having to make estimated payments. However, if your nonwage income is substantial, you will have to make estimated payments to avoid a penalty and/or interest.

The government requires that taxes are withheld or paid quarterly during the tax year because it uses tax revenues to finance its expenditures, so it needs a steady and predictable cash flow. Steady payments also greatly decrease the risk of taxes being uncollectible. State and local income taxes must also be paid during the tax year and are similarly withheld from wages or paid quarterly.

Besides income taxes, other taxes are withheld from your wages: payments for Social Security and Medicare. Social Security or the Federal Insurance Contributions Act (FICA) and Medicare are federal government programs. Social Security is insurance against loss of income due to retirement, disability, or loss of a spouse or parent. Individuals are eligible for benefits based on their own contributions—or their spouse's or parents'—during their working lives, so technically, the Social Security payment withheld from your current wages is not a tax but a contribution to your own deferred income. Medicare finances health care for the elderly. Both programs were designed to provide minimal benefits to those no longer able to sell their labor in exchange for wage income. In fact, both Social Security and Medicare function as "pay-as-you-go" systems, so your contributions pay for benefits that current beneficiaries receive.

FIGURE 6.6

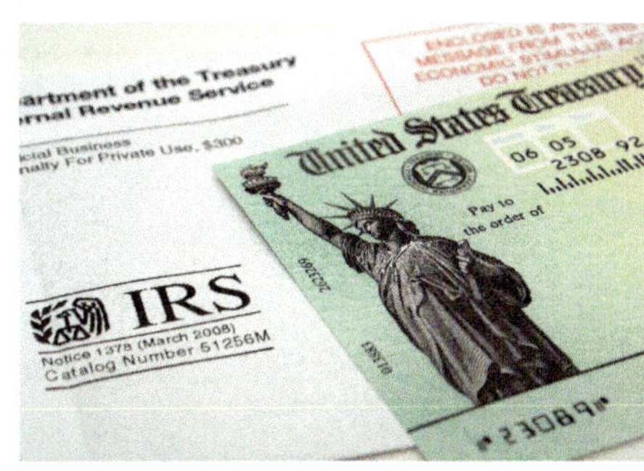

If you have paid more during the tax year than your actual obligation, then you are due a refund of the difference. You may have that amount directly deposited to a bank account, or the government will send you a check.

If you have paid less during the tax year than your actual obligation, then you will have to pay the difference (by check or credit card) and you may have to pay a penalty and/or interest, depending on the size of your payment.

The deadline for filing income tax returns and for paying any necessary amounts is April 15, following the end of the tax year on December 31. You may file to request an extension of that deadline to August 15. Should you miss a deadline without filing for an extension, you will owe penalties and interest, even if your actual tax obligation results in a refund. It really pays to get your return in on time.

Key Takeaways

- The most relevant tax for financial planning is the income tax, as it affects the taxpayer over an entire lifetime.
- Different kinds of income must be defined and declared on specific income schedules and are subject to tax.
- Deductions and exemptions reduce taxable income.
- Credits reduce tax obligations.
- Payments are made throughout the tax year through withholding from wages or through quarterly payments.

Exercises

1. What are the 10 "rights" of the "Taxpayer Bill of Rights" (https://www.irs.gov/taxpayer-bill-of-rights)? Discuss with your classmates why these "rights" may have been formally adopted by the IRS.
2. Download and study the following schedules or their equivalent for the current year. In what circumstances would you have to file each one? Tentatively fill out any schedules that apply to you for the current year.
   - Schedules A: http://www.irs.gov/pub/irs-pdf/f1040sa.pdf
   - Schedules B: http://www.irs.gov/pub/irs-pdf/f1040sb.pdf
   - Schedule C: http://www.irs.gov/pub/irs-pdf/f1040sc.pdf
   - Schedule D: http://www.irs.gov/pub/irs-pdf/f1040sd.pdf
   - Schedule E: http://www.irs.gov/pub/irs-pdf/f1040se.pdf
   - Schedule F: http://www.irs.gov/pub/irs-pdf/f1040sf.pdf
3. Find answers to the following questions at http://www.finaid.org/scholarships/taxability.phtml. Then check to see if the 2017 Tax Cuts and Jobs Act changes any of your answers.
   a. Is financial aid for college subject to federal income tax?
   b. Can federal and state education grants be taxed as income?
   c. Are student loans taxable?
   d. When is a scholarship tax exempt?
   e. Do you have to be in a degree program to qualify for tax exemption?
   f. When can the cost of textbooks be deducted from gross income for tax reporting purposes?
   g. Can the amount of a scholarship used for tuition be deducted?
   h. Can living expenses while on scholarship be deducted?
   i. Is the income and stipend from a teaching fellowship or research assistantship tax exempt?
   j. Are the tuition, books, and stipends of ROTC students tax exempt?

6.4 Record Keeping, Preparation, and Filing

Learning Objectives

1. Identify sources of tax information.
2. Explain the importance of verifiable records and record keeping.
3. Compare sources of tax preparation assistance.
4. Trace the tax review process and its implications.

The Internal Revenue Code (IRC), the federal tax law, is written by the U.S. Congress and enforced by the Internal Revenue Service (IRS), which is a part of the U.S. Department of Treasury. The IRS is responsible for the collection of tax revenues. To collect revenues, the IRS must inform the public of tax obligations and devise data collection systems that will allow for collection and verification of tax information so that collectible revenues can be verified. In other words, the IRS has to figure out how to inform the public and collect taxes while also collecting enough information to be able to check that those taxes are correct.

To inform the public, the IRS has published over 2,100 separate publications covering various aspects of the tax code. There are more than 1,300 forms and accompanying instructions to file complete tax information, although most taxpayers actually file about half a dozen forms each year. In addition, the IRS provides a website (http://www.irs.gov) and telephone support to answer questions and assist in preparing tax filings.

By far, most income taxes from wages are collected through withholding as earned. For most taxpayers, wages represent the primary form of income, and thus most of their tax payments are withheld or paid as wages are earned. Still, everyone has to file to summarize the details of the year's incomes for the IRS and to calculate the final tax obligation. In 2015 (the last year for which figures are available), the IRS collected over 150 million individual tax returns representing almost $1.5 trillion in income tax revenue.[2]

Keeping Records

The individual filer must collect and report the information on tax forms and schedules. Fortunately, this is not as difficult as the volume of data would suggest. Employers are required to send Form W-2 to each employee at the end of the year, detailing the total wages earned and taxes and contributions withheld. If you have earned other kinds of income, your clients, customers, retirement fund, or other source of income may have to file a Form 1099 to report that income to you and to the IRS. Interest and dividend income is also reported by the bank or brokerage firm on Form 1099. The W-2 and the Form 1099 are reported to both the IRS and you.

The system for filing tax information has purposeful redundancies. Where possible, information is collected independently from at least two sources, so it can be verified. For example, your wage data is collected both from you and from your employer, your interest and dividend incomes are reported by both you and the bank or brokerage that paid them, and so on. Those redundancies, wherever practical, allow for a system of cross-references so that the IRS can check the validity of the data it receives.

Incomes may be summarized and reported to you, but only you know your expenses. Expenditures are important if they are allowed as deductions, such as charitable gifts, medical and dental expenses, and so on, so data should be collected throughout the tax year. If you do nothing more than keep a checkbook, then you will have to go through it and identify the deductible expenses for the tax year. Financial software applications will make that task easier; most allow you to flag deductible expenses in your initial setup.

You should also keep receipts of purchases that may be deductible; credit or debit card statements and bank statements provide convenient backup proof of expenditures. Proof is needed in the event the IRS questions the accuracy of your return.

Tax Preparation and Filing

After you have collected the information you need, you fill out the forms. The tax code is based on the idea that citizens should create revenues for the government based on their ability to pay—and the tax forms follow that logic. Most taxpayers need to complete only a few schedules and forms to supplement their Form 1040. Most taxpayers have the same kinds of taxable events, incomes, and deductions year after year and file the same kinds of schedules and forms.

Many taxpayers prefer to consult a professional tax preparer. Professional help is useful if you have a relatively complicated tax situation: unusual sources of income or expenditures that may be deductible under unusual circumstances. Some taxpayers use a tax preparer simply to protect against making a mistake and having the error, however, innocent, prove costly to fix. Fees for tax preparers depend on how complex your return is, the number of forms that need to be completed, and the type of professional you consult.

Professional tax preparers may be lawyers, accountants, personal financial planners, or tax consultants. You may have an ongoing relationship with your tax preparer who may also be your accountant or financial planner, working with you on other financial decisions. Or you may consult a tax preparer simply on tax issues. You may want your tax preparer to fill out and file the forms for you, or you may be looking for advice about future financial decisions that have tax consequences. Tax preparers may be independent practitioners who work during tax season, or employees of a national chain that provide year-round tax services.

There is no standard certification to be a professional tax preparer. An enrolled agent (EA) is someone who has successfully passed training courses offered by the IRS. A certified public accountant (CPA) has specific training and experience in accounting. When looking for a tax preparer, your lawyer, accountant, or financial planner may be appropriate or may be able to make a recommendation. If your information is fairly straightforward, you may minimize costs by using a preparer who simply does taxes. If your situation involves more complications, especially involving other entities such as businesses or trusts, or unusual circumstances such as a gain, gift, or distribution, you may want to consult a professional with a range of expertise, such as an accountant or a lawyer who specializes in taxes. Many professionals also offer a "guarantee," that is, they will also help you if the information on your return is later questioned by the IRS.

FIGURE 6.7

© Shutterstock, Inc.

Whether you prepare your tax return by yourself or with a professional, it is you who must sign the return and assume responsibility for its details. You should be sure to review your return with your tax preparer so that you understand and can explain any of the information found on it. You should question anything that you cannot understand or that seems contrary to your original information. You should also know your tax return because understanding how and why tax obligations are created or avoided can help you plan for tax consequences in future financial decisions.

You may choose to prepare the return yourself using a tax preparation software application. There are many available, and several that are compatible with personal financial software applications, enabling you to download or transfer data from your financial software directly into the tax software. Software applications are usually designed as a series of questions that guide you through Form 1040 and the supplemental schedules, filling in the data from your answers. Once you have been through the "questionnaire," it tells you the forms it has completed for you, and you can simply print them out to submit by mail or "e-file" them directly to the IRS. Most programs also allow you to enter data into the individual forms directly.

The IRS offers access to Free File software that helps those with limited income fill out the forms and e-file their taxes. Those with more income can use the Free File Fillable Forms, which offer access to free forms with a fee for e-filing.[3] Many tax preparation software packages are available, and many are reviewed in the business press or online. Some popular programs include the following (see http://tax-software-review.toptenreviews.com):

- Turbo Tax
- Tax Act
- Credit Karma Tax
- Free Tax USA
- TaxSlayer

Software can be useful in that it automatically calculates unusual circumstances, limitations, or exceptions to rules using your complete data. Some programs even prompt you for additional information based on the data you submit. Overlooking exceptions is a common error that software programs can help you avoid. The programs have all the forms and schedules, but if you choose to file hard copy versions, you can download them directly from the IRS website, or you can call the IRS and request that they be sent to you. Once your return is completed, you must file it with the IRS, either by mail or by e-file, which has become increasingly popular.

Following Up

After you file your tax return, it will be processed and reviewed by the IRS. If you are owed a refund, it will be mailed to you or direct deposited to an account you specify; if you made a payment, it will be received by the U.S. Treasury. The IRS reviews returns for accuracy, based on redundant reporting and its "sense" of your data. For example, the IRS may investigate any discrepancies between the wages you report and the wages your employer reports. As another example, if your total wages are $23,000 and you show a charitable contribution of $20,000, the IRS may investigate because that contribution seems too high for your income—although there may be an explanation.

The IRS may follow up by mail or by a personal interview. It may just ask for verification of one or two items, or it may conduct a full **audit**—a thorough financial investigation of your return. In any case, you will be asked to produce records or receipts that will verify your reported data. Therefore, it is important to save a copy of your return and the records and receipts that you used to prepare it. The IRS[4] has the following recommendations for the number of years to save your tax data. Specifically written for the self employed, they are a pretty good guideline for all:

audit

A review of tax calculations and obligations performed by the Internal Revenue Service (IRS).

1. If you owe additional tax and situations 2, 3, and 4 below do not apply to you, keep records for three years.
2. If you do not report income that you should report, and it is more than 25% of the gross income shown on your return, keep records for six years.
3. If you file a fraudulent return, keep records indefinitely.

4. If you do not file a return, keep records indefinitely.
5. If you file a claim for credit or refund after you file your return, keep records for three years from the date you filed your original return or two years from the date you paid the tax, whichever is later.
6. If you file a claim for a loss from worthless securities or bad debt deduction, keep records for seven years.
7. Keep all employment tax records for at least four years after the date that the tax becomes due or is paid, whichever is later.

If you have a personal interview, your tax preparer may accompany you to help explain and verify your return. Ultimately, however, you are—and will be held—responsible. If you have made errors, and if those errors result in a larger tax obligation (if you owe more), you may have to pay penalties and interest in addition to the tax you owe. You may be able to negotiate a payment schedule with the IRS.

The IRS randomly chooses a certain number of returns each year for review and possible audit even where no discrepancies or unusual items are noticed. The threat of a random audit may deter taxpayers from cheating or taking shortcuts on their tax returns. Computerized record keeping has made it easier for both taxpayers and the IRS to collect, report, and verify tax data.

Filing Strategies

tax avoidance

The legal attempt to minimize tax obligations.

tax evasion

The illegal attempt to report financial information fraudulently to minimize tax obligations.

Most citizens recognize the need to contribute to the government's revenues but want to avoid paying more than they need to. **Tax avoidance** is the practice of ensuring that you have no excess tax obligations. Strategies for minimizing or avoiding tax obligations are perfectly legal. However, **tax evasion**—fraudulently reporting tax obligations, for example, by understating incomes and gains or overstating expenses and losses—is illegal.

FIGURE 6.8

Timing can affect the value of taxable incomes or deductible expenses. If you anticipate a significant increase in income—and therefore in your tax rate—in the next tax year, you may try to defer a deductible expense. When you have more income and it is taxed at a higher rate, a deductible expense may be worth more as a tax savings to offset your income. For example, if your tax rate is 20% and your deductible expense of $100 saves you from paying taxes on $100, then it saves you $20 in taxes. If your tax rate is 35%, that same $100 deductible saves you $35. Likewise, if you anticipate a decrease in income that will decrease your tax rate, you may want to defer receipt of income until the next year when it will be taxed at a lower rate. In addition, some kinds of incomes are taxed at different rates than others, so how your income is created may bear on how much tax it creates.

The definition of expenses and the way you claim them can affect the tax they save. You may be able to deduct more expenses if you itemize your deductions than if you do not, or it may not make a difference. Also, there may be some discretion in classifying expenses. For example, suppose you are a high school Spanish teacher. You also tutor students privately. You buy Spanish books to improve your own language skills and to keep current with the published literature. Are the costs of those books an unreimbursed employee expense related to your job as a teacher, or are they an expense of your private tutoring business?

They may be both, but if you classify it as an employment-related expense, you cannot deduct it, whereas if it is a cost of your tutoring business, you may be able to fully expense it from your business income.

An income that is not taxed or taxed at a lower rate is more valuable than an income that is taxed or taxed at a higher rate. An expense that is fully deductible is more valuable than an expense that is not. Taxes deferred—by delaying income or accelerating expense—create more liquidity and thus more value. However, taxable income is still income, and a deductible expense is still an expense. Tax consequences should not obscure the benefits of enjoying income and the costs of incurring expenses.

There are many ideas about how to avoid an audit or what will trigger one: certain kinds of incomes or expenses, or filing earlier or later, for example. In truth, with the increased sophistication of computerization, the review process is much better at noticing real discrepancies and at choosing audits randomly. Time and effort (and cost) invested in outsmarting a possible audit is usually wasted. The best protection against a possible audit is to have verification—a receipt or a bill or a canceled check—for all the incomes and expenses that you report.

Key Takeaways

- Tax code information is available from the Internal Revenue Service.
- Verifiable records must be kept for all taxable incomes and expenses or other taxable events and activities.
- Professional tax assistance and tax preparation software are readily available.
- The Internal Revenue Service reviews tax returns for errors and may follow up through an informal or formal audit process.
- Tax avoidance is the legal practice of minimizing tax obligations.
- Tax evasion is the illegal process of fraudulently presenting information used in calculating tax obligations.
- Tax avoidance strategies can involve the timing of incomes and/or expenses to take advantage of changing tax circumstances.

Exercises

1. Read the article, "Policy Basics: Where Do Our Federal Tax Dollars Go" (Center on Budget and Policy Priorities, accessed July 3, 2018) at http://www.cbpp.org/cms/index.cfm?fa=view&id=1258. In the last year, what were the federal government's three largest expenditures of tax dollars?
2. Gather a current sample of the kind of records you will use to calculate your tax liability this year and to verify your tax return. List each type of record and identify exactly what information it will give you, your tax preparer, and the IRS about your tax situation. What additional records will you need that are not yet in your possession?
3. Compare and contrast tax preparation software at sites such as http://financialplan.about.com/od/software/tp/TPTaxSoftware.htm and https://www.consumerreports.org/taxes/how-to-choose-the-right-do-it-yourself-tax-software/. What are the chief differences among the top three or four programs? Also check out the IRS Free File program at http://www.irs.gov/efile. Would you quality for Free File?
4. According to the article, "12 Questions to Ask When Choosing a Tax Preparer" (https://www.forbes.com/sites/kellyphillipserb/2016/01/18/12-questions-to-ask-when-choosing-a-tax-preparer/#42919d82592f), what should you look for in a professional tax preparation service provider?
5. Research how can you reduce your tax liability and/or avoid paying taxes when you file this year. Work with classmates to develop a tip sheet for students on tax avoidance.

6.5 Taxes and Financial Planning

Learning Objectives

1. Trace the tax effects of life stages and life changes.
2. Identify goals and strategies that provide tax advantages.
3. Identify tax advantages that may be useful in pursuing your goals.
4. Discuss the relationship of tax considerations to financial planning.

You may anticipate significant changes in income or expenses based on a change of job or career, or a change of life stage or lifestyle. Not only may the amounts of income or expenses change, but the kinds of incomes or expenses may change as well. Planning for those changes in relation to tax obligations is part of personal financial planning.

Tax Strategies and Life Stages

Tax obligations change more broadly as your stage of life changes. Although everyone is different, there is a typical pattern to aging, earning, and taxes, as shown in Table 6.3.

TABLE 6.3 Life Stages and Tax Implications

	Young Adulthood	Middle Adulthood	Older Adulthood	Retirement
Source of Income	Wages	Wages/Investment	Wages/Investment	Investment
Asset Base	None	Accumulating	Growing	Depleting
Adjusted Gross Income	Low	Higher	Highest	Lower
Deductions, Exemptions	Low	Higher	High	Low

In young adulthood, you rely on income from wages, and you usually have yet to acquire an asset base, so you have little income from interest, dividends, or capital gains. Your family structure does not include dependents, so you have few deductions but also low taxable income.

As you progress in your career, you can expect wages, expenses, and dependents to increase. You are building an asset base by buying a home, possibly saving for your children's education, or saving for retirement. Because those are the kinds of assets encouraged by the government, they not only build wealth but also create tax advantages: the retirement or education savings exemptions or a possible mortgage interest deduction.

In older adulthood, you may begin to build an asset base that creates taxable income such as interest, dividends, or rental income. In retirement, most people can anticipate a significant decrease in income from wages and a significant increase in reliance on incomes from investments such as interest, dividends, and gains. Some of those assets may be in retirement savings accounts, such as an individual retirement account (IRA) or 401(k), that created tax advantages while growing but will create tax obligations as income is drawn from them.

FIGURE 6.9

© Shutterstock, Inc.

Generally, you can expect your income to increase during your middle adult life, but that is when many people typically have dependents and are more likely to have deductions to offset increased tax obligations. As you age, and especially when you retire, you can expect less income and your deductions may also change, for example, you can expect fewer dependents but more medical expenses.

The bigger picture is that at the stages of your life when income is increasing, so are your deductions and exemptions. Although your incomes and your tax obligations change over your lifetime, your taxes should remain somewhat stable relative to your ability to pay.

The tax consequences of such changes should be anticipated and considered as you evaluate choices for financial strategies. Because the tax code is a matter of law it does change, but because it is also a matter of politics, it changes slowly and only after much public discussion. You can usually be aware of any tax code changes far enough in advance to incorporate them into your planning.

Tax Strategies and Personal Financial Planning

Tax advantages are sometimes created for personal financial strategies as a way of encouraging certain personal goals. In the United States, as in most developed economies, certain goals such as retirement savings, and education and health financing are seen as personal goals that benefit society as well as the individual.

In most cases, tax advantages are created to encourage progress toward those goals. For example, retirement saving is encouraged, so some savings plans such as an IRA or a **defined contribution** plan such as a 401(k) or a 403b (so named for the sections of the Internal Revenue Code that define them) create tax advantages. The deposits made to those plans may be used to reduce taxable income, although there are limits to the amount of those deposits. There are also retirement savings strategies that do not create tax advantages, such as saving outside of a tax-advantaged account. There are limited tax-advantaged savings accounts for education savings and health care expenses as well.

defined contribution
A tax-advantaged pension plan, such as a 401(k), that both employer and employee may contribute to and that does not pay an obligated or defined benefit at maturity.

Where you have a choice, it makes sense to use a strategy that will allow you to make progress toward your goal and realize a tax advantage. Taxes affect the value of your alternatives, so recognizing tax implications should inform your choices. Your enthusiasm for the tax advantage should not define your goals, however.

FIGURE 6.10

Unanticipated events such as an inheritance, a gift, lottery winnings, or medical expenses can also have tax consequences. They are often unusual events (and therefore unanticipated) and may be unfamiliar and financially complicated. In those circumstances, it may be wise to consult an expert.

Your financial plans should reflect your vision for your life: what you want to have, how you want to get it, how you want to protect it. You will want to be aware of tax advantages or disadvantages, but tax consequences should not drive your vision. You would not save for retirement only to deduct the contribution, for example. However, since you must save for retirement, you can plan to do so in the most tax-advantageous way.

As Supreme Court Justice Oliver Wendell Holmes, Jr., said, "Taxes are what we pay for a civilized society."[5]http://www.treasury.gov/resource-center/faqs/Taxes/Pages/taxes-society.aspx (accessed August 6, 2014). Like any costs, you want to minimize your tax costs of living and of life events, but tax avoidance is only a means to an end. You should make your life choices for better reasons than avoiding taxes.

> *"Friends and neighbors complain that taxes are indeed very heavy, and if those laid on by the government were the only ones we had to pay, we might more easily discharge them; but we have many others, and much more grievous to some of us. We are taxed twice as much by our idleness, three times as much by our pride, and four times as much by our folly...."*
>
> — Benjamin Franklin, *The Way to Wealth* (1758)[6]

Key Takeaways

- Tax strategies may change as life stages and family structure changes.
- Some personal finance goals may be pursued in a more or less tax-advantaged way, so you should evaluate the tax effects on your alternatives.
- Tax strategies are a means to an end, that is, to achieve your personal finance goals with a minimum of cost.

Exercises

1. Review your list of personal financial goals. For each goal, how does the U.S. Tax Code help or hinder you in achieving it?
2. Investigate tax strategies that would benefit you in your present life stage. Begin your online research at this comprehensive list of tax links: http://www.el.com/elinks/taxes/. What tax strategies would benefit you in your next life stage? Share your findings and strategies with others in your life stage.
3. What does Benjamin Franklin mean in his statement about taxation? What advice is implied and how would you apply that advice to your financial planning?

Endnotes

1. The Tax Foundation, "2018 Tax Brackets (Updated)," *Fiscal Facts*, No. 567, January 2018. https://files.taxfoundation.org/20180207142513/Tax-Foundation-FF567-Updated.pdf (accessed July 3, 2018).
2. U.S. Department of the Treasury, Internal Revenue Service, "SOI Tax Stats - Individual Income Tax Returns Publication 1304," https://www.irs.gov/statistics/soi-tax-stats-individual-income-tax-returns-publication-1304-complete-report#_pt3 (accessed July 3, 2018).
3. U.S. Department of the Treasury, Internal Revenue Service, https://www.irs.gov/filing/free-file-do-your-federal-taxes-for-free (accessed July 3, 2018).
4. U.S. Department of the Treasury, Internal Revenue Service, "How Long Should I Keep Records," https://www.irs.gov/businesses/small-businesses-self-employed/how-long-should-i-keep-records (accessed September 13, 2018).
5. U.S. Department of the Treasury, "Taxes and Society," Resource Center,
6. Benjamin Franklin, quoted in Jeffrey Yablon, "As Certain as Death—Quotations about Taxes," Tax Analysts, April 12, 2010, https://taxprof.typepad.com/files/yablon.pdf (accessed November 16, 2018).

CHAPTER 7

Financial Management

7.1 Introduction

Financial management is about managing the financing for consumption and investment. You have two sources for money: yourself or someone else. You need to decide when to use whose money and how to do so as efficiently as possible: maximizing benefit and minimizing cost. As with all financial decisions, you also need to think about the strategic consequences for future decisions.

You can use your own money as a source of financing if your income is at least equal to your living expenses. If it is more, you have a budget surplus that can be saved and used as a source of future financing while earning income at the same time. If your own income is less than the expenses, you have a budget deficit that will require another external source of financing—someone else's money—that will add an expense. Ideally, you want to avoid the additional expense of borrowing and instead create the additional income from saving. The budgeting techniques discussed in Chapter 5 are helpful in seeing this picture more clearly.

Your ability to save will vary over your lifetime, as your family structure, age, career choice, and health will change. Those "micro" factors determine your income and expenses and thus your ability to create a budget surplus and your own internal financing. Likewise, your need to use external financing, such as credit or debt, will vary with your income, expenses, and ability to save.

FIGURE 7.1

© Shutterstock, Inc.

At times, unexpected change can turn a budget surplus into a budget deficit as, for example, with a sudden job loss or increased health expenses, and a saver can reluctantly become a borrower. Being able to recognize that change and understand the choices for financing and managing cash flow will help you create better strategies.

Financing can be used to purchase a long-term asset that will generate income, reduce expense, or create a gain in value, and it may be useful when those benefits outweigh the cost of the debt. The benefit of long-term assets is also influenced by personal factors. For example, a house may be more useful, efficient, and valuable when families are larger.

Macroeconomic factors, such as the economic cycle, employment, and inflation, should bear on your financing decisions as well. Your incomes and expenses are affected by the economy's expansion or contraction, especially as it affects your own employment or earning potential. Inflation or deflation, or an expected devaluation or appreciation of the currency, affects interest rates as both lenders and borrowers anticipate using or returning money that has changed in value.

Financial management decisions become more complicated when the personal and macroeconomic factors become part of the decision process, but the result is a more realistic evaluation of alternatives and a better strategy that leaves more choices open in the future. Financial management decisions, however, are difficult because of their complexity and because the way you can finance your assets and expenses—your lifestyle—determines the life that you live. The stakes are high.

7.2 Your Own Money: Cash

Learning Objectives

1. Identify the cash flows and instruments used to manage income deposits and expense payments.
2. Explain the purpose of checkbook balancing.

checking account

A bank account that is used to facilitate payment by check.

direct deposit

An automatic deposit of income directly to the receiver's designated bank account; it is widely used by employers and government agencies.

automatic payments

A direct payment of an expense or a debt payment made as an electronic transfer of funds from the payer's bank account to the payee's.

debit card

A card that allows point-of-sale payment as an electronic transfer of funds from the payer's bank account to the payee's at the time of sale.

ATM (automated teller machine) card

A card allowing direct access to a bank account through an automated teller machine (ATM), most often used to access cash without having to go to the bank housing the account.

Most people use a **checking account** as their primary means of managing cash flows for daily living. Incomes from wages and perhaps from investments are deposited to this account, and expenses are paid from it. The actual deposit of paychecks and writing of checks, however, has been made somewhat obsolete as more cash flow services are provided electronically.

When incoming funds are distributed regularly, such as a paycheck or a government distribution, **direct deposit** is preferred. For employers and government agencies, it offers a more efficient, timely, and secure method of distributing funds. For the recipient, direct deposit is equally timely and secure and can allow for a more efficient dispersal of funds to different accounts. For example, you may have some of your paycheck directly deposited to a savings account, while the rest is directly deposited to your checking account to pay living expenses. Because you never "see" the money that is saved, it never passes through the account that you "use," so you are less likely to spend it.

Withdrawals or payments have many electronic options. **Automatic payments** may be scheduled to take care of a periodic payment (i.e., same payee, same amount) such as a mortgage or car payment. They may also be used for periodic expenses of different amounts—for example, utility or telephone expenses. A **debit card** may be used to directly transfer funds at the time of purchase; money is withdrawn from your account and transferred to the payee's with one quick swipe at checkout. An **ATM (automated teller machine) card** offered by a bank allows for convenient access to the cash in your bank accounts through instant cash withdrawals.

The bank clears these transactions as it manages your account, providing statements of your cash activities, usually monthly and online. When you reconcile your record keeping (i.e., your checkbook or software accounts) with the bank's statement, you are balancing your checking account. This ensures that your records and the bank's records are accurate and that your information and account balance and the bank's are up to date. Banks do make mistakes, and so do you, so it is important to check and be sure that the bank's version of events agrees with yours.

Key Takeaways

- A checking account is the primary cash flow management tool for most consumers, providing a way to pay for expenses and store cash until it is needed.
- Balancing your checkbook reconciles your personal records with the bank's records of your checking account activity.

Exercises

1. In My Notes or your personal finance journal, inventory in detail all the vehicles you use for managing your cash flows. Include all your accounts that are mediated through banks and finance companies. Also, list your cards issued by banks, such as debit or ATM cards, and identify any direct deposits and automatic payments that are made through your savings and checking accounts. How might you further enhance your cash management through the use of banking tools?
2. Does your bank offer online banking services, such as electronic bill payment? View your bank and others (such as https://home.capitalone360.com/) online to learn more about Internet banking. What products and services do online branches and banks offer? Do you (or would you) use those products and services? Why (or why not)? Discuss online banking with classmates. What do they identify as the main benefits and risks of electronic banking?

7.3 Your Own Money: Savings

Learning Objectives

1. Identify the markets and institutions used for saving.
2. Compare and contrast the instruments used for saving.
3. Analyze a savings strategy in terms of its liquidity and risk.

When incomes are larger than expenses, there is a budget surplus, and that surplus can be saved. You could keep it in your possession and store it for future use, but then you have the burden of protecting it from theft or damage. More importantly, you create an opportunity cost. Because money trades in markets and liquidity has value, your alternative is to lend that liquidity to someone who wants it more than you do at the moment and is willing to pay for its use. Money sitting idle is an opportunity cost.

The price that you can get for your money has to do with supply and demand for liquidity in the market, which in turn has to do with a host of other macroeconomic factors. It also has a lot to do with time, opportunity cost, and risk. If you are willing to lend your liquidity for a long time, then the borrower has more possible uses for it, and increased mobility increases its value. However, while the borrower has more opportunity, you (the seller) have more opportunity cost because you give up more choices over a longer period of time. That also creates more risk for you, since more can happen over a longer period of time. The longer you lend your liquidity, the more compensation you need for your increased opportunity cost and risk.

Savings Markets

money market

A market where short-term liquidity is traded.

capital market

A market where long-term liquidity is traded.

The markets for liquidity are referred to as the **money markets** and the **capital markets**. The money markets are used for relatively short-term, low-risk trading of money, whereas the capital markets are used for relatively long-term, higher-risk trading of money. The different time horizons and risk tolerances of the buyers, and especially the sellers, in each market create different ways of trading or packaging liquidity.

When individuals are saving or investing for a long-term goal (e.g., education or retirement) they are more likely to use the capital markets; their longer time horizon allows for greater use of risk to earn return. Saving to finance consumption relies more on trading liquidity in the money markets because there is usually a shorter horizon for the use of the money. Also, most individuals are less willing to assume opportunity costs and risks when it comes to consumption, thus limiting the time that they are willing to lend liquidity.

When you save, you are the seller or lender of liquidity. When you use someone else's money or when you borrow, you are the buyer of liquidity.

Savings Institutions

intermediary

A third party that facilitates trade between two parties. In financial services, a bank is an intermediary between lenders and borrowers.

For most individuals, access to the money markets is done through a bank. A bank functions as an **intermediary** or "middleman" between the individual lender of money (the saver) and the individual borrower of money.

For the saver or lender, the bank can offer the convenience of finding and screening the borrowers, and of managing the loan repayments. Most important, a bank can guarantee the lender a return: the bank assumes the risk of lending. For the borrowers, the bank can create a steady supply of surplus money for loans (from the lenders), and arrange standard loan terms for the borrowers.

Banks create other advantages for both lenders and borrowers. Intermediation allows for the amounts loaned or borrowed to be flexible and for the maturity of the loans to vary. That is, you don't have to lend exactly the amount someone wants to borrow for exactly the time she or he wants to borrow it. The bank can "disconnect" the lender and borrower, creating that flexibility. By having many lenders and many borrowers, the bank diversifies the supply of and demand for money, and thus lowers the overall risk in the money market.

The bank can also develop expertise in screening borrowers to minimize risk and in managing and collecting the loan payments. In turn, that reduced risk allows the bank to attract lenders and diversify supply. Through diversification and expertise, banks ultimately lower the cost of lending and borrowing liquidity. Since they create value in the market (by lowering costs), banks remain as intermediaries or middlemen in the money markets.

There are different kinds of banks based on what kind of brokering of money the bank does. Those differences have become less distinct as the banking industry consolidates and strives to offer more universal services. Decreasing bank regulation, increasing globalization, and improving technology have all contributed to that trend. Different kinds of banks are listed below.

- Retail banks have focused on consumer saving and borrowing.
- Commercial banks have focused on operating cash flow management for businesses.
- Investment banks have focused on long-term financing for businesses.

Retail banks are commonly known as thrift institutions, savings banks, savings and loan associations, or mutual savings banks and are usually private or public corporations. **Credit unions** function similarly, but are cooperative membership organizations, with depositors as members.

credit union

A retail banking institution that is either depositor- or member-owned. Membership is usually defined and limited to affiliation with a particular group—for example, state or union employees, or a religious or social affiliation.

In addition to banks, other kinds of intermediaries for savers include pension funds, life insurance companies, and investment funds. They focus on saving for a particular long-term goal. To finance consumption, however, most individuals primarily use banks.

Some intermediaries have moved away from the "bricks-and-mortar" branch model and now operate as online banks, either entirely or in part. There are cost advantages for the bank if it can use online technologies in processing saving and lending. Those cost savings can be passed along to savers in the form of higher returns on savings accounts or lower service fees. Most banks offer online and, increasingly, mobile account access, via cell phone or smartphone. Intermediaries operating as finance companies offer similar services.

Because their role as intermediaries is critical to the flow of funds, banks are regulated by federal and state governments. Since the bank failures of the Great Depression, bank deposits are federally insured (up to $250,000) through the FDIC (Federal Deposit Insurance Corporation). Since the financial crisis of 2007–2009, bank money market funds also are insured. Credit union accounts are similarly insured by the National Credit Union Agency or NCUA, also an independent federal agency. In choosing an intermediary, savers should make sure that accounts are FDIC or NCUA insured.

Saving Instruments

Banks offer many different ways to save your money until you use it for consumption. The primary difference among the accounts offered to you is the price that your liquidity earns, or the compensation for your opportunity cost and risk, which in turn depends on the degree of liquidity that you are willing to give up. You give up more liquidity when you agree to commit to a minimum time or amount of money to save or lend.

For the saver, a **demand deposit** (e.g., checking account) typically earns no or very low interest but allows complete liquidity on demand. Checking accounts that do not earn interest are less useful for savings and more useful for cash management. Some checking accounts do earn some interest, but often require a minimum balance. **Time deposits**, or savings accounts, offer minimal interest or a bit more interest with minimum deposit requirements.

demand deposit

Accounts from which withdrawals may be made "on demand," such as a checking account.

time deposits

An account from which withdrawals are made over time, or funds that are deposited for a time.

FIGURE 7.2

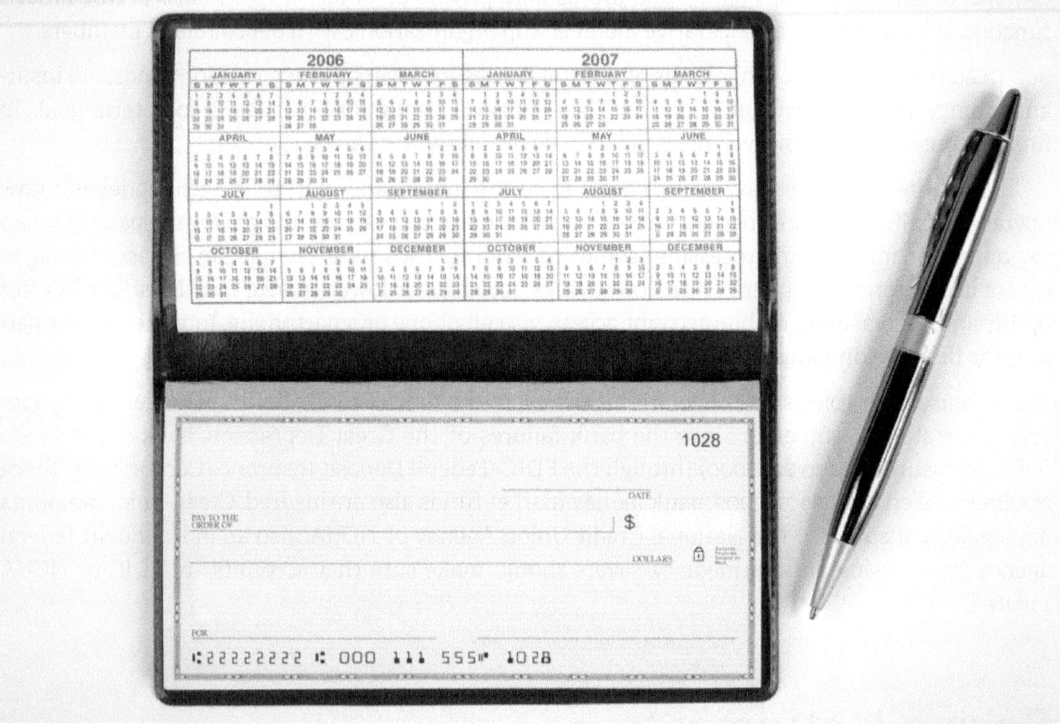

© Shutterstock, Inc.

certificate of deposit (CD)

A savings instrument requiring a minimum sacrifice of liquidity, either as a minimum deposit amount or a minimum time deposited, in exchange for a higher rate of earnings.

money market mutual fund (MMMF)

A savings instrument invested in the money markets.

If you are willing to give up more liquidity, **certificates of deposit (CDs)** offer a higher price for liquidity but extract a time commitment enforced by a penalty for early withdrawal. They are offered for different maturities, which are typically from six months to five years, and some have minimum deposits as well. Banks also can offer investments in **money market mutual funds (MMMFs)**, which offer a higher price for liquidity because your money is put to use in slightly higher-risk investments, such as Treasury bills (short-term government debt) and commercial paper (short-term corporate debt).

Compared to the capital markets, the money markets have very little risk, so MMMFs are considered very low-risk investments. The trade-offs between liquidity and return are seen in Table 7.1.

TABLE 7.1 Savings Products versus Liquidity and Risk

	Less	More
Time Commitment	Checking, savings, MMMFs	CDs
Risk	Checking, savings, CDs	MMMFs
Interest Earned	Checking, savings	MMMFs, CDs

annual percentage rate (APR)

The annual rate of interest on credit or debt.

As long as your money remains in your account, including any interest earned while it is there, you earn interest on that money. If you do not withdraw the interest from your account, it is added to your principal balance, and you earn interest on both. This is referred to as earning interest on interest, or compounding. The rate at which your principal compounds is the **annual percentage rate (APR)** that your account earns.

You can calculate the eventual value of your account by using the relationships of time and value that we looked at in Chapter 4—that is,

$$FV = PV \times (1 + r)^t,$$

where FV = future value, PV = present value, r = rate, and t = time. The balance in your account today is your present value, PV; the APR is your rate of compounding, r; the time until you will withdraw your funds is t. Your future value depends on the rate at which you can earn a return or the rate of compounding for your present account.

If you are depositing a certain amount each month or with each paycheck, that stream of cash flows is an annuity. You can use the annuity relationships discussed in Chapter 4 to project how much the account will be worth at any point in time, given the rate at which it compounds. Many financial calculators—both online and handheld—can help you make those calculations.

Ideally, you would choose a bank's savings instrument that offers the highest APR and most frequent compounding. However, interest rates change, and banks with savings plans that offer higher yields often require a minimum deposit, minimum balance, and/or a maintenance fee. Also, your interest from savings is taxable, as it is considered income. As you can imagine, however, with monthly automatic deposits into a savings account with compounding interest, your wealth can grow safely.

Savings Strategies

Your choice of savings instrument should reflect your liquidity needs. In the money markets, all such instruments are relatively low risk, so return will be determined by opportunity cost.

You do not want to give up too much liquidity and risk being caught short because then you will have to become a borrower to make up that shortfall, which will create additional costs. If you cannot predict your liquidity needs or you know they are immediate, you should choose products that will least restrict your liquidity choices. If your liquidity needs are more predictable or longer term, you can give up liquidity without creating unnecessary risk and can therefore take advantage of products, such as CDs, that will pay a higher price.

Your expectations of interest rates will contribute to your decision to give up liquidity. If you expect interest rates to rise, you will want to invest in shorter-term maturities, so as to regain your liquidity in time to reinvest at higher rates. If you expect interest rates to fall, you would want to invest in longer-term maturities so as to maximize your earnings for as long as possible before having to reinvest at lower rates.

One strategy to maximize liquidity is to diversify your savings in a series of instruments with differing maturities. If you are using CDs, the strategy is called "CD laddering." For example, suppose you have $12,000 in savings earning 0.50% annually. You have no immediate liquidity needs but would like to keep $1,000 easily available for emergencies. If a one-year CD is offering a 1.5% return, the more savings you put into the CD, the more return you will earn, but the less liquidity you will have.

A "laddering" strategy allows you to maximize return and liquidity by investing $1,000 per month in a one-year CD. After 12 months, all your savings is invested in 12 CDs, each earning 1.5%. But because one CD matures each month, you have $1,000 worth of liquidity each month. You can keep the strategy going by reinvesting each CD as it matures. Your choices are shown in Table 7.2.

TABLE 7.2 CD Laddering Strategy

CD Strategy	Amount in CDs	Amount Liquid	Earnings	Interest Rate
All in savings account	0	12,000	60	0.50%
All in CDs without laddering	12,000	0	180	1.50%
Monthly deposits to laddered CDs, without reinvesting	11,000	1,000	165	1.50%
Monthly deposits to laddered CDs, with reinvesting	12,000	0	180	1.50%

A laddering strategy can also reflect expectations of interest rates. If you believe that interest rates or the earnings on your money will increase, then you don't want to commit to the currently offered rates for too long. Your laddering strategy may involve a series of relatively short-term (less than one year) instruments. On the other hand, if you expect interest rates to fall, you would want to weight your laddering strategy to longer-term CDs, keeping only your minimum liquidity requirement in the shorter-term CDs.

FIGURE 7.3

© Shutterstock, Inc.

The laddering strategy is an example of how diversifying maturities can maximize both earnings and liquidity. In order to save at all, however, you have to choose to save income that could otherwise be spent, suffering the opportunity cost of everything that you could have had instead. Saving is delayed spending, often seen as a process of self-denial.

One saving strategy is to create regular deposits into a separate account such that you might have a checking account from which you pay living expenses and a savings account in which you save.

This is easier with direct deposit of wages, since you can have a portion of your disposable income go directly into your savings account. Saving becomes effortless, while spending actually requires a more conscious effort.

Some savings accounts need to be "segregated" because of different tax consequences—a retirement or education account, for example. In most cases, however, separating accounts by their intended use has no real financial value, although it can create a psychological benefit. Establishing a savings vehicle has a very low cost, if any, so it is easy to establish as many separate funds for saving as you find useful.

Key Takeaways

- Banks serve to provide the consumer with excess cash by having the cash earn money through savings until the consumer needs it.
- Banking institutions include retail, commercial, and investment banks.
- Consumers use retail institutions, including the following:
  - Savings banks
  - Mutual savings banks
  - Savings and loan associations
  - Credit unions
- Savings instruments include the following:
  - Demand deposit accounts
  - Time deposit accounts
  - Certificates of deposit
  - Money market mutual fund accounts
- A savings strategy can maximize your earnings from savings.

Exercises

1. Record your experiences with certificates of deposit (CDs) and money market mutual funds (MMMFs). What are the benefits and drawbacks of these instruments for saving? Compared to savings accounts, what are their implications for liquidity and risk? What are their implications for cost and return? What advice would you give to someone who saves by keeping money in a piggy bank?

2. You have $10,000 to deposit. You want to save it, earning interest by loaning its use in the money market to your bank. You anticipate you will need to replace your washing machine within the year, however, so you don't want to surrender all your liquidity all at once. What is the best way to save your money that will give you the greatest increase in wealth without too much risk and while still retaining some liquidity? Explain your reasons for your choice of a solution.
3. Read the article "9 Handy Financial Rules of Thumb" at http://business.time.com/2012/12/28/9-handy-financial-rules-of-thumb/. Which of these ideas, if any, have you tried or thought about in your own work to make ends meet? What are some other strategies you have tried for living frugally to achieve a particular financial goal? Share these strategies with classmates.
4. Go online to experiment with compound interest calculators (e.g., see http://www.moneychimp.com/calculator/compound_interest_calculator.htm or http://www.webmath.com/compinterest.html). Use real numbers based on your actual or projected savings. For example, based on what you have in savings now, how much could you have in five years? To see the effects of compounding, compare your results with the same calculation for simple interest (rather than compounded interest), using the calculator at http://www.webmath.com/simpinterest.html.

7.4 Other People's Money: Credit

Learning Objectives

1. Identify the different kinds of credit used to finance expenses.
2. Analyze the costs of credit and their relationships to risk and liquidity.
3. Describe the credit rating process and identify its criteria.
4. Identify common features of a credit card.
5. Discuss remedies for credit card trouble.
6. Summarize government's role in protecting lenders and borrowers.

"Credit" derives from the Latin verb *credere* (to believe). It has several meanings as a verb in common usage—to recognize with respect, to acknowledge a contribution—but in finance, it generally means to allow delayed payment.

Both credit and debt are forms of borrowing. Credit is distinguished from debt in both its purpose and duration or timing, although in casual conversation the words are used interchangeably. Credit is used to purchase goods and services, to finance living expenses, or to make payments more convenient by delaying them for a relatively short time. Debt, on the other hand, is used to finance the purchase of assets—such as a car or a home—rather than to delay payment of recurring expenses.

The costs of credit and of debt are likewise different, given their different uses and time horizons. Often, people get into some trouble when they cannot distinguish between the two and choose the wrong form of financing at the wrong time. Table 7.3 distinguishes credit from debt.

TABLE 7.3 Credit versus Debt

	Credit	Debt
Finances	Living expenses	Assets
Maturity	Short-term	Long-term

Kinds of Credit

installment credit

A form of credit used to purchase consumer durables, usually issued by one vendor for one item.

default risk

The risk that a borrower will not be able to meet interest obligations or principal repayment.

revolving credit

A form of credit used to purchase consumer durables issued by a bank of finance company to purchase many items from many vendors.

charge card

Revolving credit that must be periodically paid in full.

credit card

Revolving credit that may not be paid in full, creating an interest expense.

credit cycle

The time period for extending and paying credit.

Credit is issued either as installment credit or as revolving credit. **Installment credit** is typically issued by one vendor, such as a department store, for a specific purchase. The vendor screens the applicant and extends credit, bearing the **default risk**, or risk of nonpayment. Payments are made until that amount is paid for. Payments include a portion of the cost of the purchase and the cost of the credit itself, or interest.

Installment credit is an older form of credit that became popular for the purchase of consumer durables (i.e., furniture, appliances, electronics, or household items) after the First World War. This form of credit expanded as mass production and invention made consumer durables such as radios and refrigerators widely available. (Longer-term installment purchases for bigger-ticket assets, such as a car or property, are considered debt.)

Revolving credit extends the ability to delay payment for different items from different vendors up to a certain limit. Such credit is lent by a bank or finance company, typically through a **charge card** or a **credit card**. The charge card balance must be paid in full in each period or **credit cycle**, while the credit card balance may not be, requiring only a minimum payment.

The credit card is a more recent form of credit, as its use became widely practical only with the development of computing technology. The first charge card was the Diners' Club card, issued in 1950. The first credit card was the Bank Americard (now called Visa), issued by Bank of America in 1958, which was later followed by MasterCard in 1966. Retailers can also issue revolving credit (e.g., a store account or credit card) to encourage purchases.

Credit cards are used for convenience and security. Merchants worldwide accept credit cards as a method of payment because the issuer (the bank or finance company) has assumed the default risk by guaranteeing the merchants' payment. Use of a credit card abroad also allows consumers to incur less transaction cost.

This universal acceptance allows a consumer to rely less on cash, so consumers can carry less cash, which could be lost or stolen. Credit card payments also create a record of purchases, which is convenient for later record keeping. When banks and finance companies compete to issue credit, they often offer gifts or rewards to encourage purchases.

Credit cards create security against cash theft, but they also create opportunities for credit fraud and even for identity theft. A lost or stolen credit card can be used to extend credit to a fraudulent purchaser. It can also provide personal information that can then be used to assume your financial identity, usually without your knowing it. Therefore, handle your credit cards carefully and be aware of publicized fraud alerts. Check your credit card statements for erroneous or fraudulent charges and notify the issuer immediately of any discrepancies, especially if the card is lost or stolen. Failure to do so may leave you responsible for purchases you did not make—or enjoy.

Costs of Credit

Credit has become a part of modern transactions, largely enabled by technology, and a matter of convenience and security. It is easy to forget that credit is a form of borrowing and thus has costs. Understanding those costs helps you manage them.

Because consumer credit is all relatively short term, its cost is driven more by risk than by opportunity cost, which is the risk of default or the risk that you will fail to repay the amounts advanced to you. The riskier the borrower seems to be, the fewer the sources of credit. The fewer sources of credit available to a borrower, the more credit will cost.

FIGURE 7.4

© Shutterstock, Inc.

Measuring Risk: Credit Ratings and Reports

How do lenders know who the riskier borrowers are?

Credit rating agencies specialize in evaluating borrowers' credit risk or default risk for lenders. That evaluation results in a **credit score**, which lenders use to determine their willingness to lend and their price.

credit rating

An analysis of personal creditworthiness based on income, current credit and debt, and credit history. The assessment is done by a credit rating agency that makes the credit report available to lenders.

credit score

A numerical score that rates personal creditworthiness in the credit rating process.

If you have ever applied for consumer credit (a revolving, installment, or personal loan), you have been evaluated and given a credit score. The information you write on your credit application form, such as your name, address, income, and employment, is used to research the factors for calculating your credit score, also known as a FICO (Fair Isaac Corporation) score, named after the company that developed it.

In the United States, there are currently three major credit rating agencies: Experian, Equifax, and TransUnion. Each calculates your score a bit differently, but the process is common. They assign a numerical value to five characteristics of your financial life and then compile a weighted average score. Scores range from 300 to 900; the higher your score, the less risky you appear to be. The five factors that determine your credit score are:

1. your payment history,
2. amounts you currently owe,
3. the length of credit history,
4. new credit issued to you,
5. the types of credit you have received.

The rating agencies give your payment history the most weight, because it indicates your risk of future defaults. Do you pay your debts? How often have you defaulted in the past?

The credit available to you is reflected in the amounts you currently owe or the credit limits on your current accounts. These show how dependent you are on credit and whether or not you are able to take on more credit. Generally, your outstanding credit balances should be no more than 25 percent of your available credit.

The length of your credit history shows how long you have been using credit successfully; the longer you have been doing so, the less risky a borrower you are, and the higher your score becomes. Credit rating agencies pay more attention to your more recent credit history and also look at the age and mix of your credit accounts, which show your consistency and diversification as a borrower.

FIGURE 7.5

© 2010 Jupiterimages Corporation

The credit rating process is open to manipulation and misinterpretation. Many people are shocked to discover, for example, that simply canceling a credit card, even for a dormant or unused account, lowers their credit rating by shortening their credit history and decreasing the diversity of their accounts. Yet, it may make sense for a responsible borrower to cancel a card. Credit reports may also contain errors that you should correct by disputing the information.

You should know your credit score. Even if you haven't applied for new credit, you should check on it annually. Each of the three agencies is required to provide your score once per year for free and to correct any errors that appear—and they do—in a timely way. If you should find an error in your report, you should immediately contact the agency and follow up until the report is corrected.

Order your free annual credit report from the three credit reporting agencies at https://www.annualcreditreport.com/cra/index.jsp. (Beware of any other websites called "annual credit report" as these may be impostors.) It is important to check your score regularly to check for those errors. Knowing your score can help you to make financing decisions because it can help you to determine your potential costs of credit. It can also alert you to any credit or identity theft of which you otherwise are unaware.

identity theft

A fraud that occurs when the identity is used to access or create accounts for financial gain.

Identity theft is a growing problem. Financial identity theft occurs when someone poses as you based on having personal information, such as your Social Security number, driver's license number, bank account number, or credit card numbers. The impostor uses your identity to either access your existing accounts (withdrawing funds from your checking account or buying things with your credit card) or to establish new accounts in your name and use those.

The best protection is to be careful how you give out public information. Convenience encourages more and more transactions by telephone and Internet, but you still need to be sure of whom you are talking to before giving out identifying data.

As careful as you are, you cannot protect yourself completely. However, checking your credit report regularly can flag any unfamiliar or unusual activity carried out in your name. If you suspect that your personal information has been breached, you can ask the credit reporting agencies to issue a fraud alert. Fraud alert messages notify potential credit grantors to verify your identification by contacting you before extending credit in your name in case someone is using your information without your consent. That way, if a thief is using your credit to establish new accounts (or buy a home, a car, or a boat) you will know it. If a stronger measure is needed, you can order a credit freeze that will prevent anyone other than yourself from accessing your credit file.

Using a Credit Card

grace period

The time between the purchase date and the date that interest is charged on revolving credit.

Credit cards issued by a bank or financing company are the most common form of revolving credit. This often has costs only after a repayment deadline has passed. For example, many credit cards offer a **grace period** between the time of the credit purchase or "charge" and the time of payment, assuming your beginning balance is zero. If you pay before interest is applied, you are using someone else's money to make your purchases at no additional cost. In that case, you are using the credit simply as a cash management tool.

Credit cards are effective as a cash management tool. They can be safer to use than cash, especially for purchasing pricier items. Payment for many items can be consolidated and made monthly, with the credit card statement providing a detailed record of purchases. If you carry more than one card, you might use them for different purposes. For example, you might use one card for personal purchases and another for work-related expenses. Credit cards also make it convenient to buy on impulse, which may cause problems.

Problems arise if you go beyond using your card as a cash management tool and use it to extend credit or to finance your purchases past the payment deadline. At that point, interest charges begin to accrue. Typically, that interest is expensive—perhaps only a few percentage points per month, but compounding to a large annual percentage rate (APR).

Credit card APRs today may start with 0% for introductory offers and range from 8.75% to more than 20%. These rates may be fixed or variable, but in any case, when you carry a balance from month to month, this high interest is added to what you owe.

As an example, if your credit card charges interest of 1.5% per month, that may not sound like much, but it is an annual percentage rate of 18% (1.5% per month × 12 months per year). To put that in perspective, remember that your savings account is probably earning only around 1% to 3% *per year*. Consumer credit thus is an expensive way to finance consumption. Consumers tend to rely on their cards when they need things and lack the cash, and this can quickly lead to credit card debt.

According to recent surveys, 56% of college students have a credit card, and of those, about 63% pay their balance in full every month. The average student credit card monthly balance is $906.[1]

Choosing a Credit Card

You should shop around for credit just as you would shop around for anything that you might purchase with it: compare the features and the costs of each credit card.

Features of the credit include the credit limit (or how much credit will be extended), the grace period, purchase guarantees, liability limits, and consumer rewards. Some cards offer a guarantee for purchases; if you purchase a defective item, you can have the charge "stopped" and removed from your credit card bill. Liability limits involve your responsibilities should your card be lost or stolen.

Consumer rewards may be offered by some credit cards, usually by rewarding "points" for dollars of credit. The points may then be cashed in for various products. Sometimes the credit card is sponsored by a certain retailer and offers rewards redeemable only through that store. A big sponsor of rewards has been the airline industry, commonly offering "frequent flyer miles" through credit cards as well as actual flying. Be aware, however, that many reward offers have limitations or conditions on redemption. In the end, many people never redeem their rewards.

Creditors charge fees for extending credit. There is the APR on your actual credit, which may be a fixed or adjustable rate. It may be adjustable based on the age of your balance—that is, the rate may rise if your balance is over 60 days or 90 days. There may also be a late fee charged in addition to the actual interest. The APR may also adjust as your balance increases, so that even if you stay within your credit limit, you are paying a higher rate of interest on a larger balance.

There are also fees on cash advances and on balance transfers (i.e., having other credit balances transferred to this creditor). These can be higher than the APR and can add a lot to the cost of those services. You should be aware of those costs when making choices. For example, it can be much cheaper to withdraw cash from an ATM using your bank account's debit or ATM card than using a cash advance from your credit card.

Many credit cards charge an annual fee just for having the credit card, regardless of how much it is used. Many do not, however, and it is worth looking for a card that offers the features that you want with no annual fee.

How you will use the credit card will determine which features are important to you and what costs you will have to pay to get them. If you plan to use the credit card as a cash management tool and pay your balance every month, then you are less concerned with the APR and more concerned about the annual fee, or the cash advance charges. If you sometimes carry a balance, then you are more concerned with the APR.

It is important to understand the costs and responsibilities of using credit—and it is very easy to overlook them.

Installment Credit

Retailers also may offer credit, usually as installment credit for a specific purchase, such as a flat screen TV or baby furniture. The cost of that credit can be hard to determine, as the deal is usually offered in terms of "low, low monthly payments of only..." or "no interest for the first six months." To find the actual interest rate you would have to use the relationships of time and value. Ideally, you would pay in as few installments as you could afford and would pay all the installments in the shortest possible time.

FIGURE 7.6

© Shutterstock, Inc.

Retailers usually offer credit for the same reason they offer home delivery—as a sales tool—because most often, customers would be hesitant or even unable to make a durable goods purchase without the opportunity to buy it over time. For such retailers, the cost of issuing and collecting credit and its risk are operating costs of sales. The interest on installment credit offsets those sales costs. Some retailers sell their installment receivables to a company that specializes in the management and collection of consumer credit, including the repossession of durable goods.

Personal Loans

Aside from installment credit and rotating credit, another source of consumer credit is a short-term personal loan arranged through a bank or finance company. Personal loans used as credit are all-purpose loans that may be "unsecured"—that is, nothing is offered as collateral—or "secured." Personal loans used as debt financing are discussed in the next section. Personal loans used as credit are often costly and difficult to secure, depending on the size of the loan and the bank's risks and costs (screening and paperwork).

A personal loan may also be made by a private financier who holds personal property as collateral, such as a pawnbroker in a pawnshop. Typically, such loans are costly, usually result in the loss of the property, and are used by desperate borrowers with no other sources of credit. Today, many "financiers" offer personal loans online at very high interest rates with no questions asked to consumers with bad credit. This is a contemporary form of "loan sharking," or the practice of charging a very high and possibly illegal interest rate on an unsecured personal loan. Some loan sharks have been known to use threats of harm to collect what is owed.

One form of high-tech loan sharking growing in popularity on the Internet today is the "**payday loan**," which offers very short-term small personal loans at high interest rates. The amount you borrow, usually between $500 and $1,500, is directly deposited into your checking account overnight, but you must repay the loan with interest on your next payday. The loan thus acts as an advance payment of your wages or salary, so when your paycheck arrives, you have already spent a large portion of it, and maybe even more because of the interest you have to pay. As you can imagine, many victims of repeated payday loans fall behind in their payments, cannot meet their fixed living expenses on time, and end up ever deeper in debt.

payday loan
A small, short-term personal loan that charges a high rate of interest.

Personal loans are the most expensive way to finance recurring expenses, and almost always create more expense and risk—both financial and personal—for the borrower.

Credit Trouble and Protections

As easy as it is to use credit, it is even easier to get into trouble with it. Because of late fees and compounding interest, if you don't pay your balance in full each month, it quickly multiplies and becomes more difficult to pay. It doesn't take long for the debt to overwhelm you.

If that should happen to you, the first thing to do is to try to devise a realistic budget that includes a plan to pay off the balance. Contact your creditors and explain that you are having financial difficulties and that you have a plan to make your payments. Don't wait for the creditor to turn your account over to a debt collector; be proactive in trying to resolve the debt. If your account has been turned over to a collector, you do have some protections: the Fair Debt Collection Practices (federal) law keeps a collector from calling you at work, for example, or after 9 p.m.

You may want to use a credit counselor to help you create a budget and negotiate with creditors. Many counseling agencies are nonprofit organizations that can also help with debt consolidation and debt management. Some "counselors" are little more than creditors trying to sell you more credit, however, so be careful about checking their credentials before you agree to any plan. What you need is more realistic credit, not more credit.

As a last resort, you may file for personal bankruptcy, which may relieve you of some of your debts, but will blemish your credit rating for 10 years, making it very difficult—and expensive—for you to use any kind of credit or debt. Federal bankruptcy laws allow you to file under Chapter 7 or under Chapter 13. Each allows you to keep some assets, and each holds you to some debts. Chapter 7 requires liquidation of most of your assets, while Chapter 13 applies if you have some income. It gets complicated, and you will want legal assistance, which may be provided by your local Legal Aid Society. The effects of a bankruptcy can last longer than your debts would have, however, so it should never be seen as an "out" but really as a last resort.

Modern laws and regulations governing the extension and use of credit and debt try to balance protection of the lender and of the borrower. They try to insure that credit or debt is used for economic purposes and not to further social or political goals. They try to balance borrowers' access to credit and debt as tools of financial management with the rights of property owners (lenders).

In the United States, federal legislation reflects this balance of concerns. Major federal legislation in the United States is shown in Table 7.4.

TABLE 7.4 Major U.S. Federal Legislation: Credit and Debt

Legislation	Effective	Major Purpose
Truth in Lending Act	1969, 1971, 1982	Disclosure of credit terms, interest rates
Fair Credit Reporting Act	1971	Disclosure of credit reporting process (credit scoring)
Fair Credit Billing Act	1975	Procedures for billing disputes, error resolution
Equal Credit Opportunity Act	1975,1977	Prohibits discrimination and specifies procedures for extending or denying credit
Fair Debt Collection Practices Act	1978	Procedures for debt collection
Consumer Credit Reporting Reform Act	1997	Accountability in credit reporting and scores

In addition, many states have their own legislation and oversight. Not coincidentally, most of these laws were written after use of credit cards, and thus credit, became widespread. The set of laws and regulations that governs banking, credit, and debt markets has evolved over time as new practices for trading money are invented and new rules are seen as necessary. You should be aware of the limitations on your own behavior and on others as you trade in these markets.

If you feel that your legal rights as a borrower or lender have been ignored and that the offender has not responded to your direct, written notice, there are local, state, and national agencies and organizations for assistance. There are also organizations that help borrowers manage credit and debt.

Laws and regulations can govern how we behave in the credit and debt markets, but not whether we choose to participate as a lender or as a borrower: whether we use credit to manage cash flow or to finance a lifestyle, whether we use debt to finance assets or lifestyle, and whether we save. Laws and regulations can protect us from each other, but they cannot protect us from ourselves.

Key Takeaways

- Credit is used as a cash management tool or as short-term financing for consumption.
- Credit may be issued as revolving credit (credit cards), installment credit, or personal loans.
- Credit can be a relatively expensive method of financing.
- Credit accounts differ by the following features:
  - Credit limit
  - Grace period
  - Purchase guarantees
  - Liability limits
  - Consumer rewards
- Credit accounts charge fees, such as the following:
  - Annual percentage rate (APR)
  - Late fees
  - Balance transfer fees
  - Cash advance fees
- Credit remedies include the following:

- Renegotiation
- Debt consolidation
- Debt management
- Bankruptcy
- Modern laws governing the uses of credit and debt try to balance protection of borrowers and lenders.

Exercises

1. Read the statistics about personal credit card debt at https://www.creditcards.com/credit-card-news/credit-card-statistics.php. Record in My Notes or in your personal finance journal all the facts that pertain especially to you in your present financial situation. What facts did you find most surprising or most disturbing? Share your observations about these data with your classmates.
2. Investigate online the sources and processes of debt consolidation. Sample the websites of debt consolidation businesses offering "free" advice and services (e.g., http://www.debtconsolidationcare.com/). Are they free? Now visit the National Center for Credit Counseling (NFCC) at http://www.nfcc.org/. When seeking advice about your credit, why might you want to use an NFCC advisor or consumer center?
3. Read the MSN Money Central article "Your Three Worst Debt Consolidation Moves" at http://www.finweb.com/banking-credit/3-worst-debt-consolidation-strategies.html#axzz2a5TAQSFG. According to this article, what are the three worst moves you can make to manage your debt? How can you consolidate your debt on your own?
4. Go to the U.S. Department of Education site on loan consolidation at https://studentloans.gov/myDirectLoan/index.action. How can you consolidate your federal loans directly online with the U.S. government? Use the worksheets at this site to explore your real or hypothetical options as the recipient of federal student loans. For example, what would be the direct consolidation interest rate on your current federal student loans, and what would your payments be?
5. What is your credit rating or credit score? Apply for your three credit reports from Equifax (http://www.equifax.com), TransUnion (http://www.transunion.com), and Experian (http://www.experian.com). You can apply for all three at once from one source for free once each year, at https://www.annualcreditreport.com/. To ensure that you go to the legitimate site, type this URL directly into the address bar in your browser window.
    a. How do the three reports vary? Is the information accurate?
    b. How can you correct the information? For example, see https://www.equifax.com/personal/education/credit/report/video/credit-dispute-process/.
    c. What are your rights regarding your credit reports? Read about your rights at http://www.ftc.gov/bcp/menus/consumer/credit/rights.shtm. What does the video on that site warn you against? You will find a summary of your rights under the Fair Credit Reporting Act at http://www.ftc.gov/bcp/edu/pubs/consumer/credit/cre35.pdf. Find out if your state guarantees other rights or additional protections. Take steps now to correct your credit reports.
6. Research online how you can repair your credit history and improve your credit rating. Go to http://www.ftc.gov/bcp/edu/pubs/consumer/credit/cre13.shtm, and see http://www.ehow.com/how_4757_repair-credit-history.html.

7.5 Other People's Money: An Introduction to Debt

Learning Objectives

1. Define debt and identify its uses.
2. Explain how default risk and interest rate risk determine the cost of debt.
3. Analyze the appropriate uses of debt.

Debt is long-term credit, or the ability to delay payment over several periods. Credit is used for short-term, recurring expenses, whereas debt is used to finance the purchase of long-term assets. Credit is a cash management tool used to create security and convenience, whereas debt is an asset management tool used to create wealth. Debt also creates risk.

Two most common uses of debt by consumers are car loans and mortgages. They are discussed much more thoroughly in Chapter 8 and Chapter 9. Before you get into the specifics, however, it is good to know some general ideas about debt.

Usually, the asset financed by the debt can serve as collateral for the debt, lowering the default risk for the lender. However, that security is often outweighed by the amount and maturity of the loan, so default risk remains a serious concern for lenders. Whatever concerns lenders will be included in the cost of debt, and so these things should also concern borrowers.

interest rate risk

The risk that a bond's market value will be affected by a change in interest rates.

Lenders face two kinds of risk: default risk, or the risk of not being paid, and **interest rate risk**, or the risk of not being paid enough to outweigh their opportunity cost and make a profit from lending. Your costs of debt will be higher than the lender's cost of risk. When you lower the lender's risk, you lower your cost of debt.

Costs of Debt

Default Risk

Lenders are protected against default risk by screening applicants to try to determine their probability of defaulting. Along with the scores provided by credit rating agencies, lenders evaluate loan applicants on "the five C's": character, capacity, capital, collateral, and conditions.

Character is an assessment of the borrower's attitude toward debt and its obligations, which is a critical factor in predicting timely repayment. To deduce "character," lenders can look at your financial stability, employment history, residential history, and repayment history on prior loans.

Capacity represents your ability to repay by comparing the size of your proposed debt obligations to the size of your income, expenses, and current obligations. The larger your income is in relation to your obligations, the more likely it is that you are able to meet those obligations.

Capital is your wealth or asset base. You use your income to meet your debt payments, but you could use your asset base or accumulated wealth as well if your income falls short. Also, you can use your asset base as collateral.

Collateral insures the lender against default risk by claiming a valuable asset in case you default. Loans to finance the purchase of assets, such as a mortgage or car loan, commonly include the asset as collateral—the house or the car. Other loans, such as a student loan, may not specify collateral but instead are guaranteed by your general wealth.

Conditions refer to the lender's assessment of the current and expected economic conditions that are the context for this loan. If the economy is contracting and unemployment is expected to rise, that may affect your ability to earn income and repay the loan. Also, if inflation is expected, the lender can expect that (1) interest rates will rise and (2) the value of the currency will fall. In this case, lenders will want to use a higher interest rate to protect against interest rate risk and the devaluation of repayments.

Interest Rate Risk

Because debt is long term, the lender is exposed to interest rate risk, or the risk that interest rates will fluctuate over the maturity of the loan. A loan is issued at the current interest rate, which is "the going rate" or current equilibrium market price for liquidity. If the interest rate on the loan is fixed, then that is the lender's compensation for the opportunity cost or time value of money over the maturity of the loan.

If interest rates increase before the loan matures, lenders suffer an opportunity cost because they miss out on the extra earnings that their cash could have earned had it not been tied up in a fixed-rate loan. If interest rates fall, borrowers will try to refinance or borrow at lower rates to pay off this now higher-rate loan. Then the lender will have its liquidity back, but it can only be re-lent at a newer, lower price and create earnings at this new, lower rate. So the lender suffers the opportunity cost of the interest that could have been earned.

Why should you, the borrower, care? Because lenders will have you cover their costs and create a loan structured to protect them from these sorts of risks. Understanding their risks (looking at the loan agreement from their point of view) helps you to understand your debt choices and to use them to your advantage.

Lenders can protect themselves against interest rate risk by structuring loans with a penalty for early repayment to discourage refinancing or by offering a **floating-rate loan** instead of a **fixed-rate loan**. With a floating-rate loan, the interest rate "floats" or changes, usually relative to a benchmark such as the **prime rate**, which is the rate that banks charge their very best (least risky) borrowers. The floating-rate loan shifts some interest rate risk onto the borrower, for whom the cost of debt would rise as interest rates rise. The borrower would still benefit, and the lender would still suffer from a fall in interest rates, but there is less probability of early payoff should interest rates fall. Mainly, the floating-rate loan is used to give the lender some benefit should interest rates rise. Figure 7.7 shows the extent and frequency of fluctuations in the prime rate from 1955 to 2018.

floating-rate loan

A loan for which the interest rate can change, usually periodically and relative to a benchmark rate such as the prime rate.

fixed-rate loan

A loan for which the interest rate remains constant over the maturity of the loan.

prime rate

A benchmark interest rate understood to be the rate that major banks charge corporate borrowers with the least default risk.

FIGURE 7.7 U.S. Prime Rate, 1955-2018

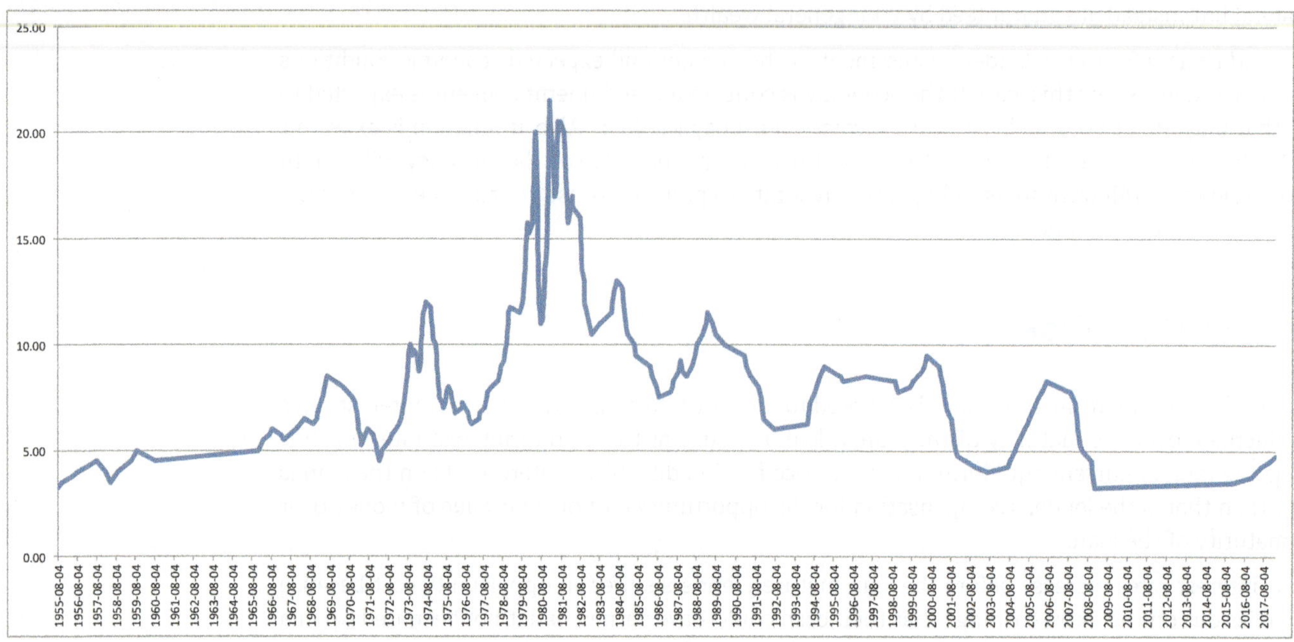

Based on data from FRED, Federal Reserve Bank of St. Louis; https://fred.stlouisfed.org/series/PRIME, accessed May 26, 2018.

Borrowers may be better off having a fixed-rate loan and having stable and predictable payments over the life of the loan. The better or more creditworthy a borrower you are, the better the terms and structure of the loan you may negotiate.

Uses of Debt

Debt should be used to finance assets rather than recurring expenses, which are better managed with a combination of cash and credit. The maturity of the financing (credit or debt) should match the useful life of the purchase. In other words, you should use shorter-term credit for consumption and longer-term debt for assets.

If you finance consumption with longer-term debt, then your debt will outlive your expenses; you will be continuing to pay for something long after it is gone. If you finance assets with short-term debt, you will be making very high payments, both because you will be repaying over a shorter time and so will have fewer periods in which to repay, and because your cost of credit is usually higher than your cost of debt. For example, annual credit card rates are typically higher than mortgage rates.

FIGURE 7.8

© Shutterstock, Inc.

Borrowers may be tempted to finance asset purchases with credit, however, to avoid the more difficult screening process of debt. Given the more significant investment of time and money in debt, lenders screen potential borrowers more rigorously for debt than they do for credit. The transaction costs for borrowing with debt are therefore higher than they are for borrowing with credit. Still, the higher costs of credit should be a caution to borrowers.

The main reason not to finance expenses with debt is that expenses are expected to recur, and therefore the best way to pay for them is with a recurring source of financing, such as income. The cost of credit can be minimized if it is used merely as a cash management tool, but if it is used as debt and if interest costs are allowed to accrue, then it becomes a very costly form of financing because it creates new expense (interest) and further obligates future income. In turn, that limits future choices, creating even more opportunity cost.

Credit is more widely available than debt and therefore is a tempting source of financing. It is a more costly financing alternative, however, in terms of both interest and opportunity costs.

Key Takeaways

- Debt is an asset management tool used to create wealth.
- Costs of debt are determined by the lender's costs and risks, such as default risk and interest rate risk.
- Default risk is defined by the borrower's ability to repay the interest and principal.
- Interest rate risk is the risk of a change in interest rates that affects the value of the loan and the borrower's behavior.
- Debt should be used to purchase assets, not to finance recurring expenses.

Exercises

1. Identify and analyze your debts. What assets secure your debts? What assets do your debts finance? What is the cost of your debts? What determined those costs? What risks do you undertake by being in debt? How can being in debt help you build wealth?
2. Are you considered a default risk? How would a lender evaluate you based on "the five C's" of character, capacity, capital, collateral, and conditions? Write your evaluations in your personal finance journal or My Notes. How could you plan to make yourself more attractive to a lender in the future?
3. Discuss with classmates the Tim Clue video on debt at http://www.youtube.com/watch?v=l5bbvMR8Ee4. What makes this comedy spot funny? What makes it not funny? What does it highlight about the (in)appropriate uses of debt?

Endnotes

1. Daniel P. Ray and Yasmin Ghahremani, "Credit Card Statistics, Industry Facts, Debt Statistics," https://www.creditcards.com/credit-card-news/credit-card-statistics.php (accessed May 27, 2018).

CHAPTER 8
Consumer Strategies

8.1 Introduction

Reva, Burt, and Kim are all students at the local state college. All are living at home to save money while in school, and all are working at least one job to pay tuition. Between their paychecks and financial aid, they can get by, but not by much.

Living in a city with public transportation, none of them needs a car, but Reva keeps an old beater in her dad's garage. The ace of her tech classes in high school, Reva loves to get under the hood.

Burt loves nothing more than to get lost in the world of games; he is hoping that his degree in digital media will lead to a career developing games and applications for a growing market. Whenever he can, he upgrades his tablet and smartphone with the latest apps.

Kim is hoping to go into business as a fashion designer and is getting a head start by joining the campus business club. Wanting to make a good impression, Kim is careful to maintain a fashionable yet professional wardrobe.

FIGURE 8.1

© Shutterstock, Inc.

All three are consumers and will be all their lives. All three make consumption decisions based on their financial and strategic goals, on their personal tastes and lifestyle, and on their professional choices. Their choices are very different and have different financial consequences. While there are many aspects of your humanity that define you, the things that you choose to surround yourself with—or not—may define your ultimate happiness. You need strategies.

8.2 Consumer Purchases

Learning Objectives

1. Trace the prepurchase, purchase, and postpurchase steps in consumer purchases.
2. Demonstrate the use of product-attribute scoring in identifying the product.
3. Compare and contrast features of different consumer markets.
4. Analyze financing choices and discuss their impact on purchasing decisions.
5. Discuss the advantages of consumer strategies using branding, timing, and transaction costs.
6. Identify common consumer scams, strategies, and remedies.

Consumer purchases refer to items used in daily living, for example, clothing, food, electronics, appliances. They are the purchases that most intimately frame your life: you live with these items and use them every day. They are an expression and a reflection of you, your tastes, and your lifestyle choices. Your spending decisions reflect your priorities. Maybe you take pride in your car or your clothes or your kitchen appliances or your latest device. Or maybe you spend whatever you can on travel or on your passion for hiking. Those very personal tastes will frame your spending choices.

Consumer purchases should fit into your budget. By making an operating budget, you can plan to consume and to finance your consumption without creating extra costs of borrowing. You can plan to live within your income. At times, you may have unexpected changes, such as a loss of a job or change in health, that put your nondiscretionary needs temporarily beyond your means. Ideally, you would want to have a cushion to tide you over until you can adjust your spending to fit your income.

A budget can also show you just how fast some "small luxuries" can add up. Stopping for a latte on your way to work or school every day ($4.95) adds up to $25 per week, or about $1,300 per year. That money may be better used to finance a bigger ticket item that you then would not have to finance with debt. With the budget to help you put expenses into perspective, you can make better purchasing decisions.

Purchasing decisions are always limited by the income available, and that means making choices. Your choices of what, where, when, and even how to buy will affect the amount you spend and the utility—the joy or regret—you ultimately get out of your purchase.

Shopping is a process. You decide what you want, then have to make more specific decisions:

- Should you buy more—and pay more—but get a cheaper unit price?
- Should you buy locally or remotely, via catalogue or Internet?
- Should you pay more for a well-known brand, or buy the generic?
- Should you look for a guarantee or warranty or consider long-term repair costs?
- Should you consider resale value?
- Should you pay cash or use credit? If you pay through credit, is it store credit, your own credit card, or a loan?

FIGURE 8.2

© Shutterstock, Inc.

Each of these decisions creates a trade-off. For example, it may be more convenient—and quicker—to shop locally, but there may be lower prices and a better selection of products online. Or you may find lower prices online but have a harder time getting repairs done if you haven't bought locally.

Some of your purchases involve few conscious decisions—for example, groceries—because you buy them repeatedly and often. Other purchases involve more decisions because they are made less often and involve costlier items such as a car. When you have to live with your decision for years instead of days, you tend to make it more carefully.

The decision process can be broken down into the following steps:

- Before you buy or "prepurchase,"
  - identify the product: compare attributes;
  - identify the market: compare price, delivery (return), convenience;
  - identify the financing.
- As you buy,
  - negotiate attributes: color, delivery, style;
  - negotiate price and purchase costs;
  - negotiate payment.
- After you buy, or "postpurchase," consider
  - maintenance;
  - how to address dissatisfaction.

Before You Buy: Identify the Product

What do you want? What do you want it to do for you? What do you want to gain by having it or using it or wearing it or driving it or playing with it or...? You buy things hoping to solve a need in your life. The more specifically you can define that need, the more accurately you can identify something to fill it. If your purchase is inappropriate for your need, you will not be happy with it, no matter how good it is. And because your budget is limited, you want to minimize your opportunity cost and **buyer's remorse**, or regret at not making a better purchase, in order to use your limited income most efficiently.

buyer's remorse

Regret following a purchase, especially common with an impulse purchase.

Sometimes you can identify a need but have no idea what kinds of products may fill it. This is especially true for infrequent needs or purchases. For example, you may decide you need to get away and take a long weekend. To do it cheaply, you decide to go hiking and camping. To make it more fun, you decide to go to an area where you've never been before. You may not be aware of the camping options available in that area, however, or of equally cheap alternatives such as hostels, bed and breakfasts, or other accommodations. When you find that you have a range of choices, you can compare them and choose one that offers the most satisfaction.

Once you have identified the product, you can compare the attributes of those products. What characteristics do you require or want? How are you going to use the product? For example, do you need cooking facilities, access to a shower, a safe but scenic location, opportunities to meet other hikers, and so on? What attributes are important to you and what are available?

Sig is looking for a new computer keyboard, a hot gaming keyboard that can also be comfortable for writing college papers. Sig begins to research keyboards and finds over five hundred models from over fifty brands with different designs, attributes, and functions offered at a range of prices. He decides to try to filter his choices by looking only at gaming keyboards, which narrows it down to about eighty models.

FIGURE 8.3

Noticing that most of the keyboards range in price from $25-$50, he decides to look in the $50-$100 range, figuring he'll get a slightly higher-end product, but not an outrageously expensive one. This narrows his search to 25 models.

None of the models has all the attributes that Sig desires. It's a trade-off: he can have some features, but not others. He decides to try to organize his research by creating a table ranking the product attributes in order of importance, and then scoring each model on each attribute (on a scale of one to ten), eventually coming up with an overall score for each model. Table 8.1 shows scoring for three models.

TABLE 8.1 Sig's Product-Attribute Scoring

		VTK		TKG		GBY	
Attribute	**Weight (%)**						
Backlit	25	8	2.00	10	2.50	9	2.25
Wireless	25	9	2.25	10	2.50	0	0.00
Programmable G-keys	25	2	0.50	10	2.50	5	1.25
Game panel	8	7	0.56	1	0.08	5	0.40
Touch	5	8	0.40	1	0.05	10	0.50
Media controls	5	7	0.35	1	0.05	10	0.50
Ergonomic design	5	7	0.35	1	0.05	10	0.50
Warranty	2	0	0.00	0	0.00	10	0.20
Weighted Average Score	**100**		**6.34**		**7.72**		**5.55**

Multiplying each attribute's weight by its score gives its weighted score, then adding up each weighted score gives the total score for the product. Based on this attribute analysis, Sig would choose TKG, which has the highest overall score.

In the case of an asset purchase, you may eventually think of reselling the item, so the ease and/or costs of doing so may figure into your prebuying evaluation. You may decide to go with a "better" product—a more recognizable or popular brand, for example—that may have a higher resale value. You also need to consider the market for used or preowned products: if there is one, how liquid the market is, or how easy it is to use. If the market is not very liquid, then the transaction costs of selling in the used product market may be significant, and you may be disappointed with the result.

The more choices you have, the better your chances of finding satisfaction. The more products there are to satisfy your need, and the more attributes those products offer, the more likely you are to find what "works" for you. Sometimes you need to be a bit creative in thinking about your alternatives, especially with limited resources.

Sources of product information include the manufacturer, retailer, and other consumers. Certain information must be provided for certain products by law. For example, food ingredients must be labeled, and perishable products dated. Appliances almost always come with operating and care instructions that can give you an idea of their ongoing maintenance costs as well as operating features.

The Internet has made it easy to research products online and to become a much better informed consumer. You can do lots of research online, even if you actually purchase locally. A feature of many online stores and consumer discussions is product reviews, where consumers give feedback on their satisfaction with the product. Such reviews can balance the information from the manufacturer and retailer, who want to inform consumers to encourage them to buy.

Other sources of information are magazines and trade journals (such as *Consumer Reports*, both in print and online), which have articles and ratings on products as well as ads. Your research may also involve actual or virtual window shopping, like going to stores to examine the products you are thinking of buying.

Before You Buy: Identify the Market

Your market may be local, national, or international, with advantages and disadvantages to each. Generally, a larger market (more vendors) will offer more variation and selection of product attributes.

As with any market, the real determinant of how your market works is competition. The more vendors there are, the more they compete for your business, and the more likely you will find options for purchasing convenience, product attributes, and price.

broker

An intermediary that acts as an agent for buyers or sellers to arrange a trade.

In markets where vendors are so plentiful that your problem is filtering rather than finding information, there are middlemen to provide that service. An example is the budget travel businesses with websites that make it convenient to research and buy flights, rental cars, and hotel accommodations. Middlemen or **brokers** exist in markets where they can add value to your purchasing process, either by providing information in the prepurchase stage or by providing convenience during the purchase. The more they can reduce the cost of a "bad" decision—e.g., a difficult flight schedule, an expensive car rental, an uncomfortable hotel accommodation—the more valuable they are. They can add more value in markets where you have too little or too much information or less familiarity with products or vendors. Generally, the more expensive the product or the less frequent the purchase, the more likely you are to find a middleman to make it easier.

Some products have a "new" and a "used" market, such as durable goods and some consumer goods like textbooks, vintage clothing, and yard sale goods. Evaluating the quality of a used or pre-owned product can require more research, information, and expertise, because the effect of its past use on its future value can be hard to estimate. Used products are almost always priced less than new products, unless they have become "collectibles" that can store value. The trade-off is that used products offer less reliable or predictable future performance and may lack attributes of newer models.

Different kinds of stores often offer the same products at different prices. Convenience stores, for example, typically charge higher prices than grocery stores but may be in more convenient locations and open at more convenient hours. Smaller boutique stores cannot always realize the economies of scale in administrative costs or in inventory management that are available to a larger store or a chain of stores. For those reasons prices tend to be higher at a smaller store. Boutiques often offer more amenities and a higher level of customer service to be competitive. You may also shop at a specialty store when you need a certain level of expertise or assistance in making a purchase.

Cooperative stores are owned and managed collectively and may provide goods or services that would not otherwise be available. Shopping is usually open to anyone, but members are eligible for discounts, depending on their participation in the store's operations or management. The members own the store, so they can forgo corporate profits for consumer discounts.

Increasingly, merchandise of all kinds may be bought directly from the manufacturer, often through a catalogue or online. The shopping experience is very different (you can't try on the sweater or see how the keyboard feels), but if you are well informed about the product, you may be comfortable buying it. Internet shopping has become a popular convenience and retailers are continuously improving the online shopping experience.

Auctions are becoming increasingly popular, especially online auctions at eBay and similar sites. Auctions are open negotiations between buyers and sellers and offer dynamic pricing. They also offer uncertainty, as the price and even the eventual purchase are risky—you may lose the auction and not get the item. Auctions are used most often for resales and for assets such as homes, cars, antiques, art, and collectibles. The popularity of online auctions can lead to more buyers, bringing more competition and thus higher prices after the bidding ends.

Before You Buy: Identify the Financing

Most consumer purchases are for consumable goods or services and are budgeted from current income. You pay by using cash or a debit card or, if financed, by using a credit card for short-term financing. Such purchases—food, clothing, transportation, and so on—should be covered by recurring income because they are recurring expenses. You need to be able to afford them. As you read in

Chapter 7, consumers who use debt to finance consumption can quickly run into trouble because they add the cost of debt to their recurring expenses, which are already greater than their recurring income.

Unless financed by savings, durable goods such as appliances, household wares, or electronics are often bought on credit, as they are costlier items infrequently purchased. Assets such as a car or a home may be financed using long-term debt, such as a car loan or a mortgage, although they also require some down payment of cash.

The use of middlemen or brokers to find and buy an item also contributes to the cost of a purchase because of the fees you pay for the service.

Products and preferred financing sources are shown in Table 8.2.

TABLE 8.2 Products and Preferred Financing Sources

	Consumer Goods	Durable Goods	Assets
Cash, Income	√	√	
Savings		√	√
Credit		√	
Debt			√

As You Buy: The Purchase

Having done your homework and made your choice, you are ready to purchase. In some cases, you may be able to make specific arrangements with vendors as to convenience, price, delivery, and even financing.

In Western cultures, prices for consumer goods are usually not negotiable; consumers expect to pay the price on the price tag. In other cultures, however, haggling over price is common and expected, which often surprises travelers abroad.

Durable goods and asset purchases typically offer more purchase options than consumer goods, usually as an incentive to buyers. Vendors may offer free delivery or free installation, product guarantees, or financing arrangements, such as "no payments for six months" or "0% financing." Offers may be enhanced periodically to "move the merchandise," when prices may also be discounted. Sales, "special offers," or "low, low prices" may be used to sell merchandise that is about to be replaced by a newer model. If those product cycles are seasonal and predictable, you may be able to schedule your purchase to take advantage of discounts.

Or you may decide to wait and pay full price for the newer model to avoid purchasing a product that is about to become outdated.

The more the purchase process allows for negotiation, the more possibility there is for consumers to enhance satisfaction. However, the negotiation process can go the other way too: it allows more opportunity for the vendor to negotiate an advantage. The better-informed consumer is more likely to negotiate a more satisfying purchase, so it is important to be thorough in the prepurchase research.

A purchase may have transaction costs such as sales tax or delivery charges. For higher-priced products such as durables and assets, those transaction costs can add up, so you should figure them into your overall cost of the purchase.

Financing costs can also be significant if debt financing is used. Debt is long term and is a significant commitment as well. It may pay to compare financing rates and terms just as you would for the product itself, or you may be able to use financing costs as a negotiating chip in your price negotiations.

After You Buy

Now you can enjoy your purchase. Some products require maintenance and periodic repair to remain useful. You should research those additional costs before buying because after the purchase you are committed to those activities.

FIGURE 8.4

© Shutterstock, Inc.

If you are not satisfied due to a product defect, you can contact the retailer or manufacturer. If there is a warranty, the retailer or manufacturer will either fix the defect or replace the item. Many manufacturers and retailers will do so even if there is no warranty to maintain good customer relations and enhance their brand's reputation. An Internet search will usually turn up contact information for a product's customer service team.

There are also federal and state consumer protection laws that cover a seller's responsibilities after a sale. In the United States, the Federal Trade Commission (FTC) Bureau of Consumer Protection has the most direct responsibility for consumer issues. At the state level, the office of the attorney general usually has a consumer protection division. Locally, you can also contact your chamber of commerce or Better Business Bureau (BBB) for more information.

You can also resort to the judicial system for compensation. For limited claims, you can file in small claims court. Claim limits vary by state, but range between $500 and $10,000. Small claims court is a less formal and costly process than filing a suit. At the other end of the spectrum is the class-action suit in which many plaintiffs pursue the same complaint, sharing the costs and the awards of the lawsuit.

Consumer Strategies

The advertising industry is proof of the importance of "branding." Customer brand loyalty is a real phenomenon. In 2017, $591 billion was spent on advertising worldwide, with the automotive, personal care, and food industries leading the pack.[1] Producers go to great expense to brand their products. When in doubt, consumers tend to choose a familiar brand. Once disappointed by a brand, consumers tend to avoid it. For some products, there are alternative private-label or store-label brands applied to many products but sold by one store or chain. The store brand is usually a cheaper alternative and often, although not always, of comparable quality. This is a widespread practice in the food industry with grocery store brands. Shopping for the store brand can often yield significant savings.

Aiden's purchase comes with a two-year manufacturer's guarantee, but the salesperson is encouraging her to buy an extended warranty. She is already paying more than she wanted to for a high-quality machine, and the extended warranty adds nearly $100 to the purchase price. She decides to forgo the extra protection, reasoning that most repairs, if needed after two years, would cost less than that anyway.

An offer of a warranty with purchase can be valuable if it lowers the expected maintenance or repair costs of the product. Sometimes a product is offered with a warranty at a higher price; sometimes you can purchase an optional warranty for an additional cost. If the cost of a malfunction is low, then the warranty is probably not worth it.

Price advantages can sometimes come through timing. Seasonally updated products or models can force retailers to discount old inventory to get it off the shelves before the new inventory arrives. Automobiles, for example, have a one-year product cycle, as do many electronics and peripherals.

Some products are naturally dated, such as calendars or tax preparation software, and so may be discounted as they near their expiration date. However, that is because they have less and less usefulness and may not be worth buying at all.

Commodities prices can fluctuate depending on the season or the weather, and although you may not have a choice of when to buy gas for your car, some products do offer you a choice. Tomatoes in January are more expensive than in August, for example; eating fresh foods seasonally can create savings.

Price can also be affected by transaction costs, or the costs of making the purchase. They can be included in the price or may be listed separately. Larger and more expensive items tend to have more transaction costs such as delivery and storage. Sales tax, which is a percentage of the price, may be required, and the higher the item's price, the more sales tax you will pay. Asset purchases also involve a legal transfer of ownership and often the costs of acquiring financing, which add to their costs. Sometimes, to entice a purchase, the seller may agree to bear some or all of the transaction costs.

Retailers change prices based on buyers' needs. They practice **price discrimination**, or the practice of charging a different price for the same product, when different consumers have different need of a product. Airlines are a classic example, charging less for a ticket bought weeks in advance than for the same flight if the ticket is bought the day before. Someone who purchases weeks ahead is probably a leisure traveler, has more flexibility, and is more sensitive to price. Someone who books one day ahead is probably a business traveler, has little flexibility, and is not so sensitive to price. The business traveler, in this case, is willing to pay more, so the airline will charge that person more.

price discrimination

The practice of offering the same product at a different price, depending on customer needs.

Retailers also offer discounts, sales, or "deals" to attract consumers who otherwise would not be shopping. Sometimes these are seasonal and predictable, such as in January, when sales follow the big holiday shopping season. Sometimes sales are not sales at all, but prices are "discounted" relative to new higher prices that will soon take effect. **Quantity discounts**, a lower unit price for a higher volume purchased, may be available for customers buying larger quantities, although sometimes the opposite is true—that is, the smaller package offers a smaller unit price. While it may be cheaper to buy a year's worth of goods at one time, you then create storage costs and sacrifice liquidity, which you should weigh against your cost savings.

quantity discounts

The practice of offering a different unit price for the same product, depending on quantity purchased.

In short, sellers want to sell and will use price to make products more attractive. As a buyer, you need to recognize when that attraction offers real value.

Scams: Caveat Emptor (Buyer Beware)

Unfortunately the world of commerce includes people with less-than-honorable intentions. You likely have been taken advantage of once or twice or have fallen victim to a **scam**, or a fraudulent business activity or swindle. Technology has made it easier for con artists to steal from more people, contacting them by telephone or by e-mail (phishing). The details of the scam vary, but the pattern is much the same: the fraud sets up a scenario that requires the victim to send money or to divulge financial or personal information, such as bank account, Social Security (federal ID), or credit card numbers, which can then be used to access accounts. Here are some examples of typical "scam" approaches:

scam

A scam (confidence game or con) is a fraud based on trust.

FIGURE 8.5

© Shutterstock, Inc.

- This car has never been in an accident.
- You've just won....
- Your account information needs to be updated.
- This stock is at 50 cents, and it's going to 5 or 6 bucks this week. Buy now!
- You don't need a physical to qualify for this low-cost health insurance!
- I'll be back sometime soon to finish your roof.
- This investment provides guaranteed high returns and low risk.
- I'm a political refugee. Help me move millions out of my former country into your bank account.
- I wouldn't go on vacation without this car repair.

The best way to protect yourself from scams is to be as informed as possible. Do your homework. If you feel like you are in over your head, call on a friend or family member to help you or to speak for you in negotiations. There are a number of nonprofit and government agencies that you can ask about the legitimacy of an idea or an arrangement. There are also some proven ways to try to protect yourself:

- Never give anyone personal and/or financial information when solicited by telephone or Internet. Legitimate business interests do not do that. When in doubt, contact the organization to verify its identity.
- Get a second opinion, especially when advised to do costly repairs.
- Check the credentials of prospective workers or service providers; most are certified, licensed, or recognized by a professional organization or trade group (e.g., auto mechanics may be endorsed by the American Automobile Association [AAA]).
- If you have doubts about a professional's credentials, such as an accountant, doctor, or architect, call the local professional society or trade group and ask about previous complaints lodged against him or her.
- Get a written estimate, specifying the work to be done, the materials to be used, the estimated labor costs, the estimated completion date, and the estimated total price. Ask the vendor to provide proof of insurance.

If you do get "scammed," it is your civic duty to complain to your state's consumer division in the attorney general's office and, if advised, to federal regulators at the Federal Trade Commission (FTC). That is the only way to stop and expose such frauds and to keep others from becoming victims. As the saying goes, "If it sounds too good to be true, it probably is."

Key Takeaways

- The consumer purchase process involves
  - Prepurchase
    - Identifying the product
    - Identifying the market
    - Identifying the financing
  - Purchase
    - Negotiating the purchase price and terms of sale
  - Postpurchase
    - Ensuring satisfaction
- Attribute scoring can be used to help identify the product.
- A product may be sold in different markets that may affect the cost of the purchase.
- Financing choices can affect the cost of the purchase.

- Strategies such as maximizing the advantages of branding, timing, and transaction costs can benefit consumers.
- There are common features of scams and also legal protections and remedies.

Exercises

1. Identify the last three items (consumer goods and durable goods) you purchased. Alternatively, select any three items you purchased during the last two months. Choose diverse items and analyze each item in terms of the following factors:
   a. Why did you buy that item? How did you decide what to get?
   b. What attributes proved most important in narrowing your choices? Create an attribute analysis chart for each item.
   c. Where did you get your information about the item?
   d. Where did you go to buy the item?
   e. In what kind of market did you make your purchase?
   f. Where did the money come from for your purchase?
   g. How much did you pay for the item, and how did you pay for it?
   h. How would you rate your satisfaction with your purchase?
   i. If or when you purchase that type of item again, what might you do differently?
2. In My Notes or your personal finance journal, record your favorite strategies for making purchases. Include a specific recent example of how you used each strategy. Your strategies may relate to bargain shopping, high-end shopping, warranties, store brands, coupons, discounts, rebates, seasonal shopping, expiry shopping, bulk buying, cooperative buying, special sales, or other practices. Share your consumer success stories with classmates and add at least one new idea to your list.
3. Have you ever been the victim of a consumer scam? What scams have you been exposed to that you managed to avoid? Describe your experiences in My Notes or your personal finance journal. Find out how many complaints of fraud the Federal Trade Commission received from consumers in its most recent reporting year (e.g., see http://www.ftc.gov/). What were the most common fraud complaints?
4. How informed are you about your rights as a consumer in your state and as a citizen of the United States? For example, what are your rights in returning unwanted purchases and recalled items? In moving your household? In buying food? In having access to electricity? Research a topic relevant to your personal situation from the comprehensive list at the Federal Trade Commission's Consumer Guides and Protections for Citizens: http://www.usa.gov/Citizen/Topics/Consumer_Safety.shtml. How will what you learn guide you in your next related purchase or in taking some other action? Visit the following websites to learn more about the information and protections available to you as a consumer. What services do the organizations and agencies provide? What should you do if you have a complaint as a consumer or suspect you are being scammed?
   a. Better Business Bureau (http://www.bbb.org)
   b. Federal Trade Commission (http://www.ftc.gov)
   c. Consumer protection laws about making purchases (http://www.ftc.gov/bcp/menus/consumer/shop.shtm)

8.3 A Major Purchase: Buying a Car

Learning Objectives

1. Show how the purchasing process (identifying the product, the market, and the financing) may be applied to a car purchase.
2. Explain the advantages (and disadvantages) of leasing versus borrowing as a form of financing.
3. Analyze all the costs associated with car ownership.
4. Define "lemon laws."

Many adults will buy a car several times during their lifetimes. A car is a major purchase. Its price can be as much as or more than one year's disposable income. Its annual operating costs can be substantial, including the cost of fuel, legally mandated insurance premiums, and registration fees, as well as maintenance and perhaps repairs and storage (parking). A car is not only a significant purchase, but also an ongoing commitment.

In the United States, people spend a considerable amount of time in their cars, commuting to work, driving their children to school and various activities, driving to entertainment and recreational activities, and so on. Most people want their car to provide not only transportation but also comforts and conveniences. You can apply the purchasing model, described earlier in this chapter, to the car purchase.

FIGURE 8.6

© Shutterstock, Inc.

First, you identify the need: What is your goal in owning a car? What needs will it fulfill? Here are some further questions to consider:

- What kind of driving will you use the car for? Will you depend on it to get you to work, or will you use it primarily for weekend getaways?
- Do you need carrying capacity (for passengers or "stuff") or hauling capacity?
- Do you live in a metropolitan area where you will be driving shorter distances at lower speeds and often idling in traffic?
- Do you live in a more rural area where you will be driving longer distances at faster speeds?
- Do you live in a climate where winter or a rainy season would make traction and storage an issue?
- How much time will you spend in the car every day?
- How many miles will you drive each year?
- How long do you expect to keep the car?
- Do you expect to resell or trade in the car?

Your answers to these questions will help you identify the product you want.

Identify the Product

Answering these questions can help identify the attributes you value in a car, based on how you will use it. Cars have many features to compare. The most critical (in no particular order) are shown in Table 8.3.

TABLE 8.3 Automobile Attributes and Relevance

Automobile Attribute	Relevance
Fuel or Energy Efficiency	Determines the costs and convenience of operating the car, a major component of your annual operating expense. Energy efficiency may also relate to growing demand for "green" cars or hybrids. An environmentally friendly car may in itself be an attribute you care about when deciding to buy a car.
Size and "Horsepower"	Determined by your need to carry passengers and "stuff." Size may also refer to engine size, which affects fuel or energy efficiency.
Condition	New, floor model, or used. Physical condition and odometer readings on trade-ins are major attributes in the used car market.
Performance Quality	Usually described in terms of the car's acceleration (0 to 60 miles per hour in *x* seconds), but also in terms of the availability of four-wheel drive and the quality of the steering system, braking system, suspension, and transmission—all of which affect the ease and utility of driving the car and its expected maintenance and repair costs.
Entertainment Features	As more people spend more time in their cars, features such as DVD players and monitors have joined radios, CD players, and cup holders as desirable features. Plug-in capacity for cell phones and laptops has also become a critical feature for many consumers.
Navigation Features	Innovations such as real-time GPS systems with digital road maps are rapidly becoming standard.

Automobile Attribute	Relevance
Safety Features	Many safety features are mandated, but distinctive safety features are offered, including, for example, electronic locking systems, built-in security alarms, built-in child restraints, and reverse sonar.
Appearance and Comfort	For some buyers the color, shape, and fittings of a car and its interior are important attributes.
Reliability	Reliability refers to expected mileage and performance over time in all conditions, as well as to future maintenance and repair costs.
Make	Some buyers prefer particular brands or styles of cars and remain loyal to them.

Based on information from Consumer Reports, "A Guide to New Car Ratings and Reviews," https://www.consumerreports.org/cro/2012/04/a-guide-to-new-car-ratings-and-reviews/index.htm (accessed October 2, 2018).

All these attributes affect price, and you may think of others. Product attribution scoring can help you identify the models that most closely fit your goals.

Mary lives on a dirt road in a rural area; she drives about 18,000 miles per year, commuting to her job as an accountant at the corporate headquarters of an auto parts chain and taking her kids to school. She is also a pretty good car mechanic and does basic maintenance herself.

John lives in the city; he walks or takes a bus to his job as a market researcher for an ad agency, but keeps a car to visit his parents in the suburbs. He drives about 5,000 miles per year, often crawling in traffic. All John knows about a car is that the key goes in the ignition and the fuel goes in the tank.

John and Mary would rate these attributes very differently, and their scoring of the same models would have very different results.

Mary may value fuel efficiency more, as she drives more (and so purchases more fuel). Driving often and with her children, she may rank size, safety, and entertainment features higher than John would, who is in his car less frequently and alone. Mary relies on the car to get to work, so reliability would be more important for her than for John, who drives only for recreational visits. But Mary also knows that she can maintain and repair some things herself, which makes that less of a factor.

Car attributes are widely publicized by car dealers and manufacturers, who are among the top advertisers globally year after year. You can visit dealerships in your area or manufacturers' websites. Using the Internet is a more efficient way of narrowing your search. Specialized print and online magazines, such as *Car and Driver*, *Road and Track*, and Edmunds.com, offer detailed discussions of model attributes and their actual performance. *Consumer Reports* also offers ratings and reviews and also provides data on frequency of repairs and annual maintenance costs.

You want to be sure to consider not only the price of buying the car, but also the costs of operating it. Fuel, maintenance, repair, insurance, property taxes, and registration may all be affected by the car's attributes, so you should consider operating costs when choosing the product. For example, routine repairs and maintenance are more expensive for some cars. A more fuel-efficient car can significantly lower your fuel costs. A more valuable car will cost more to insure and will mean higher property (or excise) taxes. Moreover, the costs of fuel, maintenance, insurance, registration, and perhaps property tax on the car will be ongoing expenses—you want to buy a car you can afford *and* afford to drive.

If you are buying a new car, you know its condition, and so you can predict annual maintenance and repair costs and the car's longevity by the history for that model. Depending on how long you expect to own the car, you may also be concerned with its predicted resale value.

Used cars are generally less expensive than new. A used car has fewer miles left in it. Its condition is less certain: you may not know how it has been driven or its repair and maintenance history. This makes it harder to predict annual maintenance and repair costs. Typically, since it is already used when you buy it, you expect little or no resale value. You can gain a significant price savings in the used car market, and there are good used cars for sale. You may just have to look a bit harder to find one.

The National Automobile Dealers Association (NADA) offers a checklist for used vehicle inspection when buying a used car. The NADA also publishes guidebooks on used car book values (see http://www.nadaguides.com). Items to inspect in your exterior, interior, and engine checks are outlined in Table 8.4.

TABLE 8.4 Used Car Buyer's Checklist

Exterior	Interior	Engine
Alignment	Carpets, upholstery	Belts and hoses
Doors	Instruments and controls	Battery
Lights	Trunk	Exhaust
Mirrors	Seats	Fluids
Paint	Safety features	Idling
Panels, bumpers, trim	Comfort	Driving
Shock		
Windshields, windows		

Source: National Automobile Dealers Association, "NADA Guides," http://www.nadaguides.com (accessed May 26, 2018).

The condition of exterior and interior features can indicate past accidents, repairs, or lack of maintenance that may increase future operating expenses, or just driving habits that have left a less attractive or less comfortable vehicle.

Services like Carfax (http://www.carfax.com) provide research on a vehicle's history based on its VIN (vehicle identification number), including any incidence of accidents, flooding, frame damage, or airbag deployment, the number and type of owners (was it a rental or commercial vehicle?), and the mileage. All these events affect your expectations of the vehicle's longevity, maintenance and repair costs, resale value, and operating costs, which can help you calculate its value and usefulness.

Unless you are an expert yourself, you should always have a trained mechanic inspect a used vehicle before you buy it. With cars, as with any item, the better informed you are, the better you can do as a consumer. Given the cost of a car and its annual expense, there is enough at stake with this purchase to make you cautious.

Identify the Market

New cars are sold through car dealerships. The dealer has a contract with the manufacturer to sell its cars in the retail market. Dealers may also offer repair and maintenance services as well as parts and accessories made especially for the models it sells.

New car dealers may also resell cars that they get as trade-ins, especially of the same models they sell new. Used car dealers typically buy cars through auctions of corporate, rental, or government cars.

FIGURE 8.7

© Shutterstock, Inc.

Individuals selling a used car can also do so through networking—in an online auction such as eBay, a virtual bulletin board such as Craig's List, or the bulletin board in the local college snack bar. Dealers will have more information about the market, especially about the supply of cars and price levels for them.

Some people prefer a new car, with its more advanced features and more certain quality, but a used car may be a viable substitute for many purchasers. Many people buy used cars while their incomes are lower, especially in the earlier stages of their adult (working) life. As income rises and concern for convenience, reliability, and safety increases with age and family size, consumers may move into the new car market.

While they are two very different markets, the markets for new and used cars are related. Supply of and demand for new cars affect price levels in the new car market, but also in the used car market. For example, when new car prices are high, more buyers seek out used cars, and when prices for new cars seem low, some used car buyers may turn to the new car market.

Demand for cars is affected by macroeconomic factors such as business cycles and inflation. If there is a recession and a rise in unemployment, incomes drop. Demand for new cars will fall. Many people will decide to keep driving their current vehicle until things pick up, unwilling to purchase a long-term asset when they are uncertain about their job and paycheck. That slowing of demand may lower car prices, but will also lower the resale or trade-in value of the current vehicle. For first-time car buyers, that may be a good time to buy.

If there is inflation, it will push up interest rates because the price of borrowing money rises with other prices. Since many people borrow when purchasing a car, that will make the borrowing, and so the purchase, more costly, which will discourage demand.

When the economy is expanding, on the other hand, and inflation and interest rates are low, demand for new cars rises, pushing up prices. In turn, prices are kept in check by competition. As demand for new cars rises, demand for used cars may fall, causing the supply of used cars to rise as more people trade in their cars to buy a new one. They trade them in earlier in the car's life, so the quality of the used cars on the market rises. This may be a good time to buy a used car.

Identify the Financing: Loans and Leases

The cost of a car is significant. Car purchases usually require financing through a loan or a lease. Each may require a down payment, which you would take out of your savings. That creates an opportunity cost of losing the return you could have earned on your savings. You also lose liquidity: you are taking cash, a liquid asset, and trading it for a car, a not-so-liquid asset.

Your opportunity cost and the cost of decreasing your liquidity are costs of buying the car. You can reduce those costs by borrowing more (and putting less money down), but the more you borrow, the higher your costs of borrowing. If you trade in a vehicle, dealers will often use the trade-in value as the down payment and will sell the car to you with "no money down."

Car loans are available from banks, credit unions, consumer finance companies, and the manufacturers themselves. Be sure to shop around for the best deal, as rates, maturity, and terms can vary. If you shop for the loan before shopping for the car, then the loan negotiation is separate from the car purchase negotiation. Both may be complex deals, and there are many trade-offs to be made. The more separate—and simplified—each negotiation is, the more likely you will be happy with the outcome.

Loans differ by interest rate or annual percentage rate (APR) and by the time to maturity. Both will affect your monthly payments. A loan with a higher APR is costing you more and, all things being equal, will have a higher monthly payment. A loan with a longer maturity will reduce your monthly payment, but if the APR is higher, it is actually costing you more. Loan maturities may range from one to five years; the longer the loan, the more you risk ending up with a loan that's worth more than your car.

Rebecca buys a used Ford for $6,000, with $1,000 cash down from savings and a Ford-financed loan at 7.2% APR, on which she pays $115 per month for 48 months. She could have gotten a 24-month loan, but she wanted to have smaller monthly payments. After only 25 months, she totals her car in a collision but luckily escapes injury. Now she needs another car. The Ford has no trade-in value, her insurance benefit won't be enough to cover the cost of another car, and she still has to pay off her loan regardless. Rebecca is out of luck because her debt outlived her asset. If your debt outlives your asset, your ability to get financing when you go to replace that vehicle will be limited, because you still have the old debt to pay off and now are looking to add a new debt—and its payments—to your budget. Rebecca will have to use more savings and may have to pay more for a second loan, if she can get one, increasing her monthly payments or extending her debt over a longer period of time.

An alternative to getting a car loan is leasing a car. Leases are a common way of financing a car purchase. A **lease** is a long-term rental agreement with a **buyout option** at maturity. Typically, at the end of the lease, usually three or four years, you can buy the car outright for a certain amount, or you can give it back (and buy or lease another car), which removes the risk of having an asset that outlives its financing. Leases specify an annual mileage limit, that is, the number of miles that you can drive the car in a year before incurring additional costs. Leases also specify the monthly payment and requirements for routine maintenance that will preserve the car's value.

lease

A rental agreement used as a form of financing for automobile purchases.

buyout option

A feature of a lease that offers the option to buy the asset financed by the lease at the end of the lease term.

So, lease or borrow? The price of the car should be the same regardless of how it is financed—the car should be worth what it's worth, no matter how it is paid for. The cost of borrowing, in percentage terms, is the interest rate or APR of the loan. The costs of leasing, in dollars, are the down payment, the lease payments, and the buyout. Since the price of the car itself is the same in either case, the present value of all the lease costs should be the same as the price of the car. You can use what you know about the time value of money to calculate the discount rate that produces that price; that is the equivalent annual cost of the lease, in percentage terms.

For example, you want to buy a car with a price of $19,000. You can get a car loan with an APR of 6.5% from your bank. You are offered a lease requiring a down payment of $2,999, monthly payments of $359 for three years, and a final buyout of $5,000. The APR of the lease is actually 5.93%, which would make it the cheaper financing alternative.

FIGURE 8.8

In general, the longer you intend to keep the car, the less sense it makes to lease. If you typically drive a car "into the ground," until it costs more to repair than replace it, then you are better off borrowing and spreading the costs of financing over a longer period. On the other hand, if you intend to keep the car only for the term of the lease and not to exercise the buyout option, then it is usually more cost effective to lease. You also need to consider whether or not you are likely to stay within the mileage limits of the lease, as the mileage penalties can add significantly to your costs.

Some people will say that they like to borrow and then "own" in order to have an asset that can store value or "build equity." Given the unpredictable nature of the used car market, however, a car is really not an asset that can be counted on to store value. Thinking of a car as something that you will use up (although over several years) rather than as an asset you can preserve or save will help you make better financial decisions.

When you are buying a car, you want to minimize the cost of both the car and the financing. If you are purchasing both the car and the financing from the same dealer, you should be careful to discuss them separately. Car dealers, who offer loans and leases as well as cars, often combine the three discussions, offering a break on the financing to make the car more affordable, or offering a break on the car to make the financing more affordable. To complicate matters further, they may also offer a rebate on a certain model or with a certain lease. The more clearly you can separate which costs belongs to which—the car or the financing—the more clearly you can understand and minimize your costs.

Purchase and Postpurchase

A car purchase requires significant prepurchase activities. Once you have identified and compared appropriate car attributes, a seller, and financing options, all you have to do is drive away, right? Not quite.

manufacturer's suggested retail price (MSRP)

The "sticker price" for an item.

Car purchases are one instance where the buyer is expected to haggle over price. The sticker price is the **manufacturer's suggested retail price (MSRP)** for that vehicle model with those features. Dealers negotiate many of the factors that ultimately determine the value of the purchase: the optional features of the car, the warranty terms, service discounts on routine maintenance, financing terms, rebates, trade-in value for your old car, and so on.

As more of these factors are discussed at once, the negotiation becomes more and more complex. You can help yourself by keeping the negotiations as simple as possible: negotiate one thing at a time, settle on that, and then negotiate the next factor. Keep track of what has been agreed to as you go along. When each factor has been negotiated, you will have the package deal.

Your ability to get a satisfying deal rests on your abilities as a negotiator. For this reason, many people who find that process distasteful or suspect that their skills are lacking find the car purchasing process distasteful. Dealers know this, and some will try to attract customers by being more transparent about their own costs and about prices. Some even promise the "no-dicker sticker" sale with no haggling over price at all.

As with any product in any market, the more information you have, the better you can negotiate. The more thorough your prepurchase activities, the more satisfying your purchase will be.

While you own the car, you will maximize the benefits enjoyed by operating the vehicle safely and by keeping it in good condition. Routine maintenance (e.g., replacing fluids, rotating tires) can ensure the quality and longevity of your vehicle. New cars come with owner's manuals that detail a schedule of service requirements and good driving practices for your vehicle. You will be required to keep the car legally insured and registered with the state where you reside, and you must maintain a valid license to drive.

warranty

A manufacturer's guarantee of product performance for a period of time.

New cars, and some used cars, are sold with a **warranty**, which is a promise about the quality of the product, made for a certain period of time. The terms and covered repair costs may vary. You should understand the terms of the warranty, especially if something covered should need servicing, so that you know what repairs you would have to pay. The manufacturer, and sometimes the seller, issues the warranty. If you have questions about the warranty after purchasing, it may be best to contact the manufacturer directly.

If you are dissatisfied with your purchase (and the fault seems to be with the car), your first step should be a conversation with your dealer. If the problem is not addressed, you can contact the automobile company directly; its website will provide you with a customer service contact. If the dealer and the manufacturer refuse to make good, you should contact your state's consumer affairs division in the attorney general's office. In some states, there are entire state agencies or departments devoted to auto purchases.

FIGURE 8.9

© Shutterstock, Inc.

For his first car, Ray bought a ten-year-old coupe with only 60,000 miles on it for a price that seemed too good to be true. The seller said the good price was in exchange for getting payment in full in cash. The car broke down right away, however, and within two weeks died of a cracked block. When Ray complained, the seller claimed he didn't know about the cracked block and pointed out that there was no warranty on the car, so Ray was out of luck. Fortunately, Ray had read that a defective car, referred to as a "lemon," is covered under laws that protect consumers who unknowingly purchase a car that proves to be defective. **Lemon laws** regulate sales terms, purchase cancellation conditions, and warranty requirements. These laws are enforced on both the federal and state levels in the United States. Other consumer protection laws apply specifically to motor vehicles and vary by state. Ray learned that laws in his state include used cars as well as new ones, and when he told the seller, he was able to get most of his cash back.

lemon laws

Federal and state laws protecting consumers against products that repeatedly fail to meet standards of performance. The federal Magnuson-Moss Warranty Act was enacted in 1975.

Key Takeaways

- The purchase process may be applied to a car purchase.
- Attribute scoring may be helpful to identify the product.
- Common car financing is through a loan or a lease.
- A warranty guarantees minimal satisfaction with performance attributes.
- Laws protect consumers who are dissatisfied with their car purchases or unknowingly buy defective cars.

Exercises

1. Perform an attribute analysis for your next new or used car. Go online to research cars with the attributes you have prioritized, and find where you could buy what you want locally. Then

research the dealership, including a quick check at the Better Business Bureau website or your local chamber of commerce to learn if there have been many consumer complaints. After researching the product, the market, and the price, visit a dealership, preferably with a classmate or partner, for the experience of getting information and practicing your negotiation skills (but without making any commitments, unless you really are in the market for a car at this time).

2. How will you finance a car? Play with the Car Loan Calculator at http://www.edmunds.com/apps/calc/CalculatorController. First identify a sample of new or used cars you would like to own, and for each choice calculate what your down payment, monthly loan payments, and term of payment would be. How much would you need to buy a car and where would you get that money? How much could you afford to pay each month and for how long? How could you modify your budget to accommodate car payments?
3. For a car you would like to drive, calculate and compare what it would cost you to buy it and to lease it. Use the Lease versus Buy Calculator at http://www.leaseguide.com/leasevsbuy.htm. What would be the advantages of owning the car? What would be the advantages of leasing it? For your lifestyle, needs, and uses of a vehicle, should you buy or lease?
4. Check the lemon laws in your state at Lemon Law America's website: http://www.lemonlawamerica.com/. Click on your state on the map. What conditions do your state lemon laws cover? Some states do not cover used or leased cars under lemon laws. Under federal laws, if you buy a used car "as is," do you still retain rights under the lemon laws? Under federal lemon laws, in what situations, when the seller does not divulge the information, may you be able to get your money back on a car?

Endnotes

1. https://www.statista.com/statistics/273288/advertising-spending-worldwide/ (accessed May 26, 2018).

CHAPTER 9

Buying a Home

9.1 Introduction

Be it ever so humble, the "biggest" purchase you ever make may be your home. Unlike most other consumer purchases, a home is expected to be more than a living space; it is also an asset that stores and increases value. The house has a dual financial role as both a nest *and* a nest egg.

There are substantial annual operating expenses for repairs and maintenance, insurance, and taxes. Maintenance preserves a home's value, insurance protects that value, and taxes for community services both enhance and secure its value.

FIGURE 9.1

© Shutterstock, Inc.

A home purchase is typically financed with debt that creates a significant monthly expense, the mortgage payment, in your budget. A mortgage is a long-term debt that obligates your cash flows for a long time, and, depending on fluctuations in the housing market and the value of your home, can even affect your future mobility.

Your choice of home reflects personal factors in your life. These factors include your personal tastes, your age and stage of life, your family size and circumstances, your health, and your career choices. These factors are reflected in your decision to own a home, as well as in the location, size, and use of your home.

9.2 Identify the Product and the Market

Learning Objectives

1. Describe the different building structures for residential dwellings.
2. Describe the different ownership structures for residential dwellings.
3. Identify the factors used by lenders to evaluate borrowers for mortgage credit.
4. Identify the components of the mortgage affordability calculation and calculate estimated mortgage affordability.
5. Identify the components of a buyer's inspection checklist.
6. Explain the potential effects of business cycles, unemployment, and inflation on the housing market.
7. Analyze the effects of the demand for housing financing on the housing market.

Renting a Home

If you have already decided on a goal of home ownership, you have already compared the costs and benefits of the alternative, which is renting. Renting requires relatively few initial legal or financial commitments. The renter signs a lease that spells out the conditions of the rental agreement: term, rent, payments and fees, restrictions such as pets or smoking, and charges for damages. A renter is usually required to give the landlord a security deposit to cover the landlord's costs of repairs or cleaning, as necessary, when the tenant moves out. If the deposit is not used, it is returned to the departing tenant (although without any interest earned).

Some general advantages and disadvantages of renting and owning are shown in Table 9.1.

TABLE 9.1 Renting versus Owning

	Advantage	Disadvantage
Renting	• Limited financial obligation • Limited maintenance expenses • More liquidity • More mobility	• No equity growth or store of value • Lifestyle limitations (e.g., pets, smoking) • Decorating/renovating limitations • Less predictable housing expense
Owning	• Store of value and possible equity growth • Lifestyle choices • Decorating/renovating choices • Pride of ownership • Tax deduction for mortgage interest • More predictable housing expenses	• Substantial financial obligation • Significant annual expenses • Less liquidity • Less mobility

The choice of whether to rent or to own follows the pattern of life stages. People rent early in their adult lives because they typically have fewer financial resources and put a higher value on mobility, usually to keep more career flexibility. Since incomes are usually low, any tax advantages of ownership don't have much benefit.

As family size grows, the quality of life for dependents typically takes precedence, and a family looks for the added space and comfort of a home and its benefits as an investment. This is the mid-adult stage of accumulating assets and building wealth. As income rises, tax benefits becomes more valuable, too.

Often, in retirement, with both incomes and family size smaller, older adults will downsize to an apartment, shedding responsibilities and financial commitments.

Home ownership decisions vary: some people just never want the responsibilities of ownership, while some just always want a place of their own.

Finding an apartment is much like finding a home in terms of assessing its attributes, comparing choices, and making a choice. Landlords, property managers, and agents all rent properties and use various media to advertise an available space. Since the rent for an apartment is a regular expense, financed from current income (not long-term debt), you need to find only the apartment and not the financing, which simplifies the process considerably.

Assessing Attributes

Once you decide to own your home, you must choose the home to own, considering the different kinds of homes and of home ownership.

There are single- and multiple-unit dwellings, for example. A **multiple-unit dwelling** can be used to create rental income or to house extended family members, but this choice imposes the responsibilities of being a landlord and also limits privacy.

multiple-unit dwelling

A residential building including more than one housing unit, such as a duplex, triplex, or apartment building.

FIGURE 9.2

© Shutterstock, Inc.

There are previously owned, new, and custom-built homes. Previously owned homes may require some renovation to make them comfortably modern and convenient. New and custom-built homes typically have more modern features and conveniences and require less maintenance and repair expense. Custom-built homes are built to the homeowners' specifications.

Sales of existing single-family homes far outnumber sales of new and custom homes. In April 2018, for example, 4,840,000 existing single-family homes were sold compared to 662,000 new homes.[1]

Mobile homes are large trailers fitted with utilities connections, which can be installed on permanent sites and used as residences. A mobile home may also be situated in a trailer park or mobile home community where the owner rents the lot where it sits. Mobile homes are often referred to as manufactured homes, and other examples of manufactured homes are prefabricated or modular homes, which are moved to a foundation site by trailer and then assembled.

mobile homes

A manufactured home, usually under 1,000 sq. ft. in size.

condominium (condo)

An ownership arrangement where individual housing units are owned by individual owners, while common spaces are owned by the condominium association of unit owners.

cooperative housing (coop)

An ownership arrangement where the right to inhabit living space is claimed by the purchase of shares in the cooperative ownership of a multi-unit dwelling.

In a **condominium**, the homeowner owns a unit in a multiple-unit dwelling, but the common areas of the building are owned and managed by the condominium owners' association. Condo owners pay a fee to cover the costs of overall building maintenance and operating expenses for common areas.

Cooperative housing is a unit in a building or complex owned by a nonprofit association or a corporation for the residents' use. Residents do not own the units, but rather own shares in the cooperative association, which entitles them to the right to dwell in its housing units.

FIGURE 9.3

Personal factors such as your age, family size, health, and career help you to answer some of the following key questions:

- How large should the house be? How many bedrooms and bathrooms?
- Which rooms are most important: kitchen, family room, or home office?
- Do you need parking or a garage?
- Do you need storage space?
- Do you need disability accommodation?
- Do you want outside space: a yard, patio, or deck?
- How important is privacy?
- How important is energy efficiency and other "green" features?
- How important are design features and appearance?
- How important is location and environmental factors?
- Proximity to work? Schools? Shopping? Family and friends?

After ranking the importance of such attributes, you can use an attribute-scoring matrix to score your choices. After understanding exactly what you are looking for in a home, you should begin to think about how much house you can afford.

Assessing Affordability

Before looking for a house that offers what you want, you need to identify a price range that you can afford. Most people use financing to purchase a home, so your ability to access financing or get a loan will determine the price range of the house you can buy. Since your home and your financing are long-term commitments, you need to be careful to try to include future changes in your thinking.

For example, Jill and Jack are both 25 years old, newly married, and looking to buy their first home. Both work and earn good incomes. The real estate market is strong, especially with mortgage rates relatively low. They buy a two-bedroom condo in a new development as a starter home.

Fast-forward five years. Jill is expecting their second child; while the couple is happy about the new baby, neither can imagine how they will all fit in their already cramped space. They would love to sell the condo and purchase a larger home with a yard for the kids, but the real estate market has slowed, mortgage rates have risen, and a plant closing last year has driven up unemployment in their area. Jill hasn't worked outside the home since their first child was born two years ago—they are just getting by on one salary and a new baby will increase their expenses—making it even more difficult to think about financing a larger home.

A lender will look at your income, your current debts, and credit history to assess your ability to assume a mortgage. As discussed in Chapter 7, your credit score is an important tool for the lender, who may also request verification of employment and income from your employer.

Lenders do their own calculations of how much debt you can afford, based on a reasonable percentage, usually about 33%, of your monthly gross income that should go toward your monthly housing costs, or **principal, interest, taxes, and insurance (PITI)**. If you have other debts, your PITI plus your other debt repayments should be no more than about 38% of your gross income. Those percentages will be adjusted for income level, credit score, and amount of the down payment.

principal, interest, taxes, and insurance (PITI)

Principal, interest, taxes, and insurance are the costs of home ownership. PITI is usually calculated on a monthly basis in the process of determining the affordability of a mortgage.

Say the lender assumes that 38% of your monthly gross income (annual gross income divided by 12) should cover your PITI plus any other debt payments. Subtracting your other debt payments and estimated cost of taxes and insurance leaves you with a figure for affordable monthly mortgage payments. Dividing that figure by the mortgage factor for your mortgage's maturity and mortgage rate shows the affordable mortgage overall. (The mortgage factor is the payment per $1,000 of mortgage principal, based on the interest rate and term of the mortgage.) Knowing what percentage your mortgage will be of the home's purchase price, you can calculate the maximum purchase price of the home that you can afford. That affordable home purchase price is based on your gross income, other debts, taxes, insurance, mortgage rate, mortgage maturity, and down payment.

Table 9.2 shows an example of this calculation for a 30-year, 6.5% mortgage.

TABLE 9.2 Mortgage Affordability Calculation

1. Gross Annual Income	60,000	
2. Gross Monthly Income	5,000	= 60,000 ÷ 12
3. PITI + Other Debt Payments	1,900	= 38% of 5,000
4. Other Debt Payments	200	= your estimate
5. Affordable Monthly PITI	1,700	= (3) – (4)
6. Monthly Taxes + Insurance	700	= your estimate
7. Affordable Monthly Mortgage Payment	1,000	= (5) – (6)
8. Mortgage Factor	6.32	= mortgage factor
9. Affordable Mortgage	158,228	= (7) ÷ (8) × 1,000
10. Down Payment as % of Purchase Price	20%	= your estimate
11. Mortgage as % of Purchase Price	80%	= 1 – (10)
12. Affordable Purchase Price	197,785	= (9) ÷ (11)

These kinds of calculations give both you and your lender a much clearer idea of what you can afford. You may want to sit down with a potential lender and have this discussion before you do any serious house hunting, so that you have a price range in mind before you shop. Mortgage affordability calculators are also available online.

Searching for a Home

After understanding exactly what you are looking for in a home and what you can afford, you can organize your efforts and begin your search.

Typically, buyers use a **realtor** and realty listings to identify homes for sale. A real estate broker can add value to your search by providing information about the house and property, the neighborhood and its schools, recreational and cultural opportunities, and costs of living.

realtor

A salesperson for real estate, usually hired by the seller to help price, advertise, and show the property and negotiate the actual sale.

Remember, however, that the broker or its agent, while helping you gather information and assess your choices, is working for the sellers and will be compensated by the seller when a sale is made. Consider paying for the services of a buyer's agent, a fee-based real estate broker who works for the buyer to identify choices independently of the purchase. The real estate industry is regulated by state and federal laws as well as by self-regulatory bodies, and real estate agents must be licensed to operate.

Increasingly, sellers are marketing their homes directly to save the cost of using a broker. A real estate broker typically takes a negotiable amount up to 6% of the purchase price, from which it pays a commission to the real estate agent. "For sale by owner" sites on the Internet can make the exchange of housing information easier and more convenient for both buyers and sellers. For example, websites such as Picketfencepreview.com serve home sellers and buyers directly. Keep in mind, however, that sellers acting as their own brokers and agents are not licensed or regulated and may not be knowledgeable about federal and state laws governing real estate transactions, potentially increasing your risk.

After you narrow your search and choose a prospective home in your price range, you have the home inspected to assess its condition and project the cost of any repairs or renovations. Many states require a home inspection before signing a purchase agreement or as a condition of the agreement. A standard home inspection checklist, based on information from the National Association of Certified Home Inspectors, is shown in Table 9.3.

TABLE 9.3 Standard Home Inspection Checklist

Structural Elements	• Foundation, floors, walls, ceilings, roof
Exterior Elements	• Siding, fascia, trim, windows, doors • Elevation, drainage, landscaping, pool • Driveways, sidewalks
Roof and Attic	• Framing, ventilation, flashing, gutters
Plumbing	• Pipes: potable, drain, waste, vent • Toilets, showers, sinks, faucets, traps
Electrical	• Main panel, circuit breakers, wiring, fixtures
Systems	• Furnace, water heater, air conditioner, ducts, chimney, sprinklers
Outdoor Buildings	• Garage, tool shed, pool house

Based on information from the National Association of Certified Home Inspectors, https://www.nachi.org/sop.htm (accessed October 2, 2018).

As with a car, it is best to hire a professional such as a structural engineer, contractor, or licensed home inspector to do the home inspection. (For example, see the website of the American Association of Home Inspectors at http://www.ashi.org/.) A professional will be able to spot not only potential problems but also evidence of past problems that may have been fixed improperly or that may recur—for example, water in the basement or leaks in the roof. If there are problems, you will need an estimate for the cost of fixing them. If there are significant and immediate repair or renovation costs projected by the home's condition, you may try to reduce the purchase price of the property by those costs. You don't want any surprises after you buy the house, especially costly ones.

lien

An interest in a property granted to secure payment of debt.

You will also want to do a title search, as required by your lender, to verify that there are no **liens** or claims outstanding against the property. For example, the previous owners may have had a dispute with a contractor and never paid his bill, and the contractor may have filed a lien or a claim against the property that must be resolved before the property can change hands. There are several other kinds of liens; for example, a tax lien is imposed to secure payment of overdue taxes.

A lawyer or a title search company can do the search, which involves checking the municipal or town records where a lien would be filed. A title search will also reveal if previous owners have deeded any rights—such as development rights or water rights, for example, or grants of right-of-way across the property—that would diminish the property's value.

Identifying the Market

Housing costs are determined by the price of the house and by the price of the debt that finances the house. House prices are determined by forces of supply and demand, which in turn are determined by macroeconomic circumstances.

When the economy is contracting and incomes are decreasing, and especially if unemployment rises and incomes become uncertain, buyers are hesitant to add the significant financial responsibility of new debt to their budgets. They tend to continue with their present arrangements or may try to move into cheaper housing, downsizing to a smaller house, an apartment, or condo to decrease operating expenses. When the economy is expanding, on the other hand, expectations of rising incomes may encourage buyers to be bolder with their purchasing decisions.

A house represents not only a housing expense but also an investment that can serve as a store of wealth. In theory, if a contraction creates a market with declining asset values, investors will seek out alternative investments, abandoning that market. In other words, if house prices decline, the house's value as an investment will decline. Investors will seek other assets in which to store wealth to avoid the opportunity cost of making an investment that does not generate returns.

Housing markets are local, however. If the local economy is dominated by one industry or by one large employer, the housing market will be sensitive to the fate of that industry or employer. If a location has value independent of the local economy, such as value as a vacation or retirement location, that value can offset local concerns. In that case, housing prices may be less sensitive to the local economy.

Since a house is an investment, the home buyer is concerned about its expected future value. Future value is not easy to predict, however, as housing markets have some volatility. In extreme periods, for example between 2004 and 2009, there was extreme volatility (read more on the real estate bubble in Chapter 13). Thus, depending on how long you intend to own the home, it may or may not be realistic to try to predict price trends based on macroeconomic cycles or factors. Some areas may seem to be always desirable, such as Manhattan or Malibu, California, but a severe economic shock or boom can affect prices in those areas as well.

Figure 9.4 shows housing prices in the United States from 1963-2018 in inflation-adjusted dollars.

FIGURE 9.4 U.S. Housing Prices, 1963-2018 (Inflation-Adjusted Dollars)

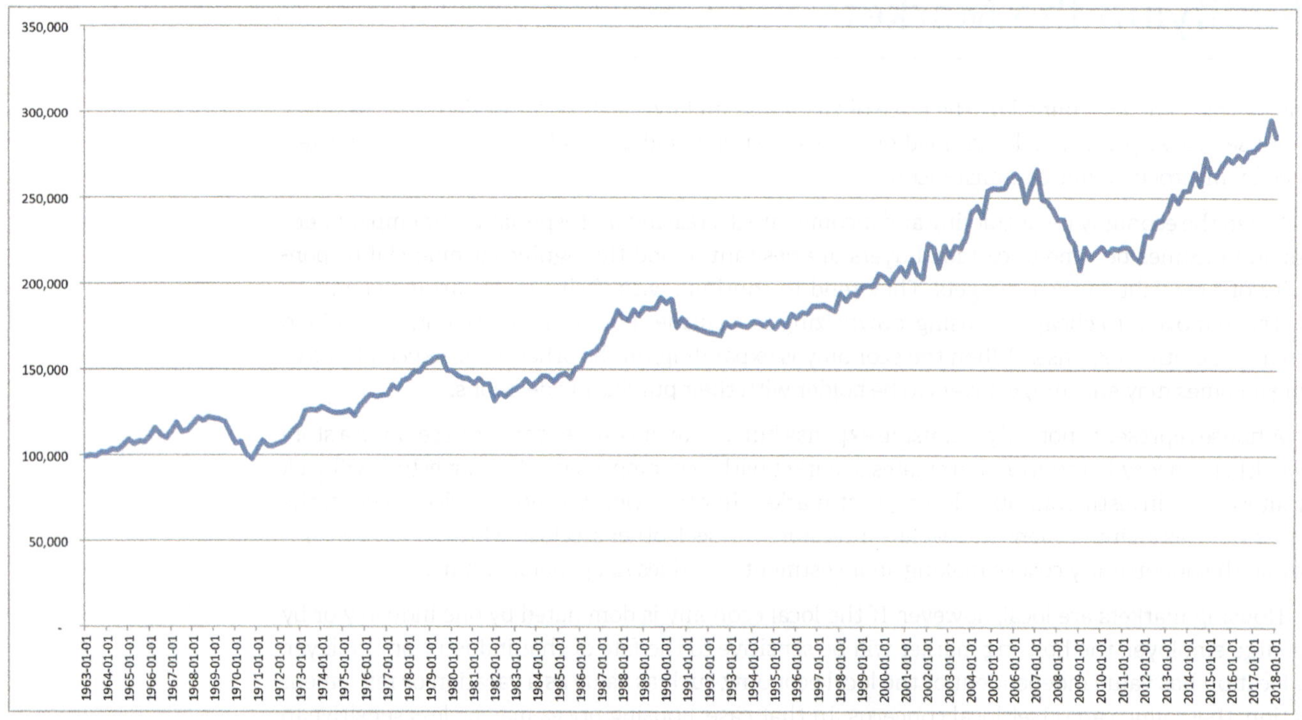

Based on data from FRED, Federal Reserve Bank of St. Louis; https://fred.stlouisfed.org/series/MSPUS, accessed May 26, 2018.

The data in Figure 9.4 show a steady trend of increasing value, suggesting that a house may be used to store value, and even generate a real increase in wealth. It seems that over the very long term, housing prices are not highly sensitive to economic cycles, population growth, building costs, or even interest rates.

The long-term trend is gradual, but there are periods when housing prices increase faster or even decrease. From the early 2000s, housing prices soared. Most economists attribute this to a sustained period of low unemployment rates, low mortgage rates, and economic growth. As bubbles do, this one eventually burst in 2007 as the economy slumped into a recession. Housing demand and prices fell, even with low mortgage rates, creating a real buyer's market. Many economists attribute the severity of the slump to the banking crisis that froze the credit markets because most housing purchases are financed with debt. The trend since 2011 shows rising housing prices.

The ability to buy a house rests on the ability to finance the purchase, to provide a down payment, and to borrow. That ability is determined by the buyer's personal situation (e.g., stability of employment or income, credit history) and by macroeconomic events such as interest rate levels, expected inflation, and liquidity in the credit markets. If interest rates and inflation are low and there is liquidity in the credit markets, it will be easier for buyers to borrow than if inflation and interest rates are high and the credit market is illiquid. Demand for housing thus relies on the availability of credit for the housing market.

Key Takeaways

- Different building structures are
  - single-unit or multiple-unit dwellings or mobile homes;
  - previously owned, new, or custom built.

- Different ownership structures include
  - conventional ownership,
  - condominium,
  - cooperative housing.
- The buyer's inspection checklist includes
  - structural elements;
  - exterior elements;
  - systems for plumbing, electrical, heating/cooling;
  - outdoor buildings and features.
- Lenders assess income, current debts, and credit history to determine the creditworthiness of borrowers.
- A mortgage affordability estimate uses an estimate of PITI and other debt payments as a percentage of gross monthly income and of the down payment as a percentage of the purchase price.
- Housing prices may be affected by business cycles as they affect
  - unemployment and income levels;
  - inflation, which affects not only the cost of houses but also interest rates and the cost of home financing.
- Housing prices are affected by the availability of home financing, which in turn depends on
  - interest rates and inflation,
  - liquidity in the credit markets.

Exercises

1. Perform an attribute analysis of your projected wants and needs as a homeowner. Begin by prioritizing the following personal and microeconomic factors in terms of their importance to you in deciding when to buy a home.
   - How large should the house be? How many bedrooms and bathrooms?
   - Which rooms are most important: kitchen, family room, or home office?
   - Do you need parking or a garage?
   - Do you need storage space?
   - Do you need disability accommodation?
   - Do you want outside space: a yard, patio, deck?
   - How important is privacy?
   - How important is energy efficiency or other "green" features?
   - How important are design features and appearance?
   - How important is location and environmental factors?
   - Proximity to work? Schools? Shopping? Family and friends?
2. In your journal or My Notes describe hypothetically your first or next home that you think you would like to own, including its location and environment. Predict how much you think it might cost to own such a home in your state. Then look through realty news and ads to find the asking prices for homes or housing units similar to the one you described. How accurate is your prediction?
3. Do you live in a dorm or at home with parents or other relatives? What needs to happen for you to have a place of your own? Research websites that aid students in finding independent housing, such as http://collegelife.about.com/od/livingoffcampus/ht/Apartments.htm. Develop a flexible plan and timetable for finding and financing a place of your own and record it in your personal finance journal.

4. Investigate the real estate market in your area. How do local housing availability and pricing differ from other cities and towns, counties, and states? Use online resources to find this information, such as HousingPredictor.com, which provides independent real estate market forecasts for local housing markets for all fifty United States, or RealtyTimes.com, an industry news source that likewise analyzes local real estate markets nationwide. How stable or volatile is your real estate market? Is it a buyer's market or a seller's market, and what does that mean? To what local factors do you attribute the differences you find? Share your findings with classmates.
5. Identify and analyze the macroeconomic factors that are affecting your local real estate market. In what ways or to what extent does your local economy reflect macroeconomic factors in the national economy? According to the National Association of Realtors (http://www.realtor.org/research-and-statistics/research-reports), what are the most important present trends in the real estate market? If you were shopping for a new or existing home today, or were planning to build, how would each macroeconomic factor and each trend you identify likely affect your choices? Record your answers in My Notes or your personal finance journal.
6. Read the article "Top 10 Real Estate Tips for the Fall" at http://www.bankrate.com/finance/real-estate/tips. What does it mean when it describes the current housing market as a "seller's market"? What are the four things to ask the seller about when buying a home, and what do you do if you don't get an answer?

9.3 Identify the Financing

Learning Objectives

1. Define the effects of the down payment on other housing costs.
2. Calculate the monthly mortgage payment, given its interest rate, maturity, and principal balance.
3. Distinguish between a fixed-rate and an adjustable-rate mortgage and explain their effects on the monthly payment and interest rate.
4. Distinguish between a rate cap and a payment cap, and explain their uses and risks.
5. Determine the effect of points on the monthly mortgage payment.
6. Identify potential closing costs.

foreclosure

The repossession of real property by a lender after a default on the mortgage by the borrower, assuming the real property has acted as collateral for the financing.

Just as your house may be your most significant purchase, your mortgage may be your most significant debt. The principal may be many times one year's disposable income and may need to be paid over 15 or 30 years. The house secures the loan, so if you default or miss payments, the lender may **foreclose** on your house or claim ownership of the property, evict you, and resell the house to recover what you owed. You may lose not only your house but also your home.

Banks, credit unions, finance companies, and mortgage finance companies sell mortgages. They profit by lending and competing for borrowers. It makes sense to shop around for a mortgage, as rates and terms (i.e., the borrowers' costs and conditions) may vary widely. The Internet has made it easy to compare; a quick search for "mortgage rates" yields many websites that provide national and state averages, lenders in your area, comparable rates and terms, and free mortgage calculators.

You may feel more comfortable getting your mortgage through your local bank, which may process the loan and then sell the mortgage to a larger financial institution. The local bank usually continues to service the loan, to collect the payments, but those cash flows are passed through to the financial institution (usually a much larger bank) that has bought the mortgage. This secondary mortgage market allows your local bank to have more liquidity and less risk, as it gets repaid right away, allowing it to make more loans. As long as you continue to make your payments, your only interaction is with the bank that is servicing the loan. Alternatively, local banks may earmark a percentage of mortgages to keep "in house" rather than sell.

FIGURE 9.5

Keep in mind that the costs discussed in this chapter, associated with various kinds of mortgages, may change. The real estate market, government housing policies, and government regulation of the mortgage financing market may change at any time. When it is time for you to shop for a mortgage, therefore, be sure you are informed of current developments.

Down Payment

Mortgages require a **down payment**, or a percentage of the purchase price paid in cash upon purchase. Most buyers use cash from savings, the proceeds of a house they are selling, or a family gift.

down payment

The share of the purchase price paid in cash at the time of purchase; also called earnest money.

The size of the down payment does not affect the price of the house, but it can affect the cost of the financing. For a given house price, the larger the down payment, the smaller the mortgage and, all things being equal, the lower the monthly payments. An example of different down payments and their effects on the monthly mortgage payment for a 30-year mortgage is shown in Table 9.4.

TABLE 9.4 Down Payment and Monthly Payment

Purchase price	% down	Mortgage	Mortgage rate	Mortgage payment
250,000	5%	237,500	5%	1,274.95
250,000	10%	225,000	5%	1,207.85
250,000	20%	200,000	5%	1,073.64
250,000	30%	175,000	5%	939.44
250,000	40%	150,000	5%	805.23
250,000	50%	125,000	5%	671.03

private mortgage insurance

Insurance that insures the lender against any losses incurred by the costs of a loan default.

closing costs

Transaction costs of the home purchase, including appraisal fees, title, additional fees, and title insurance; closing costs are paid at the closing or purchase of the home.

Usually, if the down payment is less than 20% of the property's sale price, the borrower has to pay for **private mortgage insurance**, which insures the lender against the costs of default. A larger down payment eliminates this expense for the borrower.

The down payment can offset the annual cost of the financing, but it creates opportunity cost and decreases your liquidity as you take money out of savings. Cash will also be needed for the **closing costs** or transaction costs of this purchase or for any immediate renovations or repairs. Those needs will have to be weighed against your available cash to determine the amount of your down payment.

Monthly Payment

The monthly payment is the ongoing cash flow obligation of the loan. If you don't pay this payment, you are in default on the loan and may eventually lose the house with no compensation for the money you have already put into it. Your ability to make the monthly payment determines your ability to keep the house.

fixed-rate mortgage

A mortgage loan with a fixed interest rate over the life of the loan.

The interest rate and the maturity (duration of the mortgage) determine the monthly payment amount. With a **fixed-rate mortgage**, the interest rate remains the same over the entire maturity of the mortgage, and so does the monthly payment. Conventional mortgages are fixed-rate mortgages for 30, 20, or 15 years.

The longer the maturity, the greater the interest rate, because the lender faces more risk the longer it takes for the loan to be repaid.

A fixed-rate mortgage is structured as an annuity: regular periodic payments of equal amounts. Some of the payment is repayment of the principal and some is for the interest expense. As you make a payment, your balance gets smaller, and so the interest portion of your next payment is smaller, and the principal payment is larger. In other words, as you continue making payments, you are paying off the balance of the loan faster and faster and paying less and less interest.

mortgage amortization

A schedule of mortgage payments showing the amounts of each payment that pay interest and that pay principal.

An example of a **mortgage amortization**, or a schedule of interest and principal payments over the life of the loan, is shown in Table 9.5. The mortgage has a 30-year, 6.5% fixed-rate with a principal amount of $200,000. Only the first two years are shown, but the calculations could continue to show the amortization over the term of the mortgage.

TABLE 9.5 Mortgage Amortization Table for a 30-year, 6.5%, $200,000 mortgage

Month	Payment amount	Interest expense	Principal paid	Balance
0	1,264.14			200,000.00
1	1,264.14	1,083.33	180.80	199,819.20
2	1,264.14	1,082.35	181.78	199,637.42
3	1,264.14	1,081.37	182.77	199,454.65
4	1,264.14	1,080.38	183.76	199,270.89
5	1,264.14	1,079.38	184.75	199,086.14
6	1,264.14	1,078.38	185.75	198,900.39
7	1,264.14	1,077.38	186.76	198,713.63
8	1,264.14	1,076.37	187.77	198,525.86
9	1,264.14	1,075.35	188.79	198,337.07
10	1,264.14	1,074.33	189.81	198,147.26
11	1,264.14	1,073.30	190.84	197,956.42
12	1,264.14	1,072.26	191.87	197,764.55
13	1,264.14	1,071.22	192.91	197,571.64
14	1,264.14	1,070.18	193.96	197,377.68
15	1,264.14	1,069.13	195.01	197,182.67
16	1,264.14	1,068.07	196.06	196,986.61
17	1,264.14	1,067.01	197.13	196,789.49
18	1,264.14	1,065.94	198.19	196,591.29
19	1,264.14	1,064.87	199.27	196,392.03
20	1,264.14	1,063.79	200.35	196,191.68
21	1,264.14	1,062.70	201.43	195,990.25
22	1,264.14	1,061.61	202.52	195,787.73
23	1,264.14	1,060.52	203.62	195,584.11
24	1,264.14	1,059.41	204.72	195,379.39

In the early years of the mortgage, your payments are mostly interest, while in the last years they are mostly principal. It is important to distinguish between them because the mortgage interest may be tax deductible. That tax benefit is greater in the earlier years of the mortgage, when the interest expense is larger.

Monthly mortgage payments can be estimated using the **mortgage factor**. The mortgage factor is a calculation of the payment per $1,000 of the mortgage loan, given the interest rate and the maturity of the mortgage. Mortgage factors for 30-, 20-, and 15-year mortgages are shown in Table 9.6.

mortgage factor
The mortgage payment per $1,000 of principal.

TABLE 9.6 Mortgage Factors for Different Interest Rates and Mortgage Terms

		Mortgage factor		
Mortgage amount	**Mortgage rate**	**30-year**	**20-year**	**15-year**
1,000	4.00%	4.77	6.06	7.40
1,000	4.50%	5.07	6.33	7.65
1,000	5.00%	5.37	6.60	7.91
1,000	5.50%	5.68	6.88	8.17
1,000	6.00%	6.00	7.16	8.44
1,000	6.50%	6.32	7.46	8.71
1,000	7.00%	6.65	7.75	8.99
1,000	7.50%	6.99	8.06	9.27
1,000	8.00%	7.34	8.36	9.56
1,000	8.50%	7.69	8.68	9.85
1,000	9.00%	8.05	9.00	10.14
1,000	9.50%	8.41	9.32	10.44
1,000	10.00%	8.78	9.65	10.75

The monthly payment can be calculated as:

$$\frac{\text{Mortgage factor} \times \text{Principal}}{1,000}$$

So, if you were considering purchasing a house for $250,000 with a $50,000 down payment and financing the remaining $200,000 with a 30-year, 6.5% mortgage, then your monthly mortgage payment would be:

$$\frac{6.32 \times 200,000}{1,000} = 1,264$$

If you used a 15-year mortgage, your monthly payment would be:

$$\frac{8.71 \times 200,000}{1,000} = 1,742$$

If you got the 30-year mortgage but at a rate of 6%, your monthly payment would be $1,200.

Potential lenders and many websites provide mortgage calculators to do these calculations, so you can estimate your monthly payments for a fixed-rate mortgage if you know the mortgage rate, the term to maturity, and the principal borrowed.

Mortgage Designs

So far, the discussion has focused on fixed-rate mortgages, that is, mortgages with fixed or constant interest rates, and therefore payments, until maturity. With an **adjustable-rate mortgage (ARM)**, the interest rate—and the monthly payment—can change. If interest rates rise, the monthly payment will increase, and if they fall, it will decrease. By federal law, increases in ARM interest rates cannot rise more than 2% at a time, but even with this **rate cap**, homeowners with ARMs are at risk of seeing their monthly payment increase. Borrowers can limit this interest rate risk with a payment cap, which, however, introduces another risk.

adjustable-rate mortgage (ARM)
A mortgage loan with a floating or adjustable rate of interest.

rate cap
A limit on the potential adjustment to the mortgage interest rate.

FIGURE 9.6

A **payment cap** limits the amount by which the payment can increase or decrease. That sounds like it would protect the borrower, but if the payment is capped and the interest rate rises, more of the payment pays for the interest expense and less for the principal payment, so the balance is paid down more slowly. If interest rates are high enough, the payment may be too small to pay all the interest expense, and any interest not paid will add to the principal balance of the mortgage.

payment cap
A limit to the potential adjustment to the mortgage payment.

In other words, instead of paying off the mortgage, your payments may actually increase your debt, and you could end up owing more money than you borrowed, even though you make all your required payments on time. This is called negative amortization. You should make sure you know if your ARM mortgage is this type of loan. You can voluntarily increase your monthly payment amount to avoid the negative effects of a payment cap.

Adjustable-rate mortgages are risky for borrowers. ARMs are usually offered at lower rates than fixed-rate mortgages, however, and may be more affordable. Borrowers who expect an increase in their disposable incomes, which would offset the risk of a higher payment, or who expect a decrease in interest rates, may prefer an adjustable-rate mortgage, which can have a maturity of up to forty years. Otherwise, a fixed-rate mortgage is better.

balloon mortgage

A mortgage that offers a shorter maturity but with lower payments and a large principal balance due at maturity.

home equity loan

A loan secured by home equity value.

home equity line of credit (HELOC)

A loan secured by home equity value, structured such that principal may be borrowed only as needed, and interest paid only on the balance outstanding.

reverse mortgage

A loan secured by equity value, most often used for elderly homeowners to extract equity value while retaining home ownership. Typically, the loan balance is payable at the home owner's death.

points

One percent of the mortgage value, used as prepaid interest paid at time of purchase.

There are mortgages that combine fixed and variable rates—for example, offering a fixed rate for a specified period of time, and then an adjustable rate. Another type of mortgage is a **balloon mortgage** that offers fixed monthly payments for a specified period, usually three, five, or seven years, and then a final, large repayment of the principal. There are option ARMs, where you pay either interest only or principal only for the first few years of the loan, which makes it more affordable. While you are paying interest only, however, you are not accumulating equity in your investment.

As an asset, a house may be used to secure other types of loans. A **home equity loan** or a second mortgage allows a homeowner to borrow against any equity in the home. A home improvement loan is a type of home equity loan. A **home equity line of credit (HELOC)** allows the homeowner to secure a line of credit, or a loan that is borrowed and paid down as needed, with interest paid only on the outstanding balance. A **reverse mortgage** is designed to provide homeowners with high equity a monthly income in the form of a loan. Essentially, a reverse mortgage is a loan against your home that you do not have to pay back for as long as you live there. To be eligible for most reverse mortgages, you must own your home and be 62 years of age or older. You or your estate repays the loan when you sell the house or die.

Points

Points are another kind of financing cost. One point is 1% of the mortgage. Points are paid to the lender as a form of prepaid interest when the mortgage originates and are used to decrease the mortgage rate. In other words, paying points is a way of buying a lower mortgage rate.

In deciding whether it is worth it to pay points, you need to think about the difference that the lower mortgage rate will make to your monthly payment and how long you will be paying this mortgage. How long will it take for the points to pay for themselves in reduced monthly payments? For example, suppose you have the following choices for a 30-year, fixed rate, $200,000 mortgage: a mortgage rate of 6.5% with no points or a rate of 6% with 2 points.

First, you can calculate the difference in your monthly payments for the two different situations. Using the mortgage factor for a 30-year mortgage, the monthly payment in each case would be the mortgage factor × $200,000 ÷ 1,000 or:

Points	Mortgage rate	Mortgage factor	Monthly payment
0	6.50%	6.32	1,264
2	6.00%	6.00	1,200

Paying the two points buys you a lower monthly payment and saves you $64 per month. The two points cost $4,000 (2% of $200,000). At the rate of $64 per month, it will take 62.5 months ($4,000 ÷ 64) or a little over five years for those points to pay for themselves. If you do not plan on having this mortgage for that long, then paying the points is not worth it. Paying points has liquidity and opportunity costs up front that must be weighed against its benefit. Points are part of the closing costs, but borrowers do not have to pay them if they are willing to pay a higher interest rate instead.

Closing Costs

Other costs of a house purchase are transaction costs, that is, costs of making the transaction happen that are not direct costs of either the home or the financing. These are referred to as closing costs, as they are paid at the closing, the meeting between buyer and seller where the ownership and loan documents are signed and the property is actually transferred. The buyer pays these closing costs, including the appraisal fee, title insurance, and filing fee for the deed.

The lender will have required an independent **appraisal** of the home's value to make sure that the amount of the mortgage is reasonable given the value of the house that secures it. The lender will also require a **title search** and contract for **title insurance**. The title company will research any claims or liens on the deed; the purchase cannot go forward if the deed may not be freely transferred. Over the term of the mortgage, the title insurance protects against flaws not found in the title and any claims that may result. The buyer also pays a fee to file the property deed with the township, municipality, or county. Some states may also have a **property transfer tax** that is the responsibility of the buyer.

Closings may take place in the office of the title company handling the transaction or at the registry of deeds. Closings also may take place in the lender's offices, such as a bank or an attorney's office and usually are mediated between the buyer and the seller through their attorneys. Lawyers who specialize in real estate ensure that all legal requirements are met and all filings of legal documents are completed. For example, before signing, home buyers have a right to review a U.S. Housing and Urban Development (HUD) Settlement Statement 24 hours prior to the closing. This document, along with a truth-in-lending disclosure statement, sets out and explains all the terms of the transaction, all the costs of buying the house, and all closing costs. Both the buyer and the seller must sign the HUD document and are legally bound by it.

appraisal

An opinion of the market value of a property done by a professional appraiser who is familiar with the real estate market and with housing, and who has been certified to do appraisals.

title search

A search of public records to determine if there are any restrictions or allowances on the property to be purchased, or any liens, or debts such as a mortgage balance, overdue taxes, a mechanic's lien, and so on, that must be paid if the property is sold.

title insurance

Insurance purchased by the purchaser of the property that insures against any omission from the title search.

property transfer tax

A tax on the transfer of title to property; a transaction cost of purchasing property.

Key Takeaways

- The percentage of the purchase price paid upfront as the down payment will determine the amount that is borrowed. That principal balance on the mortgage, in turn, determines the monthly mortgage payment.
- A larger down payment may make the monthly payment smaller but creates the opportunity cost of losing liquidity.
- A fixed-rate mortgage is structured as an annuity; the monthly mortgage payment can be calculated from the mortgage rate, the maturity, and the principal balance on the mortgage.
- A fixed-rate mortgage has a fixed mortgage rate and fixed monthly payments.
- An adjustable-rate mortgage may have an adjustable mortgage rate and/or adjustable payments.
- A rate cap or a payment cap may be used to offset the effects of an adjustable-rate mortgage on monthly payments.
- Points are borrowing costs paid upfront (rather than over the maturity of the mortgage).
- Closing costs are transaction costs such as an appraisal fee, title search and title insurance, filing fees for legal documents, transfer taxes, and sometimes realtors' commissions.

Exercises

1. You are considering purchasing an existing single family house for $200,000 with a 20% down payment and a 30-year fixed-rate mortgage at 5.5%.
   a. What would be your monthly mortgage payment?
   b. If you decided to buy two points for a rate of 5%, how much would you save in monthly payments? Would it be worth it to buy the points? Why, or why not?
   c. When should you consider an adjustable-rate mortgage?
2. Review the explanation of adjustable-rate mortgages on the consumer guide site of the U.S. Federal Reserve (the Fed) at https://www.federalreserve.gov/pubs/arms/armstext_cover2005.pdf. According to the Fed, why should you be cautious about adjustable-rate

mortgages? Download the "Mortgage Shopping Worksheet" at this website as a guide to comparing features of ARMs with lenders.

3. Do you presently rent or own your home or apartment? What are your housing costs? What percent of your income is taken up in housing costs? If your housing is costing you more than a third of your income, what could you do to reduce that cost? Record your alternatives in your personal finance journal.
4. As a prospective homeowner, what would be your estimated PITI? Would a bank consider that you qualify for a mortgage loan at this time? Why or why not? What criteria do lenders use to determine your eligibility for a home mortgage?
5. Can you afford a mortgage now? How much of a mortgage could you afford? Answer these questions using online mortgage affordability calculators, found, for example, at http://www.bankrate.com/calculators/mortgages/new-house-calculator.aspx, and https://www.msn.com/en-us/money/tools. If you cannot afford a mortgage now, how would your personal situation and/or your budget need to change to make that possible? Establish home affordability as a goal in your financial planning. Write in My Notes or your personal finance journal how and when you expect you will reach that goal.
6. Read about the closing process at http://mortgage.lovetoknow.com/The_Closing_Process_When_Buying_a_House. According to Love to Know, who attends the closing? What legal documents are processed at the closing?
7. Review local real estate, condo, or apartment listings in the price range you have now determined is truly affordable for you. For learning purposes, choose a home you would like to own and clip the ad with photo to put in your personal finance journal. Record the purchase price, the down payment you would make, the mortgage amount you would seek, the current interest rates on a mortgage loan for fixed- and adjustable-rate mortgages for various periods or maturities, the type of mortgage you would prefer, the rate and maturity you would seek, the points you would buy (if any), the amount of monthly mortgage payments you would expect to make, and the names of lenders you would consider approaching first.

9.4 Purchasing and Owning Your Home

Learning Objectives

1. Identify the components of a purchase and sale agreement.
2. Explain the importance of a capital budget in determining capital spending priorities.
3. Identify the financing events you may encounter during the maturity of a mortgage.
4. Define the borrower's and the lender's responsibilities to the mortgage.
5. Explain the consequences of default and foreclosure.

The Purchase Process

Now that you've chosen your home and figured out the financing, all that's left to do is sign the papers, right?

Once you have found a house, you will make an offer to the seller, who will then accept or reject your offer. If the offer is rejected, you may try to negotiate with the seller or you may decide to forgo this purchase. If your offer is accepted, you and the seller will sign a formal agreement called a **purchase and sale agreement**, specifying the terms of the sale. You will be required to pay a nonrefundable deposit, or **earnest money**, when the purchase and sale agreement is signed. That money will be held in **escrow** or in a restricted account and then applied toward the closing costs at settlement.

purchase and sale agreement

The legally binding agreement that sets the terms of the property transaction as agreed to by buyer and seller.

earnest money

A nonrefundable deposit paid by the buyer to the seller at the time of the purchase and sale agreement then applied toward the closing costs.

escrow

A restricted account used for the earnest money until closing.

conveyances

Any agreements regarding property features also included in the transaction, such as appliances, satellite dishes, and so on.

The purchase and sale agreement will include the following terms and conditions:

- A legal description of the property, including boundaries, with a site survey contingency
- The sale price and deposit amount
- A mortgage contingency, stating that the sale is contingent on the final approval of your financing
- The closing date and location, mutually agreed upon by buyer and seller
- **Conveyances** or any agreements made as part of the offer—for example, an agreement as to whether the kitchen appliances are sold with the house
- A home inspection contingency specifying the consequences of a home inspection and any problems that it may find, if not already completed and included in the price negotiation
- Possession date, usually the closing date
- A description of the property insurance policy that will cover the home until the closing date

Property disclosures of any problems with the property that must be legally disclosed, which vary by state, will also be included. Lead-paint disclosure is a federal mandate for any housing built before 1978.

After the purchase and sale agreement is signed, any conditions that it specified must be fulfilled before the closing date. If those conditions are the seller's responsibility, you will want to be sure that they have been fulfilled before closing. Read all the documents before you sign them and get copies of everything you sign. Do not hesitate to ask questions. You may live with your mortgage, and your house, for a long time.

Capital Expenditures

A house and property need care; even a new home will have repair and maintenance costs. These costs are now a part of your living expenses or operating budget.

If you have purchased a home that requires renovation or repair, you will decide how much of the work you can do immediately and how much can be done on an annual basis. A capital budget is helpful to project these capital expenditures and plan the income or savings to finance them. You can prioritize these costs by their urgency and by how they will be done.

FIGURE 9.7

© 2010 Jupiterimages Corporation

For example, Sally and Chris just closed on an older home and are planning renovations. During the home inspection, they learned that the old stone foundation would need some work. They would like to install more energy-efficient windows, paint the walls, and strip and refinish the old, wood floors.

Their first priority should be the foundation on which the house rests. The windows should be the next on the list, as they will not only provide comfort but also reduce the heating and cooling expenses. Cosmetic repairs such as painting and refinishing can be done later. The walls should be done first (in case any paint drips on the floors) and then the floors.

Renovations should increase the resale value of your home. It is tempting to customize renovations to suit your tastes and needs, but too much customization will make it more difficult to realize the value of those renovations when it comes time to sell. You will have a better chance of selling the house at a higher price if there is more demand for it, if it appeals to as many potential buyers as possible. The more customized or "quirky" a house is, the less broad its appeal may be.

Early Payment

early payment

Redemption or paying back the mortgage loan before its maturity.

refinancing

Attaining a new mortgage and simultaneously paying off the old mortgage.

early payment penalty

A cash penalty for the borrower for an early payment; this clause is not included in all mortgages.

Two financing decisions may come up during the life of a mortgage: **early payment** and **refinancing**. Some mortgages have an **early payment penalty** that fines the borrower for repaying the loan before it is due, but most do not. If your mortgage does not, you may be able to pay it off early (before maturity) either with a lump sum or by paying more than your required monthly payment and having the excess payment applied to your principal balance.

If you are thinking of paying off your mortgage with a lump sum, then you are weighing the value of your liquidity, the opportunity cost of giving up cash, against the cost of the remaining interest payments. The cost of giving up your cash is the loss of any investment return you may otherwise have from it. You would compare that to the cost of your mortgage, or your mortgage rate, less any tax benefit that it provides.

For example, suppose you can invest cash and earn a return of 10%. Your mortgage rate is 6%, and your tax rate is 25%. (For simplicity, assume that your mortgage interest is not tax deductible.) Your mortgage costs you 6% per year but after taxes, your investment earns 7.5%, or 75% of 10%. Since your cash is worth more to you as a investment where it nets 7.5% than it costs you in mortgage interest (6%), you should leave it invested and pay your mortgage incrementally as planned.

On the other hand, if your investment earns 2%, but your mortgage rate is 8% and you are in the 25% tax bracket, then the cost of your mortgage (8%) is more than your cash can earn (1.5%). You would be better off using the cash to pay off your mortgage and eliminating that interest cost.

You also need to weigh the use of your cash to pay off the mortgage versus other uses of that cash. For example, suppose you have some money saved. It is earning less than your after-tax mortgage interest, so you are thinking of paying down the mortgage. However, you also know that you will need a new car in two years. If you use that money to pay down the mortgage now, you won't have it to pay for the car two years from now. You could get a car loan to buy the car, but the interest rate on that loan will be higher than the rate on your mortgage. If paying off your mortgage debt forces you to use more expensive debt, then it is not worth it.

One way to pay down a mortgage early without sacrificing too much liquidity is by making a larger monthly payment. The excess over the required amount will be applied to your principal balance, which then decreases faster. Since you pay interest on the principal balance, reducing it more quickly would save you some interest expense. If you have had an increase in income, you may be able to do this fairly "painlessly," but then again, there may be a better use for your increased cash flow.

Over a mortgage term as long as 30 years, interest expense can be substantial—more than the original balance on the mortgage. However, that choice must be made in the context of the value of your alternatives.

Refinancing

You may think about refinancing your mortgage if better mortgage rates are available. Refinancing means borrowing a new debt or getting a new mortgage and repaying the old one. It involves closing costs: the lender will want an updated appraisal, a title search, and title insurance. It is valuable to refinance if the mortgage rate will be so much lower that your monthly payment will be substantially reduced. That in turn depends on the size of your mortgage balance.

FIGURE 9.8

If interest rates are low enough and your home has appreciated so that your equity has increased, you may be able to refinance and increase the principal balance on the new mortgage without increasing the monthly payment over your old monthly payment. If you do that, you are withdrawing equity from your house, and you are not allowing it to perform as an investment, that is to store your wealth.

If you would rather take gains from the house and invest them differently, that may be a good choice. But if you want to take gains from the house and use those for consumption, then you are reducing the investment returns on your home. You are also using nonrecurring income to finance recurring expenses, which is not sustainable. There is also a danger that property values will decrease and you will be left with a mortgage worth more than your home.

Default, Foreclosure, and Fraud

If you have a change of circumstances—for example, you lose your job in an economic downturn, or you have unexpected health care costs in your family—you may find that you are unable to meet your mortgage obligations as planned: to make the payments. A mortgage is secured by the property it financed. If you miss payments and default on your mortgage, the lender has recourse to foreclose on your property, to evict you and take possession of your home, and then to sell it or lease it to recover its investment. Under normal circumstances, lenders incur a cost in repossessing a home, and usually lose money in its resale. It may be possible to renegotiate terms of your mortgage to forestall foreclosure. You may want to consult with a legal representative, or to contact federal and/or state agencies for assistance.

You may believe you are having trouble meeting your mortgage obligations because they are not what you thought they would be. Lenders profit by lending. When you are borrowing, it is important to understand the terms of your loan. If those terms will adjust under certain conditions, you must understand what could happen to your payments and to the value of your home. It is your responsibility to understand these conditions. However, the lender has a responsibility to disclose the lending arrangement and all its costs, according to federal and state laws (which vary by state). If you believe that all conditions and terms of your mortgage were not fairly disclosed, you should contact your state banking regulator or the U.S Department of Housing and Urban Development (HUD). There are also consumer advocacy groups that will help clarify the laws and explore any legal recourse you may have.

mortgage fraud

Intentional misrepresentation or omission of facts perpetrated by a borrower in the process of obtaining mortgage financing.

Just as your lender has a legal obligation to be forthcoming and clear with you, you have an obligation to be truthful. If you have misrepresented or omitted facts on your mortgage application, you can be held liable for mortgage fraud. For example, if you have overstated your income, misled the lender about your employment or your intention to live in the house, or have understated your debts, you may be prosecuted for **mortgage fraud**. Other forms of mortgage fraud are more elaborate, such as inflating the appraisal amount in order to borrow more.

Mortgage fraud can be perpetrated by the borrower, appraiser, or loan officer who originates the loan. During the recent housing bubble, mortgage fraud was aggravated by low interest rates that encouraged more borrowing and lending, often when it was less than prudent to do so. Mortgage fraud in the United States spiked in the run up to the 2007 bursting of the housing bubble. In response, the U.S. government enacted the Fraud and Enforcement Recovery Act of 2009, which strengthened criminal enforcement of fraud laws.

Key Takeaways

- The purchase and sale agreement details the conditions of the sale.
- Conditions of the purchase and sale agreement must be met before the closing.
- A capital budget can help you prioritize and budget for capital expenditures.
- Early payment is the trade-off of interest expense versus the opportunity cost of losing liquidity.
- Refinancing is the trade-off between lower monthly payments and closing costs.
- Both borrowers and lenders have a responsibility to understand the terms of the mortgage.
- Buyers, sellers, lenders, and brokers must be alert to predatory lending, real estate scams, and possible cases of mortgage fraud.
- Default may result in the lender foreclosing on the property and evicting the former homeowner.

Exercises

1. Read about home purchase agreements at http://real-estate.lawyers.com/residential-real-estate/home-purchase-agreements.html, and view the standard purchase and sale agreement form at https://www.lawdepot.com/contracts/real-estate-purchase-agreement/?loc=US#.Wwr4Y1MvxsY. For comparison, find a sample purchase and sale agreement for your state.
2. According to this chapter, what information is included in a purchase and sale agreement?
3. Use the mortgage refinancing calculator at Bankrate.com (http://www.bankrate.com/calculators/mortgages/refinance-calculator.aspx) to find out if you would save money by refinancing your real or hypothetical mortgage at this time. What factors should you take into consideration when deciding to refinance?
4. Sample consumer advocacy groups online at http://homeownersconsumercenter.com/. What kinds of help can you get through such organizations?
5. What constitutes mortgage fraud? Find out at https://www.thebalance.com/how-to-avoid-mortgage-fraud-1798419. Discuss with others taking this course the common ways that homebuyers can become involved both directly and indirectly in mortgage or real estate fraud.
6. Survey the Department of Housing and Urban Development website on how to avoid foreclosure at https://www.hud.gov/faqs/foreclose. Inferring from information on this site, what are ten steps people should take to avoid foreclosure?

Endnotes

1. National Association of Realtors, Existing Single-Family Home Sales [EXSFHSUSM495S], retrieved from FRED, Federal Reserve Bank of St. Louis; https://fred.stlouisfed.org/series/EXSFHSUSM495S (accessed June 16, 2018).

CHAPTER 10

Personal Risk Management: Insurance

10.1 Introduction

Life is full of risks. You can try to avoid them or reduce their likelihood and consequences, but you cannot eliminate them. You can, however, pay someone to share them. That is the idea behind insurance.

There are **speculative risks**, that is, risks that offer a chance of loss or gain, such as developing a "killer app" that may or may not sell or investing in a corporate stock that may or may not provide good returns. Such risks can be avoided simply by not participating. They are almost always uninsurable.

speculative risks

Intended risk that offers a chance of loss or gain.

There are **pure risks** of accidental or unintentional events, such as a car accident or an illness. Pure risks are insurable because their probabilities can be calculated precisely enough for the risk to be quantified, which means it can be priced, bought, and sold.

FIGURE 10.1

© Shutterstock, Inc.

Risk shifting is the process of selling risk to someone who then assumes the risk and its consequences. Why would someone buy your risk? Because in a large enough market, your risk can be diversified, which minimizes its cost. You are selling risk when you buy insurance.

Insurance can be purchased for your property and your home, your health, your employment, and your life. In each case, you weigh the cost of the consequence of a risk that may never actually happen against the cost of insuring against it. Deciding what and how to insure is really a process of deciding what the costs of loss would be and how willing you are to pay to get rid of those risks.

pure risks

The risk of accidental or unintentional events.

risk shifting

Selling risk to avoid bearing the full consequence of unintentional events.

The costs of insurance can also be lowered through risk avoidance or reduction strategies. For example, installing an alarm system in your home may reduce homeowners' insurance premiums because that reduces the risk of theft. Of course, installing an alarm system has a cost too. Risk management is the strategic trade-off of the costs of reducing, assuming, and shifting risks.

10.2 Insuring Your Property

Learning Objectives

1. Describe the purpose of property insurance.
2. Identify the causes of property damage.

3. Compare the kinds of homeowner's insurance coverage and benefits.
4. Analyze the costs of homeowner's insurance.
5. Compare the kinds of auto insurance to cover bodily injury and property damage.
6. Explain the factors that determine auto insurance costs.
7. Analyze the factors used in determining the risks of the driver, the car, and the driving region.

Property insurance is ownership insurance: it insures that the rights of ownership conferred upon you when you purchased your property will remain intact. Typically, property insurance covers loss of use from either damage or theft; loss of value, or the cost of replacement; and liability for any use of the property that causes damage to others or others' property. For most people, insurable property risks are covered by insuring two kinds of property: car and home.

Loss of use and value can occur from hazards such as fire or weather disasters and from deliberate destruction such as vandalism or theft. When replacement or repair is needed to restore usefulness and value, that cost is the cost of your risk. For example, if your laptop crashes, you not only have the cost of replacing or repairing it, but also the cost of being without your laptop for however long that takes. Insuring your laptop shares that risk (and those costs) with the insurer.

Liability is the risk that your use of your property will injure someone or something else. Ownership implies control of, and therefore responsibility for, property use.

For example, you are liable for your dog's attack on a pedestrian and for your fallen tree's damage to a neighbor's fence. You also are liable for damage a friend causes while driving your car with your permission and for injury to your invited guests who trip over your lawn ornament, fall off your deck, or leave your party intoxicated.

FIGURE 10.2

Legal responsibility can be from:

- **negligence**, or the failure to take usual precautions;
- **strict liability**, or responsibility for intentional or unintentional events;
- **vicarious liability**, or responsibility for someone else's use of your possessions or someone else's activity for which you are responsible.

negligence

Failure to take ordinary precautions.

strict liability

Responsibility for intentional or unintentional events.

vicarious liability

Responsibility for another's use of your possessions, or for another's actions, under certain circumstances.

Home Insurance Coverage

Homeowner's insurance insures both the structure and the personal possessions that make the house your home. Renter's insurance protects your possessions even if you are not the owner of your dwelling. You may not think you need insurance until you are the homeowner, but even when you don't need to insure against possible damage or liability for your dwelling, you can still insure your possessions. Even if your furniture came from your aunt's house or a yard sale, it could cost a lot to replace. About 96% of all homeowners have homeowners' insurance, but only about 41% of all renters have renters' insurance.[1]https://www.iii.org/fact-statistic/facts-statistics-homeowners-and-renters-insurance (accessed June 17, 2018)

If you have especially valuable possessions such as jewelry or fine musical instruments, you may want to insure them separately to get enough coverage for them. Such items are typically referred to as **listed property** and are insured as **endorsements** added on to a homeowners' or renter's policy. Items should be appraised by a certified appraiser to determine their replacement or insured value.

listed property

Valuable property insured separately under a homeowner's policy.

endorsements

The clause of a homeowner's policy insuring listed property.

A good precaution is to have an up-to-date inventory of your possessions such as furniture, clothing, electronics, and appliances, along with photographs or video showing these items in your home. That inventory should be kept somewhere else, such as a safe deposit box. If the house suffered damage, you would then have the inventory to help you document your losses.

A homeowners' policy covers damage to the structure itself as well as any outbuildings on the property and, in some cases, even the landscaping or infrastructure on the grounds, such as a driveway.

A homeowners' policy does not cover:

- animals;
- property of renters, or property kept in an apartment regularly rented;
- business property, even if the business is conducted on the residential premises.

According to information from the Insurance Information Institute, an insurance industry data and research company, hazards covered by the homeowner's policy include[2]

- fire or lightning;
- windstorm or hail;
- explosion;
- riot or civil commotion;
- damage caused by aircraft;
- damage caused by vehicles;
- smoke;
- vandalism or malicious mischief;
- theft;
- volcanic eruption;
- falling objects;

- weight of ice, snow, or sleet;
- accidental discharge or overflow of water or steam from within a plumbing, heating, air conditioning, or automatic fire-protective sprinkler system, or from a household appliance;
- sudden and accidental tearing apart, cracking, burning, or bulging of a steam or hot water heating, air conditioning, or automatic fire-protective system;
- freezing of a plumbing, heating, air conditioning, or automatic fire-protective sprinkler system, or of a household appliance;
- sudden and accidental damage from artificially generated electrical current (does not include loss to a tube, transistor, or similar electronic component).

Note that floods and earthquakes are not covered. A homeowner in a flood- or earthquake-prone area may buy special coverage, either from a private insurer or from a federal or state program.

Homeowners' insurance covers the less direct costs of hazards as well. For example, the costs of removing damaged goods or temporary repairs are covered. The cost of temporary housing and extra living expenses while repairs are made is covered, although usually for a limited time or amount.

umbrella policy

Personal liability insurance in attached to a homeowner's policy.

Homeowners' policies cover liability for injuries on the property and for injuries that the homeowner may accidentally inflict. You may also want to add an **umbrella policy** that covers personal liabilities such as slander, libel, and defamation of character. An umbrella policy may also extend over other assets, such as vehicles or rentals covered by other insurance carriers. If you participate in activities where you are assuming responsibilities for others—you are taking the Cub Scout pack out for a hike, for example, or volunteering at your local recycling center—you may want such extended liability coverage available through your homeowners' policy (also available separately).

Home Insurance Coverage: The Benefit

FIGURE 10.3

© 2010 Jupiterimages Corporation

actual cash value

Market value of insured property at time of loss.

replacement cost

Cost of replacing insured property at time of loss.

Home insurance policies automatically cover your possessions for up to 40% of the house's insured value. You can buy more coverage if you think they are worth more. The benefits are specified as either **actual cash value** or **replacement cost**. Actual cash value tries to estimate the actual market value of the item at the time of loss, so it accounts for the original cost less any depreciation that has occurred. Replacement cost is the cost of replacing the item. For most items, the actual cash value is less.

For example, say your policy insures items at actual cash value. You are claiming the loss of a 10-year-old washer and dryer that were ruined when a pipe burst and your basement flooded. Your coverage could mean a benefit of $100 (based on the market price of 10-year-old appliances). However, to replace your appliances with comparable new ones could cost $1,000 or more.

The actual cash value is almost always less than the replacement value, because prices generally rise over time and because items generally depreciate (rather than appreciate) in value. A policy that specifies benefits as replacement costs offers more actual coverage. **Guaranteed replacement costs** are the full cost of replacing your items, while **extended replacement costs** are capped at some percentage—for example, 125% of actual cash value.

guaranteed replacement cost
The full cost of replacing insured items at time of loss.

extended replacement cost
Insured amount capped at a specified percentage of actual cash value.

Home Insurance Coverage: The Cost

You buy home insurance by paying a premium to the insurance company. The insurance purchase is arranged through a broker, who may represent more than one insurance company. The broker should be knowledgeable about various policies, coverage, and premiums offered by different insurers.

The amount of the premium is determined by the insurer's risk—the more risk, the higher the premium. Risk is determined by

- the insured (the person buying the policy),
- the property insured,
- the amount of coverage.

To gauge the risk of the insured, the insurer needs information about your personal circumstances and history, the nature of the property, and the amount of coverage desired for protection. This information is summarized in Table 10.1.

TABLE 10.1 Factors That Determine Insurance Premiums

Insured	Property	Coverage
Employment	Age	Actual cash value
Marital status	Size	Replacement cost
Criminal record	Location	Endorsements for listed property
Credit history	Proximity to fire/police services	Umbrella for personal liability
Insurance claim history	Building materials	
	Number of occupants	
	Heating system	

Based on information from https://www.investopedia.com/insurance/homeowners-insurance-guide/ (accessed October 2, 2018).

Insurers may offer discounts for enhancements that lower risks, such as alarm systems or upgraded electrical systems. (Smoke detectors are required by law in every state.) You also may be offered a discount for being a loyal customer, for example, by insuring both your car and home with the same company. Be sure to ask your insurance broker about available discounts for the following:

- Multiple policies (with the same insurer)
- Fire extinguishers
- Sprinkler systems
- Burglar and fire alarms
- Deadbolt locks and fire-safe window grates
- Longtime policyholder
- Upgrades to plumbing, heating, and electrical systems

The average premium for homeowners' insurance in 2015 in the United States was $1,173 a year. That year, Oregon homeowners paid the lowest average premium, $643, and Florida homeowners paid the highest, $1,993 .[3]https://www.iii.org/fact-statistic/facts-statistics-homeowners-and-renters-insurance (accessed June 17, 2018). Premiums can vary, even for the same levels of coverage for the same insured. You should compare policies offered by different insurers to shop around for the best premium for the coverage you want.

Insuring Your Car

If you own and drive a car, you must have car insurance. Your car accident may affect not only you and your car but also the health and property of others. A car accident often involves a second party, and so legal and financial responsibility must be assigned and covered by both parties. In the United States, financial responsibility laws in each state mandate minimal car insurance, although what's "minimal" varies by state.

Conventionally, a victim or plaintiff in an accident is reimbursed by the driver at fault or by his or her insurer. Fault has to be established, and the amount of the claim agreed to. In practice, this has often been done only through extensive litigation.

no-fault insurance

A system of auto insurance where the insured's insurance covers physical and property damage and liability, regardless of "fault" determined.

Some states in the United States and provinces in Canada have adopted some form of **no-fault insurance**, in which, regardless of fault, an injured driver's own insurance covers his or her damages and injuries, and a victim's ability to sue the driver-at-fault is limited. The idea is to lower the incidence of court cases and speed up compensation for victims. Twelve states and Puerto Rico currently have compulsory no-fault auto insurance, in which personal injury protection (PIP) is required. Eleven other states use no-fault as add-on or optional insurance.[4] https://www.iii.org/article/background-on-no-fault-auto-insurance (accessed June 17, 2018). The remaining states in the United States use the conventional tort system (suing for damages in court). Understanding the laws of the state where you drive will help you to make better insurance decisions.

Auto Insurance Coverage

Auto insurance policies cover two types of consequences: bodily injury and property damage. Each covers three types of financial losses. Table 10.2 shows these different kinds of coverage.

TABLE 10.2 Automobile Insurance Coverage

Bodily Injury	Property Damage
Bodily injury liability	Property damage liability
Medical payments	Collision
Uninsured motorist protection	Comprehensive physical damage

Bodily injury liability refers to the financial losses of people in the other car that are injured in an accident you cause, including their medical expenses, loss of income, and your legal fees. Injuries to people in your car or to yourself are covered by **medical payments coverage**. **Uninsured motorist protection** covers your injuries if the accident is caused by someone with insufficient insurance or by an unidentified driver.

Property damage liability covers the costs to other people's property from damage that you cause, while **collision** covers the costs of damage to your own property. Collision coverage is limited to the market value of the car at the time, usually defined by the National Automobile Dealers Association's (NADA) *Official Used Car Guide* or "blue book" (http://www.nada.org). To reduce their risk, the lenders financing your car loan will require that you carry adequate collision coverage. **Comprehensive physical damage** covers your losses from anything other than a collision, such as theft, weather damage, acts of nature, or hitting an animal.

Auto insurance coverage is limited, depending on the policy. The limits are typically stated in numbers representing thousands of dollars. For example, 100/300/50 means that $100,000 is the limit on the payment to one person in an accident; $300,000 is the limit on the amount paid in total (for all people) per accident; and $50,000 is the limit on the amount of property damage liability that can be paid out.

Here's an example of how it all works. Kit is driving home one night from a late shift at the convenience store where he works. Sleepy, he drifts into the other lane of the two-lane road and hits an oncoming car driven by Ray. Both Kit and Ray are injured, and both cars are damaged. Table 10.3 shows how Kit's insurance will cover the costs.

TABLE 10.3 Auto Insurance Coverage Example

Type of Insurance	Costs Covered
Bodily injury liability	Ray's medical bills and lost wages
Medical payments coverage	Kit's medical bills
Property damage liability	Repairs to Ray's car
Collision	Repairs to Kit's car

bodily injury liability

Responsibility for financial losses from injuries sustained in an accident for people outside of the car of the driver at fault.

medical payments coverage

Responsibility for financial losses from injuries sustained in an accident for people inside the car of the driver at fault.

uninsured motorist protection

Coverage of financial losses from injuries sustained in an accident if the driver at fault has insufficient insurance.

property damage liability

Responsibility for damage to property owned by people other than the driver at fault.

collision

Responsibility for damage to the property of the driver at fault.

comprehensive physical damage

Coverage for damage from hazards.

Auto Insurance Costs

As with any insurance, the cost of having an insurer assume risk is related to the cost of that risk. The cost of auto insurance is related to three factors that create risk: the car, the driver, and the driving environment—the region or rating territory.

The model, style, and age of the car determine how costly it may be to repair or replace and therefore the potential cost of damage or collision. The higher that cost is, the higher the cost of insuring the car. For example, a new luxury car will cost more to insure than a 10-year-old sedan. Also, different models have different safety features that may lower the potential cost of injury to passengers, and those features may lower the cost of insurance. Different models may come with different security devices or be more or less attractive to thieves, affecting the risk of theft.

The driver is an obvious source of risk as the operator of the car. Insurers use various demographic factors such as age, education level, marital status, gender, and driving habits to determine which kinds of drivers present more risk. Not surprisingly, young drivers (ages 16-24) of both sexes and elderly drivers (over 70) are the riskiest. Twice as many males as females die in auto accidents, but more females suffer injuries.[5]http://www.disastercenter.com/traffic (accessed June 17, 2018). Nationally, in 2017, there were about 12.28 fatalities for every 100,000 people in the United States.[6]

Your driving history and especially your accident claim history can affect your premiums, as well as your criminal record and credit score. In some states, an accident claim can double your cost of insurance over a number of years. Your driving habits—whether or not you use the car to commute to work, for example—can affect your costs as well. Some states offer credits or points that reduce your premium if you have a safe driving record, are a member of the American Automobile Association (AAA), or have passed a driver education course.

Where you live and drive also matters. Insurers use police statistics to determine rates of traffic accidents, auto theft, and vandalism, for example. If you are in an accident-prone area or higher crime region, you may be able to offset those costs by installing safety and security features to your car.

Premium rates vary, so you should always shop around. You can shop through a broker or directly. Online discount auto insurers have become increasingly popular in recent years. Their rates may be lower, but the same cautions apply as for other high-stakes transactions conducted online.

Also, premiums are not the only cost of auto insurance. You should also consider the insurer's reliability in addressing a claim. Chances are you rely on your car to get to school, to work, or for your daily errands or recreational activities. Your car is also a substantial investment, and you may still be paying off debt from financing your car. Losing your car to repairs and perhaps being injured yourself is no small inconvenience and can seriously disrupt your life. You want to be working with an insurer who will cooperate in trying to get you and your car back on the road as soon as possible. You can check your insurer's reputation by the record of complaints against it, filed with your state's agency of banking and insurance, or with your state's attorney general's office.

Key Takeaways

- Property insurance is to insure the rights of ownership and to protect against its liabilities.
- Property damage can be caused by hazards or by deliberate destruction, such as vandalism or theft.
- Homeowner's policies insure structures and possessions for actual cash value or replacement cost; an umbrella policy covers personal liability.
- The cost of homeowner's insurance is determined by the insured, the property insured, and the extent of the coverage and benefits.
- Auto insurance coverage insures bodily injury through
    - bodily injury liability,
    - medical payments coverage,
    - uninsured motorist protection.
- Auto insurance coverage insures property damage through
    - property damage liability,
    - collision,
    - comprehensive physical damage.
- Auto insurance costs are determined by the driver, the car, and the driving region.
- The risk of the driver is determined by demographics, credit history, employment history, and driving record.
- The risk of the car is determined by its cost; safety and security features may lower insurance costs.
- The risk of the driving region is determined by statistical incident histories of accidents or thefts.

Exercises

1. In your personal finance journal or My Notes, record or chart all the insurances you own privately or through a financial institution and/or are entitled to through your employer. In each case, what is insured, who is the insurer, what is the term, what are the benefits, and what is your premium or deduction? Research online to find the details. Then analyze your insurance in relation to your financial situation. How does each type of insurance shift or reduce your risk or otherwise help protect you and your assets or wealth?
2. Conduct and record a complete inventory of all your personal property. State the current market value or replacement cost of each item. Then identify the specific items that would cause you the greatest difficulty and expense if they were lost, damaged, or stolen.
3. How would a renter's insurance policy help protect your property? What do such policies cover? See http://www.insure.com/articles/homeinsurance/renters.html, for example, and https://www.thebalance.com/before-you-buy-renter-s-insurance-2385647. How much would it cost you to insure against the loss of just your laptop or desktop computer (see, for example, http://www.nssi.com)?
4. How do auto insurance rates in your state compare with rates in other states? Rates are based partly on the rates of accidents, injuries, and deaths in your state. Look at your state statistics concerning highway fatalities from the National Highway Traffic Safety Administration at https://cdan.nhtsa.gov/STSI.htm. What minimum auto insurance must you carry by law in your state? You will find state-by-state minimum car insurance data at http://personalinsure.about.com/cs/vehicleratings/a/blautominimum.htm. What optional insurance do you carry over the minimum, and why? What do you pay for car insurance, and how can you reduce your premium?
5. What does the National Association of Insurance Commissioners (http://www.naic.org/index_about.htm) do to protect consumers of insurance products? How would you contact your state's insurance department office, and what could you learn there (see http://www.usa.gov/directory/stateconsumer/index.shtml)?

10.3 Insuring Your Health

Learning Objectives

1. Define basic health care coverage and major medical insurance.
2. Identify the insured's responsibility for costs.
3. Describe the structure of health maintenance organizations.
4. Distinguish the different accounts for private health care financing.
5. Distinguish the different programs for public health care financing.
6. Describe the standards of the Patient's Bill of Rights.
7. Explain the goals of the Affordable Care Act.
8. Explain the purpose of long-term care insurance.

Melissa is a medical transcriptionist who runs a cleaning service on the side. She usually clears about $24,000 per year from the cleaning service, and has come to rely on that money. One day, Melissa slips on a wet floor. She is taken by ambulance to the local hospital, where she is treated for a badly broken wrist and released the next day. Melissa can't clean for about eight weeks, losing close to $4,000 in earnings.

FIGURE 10.4

Joaquin Barbara / Shutterstock.com

Soon, medical bills start to arrive. Melissa is not concerned, because she has health insurance through her job as a medical transcriptionist. She is surprised to find out, however, that some of the costs of this accident are not covered, that she has a significant deductible, and that she'll also have to pay the difference between what the doctors billed and what the insurance will pay. Not only did she lose substantial cleaning earnings, but her out-of-pocket costs are mounting as well. This accident is beginning to be very costly.

Melissa is discovering that health insurance is a complicated business. The time to understand your health coverage is before you need it. When you are recovering from an accident or illness, you should not be concerned with your medical bills, yet you may have to be.

According to the Henry J. Kaiser Family Foundation's "2017 Employer Health Benefits Survey," Melissa's experience is typical. Even when employers provide some health insurance, "[a] large majority of covered workers have cost sharing when they visit an emergency room. In 2017, 58% of workers have a copayment for emergency room visits and 32% have a coinsurance." In addition, "the share of covered workers enrolled in a plan with a general annual deductible has increased significantly over time: from 59% in 2007, to 72% in 2012, to 81% in 2017, as have the average deductible amounts for covered workers in plans with deductibles: from $616 in 2007, to $1,097 in 2012, to $1,505 in 2017."[7]

The rate of increase in health insurance costs is also concerning: "The average annual premiums in 2017 are $6,690 for single coverage and $18,764 for family coverage ... . The average family premium has increased 55% since 2007 and 19% since 2012."[8] In other words, even where employers "provide" health insurance as an employee benefit, workers are paying an increasing share of the costs and the costs are increasing.

Even if you think those numbers are exaggerated, it's still sobering, because no matter how much you try to take care of yourself and to be careful, no one can evade the pure risk of injury or illness. All you can do is try to shift that risk in a way that makes sense for your financial health.

Because of the increasing costs of health care and the increasing complexities of paying for them, the markets for and financing of health care and health insurance are much discussed and debated in the United States, especially the roles of the federal government and insurance providers. Regardless of the ultimate outcome of this debate, momentum is building for change. You should be aware of changes as they occur, so you can incorporate those changes into your budget and financial plans.

Health Insurance Coverage

There are many different kinds of coverage and plans for health insurance. You may have group health insurance offered as an employee benefit or as a member of a professional association. Group plans have lower costs, because the group has some bargaining power with the insurer and can generally secure lower rates for its members. But group plans are not necessarily comprehensive, so you may want to supplement the group coverage with a supplemental health insurance policy, available to individuals and families.

Sufficient coverage should include **basic insurance** and major medical insurance. A basic insurance policy will cover physician expense, surgical expense, and hospital expense.

basic insurance
Health insurance that covers the costs of physician expenses, surgical expenses, and hospital expenses.

- Physician expenses include nonsurgical treatments and lab tests.
- Surgical expenses include surgeons' fees.
- Hospital expenses include room and board and other hospital charges.

Frequently, these coverages are capped or limited. For example, hospital expense coverage is typically limited to a certain amount per day or a certain number of days per incident. Surgeons' fees are often capped.

The three basic coverages are usually combined under one policy. In addition, health insurance is completed by **major medical insurance**, which covers the costs of a serious injury or illness. Depending on the extent and the nature of your illness or injury, medical bills can quickly exceed your basic coverage limits, so major medical can act as an extension to those limits, saving you from potential financial distress.

FIGURE 10.5

© Shutterstock, Inc.

Dental insurance also supplements your basic insurance, usually providing reimbursement for preventative treatments and some partial payment of restorative dental services such as fillings, root canals, crowns, extractions, bridgework, and dentures. Vision insurance provides for eye care, including exams and treatment for eye diseases, as well as for corrective lenses. Depending on your basic coverage limits, dental and vision care could be important for you.

Another feature of basic coverage is a prescription drug plan. Prescriptions may be covered entirely or with a co-pay, or only if the generic version of the drug is available. Your insurer should provide a **formulary** or a list of drugs that are covered. Depending on your plan, prescription coverage may be available only as a supplement to your basic coverage.

major medical insurance
Insurance for the costs of serious injury or illness.

formulary
A list of drugs covered by an insurer under a prescription drug plan.

Health Insurance Costs

As health care costs and insurance premiums rise, insurers add cost offsets to make their policies more affordable. Those offsets may include the following:

deductibles

Costs paid by the insured before the insurer provides coverage.

co-pays

Partial payment for certain costs, made by the insured.

coinsurance

Shared payments by insured and insurer.

- **Deductibles**—an amount payable by the insured before any expenses are assumed by the insurer.
- **Co-pays**—partial payment for certain costs, for example, for physician's visits or prescriptions.
- **Coinsurance**—shared payments of expenses by insured and insurer.

Each of these payment features represents responsibilities of the insured, that is, your out-of-pocket costs. The more costs you shoulder, the less risk to the insurer, and so the less you pay for the insurance policy. Making you responsible for initial costs also discourages you from seeking health care more than is necessary or from submitting frivolous health care claims.

Costs vary with coverage, coverage limits, and offsets, and they vary widely between insurers. You should be well informed as to the specifics of your coverage, and you should compare rates before you buy. An insurance broker can help you to do this, and there are websites designed to help you explore the available options, especially the health insurance exchanges created under the Affordable Care Act (discussed in this chapter). See, for example, the health insurance consumer guide and resource links https://www.consumerreports.org/health-insurance/guide-to-health-insurance/ or https://advantages.aarp.org/en/healthcare-insurance/healthcare-tools-resources.html.

Health Insurance and Health Care

Health insurance is sold through private insurers, nonprofit service plans, and managed care organizations. Private insurers sell most of their plans to employers as group plans. Individuals are far more likely to purchase insurance through a service plan or managed care.

Private (for-profit) plans in most states are underwritten based on your age, weight, smoking status, and health history and are generally more expensive than other types of plans. You may have to take a medical exam, and specific preexisting conditions—such as asthma, heart disease, anxiety, or diabetes—could be used as grounds for increasing the cost of your premium, based on your higher risk. Nevertheless, federal and state laws protect you from being denied health care coverage because of any preexisting condition.

A service plan such as Blue Cross/Blue Shield, for example, consists of regional and state-based nonprofit agencies that sell both group and individual policies. More than half of the health insurance companies in the United States are nonprofits, including, for example, Health Care Service Corporation and Kaiser Permanente, among the largest health insurers in the United States.

managed care organizations

Organizations or networks of health care providers based on the principle of providing preventative care in order to better health and lower costs of health care. Such organizations also provide for emergency and special treatment services under various systems.

Managed care organizations became popular in the last 30 years or so with the idea that providing preventative care would lower health care costs. Managed care takes the following forms:

- Health maintenance organizations
- Preferred provider organizations
- Exclusive provider organizations
- Point-of-service plans
- Traditional indemnity plans

The two most familiar kinds of managed care are health maintenance organizations (HMOs) and preferred provider organizations (PPOs). A **health maintenance organization** directly hires physicians to provide preventative, basic, and supplemental care. Preventative care should include routine exams and screening tests and immunizations. Basic care should include inpatient and outpatient treatments, emergency care, maternity care, and mental health and substance abuse services. As with any plan, the details for what defines "basic care" will vary, and you should check the fine print to make sure that services are provided. For example, the plan may cover inpatient hospitalizations for a limited number of days in case of a physical illness, but inpatient hospitalization for a more limited number of days for a mental illness.

health maintenance organizations (HMOs)

An organization to provide "managed care" through reliance on primary care physicians and a network of specialists, with an emphasis on preventative care.

Supplemental care typically includes the cost of vision and hearing care, prescriptions, prosthetics devices, or home health care. Some or all of this coverage may be limited, or may be available for an added premium. The premium paid to the HMO is a fixed, monthly fee, and you must seek care only within the HMO's network of care providers.

The most serious constraint of HMOs is the limited choice of doctors and the need to get a referral from your primary care physician (PCP) to obtain the services of any specialist. Depending on where you live and the availability of medical practitioners, this may or may not be an issue for you, but before joining an HMO, you should consider the accessibility and convenience of the care that you are allowed, as well as the limitations of the coverage. For example, if you are diagnosed with a serious disease or need a specific surgical technique, is there an appropriate specialist in the network that you can consult? Suppose you want a second opinion? The rules differ among HMOs, but these are the kinds of questions you should be asking. You should also be familiar with the HMO's appeal procedures for coverage denied.

The **preferred provider organization (PPO)** has a different arrangement with affiliated physicians: it negotiates discounted rates directly with health care providers in exchange for making them the "preferred providers" for members seeking care. Care by physicians outside the network may be covered, but with more limitations, or higher co-pays and deductibles. In exchange for offering the flexibility of more choices of provider, the PPO charges a higher premium. Services covered are similar to those covered by an HMO.

preferred provider organization (PPO)

A type of managed care in which physicians, hospitals, and other care providers contract with an insurer to provide care at reduced rates upon referral from the insured's primary care physician. Unlike the HMO, out-of-network providers may be used.

The exclusive provider organization works much like the PPO, except that out-of-network services are not covered at all and become out-of-pocket expenses for the insured.

The **point-of-service (POS)** plan also uses a network of contracted, preferred providers. As in an HMO, you choose a primary care physician who then controls referrals to specialists or care beyond preventative and basic care. As in the PPO, out-of-network services may be used, but their coverage is more limited and you pay higher out-of-pocket expenses for co-pays and deductibles.

point-of-service (POS)

A type of managed care in which physicians, hospitals, and other care providers contract with an insurer to provide care at reduced rates upon referral from the insured's primary care physician. Unlike the HMO, out-of-network providers may be used, but on a limited basis.

Table 10.4 shows the differences in managed care options.

TABLE 10.4 Managed Care Choices

Health Maintenance Organization	Preferred Provider Organization	Exclusive Provider Organization	Point-of-Service Organization
Physicians are hired	Physicians are contracted	Physicians are contracted	Physicians are contracted
No out-of-network care	Out-of-network care	No out-of-network care	Out-of-network care
Primary care physician			Primary care physician

Private Health Care Financing

In the United States, if someone is not self-insured or uninsured, health insurance coverage is paid for, at least in part, by the employer. As health care costs have risen, employers in all industries have increasingly noted that this cost makes them less competitive in global markets. As an incentive to have more people paying the costs of health care themselves and to be less dependent on employers, the federal government has created tax deductions for savings earmarked for use in paying for health costs. These savings plans are known as flexible spending accounts (FSAs), health reimbursement accounts (HRAs), and health savings accounts (HSAs).

flexible spending account

An account created with regular payroll deductions by an employee to finance supplemental health care costs. Money must be expended within a specified time period or forfeited ("use it or lose it").

health reimbursement account

An employer-owned and -funded account to finance employee health care costs, with the employee choosing the type of coverage.

health savings accounts (HSA)

Individually owned and financed savings accounts that may be used to finance health care costs with tax deductible contributions.

A **flexible spending account** is used to supplement your basic coverage. It is offered by employers and funded by employees: you may have a tax-exempt deduction made from your paycheck to your flexible spending account. The money from your FSA may be used for care expenses not normally covered by your plan—for example, orthodontia, elder care, or child care. At the end of the year, any money remaining in your account is forfeited; that is, it does not roll over into the next year. Unless you can foresee expenses within the coming year, flexible spending may not be worth the tax break.

A **health reimbursement account** is an account funded by employers. The amount is used to pay the premiums for basic coverage with a high deductible, and any money left over may be used for other health expenses, or, if unused, a limited amount may be carried over to the next year. The account is yours until you leave your job, when it reverts back to your employer.

A **health savings account** (HSA) allows a tax-deductible contribution from your paycheck to pay the premiums for catastrophic coverage with a high deductible and whatever out-of-pocket health care costs you may have. It is employee funded, employee managed, and employee owned. Thus, it is yours, and you may take it with you when you change jobs.

Table 10.5 shows the differences between these accounts.

TABLE 10.5 Differences in Private Funding of Health Care

FSA	HRA	HSA
Funded by employee	Funded by employer	Funded by employee
Use for 1 year	Use until leave employment	No time limit on use
Contributions not taxed		Contributions not taxed

A health savings account shifts the responsibility for health insurance from the employer to the employee, although it still gives the employee access to lower group rates on premiums. If you are relatively young and healthy, and your healthcare need is usually just an annual physical, this seems like an advantageous plan. However, remember that the idea of insurance is to shift risk away from you, to pay someone to assume the risk for you. With a high deductible policy, you are still bearing a lot of risk. If that risk has the potential to cause a financial disaster, it's too much.

If you have employer-sponsored health insurance and you leave your job, you may be entitled to keep your insurance for 18 months (or more under certain circumstances). Under the 1985 Consolidated Budget Omnibus Reconciliation Act (COBRA), an employee at a company with at least 20 employees who notifies the employer of his or her intention to maintain health care coverage is entitled to do so provided the employee pays the premiums. Some states extend this privilege to companies with less than 20 employees, so you should check with your state's insurance commissioner. You may also be able to convert your group coverage into an individual policy, although with more costly premiums.

The Health Insurance Portability and Accountability Act (HIPAA) of 1996 addresses issues of transferring coverage, especially as happens with a change of jobs. It credits an insured for previous periods of insurance coverage that can be used to offset any waiting periods for coverage of preexisting conditions. In other words, it makes it easier for someone who is changing jobs to maintain continuous coverage of chronic conditions or illnesses.[9]https://www.hhs.gov/hipaa/for-individuals/guidance-materials-for-consumers/index.html (accessed June 17, 2018). (For more information, research the U.S. Department of Health and Human Services at http://www.hhs.gov; see, for example, https://www.hhs.gov/hipaa/for-individuals/guidance-materials-for-consumers/index.html.)

Public Health Care Financing

The federal government, in concert with state governments, provides two major programs to the general public for funding health care: Medicare and Medicaid. The federal government also provides services to veterans of the armed forces, and their spouses and dependents, provided they use veterans' health care facilities and providers (see http://www.va.gov).

Medicare was established in 1965 to provide minimal health care coverage for the elderly—that is, anyone over the age of 65. Medicare offers hospital (Part A), medical (Part B), combined medical and hospital (Part C), and prescription coverage (Part D), as outlined in Table 10.6.

Medicare

A federal program financing health care costs with eligibility based on age (for those over age 65).

TABLE 10.6 Medicare Plans and Coverage

Part A	Hospital	Compulsory	Choice of doctors
Part B	Medical	Optional	Choice of doctors
Part C	Hospital and medical	Optional	HMO or PPO
Part D	Prescriptions	Optional	Purchased through an approved insurer
Medigap	Supplemental	Optional	Individual policies differ

Medicare is really a combination of privately and publicly funded health care; the optional services all require some premium paid by the insured. You may not need Medicare's supplemental plans if you have access to supplemental insurance provided by your former employer or by membership in a union or professional organization.

FIGURE 10.6

Medicare does not cover all services. For example, it does not cover dental and vision care, private nursing care, unapproved nursing home care, care in a foreign country, and optional or discretionary (unnecessary) care.

Medicare also determines the limits on payments for services, but physicians may charge more than that for their services (within limits determined by Medicare). You would be responsible for paying the difference. For these reasons, it is advisable to have supplemental insurance.

Marley thought she didn't need to know anything about Medicare, being young, single, and healthy, but then her 66-year-old father developed a debilitating illness, requiring not only medical care but also assistance with many of his daily living activities. Suddenly, Marley was shouldering the responsibility of arranging her father's care and devising a strategy for financing it. She quickly learned about the care and limits of coverage offered by various Medicare plans.

Medicaid was also established in 1965 to provide health care based on income eligibility. It is administered by each state following broad federal guidelines and is jointly financed by the state and federal government. This means that states differ somewhat in the benefits or coverage they offer. If someone is covered by both Medicaid and Medicare, Medicaid pays for expenses not covered by Medicare, such as co-pays and deductibles. Medicaid pays for about 60% of all long-term care costs in the United States.[10]https://www.kff.org/infographic/medicaids-role-in-nursing-home-care/ (accessed June 17, 2018).

Medicaid

A federal program financing health care costs with eligibility based on income.

Health Insurance Regulation

Over the last half century, medical knowledge and technology have made medical care much more effective—and expensive. In response to the increasing cost of medical care, health insurance providers tried to minimize their payouts by adding conditions to coverage that exempted them from certain risks. Such exemptions included limits on lifetime payouts, limits on coverage of pre-existing conditions, or age limits for coverage of dependents. They also raised premiums, making any health insurance too expensive for many. Meanwhile, as it became more expensive, many employers who had been buying health insurance coverage for employees as a benefit stopped providing insurance.

The result was a growing number of uninsured people in the United States. This shifted health care costs, either through public financing such as Medicaid or through cost-sharing with the insured. Those who still had insurance paid even more to "cover" a provider's costs of caring for those who had none, or public financing was left to pay. In response, the U.S. government took steps to lower the cost of insurance and encourage more self-insurance by limiting the exemptions that insurers can claim and by making it easier for people to shop for health insurance.

In 2010, the federal government passed a law known as the Patient Protection and Affordable Care Act. Because the law required major changes for insurers and for individuals, it was designed to be implemented gradually over a period of years. The law has two goals: to create minimum standards for insurance coverage that protects the insured and to make it easier—and cheaper—for people to buy insurance.

Provisions of the law, known as the "Patient's Bill of Rights," took effect almost immediately after the act was signed. These are consumer protection rules for individuals that buy private health insurance. They are an attempt to set minimum standards of coverage for health insurance, focusing on the exemptions and limits of coverage that insurers claimed in order to minimize their risk of payout. These "rights" include the following:

- Children cannot not be excluded from health care coverage due to a preexisting condition.
- Children can be covered under a parent's health insurance until age 26.
- Claimants can appeal coverage decisions made by an insurer.
- There can be no lifetime or yearly limits on coverage for a specific condition.
- The individual's choice of doctors must be protected.
- Preventative and emergency care must be covered.
- Health care premiums must be used mostly to pay for health care costs.

In the long term, the Affordable Care Act is designed to make it cheaper and easier for individuals to buy health insurance by creating "exchanges" or central markets where consumers can shop for insurance. Health insurers have to provide certain information to consumers, who can then shop among different kinds of health insurance coverage and compare the plans offered by different vendors. This should make health insurers more competitive and consumers more likely to pay a more reasonable price for the coverage that they need, depending on their health, age, and family situation.

The Affordable Care Act of 2010 also has provisions that are designed to make health insurance coverage cheaper by making it mandatory for everyone to have some kind of minimal coverage. This means that if you do not have health insurance sponsored by your employer or are not eligible for health insurance under a public program, such as Medicare or Medicaid, you will have to purchase your own insurance coverage or pay a penalty. The benefits of this should be twofold:

- It minimizes the number of uninsured people and the cost of their health care.
- It minimizes the cost to the insurer by adding more people to diversify its risks, and those cost savings can be passed along to the insured.

This particular provision of the law was quite controversial, because it required people who may not otherwise choose to purchase health insurance to do so. It was repealed as part of the Tax Cuts and Jobs Act of 2017; the repeal takes effect in 2019.

While health care has long been regulated, the Affordable Care Act is an attempt to regulate the market for health insurance by setting standards to protect the insured and by making the marketplace more competitive, thus lowering costs for all. Its major provisions guarantee minimal standards of coverage in the Patient's Bill of Rights and allow for more competition in the market for health care insurance through the health care exchanges set up by the federal or state governments.

Long-Term Care Insurance

Long-term care insurance is designed to insure your care should you be chronically unable to care for yourself. "Care" refers not to medical care, but to care of "activities of daily living" (ADLs) such as bathing, dressing, toileting, eating, and mobility, which may be impaired due to physical or mental illness or injury.

long-term care insurance

Insurance to provide for permanent assistance with activities of daily living in the event of disabling injury or illness.

Long-term care coverage is offered as either indemnity coverage or "expense incurred" policies. With an indemnity policy, you will be paid a specified benefit amount per day regardless of your costs incurred. With an "expense incurred" policy, you will be reimbursed for your actual expenses incurred. Both types of policies can have limits, either for dollar amounts per day, week, or month or for the number of days or years of coverage. Newer policies are designed as integrated policies, offering pooled benefits and specifying a total dollar limit of benefits that may be used over an unspecified period.

Need for long-term care is anticipated in older age, although anyone of any age may need it. When you buy the policy, you may be far away from needing the coverage. For that reason, many policies offer benefit limits indexed to inflation, to account for cost increases that happen before you receive benefits.

The cost of a long-term care policy varies with your age, coverage, policy features such as inflation indexing, and current health. As with any insurance purchase, you should be as informed as possible, comparing coverage and costs before buying.

Key Takeaways

- Basic health care coverage is for physician expenses, surgical expenses, and hospital expenses; major medical insurance extends basic insurance in case of serious illness or injury.
- The insured's responsibility for costs can be structured as:
    - deductibles,
    - co-pays,
    - coinsurance.
- Health insurance is sold through private insurers, nonprofit service plans, and managed care organizations, that may be structured as:
    - health maintenance organizations,
    - preferred provider organizations,
    - exclusive provider organizations,
    - point-of-service plans,
    - traditional indemnity plans.
- Private health care financing may be supplemented by
    - flexible spending accounts (FSAs),
    - health reimbursement accounts (HRAs),
    - health savings accounts (HSAs).
- Public health care financing is provided by federal programs: Medicare and Medicaid.
- The Affordable Care Act and the Patient's Bill of Rights are designed to:
    - require health insurers to provide minimal standards of coverage;
    - create insurance markets that are more accessible, informative, and competitive for consumers;
    - decrease the number and cost of the uninsured.
- Long-term care insurance provides for the costs of assistance with activities of daily living.

Exercises

1. What health insurance do you have, directly or as a participant in someone else's health insurance policy (such as a spouse)? Identify the type of insurance in terms of the information presented in this chapter, and list the advantages and disadvantages of carrying this type of health insurance. Are you satisfied with the benefits and coverage in your plan? What would you change? What do you or the insured pay for health insurance each month, and how is it paid? Based on your research on health insurance, how might you try to change the way you fill this need in the future?
2. What is the Health Insurance Portability and Accountability Act (HIPPAA) Security Rule, and why was the law enacted? Find out at https://www.hhs.gov/hipaa/for-professionals/security/laws-regulations/index.html.
3. View a classic *Saturday Night Live* video at https://www.nbc.com/saturday-night-live/video/old-glory-insurance/n10766. Discuss with your class what is and what is not so funny about this video. What criticisms of the insurance market are implied?
4. The Affordable Care Act was—and still is—controversial. What are the advantages and disadvantages of it for you given your current health, age, income, and family situation? Discuss with your classmates ... It should be a lively discussion.

10.4 Insuring Your Income

Learning Objectives

1. Describe the purposes, coverage, and costs of disability insurance.
2. Compare the appropriate uses of term life and whole life insurance.
3. Explain the differences among variable, adjustable, and universal whole life policies and the use of riders.
4. List the factors that determine the premiums for whole life policies.
5. Describe the purposes, coverage, and costs of unemployment insurance.

As you have learned, assets such as a home or car should be protected from the risk of a loss of value, because assets store wealth, so a loss of value is a loss of wealth.

Your health is also valuable, and the costs of repairing it in the case of accident or illness are significant enough that it also requires insurance coverage. In addition, however, you may have an accident or illness that leaves you permanently impaired or even dead. In either case, your ability to earn income will be restricted or gone. Thus, your income should be insured, especially if you have dependents who would bear the consequences of losing your income. Disability insurance and life insurance are ways of insuring your income against some limitations.

Disability Insurance

disability insurance

Insurance to protect the insured against the risk of being unable to earn wages or salary as a result of injury or illness.

Disability insurance is designed to insure your income should you survive an injury or illness impaired. The definition of "disability" is a variable feature of most policies. Some define it as being unable to pursue your regular work, while others define it more narrowly as being unable to pursue any work. Some plans pay partial benefits if you return to work part-time, and some do not. As always, you should understand the limits of your plan's coverage.

The costs of disability insurance are determined by the features and/or conditions of the plan, including the following:

- Waiting period
- Amount of benefits
- Duration of benefits
- Cause of disability
- Payments for loss of vision, hearing, speech, or use of limbs
- Inflation-adjusted benefits
- Guaranteed renewal or noncancelable clause

In general, the greater the number of these features or conditions that apply, the higher your premium.

All plans have a waiting period from the time of disability to the collection of benefits. Most are between 30 and 90 days, but some are as long as 180 days. The longer the waiting period is, generally, the less the premium.

Plans also vary in the amount and duration of benefits. Benefits are usually offered as a percent of your current wages or salary. The more the benefits or the longer the insurance pays out, the higher the premium. Some plans offer lifetime benefits, while others end benefits at age 65 (the age of Medicare eligibility).

In addition, some plans offer benefits in the following cases, all of which carry higher premiums:

- Disability due to accident or illness
- Loss of vision, hearing, speech, or the use of limbs, regardless of disability
- Benefits that automatically increase with the rate of inflation
- Guaranteed renewal, which insures against losing your coverage if your health deteriorates

You may already have some disability insurance through your employer, although in many cases the coverage is minimal. You may also be eligible for Social Security benefits from the federal government or workers' compensation benefit from your state if the disability is due to an on-the-job accident. Other providers of disability benefits include the following:

- The Veterans' Administration (if you are a veteran)
- Automobile insurance (if the disability is due to a car accident)
- Labor unions (if you are a member)
- Civil service provisions (if you are a government employee)

You should know the coverage available to you and if you find it's not adequate, supplement it with private disability insurance.

Life Insurance

life insurance

Insurance to compensate beneficiaries against the financial consequences of the death of the insured.

Life insurance is a way of insuring that your income will continue after your death. If you have a spouse, children, parents, or siblings who are dependent on your income or care, your death would create new financial burdens for them. To avoid that, you can insure your dependents against your loss, at least financially.

There are many kinds of life insurance policies. Before purchasing one, you should determine what it is you want the insurance to accomplish for your survivors. What do you want it to do?

- Pay off the mortgage?
- Put your kids through college?
- Provide income so that your spouse can be home with the kids and not be forced into the workplace?
- Provide alternative care for your elderly parents or dependent siblings?
- Cover the costs of your medical expenses and funeral?
- Avoid estate taxes?

These are uses of life insurance. Your goals for your life insurance will determine how much benefit you need and what kind of policy you need. Weighed against that are its costs—the amount of premium that you pay and how that fits into your current budget.

Sam and Maggie have two children, ages three and five. Maggie works as a credit analyst in a bank. Sam looks after the household and the children and Maggie's elderly mother, who lives a couple of blocks away. He does her grocery shopping, cleans her apartment, does her laundry, and runs any errands that she may need done. Sam and Maggie live in a condo they bought, financed with a mortgage. They have established college savings accounts for each child, and they try to save regularly.

FIGURE 10.7

Sam and Maggie need to insure both their lives, because the loss of either would cause the survivors financial hardship. With Maggie's death, her earnings would be gone, which is how they pay the mortgage and household expenses and save for their children's education. Insurance on her life should be enough to pay off the mortgage and fund their children's college educations, while providing for the family's living expenses, unless Sam returns to the workforce. With Sam's death, Maggie would have to hire someone to keep house and care for their children, and also someone to keep her mother's house and provide care for her. Insurance on Sam's life should be enough to maintain everyone's quality of living.

Term Insurance

whole life

Life insurance providing coverage until the insured's death; it can also be used as an investment instrument.

term insurance

Life insurance providing coverage for a specified period of time.

Maggie's income provides for three expenditures: the mortgage, education savings, and living expenses. While living expenses are an ongoing or permanent need, the mortgage payment and the education savings are not: eventually, the mortgage will be paid off and the children educated. To cover permanent needs, Maggie and Sam should consider permanent insurance, also known as **whole life**, straight life, or cash value insurance. To insure those two temporary goals of paying the mortgage and college tuitions, Maggie and Sam could consider temporary or term insurance.

Term insurance is insurance for a limited time period, usually one, five, ten, or twenty years. After that period, the coverage stops. It is used to cover financial needs for a limited time period—for example, to cover the balance due on a mortgage, or education costs. Premiums are lower for term insurance, because the coverage is limited. The premium is based on the amount of coverage and the length of the time period covered.

A term insurance policy may have a renewability option, so that you can renew the policy at the end of its term, or it may have a conversion option, so that you can convert it to a whole life policy and pay a higher premium. If it is multiyear level term or straight term, the premium will remain the same over the term of coverage.

Decreasing term insurance pays a decreasing benefit as the term progresses, which may make sense in covering the balance due on a mortgage, which also decreases with payments over time. On the other hand, you could simply buy a one-year term policy with a smaller benefit each year and have more flexibility should you decide to make a change.

A return-of-premium (ROP) term policy will return the premiums you have paid if you outlive the term of the policy. On the other hand, the premiums on such policies are higher, and you may do better by simply buying the regular term policy and saving the difference between the premiums.

Term insurance is a more affordable way to insure against a specific risk for a specific time. It is pure insurance, in that it provides risk shifting for a period of time, but unlike whole life, it does not also provide a way to save or invest.

Whole Life Insurance

Whole life insurance is permanent insurance. That is, you pay a specified premium until you die, at which time your specified benefit is paid to your beneficiary. The amount of the premium is determined by the amount of your benefit and your age and life expectancy when the policy is purchased.

cash surrender value

The value of a whole life policy—the cash available for the policyholder—if the policy is canceled before the death of the insured.

Unlike term insurance, where your premiums simply pay for your coverage or risk shifting, a whole life insurance policy has a **cash surrender value** or cash value that is the value you would receive if you canceled the policy before you die. You can "cash out" the policy and receive that cash value before you die. In that way, the whole life policy is also an investment vehicle; your premiums are a way of saving and investing, using the insurance company as your investment manager.

Whole life premiums are more than term life premiums because you are paying not only for risk shifting but also for investment management.

A **variable life** insurance policy has a minimum death benefit guaranteed, but the actual death benefit can be higher depending on the investment returns that the policy has earned. In that case, you are shifting some risk, but also assuming some risk of the investment performance.

An **adjustable life** policy is one where you can adjust the amount of your benefit, and your premium, as your needs change.

A **universal life** policy offers flexible premiums and benefits. The benefit can be increased or decreased without canceling the policy and getting a new one (and thus losing the cash value, as in a basic whole life policy). Premiums are added to the policy's cash value, as are investment returns, while the insurer deducts the cost of insurance (COI) and any other policy fees.

When purchased, universal life policies may be offered with a single premium payment, a fixed (and regular) premium payment until you die, or a flexible premium where you can determine the amount of each premium, so long as the cash value in the account can cover the insurer's COI.

Figure 10.8 shows the life insurance options.

variable life

Life insurance that provides a guaranteed minimum benefit with potential to be greater depending on investment performance.

adjustable life

Benefits and premium can be adjusted without cancellation of the policy.

universal life

Benefits and premiums are flexible, in terms of both timing and amounts.

FIGURE 10.8 Life Insurance Options

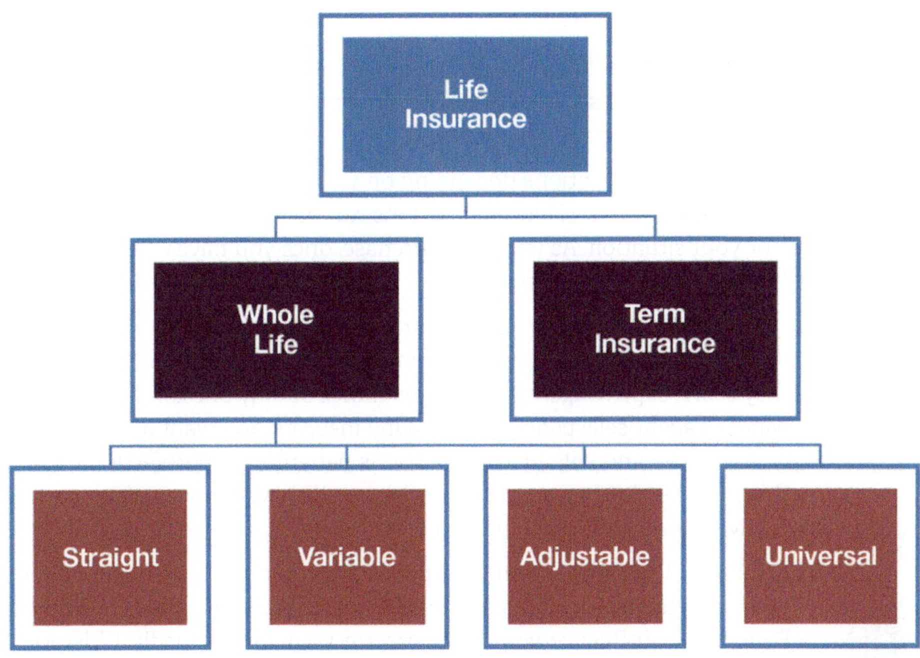

So, is it term or whole life? When you purchase a term life policy, you purchase and pay for the insurance only. When you purchase a whole life policy, you purchase insurance plus investment management. You pay more for that additional service, so its value should be greater than its cost (in additional premiums). A whole life policy is valuable to you only if the insurer is a better investment manager than you could have otherwise ... and there are many choices for investment management. Thus, the additional cost of a whole life policy must be weighed against your choices among investment vehicles. If it's better than your other choices, then you should buy the whole life. If not, then buy term life and save or invest the difference in the premiums.

Choosing a Policy

rider

A clause to a policy that adds specific benefits under specific conditions.

All life insurance policies have basic features, which then can be customized with a **rider**—a clause that adds benefits under certain conditions. The standard features include provisions that protect the insured and beneficiaries in cases of missed premium payments, fraud, or suicide. There are also loan provisions granted, so that you can borrow against the cash value of a whole life policy.

Riders are actually extra insurance that you can purchase to cover less common circumstances. Commonly offered riders include:

- a waiver of premium payment if the insured becomes completely disabled;
- a double benefit for accidental death;
- guaranteed insurability allowing you to increase your benefit without proof of good health;
- cost of living protection that protects your benefit from inflation;
- accelerated benefits that allow you to spend your benefit before your death if you need to finance long-term care.

Finally, you need to consider the settlement options offered by the policy: the ways that the benefit is paid out to your beneficiaries. The three common options are:

- as a lump sum, paid out all at once;
- in installments, paid out over a specified period;
- as interest payments, so that a series of interest payments is made to the beneficiaries until a specified time when the benefit itself is paid out.

You would choose the various options depending on your beneficiaries and their anticipated needs. Understanding these features, riders, and options can help you to identify the appropriate insurance product for your situation. As with any purchase, once you have identified the product, you need to identify the market and the financing.

FIGURE 10.9

© Shutterstock, Inc.

Many insurers offer many insurance products, usually sold through brokers or agents. Agents are paid on commission, based on the amount of insurance they sell. A captive agent sells the insurance of only one company, while an independent agent sells policies from many insurers. You want a licensed agent that is responsive and will answer questions patiently and professionally. If you die, this may be the person your survivors will have to depend on to help them receive their benefits in a difficult time.

You will have to submit an application for a policy and may be required to have a physical exam or release medical records to verify your physical condition. Factors that influence your riskiness are your family medical history, age and weight, and lifestyle choices such as tobacco, alcohol, and drug use. Your risks will influence the amount of your premiums.

Having analyzed the product and the market, you need to be sure that the premium payments are sustainable for you, that you can add the expense in your operating budget without creating a budget deficit.

Life Insurance as a Financial Planning Decision

Unlike insuring property and health, life insurance can combine two financial planning functions: shifting risk and saving to build wealth. The decision to buy life insurance involves thinking about your choices for both and your opportunity cost in doing so.

Life insurance is about insuring your earnings even after your death. You can create earnings during your lifetime by selling labor or capital. Your death precludes your selling labor or earning income from salary or wages, but if you have assets that can also earn income, they may be able to generate some or even enough income to insure the continued comfort of your dependents, even without your salary or wages.

In other words, the larger your accumulated asset base, the greater its earnings, and the less dependent you are on your own labor for financial support. In that case, you will need less income protection and less life insurance. Besides life insurance, another way to protect your beneficiaries is to accumulate a large enough asset base with a large enough earning potential.

If you can afford the life insurance premiums, then the money that you will pay in premiums is currently part of your budget surplus and is being saved somehow. If it is currently contributing to your children's education savings or to your retirement plan, you will have to weigh the value of protecting current income against insuring your children's education or your future income in retirement. Or that surplus could be used toward generating that larger asset base.

These are tough decisions to weigh because life is risky. If you never have an accident or illness and simply go through life earning plenty and paying off your mortgage and saving for retirement and educating your children, then are all those insurance premiums just wasted? No. Since your financial strategy includes accumulating assets and earning income to satisfy your needs now or in the future, you need to protect those assets and income, at least by shifting the risk of losing them through a chance accident. At the same time, you must make risk-shifting decisions in the context of your other financial goals and decisions.

Public Employment Insurance

Just as there is public health insurance that you may use under certain circumstances, there is also public insurance that covers a loss of income under certain conditions. This allows workers "who become unemployed through no fault of their own, and meet certain other eligibility requirements"[11] to collect a limited amount of money for a limited amount of time as a replacement for their lost income from wages.

The Federal-State Unemployment Insurance Program is administered by each state in compliance with federal guidelines. The benefit qualifications, amounts, and term of benefit eligibility are determined by each state, and can vary greatly. Most states finance unemployment benefits by a tax on employers, usually related to an employer's rate of involuntary employee turnover.

Unemployment insurance is designed to temporarily help employees who lose their jobs—and incomes—through forces beyond their control, such as layoffs, plant closings, business bankruptcies, and natural disasters. You will not qualify for benefits if you are fired for cause or leave your job voluntarily. Depending on the state you live in, you may not qualify if you have not been employed long, or if you are not actively searching for a job while unemployed. "Collecting unemployment" is not a desirable outcome of a job experience, but it can be a useful, temporary safety net if things do not work out as planned.

Key Takeaways

- Disability insurance insures your income against an accident or illness that leaves your earning ability impaired.
- Disability insurance coverage and costs vary.
- Life insurance is designed to protect dependents against the loss of your income in the event of your death.
- Term insurance provides life insurance coverage for a specified period of time.
- Whole life insurance provides life insurance coverage until the insured's death.

- Whole life insurance has a cash surrender value and thus can be used as an investment instrument as well as a way of shifting risk.
- Variable, adjustable, and universal life policies offer more flexibility of benefits and premiums.
- Riders provide more specific coverage.
- Premiums are determined by the choice of benefits and riders and the risk of the insured, as assessed by medical history and lifestyle choices.
- Unemployment insurance is designed to temporarily help employees who lose their jobs through forces beyond their control.

Exercises

1. Find out about workers' compensation at http://www.dol.gov/owcp/. What does the federal Office of Workers' Compensation Programs do, and what specific disabilities are covered in the programs that the OWCP administers? Find out what programs are available in your state for workers' compensation covering industrial and workplace accidents at http://www.workerscompensation.com/workers_comp_by_state.php. What is the role of the U.S. Department of Labor's Occupational Safety & Health Administration (OSHA) in preventing workplace illness and injury? Find out at http://www.osha.gov/.
2. Find information about unemployment compensation at http://www.dol.gov/dol/topic/unemployment-insurance/ and then search for information about your state's unemployment insurance. Would you qualify for unemployment insurance if you lost your job involuntarily? See if you can find answers to the following questions.
   a. If you are involuntarily unemployed, how much of your wages would the federal and state unemployment compensation programs replace?
   b. Are you entitled to unemployment compensation if you choose to be unemployed temporarily?
   c. Does it matter what kind of a job you have or how much income you earn?
   d. What does it mean to be involuntarily unemployed?
   e. Where does the money come from?
   f. If you have seasonal employment, can you collect unemployment to cover the off-season?
   g. If you are eligible, how long can you collect unemployment?
   h. Is the money you receive from unemployment compensation taxable?
3. Read advice on choosing insurance from The Motley Fool at https://www.fool.com/retirement/2017/10/30/do-i-need-life-insurance.aspx?. What are two situations in which purchasing life insurance might not be a good choice for you? According to the Insurance Information Institute (https://www.iii.org/article/how-do-i-pick-life-insurance-company), what factors should you consider when choosing a life insurance company?

Endnotes

1. Insurance Information Institute, "Homeowners and Renters Insurance,"
2. Insurance Information Institute, "Which Disasters are Covered by Homeowners Insurance?" https://www.iii.org/article/which-disasters-are-covered-by-homeowners-insurance (accessed September 13, 2018).
3. Insurance Information Institute, "Homeowners and Renters Insurance,"
4. Insurance Information Institute, "Background on: No-fault insurance,"
5. U.S. Census Bureau, The Disaster Center, "The Disaster Center's Motor Vehicle Accident Death and Injury Data Index,"
6. The Insurance Journal, https://www.insurancejournal.com/news/national/2018/02/16/480956.htm (accessed June 17, 2018).
7. The Kaiser Family Foundation, "2017 Employer Health Benefits Survey," https://www.kff.org/health-costs/report/2017-employer-health-benefits-survey/, (accessed June 17, 2018).
8. The Kaiser Family Foundation, "2017 Employer Health Benefits Survey," https://www.kff.org/health-costs/report/2017-employer-health-benefits-survey/, (accessed June 17, 2018).
9. Centers for Medicare and Medicaid Services, U.S. Department of Health and Human Services, "HIPAA—General Information."
10. The Henry J. Kaiser Family Foundation, "Medicaid's Role in Nursing Home Care," June 20, 2017.
11. U.S. Department of Labor, https://www.dol.gov/general/topic/unemployment-insurance (accessed June 19, 2018).

CHAPTER 11
Personal Risk Management: Retirement and Estate Planning

11.1 Introduction

While insurance is about protecting what you have, retirement and estate planning is about protecting what you may have in the future. Insuring what you have means finding the best way to protect it. Retirement planning, on the other hand, means finding the best way to protect the life that you'd like to be living after you stop earning income from employment. Estate planning involves protecting what you have even after your death. So retirement planning and estate planning are plans to create and then protect an accumulation of wealth.

Both types of planning also require you to ask yourself some questions that you really can't answer:

- What will my life be like when I retire?
- Will I have a spouse or partner?
- Dependents?
- A home?
- A mortgage?
- Will I be disabled?
- Where will I live?
- What will I do?
- What would I like to do?
- When I die, will I have a taxable estate?

Planning, especially for retirement, should start as early as possible, allowing the most time for savings to occur and accrue. Ironically, that's when it is hardest to try to imagine answers to these questions. Understanding the practical means to planning and saving for retirement can help you get started. If your plans are flexible, they can adapt to the unexpected as it happens, which it inevitably will.

11.2 Retirement Planning: Projecting Needs

Learning Objectives

1. Identify the factors required to estimate savings for retirement.
2. Estimate retirement expenses, length of retirement, and the amount saved at retirement.
3. Calculate relationships between the annual savings required and the time to retirement.

Retirement planning involves the same steps as any other personal planning: figure out where you'd like to be and then figure out how to get there from where you are. More formally, the first step is to define your goals, even if they are no more specific than, "I want to be able to afford a nice life after I stop getting a paycheck." But what is a "nice life," and how will you pay for it?

It may seem impossible or futile to try to project your retirement needs given that there are so many uncertainties in life and retirement may be far away. But that shouldn't keep you from saving. You can try to save as much as possible for now, with the idea that your plans will clarify as you get closer to your retirement, so whatever money you have saved will give you a head start.

FIGURE 11.1

© Shutterstock, Inc.

Chris and Sam were young urban professionals until their children were born. Tired of pushing strollers through the subways, they bought a home in the suburbs. They are happy to provide a more idyllic lifestyle for their kids but miss the "buzz" and convenience of their urban lifestyle. When their children are on their own and Chris and Sam are ready to retire, they would like to sell their home and move back into the city.

Chris and Sam are planning to use the value of their house to finance a condo in the city, but they also know that real estate prices are often higher in the more desirable urban areas and that living expenses may be higher in the future. Now in their mid-30s, Chris and Sam are planning to retire in 30 years.

Chris and Sam need to project how much money they will need to have saved by the time they wish to retire. To do that, they need to project both their future capital needs (to buy the condo) and their future living expenses in retirement. They also need to project how long they may live after retirement, or how many years' worth of living expenses they will need, so that they won't outlive their savings.

They know that they have 30 years over which to save this money. They also know, as explained in Chapter 4, that time affects value. Thus, Sam and Chris need to project the rate of compounding for their savings, or the rate at which time will affect the value of their money.

To estimate required savings, in other words, you need to estimate the following:

- Expenses in retirement
- The duration of retirement
- The return on savings in retirement

As difficult as these estimations seem, because it is a long time until retirement and a lot can happen in the meantime, you can start by using what you know about the present.

Estimating Annual Expenses

One approach is to assume that your current living expenses will remain about the same in the future. Given that over the long run, inflation affects the purchasing power of your income, you factor in the effect inflation may have so that your purchasing power remains the same.

For example, say your living expenses are around $25,000 per year and you'd like to have that amount of purchasing power in retirement as well. Assuming your costs of living remain constant, if you are 30 years from retirement, how much will you be spending on living expenses then?

The overall average historic annual rate of inflation in the United States is about 3.7%,[1] so you would have to spend

$$25,000 \times (1.037)^{30} = 74,353.72$$

per year to maintain your standard of living 30 years from now. Put another way, 30 years from now, $1.00 will buy only about 34 *cents* worth of today's expenses. (This calculation comes from the relationship of time and value, studied in Chapter 4.) In this case, $25,000 is the present value of your expenses, and you are looking for the future value, given that your expenses will appreciate at a rate of 3.7% per year for 30 years.

As you can see, you would need about three times your current spending just to live the life you live now. Fortunately, your savings won't be just "sitting there" during that time. They, too, will be compounding to keep up with your needs.

You may use your current expenses as a basis to project a more or less expensive lifestyle after retirement. You may anticipate expenses dropping with fewer household members and dependents, for example, after your children have grown. Or you may wish to spend more and live a more comfortable life, doing things you've always wanted to do. In any case, your current level of spending can be a starting point for your estimates.

Estimating Length of Retirement

How much you need to have saved to support your annual living expenses after retirement depends on how long those expenses continue or how long you'll live after retirement. In the United States, life expectancy at age 65 has increased dramatically in the last century, from 12 to 18 years for males and from 15 to 20 years for females, due to increased access to health care, medical advances, and healthier lives before age 65.[2] Figure 11.2 shows how life expectancy has increased since 1900, and projects it going forward.

FIGURE 11.2 Life Expectancy at Age 65 in the United States

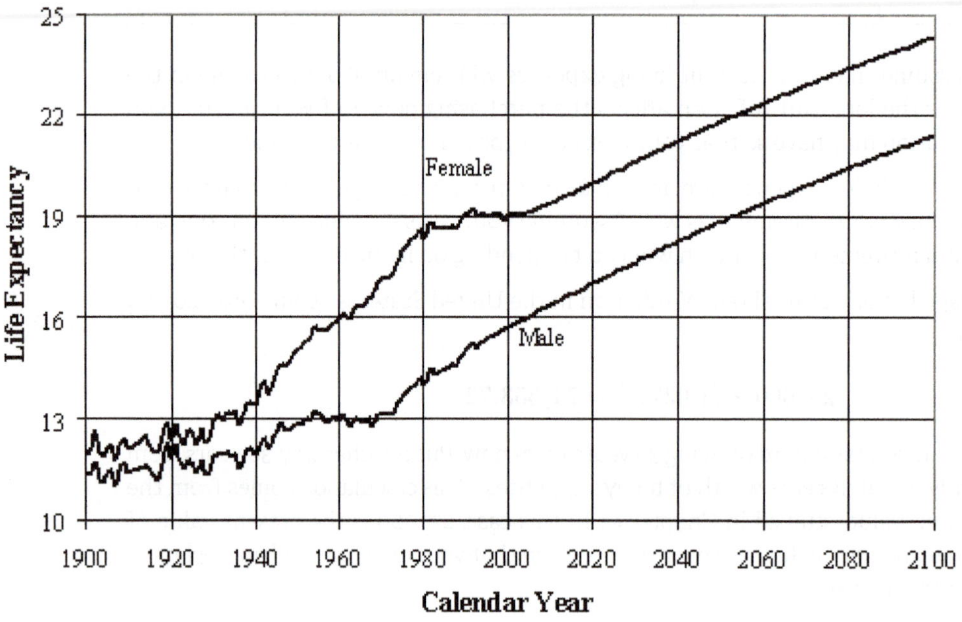

U.S. Social Security Administration, Actuarial Study No. 116, https://www.ssa.gov/oact/NOTES/as116/as116_V.html (accessed June 19, 2018).

If life expectancy continues to increase at these rates, in 40 years your life expectancy at age 65 could be 19 to 22 years. In that case, your retirement savings will have to provide for your living expenses for at least couple of decades. Put another way, at age 35 you have 30 years to save enough to support you for 20 years after that, and probably for even longer.

Estimating the Amount Needed at Retirement

You can use what you know about time and value (from Chapter 4) to estimate the amount you would need to have saved up by the time you retire. Your annual expenses in retirement are really a series of cash flows that will grow by the rate of inflation. At the same time, your savings will grow by your rate of return, even after you are making withdrawals to cover your expenses.

Say that when you retire, you have your retirement funds invested so they are earning a return of 5% per year. Assume an annual inflation rate of 3.7% and that your annual expenses when you retire are $75,000.

Table 11.1 shows what your situation would look like.

TABLE 11.1 Estimated Savings at Retirement

Years after Retirement	Annual Expenses	Present Value at Retirement if Return on Savings =	
		5%	2%
0	75,000.00	75,000.00	75,000.00
1	77,775.00	74,071.43	76,250.00
2	80,652.68	73,154.35	77,520.83
3	83,636.82	72,248.63	78,812.85
4	86,731.39	71,354.13	80,126.39
5	89,940.45	70,470.69	81,461.83
6	93,268.24	69,598.20	82,819.53
7	96,719.17	68,736.51	84,199.86
8	100,297.78	67,885.48	85,603.19
9	104,008.80	67,045.00	87,029.91
10	107,857.12	66,214.92	88,480.41
11	111,847.84	65,395.11	89,955.08
12	115,986.21	64,585.46	91,454.33
13	120,277.69	63,785.83	92,978.57
14	124,727.97	62,996.10	94,528.21
15	129,342.90	62,216.15	96,103.68
16	134,128.59	61,445.85	97,705.41
17	139,091.35	60,685.10	99,333.83
18	144,237.73	59,933.76	100,989.40
19	149,574.53	59,191.72	102,672.56
20	155,108.78	58,458.87	104,383.76
21	160,847.81	57,735.09	106,123.49
22	166,799.18	57,020.28	107,892.22
23	172,970.75	56,314.31	109,690.42
24	179,370.66	55,617.09	111,518.60
25	186,007.38	54,928.49	113,377.24
26	192,889.65	54,248.43	115,266.86
27	200,026.57	53,576.78	117,187.97
28	207,427.55	52,913.45	119,141.11
29	215,102.37	52,258.33	121,126.79
30	223,061.16	51,611.32	123,145.57
Total at Retirement		**1,940,696.86**	**3,011,879.92**

The amount you need at retirement varies with the expected rate of return on your savings. While you are retired, you will be drawing income from your savings, but your remaining savings will still be earning a return. The more return your savings can earn while you are retired, the less you have to have saved by retirement. The less return your savings can earn in retirement, the more you need to have saved *before* retirement.

In Table 11.1, the total amount needed at retirement is only about $1.94 million if your remaining savings will earn 5% while you are retired, but if that rate of return is only 2%, you would have to begin retirement with over $3 million.

Let's assume your return on savings is 5%. If you want to have $1,940,697 in 30 years when you retire, you could deposit $449,034 today and just let it compound for 30 years without a withdrawal.

$$\frac{1,940,697}{(1.05)^{30}} = 449,034$$

But if you plan to make an annual investment in your retirement savings, how much would that have to be?

Estimating the Annual Savings for Retirement

In the example above, if you make regular annual deposits into your retirement account for the next 30 years, each deposit would have to be $29,210, assuming that your account will earn 5% for 30 years and you want to have $1,940,697 when you retire. You can calculate this annual deposit as the cash flow of an annuity (discussed in Chapter 4.)

$$FV_{Annuity} = CF\left[\frac{(1+r)^t - 1}{r}\right]$$

$$1,940,697 = 29,210\left[\frac{(1.05)^{30} - 1}{0.05}\right]$$

If the rate of return for your savings is less, you would have to save more to have more at retirement. If your retirement savings can earn only 2%, for example, you would have to deposit $47,838 per year to have $1,940,697 when you retire. Your retirement account grows through your contributions and through its own earnings. The more your account can earn before you retire, the less you will have to contribute to it. On the other hand, the more you can contribute to it, the less it has to earn.

The time you have to save until retirement can make a big difference to the amount you must save every year. The longer the time you have to save, the less you have to save each year to reach your goal. Table 11.2 shows this idea as applied to the example above, assuming a 5% return on savings and a goal of $1,940,697.

TABLE 11.2 Time to Retirement and Annual Savings Required

Years to Retirement	Annual Savings Required	Funds at Retirement	Annual Return on Savings
15	89,936.00	1,940,697	5%
30	29,210.00	1,940,697	5%
40	16,065.00	1,940,697	5%

The longer the time you have to save—the sooner you start saving—the less you need to save each year. Chris and Sam are already in their 30s, so they figure they have 30 years to save for retirement. Had they started in their 20s and had 40 years until retirement, they would not have to save so much each year. If they wait until they are around 50, they will have to save a lot more each year. The more you have to save, the less disposable income you will have to spend on current living expenses, making it harder to save. Clearly, saving early and regularly is the superior strategy.

When you make these calculations, be aware that you are using estimates to figure the money you'll need at retirement. You use the *expected* inflation rate, based on its historic average, to estimate annual expenses, historical statistics on life expectancy to *estimate* the duration of your retirement, and an *estimate* of future savings returns. Estimates must be adjusted because things change. As you progress toward retirement, you'll want to reevaluate these numbers at least annually to be sure you are still saving enough.

Key Takeaways

- To estimate required savings at retirement, you need to estimate:
  - expenses in retirement, based on lifestyle and adjusted for inflation;
  - the duration of retirement, based on age at retirement and longevity;
  - the return on savings in retirement.
- You must save more for retirement if:
  - expenses are higher,
  - duration of retirement is longer,
  - the return on savings in retirement is less.
- To estimate annual savings for retirement, you need to estimate:
  - required savings at retirement;
  - time until retirement;
  - return on savings until retirement.

Exercises

1. Write in your personal finance journal or My Notes your ideas and expectations for your retirement. At what age do you want to retire? How many years do you have to prepare before you reach that age? Will you want to stop working at retirement? Will you want to have a retirement business or start a new career? Where and how would you like to live? How do you think you would like to spend your time in retirement? How much have you saved toward retirement so far?
2. Experiment with the retirement planning calculator at MSN Money (http://money.msn.com/retirement/retirement-calculator.aspx). What will you have saved for retirement by the time you retire? What will you need to live in retirement without income from employment? How old will you be when your retirement savings run out? Run several combinations of estimates to get an idea of how and why you should plan to save for retirement. Then, take the quiz at http://www.kiplinger.com/quiz/retirement/T047-S001-are-you-saving-enough-for-retirement-quiz/index.html, and see how you do.

11.3 Retirement Planning: Ways to Save

Learning Objectives

1. Compare and contrast employer, government, and individual retirement plans.
2. Explain the differences between a defined benefit plan and a defined contribution plan.
3. Summarize the structure and purpose of Social Security.
4. Identify the differences between a Traditional IRA and a Roth IRA.
5. Identify retirement plans for the self-employed.

While knowing the numbers clarifies the picture of your needs, you must reconcile that picture with the realities that you face now. How will you be able to afford to save what you need for retirement?

There are several savings plans structured to help you save—some offer tax advantages, some don't—but first you need to make a commitment to save.

Saving means not spending a portion of your disposable income. It means delaying gratification or putting off until tomorrow what you could have today. That is often difficult, as you have many demands on your disposable income. You must weigh the benefit of fulfilling those demands with the cost of not saving for retirement, even though benefit in the present is much easier to credit than benefit in the future. Once you resolve to save, however, employer, government, and individual retirement plans are there to help you.

Employer Retirement Accounts

Employers may sponsor pension or retirement plans for their employees as part of the employees' total compensation. There are two kinds of employer-sponsored plans: defined benefit plans and defined contribution plans.

defined benefit plan

A pension plan sponsored by an employer in which the employer commits to providing a specific amount of benefit based on wages and tenure to retired employees.

pension plan

An employer-sponsored, defined benefit plan providing a regular, specified amount of pension, based on wages and years of service.

A **defined benefit plan** is a retirement plan, sometimes called a **pension plan**, funded by the employer, who promises the employee a specific benefit upon retirement. The "employer" can be a corporation, labor union, government, or other organization that establishes a retirement plan for its employees. In addition to or instead of a defined benefit plan, an employer may also offer a profit-sharing plan, a stock bonus plan, an employee stock ownership plan (ESOP), a thrift plan, or other plan. Each type of plans has advantages and disadvantages for employers and employees, but all are designed to give employees a way to save for the future and employers a way to attract and keep employees.

The payout for a defined benefit plan is usually an annual or monthly payment for the remainder of the employee's life. In some defined benefit plans, there is also a spousal or survivor's benefit. The amount of the benefit is determined by your wages and length of service with the company.

Many defined benefit plans are structured with a **vesting** option that limits your claim on the retirement fund until you have been with the company for a certain length of time. For example, Paul's employer has a defined benefit plan that provides for Paul to be 50% vested after five years and fully vested after seven years. If Paul were to leave the company before he had worked there for five years, none of his retirement fund would be in his account. If he left after six years, half his fund would be kept for him; after 10 years, all of it would be.

vesting
The process of earning full ownership in an employer-sponsored retirement plan according to length of service.

With a defined benefit plan, your income in retirement is constant or "fixed," and it is the employer's responsibility to fund your retirement. This is both an advantage and a disadvantage for the employee. Having your employer fund the plan is an advantage, but having a fixed income in retirement is a drawback during periods of inflation, when the purchasing power of each dollar declines. In some plans, that drawback is offset by automatic cost of living increases.

Defined benefit plans also carry some risk. Most companies reserve the right to change or discontinue their pension plans. Furthermore, the pension payout is only as good as the company that pays it. If the company defaults, its pension obligations may be covered by the **Pension Benefit Guaranty Corporation (PBGC)**, an independent federal government agency. If not, employees are left without the benefit. Even if the company is insured, the PBGC may not cover 100% of employees' benefits.

Pension Benefit Guaranty Corporation (PBGC)
An agency of the federal government that guarantees defined benefit pensions in the case of employer default.

FIGURE 11.3

Founded in 1974, the PBGC is funded by insurance premiums paid by employers who sponsor defined benefit plans. If a pension plan ends, e.g., through the employer's bankruptcy, the PBGC assumes pensions payments up to a limit per employee. In 2017, the PBGC paid $5.841 billion in benefits to approximately 903,000 retirees.[3] There is some concern, however, that the PBGC will not be able to fully fund its obligations in the future.

defined contribution retirement plans

A pension plan sponsored by an employer in which the employer commits to providing a specific amount of contribution to a retirement account owned by an active employee.

To avoid the responsibility for employee retirement funds, more and more employers sponsor **defined contribution retirement plans**. Under defined contribution plans, each employee has a retirement account, and both the employee and the employer may contribute to the account. The employer may contribute up to a percentage limit or offer to match the employee's contributions, up to a limit. With a matching contribution, if employees choose not to contribute, they lose the opportunity of having the employer's contribution as well as their own. The employee makes untaxed contributions to the account as a payroll deduction, up to a maximum limit specified by the tax code. The maximum for defined contribution plans' employer contribution is 25% of the employee's compensation, with a cap in 2018 of $55,000. The employee can make a maximum contribution of $18,500 (or $24,500 for people over age 50) in 2018.

401(k) plans

An employer-sponsored defined contribution plan. Contributions may be made by employer, employee, or both. The employee's contributions are tax deferred until distribution after age 59.5 and are limited by the Internal Revenue Code.

Defined contribution plans have become increasingly popular since Section 401(k) was introduced into the tax code in 1978. The **401(k) plans**—or 403b plans for employees of nonprofits and 457 plans for employees of government organizations—offer employees a pretax (or tax-deferred) way to save for retirement to which employers can make a tax-deductible contribution.

The advantages of a 401(k) for the employee are the plan's flexibility and portability and the tax benefit. A defined contribution account belongs to the employee and can go with the employee when he or she leaves that employer. For the employer, there is the lower cost and the opportunity to shift the risk of investing funds onto the employee. There is a ceiling on the employer's costs: either a limited matching contribution or a limit set by the tax code.

The plan offers a selection of investments, but the employee chooses how the funds in his or her account are diversified and invested. Thus, the employee assumes the responsibility—and risk—for investment returns. The employer's contributions are a benefit to the employee. Employers can also make a contribution with company stock, which can create an undiversified account. A retirement portfolio consisting only of your company's stock exposes you to market risk should the company not do well, in which case, you may find yourself losing both your job and your retirement account's value.

U.S. Government Retirement Accounts

"We can never insure one hundred percent of the population against one hundred percent of the hazards and vicissitudes of life. But we have tried to frame a law which will give some measure of protection to the average citizen and to his family against the loss of a job and against poverty-ridden old age .... It is, in short, a law that will take care of human needs and at the same time provide for the United States an economic structure of vastly greater soundness."

— Franklin D. Roosevelt, August 14, 1935[4]

Social Security

The mandatory retirement program sponsored by the U.S. government to provide supplemental retirement income. It is funded by a tax (FICA) paid by employers and employees and by self-employed individuals who act as both employer and employee.

The federal government offers a mandatory retirement plan for all citizens, except federal government employees and railroad workers, known as **Social Security**. Social Security is funded by a mandatory payroll tax shared by employee and employer, commonly referred to as "FICA" for the Federal Insurance Contributions Act. Social Security was signed into law by President Franklin D. Roosevelt in 1935 to provide benefits for old age and survivors and disability insurance (OASDI) for workers. The Social Security Administration (SSA) was established to manage these "safety nets."

Data provided by the SSA from December 2016 show that about 60,907,000 beneficiaries receive an average monthly benefit of $1,232.25. The federal government's annual payment of benefits totaled $911.54 billion for 2016. Most of the beneficiaries are retirees (68%) or their spouses and children (5%), but there are also survivors, widows, and orphans receiving about 10% of benefits and disabled workers and their spouses and children receiving approximately 17% of benefits.[5]

FIGURE 11.4 President Franklin D. Roosevelt Signing the Social Security Act, August 14, 1935

Library of Congress photo, "Signing the Social Security Act of 1935," LC-US262-123278, http://www.ssa.gov/history/fdrsign.html (accessed May 1, 2009).

Social Security is not an automatic benefit but an entitlement. To qualify for benefits, you must work and contribute FICA taxes for 40 quarters (10 years). Retirement benefits may be claimed as early as age 62, but full benefits are not available until age 67 for workers born in 1960 or later. If you continue to earn wage income after you begin collecting Social Security but before you reach full retirement age, your benefit may be reduced. Once you reach full retirement age, your benefit will not be reduced by additional wage income, but a larger portion of your benefit may be taxable.

The amount of your benefit is calculated based on the amount of FICA tax paid during your working life and your age at retirement. Up to 85% of individual Social Security benefits may be taxable, depending on other sources of income.[6] Each year, the SSA provides each potential, qualified beneficiary with a projection of the expected monthly benefit amount (in current dollars) for that individual based on the individual's wage history.

Social Security benefits represent a large expenditure by the federal government, so the program is often the subject of debate. Economists and politicians disagree on whether the system is sustainable. As the population ages, the ratio of beneficiaries to workers increases—that is, there are more retirees collecting benefits relative to the number of workers who are paying into the system.

Many reforms to the system have been suggested, such as extending the eligibility age, increasing the FICA tax to apply to more income (right now it applies only to a limited amount of wages, but not to income from interest, dividends, or investment gains), or having workers manage their Social Security accounts the same way they manage 401(k) plans. Some of these proposals are based on economics, some on politics, and some on social philosophy. Despite its critics, Social Security remains a popular program that many Americans have come to rely on. You should, however, be aware that Social Security can be amended and faces possible underfunding.

FIGURE 11.5

© Shutterstock, Inc.

Keep in mind that in 1935 when Social Security was created, life expectancy for American males was only 65, the age of Social Security eligibility. Social Security was never meant to be a retirement income, but rather a supplement to those who outlived their life expectancy, merely "some measure of protection against ... poverty-ridden old age."[7]

As part of the Federal Employees Retirement System (FERS), the U.S. government also offers special retirement plans to its employees, including a Thrift Savings Plan (TSP) for civilians employed by the United States and members of the uniformed services (i.e., Army, Navy, Air Force, Marine Corps, Coast Guard, National Oceanic and Atmospheric Administration, and Public Health Service).

FIGURE 11.6

© Shutterstock, Inc.

Federal, state, and local government plans, plans for public school teachers and administrators, and church plans are exempt from the rules of the Employee Retirement Income Security Act of 1974 (ERISA) and from some rules that govern retirement plans of private employers under the Internal Revenue Code. In some states, public school teachers pay into a state retirement system and do not pay federal Social Security taxes (or receive Social Security benefits) for the years they are working as teachers.

Nevertheless, there are many plans for public employees that are defined benefit plans providing annuities upon retirement, similar to but separate from plans for employees in the private sector.

Individual Retirement Accounts

Any individual can save for retirement without a special "account," but since the government would like to encourage retirement savings, it has created tax-advantaged accounts to help you do so. Because these accounts provide tax benefits as well as some convenience, it is best to use them first in planning for retirement, although their use may be limited.

Individual retirement accounts (IRAs) were created in 1974 by ERISA. They were initially available only to employees not covered by an employer's retirement plan. In 1981, participation was amended to include everyone under the age of 70.5.[8] IRAs are personal investment accounts, and as such may be invested in a wide range of financial products: stocks, bonds, certificate of deposits (CDs), mutual funds, and so on. Types of IRAs differ in terms of tax treatment of contributions, withdrawals, and in the limits of contributions.

The **Traditional IRA** is an account funded by tax-deductible and/or nondeductible contributions. Deductible contributions are taxed later as funds are withdrawn, but nondeductible contributions are not. In other words, you either pay tax on the money as you put it in, or you pay tax on it as you take it out.

Traditional IRA

An individual retirement account for which contributions are tax deductible and withdrawals are taxed.

A great advantage of a Traditional IRA is that principal appreciation (interest, dividend income, or capital gain) is not taxed until the funds are withdrawn. Withdrawals may begin without penalty after the age of 59.5. Funds may be withdrawn before age 59.5, but with penalties and taxes applied. Contributions may be made until age 70.5, at which time required minimum distributions (withdrawals) of funds must begin.

Because they create tax advantages, tax-deductible contributions to a Traditional IRA are limited. That limit on deductible contributions becomes smaller (the tax benefit is phased out) as income rises. If you (or your spouse) are eligible to save through a tax-advantaged retirement plan with your employer, the Internal Revenue Service (IRS) provides a worksheet to calculate how much of your contribution is taxable with your personal income tax return (Form 1040).

For the **Roth IRA**, created in 1997, contributions are not tax deductible, but withdrawals are not taxed. You can continue to contribute at any age, and you do not have to take any minimum required distribution. The great advantage of a Roth IRA is that capital appreciation is not taxed.

Roth IRA

An individual retirement account for which contributions are not deductible but withdrawals are not taxed.

As with the Traditional IRA, contributions may be limited depending on your income. If you have both a Traditional and a Roth IRA, you may contribute to both, but your combined contribution is limited.

Table 11.3 is an adaptation of a guide provided by the IRS to show the key differences between a Traditional and a Roth IRA.[9]

TABLE 11.3 Differences between Traditional and Roth IRAs

	Traditional IRA	Roth IRA
Age limit to create the IRA?	Yes, 70½	No
Age limit to contribute?	Yes, 70½	No
Tax-deductible contributions allowed?	Yes	No
Tax-deductible contributions limited?	Yes, by income	N/A
Nondeductible contributions allowed?	Yes	Yes
Nondeductible contributions limited?	Yes	Yes
Withdrawals are taxed?	Yes, of deductible contributions	No
Minimum required distribution?	Yes	No
Age of mandatory distribution?	70½	None
Minimum age for distribution?	Yes, 59½	Yes, 59½

rollover

A retirement plan that may accept or distribute funds from another qualified retirement account without tax consequence or penalty.

transfer

The movement of funds in a tax-advantaged retirement account from one trustee or asset manager to another that is not considered a withdrawal or distribution of funds.

simplified employee pension (SEP)

A retirement plan for employers with less than one hundred employees or for the self-employed, usually using individual IRAs (SEP-IRAs) as retirement accounts.

savings income match plan for employees (SIMPLE)

A retirement plan for employers with less than one hundred employees or for the self-employed.

Keogh Plan

A tax-advantaged retirement plan for the self-employed.

A **rollover** is a distribution of cash from one retirement fund to another. Funds may be rolled into a Traditional IRA from an employer plan (401(k), 403b, or 457) or from another IRA. You may not deduct a rollover contribution (since you have already deducted it when it was originally contributed), but you are not taxed on the distribution from one fund that you immediately contribute to another. A **transfer** moves a retirement account, a Traditional IRA, from one trustee or asset manager to another. Rollovers and transfers are not taxed if accomplished within 60 days of distribution.

Self-Employed Individual Plans

People who are self-employed wear many hats: employer, employee, and individual. To accommodate them, there are several plans that allow for deductible contributions.

A **simplified employee pension (SEP)** is a plan that allows an employer with few or even no other employees than himself or herself to contribute deductible retirement contributions to an employee's Traditional IRA. Such an account is called a SEP-IRA and is set up for each eligible employee. Contributions are limited: in any year they can't be more than 25% of salary or $55,000 (in 2018), whichever is less. If you are self-employed and contributing to your own SEP-IRA, the same limits apply, but you must also include any other contributions that you have made to a qualified retirement plan.[10]

A **savings income match plan for employees (SIMPLE)** is a plan where employees make salary-reduction (before-tax) contributions that the employer matches. If the contributions are made to a Traditional IRA, the plan is called a SIMPLE IRA plan. Any employer with fewer than 100 employees who were paid at least $5,000 in the preceding year may use a SIMPLE plan. There are also SIMPLE 401(k) plans. Deductible contributions are limited to $12,500 in 2018 .[11]

A **Keogh Plan** is another retirement vehicle for small or self-employers. It can be a defined benefit or a defined contribution qualified plan with deductible contribution limits.

Key Takeaways

- Retirement plans may be sponsored by employers, government, or individuals.
- Defined benefit plans differ from defined contribution plans in that the benefit is a specified amount that the employer is liable for. In a defined contribution plan, the benefit is not specified, and the employee is responsible for the accumulation in the plan.
- Social Security is an entitlement financed by payroll taxes and designed to supplement employer retirement plans or individual retirement plans.
- Traditional and Roth IRAs differ by the taxable nature of contributions and withdrawals and by the age limits of contributions and withdrawals.
- Retirement plans for the self-employed are designed for those who are both employee and employer.

Exercises

1. Do you participate in an employer-sponsored retirement savings plan? If so, what kind of plan is it, and what do you see as the benefits and drawbacks of participating? If you contribute to your plan, how did you decide how much to contribute? Could you contribute more? In searching for your next good job, what kind of retirement plan would you prefer to find in the new employer's benefit package, and why?

2. As part of your planning, how can you estimate what you can expect from Social Security as a contribution to your retirement income? Find this answer by going to http://www.ssa.gov/retire2. Using the menus at this site, find out your retirement age. How many credits toward Social Security do you have now? How many do you expect to accumulate over your working life? Use one of the benefit calculators to find your estimated Social Security benefit. How much could you receive monthly? Would you be able to live on your Social Security alone? How much more would you need to save for? What would happen if you continued to work or went back to work after taking your retirement benefit? What would happen if you took your benefit before your full retirement age?
3. Will your career path lead you to employment through government at the local, state, or federal level (for example, in education, law enforcement, or public health)? How are retirement plans for government employees different from the plans described in this section? Find answers to this question at http://www.opm.gov/RETIRE/.
4. What individual retirement account(s) do you have? Which type of IRA, if any, would be best for you, and why? Why might it be a good idea to have an IRA as a means of funding your retirement along with other means? According to the Motley Fool article, "All About IRAs" at http://www.fool.com/Money/AllAboutIRAs/AllAboutIRAs.htm, what are the chief advantages of IRAs? How many types of IRAs are there? Can you withdraw money from an IRA account? When must you take a distribution (cash out your IRA)?

11.4 Estate Planning

Learning Objectives

1. Identify the purposes, types, and components of a will.
2. Describe the roles and types of trusts and gifts.
3. Analyze the role of the estate tax in estate planning.

Your **estate** includes everything you own. Other aspects of financial planning involve creating and managing your assets while you are alive. Estate planning is a way to manage your assets after your death. Age is not really a factor, because death can occur at any time, at any age, by any cause. For survivors, death is a legal and financial event—and in some cases a taxable event—as well as an emotional one. Arranging for the disposition of your estate gives clarity and direction to those you leave behind. Your loved ones will have to deal with the emotional aftermath of your loss and will appreciate your care in planning for the legal and financial outcomes of your death.

estate

All real and personal property of a decedent at the time of death, not including properties in joint ownership or assets that pass directly to a named beneficiary.

Wills

will

A legal document detailing the disposition of assets upon death.

intestate

To die without a valid will, leaving the disposition of assets and debts to the law.

holographic will

A handwritten or oral will.

statutory will

A will written on a preprinted form.

probate

The legal process of validating a will and overseeing the orderly payment of debts and the distribution of assets.

executor

The person named in a will who administers the payments of debts and the distribution of assets, as described in the will.

Since you won't be here, you will need to leave a written document outlining your instructions regarding your estate. That is your **will**, your legal request for the distribution of your estate, that is, assets that remain after your debts have been satisfied. If you die **intestate**, or without a will, the laws of your state of legal residence will dictate the distribution of your estate.

You can write your own will so long as you are a legal adult and mentally competent. The document has to be witnessed by two or three people who are not inheriting anything under the terms of the will, and it must be dated and signed and, in some states, notarized. A **holographic will** is handwritten; it may be more difficult to validate. A **statutory will** is a preprinted will that you can buy from a store or in a software package. Consider, however, that a will is a legal document. Having it drawn up by a lawyer may better insure its completeness and validity in court.

Probate is the legal process of validating a will and administering the payment of debts and the distribution of assets by a probate court. Probate courts also distribute property in the absence of a will. Probate is not required in every case, however. Probate is not required if the deceased:

- owned assets of little value, allowing for transfer without court supervision;
- owned assets jointly with or "payable on death" to another person;
- owned assets naming another person as beneficiary;
- held all assets in a living trust (a legal entity for managing assets on behalf of beneficiaries).

Besides the details of "who gets what," a will should name an **executor**, the person or persons who will administer the payment of your debts and the distribution of your remaining assets, according to your wishes as expressed in your will. If you have legal dependents, your will should name a guardian for them. You may also include a "letter of last instruction" stating the location of important documents, safe deposit keys, and bank accounts and specifying your funeral arrangements.

FIGURE 11.7 Will's Will

The will of William Shakespeare, signed March 25, 1616.

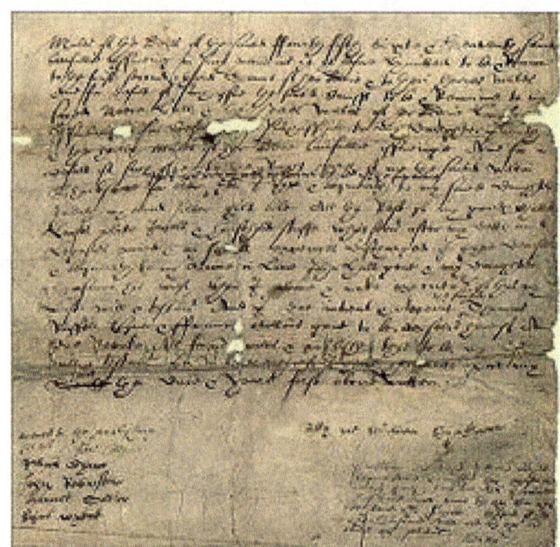

https://en.wikipedia.org/wiki/Shakespeare's_will#/media/File:Shakespeare-Testament.jpg, accessed July 25, 2018. This file has been identified as being free of known restrictions under copyright law, including all related and neighboring rights.

There are several types of wills. A **simple will** leaves everything to a spouse. For comparatively small estates that are not taxable, a simple will may be the most appropriate kind. A **traditional marital share will** will leave one half of the estate to a spouse and the other half to others, usually children. This may lower any tax burden on your estate and/or your spouse.

A **stated dollar amount will** allows you to leave specific amounts to beneficiaries. One drawback of this type of will is that the stated amounts may be reasonable when your will is drawn up but may not reflect your intentions at the time of your death, perhaps many years later. For that reason, rather than specifying specific amounts, it may be better to specify percentages of your asset values you would like each beneficiary to have.

You may change or rewrite your will at any time, but you should definitely do so as your life circumstances change, especially with events such as marriage or divorce, the birth of a child, and the acquisition of significant assets, such as a house. If the changes in your circumstances are substantial, you should create a new will.

It is possible that you will become mentally or physically disabled before you die and unable to direct management of your assets. To prepare for this possibility, you may create a **living will** with instructions for your care in that event. You may appoint someone—usually a spouse, child, or sibling—who would have **power of attorney**: that is, the right to act on your behalf, especially as regards financial and legal decisions. That power may be limited or unlimited (such as a "durable power of attorney") and is restricted to certain acts or dependent on certain circumstances.

Along with granting power of attorney, your living will may include a health care proxy, requesting that medical personnel follow the instructions of a designated family member who expresses your wishes concerning your end-of-life treatment. Many people request, for example, that they not be revived or sustained if they cannot experience some quality of life. Be sure to update your living will, however, as over time your views may change and as medical and technological advances change our notions of "quality of life."

simple will

A will leaving all property to a spouse.

traditional marital share will

A will leaving one-half of the estate to the surviving spouse.

stated dollar amount will

A will leaving a specific monetary amount to each beneficiary.

living will

A document conveying your intentions for your personal care and management of your assets should you become unable to do so before your death.

power of attorney

The legal right to act on your behalf should you become unable to do so before your death.

FIGURE 11.8

Trusts and Gifts

trust

A legal entity created to own and manage assets for the benefit of beneficiaries.

testamentary trust

A trust created by a will that becomes effective upon the death of the grantor.

living trust

A trust created while the grantor is alive.

revocable living trust

A trust created while the grantor is living that may be revoked or changed by the grantor; therefore, ownership of the grantor's assets remains under the control of the grantor.

irrevocable living trust

A trust created while the grantor is living, that may not be revoked or changed by the grantor. The trust is considered a legal entity, and ownership of the grantor's assets is transferred to the trust.

A **trust** is a legal entity created by a trustor, or grantor, who owns assets managed by a trustee or trustees for the benefit of a beneficiary or beneficiaries. A **testamentary trust** may be established by a will so that beneficiaries who are unable to manage assets (minor children or disabled dependents) can benefit from the assets but have them managed for them. A **living trust** is established while the grantor is alive. Unlike a will, it does not become a matter of public record upon your death. A **revocable living trust** can be revoked by the grantor, who remains the owner of the assets, at any time. Such a trust avoids the probate process but may not shield assets from estate taxes. An **irrevocable living trust** cannot be changed; the grantor gives up ownership of his or her assets, which passes to the trust, avoiding probate and estate taxes. However, the trust then becomes a separate taxable entity and pays tax on its accumulated income.

Another way to avoid probate and estate taxes is to gift assets to your beneficiaries while you are alive. Ownership of the assets passes to the beneficiaries at the time of the gift, so the assets are no longer included in your estate. The federal government and many state governments levy a gift tax for gifts exceeding certain limits. In 2018, the annual exclusion from federal tax was $15,000 per recipient, for example. Also, the federal government does not tax gifts to spouses and to pay others' medical bills or tuitions.

FIGURE 11.9

© Shutterstock, Inc.

There are limits to this kind of tax-free distribution of funds, however. For example, the federal government considers any "gift" you make within three years prior to your death as part of your taxable estate. Gifting nevertheless is a way to reduce the value of an estate. Some parents also prefer to make funds available or to gift them to their children when the children need them more—for example, earlier in their adult lives when they may not have accrued enough wealth to make a down payment on a house.

Most trusts, whether testamentary or living, revocable or irrevocable, are created to avoid either the probate process or estate taxes or both. The probate process can be long and costly and therefore a burden for your executor, your beneficiaries (who may have to wait for their distributions), and your estate.

Estate Taxes

Estate taxes diminish the value of your estate that will be distributed to your beneficiaries. For that reason, one of the purposes of estate planning is to try to minimize those taxes.

The federal estate tax is a tax on your right to transfer property at your death. In 2018, you are required to file an estate tax return if the taxable estate is valued at $5,490,000 or more.[12] In states with estate taxes, you must file a return if the taxable estate value is greater than a specified amount, depending on the state. The estate tax is the subject of much political debate, so those filing limits are subject to change.

A taxable estate is the gross estate less allowable deductions. The tax law defines the gross estate as the following:

- The value of all property in which you had an ownership interest at the time of death
- Life insurance proceeds payable to your estate or, if you owned the policy, to your heirs
- The value of certain annuities payable to your estate or your heirs
- The value of certain property you transferred within three years before your death.[13]

Allowable deductions include debts that you owed at the time of death, including mortgage debt, your funeral expenses, the value of property passing directly to your surviving spouse (the marital deduction), charitable gifts, and the state estate tax.[14]

In the United States, only about 2 of every 1,000 estates will pay federal estate tax, and estate taxes collected are less than 1% of the total tax revenues collected.[15]

While estate taxes tax your assets in your estate, inheritance taxes tax your assets in the hands of your beneficiaries. Because of the costs involved, beneficiaries may not be able to afford to inherit or preserve wealth within the family. For this reason and others, many states have redefined or repealed their inheritance tax laws.

Estate taxes also can be more costly to beneficiaries if assets are not liquid. For example, if a large portion of the value of your taxable estate is in your home or business, your survivors may be required to liquidate or sell assets just to pay the estate taxes. To avoid that, some estate plans include purchasing a life insurance policy for the anticipated amount of the estate tax, thus providing a source of liquid funds or cash for tax payment.

Minimizing taxes owed is a goal of estate planning, but not the only goal. Your primary objective is to see that your dependents are provided for by the distribution of your assets and that your assets are distributed as you would wish were you still there to distribute them yourself.

Key Takeaways

- A will describes your wishes for the distribution of your assets (the estate) after your death.
- Probate courts distribute assets in the absence of a will and administer wills in estates with assets valued above a certain (variable) dollar amount.
- There are many kinds of wills, including
  - the simple will,
  - the traditional marital share will,
  - the stated dollar amount will.

- Living wills, with power of attorney and health care proxy, provide medical directives, empower someone to manage your estate while you are still alive, and authorize someone to make decision about your health and end-of-life care.
- Trusts are used to provide the benefits of assets for beneficiaries without them assuming responsibility for asset management.
- There are testamentary and living trusts, revocable and irrevocable trusts. Setting up and administering trusts involves some considerable expense.
- Creating trusts and giving gifts are ways to reduce the taxable value of an estate.
- Estate planning should try to minimize the federal and state tax obligations of estate disposition.

Exercises

1. What are the estate tax laws in your state? How does your state treat inheritance taxes and estate taxes? Find answers to these questions by visiting https://taxfoundation.org/state-estate-tax-inheritance-tax-2018/.
2. Draft a holographic will or use a form for a statutory will recognized in your state. Start by reviewing your balance sheet, showing your assets, liabilities, net worth, and inventory of personal and household property. Think about how you would want your estate to be distributed upon your death. Identify an executor. Sample the free forms and advice for writing a will at https://www.free-legal-document.com/ and http://www.alllaw.com/forms/wills_and_trusts/last_will_and_testam/. Find out what kind of document your state requires for a "last will and testament" at http://www.legalzoom.com/wills-guide/last-wills-state-requirements.html. According to the article "4 Things You Should Know Before You Make Your Own Will" (http://time.com/money/4443349/do-it-yourself-will/), why and when should you have a lawyer draw up your will or review a will you have written yourself?
3. Consider drafting a living will. What should be in a living will? See http://www.alllaw.com/articles/wills_and_trusts/article7.asp. What form for a living will does your state recognize as legal (see https://estate.findlaw.com/living-will/living-wills-state-laws.html)? What is the purpose of the U.S. Living Will Registry?
4. When and why might you want to create a living trust as an alternative to a will? See http://www.investopedia.com/articles/pf/06/revocablelivingtrust.asp. According to the National Consumer Law Center, what questions should you ask to avoid becoming a victim of living trust scams? See https://www.nclc.org/images/pdf/older_consumers/consumer_concerns/cc_avoiding_living_trust_scams.pdf

Endnotes

1. Based on data from the Bureau of Labor Statistics, U.S. Department of Labor, http://www.bls.gov (accessed May 8, 2018).
2. Centers for Disease Control and Prevention, "Table 15. Life Expectancy at Birth, at Age 65, and at Age 75, by Sex, Race, and Hispanic Origin: United States, Selected Years 1950–2015," https://www.cdc.gov/nchs/data/hus/2016/015.pdf (accessed June 19, 2018).
3. The Pension Benefit Guaranty Corporation, "Annual Report, 2017," https://www.pbgc.gov/about/annual-reports/pbgc-annual-report-2017 (accessed June 20, 2018).
4. Franklin D. Roosevelt, "Statement on Signing the Social Security Act," August 14, 1935, http://www.ssa.gov/history/fdrsignstate.html (accessed June 28, 2014).
5. Based on data from U.S. Social Security Administration, "Fast Facts and Figures about Social Security 2017," https://www.ssa.gov/policy/docs/chartbooks/fast_facts/2017/fast_facts17.html#contributions (accessed June 20, 2018).
6. IRS Form 1040 Instructions 2017, p. 30, https://www.irs.gov/pub/irs-pdf/i1040gi.pdf, accessed June 20, 2018.
7. Social Security Administration archives, "Presidential Statement Signing the Social Security Act. August 14, 1935," http://www.socialsecurity.gov/history/fdrstmts.html#signing (accessed November 23, 2009).
8. Wikipedia, "Individual Retirement Account," http://en.wikipedia.org/wiki/Individual_retirement_account (accessed May 23, 2012).
9. U.S. Department of the Treasury, Publication 590, Internal Revenue Service, 2017.
10. U.S. Department of the Treasury, Publication 560, Internal Revenue Service, 2017.
11. U.S. Department of the Treasury, Publication 560, Internal Revenue Service, 2017.
12. U.S. Department of the Treasury, IRS Form 706 Instructions, www.irs.gov (accessed June 23, 2018).
13. U.S. Department of the Treasury, IRS Form 706, Internal Revenue Service, 2018 (accessed June 23, 2018).
14. U.S. Department of the Treasury, Form 706, Internal Revenue Service, 2018 (accessed June 23, 2018).
15. Center on Budget and Policy Priorities, https://www.cbpp.org (accessed June 23, 2018).

CHAPTER 12

Investing

12.1 Introduction

When people have too much money to spend immediately—that is, a surplus of disposable income—they become savers or investors. They transfer their surplus to individuals, companies, or governments that have a shortage or too little money to meet immediate needs. This is almost always done through an intermediary—a bank or broker—who can match up the surpluses and the shortages. If the capital markets work well, those who need money can get it, and those who can defer their need can try to profit from that deferral. When you invest, you are transferring capital to those who need it on the assumption that they will be able to return your capital when you need or want it and that they will also pay you for its use in the meantime.

FIGURE 12.1

© Shutterstock, Inc.

Saving to build wealth is investing. Investing happens over your lifetime. In your early adult years, you typically have little surplus to invest. Your first investments are in your home (although primarily financed with the debt of your mortgage) and then perhaps in planning for your children's education or for your retirement.

After a period of just paying the bills, making the mortgage, and trying to put something away for retirement, you may have the chance to accumulate wealth. Your income increases as your career progresses. You have fewer dependents (as children leave home), so your expenses decrease. You begin to think about your investment options. You have already been investing—in your home and retirement—but those investments have been prescribed by their specific goals.

You may reach this stage earlier or later in your life, but at some point, you begin to think beyond your immediate situation and look to increase your real wealth and to your future financial health. Investing is about that future.

12.2 Investments and Markets: A Brief Overview

Learning Objectives

1. Identify the features and uses of issuing, owning, and trading bonds.
2. Identify the uses of issuing, owning, and trading stocks.
3. Identify the features and uses of issuing, owning, and trading commodities and derivatives.

4. Identify the features and uses of issuing, owning, and trading mutual funds, including exchange-traded funds and index funds.
5. Describe the reasons for different instruments in different markets.

Before looking at investment planning and strategy, it is important to take a closer look at the galaxy of investments and markets where investing takes place. Understanding how markets work, how different investments work, and how different investors can use investments is critical to understanding how to begin to plan your investment goals and strategies.

You have looked at using the money markets to save surplus cash for the short term. Investing is primarily about using the capital markets to invest surplus cash for the longer term. As in the money markets, when you invest in the capital markets, you are selling liquidity.

The capital markets developed as a way for buyers to buy liquidity. In Western Europe, where many of our ideas of modern finance began, those early buyers were usually monarchs or members of the nobility, raising capital to finance armies and navies to conquer or defend territories or resources. Many devices and markets were used to raise capital,[1] but the two primary methods that have evolved into modern times are the stock and bond markets. (Both are discussed in greater detail in Chapter 15 and Chapter 16, but a brief introduction is provided here to give you the basic idea of what they are and how they can be used as investments.)

In the United States, more than half (51.9%) of all adults owned stocks or bonds in 2016, most through retirement accounts. Only 1.2% of all households directly own bonds, while 13.9% of all households directly owned stocks. [2]

FIGURE 12.2 Amsterdam Stock Exchange

The Amsterdam Stock Exchange was established following the success of the Dutch East India Company, the first company in the world to issue publicly traded stock. Founded in 1602, the company paid annual dividends for nearly 200 years based on its near monopoly of the Indonesian spice trade.

Bonds and Bond Markets

Bonds are debt. The bond issuer borrows by selling a bond, promising the buyer regular interest payments and then repayment of the principal at maturity. If a company wants to borrow, it could just go to one lender and borrow. But if the company wants to borrow a lot, it may be difficult to find any one investor with the capital and the inclination to make a large loan—and take that large risk—on only one borrower. In this case the company may need to find a lot of lenders who will each lend a little money, and this is done through selling bonds.

A bond is a formal contract to repay borrowed money with interest (often referred to as the coupon) at fixed intervals. Corporations and governments (e.g., federal, state, municipal, and foreign) borrow by issuing bonds. The interest rate on the bond may be a **fixed interest rate** or a **floating interest rate** that changes as underlying interest rates—rates on debt of comparable companies—change. (Underlying interest rates include the prime rate that banks charge their most trustworthy borrowers and the target rates set by the Federal Reserve Bank.)

There are many features of bonds other than the principal and interest, such as the **issue price** (the price you pay to buy the bond when it is first issued) and the **maturity date** (when the issuer of the bond has to repay you). Bonds may also be "callable": **redeemable** before **maturity** (paid off early). Bonds may also be issued with various **covenants** or conditions that the borrower must meet to protect the bondholders, the lenders. For example, the borrower, the bond issuer, may be required to keep a certain level of cash on hand, relative to its short-term debts, or may not be allowed to issue more debt until this bond is paid off.

Because of the diversity and flexibility of bond features, the bond markets are not as transparent as the stock markets; that is, the relationship between the bond and its price is harder to determine. This may be a reason that many fewer households prefer to invest in bonds. However, the bond markets are used to raise much more capital than the stock markets are. In 2016, the U.S. corporate bond market raised about $1.5 trillion in new corporate debt, while the U.S. equity markets raised about $17.8 billion in new capital.[3]

U.S. Treasury bonds are auctioned regularly to banks and large institutional investors by the Treasury Department, but individuals can buy U.S. Treasury bonds directly from the U.S. government (http://www.treasurydirect.gov). To trade any other kind of bond, you have to go through a broker. The brokerage firm acts as a principal or dealer, buying from or selling to investors, or as an agent for another buyer or seller.

Stocks and Stock Markets

Stocks or equity securities are shares of ownership. When you buy a share of stock, you buy a share of the corporation. The size of your share of the corporation is proportional to the size of your stock holding. Since corporations exist to create profit for the owners, when you buy a share of the corporation, you buy a share of its future profits. You are literally sharing in the fortunes of the company.

bonds

Publicly issued and traded long-term debt used by corporations and governments.

fixed interest rate

A bond interest rate that does not change over time, from issuance to maturity.

floating interest rate

A bond interest rate that changes over time, usually related to a benchmark rate such as the U.S. discount rate or prime rate.

issue price

The original market price of a bond at issuance.

maturity date

Date at which a bond matures, or the end of the bond's term, when the bond must be redeemed.

redeemable

A bond that is eligible for redemption.

maturity

The date on which payment of a financial obligation is due, such as bond redemption date.

bond covenant

A condition placed on bond issuers (borrowers) to protect bondholders (lenders).

stock

Shares issued to account for ownership, as defined by owners' contributions to a corporation.

FIGURE 12.3 Shanghai Stock Exchange, China

The Shanghai Stock Exchange (SSE), one of three exchanges in China, is not open to foreign investors. It is the sixth largest stock exchange in the world. The other exchanges in China are the Shenzhen Stock Exchange (SZSE) and the Hong Kong Stock Exchange (HKE). The Hang Seng is an index of Asian stocks on the HKE that is popular with investors interested in investing in Asian companies.

© Baycrest Gallery, used by permission

Unlike bonds, however, shares do not promise you any returns at all. If the company does create a profit, some of that profit may be paid out to owners as a **dividend**, usually in cash but sometimes in additional shares of stock. The company may pay no dividend at all, however, in which case the value of your shares should rise as the company's profits rise. But even if the company is profitable, the value of its shares may not rise, for a variety of reasons having to do more with the markets or the larger economy than with the company itself. Likewise, when you invest in stocks, you share the company's losses, which may decrease the value of your shares.

Corporations issue shares to raise capital. When shares are issued and traded in a public market such as a **stock exchange**, the corporation is "publicly traded." There are many stock exchanges in the United States and around the world. The two best known in the United States are the New York Stock Exchange (now NYSE Euronext), founded in 1792, and the NASDAQ, a computerized trading system managed by the National Association of Securities Dealers (the "AQ" stands for "Automated Quotations"). In 2017, there were 4,336 publicly traded corporations with stock listed on exchanges in the United States, representing a total value of more than $32.12 trillion.[4]

Only members of an exchange may trade on the exchange, so to buy or sell stocks, you must go through a broker who is a member of the exchange. Brokers also manage your account and offer varying levels of advice and access to research. Most brokers have online access to trading systems for retail investors. Some discount brokers offer minimal advice and research along with minimal trading commissions and fees.

dividend

A share of corporate profit distributed to shareholders, usually as cash or corporate stock.

stock exchange

An organized market for the trading of corporate shares conducted by members of the exchange.

commodities

Raw materials—natural resources or agricultural products—used as inputs in processing goods and services.

Commodities and Derivatives

Commodities are resources or raw materials, including the following:

- Agricultural products (food and fibers), such as soybeans, pork bellies, and cotton
- Energy resources such as oil, coal, and natural gas
- Precious metals such as gold, silver, and copper
- Currencies, such as the dollar, yen, and euro.

Commodity trading was formalized because of the risks inherent in producing commodities—raising and harvesting agricultural products or natural resources—and the resulting volatility of commodity prices. As farming and food production became mechanized and required a larger investment of capital, commodity producers and users wanted a way to reduce volatility by locking in prices over the longer term.

The answer was futures and forward contracts. **Futures** and **forward contracts** are a form of **derivatives**, the term for any financial instrument whose value is derived from the value of another security. For example, suppose it is now July 2020, and you are the manager of a food manufacturer that uses wheat as an input to production. If you know that you will want to have wheat in May 2021, you could wait until May 2021 and buy the wheat at the market price, which is unknown in July 2020. Or you could buy it now, paying today's price, and store the wheat until May 2021. Doing so would remove your future price uncertainty, but you would incur the cost of storing the wheat.

futures

A publicly traded contract to buy or sell an asset at a specified time and price in the future.

forward contracts

A private contract to buy or sell an asset at a specified time and price in the future.

derivatives

Financial instruments such as options, futures, forwards, securitized assets, and so on whose value is derived from the value of another asset.

Alternatively, you could buy a futures contract for May 2021 wheat in July 2020. You would be buying May 2021 wheat at a price that is now known to you (as stated in the futures contract), but you will not take delivery of the wheat until May 2021. The value of the futures contract to you is that you are removing the future price uncertainty without incurring any storage costs. In July 2020, the value of a contract to buy May 2021 wheat depends on what the price of wheat actually turns out to be in May 2021.

Forward contracts are traded privately, as a direct deal made between the seller and the buyer, while futures contracts are traded publicly on an exchange such as the Chicago Mercantile Exchange (CME) or the New York Mercantile Exchange (NYMEX).

When you buy a forward contract for wheat, for example, you are literally buying future wheat, wheat that doesn't yet exist. Buying it now, you avoid any uncertainty about the price, which may change. Likewise, by writing a contract to sell future wheat, you lock in a price for your crop or a return for your investment in seed and fertilizer.

Futures and forward contracts proved so successful in shielding against some risk that they are now written for many more types of "commodities," such as interest rates and stock market indices. More kinds of derivatives have been created as well, such as options. **Options** are the right but not the obligation to buy or sell at a specific price at a specific time in the future. Options are commonly written on shares of stock as well as on stock indices, interest rates, and commodities.

options

The right but not the obligation to buy or sell at a specific price at a specific time in the future; commonly written on shares of stock as well as on stock indices, interest rates, and commodities.

Derivatives such as forwards, futures, and options are used to hedge or protect against an existing risk or to speculate on a future price. For a number of reasons, commodities and derivatives are more risky than investing in stocks and bonds and are not the best choice for most individual investors.

Mutual Funds, Index Funds, and Exchange-Traded Funds

A **mutual fund** is an investment portfolio consisting of securities that an individual investor can invest in all at once without having to buy each investment individually. The fund thus allows you to own the performance of many investments while actually buying—and paying the transaction cost for buying—only one investment.

mutual fund

A portfolio of investments created by an investment company such as a brokerage or bank. It is financed as the investment company sells shares of the fund to investors. For investors, a mutual fund provides a way to achieve maximum diversification with minimal transaction costs through economies of scale.

Mutual funds have become popular because they can provide diverse investments with a minimum of transaction costs. In theory, they also provide good returns through the performance of professional portfolio managers.

index fund

A mutual fund designed to track the performance of an index for investors who seek diversification without having to select securities.

An **index fund** is a mutual fund designed to mimic the performance of an index, a particular collection of stocks or bonds whose performance is tracked as an indicator of the performance of an entire class or type of security. For example, the Standard & Poor's (S&P) 500 is an index of the 500 largest publicly traded corporations, and the famous Dow Jones Industrial Average is an index of 30 stocks of major industrial corporations. An index fund is a mutual fund invested in the same securities as the index and so requires minimal management and should have minimal management fees or costs.

Mutual funds are created and managed by mutual fund companies or by brokerages or even banks. To trade shares of a mutual fund, you must have an account with the company, brokerage, or bank. Mutual funds are a large component of individual retirement accounts and of defined contribution plans.

exchange-traded fund (ETF)

A fund that tracks an index or a commodity or a basket of assets but is traded like stocks on a stock exchange.

Mutual fund shares are valued at the close of trading each day and orders placed the next day are executed at that price until it closes. An **exchange-traded fund (ETF)** is a mutual fund that trades like a share of stock in that it is valued continuously throughout the day, and trades are executed at the market price.

FIGURE 12.4

financial engineering

The use of mathematical modeling to create and value new financial instruments and markets.

The ways that capital can be bought and sold are limited only by the imagination. When corporations or governments need financing, they invent ways to entice investors and promise them a return. The last 50 years have seen an explosion in **financial engineering**, the innovation of new financial instruments through mathematical pricing models. This explosion has coincided with the ever-expanding powers of the computer, allowing professional investors to run the millions of calculations involved in sophisticated pricing models or trading algorithms. The Internet also gives amateurs instantaneous access to information and accounts.

Much of the modern portfolio theory that spawned these innovations (i.e., the idea of using the predictability of returns to manage portfolios of investments) is based on an infinite time horizon, looking at performance over very long periods of time. This has been very valuable for institutional investors (e.g., pension funds, insurance companies, endowments, foundations, and trusts) as it gives them the chance to magnify returns over their infinite horizons.

For most individual investors, however, most portfolio theory may present too much risk or just be impractical. Individual investors don't have an infinite time horizon. You have only a comparatively small amount of time to create wealth and to enjoy it. For individual investors, investing is a process of balancing the demands and desires of returns with the costs of risk, before time runs out.

Key Takeaways

- Bonds are:
  - a way to raise capital through borrowing, used by corporations and governments;
  - an investment for the bondholder that creates return through regular, fixed or floating interest payments on the debt and the repayment of principal at maturity;
  - traded on bond exchanges through brokers.
- Stocks are:
  - a way to raise capital through selling ownership or equity;
  - an investment for shareholders that creates return through the distribution of corporate profits as dividends or through gains (losses) in corporate value;
  - traded on stock exchanges through member brokers.
- Commodities are:
  - natural or cultivated resources;
  - traded to hedge revenue or production needs or to speculate on resource prices;
  - traded on commodities exchanges through brokers.
- Derivatives are instruments based on the future, and therefore uncertain, price of another security, such as a share of stock, a government bond, a currency, or a commodity.
- Mutual funds are portfolios of investments designed to achieve maximum diversification with minimal cost through economies of scale.
  - An index fund is a mutual fund designed to replicate the performance of an asset class or selection of investments listed on an index.
  - An exchange-traded fund is a mutual fund whose shares are traded on an exchange.
- Institutional and individual investors differ in the use of different investment instruments and in using them to create appropriate portfolios.

Exercises

1. In My Notes or your personal finance journal, record your experiences with investing. What investments have you made, and how much do you have invested? What stocks, bonds, funds, or other instruments, described in this section, do you have now (or had in the past)? How were the decisions about your investments made, and who made them? If you have had no personal experience with investing, explain your reasons. What reasons might you have for investing (or not) in the future?
2. About how many stock exchanges exist in the world? Which geographic region has the greatest number of exchanges? Sample features of stock exchanges on each continent at https://www.stockmarketclock.com/exchanges. What characteristics do all the exchanges share?
3. How many stock index funds are there? How many bond index funds? Why would a brokerage offer investments in index funds to individual investors?

4. Visit the Chicago Mercantile Exchange (CME) at http://www.cmegroup.com/. What are some examples of commodities on the CME that theoretically could be part of your investment portfolio? In what energy product does the CME specialize? Could you invest in whether a foreign currency will rise or fall in relation to another currency? Could you invest in whether interest rates will rise or fall? Could you invest in how the weather will change?

12.3 Investment Planning

Learning Objectives

1. Describe the advantages of the investment policy statement as a useful framework for investment planning.
2. Identify the process of defining investor return objectives.
3. Identify the process of defining investor risk tolerance.
4. Identify investor constraints or restrictions on an investment strategy.

Allison has a few hours to kill while her flight home is delayed. She loves her job as an analyst for a management consulting firm, but the travel is getting old. As she gazes at the many investment magazines and paperbacks on display and the several screens all tuned to financial news networks and watches people hurriedly checking their stocks on their mobile phones, she begins to think about her own investments. She has been paying her bills, paying back student loans and trying to save some money for a while. Her uncle just died and left her a bequest of $50,000. She is thinking of investing it since she is getting by on her salary and has no immediate plans for this windfall.

FIGURE 12.5

investment policy statement

A structured framework for investment planning based on the investor's return objectives, risk tolerance, and constraints.

Allison is wondering how to get into some serious investing. She is thinking that since so many people seem to be interested in "Wall Street," there must be money in it. There is no lack of information or advice about investing, but Allison isn't sure how to get started.

Allison may not realize that there are as many different investment strategies as there are investors. The planning process is similar to planning a budget plan or savings plan. You figure out where you are, where you want to be, and how to get there. One way to get started is to draw up an individual investment policy statement.

Investment policy statements, outlines of the investor's goals and constraints, are popular with institutional investors such as pension plans, insurance companies, or nonprofit endowments. Institutional investment decisions typically are made by professional managers operating on instructions from a higher authority, usually a board of directors or trustees. The directors or trustees may approve the investment policy statement and then leave the specific investment decisions up to the professional investment managers. The managers use the policy statement as their guide to the directors' wishes and concerns.

This idea of a policy statement has been adapted for individual use, providing a helpful, structured framework for investment planning—and thinking. The advantages of drawing up an investment policy to use as a planning framework include the following:

- The process of creating the policy requires thinking through your goals and expectations and adjusting those to what is possible.

- The policy statement gives you an active role in your investment planning, even if the more specific details and implementation are left to a professional investment advisor.
- Your policy statement is portable, so even if you change advisors, your plan can go with you.
- Your policy statement is flexible; it can and should be updated at least once a year.

A policy statement is written in two parts. The first part lists your return objectives and risk preferences as an investor. The second part lists your constraints on investment. It sometimes is difficult to reconcile the two parts. That is, you may need to adjust your statement to improve your chances of achieving your return objectives within your risk preferences without violating your constraints.

Defining Return Objective and Risk

Defining return objectives is the process of quantifying the required annual return (e.g., 5%, 10%) necessary to meet your investment goals. If your investment goals are vague (e.g., to "increase wealth"), then any positive return will do. Usually, however, you have some specific goals—for example, to finance a child's or grandchild's education, to have a certain amount of wealth at retirement, to buy a sailboat on your 50th birthday, and so on.

Once you have defined goals, you must determine when they will happen and how much they will cost, or how much you will have to have invested to make your dreams come true. As explained in Chapter 4, the rate of return that your investments must achieve to reach your goals depends on how much you have to invest to start with, how long you have to invest it, and how much you need to fulfill your goals.

As in Allison's case, your goals may not be so specific. Your thinking may be more along the lines of, "I want my money to grow and not lose value," or, "I want the investment to provide a little extra spending money until my salary rises as my career advances." In that case, your return objective can be calculated based on the role that these funds play in your life: safety net, emergency fund, extra spending money, or nest egg for the future.

FIGURE 12.6

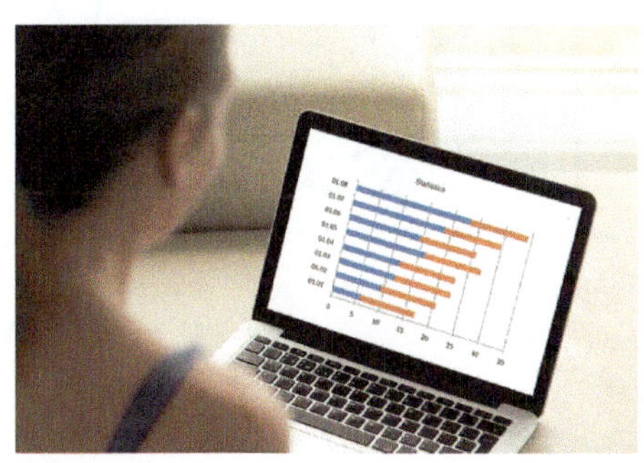

© Shutterstock, Inc.

However specific (or not) your goals may be, the quantified return objective defines the annual performance that you demand from your investments. Your portfolio can then be structured—you can choose your investments—such that it can be expected to provide that performance.

If your return objective is more than can be achieved given your investment and expected market conditions, then you know to scale down your goals, or perhaps find a different way to fund them. For example, if Allison wanted to stop working in 10 years and start her own business, she probably would not be able to achieve this goal solely by investing her $50,000 inheritance, even in a bull (up) market earning higher rates of return.

As you saw in Chapter 10 and Chapter 11, in investing there is a direct relationship between risk and return, and risk is costly. The nature of these relationships has fascinated and frustrated investors since the origin of capital markets and remains a subject of investigation, exploration, and debate. To invest is to take risk. To invest is to separate yourself from your money through actual distance—you literally give it to someone else—or through time. There is always some risk that what you get back is worth less (or costs more) than what you invested (a loss) or less than what you might have had if you had done something else with your money (opportunity cost). The more risk you are willing to take, the more potential return you can make, but the higher the risk, the more potential losses and opportunity costs you may incur.

risk tolerance

An investor's capacity for risk exposure, based on the ability and willingness to assume risk.

Individuals have different risk tolerances. Your **risk tolerance** is your ability and willingness to assume risk. Your ability to assume risk is based on your asset base, your time horizon, and your liquidity needs. In other words, your ability to take investment risks is limited by how much you have to invest, how long you have to invest it, and your need for your portfolio to provide cash—for use rather than reinvestment—in the meantime.

Your willingness to take risk is shaped by your "personality," your experiences, and your knowledge and education. Attitudes are shaped by life experiences, and attitudes toward risk are no different. Figure 12.7 shows how your level of risk tolerance develops.

FIGURE 12.7 Risk Tolerance

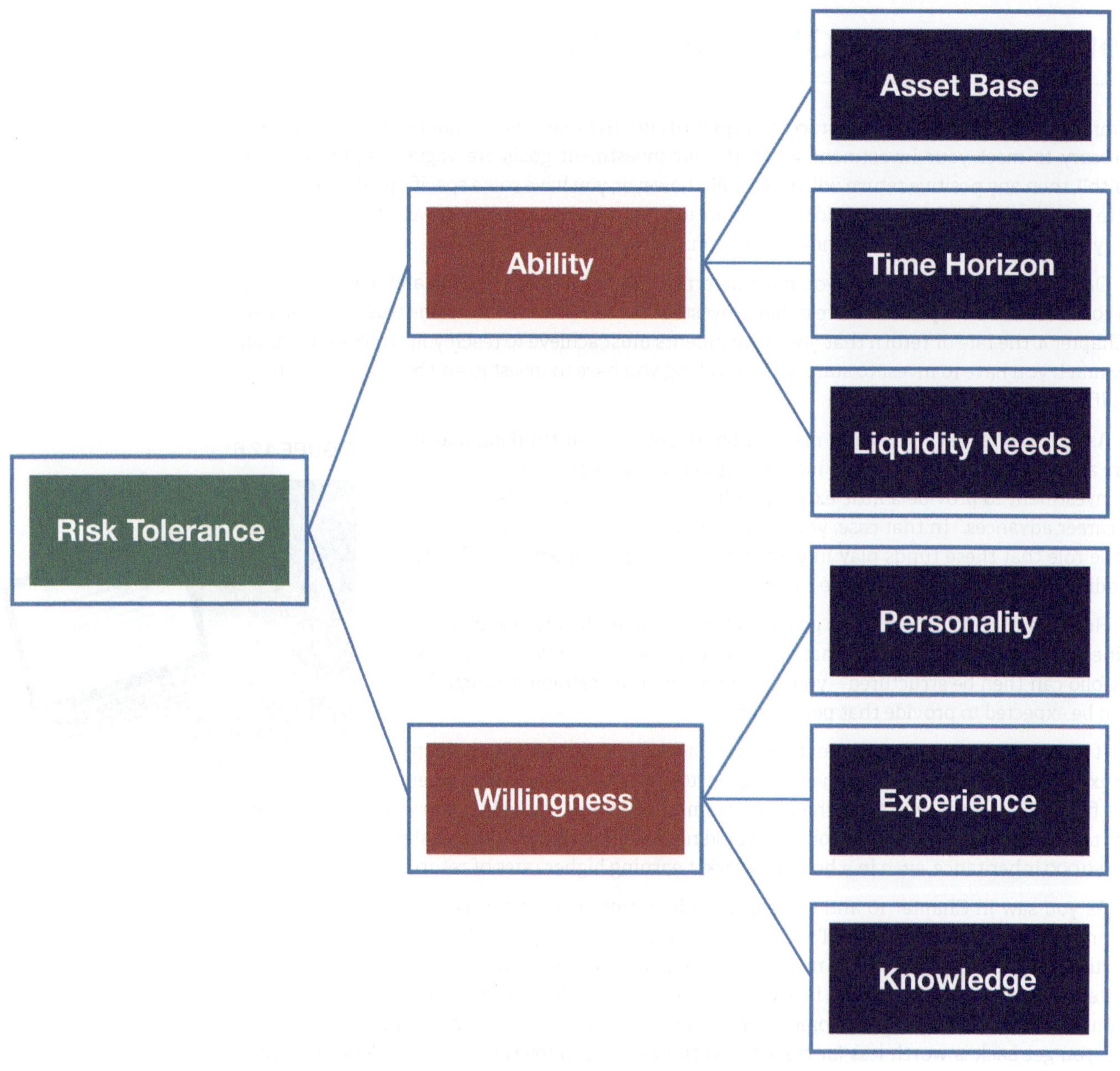

risk averse

An investor's preference to minimize exposure to risk.

Investment advisors may try to gauge your attitude toward risk by having you answer a series of questions on a formal questionnaire or by just talking with you about your investment approach. For example, an investor who says, "It's more important to me to preserve what I have than to make big gains in the markets," is relatively **risk averse**. The investor who says, "I just want to make a quick profit," is probably more of a risk seeker.

Once you have determined your return objective and risk tolerance (i.e., what it will take to reach your goals and what you are willing and able to risk to get there) you may have to reconcile the two. You may find that your goals are not realistic unless you are willing to take on more risk. If you are unwilling or unable to take on more risk, you may have to scale down your goals.

Defining Constraints

Defining constraints is a process of recognizing any limitation that may impede or slow or divert progress toward your goals. The more you can anticipate and include constraints in your planning, the less likely they will throw you off course. Constraints include the following:

- Liquidity needs
- Time available
- Tax obligations
- Legal requirements
- Unique circumstances

Liquidity needs, or the need to use cash, can slow your progress from investing because you have to divert cash from your investment portfolio in order to spend it. In addition you will have ongoing expenses from investing. For example, you will have to use some liquidity to cover your transaction costs such as brokerage fees and management fees. You may also wish to use your portfolio as a source of regular income or to finance asset purchases, such as the down payment on a home or a new car or new appliances.

While these may be happy transactions for you, for your portfolio they are negative events, because they take away value from your investment portfolio. Since your portfolio's ability to earn return is based on its value, whenever you take away from that value, you are reducing its ability to earn.

Time is another determinant of your portfolio's earning power. The more time you have to let your investments earn, the more earnings you can amass. Or, the more time you have to reach your goals, the more slowly you can afford to get there, earning less return each year but taking less risk as you do. Your time horizon will depend on your age and life stage and on your goals and their specific liquidity needs.

Tax obligations are another constraint because paying taxes takes value away from your investments. Investment value may be taxed in many ways (as income tax, capital gains tax, property tax, estate tax, or gift tax) depending on how it is invested, how its returns are earned, and how ownership is transferred if it is bought or sold.

Investors typically want to avoid, defer, or minimize paying taxes, and some investment strategies will do that better than others. In any case, your individual tax liabilities may become a constraint in determining how the portfolio earns to best avoid, defer, or minimize taxes.

Legalities also can be a constraint if the portfolio is not owned by you as an individual investor but by a personal trust or a family foundation. Trusts and foundations have legal constraints defined by their structure.

"Unique circumstances" refer to your individual preferences, beliefs, and values as an investor. For example, some investors believe in socially responsible investing (SRI), so they want their funds to be invested in companies that practice good corporate governance, responsible citizenship, fair trade practices, or environmental stewardship.

Socially responsible investment is the term for investments based on ideas about products or businesses that are desirable or objectionable. These qualities are in the eye of the beholder, however, and vary among investors. Your beliefs and values are unique to you and to your circumstances in investing and may change over time.

socially responsible investn

An investment strategy to achieve both ethical and financial goals.

divestment

The sale of an asset to reverse an invested position.

Some investors do not want to finance companies that make objectionable products or by-products or have labor or trade practices reflecting objectionable political views. ***Divestment*** is the term for taking money out of investments. Grassroots political movements often include divestiture campaigns, such as student demands that their universities stop investing in companies that do business with nondemocratic or oppressive governments.

Having mapped out your goals and determined the risks you are willing to take, and having recognized the limitations you must work with, you and/or investment advisors can now choose the best investments. Different advisors may have different suggestions based on your investment policy statement. The process of choosing involves knowing what returns and risks investments have produced in the past, what returns and risks they are likely to have in the future, and how the returns and risks are related—or not—to each other.

Key Takeaways

- The investment policy statement provides a useful framework for investment planning because:
  - the process of creating the policy requires thinking through goals and expectations and adjusting those to the possible;
  - the statement gives the investor an active role in investment planning, even if the more specific details and implementation are left to a professional investment advisor;
  - the statement is portable, so that even if you change advisors your plans can go with you;
  - the statement is flexible; it can and should be updated at least once per year.
- Return objectives are defined by the investor's goals, time horizon, and value of the asset base.
- Risk tolerance is defined by the investor's ability and willingness to assume risk; comfort with risk taking relates to personality, experience, and knowledge.
- Constraints or restrictions to an investment strategy are the investor's
  - liquidity needs,
  - time horizon,
  - tax circumstances and obligations,
  - legal restrictions,
  - unique preferences or circumstances.
- Social investment and divestment are unique preferences based on beliefs and values about desirable or objectionable industries, products, or companies.
- Your investment policy statement guides the selection of investments and development of your investment portfolio.

Exercises

1. Brainstorm with classmates expressions or homilies relating to investing, such as *you gotta pay to play*; *you gotta play to win*; *no pain, no gain*; *it takes money to make money*; and so on. What does each of these expressions really mean? How do they relate to the concepts of investment risk and return on investment? In what ways are risks and returns in a reciprocal relationship?
2. Draft an individual investment policy statement as a guide to your future investment planning. What will be the advantages of having an investment policy statement? In My Notes or your personal finance journal, record your general return objectives and specific goals at this time. What is a return objective?

3. What is your level of risk tolerance? How would you rate your risk tolerance on a five-point scale (with one indicating "most risk averse")? In your personal finance journal, record how your asset base, time horizon, and liquidity needs define your ability to undertake investment risk. Then describe the personality characteristics, past experiences, and knowledge base that you feel help shape your degree of willingness to undertake risk. Now check your beliefs by taking the Risk Tolerance Quiz at http://www.bankrate.com/finance/investing/risk-tolerance-quiz.aspx. How do the results compare with your estimate?
4. In My Notes or your personal finance journal, record the constraints you face against reaching your investment goals. With what types of constraints must you reconcile your investment planning? The more you need to use your money to live and the less time you have to achieve your goals, the greater the constraints in your investment planning. Revise your statement of goals and return objectives as needed to ensure it is realistic in light of your constraints.
5. In collaboration with classmates, conduct an online investigation into socially responsible investing. Start with the following websites:
   - http://www.socialinvest.org
   - http://www.greeninvestment.com
   - http://www.newsreview.com/sacramento/content?oid=323855

   On the basis of your investigation, outline and discuss the different forms and purposes of SRI. Which form and purpose appeal most to you and why? What investments might you make, and what investments might you specifically avoid, to express your beliefs and values? Do you think investment planning could ever have a role in bringing about social change?

12.4 Measuring Return and Risk

Learning Objectives

1. Characterize the relationship between risk and return.
2. Describe the differences between actual and expected returns.
3. Explain how actual and expected returns are calculated.
4. Define investment risk and explain how it is measured.
5. Define the different kinds of investment risk.

You want to choose investments that will combine to achieve the return objectives and level of risk that's right for you, but how do you know what the right combination will be? You can't predict the future, but you can make an educated guess based on an investment's past history. To do this, you need to know how to read or use the information available. Perhaps the most critical information to have about an investment is its potential return and susceptibility to types of risk.

Return

Returns are always calculated as annual rates of return, or the percentage of return created for each unit (as measured in currency, e.g., dollar) of original value. If an investment earns 5%, for example, that means that for every $100 invested, you would earn $5 per year, because $5 = 5% of $100.

Returns are created in two ways: the investment creates income or the investment gains (or loses) value. To calculate the annual rate of return for an investment, you need to know the income created, the gain (loss) in value, and the original value at the beginning of the year. The percentage return can be calculated as:

$$\frac{\textbf{Income} + \textbf{Gain(Loss)}}{\textbf{Beginning value}}$$

Note that

$$\textbf{Gain(Loss)} = \textbf{Ending value} - \textbf{Beginning value}$$

so if the ending value is greater than the original value, then

$$\textbf{Ending value} - \textbf{Beginning value} > 0$$

and you have a gain that adds to your return.

If the ending value is less, then

$$\textbf{Ending value} - \textbf{Beginning value} < 0$$

and you have a loss that detracts from your return.

If there is no gain or loss, if

$$\textbf{Ending value} - \textbf{Beginning value} = 0$$

then your return is simply the income that the investment created.

For example, if you buy a share of stock for $100, and it pays no dividend, and a year later the market price is $105, then your return is

$$\frac{0 + (105 - 100)}{100} = 0.05 = 5\%.$$

If the same stock paid a dividend of $2, then your return is

$$\frac{2 + (105 - 100)}{100} = 0.07 = 7\%.$$

If the information you have shows more than one year's results, you can calculate the annual return using what you learned in Chapter 4 about the relationships of time and value. For example, if an investment was worth $10,000 five years ago and is worth $14,026 today, then

$$10,000 \times (1 + r)^5 = 14,026.$$

Solving for r—the annual rate of return, assuming you have not taken the returns out in the meantime—and using a calculator, a computer application, or doing the math, you get 7%. So the $10,000 investment must have earned at a rate of 7% per year to be worth $14,026 five years later, all else being equal.

expected return

The return expected for an investment based on its average historical performance. Statistically, it is the mean or average of the investment's past performance.

While information about current and past returns is useful, investment professionals are more concerned with the **expected return** for the investment, that is, how much it may be expected to earn in the future. Estimating the expected return is complicated because many factors (i.e., current economic conditions, industry conditions, and market conditions) may affect that estimate.

For investments with a long history, a strong indicator of future performance may be past performance. Economic cycles fluctuate, and industry and firm conditions vary, but over the long run, an investment that has survived has weathered all those storms. So you could look at the average of the returns for each year. There are several ways to do the math, but if you look at the average return for different investments of the same asset class or type—e.g., stocks of large companies—you could compare what they have returned, on average, over time. Figure 12.8 shows average returns on investments in the S&P 500, an index of large U.S. companies, since 1928.

FIGURE 12.8 S&P 500 Average Annual Return, 1928-2017

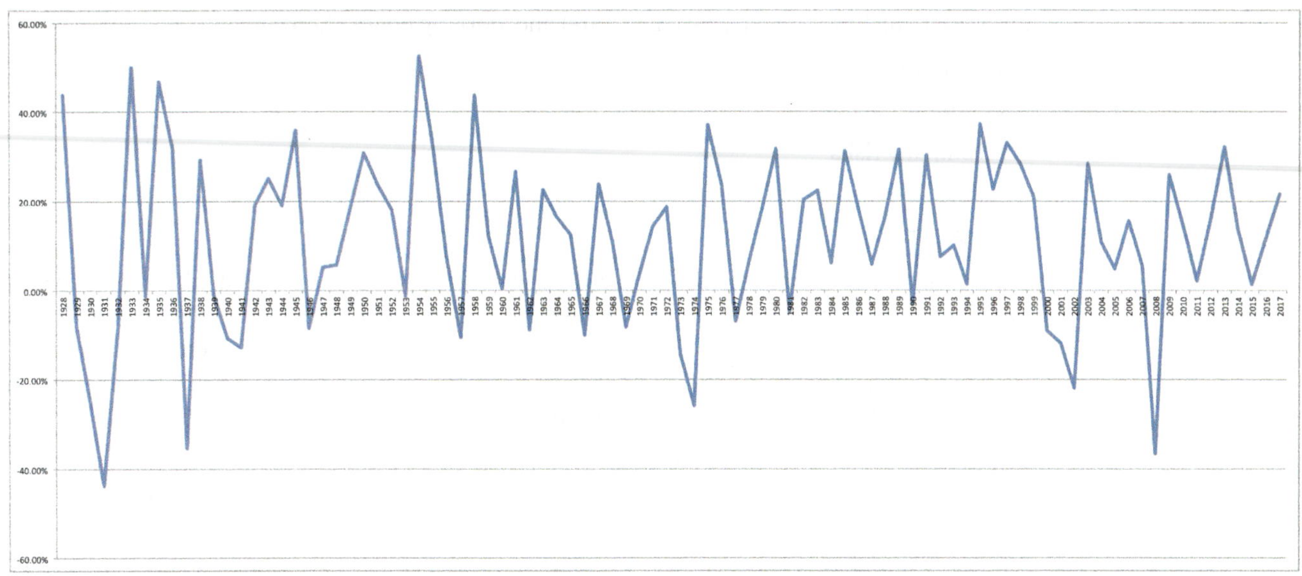

Based on data from Aswath Damodaran;http://www.stern.nyu.edu/~adamodar/pc/datasets/histretSP.xls (accessed June 3, 2018).

If the time period you are looking at is long enough, you can reasonably assume that an investment's average return over time is the return you can expect in the next year. For example, if a company's stock has returned, on average, 9% per year over the last 20 years, then if next year is an average year, that investment should return 9% again. Over the 90-year span from 1928 to 2017, for example, the average return for the S&P 500 was 11.5%. Unless you have some reason to believe that next year will *not* be an average year, the average return can be your expected return. The longer the time period you consider, the less volatility there will be in the returns and the more accurate your prediction of expected returns will be.

Returns are the value created by an investment, through either income or gains. Returns are also your compensation for investing, for taking on some or all of the risk of the investment, whether it is a corporation, government, parcel of real estate, or work of art. Even if there is no risk, you must be paid for the use of liquidity that you give up to the investment (by investing).

Returns are the benefits from investing, but they must be larger than its costs. There are at least two costs to investing: 1) the opportunity cost of giving up cash and giving up all your other uses of that cash until you get it back in the future and 2) the cost of the risk you take—the risk that you won't get it all back.

Risk

Investment risk is the idea that an investment will not perform as expected, that its actual return will deviate from the expected return. Risk is measured by the amount of volatility, that is, the difference between actual returns and average (expected) returns. This difference is referred to as the **standard deviation**. Returns with a large standard deviation (showing the greatest variance from the average) have higher volatility and are the riskier investments.

standard deviation

In finance, the statistical measure that calculates the frequency and amount by which actual returns differ from the average or expected returns.

As Figure 12.8 shows, an investment may do better or worse than its average. Thus, standard deviation can be used to define the expected range of investment returns. For the S&P 500, for example, the standard deviation from 1928 to 2013 was 19.62%. So, in any given year, the S&P 500 is expected to return, on average, 11.5%, but its return could reasonably be as high as 70.36% or as low as −47.36% based on its performance during that specific period.

What risks are there? What would cause an investment to unexpectedly over- or underperform? Starting from the top (the big picture) and working down, there are:

- economic risks
- industry risks
- company risks
- asset class risks
- market risks.

Economic risks are risks that something will upset the economy as a whole. The economic cycle may swing from expansion to recession, for example; inflation or deflation may increase, unemployment may increase, or interest rates may fluctuate. These macroeconomic factors affect everyone doing business in the economy. Most businesses are cyclical, growing when the economy grows and contracting when the economy contracts.

Consumers tend to spend more disposable income when they are more confident about economic growth and the stability of their jobs and incomes. They tend to be more willing and able to finance purchases with debt or with credit, expanding their ability to purchase durable goods. So, demand for most goods and services increases as an economy expands, and businesses expand too. An exception is businesses that are countercyclical. Their growth accelerates when the economy is in a downturn and slows when the economy expands. For example, low-priced, fast-food chains typically have increased sales in an economic downturn because people substitute fast food for more expensive restaurant meals as they worry more about losing their jobs and incomes.

FIGURE 12.9

© 2010 Jupiterimages Corporation

Industry risks usually involve economic factors that affect an entire industry or developments in technology that affect an industry's markets. An example is the effect of a sudden increase in the price of oil (a macroeconomic event) on the airline industry. Every airline is affected by such an event, as an increase in the price of airplane fuel increases airline costs and reduces profits. An industry such as real estate is vulnerable to changes in interest rates. A rise in interest rates, for example, makes it harder for people to borrow money to finance purchases, which depresses the value of real estate.

Company risk refers to the characteristics of specific businesses or firms that affect their performance, making them more or less vulnerable to economic and industry risks. These characteristics include how much debt financing the company uses, how well it creates economies of scale, how efficient its inventory management is, how flexible its labor relationships are, and so on.

asset class

A kind of investment distinguished by its uses and market (e.g., stock, bonds, fine art, real estate, currency).

The **asset class** that an investment belongs to can also bear on its performance and risk. Investments (assets) are categorized in terms of the markets they trade in. Broadly defined, asset classes include:

- corporate stock or equities (shares in public corporations, domestic, or foreign);
- bonds or the public debts of corporation or governments;
- commodities or resources (e.g., oil, coffee, or gold);
- derivatives or contracts based on the performance of other underlying assets;
- real estate (both residential and commercial);
- fine art and collectibles (e.g., stamps, coins, baseball cards, or vintage cars).

Within those broad categories, there are finer distinctions. For example, corporate stock is classified as large cap, mid cap, or small cap, depending on the size of the corporation as measured by its market capitalization (the aggregate value of its stock). Bonds are distinguished as corporate or government and as short-term, intermediate-term, or long-term, depending on the maturity date.

Risks can affect entire asset classes. Changes in the inflation rate can make corporate bonds more or less valuable, for example, or more or less able to create valuable returns. In addition, changes in a market can affect an investment's value. When the stock market fell unexpectedly and significantly, as it did in October of 1929, 1987, and 2008, all stocks were affected, regardless of relative exposure to other kinds of risk. After such an event, the market is usually less efficient or less liquid; that is, there is less trading and less efficient pricing of assets (stocks) because there is less information flowing between buyers and sellers. The loss in market efficiency further affects the value of assets traded.

As you can see, the link between risk and return is reciprocal. The eternal question for investors and their advisors is this: How can you get higher returns with less risk?

Key Takeaways

- There is a direct relationship between risk and return because investors will demand more compensation for sharing more investment risk.
- Actual return includes any gain or loss of asset value plus any income produced by the asset during a period.
- Actual return can be calculated using the beginning and ending asset values for the period and any investment income earned during the period.
- Expected return is the average return the asset has generated based on historical data of actual returns.
- Investment risk is the possibility that an investment's actual return will not be its expected return.
- The standard deviation is a statistical measure used to calculate how often and how far the average actual return differs from the expected return.
- Investment risk is exposure to:
    - economic risk,
    - industry risk,
    - company- or firm-specific risk,
    - asset class risk, or
    - market risk.

Exercises

1. Use your knowledge of U.S. history and Figure 12.8 to think about annual stock returns. For each year of negative returns, find at least two reasons outside of the financial markets that could have contributed to the negativity of returns. ... That is, what was going on to cause the decrease in stock values?
2. Find the estimated annualized rate of return for a hypothetical portfolio by using the AARP's investment return calculator at http://www.aarp.org/money/investing/investment_return_calculator/, experimenting with different figures to solve for a range of situations. Use the information on that page to answer the following questions. Can the future rate of return on an investment be estimated with any certainty? How does expected inflation affect required return? What accounts for differences between the actual return and the expected return on an investment?
3. The standard deviation on the rate of return on an investment is a measure of its volatility, or risk. What would a standard deviation of zero mean? What would a standard deviation of 100% mean?
4. What kinds of risk are included in investment risk? Go online to survey current or recent financial news. Find and present a specific example of the impact of each type of investment risk. In each case, how did the type of risk affect investment performance?

12.5 Diversification: Return with Less Risk

Learning Objectives

1. Explain the use of diversification in portfolio strategy.
2. List the steps in creating a portfolio strategy, explaining the importance of each step.
3. Compare and contrast active and passive portfolio strategies.

Every investor wants to maximize return, the earnings or gains from giving up surplus cash. And every investor wants to minimize risk because it is costly. To invest is to assume risk, and you assume risk expecting to be compensated through return. The more risk assumed, the more the promised return. So, to increase return you must increase risk. To lessen risk, you must expect less return, but another way to lessen risk is to diversify—to spread out your investments among a number of different asset classes. Investing in different asset classes reduces your exposure to economic, asset class, and market risks.

Concentrating investment concentrates risk. Diversifying investments spreads risk by having more than one kind of investment and thus more than one kind of risk. To truly diversify, you need to invest in assets that are not vulnerable to one or more kinds of risk. For example, you may want to diversify:

- between cyclical and countercyclical investments, reducing economic risk;
- among different sectors of the economy, reducing industry risks;
- among different kinds of investments, reducing asset class risk;
- among different kinds of firms, reducing company risks.

To diversify well, you have to look at your collection of investments as a whole—as a portfolio—rather than as a gathering of separate investments. If you choose the investments well, if they are truly different from each other, the whole can actually be more valuable than the sum of its parts.

Steps to Diversification

In traditional portfolio theory, there are three levels or steps to diversifying: capital allocation, asset allocation, and security selection.

capital allocation

A strategy of diversifying a portfolio between risky and riskless assets.

Capital allocation is diversifying your capital between risky and riskless investments. A "riskless" asset is the short-term (less than 90-day) U.S. Treasury bill. Because it has such a short time to maturity, it won't be much affected by interest rate changes, and it is probably impossible for the U.S. government to become insolvent—go bankrupt—and have to default on its debt within such a short time.

The capital allocation decision is the first diversification decision. It determines the portfolio's overall exposure to risk, or the proportion of the portfolio that is invested in risky assets. That, in turn, will determine the portfolio's level of return.

The second diversification decision is **asset allocation**, deciding which asset classes, and therefore which risks and which markets, to invest in. Asset allocations are specified in terms of the percentage of the portfolio's total value that will be invested in each asset class. To maintain the desired allocation, the percentages are adjusted periodically as asset values change. Figure 12.10 shows an asset allocation for an investor's portfolio.

asset allocation

The strategy of achieving portfolio diversification by investing in different asset classes.

FIGURE 12.10 Proposed Asset Allocation

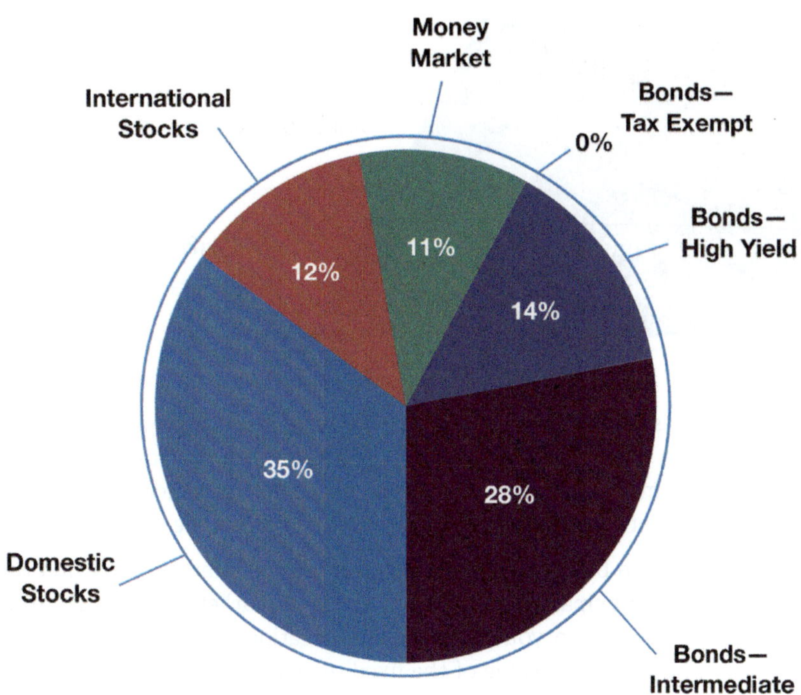

Asset allocation is based on the expected returns and relative risk of each asset class and how it will contribute to the return and risk of the portfolio as a whole. If the asset classes you choose are truly diverse, then the portfolio's risk can be lower than the sum of the assets' risks.

Security selection is the third step in diversification, choosing individual investments within each asset class. Here is the chance to achieve industry or sector and company diversification. For example, if you decided to include corporate stock in your portfolio (asset allocation), you decide which corporation's stock to invest in. Choosing corporations in different industries or companies of different sizes or ages will diversify your stock holdings. You will have less risk than if you invested in just one corporation's stock. Diversification is not defined by the number of investments but by their different characteristics and performance.

security selection

The process of choosing individual securities to be included in the portfolio.

Investment Strategies

Capital allocation decides the amount of overall risk in the portfolio; asset allocation tries to maximize the return you can get for that amount of risk. Security selection further diversifies within each asset class. Figure 12.11 demonstrates the three levels of diversification.

FIGURE 12.11 Levels of Diversification

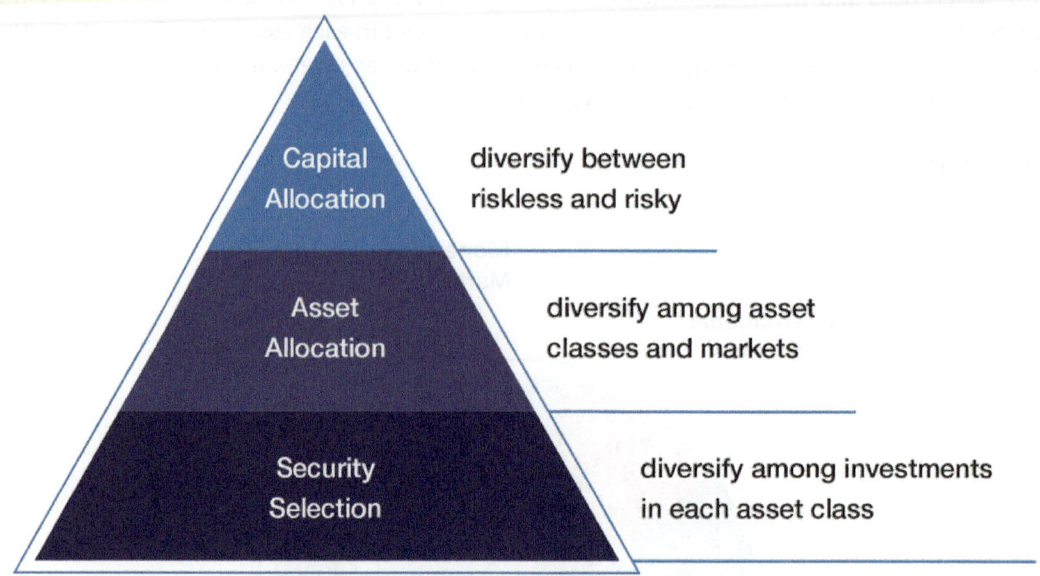

One example of an asset allocation strategy is **life cycle investing**—changing your asset allocation as you age. When you retire, for example, and forgo income from working, you become dependent on income from your investments. As you approach retirement age, therefore, you typically shift your asset allocation to less risky asset classes to protect the value of your investments.

market timing

The practice of basing investment strategy on predictions of future market changes or on asset return forecasts.

benchmark

A standard, often an index of securities, representing an industry or asset class and used as an indicator of growth potential or as a basis of comparison for similar or disparate industries or assets.

passive management

An investment strategy that does not include security selection within an asset class; the investment is expected to perform as well as the benchmark index.

active management

An investment strategy that includes security selection within an asset class in order to outperform the asset class benchmark.

Also, asset allocation can be actively managed through the strategy of **market timing**—shifting the asset allocation in anticipation of economic shifts or market volatility. For example, if you forecast a period of higher inflation, you might reduce allocation in fixed-rate bonds or debt instruments, because inflation erodes the value of the fixed repayments. Until the inflation passes, you would shift your allocation so that more of your portfolio is in stocks, say, and less in bonds.

Just as life cycle investing is a strategy for asset allocation, investing in index funds is a strategy for security selection. Indexes are a way of measuring the performance of an entire asset class by measuring returns for a portfolio containing all the investments in that asset class. Essentially, the index becomes a **benchmark** for the asset class, a standard against which any specific investment in that asset class can be measured. An index fund is an investment that holds the same securities as the index, so it provides a way for you to invest in an entire asset class without having to select particular securities. For example, if you invest in the S&P 500 Index fund, you are investing in the 500 largest corporations in the United States—the asset class of large corporations.

There are indexes and index funds for most asset classes. By investing in an index, you are achieving the most diversification possible for that asset class without having to make individual investments, that is, without having to make any security selection decisions. This strategy of bypassing the security selection decision is called **passive management**. It also has the advantage of saving transaction costs (broker's fees) because you can invest in the entire index through only one transaction rather than the many transactions that picking investments would require.

In contrast, making security selection decisions to maximize returns and minimize risks is called **active management**. Investors who favor active management feel that the advantages of picking specific investments, after careful research and analysis, are worth the added transaction costs. Actively managed portfolios may achieve diversification based on the quality, rather than the quantity, of securities selected.

It is rare, however, for active investors or investment managers to achieve superior results over time. More commonly, an investment manager is unable to achieve consistently better returns within an asset class than the returns of the passively managed index.[5]

Key Takeaways

- Diversification can decrease portfolio risk through choosing investments with different risk characteristics and exposures.
- A portfolio strategy involves:
    - capital allocation decisions,
    - asset allocation decisions,
    - security selection decisions.
- Active management is a portfolio strategy including security selection decisions and market timing.
- Passive management is a portfolio strategy omitting security selection decisions and relying on index funds to represent asset classes, while maintaining a long-term asset allocation.

Exercises

1. What is the meaning of the expressions "don't count your chickens before they hatch" and "don't put all your eggs in one basket"? How do these expressions relate to the challenge of reducing exposure to investment risks and building a high-performance investment portfolio? See what Warren Buffet has to say about diversification at https://www.youtube.com/watch?v=wbjPiYE-F4Y. According to Buffett, when can "diversification be a terrible mistake"? Discuss with your classmates whether you agree or not.
2. Draft a provisional portfolio strategy. In My Notes or your personal finance journal, describe your capital allocation decisions. Then identify the asset classes you are thinking of investing in. Describe how you might allocate assets to diversify your portfolio. Draw a pie chart showing your asset allocation. Draw another pie chart to show how life cycle investing might affect your asset allocation decisions in the future. How might you use the strategy of market timing in changing your asset allocation decisions?
3. Outline the steps you would take to select specific securities. How would you know which stocks, bonds, or funds to invest in? How are index funds useful as an alternative to security selection? What are the advantages and disadvantages of investing in an index fund such as the Dow Jones Industrial Average? (Go to http://money.cnn.com/data/markets/dow/ to find out which stocks the Dow represents.)
4. Do you favor an active or a passive investment management strategy? Why? Identify all the pros and cons of these investment strategies and debate them with classmates. What factors favor an active approach? What factors favor a passive approach? Which strategy might prove more beneficial for first-time investors?
5. Read the article, "Successful Investing: 10 Tips to Successful Investing" at http://financialhighway.com/successful-investing-10-tips-for-successful-investing. What advice does the article have for novice investors? Which of those tips are most relevant to you as a novice investor?

Endnotes

1. For a thorough history of the evolution of finance and financial instruments, see Charles P. Kindleberger, *A Financial History of Western Europe* (London: George Allen & Unwin, Ltd., 1984).
2. Jesse Bricker, Lisa J. Dettling, Alice Henriques, Joanne W. Hsu, Lindsay Jacobs, Kevin B. Moore, Sarah Pack, John Sabelhaus, Jeffrey Thompson, and Richard A. Windle, "Changes in U.S. Family Finances from 2013 to 2016: Evidence from the Survey of Consumer Finances," *Federal Reserve Bulletin*, September 2017, v. 103, No. 3, https://www.federalreserve.gov/publications/files/scf17.pdf (accessed on June 3, 2018).
3. The Securities Industry and Financial Markets Associations, "U.S. Capital Markets Deck," September 2017, https://www.sifma.org/wp-content/uploads/2016/10/US-Capital-Markets-Deck-2017-09-11-SIFMA.pdf, (accessed June 3, 2018).
4. The World Bank, "Market Capitalization of Listed Domestic Companies," https://data.worldbank.org/indicator/CM.MKT.LCAP.CD (accessed June 3, 2018).
5. Much research, some of it quite academic, has been done on this subject. For a succinct (and instructive) summary of the discussion, see Burton G. Malkiel, *A Random Walk Down Wall Street*, 10th ed. (New York: W. W. Norton & Company, Inc., 2007).

CHAPTER 13

Behavioral Finance and Market Behavior

13.1 Introduction

Much of what is known about finance and investments has come from the study of economics. Classic economics assumes that people are rational when they make economic or financial decisions. "Rational" means that people respond to incentives because their goal is always to maximize benefit and minimize costs. Not everyone shares the same idea of benefit and cost, but in a market with millions of participants, there tends to be some general consensus.

This belief in rationality leads to the idea of **market efficiency**. In an efficient market, prices reflect "fundamental value" as appraised by rational decision makers who have access to information and are free to choose to buy or sell as their rational decisions dictate. The belief in efficiency assumes that when prices do not reflect real value, people will notice and will act on the anomaly with the result that the market "corrects" that price.

market efficiency

The idea that the market works best when prices reflect all available information, implying that a market price represents an unbiased estimate with an equal chance that a good is over- or undervalued.

People are not always rational, however, and markets are not always efficient. **Behavioral finance** is the study of why individuals do not always make the decisions they are expected to make and why markets do not reliably behave as they are expected to behave. As market participants, individuals are affected by others' behavior, which collectively affects market behavior, which in turn affects all the participants in the market.

behavioral finance

The study of how cognitive and emotional factors affect economic decisions, particularly how they affect rationality in decision making.

As an individual, you participate in the capital markets and are vulnerable to the individual and market behaviors that influence the outcomes of your decisions. The more you understand and anticipate those behaviors, the better your financial decision making may be.

13.2 Investor Behavior

Learning Objectives

1. Identify and describe the biases that can affect investor decision making.
2. Explain how framing errors can influence investor decision making.
3. Identify the factors that can influence investor profiles.

Rational thinking can lead to irrational decisions if the context is misperceived or misunderstood. In addition, biases can cause people to emphasize or discount information, or can lead to too strong an attachment to an idea or an inability to recognize an opportunity. The context in which you see a decision, the mental frame you give it—the kind of decision you determine it to be—can also inhibit your otherwise objective view.[1] Learning to recognize your behaviors and habits of mind that act as impediments to objective decision making may help you to overcome them.

Biases

bias

A tendency, preference, or belief that interferes with objectivity.

One kind of investor behavior that leads to unexpected decisions is **bias**, a predisposition to a view that inhibits objective thinking. Biases that can affect investment decisions are the following:

- Availability
- Representativeness
- Overconfidence
- Anchoring
- Ambiguity aversion[2]

availability bias

In finance, an investor's tendency to base the probability of an event on the availability of information.

representativeness

The practice of stereotyping asset performance, or of assuming commonality of disparate assets based on superficial, stereotypical traits.

overconfidence

A bias in which you have too much faith in the precision of your estimates, causing you to underestimate the range of possibilities that actually exist.

anchoring

A bias in which the investor relies too heavily on limited known factors or points of reference.

ambiguity aversion

A preference for known risks over unknown risks.

Availability bias occurs because investors rely on information to make informed decisions, but not all information is readily available. Investors tend to give more weight to information that is more available and less weight to information that is brought to their attention less often. The stocks of corporations that get good press, for example, may seem to do better than those of less-publicized companies when in reality these "high-profile" companies may actually have worse earnings and return potential.

Representativeness is decision making based on stereotypes, or characterizations that are treated as "representative" of all members of a group. In investing, representativeness is a tendency to be more optimistic about investments that have performed well lately and more pessimistic about investments that have performed poorly. In your mind, you stereotype the immediate past performance of investments as "strong" or "weak." This representation then makes it hard to think of them in any other way or to analyze their potential. As a result, you may put too much emphasis on past performance and not enough on future prospects.

Objective investment decisions involve forming expectations about what will happen, making educated guesses by gathering as much information as possible and making as good use of it as possible. **Overconfidence** is a bias in which you have too much faith in the precision of your estimates, causing you to underestimate the range of possibilities that actually exist. You may underestimate the extent of possible losses, for example, and therefore underestimate investment risks. Overconfidence also comes from the tendency to attribute good results to good investor decisions and bad results to bad luck or bad markets.

Anchoring happens when you cannot integrate new information into your thinking because you are too "anchored" to your existing views. You do not give new information its due, especially if it contradicts your previous views. By devaluing new information, you tend to underreact to changes or news and become less likely to act, even when it is in your interest.

Ambiguity aversion is the tendency to prefer the familiar to the unfamiliar or the known to the unknown. Avoiding ambiguity can lead to discounting opportunities with greater uncertainty in favor of "sure things." In that case, your bias against uncertainty may create an opportunity cost for your portfolio. Availability bias and ambiguity aversion can also result in a failure to diversify, as investors tend to "stick with what they know." For example, in a study of defined contribution retirement accounts or 401(k)s, more than 53% of employees had invested in their employer's stock and about 7% had more than 80% of their retirement account invested in their employer's stock[3]—hardly a well-diversified asset allocation.

Framing

Framing refers to the way you see alternatives and define the context in which you are making a decision.[4] Your framing determines how you imagine the problem, its possible solutions, and its connection with other situations. A concept related to framing is **mental accounting**: the way individuals encode, describe, and assess economic outcomes when they make financial decisions.[5] In financial behavior, framing can lead to shortsighted views, narrow-minded assumptions, and restricted choices.

FIGURE 13.1

© Shutterstock, Inc.

Every rational economic decision maker would prefer to avoid a loss, to have benefits be greater than costs, to reduce risk, and to have investments gain value. **Loss aversion** refers to the tendency to loathe realizing a loss to the extent that you avoid it even when it is the better choice.

How can it be rational for a loss to be the better choice? Say you buy stock for $100 per share. Six months later, the stock price has fallen to $63 per share. You decide not to sell the stock to avoid realizing the loss. If there is another stock with better earnings potential, however, your decision creates an opportunity cost. You pass up the better chance to increase value in the hopes that your original value will be regained. Your opportunity cost likely will be greater than the benefit of holding your stock, but you will do anything to avoid that loss. Loss aversion is an instance where a rational aversion leads you to underestimate a real cost, leading you to choose the lesser alternative.

framing

The idea that the presentation or perception of a decision influences the decision maker.

mental accounting

A preference to segregate investment accounts by goals and constraints, rather than to perceive the entire portfolio as a whole.

loss aversion

An investor's preference to avoid losses, even when the costs outweigh the benefits, in which case it is not the rational economic choice.

Loss aversion is also a form of regret aversion. Regret is a feeling of responsibility for loss or disappointment. Past decisions and their outcomes inform your current decisions, but regret can bias your decision making. Regret can anchor you too firmly in past experience and hinder you from seeing new circumstances. Framing can affect your risk tolerance. You may be more willing to take risk to avoid a loss if you are loss averse, for example, or you may simply become unwilling to assume risk, depending on how you define the context.

Framing also influences how you manage making more than one decision simultaneously. If presented with multiple but separate choices, most people tend to decide on each separately, mentally segregating each decision.[6] By framing choices as separate and unrelated, however, you may miss making the best decisions, which may involve comparing or combining choices. Lack of diversification or overdiversification in a portfolio may also result.

Investor Profiles

An **investor profile** expresses a combination of characteristics based on personality traits, life stage, sources of wealth, and other factors. What is your investor profile? The better you can know yourself as an investor, the better investment decisions you can make.

investor profile

A combination of characteristics based on personality traits, life stage, and sources of wealth.

Researchers have identified some features or characteristics of investors that seem to lead to recognizable tendencies.[7] For example, stages of life have an effect on goals, views, and decisions, as shown in the examples in Table 13.1.

TABLE 13.1 Life Stage Profiles

Stage	Ages	Investment Goals
Starting	25-40	• Eliminating debt • Saving for capital expenditures • Investing in employee benefits
Accumulating	40-65	• Managing debt • Diversifying and building equity • Saving for retirement and estate planning
Spending	65-80	• Relying on retirement income • Reducing investment risks • Preserving value; preserving or reinvesting capital
Gifting	80+	• Eliminating risk • Distributing wealth

These "definitions" are fairly loose yet typical enough to think about. In each of these stages, your goals and your risk tolerance—both your ability and willingness to assume risk—change. Generally, the further you are from retirement and the loss of your wage income, the more risk you will take with your investments, having another source of income (your paycheck). As you get closer to retirement, you become more concerned with preserving your investments' value so that it can generate income when it becomes your sole source of income in retirement, thus causing you to become less risk tolerant. After retirement, your risk tolerance decreases even more, until the very end of your life when you are concerned with dispersing rather than preserving your wealth.

Risk tolerance and investment approaches are affected by more than age and investment stage, however. Studies have shown that the source and amount of wealth can be a factor in attitudes toward investment.[8]

Those who have inherited wealth or come to it "passively," tend to be much more risk averse than those who have "actively" created their own wealth. Entrepreneurs, for example, who have created wealth, tend to be much more willing to assume investment risk, perhaps because they have more confidence in their ability to create more wealth should their investments lose value. Those who have inherited wealth tend to be much more risk averse, as they see their wealth as a windfall that, once lost, they cannot replace.

Active wealth owners also tend to be more active investors, more involved in investment decisions and more knowledgeable about their investment portfolios. They have more confidence in their ability to manage and to make good decisions than do passive wealth owners, who haven't had the experience to build confidence.

Not surprisingly, those with more wealth to invest tend to be more willing to assume risk. The same loss of value is a smaller proportional loss for them than for an investor with a smaller asset base.

Many personality traits bear on investment behavior, including whether you generally are:

- confident or anxious,
- deliberate or impetuous,
- organized or sloppy,
- rebellious or conventional,
- an abstract or linear thinker.

What makes you make the decisions that you make? The more aware you are of the influences on your decisions, the more you can factor them into—or out of—the investment process.

Key Takeaways

- Traditional assumptions about economic decision making assert that financial behavior is rational and markets are efficient. Behavioral finance looks at all the factors that cause realities to depart from these assumptions.
- Biases that can affect investment decisions are the following:
  - Availability
  - Representativeness
  - Overconfidence
  - Anchoring
  - Ambiguity aversion
- Framing refers to the way you see alternatives and define the context in which you are making a decision. Examples of framing errors include the following:
  - Loss aversion
  - Choice segregation
- Framing is a kind of mental accounting—the way individuals classify, characterize, and evaluate economic outcomes when they make financial decisions.
- Investor profiles are influenced by the investor's
  - life stage,
  - personality,
  - source of wealth.

Exercises

1. Debate rational theory with classmates. How rational or nonrational (or irrational) do you think people's economic decisions are? What are some examples of efficient and inefficient markets, and how did people's behavior create those situations?
2. In My Notes or your personal finance journal record some examples of your nonrational economic behavior. For example, describe a situation in which you decreased the value of one of your assets rather than maintaining or increasing its value. In what circumstances are you likely to pay more for something than it is worth? Have you ever bought something you did not want or need just because it was a bargain? Do you tend to avoid taking risks even when the odds are good that you will not take a loss? Have you ever had a situation in which the cost of deciding not to buy something proved greater than buying it would have cost? Have you ever made a major purchase without considering alternatives? Have you ever regretted a financial decision to such an extent that the disappointment has influenced all your subsequent decisions?
3. Angus has always held shares of a big oil company's stock and has never thought about branching out to other companies or industries in the energy sector. His investment has done well in the past, proving to him that he is making the right decision. Angus has been reading about fundamental changes predicted for the energy sector, but he decides to stick with what he knows. In what ways is Angus' investment behavior irrational? What kinds of investor biases does his decision making reveal?
4. Read the Motley Fool's article, "What Kind of Investor are You?" and complete the interactive investor profile questionnaire at https://www.fool.com/investing/general/investor-quiz.aspx. According to this instrument, what kinds of investments should you consider? In My Notes or your personal finance journal, on the basis of what you have learned, write an essay profiling yourself as an investor. You may choose to post your investor profile and compare it with those of others taking this course. Specifically, how do you think your profile will assist you and your financial advisor or investment advisor in planning your portfolio?

13.3 Market Behavior

Learning Objectives

1. Define the role of arbitrage in market efficiency.
2. Describe the limits of arbitrage that may perpetuate market inefficiency.
3. Identify the economic and cultural factors that can allow market inefficiencies to persist.
4. Explain the role of feedback as reinforcement of market inefficiencies.

FIGURE 13.2

© Shutterstock, Inc.

Your economic behaviors affect economic markets. Market results reflect the collective yet independent decisions of millions of individuals. There have been years, even decades, when some markets have not produced expected or "rational" prices because of the collective behavior of their participants. In inefficient markets, prices may go way above or below actual value.

The **efficient market theory** relies on the idea that investors behave rationally and that even when they don't, their numbers are so great and their behavioral biases are so diverse that their irrational behaviors will have little overall effect on the market. In effect, investors' anomalous behaviors will cancel each other out. Thus, diversification (of participants) lowers risk (to the market).

Another protection of market efficiency is the tendency for most participants to behave rationally. If an asset is mispriced so that its market price deviates from its intrinsic value, knowledgeable investors will see that and take advantage of the opportunity. If a stock seems underpriced they will buy, driving prices back up. If a stock seems overpriced, they will sell, driving prices back down. These strategies are called **arbitrage**, or the process of creating investment gains from market mispricings (**arbitrage opportunities**). The knowledgeable investors who carry out market corrections through their investment decisions are called **arbitrageurs**.

efficient market theory

The idea that the market works best when prices reflect all available information, implying that the market price represents an unbiased estimate with an equal chance that a good is over- or undervalued.

arbitrage

Trading that profits from the market mispricing of assets in the capital markets.

arbitrage opportunity

A market mispricing that provides an opportunity for unusual gain or loss.

arbitrageurs

Traders who seek arbitrage opportunities.

In the 1600s in Holland, speculators and investors drove up the price of tulip bulbs far beyond their value. This inefficient market, called "tulip mania," led to a "boom" or "bubble," followed by a "bust" or "crash" when the market price was corrected. (There is more discussion of booms and busts in the next section.)

There are limits to arbitrage, however. There are times when the stock markets seem to rise or fall much more or for much longer than the dynamics of market correction would predict.

Limits of Arbitrage

Arbitrage may not work when the costs outweigh the benefits. Investment costs include transaction costs, such as brokers' fees, and risk, especially market risk.

An investor who sees an arbitrage opportunity would have to act quickly to take advantage of it, because chances are good that someone else will and the advantage will disappear along with the arbitrage opportunity. Acting quickly may involve borrowing if liquid funds are not available to invest. For this reason, transaction costs for arbitrage trades are likely to be higher (because they are likely to include interest), and if the costs are higher than the benefits, the market will not be corrected.

The risk of arbitrage is that the investor rather than the market is mispricing stocks. In other words, arbitrageurs assume that the current valuation for an asset will reverse—will go down if the valuation has gone too high, or will go up if the valuation has gone too low. If their analysis of fundamental value is incorrect, the market correction may not occur as predicted, and neither will their gains.

Most arbitrageurs are professional wealth managers. They invest for very wealthy clients with a large asset base and very high tolerance for risk. Arbitrage is usually not a sound practice for individual investors.

Causes of Market Inefficiency

Market inefficiencies can persist when they go undiscovered or when they seem rational. Economic historians point out that while every asset "bubble" is in some ways unique, there are common economic factors at work.[9] Bubbles are accompanied by lower interest rates, increased use of debt financing, new technology, and a decrease in government regulation or oversight. Those factors encourage economic expansion, leading to growth of earnings potential and thus of investment return, which would make assets genuinely more valuable.

A key study of the U.S. stock market points out that there are cultural as well as economic factors that can encourage or validate market inefficiency.[10] Examples include:

- demographic factors of the population,
- attitudes reflected in the popular culture,
- the availability of information and analyses,
- the lowering of transaction costs.

These factors all lead to increased participation in the market and a tendency to "rationalize irrationality," that is, to think that real economic or cultural changes, rather than mispricings, are changing the markets.

Sometimes mispricings occur when real economic and cultural changes are happening, however, so that what used to be seen as a mispricing is actually seen as a justifiable, fundamental value because the market itself has changed profoundly. An example is the dot-com bubble of 1990–2000, when stock prices of Internet start-up companies rose far higher than their value or earning capacity, yet investors irrationally kept investing until the first wave of start-ups failed, bursting the market bubble.

Economic and cultural factors can prolong market inefficiency by reinforcing the behaviors that created it, in a kind of feedback loop. For example, financial news coverage in the media increased during the 1990s with the global saturation of cable and satellite television and radio, as well as the growth of the Internet.[11] More information availability can lead to more availability bias. Stereotyping can develop as a result of repeated "news," resulting in representation bias, which encourages overconfidence or too little questioning or analysis of the situation. Misinterpreting market inefficiency as real changes can cause framing problems and other biases as well.

In this way, market inefficiencies can become self-fulfilling prophecies. Investing in an inefficient market causes asset values to rise, leading to gains and to more investments. The rise in asset values becomes self-reinforcing as it encourages anchoring, the expectation that asset values will continue to rise. Inefficiency becomes the norm. Those who do not invest in this market thus incur an opportunity cost. Participating in perpetuating market inefficiency, rather than correcting it, becomes the rational choice.

Reliance on media experts and informal communication or "word of mouth" reinforces this behavior to the point where it can become epidemic. It may not be mere coincidence, for example, that the stock market bubble of the 1920s happened as radio and telephone access became universal in the United States,[12] or that the stock boom of the 1990s coincided with the proliferation of mobile phones and e-mail, or that the real estate bubble of the 2000s coincided with our creation of the blogosphere.

Market efficiency requires that investors act independently so that the market reflects the consensus opinion of their independent judgments. Instead, the market may be reflecting the opinions of a few to whom others defer. Although the volume of market participation would seem to show lots of participation, few are actually participating. Most are simply following. The market then reflects the consensus of the few rather than the many; hence, the probability of mispricing rises.

It is difficult to know what is happening while you are in the middle of an inefficient market situation. It is easier to look back through market history and point out obvious panics or bubbles, but they were not so obvious to participants while they were happening. Hindsight allows a different perspective—it changes the frame—but as events happen, you can only work with the frame you have at the time.

Key Takeaways

- The diversification of market participants should increase market efficiency.
- Arbitrage corrects market mispricing.
- Arbitrage is not always possible, due to
  - transaction costs,
  - the risk of misinterpreting market mispricing.
- Market inefficiencies can persist due to economic and cultural factors, such as:
  - lowered interest rates and increased use of debt financing,
  - new technology,
  - a decrease in government regulation or oversight,
  - demographic factors,
  - attitudes as reflected in popular culture,
  - the availability of information and its analysts,
  - the lowering of transaction costs,
  - increased participation in inefficient markets.
- Market mispricings can be reinforced by feedback mechanisms, perpetuating inefficiencies.

Exercises

1. Find out more about the tulip mania at and at http://en.wikipedia.org/wiki/Tulip_mania, or http://www.investopedia.com/features/crashes/crashes2.asp. What caused mispricing in the market for tulip bulbs? What factors perpetuated the market inefficiency? What happened to burst the tulip bubble? What are some other examples from history of similar bubbles and crashes caused by inefficient markets?
2. Reflect on your impact on the economy and the financial markets as an individual, whether or not you are an investor. How does your financial behavior affect the capital markets, for example? Record your thoughts in your personal finance journal or My Notes. Share your ideas with classmates.

13.4 Extreme Market Behavior

Learning Objectives

1. Trace the typical pattern of a financial crisis.
2. Identify and define the factors that contribute to a financial crisis.

Economic forces and financial behavior can converge to create extreme markets or financial crises, such as booms, bubbles, panics, crashes, or meltdowns. These atypical events actually happen fairly frequently. Between 1618 and 1998, there were 38 financial crises globally, or one every 10 years.[13] Ten years after that, we had the real estate crash of 2007 followed closely by the credit crisis and stock market crash of 2008. As an investor, you can expect to weather as many as six crises in your lifetime.

Patterns of events that seem to precipitate and follow the crises are shown in Figure 13.3. First a period of economic expansion is sparked by a new technology, the discovery of a new resource, or a change in political balances. This leads to increased production, markets, wealth, consumption, and investment, as well as increased credit and lower interest rates. People are looking for ways to invest their newfound wealth. This leads to an asset bubble, or a rapid increase in the price of some asset—bonds, stocks, real estate, or commodities such as cotton, gold, oil, or tulip bulbs—that seems to be positioned to prosper from this particular expansion.

FIGURE 13.3 Pattern of a Financial Crisis

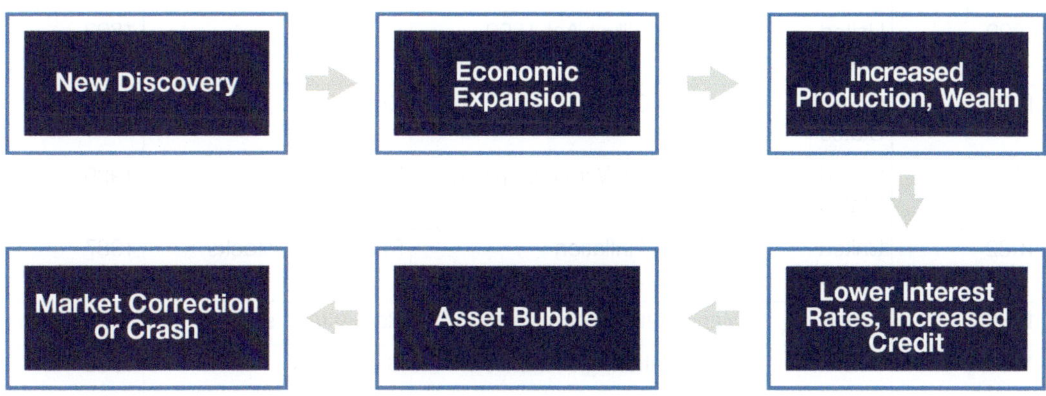

The bubble continues, reinforced by the behavioral and market consequences that it sparks until some event pricks the bubble. Then asset values quickly deflate, and credit defaults rise, damaging the banking system. Having lost wealth and access to credit, people rein in their demand for consumption and investment, further slowing the economy.

Table 13.2 shows some of the major asset bubbles since 1636 and the events that preceded them.[14]

TABLE 13.2 Major Asset Bubbles Since 1636

Bubble Began	Country	Cause of Economic Expansion	Speculative Asset	Year of Crash
1636	Netherlands	War against Spain	Exotic tulip bulbs	1637
1713	England	Treaty of Utrecht	South Sea Company stock	1720
1715	France	Death of Louis XIV	Mississippi Company stock	1720
1789	United States	Nation began	United States bonds	1792
1789	England	French Revolution	Canals	1793
1815	England	End of Napoleonic Wars	Exports	1816
1836	England	Textile boom	Cotton, railroads	1836
1836	United States	Jackson election	Cotton, land	1837
1857	England	End of the Crimean War	Railroads, wheat	1857
1863	France	Confederate defeat in the Civil War (United States)	Cotton	1864
1873	United States	Westward expansion	Railroads, land (homesteading)	1873
1890	United States	Sherman Silver Act 1890	Silver	1893
1901	United States	Panama Canal	Coffee	1907
1919	United States	Post-World War I expansion	Land, stocks	1929
1982	United States	Control of inflation	Real estate, stocks	1987
1980s	Japan	Manufacturing dominance	Real estate, stocks	1990
1997	Asia	Deregulation, globalization	Currencies	1998
1992	United States	Internet/technology	Stocks	2000
2003	United States	Monetary policy	Real estate	2007

Adapted from Charles P. Kindleberger and Robert Aliber, *Manias, Panics, and Crashes*, 5th ed. (Hoboken, NJ: John Wiley & Sons, Inc. , 2005).

In many cases, the event that started the asset speculation was not a macroeconomic event but nevertheless had consequences to the economy: the end of a war, a change of government, a change in policy, or a new technology. Often the asset that was the object of speculation was a resource for or an application of a new technology or an expansion into new territory that may have been critical to a new emphasis in the economy. In other words, the assets that became the objects of bubbles tended to be the drivers of a "new economy" at the time and thus were rationalized as investments rather than as speculation.

In all the examples listed in Table 13.2, as asset values rose—even if only on the strength of investor beliefs—speculators, financed by an expansion of credit, augmented the market and drove up asset prices even further. Many irrational financial behaviors—overconfidence, anchoring, availability bias, representativeness—were in play, until finally the market was shocked into reversal by a specific event or simply sank under its own weight.

Economists may argue that this is what you should expect, that markets expand and contract cyclically as a matter of course. In this view, a crash is nothing more than the correction for a bubble—market efficiency at work.

Examples: The Internet Stock Boom and the Crash of 1929

Much has been and will be written about a classic financial crisis, the Internet stock boom of the 1990s.[15] The asset bubble was in the stocks of emerging companies poised to take advantage of the "new economy" and its expanding markets of the new technology of the Internet.

The asset bubble grew from preceding economic events. The previous decade had seen a recovery from a major inflation and a recession in the United States in the 1970s followed by an economic expansion in the 1980s. Deregulation and new technologies had opened up the telecommunications industry. In 1989 the Soviet Union dissolved, opening markets and market economies in Eastern Europe as well as the former Soviet Union (FSU). The personal computer had taken hold and was gaining in household saturation.

This mix of relative prosperity, low inflation, new global markets, and new technology looked very promising. Classically, the economy expanded, and a new asset bubble was born.

Most Internet companies that were publicly traded were listed on the NASDAQ exchange. Figure 13.4 shows the NASDAQ composite index from 1984 to 2004.

FIGURE 13.4 NASDAQ Composite Index, 1984–2004

Based on data retrieved from Yahoo! Finance, "Historical Prices," https://finance.yahoo.com/q/hp?s=^IXIC+Historical+Prices (accessed June 3, 2018).

Between 1990 and 2000 the NASDAQ Composite Index increased ten-fold. At the height of the bubble, between 1998 and 2000, the value of the index increased 2.5 times, resulting in an average annualized return of over 58%.

Alan Greenspan, then chair of the Federal Reserve Bank, spoke to the U.S. Congress at the end of January 1999. In response to the question about how much of the stock boom was "based on sound fundamentals and how much is based on hype," Greenspan replied,

> *"First of all, you wouldn't get 'hype' working if there weren't something fundamentally, potentially sound under it. The size of the potential market is so huge that you have these pie-in-the-sky type of potentials for a lot of different [firms]. Undoubtedly, some of these small companies whose stock prices are going through the roof will succeed. And they may very well justify even higher prices. The vast majority are almost sure to fail. That's the way markets tend to work in this regard.... But there is at root here something far more fundamental—the stock market seeking out profitable ventures and directing capital to hopeful projects before profits materialize. That's good for our system. And, in fact, with all its hype and craziness, is something that, at the end of the day, is probably more plus than minus."*[16]

Greenspan implies that the bubble "with all its hype and craziness" is nothing more than business as usual in the capital markets. He sees the irrational as somewhat rational and not merely the "irrational exuberance" that he saw little more than two years earlier.[17]

Going back a bit further, the Crash of 1929 was perhaps the most profound end to an asset bubble, at least in the American psyche, as it seemed to precipitate a lengthy depression, the Great Depression. The reasons for the prolonged recession that followed the crash are complex, but the factors leading up to it illustrate a classic asset bubble.

In the decade after World War I, the U.S. economy boomed. With the war over, inflation eased and markets opened. Our manufacturing competitors in Europe had suffered losses of labor, capital, and infrastructure that allowed the United States to establish a global dominance. Technologies such as radio were changing the speed of life, while the mass production of everything from cars to appliances was changing the quality of life. Electrification and roads developed a national infrastructure. To finance the consumption of all this mass production, the idea of "store credit" was beginning to expand into the system of consumer credit that we use today. As interest rates stayed low, levels of household and corporate debt rose.

New technologies were developed by new corporations that needed mass, public financing. As more and more shares were issued, they were pitched more fervently to encourage more investment by more investors. Investing became the national pastime, share prices rose, and investors were reassured that technology had spawned a new economy to create new wealth. As in the 1990s, the mix of relative prosperity, low inflation, new global markets, and new technology looked very promising. The positive feedback loop of a classic asset bubble had been created.

After it was all over, Groucho, one of the famous Marx Brothers comedians, reflected on the rationalized irrationality of the bubble: "I would have lost more, but that was all the money I had."[18]

Given that you can expect to encounter at least a few crises during your investing lifetime, as you think about investing—creating and managing wealth—how can you protect yourself? How can you "keep your head when all about you / Are losing theirs,"[19] and is that really the right thing to do?

Key Takeaways

- Prolonged market inefficiencies can result in asset bubbles.
- Financial crises follow a typical pattern of
  - economic expansion,
  - asset bubble(s),
  - market crash(es).
- The behavior that leads to financial crises may exhibit investor biases, but to the extent that investors are responding to real changes in the economy, it is not necessarily irrational.

Exercise

1. View a flowchart of the financial crisis of 2007 by WallStats.com (http://www.wallstats.com/blog/a-visual-guide-to-the-financial-crisis/). How did the real estate market become so inefficient? What thinking does the chart identify that fed into the real estate crash? For each thought bubble on the chart, what kind of bias or framing or other mental accounting was taking place? In what ways was investor behavior irrational? On the other hand, how might you argue that investors were not deciding irrationally?

13.5 Behavioral Finance and Investment Strategies

Learning Objectives

1. Identify the factors that make successful market timing difficult.
2. Explain how technical analysis is used as an investment strategy.
3. Identify the factors that encourage investor fraud in an asset bubble.

You can apply your knowledge of findings from the field of behavioral finance in a number of ways. First, you can be alert to and counteract your natural tendencies toward investor bias and framing. For example, you can avoid availability bias by gathering news from different sources and by keeping the news in historical perspective.

A long-term viewpoint can also help you avoid anchoring or assuming that current performance indicates future performance. At the same time, keep in mind that current market trends are not the same as the past trends they may resemble. For example, factors leading to stock market crashes include elements unique to each.

Ambiguity aversion can be useful if your uncertainty is caused by a lack of information, as it can let you know when you need to do more homework. On the other hand, aversion to ambiguity can blind you to promising opportunities.

Loss aversion, like any fear, is useful when it keeps you from taking too much risk, but not when it keeps you from profitable opportunities. Using knowledge to best assess the scope and probability of loss is a way to see the loss in context. Likewise, segregating investments by their goals, risks, liquidity, and time horizons may be useful for, say, encouraging you to save for retirement or some other goal.

Your best protection against your own behavioral impulses, however, is to have a plan based on an objective analysis of goals, risk tolerance, and constraints, taking your entire portfolio into account. Review your plan at least once a year as circumstances and asset values may have changed. Having a plan in place helps you counteract investor biases.

Following your investment policy or plan, you determine the capital and asset allocations that can produce your desired return objective and risk tolerance within your defined constraints. Your asset allocation should provide diversification, a good idea whatever your investment strategy is.

Market Timing and Technical Analysis

Asset bubbles and market crashes are largely a matter of timing. If you could anticipate a bubble and invest just before it began and divest just before it burst, you would get maximum return. That sort of precise timing, however, is nearly impossible to achieve. To time events precisely, you would constantly have to watch for new information, and even then, the information from different sources may be contradictory, or there may be information available to others that you do not have. Taken together, your chances of profitably timing a bubble or crash are fairly slim.

market timing

The practice of basing investment strategy on predictions of future market changes or on asset return forecasts.

Market timing was defined in Chapter 12 as an asset allocation strategy. Because of the difficulty of predicting asset bubbles and crashes, however, and because of the biases in financial behavior, individual investors typically develop a "buy-and-hold" strategy. You invest in a diversified portfolio that reflects your return objectives and risk tolerance, and you hold on to it. You review the asset allocation periodically so it remains in line with your return and risk preferences or as your constraints shift. You rely on your plan to make progress toward your investment goals and to resist the temptations that are the subjects of the field of behavioral finance.

As you read in Chapter 12, a passive investment strategy ignores security selection by using index funds for asset classes. An active strategy, in contrast, involves selecting securities with a view to market timing in the selection of securities and asset allocation.

technical analysis

A process of estimating security value solely on the basis of past performance as an indicator of future performance.

fundamental analysis

The process of estimating security value by evaluating past performance and macroeconomic and industry factors.

An investment approach based on the idea that timing is everything is called technical analysis. **Technical analysis** involves analyzing securities in terms of their history, expressed, for example, in the form of charts of market data such as price and volume. Technical analysts are sometimes referred to as chartists. Chartists do not consider the intrinsic value of a security—a concern of **fundamental analysis**. Instead, using charts of past price changes and returns, technical analysts try to predict a security's future market movement.

Candlestick charting, with its dozens of symbols, is commonly used as a way to "see" market timing trends. It is believed to have been invented by an eighteenth-century Japanese rice trader named Homma Munehisa.[20] Although charting and technical analysis has its proponents, fundamental analysis of value remains essential to investment strategy, along with analyzing information about the economy, industry, and specific asset.

FIGURE 13.5 A Candlestick Chart Used in Technical Analysis

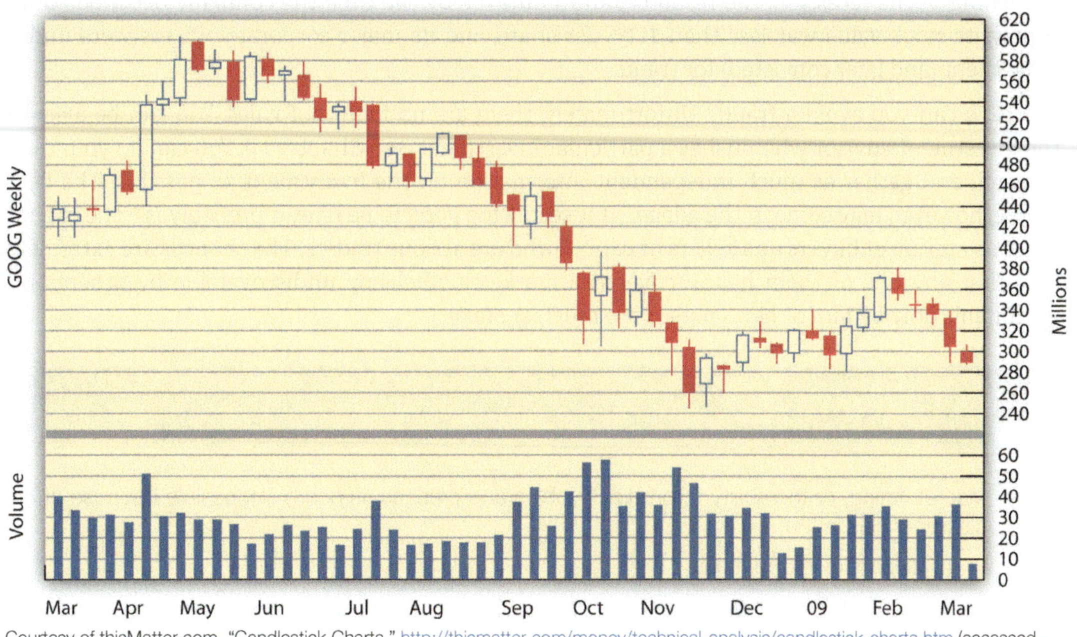

Courtesy of thisMatter.com, "Candlestick Charts," http://thismatter.com/money/technical-analysis/candlestick-charts.htm (accessed April 8, 2014).

Technical analysts use charts like the one in Figure 13.5. Each symbol annotating the graph, such as the shaded and clear "candlesticks," represents financial data. Chartists interpret the patterns they see on these charts as indicators of future price moves and returns as driven by traders' financial behavior.

Financial Fraud

Fraud is certainly not an investment strategy, but bubbles attract fraudulent schemers as well as investors and speculators. A loss of market efficiency and signs of greater investor irrationality attract con men to the markets. It is easier to convince a "mark" of the credibility and viability of a fraudulent scheme when there is general prosperity, rising asset values, and lower perceived risks.

During the post–World War I expansion and stock bubble of the 1920s, for example, Charles Ponzi created the first **Ponzi scheme**, a variation of the classic **pyramid scheme**. The pyramid scheme creates "returns" from new members' deposits rather than from real earnings in the market. The originator gets a number of people to invest, each of whom recruits more, and so on. The money from each group of investors, however, rather than being invested, is used to pay "returns" to the previous group of investors. The scheme is uncovered when there are not enough "returns" to go around. Thus, the originator and early investors may get rich, while later investors lose all their money.

Ponzi scheme

A pyramid scheme practiced by Charles Ponzi in Boston during the 1920s. The term is now commonly used to describe a pyramid scheme.

pyramid scheme

A fraud in which "returns" are created by new deposits rather than by real investment earnings.

During the prosperity of the 1980s, 1990s, and 2000s, the American financier Bernard Madoff notoriously ran a variation of the Ponzi scheme. His fraud, costing investors around the world billions of dollars, lasted through several stock bubbles and a real estate bubble before being exposed in 2008.

Fraud can be perpetrated at the corporate level as well. Enron Corporation was an innovator in developing markets for energy commodities such as oil, natural gas, and electricity. Its image was of a model corporation that encouraged bright thinkers to go "outside the box." Unfortunately, that ethos of innovation took a wrong turn when several of its corporate officers conspired to hide the company's investment risks from financing complicated subsidiaries that existed "off balance sheet." In the fall of 2001, with investor confidence shaken by the dot-com bust and the post-9/11 deepening of the recession, the fraud began to unravel. By the time the company declared bankruptcy, its stock value was less than $1.00 per share, and its major corporate officers were under indictment (and later convicted) for fraud.

How can you avoid a fraud? Unfortunately, there are no foolproof rules. You can be alert to the investment advisor who pushes a particular investment (see Chapter 14). You can do your own research and gather as much independent information on the investment as possible. The best advice, however, may come in the adage, "If it seems too good to be true, it probably is." The capital markets are full of buyers and sellers of capital who are serious traders. The chances are extremely slim that any one of them has discovered a market inefficiency undiscoverable by others and exploitable only by him or her. There is too much at stake.

Key Takeaways

- Market timing, or the ability to predict bubbles and crashes, is nearly impossible because of discrepancies in the
  - availability of information,
  - access to information,
  - interpretation of information.
- Technical analysis is a strategy based on market timing and investor sentiment.
- Asset bubbles are often accompanied by an increase in investor fraud due to the
  - loss of market efficiency,
  - increase in investor "irrationality,"
  - increase in wealth and prosperity.
- One form of financial fraud relating to market bubbles is the Ponzi scheme or pyramid scheme.

Exercises

1. Consider exploring the world of chartists at http://www.investopedia.com/articles/technical/02/121702.asp and consider trying your hand at this arcane art. You and our classmates might begin by learning how to read the charts that technical analysts use to predict price changes in the markets. For a detailed glossary of chart symbols and patterns provided by Forbes, see https://www.forbes.com/2000/06/03/feat.html#253a809d3508. What do you see as the advantages and disadvantages of technical analysis compared to fundamental analysis?
2. What is a pyramid scheme exactly? Find out at http://www.investopedia.com/articles/04/042104.asp. Have you ever participated in or invested in such a scheme? Have you ever been a victim of one? Record your answers in My Notes or your personal finance journal. According to the Investopedia article, why can it be difficult to detect a pyramid scheme? What are some possible tip-offs to this kind of fraud? Why are pyramid schemes unsustainable? Who are the victims? Draw a diagram illustrating the dynamics of pyramid schemes.
3. How are investment clubs different from pyramid schemes? Read about investment clubs at https://www.sapling.com/3505/start-investment-club. What does the U.S. Securities Exchange Commission have to say about investment clubs at http://www.sec.gov/investor/pubs/invclub.htm? Investigate further online. Would you consider joining or starting an investment club? Why, or why not? What do your classmates think about this?
4. Watch the video from PBS's Frontline "The Madoff Affair" at https://www.pbs.org/video/frontline-the-madoff-affair/. Who were Madoff's victims? Visit the support group website created for the victims at http://berniemadoffponzisupportgroup.blogspot.com/. How did Madoff defend himself? Read a *Wall Street Journal* article at http://online.wsj.com/article/

SB123111743915052731.html, explaining how Madoff's Ponzi scheme was able to succeed. How did investor biases contribute to this success? How did biases in regulatory oversight contribute to the fraud? Why did representatives and senators focus their criticism on the Securities and Exchange Commission?

Endnotes

1. Much research has been done in the field of behavioral finance over the past thirty years. A comprehensive text for further reading is by Hersh Shefrin, *Beyond Greed and Fear: Understanding Financial Behavior and the Psychology of Investing* (Oxford: Oxford University Press, 2002).
2. Hersh Shefrin, *Beyond Greed and Fear: Understanding Financial Behavior and the Psychology of Investing* (Oxford: Oxford University Press, 2002).
3. FINRA, "Putting Too Much Stock in Your Company—A 401(k) Problem," http://www.finra.org/investors/alerts/putting-too-much-stock-your-company-a-401k-problem (accessed June 3, 2018).
4. A. Tversky and D. Kahneman, "The Framing Decisions and the Psychology of Choice," *Science* 30, no. 211 (1981): 453–58.
5. R. Thaler, "Mental Accounting Matters," *Journal of Behavioral* Decision Making 12, no. 3 (1999): 183–206.
6. Hersh Shefrin, *Beyond Greed and Fear: Understanding Financial Behavior and the Psychology of Investing* (Oxford: Oxford University Press, 2002).
7. A reference for this discussion is John L. Maginn, Donald L. Tuttle, Jerald E. Pinto, and Dennis W. McLeavey, eds., *Managing Investment Portfolios: A Dynamic Process*, 3rd ed. (Hoboken, NJ: John Wiley & Sons, Inc., 2007).
8. John L. Maginn, Donald L. Tuttle, Jerald E. Pinto, and Dennis W. McLeavey, eds., *Managing Investment Portfolios: A Dynamic Process*, 3rd ed. (Hoboken, NJ: John Wiley & Sons, Inc., 2007).
9. Charles P. Kindleberger and Robert Aliber, *Manias, Panics, and Crashes*, 5th ed. (Hoboken, NJ: John Wiley & Sons, Inc., 2005).
10. Robert J. Shiller, *Irrational Exuberance*, 2nd ed. (New York: Random House, Inc., 2005).
11. Robert J. Shiller, *Irrational Exuberance*, 2nd ed. (New York: Random House, Inc., 2005).
12. See especially Robert J. Shiller, *Irrational Exuberance*, 2nd ed. (New York: Random House, Inc., 2005), 163.
13. Charles P. Kindleberger and Robert Aliber, *Manias, Panics, and Crashes*, 5th ed. (Hoboken, NJ: John Wiley & Sons, Inc., 2005).
14. Charles P. Kindleberger and Robert Aliber, *Manias, Panics, and Crashes*, 5th ed. (Hoboken, NJ: John Wiley & Sons, Inc., 2005).
15. For a wonderfully thorough and insightful start, see Robert J. Shiller, *Irrational Exuberance*, 2nd ed. (New York: Random House, Inc., 2005).
16. John Cassidy, *Dot.con* (New York: HarperCollins, 2002), 202.
17. Robert J. Shiller, *Irrational Exuberance*, 2nd ed. (New York: Random House, Inc., 2005), 1.
18. Julius Henry Marx, *Groucho and Me* (New York: Da Capo Press, Inc., 1995), 197. Originally published in 1959.
19. Rudyard Kipling, *Complete Verse* (New York: Anchor Books, 1988).
20. Gregory L. Morris, *Candlestick Charting Explained: Timeless Techniques for Trading Stocks and Futures* (New York: McGraw-Hill, 2006).

CHAPTER 14

The Practice of Investment

14.1 Introduction

Once you have developed your investment policy statement and have determined your goals, risk tolerance, and constraints, it is time to choose a strategy and to act. Whether you entrust a professional advisor or you do it yourself—or both—depends on your confidence, knowledge, and the time and effort that you want to devote to your decisions. As is true of any personal finance decision, the ultimate responsibility for and consequences of your decisions are yours alone. Whatever you decide, the more you know about the practice of investment, the better an investor you will be.

FIGURE 14.1

There are four broad areas to take into account: (1) how to find and evaluate the information you need, (2) the agents and fees involved in securities trading, (3) the ethical standards and regulatory requirements of the securities industry, and (4) the special considerations of investing internationally.

14.2 Investment Information

Learning Objectives

1. Explain how leading economic indicators are used to gauge the current economic cycle and the outlook for the economy.
2. Explain how indexes are used to gauge financial market activity and as benchmarks for asset classes and industries.
3. Identify and evaluate sources of information used to analyze and forecast corporate performance.
4. Sample and evaluate media outlets providing investment information and advice.

Investment information seems to be everywhere: in print, radio, television, and Internet—24/7 and global. Successful investors are hailed as gurus and high-profile financial news reporters become celebrities. No shortage of commentators and pundits will analyze every morsel of news, but how can you find useful investment information to make investment decisions? Even more important, how can you find useful information that you can trust based on the reliability of its source?

Your investment decisions involve capital allocation, asset allocation, and security selection. To make those decisions, you need information that will help you form an idea of the economy, industry, and security that affect your decisions. The three main kinds of information that investors use are economic indicators, market indexes, and company performance.

Economic Indicators

To gauge the economic environment or cycle, the most widely used measures are the following:

- Gross domestic product (GDP) is a common measure of the value of output.
- Inflation measures the currency's purchasing power.
- Unemployment measures the extent to which the economy creates opportunities for participation.
- Interest rates affect the future value of money.

The U.S. government tracks GDP, inflation, and unemployment through its agencies, such as the Federal Reserve Bank, the Bureau of Labor Statistics, and the National Bureau of Economic Research. Globally, the World Bank tracks similar statistics, which are widely reported in the media as recognized **benchmarks** of a nation's economic health.

benchmarks

A standard, often an index of securities, representing an industry or asset class and used as an indicator of growth potential or as a basis of comparison for similar or disparate industries or assets.

In addition, interest rates are another financial market indicator. Interest rates are tracked intently because so much capital investment, consumer investment (for houses, cars, education), and even daily consumption relies on debt financing. The prime rate, the lowest available retail interest rate, and average mortgage rates are the most commonly followed rates.

Economists look at many other factors to measure the economy. The **index of leading economic indicators**, published monthly, includes the following:

index of leading economic indicators

A set of ten economic statistics that are used to assess the potential for economic growth.

1. The length of the average workweek (in hours)
2. Initial weekly claims for unemployment compensation
3. New orders placed with manufacturers
4. The percentage of companies receiving slower deliveries from suppliers (vendor performance)
5. Contracts and orders for new plants and equipment
6. Permits for new housing starts
7. The interest rate spread (difference) between the 10-year Treasury bond and the Federal Reserve Funds rate, the "overnight rate" that banks use to lend to each other
8. The index of consumer expectations (the University of Michigan Index)
9. Change in the value of the index of stock prices (for 500 common stocks)
10. Change in the money supply.

All these measures indicate how productive the economy is, how successful it is at creating jobs and incomes, and how much benefit it can create for consumers. A decline in the leading indicators for three consecutive months is thought to be a strong sign that the economy is in a downturn or even heading toward a recession.

Market Information

The health of financial markets is gauged by the values of various securities indexes that show the growth or decline of prices in various markets. The indexes are used to gauge the movement, direction, and rate of change as well as nominal value.

Table 14.1 lists some examples of the many stock indexes and bond indexes and the publicly traded securities they track.

TABLE 14.1 Examples of Security Indexes

Stock Indexes	
Dow Jones Average (DJA)	60 leading corporations
Dow Jones Industrial Average (DJIA)	30 leading industrial corporations
S&P 500 (Standard & Poor's)	500 largest corporations (by capital value)
NASDAQ Composite	All companies listed on the NASDAQ exchange
Russell 3000	3,000 largest U.S. companies based on total market capitalization

Bond Indexes	
Dow Jones Corporate Bond Index	96 equally weighted, recently issued corporate bonds
Barclays Capital U.S. Government/Credit Bond index	U.S. government, Treasury-related, and corporate bonds
J.P. Morgan Overseas Government Bond Index	Long-term, non-U.S. government bonds
J.P. Morgan Emerging Markets Bond Index (EMBI)	Government bonds issued by emerging countries

There is an index for anything that is traded: commodities, currencies, interest rate futures, and so on. Measures of market momentum include statistics such as the percentage of stocks that advanced (increased in value) or declined (decreased in value) or the volume of shares bought and sold. If more stocks advanced than declined, for example, that may suggest optimism for the stock market.

When interpreting index information, be aware of the investments an index represents. For example, the Dow Jones Industrial Average, or "the Dow Industrials," is quoted widely and regularly as a broad indicator of stock market performance. It was started in 1896 by Charles Dow, founder of Dow Jones, Inc., and *The Wall Street Journal*. However, the Dow consists of the equity values of only 30 of the more than 4,000 publicly traded companies.

Some companies specialize in analyzing asset classes of particular securities. Two well-known analysts of mutual fund performance are Morningstar (http://www.morningstar.com), which is geared toward investors, and Lipper Research (https://www.funds.reuters.wallst.com/US/lipperResearch.asp), which is geared toward investment managers.

Indexes are used as benchmarks for an asset class or a sector of the economy. The Standard & Poor's (S&P) 500 Index is used to benchmark the performance of large company (large cap) stocks, for example, while the Dow Jones Transportation Index is used to compare the performance of the transportation industry to that of other industries.

Industry and Company Information

An industry's media is another place to research how an industry is doing. Most industries have online trade journals and magazines that can give you an idea of industry activity, optimism, and overall health. Other sources are companies that specialize in research and analysis of industry and company data, such as Hoover's (http://www.hoovers.com) or Value Line (http://www.valueline.com).

When professionals analyze a company for its investment potential, they look first at financial statements. You can access this data as well, because all publicly traded corporations must file both annual and quarterly financial reports with the U.S. Securities and Exchange Commission (SEC). Those files are then made available on the SEC's website (http://www.sec.gov/edgar) through Electronic Data Gathering and Retrieval (EDGAR), the SEC's data bank. The annual reports (10-Ks) are audited, and the quarterly reports (10-Qs) are unaudited, but both have to show the company's financial statements and report on important developments and plans or explain unusual financial results.

The 10-K and the 10-Q can give you a good sense of what and how the company has been doing or planning for the future. Even if you have trouble reading the actual financial statements, each report also includes a discussion and analysis of the company's performance and plans by its management (in prose) that can be very informative. Similar corporate information may be found in the company's annual report, which is sent to shareholders and also available on the company's website.

An annual report is a narrative of how the company is doing. It includes financial statements, dated at least two years back so that you can see the company's progress. It also includes a discussion, presented by the company's management, of the company's strategic plans, competitive environment, industry outlook, particular risk exposures, and so on. You can get a good sense of how well positioned the company is going forward from an annual report or 10-K.

Evaluating Sources of Information

Investment information is readily available. Accessing that information is easy, but evaluating its reliability may be difficult, along with knowing how to use it. It is important to distinguish between objective news and subjective commentary. A reporter should be providing unbiased information, while a commentator is providing a subjective analysis of it. A news article ideally conveys objective facts, while an editorial or opinion provides subjective commentary. Both kinds of "news" appear in all kinds of media, such as print, radio, television, and the Internet. Most print publications have continually updated websites, some with streaming video, and there are financial social networks and blogs providing online discussion and observation.

As you explore the sources of financial news, you will develop a sense for which ones are the most useful. Table 14.2 lists a selection of financial news sites to explore.

TABLE 14.2 Sample of Financial News Sources

Publication/ News Source	Website URL	About
The Economist	www.economist.com	Print and online magazine with daily comprehensive world financial news and opinion
The Wall Street Journal	www.wsj.com	Print and online newspaper with daily world news relating to business and investment
Barron's	www.barrons.com	Print and online magazine with daily news relating to stock investing
Market Watch	www.marketwatch.com	Daily online data and commentary on companies and the financial markets

Publication/ News Source	Website URL	About
Bloomberg	www.bloomberg.com	Television, radio, print, and online news with articles about companies and comprehensive data on world financial markets
Kiplinger's	www.kiplinger.com	Print and online personal finance information and advice for individual investors and small businesses
Motley Fool	www.fool.com	Financial services site offering news, investment advice, and infotainment for individual investors
CNN Money	www.money.cnn.com	Television, radio, mobile, and online business, financial, and personal finance news
Forbes Magazine	www.forbes.com	Print, online, and broadcast business news, financial news, stock market analysis, and rankings
The Street	www.thestreet.com	Online business news and personal finance and investing advice and stock picks

As you survey these news sources, be aware of features that might lead you to trust an online source of information. The following are some questions to help you evaluate the credibility of a website:[1]

1. Can the content be corroborated? (Check some of the facts.)
2. Is the site recommended by a content expert? (Look for a rating or recommendation.)
3. Is the author reputable? (Search on the author's name.)
4. Do you see the site as accurate? (Check with other sources.)
5. Was the information reviewed by peers or editors? (Read the reviews or logs.)
6. Is the author associated with a reputable organization? (Search on the organization.)
7. Is the publisher reputable? (Search on the publisher's name.)
8. Are the authors and sources identified? (Look for source citations or references.)
9. Do you see the site as current? (Check "last updated" or headline date.)
10. Do other websites link to this one? (Look for links.)
11. Is the site recommended by a generalist? (Ask a librarian.)
12. Is the site recommended by an independent subject area guide? (See site referrals.)
13. Does the domain include a trademark name? (Look for a trademark in the URL.)
14. Is the site's bias clear? (Read the "About." Look for a statement of purpose. Read the author's profile.)
15. Does the site have a professional look? (Look for a clean design and error-free writing.)

The more questions you can answer in the affirmative, the higher the credibility of the website and the more you can trust it as a source of information. The same questions can be extended to evaluate the reliability of specific online financial news sources.

Key Takeaways

- Useful investment information analyzes the current economic, industry, and company performance.
- Leading economic indicators are used to gauge the current economic cycle and the outlook for the economy.
- Indexes are used to gauge financial market activity and as benchmarks for asset classes and industries.
- Analysis and forecasting of company performance is based on publicly reported information from SEC filings and from corporate annual reports.
- Many media provide investment information and advice for both experienced and novice individual investors, and such advice is readily available online.
- The key to finding useful information is in understanding the credibility and reliability of its source.

Exercises

1. What four measures are the most important indicators of the health of the economy? What are the other leading economic indicators? Go to a financial news source to find out the status of all the economic indicators at this time. Make note of your findings and the date for purposes of comparison. How does the information inform you as an investor? Discuss with classmates the implications of the economic indicators for investing. For example, read the results of the most recent Consumer Confidence Survey at http://www.conference-board.org/data/consumerconfidence.cfm. How might these survey results inform you as an investor?
2. Read the latest summary of the index of leading economic indicators at https://www.conference-board.org/data. How might an investor use the reported information in making investment decisions? Survey the indexes listed in Table 14.1. What role might each index play in choosing assets for a portfolio?
3. Visit the SEC's EDGAR site at http://www.sec.gov/edgar.shtml. Take the tutorial to familiarize yourself with how the site works and then click on "Search for Company Filings." Input the name of a company with publicly traded stock of interest to you. Then click on the company's most recent annual report it filed with the SEC. Read the annual report in its entirety, including parts you don't understand. Jot down your questions as you read as if you are thinking of buying shares in that company. What information encourages you in that decision? What information raises questions or concerns? Go to the company's website and check its online documents, news, updates, and the current status of its stock. Are you further encouraged? Why or why not? Where can you go next to get data and commentary about the company as an investment opportunity?
4. Survey the news sources listed in Table 14.2 and number the sites to rank them in order of their usefulness to you at this time. Record in your personal finance journal or My Notes your top five sources of financial information and why you chose them.
5. Have you ever mistaken a press release or a blog for hard news when looking for information online? Read the interviews with journalists, bloggers, and others debating the reliability and accuracy of news disseminated through the Internet at http://www.pbs.org/wgbh/pages/frontline/newswar/tags/reliability.html. This PBS Frontline special delves into the questions of the credibility and reliability of news information, including financial news and blogs that we access online. Commentators include Ted Koppel, Larry Kramer, Eric Schmidt, Craig Newmark, and others. Discuss with classmates the positions taken in this debate. In My Notes or your personal finance journal, write an essay expressing your own conclusions about trusting financial information you find online and using it to make personal finance decisions.

14.3 Investing and Trading

Learning Objectives

1. Identify the important differences between types of investment agents.
2. Describe the different levels of service offered by investment agents.
3. Analyze the different fee and account structures available to investors.
4. Differentiate the types of trading orders and explain their roles in an investment strategy.

The discussion of investment so far has focused on the ideas behind your investment plan, but to be useful to you, your plan has to be implemented. You have to invest, and then, over time, trade. How do you access the capital markets? How and when do you buy, sell, or hold?

To answer these questions you need to know the types of agents who exercise trades in the financial markets; the types of services, accounts, and fees they offer; and the kinds of trading orders they execute on your behalf.

FIGURE 14.2

Agents: Brokers and Dealers

The markets or exchanges for stocks, bonds, commodities, or funds are membership organizations. Unless you are a member of the exchange, you cannot trade on the exchange without hiring an agent to execute trades for you. Trading essentially is buying and selling.

broker

An intermediary that acts as an agent for buyers or sellers to arrange a trade.

dealer

A professional investor trading for its own account.

broker-dealer

An intermediary that acts as an agent for buyers or sellers and also trades for its own account.

discretionary trading

An investor-broker relationship where the broker is empowered to make investment decisions and trades on behalf of the client.

advisory dealing

An investor-broker relationship where the broker provides advice and guidance to the client, but investment decisions remain the client's.

execution-only

An investor-broker relationship where the broker's only role is to execute trades per the investor's decisions.

As you've read in Chapter 12, a **broker** is an agent who trades on behalf of clients to fulfill client directives. A **dealer** is a firm that is trading for its own account. Many firms act as **broker-dealers**, trading on behalf of both clients and the firm's account. Many brokers, dealers, and broker-dealers are independent firms, but many are subsidiaries or operations of large investment banks, commercial banks, or investment companies.

Firms may offer different levels of brokerage services:

- **Discretionary trading** means that the broker is empowered to make investment decisions and trades on behalf of the client.
- **Advisory dealing** means that the broker provides advice and guidance to the client, but investment decisions remain with the client.
- **Execution-only** service means that the broker's only role is to execute trades per the investor's decisions.

Almost all brokerages provide online and mobile access, and most allow you to access your account information, including trading history, and to place orders and receive order confirmations online. Some discount brokers operate only online, that is, they have no retail or storefront offices at all. This allows them to lower costs and fees. Most brokerages still send out hard copies of such information as well. Some also provide research reports and tools such as calculators and data for making asset allocation decisions.

Fees

As firms offer different levels of service, their compensation or fee structures may vary. A broker is compensated for executing a trade by receiving a commission based on the volume of the security traded and its price. A discount broker may offer lower commissions on trades but may provide execution-only services.

A firm may offer all levels of service or specialize in just one. Large discount brokers such as Fidelity, Scottrade, or Charles Schwab may provide a full range of services along with execution-only services that charge lower commissions on trades. Other discount brokers and online-only brokers may charge a lower flat fee per trade, rather than a commission on the amount of the trade. Some firms charge a commission on trades and a fee for advisory or discretionary services. The fee is usually a percentage of the value of the portfolio. Some charge a flat fee for a quarterly or annual portfolio check-up and advisory services.

churning

A broker practice of executing trades for a client's account solely to create commissions for the broker.

Both the commission-based and the fee-based compensation structures have critics. The commission-based structure results in more compensation for the broker (and more cost for you) if there are a greater number of trades. This can lead some brokers to engage in excessive trading, called **churning**—an unwarranted and unnecessary amount of trading in your account for which the broker is being compensated.

On the other hand, a fee structure based on a percentage of the value of the assets under management can reward a broker for doing nothing. If the economy expands and asset values rise, the value of the portfolio—and therefore the broker's compensation—may rise without any effort on the broker's part.

The most economical recourse for an investor is to find a broker who charges a flat fee for advisory services, independent of portfolio size, and discount fees for commissions on trading. The costs of investing and trading depend on how much trading you do and how involved you are in the investment decisions. The more of the research and advisory work you do for yourself, the less your costs should be.

Brokerage Accounts

Two basic types of brokerage accounts are cash accounts or margin accounts. With a **cash account**, you can trade using only the cash you deposit into the account directly or as a result of previous trades, dividends, or interest payments. The cash account is the most common kind of brokerage account.

With a **margin account**, you may trade in amounts exceeding the cash available in the account, in effect borrowing from your broker to complete the financing of the trade. The investor is said to be "trading on margin." The broker usually requires a minimum value for a margin account and extends credit based on the value of the cash and securities in the portfolio. If your portfolio value drops below the minimum-value threshold, perhaps because securities values have dropped, then you may be faced with a **margin call**. The broker calls on you to deposit more into the account.

Investors pay interest on funds borrowed on margin. As regulated by the Federal Reserve, the amount of an investment financed by debt or bought on margin is limited. The **margin requirement** is the percentage of the investment's value that must be paid for in cash.

Custodial accounts are accounts created for minors under the federal Uniform Gifts to Minors Act (UGMA) of 1956 or the Uniform Transfers to Minors Act (UTMA) of 1986. The account is legally owned by the minor and is in his or her name, but an adult custodian must be named for the account. Otherwise, the owner of a brokerage account must be a legal adult. The account is created at a bank, brokerage firm, or mutual fund company and is managed by an adult for an underage child (as defined by the state).

Establishing a brokerage account is as easy as opening a bank account or credit card account. You will need a good credit rating, especially for a margin account, a reasonable source of income, and a minimum deposit of assets. Many brokers allow you to transfer assets from another brokerage account with minimal effort.

cash account

A brokerage account where investments are paid for from money on deposit.

margin account

A brokerage account allowing the investor to purchase securities with funds borrowed from the broker.

margin call

The requirement that an investor invest more capital to maintain the margin requirement, or the investor's equity in the investment.

margin requirement

The percentage of security value that must represent capital from the investor (as opposed to money borrowed from the broker).

custodial account

A brokerage account for a minor, established with a guardian (adult) who is authorized to make trading decisions.

Brokerage Orders

You need not be an expert in the arcane language brokers use to describe trades, so long as you understand the basic types of orders you can request. Say you want to buy 100 shares of X Corporation's common stock. You call your broker and ask the price. The broker says that at this moment, the market is "50 bid-50.25 ask." Stock exchanges are auction markets; that is, buyers bid what they are willing to pay and sellers ask what they're willing to accept. If the market is "50 bid-50.25 ask," this means that right now the consensus among buyers is that they are willing to pay $50 per share, while sellers are willing to accept $50.25. The "bid-ask spread" or difference is 25 cents.

If you then place a **market order** to buy a hundred shares, the order will be executed at the lowest asking price—the least that the seller is willing to accept. In other words, you will pay $50.25 per share, the asking price, to buy the stock.

market order

An order to trade at the market price.

limit order

A trading order to buy or sell a security at a specific price.

long position

Ownership of securities; used in the strategy of "going long," which involves buying a security so that if the price rises, its sale will create a gain.

short position

Owing securities because of having borrowed them from a broker; used in the strategy of "shorting," which involves borrowing and selling a security so that if the price falls, you can create a gain when the securities are repurchased to be returned.

stop-loss order

An order to sell a security once its price has fallen below a specified price.

stop-buy order

An order to buy a security once its price has risen above a specified price.

You could also place a **limit order** to buy the shares when the price is lower, say $45 per share (or to sell when the price is higher, say $55), specifying how long the order is in effect. If the price goes down to $45 (or up to $55) within the period of time, then your limit order will be filled, and otherwise it will not.

When you buy a security, you are said to have a **long position** in that security; you own it. You could close out your position by selling it. When you "go long" in a security, you are expecting its value to rise, so that you can buy it for a lower price and then sell it for a higher price.

Alternatively, you could create a **short position** in the security by borrowing it from your broker, selling it, and then buying it back and returning it to your broker at some specified point in the future. When you "short" a security, you are expecting its value to decrease, so that you can sell it at a high price and then buy it back at a lower price.

Other specialized kinds of orders include a **stop-loss order**, where you direct that the stock be sold when it reaches a certain price (below the current price) in order to limit your potential loss if the value decreases. You can use a **stop-buy order** to buy a stock at a certain price (above the current price) if you have "shorted" a security and want to limit your loss if its value rises.

If you are following a "buy-and-hold" strategy, you are establishing positions that you plan to hold for a long time. With this strategy you probably will do well to use a market order. Over the long term that you hold your position, the daily fluctuations in price won't matter.

Key Takeaways

- A broker trades on behalf of clients; a dealer trades for its own account, and a broker-dealer does both.
- Brokers, dealers, and broker-dealers may be independent firms or subsidiaries of investment banks, commercial banks, or investment companies.
- Firms may offer several levels of brokerage services, defining their roles as active manager, advisor, and/or traders:
    - discretionary trading,
    - advisory dealing,
    - execution only.
- Brokerage fees are based on the level of service provided and may consist of
    - commissions on trading,
    - advisory fees based on portfolio value, or
    - a flat fee for management.
- Brokerage accounts may be
    - cash accounts,
    - margin accounts, or
    - custodial accounts.
- Trading orders allow you to better execute a specific trading strategy:
    - market orders,
    - limit orders,
    - stop-loss orders, or
    - stop-buy orders.

Exercises

1. Read the information at the following sites about choosing an investment broker or brokerage firm: http://beginnersinvest.about.com/od/choosingabroker/a/brokeraccount.htm. In My Notes or your personal finance journal, record the top ten questions about a broker or brokerage that will guide your choice. What answers will you be looking for? See how the investment industry evaluates brokers at https://www.stockbrokers.com/guides/barrons-broker-survey.
2. What information (or inspiration) useful for personal finance can you get at Money Blue Book (http://www.moneybluebook.com)? How would you evaluate the Money Blue Book website as a source of financial news, information, and advice? In your opinion, how do sites such as Money Chimp (http://www.moneychimp.com/), and Get Rich Slowly (http://www.getrichslowly.org/blog/) compare?

14.4 Ethics and Regulation

Learning Objectives

1. Discuss the reasons that investing behavior may be unethical.
2. Identify the key professional responsibilities of investment agents.
3. Describe practices that investment agents should pursue or avoid to fulfill their professional responsibilities.
4. Explain how investment agents are regulated.
5. Debate the role of government oversight in the securities industry.

Financial markets, perhaps more than most, seem to seduce otherwise good citizens into unethical or even illegal behavior. There are several reasons:

1. Investing is a complex, volatile, and unpredictable process, such that the complexity of the process lowers the probability of getting caught.
2. The stakes are high enough and the probability of getting caught is low enough so that the benefits can easily seem to outweigh the costs. The benefits can even blind participants to the costs of getting caught.
3. The complexity of the situation may allow some initial success, and the unethical investor or broker becomes overconfident, encouraging more unethical behavior.
4. Employers may put their employees under pressure to act in the company's interests rather than clients' interests.

To counteract these realities there are three forces at work: market forces, professional standards, and legal restrictions. But before these topics are discussed, it is useful to review the differences between ethical and unethical, or professional and unprofessional, behaviors in this context.

Professional Ethics

Investment intermediaries or agents such as advisors, brokers, and dealers have responsibilities to their clients, their employers, and the markets. In carrying out these responsibilities, they should demonstrate appropriate professional conduct. Professional conduct is ethical, that is, it is based on moral principles of right and wrong as expressed in the profession's standards of conduct.

prudence

Acting with sound and responsible judgment; in investing, prudence implies a relative conservatism regarding risk.

due diligence

Competent and adequate research into an investment proposal to be able to project its returns and its potential risks.

front-running

An agent trading for his or her own account before executing trading orders for clients.

Brokers and advisors should always deal objectively and fairly with clients, putting clients' interests before their own. In other words, a broker should always give higher priority to the client's wealth than to his or her own. When acting on a client's behalf, a broker should always be aware of the trust that has been placed on him or her and act with **prudence** and care. The principle of **due diligence** stipulates, for example, that investment advisors and brokers must investigate and report to the investor every detail of a potential investment.

Kim, a broker at a large brokerage firm, receives an order from a client to sell shares because the client believes the stock price will drop. Kim believes the client is right and so decides to sell her own personal shares in that stock as well. She places the order to sell her shares first, so that if the price drops as she sells, her shares will be sold at a higher price. She places the order to sell the client's shares after the price has dropped. This practice of taking advantage of the client by not putting the client first is called **front-running**. According to professional ethics, Kim should be putting her client's interest—and order—ahead of her own.

Professional ethics call for brokers and advisors to disclose any potential conflicts of interest they may have. They also should be diligent and thorough when researching investments and making recommendations and should have an objective basis for their advice. Investment recommendations should be suitable for the client, and advice should be given with the best interests of the client in mind.

Shonte is a financial advisor for a large broker-dealer that has acquired a large position in a certain bond issue. It now owns a lot of bonds. Wanting to reduce the company's exposure to risk from that position, Shonte's boss suggests that she should advise her clients to add this bond to their portfolios. That way the company can use its clients to buy its bonds and reduce its position. This conduct is unethical, however. Shonte should not automatically recommend the bond to all her clients because her advice should be based solely on the individual clients' interests and needs, not the company's.

FIGURE 14.3

© Shutterstock, Inc.

An advisor or broker should:

- be forthcoming about how the investment analysis was done and the changes or events could affect the outcome;
- not present himself or herself as a "guru" with a special or secret method of divining investment opportunities;
- clearly explain the logic and grounding for all judgments and advice;
- not try to pressure you into making an investment decision or use threats or scare tactics to influence you;
- communicate regularly and clearly with you about your portfolio performance and any market or economic changes that may affect its performance.

In addition to being loyal to clients, brokers and advisors are expected to be loyal to employers, the professions, and the financial markets. Accepting side deals, gifts, or "kickbacks," for example, may damage a company's reputation, harm colleagues as well as clients, and betray the profession. Loyalty to market integrity is shown by keeping the markets competitive and fair. For example, brokers should use only information available to all. Information from private sources to which others do not have access is **inside information**, and making trades on the basis of inside information is called **insider trading**.

inside information

Information that is not publicly available that has a material effect on an investment's value.

insider trading

The illegal practice of trading securities based on nonpublic or "inside" information.

For example, Jorge, a broker, just found out from a client that the company she works for is about to be granted a patent for a new product. The information has not yet been announced publicly, but it will almost certainly increase the value of the company's stock. Jorge is tempted to buy the stock immediately, before the news breaks, both for his employer's account and his own. He would almost surely profit and gain points with his boss as well. But that would be wrong. Trading on inside information would be disloyal to the integrity of the markets, and it is illegal.

Brokers and advisors should not manipulate markets or try to influence or distort prices to mislead market participants. Attempts to do so have become more widespread with the tremendous growth of electronic communications. For example, Tom, a dealer, has just shorted a large position in a tech stock. On his widely read blog, he announces that his "research" has revealed serious weaknesses in the tech company's marketing strategy and rumors of competitors' greater advantages in the market. Tom has no factual basis for his reporting, but if his "news" causes the price of the tech stock to fall, he will profit from his short position. Tom's attempts to manipulate the market are unethical and unprofessional.

Regulation of Advisors, Brokers, and Dealers

It is often said that the financial markets are self-regulating and self-policing. Market forces may be effective in correcting or preventing unprofessional conduct, but they often are not, so there are also professional and legal sanctions.

Sanctions provide deterrence and punishment. Registered brokers and advisors, and their firms, typically are members of professional organizations with regulatory powers. For example, professional organizations have qualifications for membership and may award credentials or accreditation that their members would not want to lose.

There are many professional designations and accreditations in the investment advising and brokerage fields (Chapter 1). However, keep in mind that no professional affiliation or designation is required to give investment advice.

The U.S. securities industry is formally regulated by federal and state governments. Government sanctions and limits have been imposed gradually, usually after a major market failure or scandal, and so form a collection of rules and laws overseen by a variety of agencies.

The Securities and Exchange Commission (SEC) is a federal government agency empowered to oversee the trading of securities and the exchanges in the capital markets. It was created in 1934 in response to the behavior that precipitated the stock market crash in 1929 and the subsequent failure of the banking system. The SEC investigates illegal activities such as trading on insider information, front-running, fraud, and market manipulation.

The SEC also requires information disclosures to inform the public about companies' financial performance and business strategy. Investors must report to the SEC their intention to acquire more than 5% of a company's shares, and business executives must report to the SEC when they buy or sell shares in their own company. The SEC then tries to minimize the use of insider information by making it publicly available.

self-regulatory organizations (SROs)

A nongovernmental organization that regulates a profession or industry.

The SEC delegates authority to **self-regulatory organizations (SROs)**, such as the National Association of Securities Dealers (NASD), and the national stock exchanges, such as the New York Stock Exchange (NYSE). NASD and the exchanges uphold industry standards and compliance requirements for trading securities and operating brokerages.

In 2007, the SEC created a new SRO that reincorporated the NASD, renamed as the Financial Industry Regulatory Authority (FINRA). FINRA's job is to focus exclusively on the enforcement of rules governing the securities industry. In addition, Congress created the Municipal Securities Rulemaking Board (MSRB) as an SRO. The MSRB's job is to create rules to protect investors involved with broker-dealers and banks that trade in tax-exempt bonds and 529 college savings plans.

Figure 14.4 shows the structure of the securities industry's regulatory environment.

FIGURE 14.4 Regulatory Environment of the U.S. Securities Industry

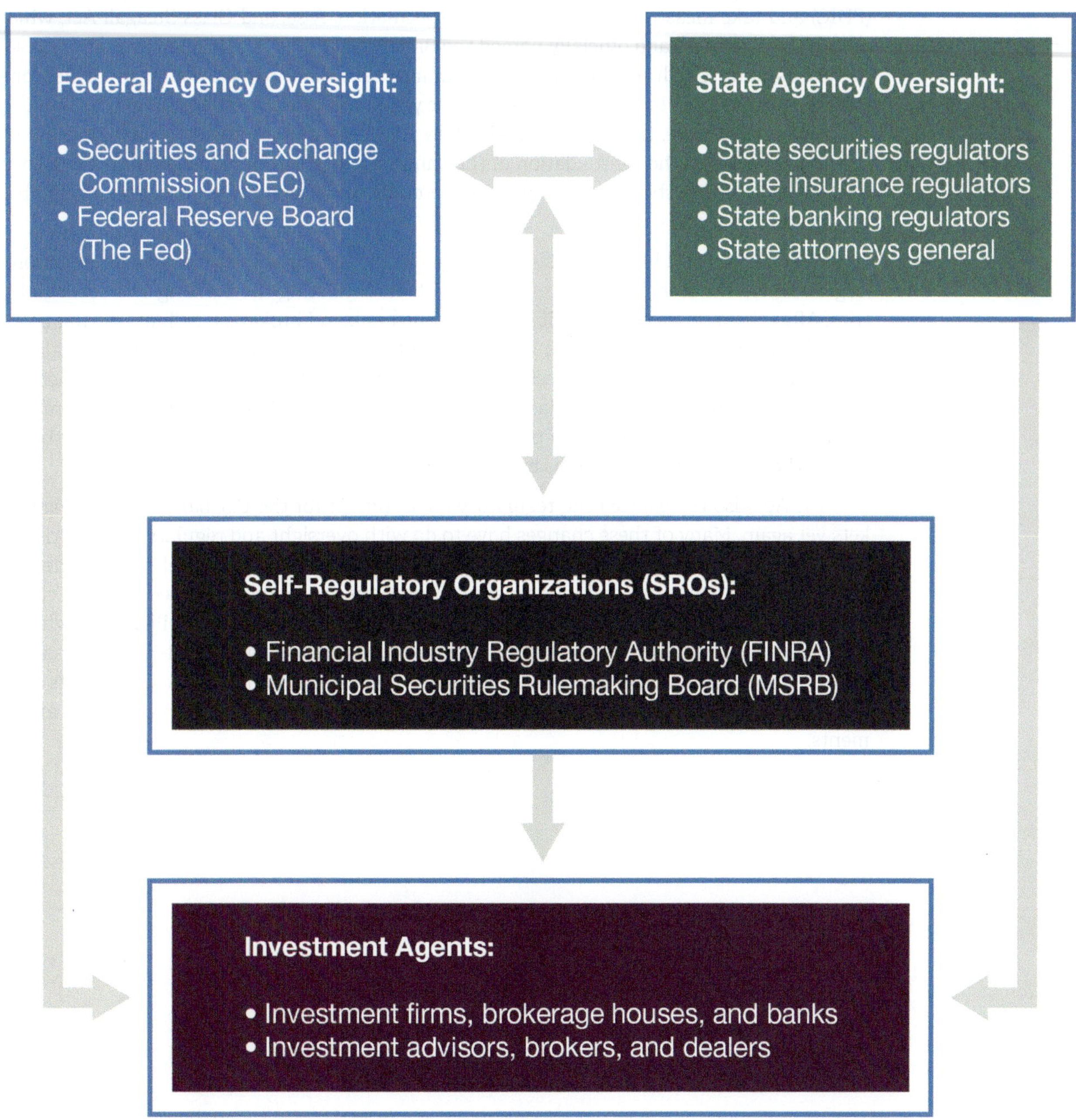

The Federal Reserve has the primary responsibility of regulating banks and the banking system. When investment brokering and advising are services of investment or commercial banks, their actions may fall under the control of both the SEC and the Fed, as well as state banking and insurance regulators. States license investment agents. Also, each state's attorney general is responsible for investigating securities violations in that state.

Government regulation of capital markets has long been a contentious issue in the United States. During periods of expansion and rising asset prices, there are fewer calls for regulation and enforcement and often more demands for less regulation and enforcement. Clients and investment agents may have fewer complaints because of investment gains and increasing earnings. When a bubble bursts or there is a true financial crisis, however, then investors demand protections and enforcement.

For example, after the stock market crash in 1929 and the widespread bank failures of 1930–1933, the Glass-Steagall Act was passed in 1933 to establish the Federal Deposit Insurance Corporation (FDIC) and take measures to reduce market speculation. A second Glass-Steagall Act, which was passed the same year and officially named the Banking Act of 1933, separated investment and commercial banking to reduce potential conflicts of interest when a bank is issuing securities for a firm that it is also lending to. In 1999, however, after years of economic expansion and at the height of the tech stock bubble, the Gramm-Leach-Bliley Act effectively repealed the Banking Act of 1933, opening the way for the consolidation of the banking industry. This consolidation led to the introduction of "one-stop-shopping" banks, which provide investment, commercial, and retail banking services all under one roof.

The financial and banking crisis that began in 2007 led to calls for increased regulation and a larger role for the federal and state governments in regulating the banking and securities industries. After the mortgage and credit crises and the bank and brokerage bailouts during 2008–2009, the federal government passed the Wall Street Reform and Consumer Protection Act, also known as "Dodd-Frank" for its main congressional sponsors, Senator Christopher Dodd of Connecticut and Representative Barney Frank of Massachusetts. The Dodd-Frank Act tries to limit the market risk created by any specific institution or investment practice, thus limiting the need for the government to bail out failing institutions by providing them with capital.

The Act also reorganized the regulatory environment for the U.S. banking and financial markets yet again. Many of these changes have to do with oversight and regulation of the risks banks and investment companies are allowed to take, both for clients and for shareholders. Other changes address disclosures banks and investment corporations are required to make, both to clients and to shareholders. Major changes include the creation of a new Financial Stability Oversight Council, an interagency overseer and coordinator for other oversight agencies. Dodd-Frank also created the Consumer Financial Protection Bureau (CFPB) to oversee consumer financial products issued by banks, insurance companies, and investment companies, particularly mortgages, credit, and investments.

Figure 14.5 shows federal agencies and their regulatory roles as created or modified by Dodd-Frank.

FIGURE 14.5 Federal Agency Oversight Roles

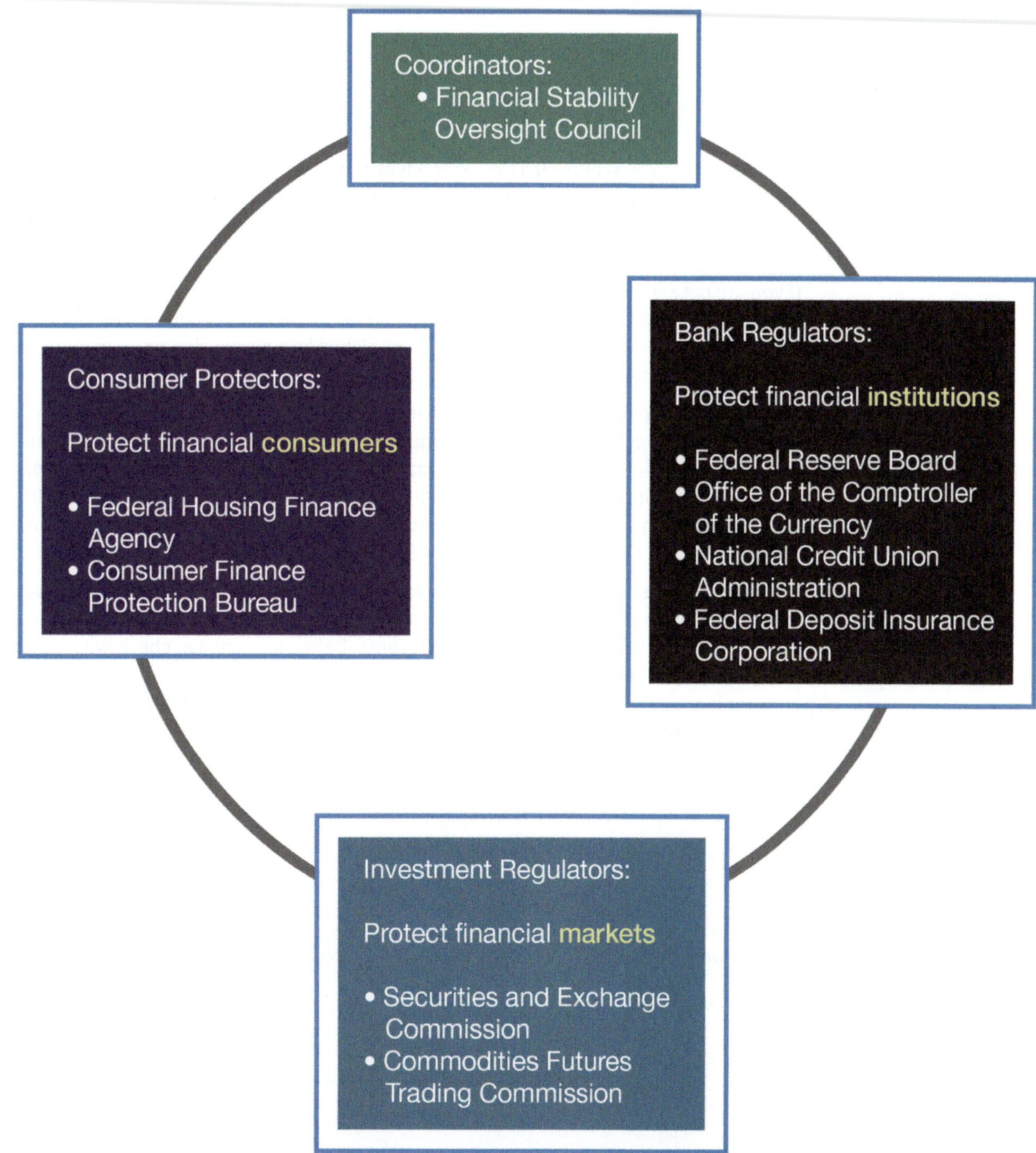

In the United States, these agencies regulate institutions (e.g., banks and brokerages), markets (e.g., a stock or bond market), and consumers of financial products (e.g., depositors and investors). Although Figure 14.5 makes it look like these functions are neatly dispersed among agencies, that is not the case, mainly because finance simultaneously takes place for all three actors: the actions of *consumers and investors* use *financial institutions* that use *markets*. Often, several agencies will be investigating or ruling on an incident or making a policy decision. Dodd-Frank does attempt to consolidate some of this activity or at least to coordinate it better.

While history shows that the kinds of regulation and amount of government oversight will vary, there clearly will always be a role for federal and state government regulators. And it will never be simple or easy.

Investor Protection

As an investor, you have recourse if a broker or advisor has been unethical, unprofessional, or criminal in his or her conduct. If the offending agent is working for a brokerage firm or bank, a complaint to a superior is sometimes all that is needed. The firm would prefer not to risk its reputation for one "bad apple."

If you are not satisfied, however, you can lodge a formal complaint with a professional organization such as the relevant SRO. The SROs have standard procedures in place and will investigate your complaint. If necessary, the offender will be punished by a suspension or permanent removal of his or her professional designation or certification.

You can also complain to the SEC, the CFPB, or a state or federal consumer protection agency; file suit in civil court; or press for a criminal complaint. Due to their complexities, investment cases are often difficult to prove, so you should consult with an attorney who is experienced with such cases. Often when a broker or advisor has used illegal practices, she or he has done so with more than one client. When you are not the only victim, the state or federal prosecutor or your lawyer may choose to bring a class-action suit on behalf of all the client-victims.

As always, the best defense is to take care in choosing an investment advisor or broker. Most investment agents are chosen by word of mouth, recommendations from trusted family members, friends, or colleagues who have been satisfied clients. Before you choose, check with the professional organization with which he or she claims affiliation or certification and review any records of past complaints or offenses. You can also check with government agencies such as your state's attorney general's office.

Your choice of advisor or broker depends largely on your expected use of services, as suggested in Table 14.3.

TABLE 14.3 Choosing an Investment Advisor or Broker

<table>
<tr><th>Your Role</th><th>Agent's Role</th><th>Type of Firm</th></tr>
<tr><td rowspan="3">You anticipate doing your own research and making your own investment decisions.</td><td rowspan="3">You want convenient access and someone to execute trades for you at a secure, accessible, and informative brokerage.</td><td>National or international firm with many branches</td></tr>
<tr><td>Internet brokerage available 24/7</td></tr>
<tr><td>Brokerage account at a one-stop shopping bank</td></tr>
<tr><td rowspan="2">You are looking for a lot of personal guidance and investment advice.</td><td rowspan="2">You want an advisor to provide independent advice on investment planning and asset allocation and a separate broker who is willing to discuss research as it relates to your plan and to implement your trades. The advisor and the broker each act as a "second opinion" to the other.</td><td>A certified financial advisor</td></tr>
<tr><td>A highly rated, stable brokerage firm or discount brokerage</td></tr>
</table>

You will be investing over a lifetime. The economic, market, and personal circumstances will change and your plans and strategies will change, but your advisors and brokers should be able to help you learn from experience and prosper from—or despite—those changes.

Key Takeaways

- Investing behavior may be unethical because:
  - its complexity lowers the probability of getting caught,
  - the stakes are high,
  - initial success may encourage more unethical behavior,
  - companies may expect that their interests have priority.
- Investment agents have responsibilities to
  - their clients,
  - employers,
  - professions,
  - markets.
- To fulfill those responsibilities, brokers should always put the interests of clients, employers, professions, and markets before their own, and should not practice:
  - front-running,
  - insider trading,
  - market manipulation.
- Regulation of investment agents comes from:
  - market forces,
  - professional associations and self-regulating organizations,
  - state and federal government oversight and enforcement agencies.
- Levels of government oversight are politically contentious and subject to change.
- Through consumer protection laws, investors have recourse for losses from unprofessional or illegal behavior. The best protection is to make good choices among financial advisors and investment brokers.

Exercises

1. Read the Securities and Exchange Commission's explanation of what it does at http://www.sec.gov/about/whatwedo.shtml. In what ways is the SEC your advocate as an investor? List your answers in your personal finance journal or My Notes. Disclosure, fair dealing, and transparency are the SEC's watchwords. What do they refer to? The SEC is a complex government agency. What are its divisions? What organizations does the SEC work with? What laws does the SEC enforce? What number can you call if you have a question or complaint about your experience as an investor?
2. Go to the SEC's site on self-regulatory organizations of the securities industry at http://www.sec.gov/rules/sro.shtml. Click on an SRO and read the new rules it is making. Discuss with classmates how you would comment on them, as you are invited to do.
3. Debate with classmates the desirability of government regulation of the financial markets at the federal, state, and organizational levels. What impacts do regulation and deregulation have on the economy, the markets, and you as an investor? What are some concrete examples of those impacts? Write an essay declaring and supporting your position on this issue.

14.5 Investing Internationally: Risks and Regulations

Learning Objectives

1. Identify the unusual risks of foreign investing compared to domestic investing.
2. Explain the role of international investments in an investment strategy.

Investing is global. While the financial markets and the capital markets may resemble a global village, it is also true that investing in assets governed by foreign standards and regulations creates additional concerns.

FIGURE 14.6

© Shutterstock, Inc.

Investments in foreign securities are used to diversify an investment portfolio's economic risk. The United States, most nations in Europe, and Japan have highly developed economies. Other economies may be developing, such as India and China; may be emerging, such as Nigeria and Bolivia; and may be using different strategies to achieve different rates of growth. The world economy is truly global, however, because although different economies may be in different stages of development, they are all intimately linked through trade.

Different economies offer different kinds of opportunities because of where they are in their progress toward free-market economic diversification and stability. Along with different opportunities, however, they also offer different risks. These risks run the gamut from the challenge of interpreting information correctly to the risk that too much or too little regulation will interfere with market forces. International investing also exposes the investor to risks relating to foreign markets, economies, currencies, and politics.

Investment Information

A general concern in international investing is the flow and quality of information. You make investment decisions by gathering and evaluating information. That information is useful to you because you know how to interpret it, and because you know the standardized way in which that information was gathered and prepared.

In the United States, financial statements are prepared using Generally Accepted Accounting Principles, or GAAP, the rules that frame accounting judgments. Those statements may then be audited by an independent certified public accountant (CPA) to assure that the accounting rules have been followed.

In other countries, however, accountants do not use GAAP. They prepare financial statements by somewhat different rules. Some of those differences relate significantly to asset valuations, a key factor in your decision to invest. When you read financial reports written for foreign companies, therefore, you need to remain mindful that they are written under different rules and may not mean the same as financial reports following the U.S. GAAP. At the very least, you should determine whether the statements you are reading were independently audited.

Other countries also have different standards and procedures for making information available to investors. One reason that the SEC requires filings of annual and quarterly reports is to make information publicly and readily available. Other countries may not have such corporate filing requirements. Information may be harder to get, and the information that you do get may not be as complete or as uniform.

Other kinds of information are also important. A good brokerage or advisory firm will have analysts and researchers "on the ground," tracking economic and cultural influences in foreign countries as well as corporations with promising earnings.

Market, Economic, and Currency Risks

Unless a foreign security is listed on an American exchange, you or your broker will have to purchase it through a foreign exchange. In the United States, a substantial volume of trade keeps markets liquid, except in relatively rare times of crisis. This may not be true on some foreign exchanges. In active major capital markets such as in Western Europe and Japan, there will be plenty of liquidity, but in some emerging markets, such as in Africa, there may not be. This means that your risk in holding an investment increases because you may find it difficult to sell when you want to, just because the market is not liquid at that time.

Market risk also affects pricing. Market liquidity and the volume of trade helps the market to function more efficiently in the pricing of assets, so you are more likely to get a favorable price when trading.

Foreign investments are often used to diversify domestic investments just because foreign economies are different. They may be in different business cycles or in different stages of development. While the United States has a long-established, developed market economy, other countries may have emerging market economies with less capitalization and less experience in market-driven economic patterns.

Other economies also have different strengths and weaknesses, sources of growth and vulnerabilities. The U.S. economy is fairly well-diversified, whereas another economy may be more dependent on fewer industries or on commodities or natural resources whose prices are volatile. Prospects for economic growth may differ based on health care and education, tax policies, and trade policies. You want to be sure your investment is in an economy that can nurture or at least accommodate growth.

currency risk

The risk that an investment denominated in a different currency will suffer a loss due to exchange rate volatility.

Perhaps the greatest risk in international investing is **currency risk**, risk to the value of the foreign currency. To invest overseas, you may have to use foreign currency, and you receive your return in foreign currency. When you change the foreign currency back into your own currency, differences in the values of the currencies—the exchange rate—could make your return more or less valuable.

Tim decides to invest in a French business when the exchange rate between the euro (France) and the dollar (U.S.) is €1.00 = $1.00. So, Tim buys €1,000 of the French company's stock for $1,000 (assuming no transaction costs for the currency exchange or for broker's fees). One year goes by and Tim decides to sell the stock. The stock is the same price, €1,000, but the exchange rate has changed. Now €1.00 = $0.87. If Tim sells his stock, even though its value has not changed, his €1,000 will only come to $870. Tim has incurred a loss, not because the value of the investment decreased, but because the value of his currency did.

The exchange rate between two currencies fluctuates, depending on many macroeconomic factors in each economy. At times there can be considerable volatility. Exchange rates are especially affected by inflation, especially when the spread in exchange rates between two countries is greater. When you are investing abroad, consider the time period you expect to hold your investment and the outlook for exchange rate fluctuations during that period.

Political Risks

Governments protect an economy and participate in it as both consumers and producers. The extent to which they do so is a major difference among governments and their economies.

The government's role in an economy influences its growth potential. When investing in a foreign company, you should consider the government's effect on its growth. Economic and political stability are important indicators for growth.

Because investing is long term, investors try to predict an investment's performance, and forecasting requires a stable context. The type of economy or government is less relevant than its relative stability. A country given to economic upheaval or with a history of weak governments or high government turnover is a less stable environment for investment.

Market-based economies thrive when markets thrive, so anything the government does to support markets will foster a better environment for investing. While some market regulation is helpful, too much may work against market liquidity and thus investors. A central bank that can encourage market liquidity and help stabilize an economy is also helpful.

In 1995 the Heritage Foundation and *The Wall Street Journal* created the Index of Economic Freedom (IEF) to try to measure a country's welcoming of investment and encouragement of economic growth. Using data from the World Bank and the International Monetary Fund (IMF), the IEF is based on 10 indicators of economic freedom that measure the governments' support and constraint of individual wealth and trade.

The resulting report is published every year. Take a look at the interactive map at the Foundation's website: https://www.heritage.org/index/heatmap. The map illustrates the Index of Economic Freedom compiled by the Heritage Foundation for 2018. The green countries, notably Hong Kong, Singapore, New Zealand, Australia, and Ireland are the most "free," and the red countries (concentrated in central and sub-Saharan Africa, parts of the Middle East, and South America) are the least.

Governments can change, peacefully or violently, slowly or suddenly, and can even change their philosophies in governing, especially as they affect participation in the global economy. Fiscal, monetary, and tax policies can change as well as fundamental attitudes toward entrepreneurship, ownership, and wealth. For example, the sudden nationalization or privatization of companies or industries can increase or decrease growth, return potential, market liquidity, volatility, and even the viability of those companies or industries. Because changes in fundamental government policies will affect the economy and its markets, you should research the country to learn as much as possible about its political risks to you as an investor.

Foreign Regulatory Environments

One of the largest political risks is regulatory risk: that a government will regulate its economy too little or too much. Too little regulation would reduce the flow of information, allowing companies to keep information from investors and to trade on inside information. A lack of regulatory oversight would also allow more unethical behavior, such as front-running and conflicts of interest.

Too much regulation, on the other hand, could stifle liquidity and also increase the potential for government corruption. The more government officials oversee more rules, the more incentive there may be for bribery, favoritism, and corruption, raising transaction costs and discouraging investment participation.

In addition to a body of laws or rules, regulation also requires enforcement and judicial processes to ensure compliance with those rules. If there is little respect for the rule of law, or if the rule of law is not consistently enforced or is arbitrarily prosecuted, then there is greater investment risk. Inappropriate levels of regulation lead to increased information costs, transaction costs, and volatility.

Often, foreign investments seem promising in part because economic growth may be higher in an emerging economy, and often, they are. Such economies can have higher levels of risk, however, because of their emergent character. Before you invest, you want to be aware of the political and regulatory environment as well as the economic, market, and investment-specific risk.

Key Takeaways

- The flow, quality, and comparability of information are concerns in international investing.
- Investing internationally may pose unusual risks compared to domestic investing, such as:
  - market or liquidity risk,
  - economic risk,
  - currency risk,
  - political risk,
  - regulatory risk.
- The Index of Economic Freedom measures a country's economic environment, growth potential, and regulatory cost, which affect investment risk.
- Greater investment risks require more research to gauge their effects on an investment opportunity and the overall investing environment.

Exercises

1. Go to the website http://www.ifrs.org. What are the International Financing Reporting Standards (IFRS)? How could the IFRS strengthen the global economy and aid investors in the international markets? Now read Investopedia's explanation of the differences between inter-

national accounting standards (IAS) and the generally accepted accounting principles (GAAP) used in the United States at http://www.investopedia.com/ask/answers/05/iasvsgaap.asp?viewed=1. What would be the advantage of every country having the same standards?

2. Use the currency converters at http://www.xe.com/ucc and https://www.oanda.com/currency/converter/ to sample differences between foreign currencies and the U.S. dollar. For example, how much is one euro worth compared to the U.S. dollar? On the foreign currency exchange what are the minimum bid and ask prices for euros? Did the price rise or fall compared to the previous day? Check foreign exchange rates at http://www.x-rates.com. Choose three currencies to compare with the American dollar (USD) and look at the tables or graphs showing the comparison history of those currencies. Which of the three currencies has been the most volatile? Which currency is presently closest to par with U.S. dollar?
3. Examine the Index of Economic Freedom at https://www.heritage.org/index/. What is economic freedom? In the 2018 index, which economies are freer than the United States? Visit the World Bank at http://www.worldbank.org and the IMF at http://www.imf.org/external/about.htm. What role do these organizations play in international finance? For example, what is the World Bank doing to help increase investment opportunities in developing countries such as the Republic of Indonesia? How does the IMF seek to strengthen the international financial markets?

Endnotes

1. Dax R. Norman, "Web Sites You Can Trust," *American Libraries* (August 2006): 36.

CHAPTER 15
Owning Stocks

15.1 Introduction

By 1976, computers had been around for decades. They were typically the size of a large room and extremely expensive. To use one, you had to learn a programming language. On April 1, 1976, Steve Jobs, Steve Wozniak, and Ron Wayne started a company to make personal computers. On January 3, 1977, Jobs and Wozniak incorporated without Wayne, buying his 10% share of the company for $800.[1] On December 12, 1980, Apple Computer, Inc., went public; its stock sold for $22 per share. Had you bought Apple's stock when the company went public and held it until December 12, 2017, you would have earned an annual return of about 17.8% (compounded and not including any dividends). To look at it another way, $1,000 invested in Apple shares when it went public would be worth about $433,618 in 2017, 37 years later.[2]

History, as much as it is a litany of wars and rulers struggling for power, is a story of invention and innovation, broadening our understanding of how the world works and, if successful, improving the quality of our lives. Theoretical milestones have to be made practical, however, to be truly effective. The steam engine, the light bulb, the telephone—and the personal computer—had to be produced and sold to be widely used and useful.

Typically, an inventor has a great idea, then teams up with—or becomes—an entrepreneur. The entrepreneur's job is to build a company that can make the invention a reality. The company needs to find the resources to make the product and sell it widely enough to pay for those resources and to create a profit, making the whole effort worthwhile. No matter how great the idea is, if it can't be done profitably, it can't be done.

As an investor, you buy stocks hoping to share in corporate profits, benefiting directly from the inventive vitality of the economy and participating in economic growth. Understanding what stocks are, where they come from, what they do, and how they have value will help you decide how to include stocks in your investment portfolio and how to use them to reach your investment goals.

15.2 Stocks and Stock Markets

Learning Objectives

1. Explain the role of stock issuance and ownership in economic growth.
2. Contrast and compare the roles of the primary and secondary stock markets.
3. Identify the steps of stock issuance.
4. Contrast and compare the important characteristics of common and preferred stock.
5. Explain the significance of American Depository Receipts for U.S. investors.

Resources have costs, so a company needs money, or capital, which is also a resource. To get that start-up capital, the company could borrow or it could offer a share of ownership, or equity, to those who chip in capital.

If the costs of debt (interest payments) are affordable, the company may choose to borrow, which limits the company's commitment to its capital contributor. When the loan matures and is paid off, the relationship is over.

FIGURE 15.1

© Shutterstock, Inc.

If the costs of debt are too high, however, or the company is unable to borrow, it seeks equity investors willing to contribute capital in exchange for an unspecified share of the company's profits at some time in the future. In exchange for taking the risk of no exact return on their investment, equity investors get a say in how the company is run.

Stock represents those shares in the company's future and the right to a say in how the company is run. The original owners—the inventor(s) and entrepreneur(s)—choose equity investors who share their ideals and vision for the company. Usually, the first equity investors are friends, family, or colleagues, allowing the original owners freedom of management. At that point, the corporation is privately held, and the company's stock may be traded privately between owners. There may be restrictions on selling the stock, often the case for a family business, so that control stays within the family.

angel investor

An individual or group providing equity financing; usually a wealthy individual.

venture capital

Private equity provided to facilitate excessive growth before the initial public offering of shares.

private equity

Equity not traded in a public market or exchange.

go public

To raise capital by issuing equity shares through a public exchange.

If successful, however, eventually the company needs more capital to grow and remain competitive. If debt is not desirable, then the company issues more equity, or stock, to raise capital. The company may seek out an **angel investor**, **venture capital** firm, or **private equity** firm. Such investors finance companies in the early stages in exchange for a large ownership and management stake in the company. Their strategy is to buy a significant stake when the company is still "private" and then realize a large gain, typically when the company goes public. The company also may seek a buyer, perhaps a competitive or complementary business.

Alternatively, the company may choose to **go public**, to sell shares of ownership to investors in the public markets. Theoretically, this means sharing control with random strangers because anyone can purchase shares traded in the stock market. It may even mean losing control of the company. Founders can be fired, as Steve Jobs was from Apple in 1985 (although he returned as CEO in 1996).

Going public requires a profound shift in the corporate structure and management. Once a company is publicly traded, it falls under the regulatory scrutiny of federal and state governments, and must regularly file financial reports and analysis. It must broaden participation on the board of directors and allow more oversight of management. Companies go public to raise large amounts of capital to expand products, operations, markets, or to improve or create competitive advantages. To raise public equity capital, companies need to sell stock, and to sell stock they need a market. That's where the stock markets come in.

Primary and Secondary Markets

The private corporation's board of directors, shareholders elected by the shareholders, must authorize the number of shares that can be publicly issued. Since issuing shares means opening up the company to more owners, or sharing it more, only the existing owners have the authority to do so. Usually, the corporation authorizes more shares than it intends to issue, so it has the option of issuing more as need be.

Those **authorized shares** are then issued through an **initial public offering (IPO)**. At that point the company goes public. The IPO is a **primary market** transaction, which occurs when the stock is initially sold and the proceeds go to the company issuing the stock. After that, the company is publicly traded; its stock is outstanding, or publicly available. Then, whenever the stock changes hands, it is a **secondary market** transaction. The owner of the stock may sell shares and realize the proceeds. When most people think of "the stock market," they are thinking of the secondary markets.

The existence of secondary markets makes the stock a liquid or tradable asset, which reduces its risk for both the issuing company and the investor buying it. The investor is giving up capital in exchange for a share of the company's profit, with the risk that there will be no profit or not enough to compensate for the opportunity cost of sacrificing the capital. The secondary markets reduce that risk to the shareholder because the stock can be resold, allowing the shareholder to recover at least some of the invested capital and to make new choices with it.

Meanwhile, the company issuing the stock must pay the investor for assuming some of its risk. The less that risk is, because of the liquidity provided by the secondary markets, the less the company has to pay. The secondary markets decrease the company's cost of equity capital.

A company hires an investment bank to manage its initial public offering of stock. For efficiency, the bank usually sells the IPO stock to institutional investors. Typically, the original owners of the corporation keep large amounts of stock as well.

What does this mean for individual investors? Some investors believe that after an initial public offering of stock, the share price will rise because the investment bank will have initially underpriced the stock in order to sell it. This is not always the case, however. Share price is typically more volatile after an initial public offering than it is after the shares have been outstanding for a while. The longer the company has been public, the more information is known about the company, and the more predictable its earnings are and thus share price.[3]

When a company goes public, it may issue a relatively small number of shares. Its **market capitalization**—the total dollar value of its outstanding shares—may therefore be small. The number of individual shareholders, mostly institutional investors and the original owners, also may be small. As a result, the shares may be "thinly traded," traded infrequently or in small amounts.

Thinly traded shares may add to the volatility of the share price. One large shareholder deciding to sell could cause a decrease in the stock price, for example, whereas for a company with many shares and shareholders, the actions of any one shareholder would not be significant. As always, diversification—in this case of shareholders—decreases risk. Thinly traded shares are less liquid and more risky than shares that trade more frequently.

authorized shares

Shares of common or preferred stock that have been authorized for issuance by a corporation's board of directors.

initial public offering (IPO)

A company's first issuance of stock for trade in the public markets. Companies issue stock publicly to attract more investors and thus more capital for the company. When a company has its IPO is it said to "go public."

primary market

The market in which the initial issuance or initial public offering of a stock occurs.

secondary market

A market in which outstanding shares are traded.

market capitalization (market cap)

The total market value of a corporation's capital.

Common, Preferred, and Foreign Stocks

A company may issue **common stock** or **preferred stock**. Common stock is more prevalent. All companies issue common stock, whereas not all issue preferred stock. The differences between common and preferred have to do with the investor's voting rights, risk, and dividends.

common stock

Equity shares representing the residual claim on the company's value.

preferred stock

Equity shares that represent a superior claim over common shares but typically do not confer voting rights.

FIGURE 15.2

© Shutterstock, Inc.

Common stock allows each shareholder voting rights—one vote for each share owned. The more shares you own, the more you can influence the company's management. Shareholders vote for the company's directors, who provide policy guidance for and hire the management team that directly operates the corporation. After several corporate scandals in the early twenty-first century, some shareholders have become more active in their voting role.

Common stockholders assume the most risk of any corporate investor. If the company encounters financial distress, its first responsibility is to satisfy creditors, then the preferred shareholders, and then the common shareholders. Thus, common stocks provide only residual claims on the value of the company. In the event of bankruptcy, in other words, common shareholders get only the residue—whatever is left after all other claimants have been compensated.

Common shareholders share the company's profit after interest has been paid to creditors and a specified share of the profit has been paid to preferred shareholders. Common shareholders may receive all or part of the profit in cash—the dividend. The company is under no obligation to pay common stock dividends, however. The management may decide that the profit is better used to expand the company, to invest in new products or technologies, or to grow by acquiring a competitor. As a result, the company may pay a cash dividend only in certain years or not at all.

Shareholders investing in preferred stock, on the other hand, give up voting rights but get less risk and more dividends. Preferred stock typically does not convey voting rights to the shareholder. It is often distributed to the "friends and family" of the original founders when the company goes public, allowing them to share in the company's profits without having a say in its management. As noted above, preferred shareholders have a superior claim on the company's assets in the event of bankruptcy. They get their original investment back before common shareholders but after creditors.

cumulative preferred shares

Preferred shares that obligate the company to pay dividends to preferred shareholders before paying any others.

Preferred dividends are more of an obligation than common dividends. Most preferred shares are issued with a fixed dividend as **cumulative preferred shares**. This means that if the company does not create enough profit to pay its preferred dividends, those dividends ultimately must be paid before any common stock dividend.

For the individual investor, preferred stock may have two additional advantages over common stock:

1. Less volatile prices
2. More reliable dividends

As the company goes through its ups and downs, the preferred stock price will fluctuate less than the common stock price. If the company does poorly, preferred stockholders are more likely to be able to recoup more of their original investment than common shareholders because of their superior claim. If the company does well, however, preferred stockholders are less likely to share more in its success because their dividend is fixed. Preferred shareholders thus are exposed to less risk, protected by their superior claim and fixed dividend. The preferred stock price reflects less of the company's volatility.

Because the preferred dividend is more of an obligation than the common dividend, it provides more predictable dividend income for shareholders. This makes the preferred stock less risky and more attractive to an investor looking for less volatility and more regular dividend income.

Table 15.1 summarizes the differences between common stock and preferred stock.

TABLE 15.1 Stock Comparisons

Characteristic	Common Stock	Preferred Stock
Voting Rights	Yes	Usually not
Downside Risk	More	Less
Upside Risk	More	Less or none
Reliability of Investment Income	Less	More
Price Volatility	More	Less

As an investment choice, preferred stock is more comparable to bonds than to common stock. Bonds also offer less volatility and more reliable income than common stock (see Chapter 16). If there is a difference in the tax rate between dividend income (from preferred stock) and interest income (from bonds), you may find a tax advantage to investing in preferred stock instead of bonds.

Corporations often issue and trade their stocks on exchanges or in markets outside their home country, especially if the foreign market has more liquidity and will attract more buyers. Many foreign corporations issue and trade stock on the New York Stock Exchange (NYSE) or on the National Association of Securities Dealers Automated Quotations (NASDAQ), for example.

Investing in foreign shares is complicated by the fact that stock represents ownership, a legal as well as an economic idea, and because foreign companies operate in foreign currencies. To get around those issues and make foreign shares more tradable, the **American Depository Receipt (ADR)** was created in 1927. U.S. banks buy large amounts of shares in a foreign company and then sell ADRs (each representing a specified number of those shares) to U.S. investors. Individual shares of the stock are called American Depository Shares, or ADSs.

American Depository Receipt (ADR)

An asset representing equity shares in a foreign corporation trading in U.S. markets.

The ADR is usually listed on a major U.S. stock exchange, such as the New York Stock Exchange, or is quoted on the NASDAQ. One ADR can represent more or less than one share of the foreign stock, depending on its price and the currency exchange rate, so that the bank issuing the ADR can "price" it according to the norms of U.S. stock markets.

In return for marketing their shares in the lucrative U.S. market, foreign companies must provide U.S. banks with detailed financial reports. This puts available foreign corporate information on par with that of U.S. companies. Because they are issued and sold in the United States on U.S. exchanges, ADRs fall under the regulatory control of the Securities and Exchange Commission (SEC) and other federal and state regulatory agencies, which also lowers risk.

ADRs provide a practical way for U.S. investors to invest in foreign corporations. Because they are denominated in U.S. dollars, they lower exchange rate or currency risk for U.S. investors. They also lower the usual risks with investing overseas, such as lack of information and too much or too little regulatory oversight.

Key Takeaways

- Companies go public to raise capital to finance growth by selling equity shares in the public markets.
- A primary market transaction happens between the original issuer and buyer.
- Secondary market transactions are between all subsequent sellers and buyers.
- The secondary market lowers risk and transaction costs by increasing liquidity.
- Shares are authorized and issued and then become outstanding or publicly available.
- Equity securities may be common or preferred stock, differing by

- the assignment of voting rights,
- dividend obligations,
- claims in case of bankruptcy,
- risk.

- Common stocks have less predictable income, whereas most preferred stocks have fixed-rate cumulative dividends.
- ADRs represent foreign shares traded in U.S. markets, lowering risks, such as currency risks, and transaction costs for U.S. investors.

Exercises

1. Read the article, "Why It's Time to Go Public..." at https://www.forbes.com/sites/valleyvoices/2018/02/23/why-its-time-to-go-public/#70201d4f694d. Why would an entrepreneur not want to cash in on his company's success? What are the counterarguments? If you were the founder of a unicorn, how would you feel? Record your thoughts in My Notes or your personal finance journal.
2. What is a venture capitalist? Watch noted venture capitalist (or VC) and entrepreneur Janet Bannister at https://www.youtube.com/watch?v=49DWESzSJew. What three top pieces of advice does she give to new ventures seeking equity investment? According to http://www.investorwords.com/212/angel_investor.html, what is an angel investor?
3. Explore Hoover's at http://www.hoovers.com/. What information about IPOs can be found there? Click on a recently listed IPO. Read about the company and click on its stock ticker symbol. What was the price per share when the company was first listed on the stock exchange? How many shares were sold? What is its price today? Where did the proceeds from the IPO sale of shares go, and where will the proceeds from sales on the secondary markets go?

15.3 Stock Value

Learning Objectives

1. Explain the basis of stock value.
2. Identify the factors that affect earnings expectations.
3. Analyze how market capitalization affects stock value.
4. Discuss how market popularity or perception of value affects stock value.
5. Explain how stocks can be characterized by their expected performance relative to the market.

The value of a stock is in its ability to create a return, to create income or a gain in value for the investor. With common stock, the income is in the form of a dividend, which the company is not obligated to pay. The potential gain is determined by estimations of the future value of the stock.

If you knew that the future value would likely be more than the current market price—over your transaction costs, tax consequences, and opportunity cost—then you would buy the stock.

If you thought the future value would be less, you would short the stock (borrow it to sell with the intent of buying it back when its price falls), or you would just look for another investment.

Every investor wants to know what a stock will be worth, which is why so many stock analysts spend so much time estimating future value. Equity analysis is the process of gathering as much information as possible and making the most educated guesses.

Corporations exist to make profit for the owners. The better a corporation is at doing that, the more valuable it is, and the more valuable are its shares. A company also needs to increase earnings, or grow, because the global economy is competitive. A corporation's future value depends on its ability to create and grow earnings.

That ability depends on many factors. Some factors are company-specific, some are specific to the industry or sector, and some are macroeconomic forces. Chapter 12 discussed these factors in terms of the risk that a stock creates for the investor. The risk is that the company will not be able to earn the expected profit.

A company's size is an indicator of its earnings and growth potential. Size may correlate with age. A large company typically is more mature than a smaller one, for example. A larger company may have achieved economies of scale or may have gotten large by eliminating competitors or dominating its market. Size in itself is not an indicator of success, but similarly sized companies tend to have similar earnings growth.[4]

Companies are usually referred to by the size of their market capitalization or market cap, that is, the current market value of the debt and equity they use to finance their assets. Common market cap categories are the sizes micro, small, mid (medium), and large, or

- micro cap, with a market capitalization of less than $300 million;
- small cap, with a market capitalization between $300 million and $2 billion;
- mid cap, with a market capitalization between $2 billion and $10 billion;
- large cap, with a market capitalization of more than $10 billion.

The market capitalization of a company—along with industry and economic indicators—is a valuable indicator of earnings potential.

The economist John Maynard Keynes (1883–1946) famously compared the securities markets with a newspaper beauty contest. You "won" not because you could pick the prettiest contestant, but because you could pick the contestant that everyone else would pick as the prettiest contestant. In other words, the stock market is a popularity contest, but the "best" stock was not necessarily the most popular.

Keynes described investing in the stock market as follows:

> *"The smart player recognizes that personal criteria of beauty are irrelevant in determining the contest winner. A better strategy is to select those faces the other players are likely to fancy. This logic tends to snowball. After all, the other participants are likely to play the game with at least as keen a perception. Thus, the optimal strategy is not to pick those faces the player thinks are prettiest, or those the other players are likely to fancy, but rather to predict what the average opinion is likely to be about what the average opinion will be."*[5]

In the stock market, the forces of supply and demand determine stock prices. The more demand or popularity there is for a company's stock, the higher its price will go (unless the company issues more shares). A stock is popular, and thus in greater demand, if it is thought to be more valuable—that is, if it has more earnings and growth potential.

FIGURE 15.3

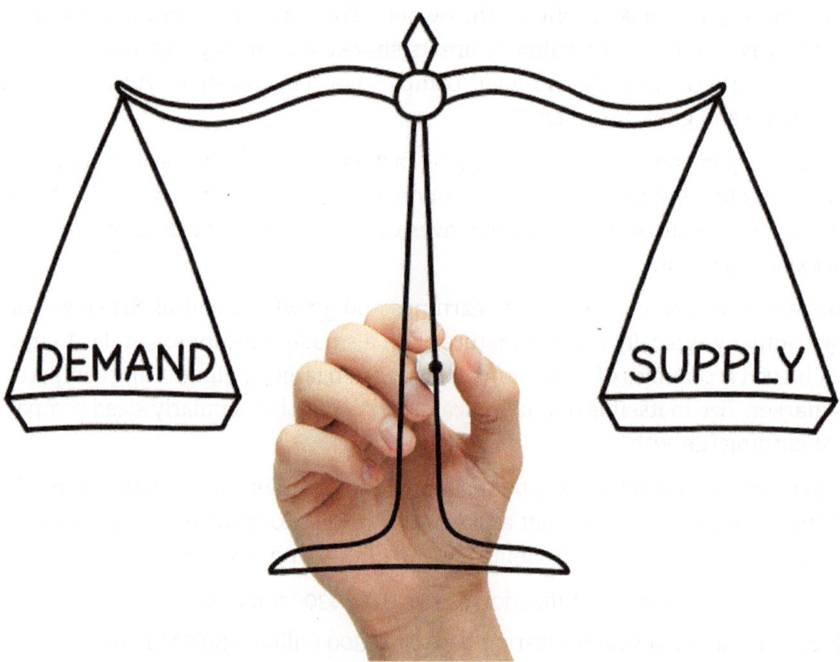

© Shutterstock, Inc.

Sometimes a company is under- or overpriced relative to the going price for similar companies. If the market recognizes the "error," the stock price should rise or fall as it "corrects" itself.

A growth stock is a stock that promises a higher rate of return because the market has underestimated its growth potential. A value stock is a stock that has been underpriced for some other reason. For example, investors may be wary of the outlook for its industry. Because it is underpriced, a value stock is expected to provide a higher-than-average return.

Stocks may be characterized by the role that they play in a diversified portfolio—and some by their colorful names—as shown in Table 15.2.

TABLE 15.2 Definitions of Stocks and Their Roles in a Portfolio

	Definition	Role
Growth Stock	Underestimated potential for growth.	Expect a higher rate of return.
Value Stock	Undervalued by the market; underpriced.	Expect a higher than average return.
Defensive Stock	Less volatility than the overall market and less sensitive to market changes.	Expect the value to fall less than the market's during a market decline.
Cyclical Stock	More volatility than the overall market and more sensitive to market changes.	When the market rises, expect the price to rise at a higher rate. When the market falls, expect the price to fall at a higher rate.
Speculative Stock	Overvalued by the market; overpriced.	Expect the price to continue rising for a time before it falls.
Blue Chip Stock	Stock of a stable, well-established, large cap company.	Expect stable returns.

	Definition	Role
Widow-and-Orphan Stock	A blue chip defensive stock.	Expect a steady dividend.
Wallflower Stock	Overlooked and therefore underpriced.	Expect the value to rise when the stock is "discovered."
Penny Stock	Low-priced stock of a small- or micro cap company.	Expect the value to rise if and when the company succeeds.

Each term in Table 15.2 names a stock's relationship to the market and to investors. For example, an investor who wants to invest in stocks but wants to minimize economic risk would include defensive stocks in the stock portfolio along with some blue chips. Implicit in that decision is each stock's potential for price growth, risk, or role in a diversified portfolio.

Key Takeaways

- A stock's value is based on the corporation's ability to create and grow profits.
- Earnings expectations are based on economic, industry, and company-specific factors.
- The size of the market capitalization affects stock value.
- A stock's market popularity or perception of value affects its value.
- Stocks can be characterized by their expected behavior relative to the market as
    - growth stocks,
    - value stocks,
    - cyclical stocks,
    - defensive stocks, or
    - other named types (e.g., blue chip stocks, penny stocks).

Exercise

1. What is a sector? Start thinking by reading "The 11 Sectors of the Stock Market" at http://etfdb.com/etf-education/the-10-sectors-of-the-stock-market/. According to this article: What are the sectors? Which of them are regarded as defensive and which as cyclical? As an investor, when might you consider defensive stocks over cyclical stocks? Choose a sector that interests you and read about small-cap, mid-cap, and large-cap companies in that sector. What are their stock prices? What do their recent price histories tell you about their perceived value in the stock market? Write your observations in My Notes or your personal finance journal and share your observations with classmates.

15.4 Common Measures of Value

Learning Objectives

1. Identify common return ratios and evaluate their usefulness.
2. Explain how to interpret dividend yield.
3. Explain the significance of growth ratios.
4. Explain the significance of market value ratios.

A corporation creates a return for investors by creating earnings. Those earnings may be paid out in cash as a dividend or retained as capital by the company. A company's ability to create earnings is watched closely by investors because the company's earnings are the investor's return.

A company's earnings potential can be tracked and measured, and several measurements are expressed as ratios. Mathematically, as discussed in Chapter 3, a ratio is simply a fraction. In investment analysis, a ratio provides a clear means of comparing values. Three kinds of ratios important to investors are return ratios, growth ratios, and market value ratios.

The ratios described here are commonly presented in news outlets and websites where stocks are discussed (e.g., http://www.nasdaq.com), so chances are you won't have to calculate them yourself. Nevertheless, it is important to understand what they mean and how to use them in your investment thinking.

Return Ratios

earnings per share (EPS)

The dollar value of the earnings per each share of common stock.

One of the most useful ratios in looking at stocks is the **earnings per share (EPS)** ratio. It calculates the company's earnings relative to the number of common shares issued: the amount of a company's profit that each outstanding share of common stock owns. The calculation lets you see how much you benefit from holding each share. Here is the formula for calculating EPS:

$$\text{EPS} = \frac{\textbf{Net income} - \textbf{Preferred stock dividends}}{\textbf{Average number of common shares outstanding}}$$

The company's earnings are reported on its income statement as net income, so a shareholder could easily track earnings growth. However, EPS allows you to make a direct comparison to other stocks by putting the earnings on a per-share basis, creating a common denominator. Earnings per share should be compared over time and also compared to the EPS of other companies.

dividends per share

The dollar value of the dividend return to each share of stock.

When a stock pays a dividend, that dividend is income for the shareholder. Investors concerned with the cash flows provided by an equity investment look at **dividends per share** or **DPS** as a measure of the company's ability and willingness to pay a dividend.

$$\text{DPS} = \frac{\textbf{Common stock dividends}}{\textbf{Average number of common shares outstanding}}$$

Another measure of the stock's usefulness in providing dividends is the **dividend yield**, which calculates the dividend as a percentage of the stock price. It is a measure of the dividend's role as a return on investment: for every dollar invested in the stock, how much is returned as a dividend, or actual cash payback? An investor concerned about cash flow returns can compare companies' dividend yields.

dividend yield

The return provided by the dividend relative to the share price, or the dividend per each dollar of investment, given its market price.

$$\text{Dividend yield} = \frac{\text{Dividend per share}}{\text{Price per share}}$$

For example, for the fiscal year ended June 30, 2017, Microsoft, Inc., paid a total annual dividend of $12,084 million, and had about 7,746 million shares outstanding; for that fiscal year, it showed earnings of $21,204 million.[6] Assuming it had not issued preferred stock and so paid no preferred stock dividends, then:

$$\text{EPS} = \frac{21,204}{7,746} = 2.74$$

$$\text{DPS} = \frac{12,084}{7,746} = 1.56$$

Microsoft earned $12,084 million, or $2.74 for each share of stock held by stockholders, of which $1.56 is actually paid out to shareholders. On June 30, 2017, the stock price closed at $67.61.[7] So if you were thinking of buying a share of Microsoft by investing $67.61, the expected cash return provided to you by the company's last dividend represents 2.3% of your investment.

$$\text{Dividend yield} = \frac{1.56}{67.61} = 2.3\%$$

Earnings either are paid out as dividends or are retained by the company as capital. That capital is used by the company to finance operations, capital investments such as new assets for expansion and growth, or repayment of debt.

The dividend is the return on investment that comes as cash while you own the stock. Some investors see the dividend as a more valuable form of return than the earnings that are retained as capital by the company. It is more liquid, since it comes in cash and comes sooner than the gain that may be realized when the stock is sold (and thus more valuable because time affects value). It is the "bird in the hand," perhaps less risky than waiting for the eventual gain from the company's **retained earnings**.

retained earnings

The portion of the company's earnings or net income that is not distributed (paid out) to owners as a dividend, but is retained as equity financing for the company.

Some investors see a high dividend yield as a sign of the company's strength, indicative of its ability to raise ample capital through earnings. Dividends are a sign that the company can earn more capital than it needs to finance operations, make capital investments, or repay debt. Thus, dividends are capital that can be spared from use by the company and given back to investors.

Other investors see a high dividend yield as a sign of weakness, indicative of a company that cannot grow because it is not putting enough capital into expansion and growth or into satisfying creditors. This may be because it is a mature company operating in saturated markets, a company stifled by competition, or a company without the creative resources to explore new ventures.

As an investor, you need to look at dividends in the context of the company and your own income needs.

Growth Ratios

The more earnings are paid out to shareholders as dividends, the less earnings are retained by the company as capital.

$$\text{Earnings} = \text{Dividends} + \text{Capital retained}$$

dividend payout rate

The percentage of earnings that is paid out as a dividend.

retention rate

The rate at which a company retains earnings for use as additional capital or the earnings retained (not paid out as dividends) as a percentage of earnings.

Since retained capital finances growth, the more earnings are used to pay dividends, the less earnings are used to create growth. Two ratios that measure a company's choice in handling its earnings are the dividend payout rate and the retention rate. The **dividend payout rate** compares dividends to earnings. The **retention rate** compares the amount of capital retained to earnings.

The dividend payout rate figures the dividend as a percentage of earnings.

$$\text{Dividend payout rate} = \frac{\text{Dividend}}{\text{Earnings}}$$

The retention rate figures the retained capital as a percentage of earnings.

$$\text{Retention rate} = \frac{\text{Capital retained}}{\text{Earnings}}$$

Because earnings = dividends + capital retained, then

$$100\% \text{ of Earnings} = \text{Dividend payout rate} + \text{Retention rate}$$

If a company's dividend payout rate is 40%, then its retention rate is 60%; if it pays out 40% of its earnings in dividends, then it retains 60% of them.

Since Microsoft had earnings of $21,204 million and dividends of $12,084 million, it must have retained $9,120 million of its earnings.

$$21,204 = 12,084 + 9,120$$

So, for Microsoft,

$$\text{Dividend payout rate} = \frac{12,084}{21,204} = 0.5699 = 57\%$$

$$\text{Retention rate} = \frac{9,120}{21,204} = 0.4301 = 43\%$$

There is no benchmark or standard dividend payout or retention ratio for every company; they vary depending on the age and size of the company, industry, and economic climate. These numbers are useful, however, to get a sense of the company's strategy and to compare it to competitors.

internal growth rate

The maximum rate of growth achieved without any issuance of debt or new equity capital.

A company's value is in its ability to grow and to increase earnings. The rate at which it can retain capital, earn it and not pay it out as dividends, is a factor in determining how fast it can grow. This rate is measured by the **internal growth rate** and the sustainable growth rate. The internal growth rate answers the question, "How fast could the company grow (increase earnings) without any new capital, without borrowing or issuing more stock?" Given how good the company is at taking capital and turning it into assets and using those assets to create earnings, the internal growth rate looks at how fast the company can grow without any new borrowing or new shares issued.

sustainable growth rate

The maximum rate of growth possible without changing the use of debt and equity capital.

The **sustainable growth** rate answers the question, "How fast could the company grow without changing the balance between using debt and using equity for capital?" Given how good the company is at taking capital and turning it into assets and using those assets to create earnings, the sustainable growth rate looks at how fast the company can grow if it uses some new borrowing, but keeps the balance between debt and equity capital stable.

Both growth rates use the retention rate as a factor in allowing growth. The fastest rate of growth could be achieved by having a 100% retention rate, that is, by paying no dividends and retaining all earnings as capital.

An investor who is not using stocks as a source of income but for their potential gain may look for higher growth rates, as evidenced by a higher retention rate and a lower dividend payout rate. An investor looking for income from stocks would instead be attracted to companies offering a higher dividend payout rate and a lower retention rate, despite lower growth rates.

Market Value Ratios

While return and growth ratios are measures of a company's fundamental value, and therefore the value of its stocks, the actual stock price is affected by the market. Investors' demand can result in underpricing or overpricing of a stock, depending on its attractiveness in relation to other investment choices or opportunity cost.

A stock's market value can be compared with that of other stocks. The most common measure for doing so is the **price-to-earnings ratio**, or P/E. Price-to-earnings ratio is calculated by dividing the price per share (in dollars) by the earnings per share (in dollars). The result shows the investment needed for every dollar of return that the stock creates.

price-to-earnings ratio (P/E)

The ratio of a stock's market value per share to its earnings per share, or the market value of one dollar of the company's earnings.

$$P/E = \frac{\text{Price per share}}{\text{Earnings per share}}$$

For Microsoft, for example, the price per share was $67.61, and the EPS was $2.74, so:

$$P/E = \frac{67.61}{2.74} = 24.68.$$

This means that the price per share was almost 25 times the earnings per share.

The larger the P/E ratio, the more expensive the stock is and the more you have to invest to get one dollar's worth of earnings in return. To get $1.00 of Microsoft's earnings, you have to invest almost $25. By comparing the P/E ratio of different companies, you can see how expensive they are relative to each other.

A low P/E ratio could be a sign of weakness. Perhaps the company has problems that make it riskier going forward, even if it has earnings now, so the future expectations and thus the price of the stock are now low. Or it could be a sign of a buying opportunity for a stock that is currently underpriced.

A high P/E ratio could be a sign of a company with great prospects for growth and so a higher price than would be indicated by its earnings alone. On the other hand, a high P/E could indicate a stock that is overpriced and has nowhere to go but down. In that case, a high P/E ratio would be a signal to sell your stock.

How do you know if the P/E ratio is "high" or "low"? You can compare it to other companies in the same industry or to the average P/E ratio for a stock index of similar companies based on company size, age, debt levels, and so on. As with any of the ratios discussed here, this one is useful in comparison.

Another indicator of market value is the **price-to-book ratio (P/B)**. Price-to-book ratio compares the price per share to the book value of each share. The **book value** is the value of the company that is reported "on the books," or the company's balance sheet, using the original values of assets, liabilities, and equity. The balance sheet does not show the market value of the company's assets. For example, it does not show what those assets could be sold for today; it shows what they were worth when the company acquired them. The book value of a company should be less than its market value, which should have appreciated over time. The company should be worth more as times goes on.

price-to-book ratio (P/B)

A ratio comparing the market value of the company to its book or "original" value.

book value

The valuation of assets, liabilities, and equity from the balance sheet; the corporation's original investment in its assets, liabilities, and equity.

$$P/B = \frac{\text{Price per share}}{\text{Book value of equity per share}}$$

As the price per share is the market value of equity per share, the P/B ratio compares the current market value of the company's equity to its book value. If that ratio is greater than one, then the company's equity is worth more than its original value, and the company has been increasing its value. If that ratio is less than one, then the company's current value is less than its original value, so the value has been decreasing. A P/B = 1 would indicate that a company has just been breaking even in terms of value over the years.

The higher the P/B ratio, the better the company has done in increasing its value over time. You can calculate the ratio for different companies and compare them by their ability to increase value.

Table 15.3 provides a summary of the return, growth, and market value ratios.

TABLE 15.3 Ratios and Their Uses

Ratio	What It Measures
Earnings per Share (EPS)	Earnings (in dollars) for every outstanding share of stock
Dividends per Share (DPS)	Dividend (in dollars) for every outstanding share of stock
Dividend Yield	Dividend (in dollars) returned for every dollar invested in the stock
Dividend Payout	Percentage of earnings paid out as dividends
Retention Rate	Percentage of earnings retained as capital
Internal Growth Rate	The fastest rate of growth without using more debt or issuing more equity
Sustainable Growth Rate	The fastest rate of growth using more debt but without changing the balance of debt and equity
Price-to-Earnings Ratio (P/E)	The market value of each dollar's worth of earnings
Price-to-Book Ratio (P/B)	The market value of the company's equity compared to its book value

Ratios can be used to compare a company with its past performance, with its competitors, or with competitive investments. They can be used to project a stock's future value based on the company's ability to earn, grow, and be a popular investment. A company has to have fundamental value to be an investment choice, but it also has to have market value to have its fundamental value appreciated in the market and to have its price reflect its fundamental value.

To go back to Keynes' analogy, it may take beauty to win a beauty contest, but beauty has to shine through to be appreciated by a majority of the judges. And beauty, as you know, is in the eye of the beholder. The more you know about how other stock market participants behold value, the better an investor you can be.

Key Takeaways

- Earnings per share (EPS) and dividends per share (DPS) indicate stock returns on investment.
- Dividend yield measures a shareholder's cash return relative to investment.
- Growth ratios such as the internal and sustainable growth rates indicate the company's ability to grow given earnings and dividend expectations.
- Market value ratios, most commonly price-to-earnings and price-to-book, indicate a stock's market popularity and its effects on its price.

Exercises

1. What do other companies' EPS tell an investor? Study the different kinds of EPS discussed at http://www.investopedia.com/articles/analyst/091901.asp. As an individual investor, explain which EPS would be most important to you.
2. Choose three companies that compete in the same industry. Compare their EPS, DPS, and P/E ratios using information from http://www.nasdaq.com. Based on these ratios, which company looks like a better long-term investment for an investor who wants income? Based on these ratios, which company looks like a better long-term investment for an investor who wants capital gains? Write a memo to investors describing and defending your choices.

15.5 Equity Strategies

Learning Objectives

1. Identify and explain the rationales behind common long-term strategies.
2. Identify and explain the rationales behind common short-term strategies.

The best stock strategy is to know what you are looking for (i.e., what kind of stock will fulfill the role you want it to play in your portfolio) and to do the analyses you need to find it. That is easier said than done, however, and requires that you have the knowledge, skill, and data for stock analysis. Commonly used general stock strategies may be long term (returns achieved in more than one year) or short term (returns achieved in less than one year), but the strategies you choose should fit your investing horizon, risk tolerance, and needs. An important part of that strategy, as with financial planning in general, is to check your stock investments and reevaluate your holdings regularly—how regularly depends on the long- or short-term horizon of your investing strategies.

Long-Term Strategies

Long-term strategies favor choosing a long-term approach to avoid the volatility and risk of market timing. For individual investors, a **buy-and-hold strategy** can be effective over the long run. The strategy is just what it sounds like: you choose the stocks for your equity investments, and you hold them for the long term. The idea is that if you choose wisely and your stocks are well diversified, over time you will do at least as well as the stock market itself. Though it suffers through economic cycles, the economy's long-term trend is growth.

buy-and-hold strategy

The long-term strategy of investing and holding without trading.

FIGURE 15.4

© Shutterstock, Inc.

By minimizing the number of transactions, you can minimize transaction costs. Since you are holding your stocks, you are not realizing gains and are not paying gains tax. Thus, even if your gross returns are not spectacular, you are minimizing your costs and maximizing net returns. This strategy is optimal for investors with a long horizon, low risk tolerance, and little need for liquidity in the short term.

dollar-cost averaging

The strategy of investing regular dollar amounts at regular intervals in one security.

Another long-term strategy is **dollar-cost averaging**. The idea of dollar-cost averaging is that you invest in a stock gradually by buying the same dollar amount of the same stock at regular intervals. This is a way of negating the effects of market timing. By buying at regular intervals, you will buy at times when the price is low and when it is high, but over time your price will average out. Dollar-cost averaging is a way of avoiding a stock's price volatility because the net effect is that you buy the stock at its average price.

An investor uses dollar-cost averaging when regular payroll deductions are made to fund defined contribution retirement plans, such as a 401(k) or a 403b. The same amount is contributed to the plan in regular intervals and is typically used to purchase the same set of specified assets.

A buy-and-hold or dollar-cost averaging strategy only makes sense over time because both assume a long-time horizon in order to "average out" volatility, making them better than other investment choices. If you have a long-term horizon, as with a retirement plan, those strategies can be quite effective. However, as the most recent decade has shown, market or economic cycles can be long too, so you need to think about whether your "long-term" horizon is likely to outlast or be outlasted by the market's cycle, especially as you near your investment goals.

Direct investment and dividend reinvestment are ways of buying shares directly from a company without going through a broker. This allows you to avoid brokerage commissions. **Direct investment** means purchasing shares from the company, while **dividend reinvestment** means having your dividends automatically invested in more shares (rather than being sent to you as cash). Dividend reinvestment is also a way of building up your equity in the stock by reinvesting cash that you might otherwise spend.

direct investment

A real estate investment in which you are the owner and manager of property.

dividend reinvestment

The practice of using dividends to automatically purchase additional shares.

The advantage of direct investment and dividend reinvestment is primarily the savings on brokers' commissions. You can also buy fractional shares or less than a whole share, and there is no minimum amount to invest, as there can be with brokerage transactions. The disadvantage is that by having funds automatically reinvested, you are not actively deciding how they should be invested and thus may be missing better opportunities.

Indexing is a passive long-term investment strategy to invest in index funds as a diversified asset rather than select stocks. Instead of choosing individual large-cap companies, for example, you could invest in Standard & Poor's (S&P) 500 Index fund, which would provide more diversification for only one transaction cost than you could get picking individual securities. The disadvantage to indexing is that you do not enjoy the potential of individual stocks producing above-average returns.

indexing

The strategy of using index funds to achieve diversification rather than specifically selecting individual securities.

Table 15.4 summarizes long-term stock strategies.

TABLE 15.4 Long-Term Stock Strategies

Strategy	Avoids Market Timing	Avoids Stock Selection	Lowers Transaction Costs	Schedules Investment (Savings)
Buy and Hold	√		√	
Dollar Cost Averaging	√		√	√
Direct Investment			√	
Dividend Reinvestment	√		√	√
Indexing		√	√	

Short-Term Strategies

Short-term stock strategies rely on taking advantage of market timing to earn above-average returns. Some advisors believe that the stock market fluctuates between favoring value stocks and favoring growth stocks. That is, the market will go through cycles when value stocks that are temporarily underpriced will outperform stocks of companies poised for higher growth, and vice versa. If true, you would want to weight your portfolio with growth stocks when they are favored and with value stocks when they are favored.

This value-growth weighting strategy relies on market timing, which is difficult for the individual investor. It also relies on correctly identifying growth and value stocks and market trends in their favor, complicating the process of market timing even further.

Day trading is a very short-term strategy of taking and closing a position in a day or two. Literally, it means buying in the morning and selling in the afternoon. Day trading became popular in the 1990s when stock prices were riding the tide of the tech stock bubble. At that time it was possible to hold a stock for just a few hours and earn a gain. Technology, especially the Internet, also

day trading

A short-term strategy for taking advantage of excessive volatility.

made real-time quotes and other market data available to individual investors at a reasonable cost. At the same time, Internet and discount brokers drove down the costs of trading.

Day trading declined, but did not die, after the tech bubble burst. It turns out that in a bubble, any strategy can make money, but when market volatility is more closely related to earnings potential and fundamental value, there is no shortcut to doing your homework, knowing as much as possible about your investments, and making strategic choices that are appropriate for you.

Key Takeaways

- Common long-term strategies try to maximize returns by:
  - minimizing transaction costs, or
  - minimizing the effects of market timing.
- Long-term stock strategies include buy and hold, dollar-cost averaging, direct investment, dividend reinvestment, and indexing.
- Common short-term strategies try to maximize return by taking advantage of market timing.

Exercises

1. Review your investing horizon, risk tolerance, and needs. In My Notes or your personal finance journal, record your ideas about the effects of your horizon, risk profile, and personal circumstances on your decisions about investing in stocks. Rank the long-term and short-term investment strategies in order of their appropriateness for you. Explain why your top-ranked strategies seem best for you at this time.
2. Survey (but do not join) websites for day traders online. Then read an article for beginning day traders at http://www.investopedia.com/articles/trading/06/DayTradingRetail.asp?viewed=1. What information in this article do you find discouraging about getting involved in day trading? Read the Securities and Exchange Commission's (SEC) page on day trading at https://www.sec.gov/reportspubs/investor-publications/investorpubsdaytipshtm.html. According to the SEC, what risks would you encounter as a "day trader"?

Endnotes

1. Ronald W. Linzmayer, *Apple Confidential: The Real Story of Apple Computer, Inc.* (San Francisco: No Starch Press, 1999).
2. Investopdia, https://www.investopedia.com/articles/active-trading/080715/if-you-would-have-invested-right-after-apples-ipo.asp (accessed June 1, 2018).
3. M. B. Lowery, M. S. Officer, and G. W. Schwert, "The Variability of IPO Initial Returns," *Journal of Finance*, http://schwert.ssb.rochester.edu/ipovolatility.htm (accessed June 9, 2009).
4. E. F. Fama and K. R. French, "The Cross-section of Expected Stock Returns," *Journal of Finance* 47 (1992): 427–86.
5. Burton G. Malkiel, *A Random Walk Down Wall Street* 10th ed. (New York: W. W. Norton & Company, Inc., 2007).
6. Based on data from NASDAQ, "Microsoft Corporation Stock Quote & Summary Data," http://www.nasdaq.com/symbol/msft (accessed June 9, 2018).
7. Yahoo! Finance, "Microsoft Corporation Historical Data," https://finance.yahoo.com/quote/msft/history?ltr=1 (accessed June 9, 2018).

CHAPTER 16

Owning Bonds

16.1 Introduction

In common parlance, a bond is an affinity between people. In science, that affinity is physically held together by an attraction of atoms. In finance, a bond is a debt agreement, holding lender and borrower together in a shared financial fate.

Investors buy bonds to participate in economic growth as lenders rather than as shareholders, with less risk and a firmer claim on assets. Bonds are issued by different kinds of organizations—by governments and government agencies as well as by corporations—giving investors different kinds of partners in growth.

Since bonds are a different form of capital than stocks, and since bond investments are made in different kinds of borrowers, bonds offer diversification from the stocks in your portfolio. Your use of bonds may change over time, as your risk tolerance or liquidity needs change.

16.2 Bonds and Bond Markets

Learning Objectives

1. Identify bond features that can determine risk and return.
2. Differentiate the roles of various U.S. government bonds.
3. List the types and features of state and municipal bonds.
4. Compare and contrast features of the corporate bond markets, the markets for corporate stock, and the markets for government bonds.
5. Explain the role of rating agencies and the process of bond rating.

Bonds are a relatively old form of financing. Formalized debt arrangements long preceded corporate structure and the idea of equity (stock) as we know it. Venice issued the first known government bonds of the modern era in 1157 to raise funds to finance a crusade against Constantinople, which included expansion of a shipyard attached to the Venetian Arsenal.[1] Private bonds are cited in British records going back to the thirteenth century.[2]

Bonds

In addition to financing government projects, bonds are used by corporations to capitalize growth. Bonds are also a legal arrangement, couched in conditions, obligations, and consequences. As a result of their legal and financial roles, bonds carry a quaint and particular vocabulary. Bonds come in all shapes and sizes to suit the needs of the borrowers and the demands of lenders. Table 16.1 lists the descriptive terms for basic bond features.

TABLE 16.1 Basic Bond Features

Bond Term	Meaning
Issuer	Borrower
Investor	Lender or creditor
Principal, Face Value, Par Value	Amount borrowed
Coupon Rate	Interest rate
Coupon	Interest payment
Maturity	Due date
Term	Time until maturity
Yield to Maturity	Annualized return on bond investment
Market Value	Current price

The **coupon** is usually paid to the investor twice yearly. It is calculated as a percentage of the **face value**—amount borrowed—so that the annual coupon = coupon rate × face value. By convention, each individual bond has a face value of $1,000. A corporation issuing a bond to raise $100 million would have to issue 100,000 individual bonds ($100,000,000 divided by $1,000 per bond). If those bonds pay a 4% coupon, a bondholder who owns one of those bonds would receive a coupon of $40 per year (1,000 × 4%), or $20 every six months.

The **coupon rate** of interest on the bond may be fixed or floating and may change. A floating rate is usually based on another interest benchmark, such as the U.S. **prime rate**, a widely recognized benchmark of prevailing interest rates.

coupon

The interest payment on a bond, specified as a feature of the bond at issuance.

face value

For a bond, the amount to be repaid to the bondholder upon redemption.

coupon rate

The interest rate offered on a bond.

prime rate

A benchmark interest rate understood to be the rate that major banks charge corporate borrowers with the least default risk.

A **zero-coupon bond** has a coupon rate of zero: it pays no interest and repays only the principal at maturity. A "zero" may be attractive to investors, however, because it can be purchased for much less than its face value. There are **deferred coupon bonds** (also called **split-coupon bonds** and issued below par), which pay no interest for a specified period, followed by higher-than-normal interest payments until maturity. There are also **step-up bonds** that have coupons that increase over time.

The face value, the principal amount borrowed, is paid back at maturity. If the bond is **callable**, it may be redeemed after a specified date but before maturity. A borrower typically "calls" its bonds after prevailing interest rates have fallen, making lower-cost debt available. Borrowers can borrow new, cheaper debt and pay off the older, more expensive debt. As an investor (lender), you would be paid back early, which sounds great, but because interest rates have fallen, you would have trouble finding another bond investment that would pay as high a rate of return.

A **convertible bond** is a corporate bond that may be converted into common equity at maturity or after some specified time. If a bond were converted into stock, the bondholder would become a shareholder, assuming more of the company's risk.

The bond may be secured by collateral, such as property or equipment, sometimes called a **mortgage bond**. If unsecured, or secured only by the "full faith and credit" of the borrower (the borrower's unconditional commitment to pay principal and interest on the debt), the bond is a **debenture**. Most bonds are issued as debentures.

A bond specifies if the borrower has more than one bond issue outstanding or more than one set of lenders to repay, which establishes the bond's seniority in relation to previously issued debt. This "pecking order" determines which lenders will be paid back first in case of default on the debt or bankruptcy. Thus, when the borrower does not meet its coupon obligations, investors holding **senior debt** as opposed to **subordinated debt** have less risk of default.

zero-coupon bond

A bond that has a coupon rate of zero, and therefore a coupon of zero. Its only cash flow return is the principal repayment at maturity.

deferred coupon bonds

Bonds whose coupon payments are deferred until a specified time.

split-coupon bonds

Deferred coupon bonds that pay no interest for a specified period, followed by higher-than-normal interest payments until maturity.

step-up bond

A bond with a floating-rate coupon that is scheduled to increase at specified intervals.

callable bond

A bond that may be redeemed before maturity.

convertible bond

A bond that may be converted to common stock under specific conditions.

mortgage bond

A bond secured by a specific asset such as real property or equipment.

debenture

A bond secured by only the "full faith and credit" of the borrower and not by any specific asset.

senior debt

A bond issue that has a superior claim in case of bankruptcy.

subordinated debt

A bond issue that has an inferior claim in case of bankruptcy.

covenant

A condition of a loan that restricts the borrower to protect the lender.

default risk

The risk that a borrower will not be able to meet interest obligations or principal repayment.

Treasury bills

Bonds issued by the U.S. government with a maturity of less than one year.

Treasury notes

Bonds issued by the U.S. government with a maturity of between one and 10 years.

Treasury bonds

Bonds issued by the U.S. government with a maturity of more than 10 years.

Treasury Inflation-Protected Securities (TIPS)

Bonds issued by the U.S. government with an adjustable face value designed to protect the bondholder against inflation risk.

revenue bond

A state or municipal bond that will be repaid from revenues of the specific project it is financing.

general obligation bond

A state or municipal bond secured only by the "full faith and credit" of the issuer.

Bonds may also come with **covenants** or conditions on the borrower. Covenants are usually attached to corporate bonds and require the company to maintain certain performance goals during the term of the loan. Those goals are designed to lower **default risk** for the lender. Examples of typical covenants are:

- dividend limits,
- debt limits,
- limits on sales of assets, and
- maintenance of certain liquidity ratios or minimum cash balances.

Corporations issue corporate bonds, usually with maturities of 10, 20, or 30 years. Corporate bonds tend to be the most "customized," with features such as callability, conversion, and covenants.

The U.S. government issues **Treasury bills** for short-term borrowing, **Treasury notes** for intermediate-term borrowing (longer than one year but less than 10 years), and **Treasury bonds** for long-term borrowing for more than 10 years. The federal government also issues **Treasury Inflation-Protected Securities (TIPS)**. TIPS pay a fixed coupon, but the principal adjusts with inflation. At maturity, you are repaid either the original principal or the inflation-adjusted principal, whichever is greater.

State and municipal governments issue revenue bonds or general obligation bonds. A **revenue bond** is repaid out of the revenue generated by the project that the debt is financing. For example, toll revenue may secure a debt that finances a highway. A **general obligation bond** is backed by the state or municipal government, just as a corporate debenture is backed by the corporation.

Interest from state and **municipal bonds** (also called "munis") may not be subject to federal income taxes. Also, if you live in that state or municipality, the interest may not be subject to state and local taxes. The tax exemption differs from bond to bond, so you should be sure to check before you invest. Even if the interest is not taxable, however, any gain (or loss) from the sale of the bond is taxed, so you should not think of munis as "tax-free" bonds.

municipal bonds or "munis"

Bonds issued by a city, town or state to finance public projects. The coupon payments may, under certain circumstances, not be subject to federal income tax for the bondholder.

Foreign corporations and governments issue bonds. You should keep in mind, however, that foreign government defaults are not uncommon: Mexico in 1994, Russia in 1998, and Argentina in 2001 are all examples. More recently, Greece, Spain, Portugal, and Italy came awfully close to defaulting in 2008–2012. Foreign corporate or sovereign debt also exposes the bondholder to currency risk, as coupons and principal will be paid in the foreign currency. Table 16.2 shows a summary of bonds and their issuers.

TABLE 16.2 Bond Issuers and Terms

		Government				Corporate
		U.S. Treasury	**State**	**Municipality**	**Foreign**	
Short-Term	**(<1 year)**	Treasury bills				Commercial paper
Intermediate-Term	**(1-10 years)**	Treasury notes	Revenue bonds or general obligation bonds	Revenue bonds or general obligation bonds	Sovereignty bonds	Bonds
Long-Term	**(>10 years)**	Treasury bonds	Revenue bonds or general obligation bonds	Revenue bonds or general obligation bonds	Sovereignty bonds	Bonds

Bond Markets

The volume of capital traded in the bond markets is far greater than what is traded in the stock markets. All sorts of borrowers issue bonds: corporations; national, state and municipal governments; and government agencies. Even small towns issue bonds to finance capital expenditures such as schools, fire stations, and roads. Each kind of bond has its own market.

Private placement refers to bonds that are issued in a private sale rather than through the public markets. The investors in privately placed bonds are institutional investors such as insurance companies, endowments, and pension funds.

private placement

An issuance of bonds through a private deal rather than through the public markets.

U.S. Treasury bonds are issued to the primary market through auctions. Participants, usually dealers or institutional investors, bid for the bonds, but no one participant is allowed to buy enough shares to monopolize the secondary market. Individuals can also buy Treasuries directly from the U.S. Treasury through its online service, called TreasuryDirect (http://www.treasurydirect.gov/).[3]

Corporate bonds are traded in over-the-counter transactions through brokers and dealers. Because the details of each bond issue may vary—maturity, coupon rate, callability, convertibility, covenants, and so on—it is hard to directly compare bond values the way stock values are compared. As a result, the corporate bond markets are less transparent to the individual investor.

To provide guidance, **rating agencies** provide bond ratings; that is, they "grade" individual bond issues based on the likelihood of default and thus the risk to the investor. Rating agencies are independent agents that base their ratings on the financial stability of the company, its business

rating agencies

Analysts of bond default risk that assign ratings to bonds.

strategy, competitive environment, outlook for the industry and the economy—any factors that may affect the company's ability to meet coupon obligations and pay back debt at maturity.

Ratings agencies such as Fitch Ratings, A. M. Best, Moody's, and Standard & Poor's (S&P) are hired by large borrowers to analyze the company and rate its debt. Moody's also rates government debt. Ratings agencies use an alphabetical system to grade bonds (shown in Table 16.3) based on the highest-to-lowest rankings of two well-known agencies.

TABLE 16.3 Bond Ratings

Standard & Poor's	Moody's	Grade	Meaning
AAA	Aaa	Investment	Risk is almost zero
AA	Aa	Investment	Low risk
A	A	Investment	Risk if economy declines
BBB	Baa	Investment	Some risk; more if economy declines
BB	Ba	Speculative	Risky
B	B	Speculative	Risky; expected to get worse
CCC	Caa	Speculative	Probable bankruptcy
CC	Ca	Speculative	Probable bankruptcy
C	C	Speculative	In bankruptcy or default
D		Speculative	In bankruptcy or default

A plus sign (+) following a rating indicates that it is likely to be upgraded, while a minus sign (-) following a rating indicates that it is likely to be downgraded.

investment grade bonds

Bonds rated BBB or Baa or higher and considered to carry insignificant default risk.

speculative grade bonds

High yield bonds rated BB or Ba or lower and considered to have significant default risk.

junk bonds

High yield bonds rated BB or Ba or lower and considered to have significant default risk.

high-yield bonds

Bonds rated BB or Ba or lower, considered to have significant default risk.

Bonds rated BBB or Baa and above are considered **investment grade bonds**, relatively low risk and "safe" for both individual and institutional investors. Bonds rated below BBB or Baa are speculative in that they carry some default risk. These are called **speculative grade bonds**, **junk bonds**, or **high-yield bonds**. Because they are riskier, speculative grade bonds need to offer investors a higher return or yield in order to be "priced to sell."

Although the term "junk bonds" sounds derogatory, not all speculative grade bonds are "worthless" or are issued by "bad" companies. Bonds may receive a speculative rating if their issuers are young companies, in a highly competitive market, or capital intensive, requiring lots of operating capital. Any of those features would make it harder for a company to meet its bond obligations and thus may consign its bonds to a speculative rating. In the 1980s, for example, companies such as CNN and MCI Communications Corporation issued high-yield bonds, which became lucrative investments as the companies grew into successful corporations.

Default risk is the risk that a company won't have enough cash to meet its interest payments and principal payment at maturity. That risk depends, in turn, on the company's ability to generate cash and profit and to grow to remain competitive. Bond-rating agencies analyze an issuer's default risk by studying its economic, industry, and firm-specific environments and estimate its current and future ability to satisfy its debts. The default risk analysis is similar to equity analysis, but bondholders are more concerned with cash flows—cash to pay back the bondholders—and profits rather than profits alone.

Bond ratings can determine the coupon rate the issuer must offer investors to compensate them for default risk. The higher the risk, the higher the coupon must be. Ratings agencies have been criticized recently for not being objective enough in their ratings of the corporations that hire them. Nevertheless, over the years, bond ratings have proven to be a fairly reliable guide for bond investors.

Key Takeaways

- Bond features that can determine risk and return include:
  - coupon and coupon structure,
  - maturity, callability, and convertibility,
  - security or debenture,
  - seniority or subordination, and
  - covenants.
- The U.S. government issues Treasury
  - bills for short-term borrowing,
  - notes for intermediate-term borrowing,
  - bonds for long-term borrowing, and
  - TIPS, which are inflation-protected.
- State and municipal governments issue
  - revenue bonds, secured by project revenues, or
  - general obligation bonds, secured by the government issuer.
- State and municipal government muni bonds may or may not have tax advantages for certain investors.
- Corporate bonds may be issued through the public bond markets or through private placement.
- U.S. government bonds are issued through auctions managed by the Federal Reserve.
- The secondary bond market offers little transparency because of the differences among bonds and the lower volume of trades.
- To help provide transparency, rating agencies analyze default risk and rate specific bonds.

Exercises

1. Explore the homepage of S&P at https://www.standardandpoors.com/en_US/web/guest/home. Access to bond ratings requires registration, but other information is readily available. How does S&P explain that its rating system does not directly measure default risk?
2. Browse the latest Fact Book from the Securities Industry and Financial Markets Association (sifma) at https://www.sifma.org/resources/archive/research/. How does the volume of bonds and stock issued compare? In the bond markets, what proportion of bonds issued were corporate or government debt? What does this tell you about how corporations and governments are raising capital? What does this tell you about their expectations for the economy, and especially for the costs of capital?
3. What is your state's bond rating? A keyword search ("[state name] bond rating") will bring up current articles on this subject in the news media. What state government activities or expenditures do the bond issues finance? What factors have caused your state's bond rating to be increased or decreased recently? How does your state's bond rating compare with ratings of other states in your region? Now find the current bond rating for your city or town.
4. In My Notes or your personal finance journal, write an explanation of why you might or might not invest in your state at this time. In general, why might you want to invest in municipal bonds? What role would bonds play in your investment portfolio?

16.3 Bond Value

Learning Objectives

1. Explain how bond returns are measured.
2. Define and describe the relationships between interest rates, bond yields, and bond prices.
3. Define and describe the risks that bond investors are exposed to.
4. Explain the implications of the three types of yield curves.
5. Assess the role of the yield curve in bond investing.

Bond-rating systems do not replace bond analysis, which focuses on bond value. Like any investment, a bond is worth the value of its expected return. That value depends on the amount expected and the certainty of that expectation. To understand a bond's value, then, is to understand the value of its return and the costs of its risks.

Bonds return two cash flows to their investors: (1) the coupon, or the interest paid at regular intervals, usually twice yearly or yearly, and (2) the repayment of the principal at maturity. The amounts are spelled out in the bond itself. The coupon rate is specified (for a fixed-rate bond) and the face value is the principal to be returned at the stated maturity.

Unlike a stock, for which the cash flows—both the amount and the timing—are "to be determined," in a bond everything about the cash flows is established at the outset. Any bond feature that makes those cash flows less certain increases the risk to the investor and thus the investor's return. If the bond has a floating-rate coupon, for example, then there is uncertainty about the amount of the coupon payments. If the bond is callable, there is uncertainty about the number of coupon payments.

Whatever the particular features of a bond, as debt instruments, bonds expose investors to specific risks. What are those risks, and what is their role is defining expectations of returns?

Bond Returns

Unlike a stock, a bond's future cash returns are known with certainty. You know what the coupon will be (for a fixed-rate bond) and you know that at maturity the bond will return its face value. For example, if a bond pays a 4% coupon and matures in 10 years, you know that you will receive $20 twice per year (20 = 4% × 1,000 × ½) for 10 years, when you will also receive the $1,000 face value at maturity. You know what you will get and when you will get it. However, you can't be sure what that will be worth to you when you do. You don't know what your opportunity cost will be at the time.

current yield

The short-term return on a bond, calculated as the coupon as a percentage of the bond price.

Investment returns are quoted as an annual percentage of the amount invested, the rate of return. For a bond, that rate is the yield. Yield is expressed in two ways: the current yield and the yield to maturity. The **current yield** is a measure of your bond's rate of return in the short term, if you buy the bond today and keep it for one year. You can calculate the current yield by looking at the coupon for the year as a percentage of your investment or the current price, which is the market price of the bond.

$$\text{Current yield} = \frac{\text{Annual coupon}}{\text{Market value}} = \frac{\text{Coupon rate} \times \text{Face value}}{\text{Market value}}$$

So, if you bought a 4% coupon bond, which is selling for $960 today (its market value), and kept it for one year, the current yield would be:

$$\frac{0.04 \times 1,000}{960} = \frac{40}{960} = 0.0417 = 4.17\%.$$

The idea of the current yield is to give you a quick look at your immediate returns (your return for the next year).

In contrast, the **yield to maturity** (YTM) is a measure of your return if you bought the bond and held it until maturity, waiting to claim the face value. That calculation is a bit more complicated because it involves the relationship between time and value (Chapter 4), since the yield is over the long term until the bond matures. You will find bond yield-to-maturity calculators online, and many financial calculators have the formulas preprogrammed.

yield to maturity
The total return on a bond, assuming it is held to maturity and that coupons may be reinvested at the same rate.

To continue the example, if you buy the bond for $960 today, you will get $20 every six months for 10 years, when you will also get $1,000. Your return will include all the coupon payments ($40 per year over 10 years) and, because you are buying the bond for less than its face value, a gain of $40 (1,000 - 960 = 40) at maturity. The values of these cash flows are affected by time because the cash flows happen at different times. The bond's yield to maturity is close to 4.5%.

Bond prices, their market values, have an inverse relationship to the yield to maturity. As the price goes down, the yield goes up, and as the price goes up, the yield goes down. This makes sense because the payout at maturity is fixed as the face value of the bond ($1,000). Thus, the only way a bond can have a higher rate of return is to have a lower price in the first place.

The yield to maturity is directly related to interest rates in general, so as interest rates increase, bond yields increase, and bond prices fall. As interest rates fall, bond yields fall, and bond prices increase. Figure 16.1 shows these relationships.

FIGURE 16.1 Bond Prices, Bond Yields, and Interest Rates

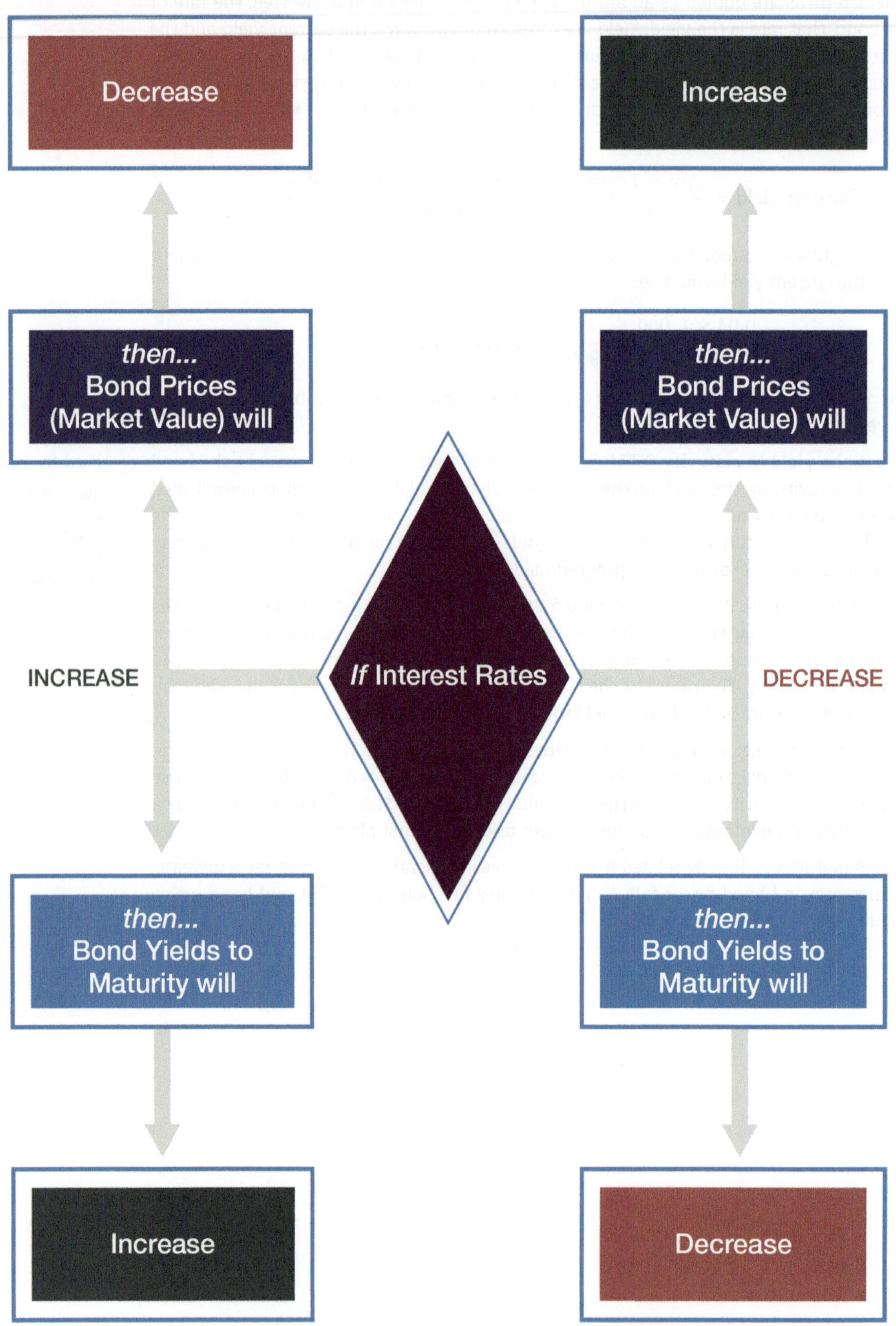

You can use the yield to maturity to compare bonds to see how good they are at creating returns. This yield holds if you hold the bond until maturity, but you may sell the bond at any time. When you sell the bond before maturity, you may have a gain or a loss, since the market value of the bond may have increased or decreased since you bought it. That gain or loss would be part of your return along with the coupons you have received over the holding period, the period of time that you held the bond.

Your **holding period yield** is the annualized rate of return that you receive depending on how long you have held the bond, its gain or loss in market value, and the coupons you received in that period. For example, if you bought the bond for $960 and sold it again for $980 after two years, your return in dollars would be the coupons of $80 ($40 per year × 2 years) plus your gain of $20 ($980 - 960), relative to your original investment of $960. Your holding period yield would be close to 5.2%.

holding period yield

The annualized return on a bond over the period it is owned.

Bond Risks

The basic risk of bond investing is that the returns—the coupon and the principal repayment (face value)—will not be repaid, or that when they are repaid, they won't be worth as much as you thought they would be. The risk that the company will be unable to make its payments is default risk—the risk that it will default on the bond. You can estimate default risk by looking at the bond rating as well as the economic, sector, and firm-specific factors that define the company's soundness.

Part of a bond's value is that you can expect regular coupon payments in cash. You could spend the money or reinvest it. There is a risk, however, that when you go to reinvest the coupon, you will not find another investment opportunity that will pay as high a return because interest rates and yields have fallen. This is called **reinvestment risk**. Your coupons are the amount you thought they would be, but they are not worth as much as you expected because you cannot earn as much from them.

reinvestment risk

The risk that a change in interest rates during the bond's term will change the earnings from reinvesting bond coupons.

If interest rates and bond yields have dropped, your fixed-rate bond, which is still paying the now-higher-than-other-bonds coupon, has become more valuable. Its market price has risen. But the only way to realize the gain from the higher price is to sell the bond, and then you won't have any place to invest the proceeds in other bonds to earn as much return.

Reinvestment risk is one facet of interest rate risk, which arises from the fundamental relationship between bond values and interest rates. **Interest rate risk** is the risk that a change in prevailing interest rates will change bond value—that interest rates will rise and the market value of the bond will fall. (If interest rates fell, the bond value would increase, which the investor would not see as a risk.)

interest rate risk

The risk that a bond's market value will be affected by a change in interest rates.

Another threat to the value of your coupons and principal repayment is inflation. **Inflation risk** is the risk that your coupons and principal repayment will not be worth as much as you thought because inflation has decreased the purchasing power or the value of the dollars you receive.

inflation risk

The risk that the value of a bond's returns will be decreased by a decrease in value of the currency of the bond's denomination.

A bond's features can make it more or less vulnerable to these risks. In general, the longer the term to maturity is, the riskier the bond is. The longer the term is, the greater the probability that the bond will be affected by a change in interest rates, a period of inflation, or a damaging business cycle.

In general, the lower the coupon rate and the smaller the coupon, the more sensitive the bond will be to a change in interest rates. The lower the coupon rate and the smaller the coupon, the more of the bond's return comes from the repayment of principal, which only happens at maturity. More of your return is deferred until maturity, which also makes it more sensitive to interest rate risk. A bond with a larger coupon provides more liquidity, over the term of the bond, and less exposure to risk. Figure 16.2 shows the relationship between bond characteristics and risks.

FIGURE 16.2 Bond Characteristics and Risks

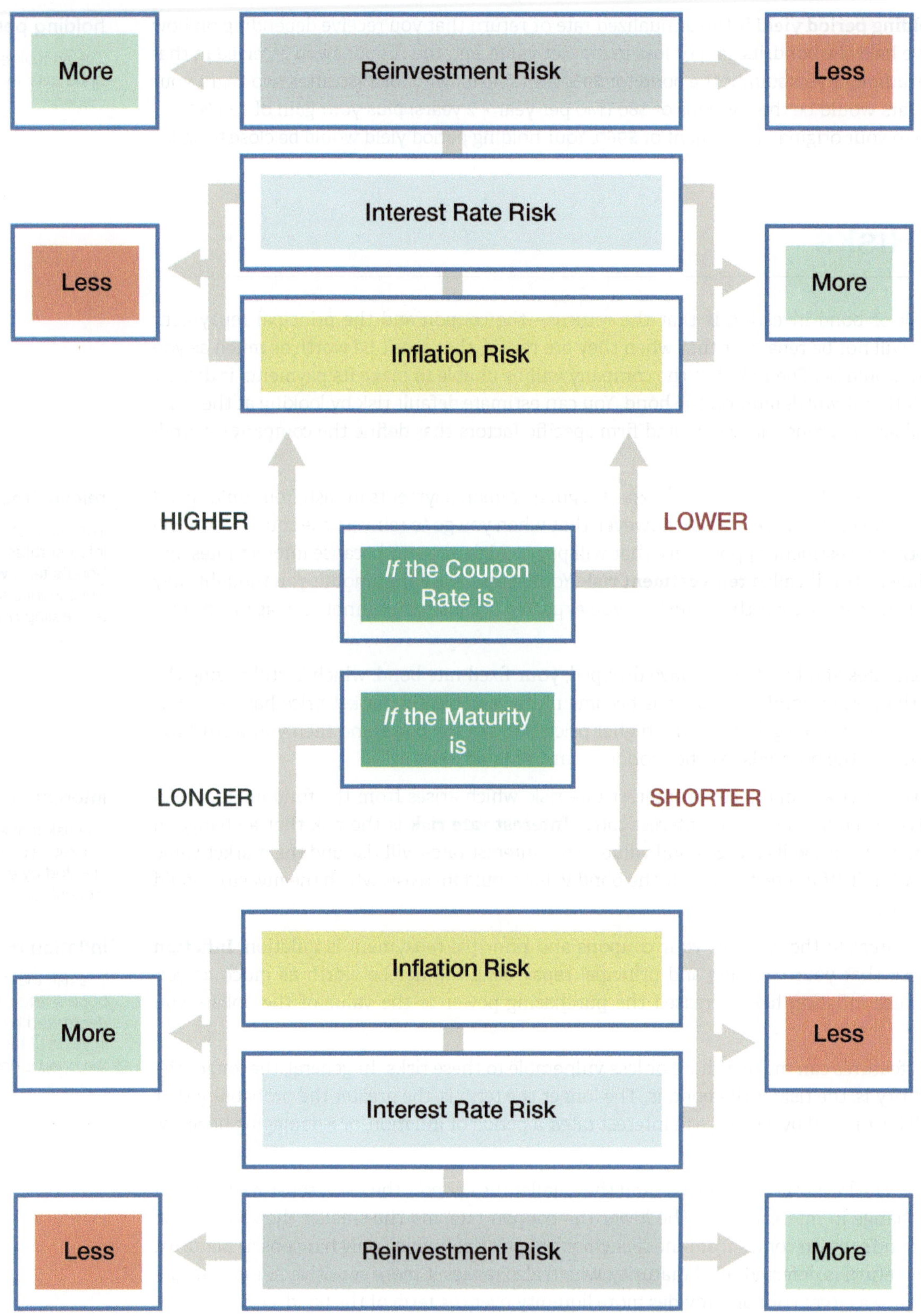

A zero-coupon bond offers the lowest coupon rate possible: zero. Investors avoid reinvestment risk since the only return—and reinvestment opportunity—comes when the principal is returned at maturity. However, a "zero" is exposed to the maximum interest rate risk because interest rates will always be higher than its coupon rate of zero. The attraction of a zero is that it can be bought for a very low price.

As a bond investor, you can make better decisions if you understand how the characteristics of bonds affect their risks and yields as you use those yields to compare and choose bonds.

Yield Curve

Interest rates affect bond risks and bond returns. If you plan to hold a bond until maturity, interest rates also affect reinvestment risk. If you plan to sell the bond before maturity, you face interest rate risk or the risk of a loss of market value. When you invest in bonds, then, you want to be able to forecast future interest rates.

Investors can get a sense of how interest rates are expected to change in the future by studying the yield curve. The **yield curve** is a graph of U.S. Treasury securities compared in terms of the yields for bonds of different maturities. U.S. Treasury securities are used because the U.S. government is considered to have no default risk, so that the yields on its bills and bonds reflect only interest rate, reinvestment, and inflation risks—all of which are reflected in expected, future interest rates.

yield curve
A graphic depiction of the term structure of interest rates.

The yield curve illustrates the **term structure of interest rates**, or the relationship of interest rates to time. Usually, the yield curve is upward sloping—that is, long-term rates are higher than short-term rates. Long-term rates indicate expected future rates. If the economy is expanding, future interest rates are expected to be higher than current interest rates because capital is expected to be more productive in the future. Future interest rates will also be higher if there is inflation because lenders will want more interest to make up for the fact that the currency has lost some of its purchasing power. Figure 16.3 shows an upward-sloping yield curve.

term structure of interest rates
A comparison of interest rates for bonds of different maturities.

FIGURE 16.3 Upward-Sloping Yield Curve

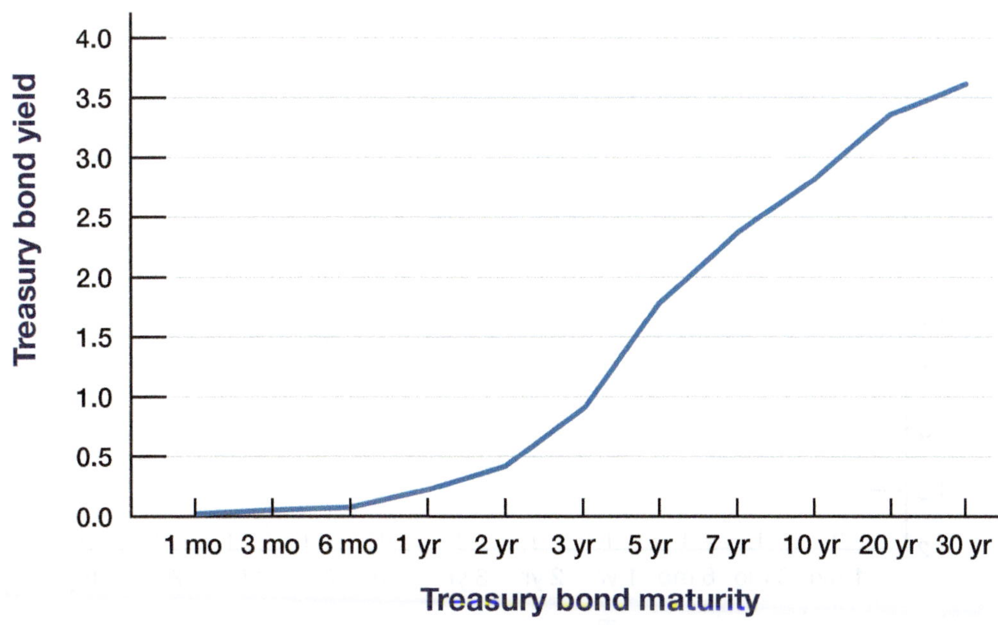

Based on date retrieved from the U.S. Department of the Treasury, "Daily Treasury Yield Curve Rates," http://www.treasury.gov/resource-center/data-chart-center/interest-rates/Pages/TextView.aspx?data=yield (accessed April 9, 2014).

Depending on economic forecasts, the yield curve can also be flat, as in Figure 16.4, or downward-sloping, as in Figure 16.5.

FIGURE 16.4 Flat Yield Curve

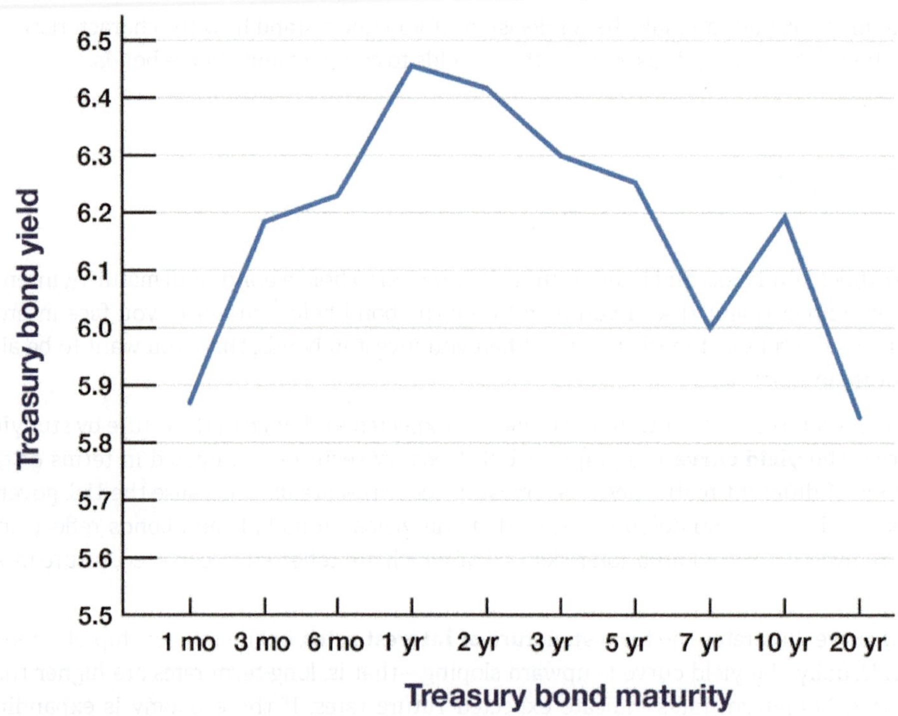

Based on date retrieved from the U.S. Department of the Treasury, "Daily Treasury Yield Curve Rates," http://www.treasury.gov/resource-center/data-chart-center/interest-rates/Pages/TextView.aspx?data=yield (accessed April 9, 2014).

FIGURE 16.5 Downward-Sloping Yield Curve

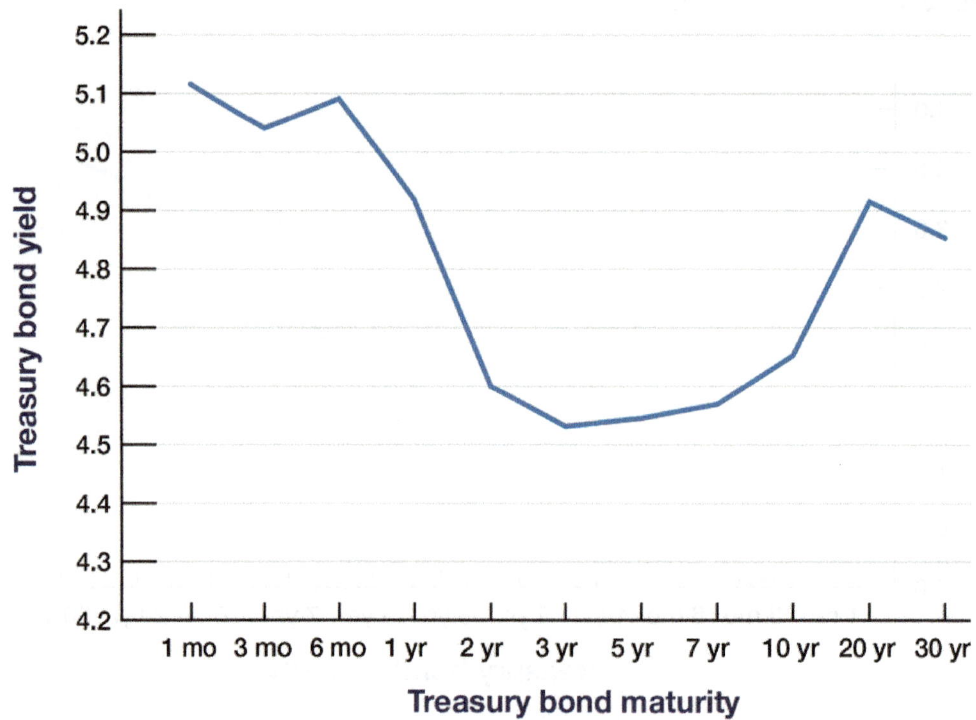

Based on data retrieved from the U.S. Department of the Treasury, "Daily Treasury Yield Curve Rates," http://www.treasury.gov/resource-center/data-chart-center/interest-rates/Pages/TextView.aspx?data=yield (accessed April 9, 2014).

A flat yield curve indicates that future interest rates are expected to be about the same as current interest rates or that capital will be about as productive in the economy as it is now. A downward-sloping yield curve shows that future interest rates are expected to be lower than current rates. This is often interpreted as a signal of a recession because capital would be less productive in the future if the economy were less productive then.

The yield curve is not perfectly smooth; it changes every day as bonds trade and new prices and new yields are established in the bond markets. It is, however, a widely used indicator of interest rate trends. It can be useful to you to know the broad trends in interest rates that the market sees.

For your bond investments, an upward-sloping yield curve indicates that interest rates will go up, which means that bond yields will go up but bond prices will go down. If you are planning to sell your bond in that period of rising interest rates, you may be selling your bond at a loss.

Because of their known coupon and face value, many investors use bonds to invest funds for a specific purpose. For example, suppose you have a child who is eight years old and you want her to be able to go to college in 10 years. You might invest in bonds that have 10 years until maturity. However, if you invest in bonds that have 20 years until maturity, they will have a higher yield (all else being equal), so you could invest less now.

You could buy the 20-year bonds but plan to sell them before maturity for a price determined by what interest rates are in 10 years (when you sell them). If the yield curve indicates that interest rates will rise over the next 10 years, then you could expect your bond price to fall, and you would have a loss when you sell the bond, which would take away from your returns.

In general, rising interest rates mean losses for bondholders who sell before maturity, and falling interest rates mean gains for bondholders who sell before maturity. Unless you are planning to hold bonds until maturity, the yield curve can give you a sense of whether you are more likely to have a gain or loss.

Key Takeaways

- All bonds expose investors to:
  - default risk (the risk that coupon and principal payments won't be made),
  - reinvestment risk (the risk that coupon payments will be reinvested at lower rates),
  - interest rate risk (the risk that changing interest rates will affect bond values),
  - inflation risk, (the risk that inflation will devalue bond coupons and principal repayment).
- Bond returns can be measured by yields.
  - The current yield measures short-term return on investment.
  - The yield to maturity measures return on investment until maturity.
  - The holding period yield measures return on investment over the term that the bond is held.
- There is a direct relationship between interest rates and bond yields.
- There is an inverse relationship between bond yields and bond prices (market values).
- There is an inverse relationship between bond prices (market values) and interest rates.
- The yield curve illustrates the term structure of interest rates, showing yields of bonds with differing maturities and the same default risk. The purpose of a yield curve is to show expectations of future interest rates.
- The yield curve may be:
  - upward sloping, indicating higher future interest rates;
  - flat, indicating similar future interest rates; or
  - downward sloping, indicating lower future interest rates.

Exercises

1. Read Investopedia's explanation of how to read a bond table at http://www.investinginbonds.com/learnmore.asp?catid=3&id=45. Why does bond and bond market information seem harder to find and understand than stock and stock market information, especially since the bond market is so much bigger than the stock market?
2. To find out more about how to use bond quotations when making investment decisions, watch the video from "Learn Bonds" at https://www.youtube.com/watch?v=imZ0tCVeOMw. As a bond investor, why would you want to know the bond spread? What does that tell you about the bond?
3. Experiment with Investopedia's yield-to-maturity calculator at http://www.investopedia.com/calculator/AOYTM.aspx. Why should you know the yield to maturity, indicated as YTM on the calculator, before investing in bonds?

16.4 Bond Strategies

Learning Objectives

1. Discuss diversification as a strategic use of bonds.
2. Summarize strategies to achieve bond diversification.
3. Define and compare matching strategies.
4. Explain life cycle investing and bond strategy.

Bonds provide more secure income for an investment portfolio, while stocks provide more growth potential. When you include bonds in your portfolio, you do so to have more income and less risk than you would have with just stocks. Bonds also diversify the portfolio. Because debt is so fundamentally different from equity, debt markets and equity markets respond differently to changing economic conditions.

Diversification Strategies

If your main strategic goal of including bonds is diversification, you can choose an active or passive bond selection strategy. As with equities, an active strategy requires individual bond selection, while a passive strategy involves the use of indexing, or investing through a broadly diversified bond index fund or mutual fund in which bonds have already been selected.

The advantage of the passive strategy is its greater diversification and relatively low cost. The advantage of an active strategy is the chance to create gains by finding and taking advantage of market mispricings. An active strategy is difficult for individual investors in bonds, however, because the bond market is less transparent and less liquid than the stock market.

If your main strategic goal of including bonds is to lower the risk of your portfolio, you should keep in mind that bond risk varies. U.S. Treasuries have the least default risk, while U.S. and foreign corporate bonds have the most. Bond ratings can help you to compare default risks.

Another way to look at the effect of default risk on bond prices is to look at spreads. A **spread** is the difference between one rate and another. With bonds, the spread generally refers to the difference between one yield to maturity and another. Spreads are measured and quoted in basis points. A **basis point** is one one-hundredth of 1%, or 0.0001 or 0.01%.

spread

A difference between two interest rates, quoted in basis points. The most commonly noted spreads are those between Treasury and corporate securities of the same maturity.

basis point

A unit of measure that is one one-hundredth of a percentage point, or 0.01 percent.

The most commonly quoted spread is the difference between the yield to maturity for a Treasury bond and a corporate bond with the same term to maturity. Treasury bonds are considered to have no default risk because it is unlikely that the U.S. government will default. Treasuries are exposed to reinvestment, interest rate, and inflation risks, however.

Corporate bonds are exposed to all four types of risk. So the difference between a 20-year corporate bond and a 20-year Treasury bond is the difference between a bond with and without default risk. The difference between their yields—the spread—is the additional yield for the investor for taking on default risk. The riskier the corporate bond is, the greater the spread will be.

Spreads generally fluctuate with market trends and with confidence in the economy or expectations of economic cycles. When spreads narrow, the yields on corporate bonds are closer to the yields on Treasuries, indicating that there is less concern with default risk. When spreads widen—as they did in the summer and fall of 2008, when the debt markets seemed suddenly very risky—corporate bondholders worry more about default risk.

As the spread widens, corporate yields rise and/or Treasury yields fall. This means that corporate bond prices (market values) are falling and/or Treasury bond values are rising. This is sometimes referred to as the "flight to quality." In uncertain times, investors would rather invest in Treasuries than corporate bonds because of the increased default risk of corporate bonds. As a result, Treasury prices rise (and yields fall) and corporate prices fall (and yields rise).

Longer-term bonds are more exposed to reinvestment, interest rate, and inflation risk than shorter-term bonds. If you are using bonds to achieve diversification, you want to be sure to be diversified among bond maturities. For example, you would want to have a mixture of short-term (less than one year until maturity), intermediate-term (two to 10 years until maturity), and long-term (more than 10 years until maturity) bonds in addition to diversifying on the basis of industries, companies, and perhaps even countries.

Matching Strategies

Matching strategies are used to create a bond portfolio that will finance specific funding needs, such as education, a down payment on a second home, or retirement. If the timing and cash flow amounts of these needs can be predicted, then a matching strategy can be used to support them. This strategy involves matching a "liability" (to yourself because you "owe" yourself the chance to reach that goal) with an asset, a bond investment. The two most commonly used matching strategies are immunization and cash flow matching.

matching strategies

Strategies used to create a bond portfolio that will finance specific funding or liquidity needs at specific times.

Immunization is designing a bond portfolio that will achieve a certain rate of return over a specific period of time, based on the idea of balancing interest rate risk and reinvestment risk.

immunization

A bond portfolio strategy designed to "immunize" or protect the portfolio from interest rate risk.

Recall that as interest rates rise, bond values decrease, but reinvested income from bond coupons earns more. As interest rates fall, bond values increase, but reinvested income from bond coupons decreases. Immunization is the idea of choosing a portfolio of bonds such that the exposure to interest rate risk is exactly offset by the exposure to reinvestment risk for a certain period of time, thus guaranteeing a minimum return over that period.[4]

In other words, the interest rate risk and the reinvestment risk cancel each other out, and the investor is left with a guaranteed return. You would use this kind of strategy when you had a liquidity need with a deadline, for example, to fund a child's higher education.

cash flow matching

A strategy of investing in bonds with maturities and face values that match anticipated cash flow amounts and timing.

Cash flow matching, also called a dedication strategy, is an alternative to immunization. It involves choosing bonds that match your anticipated cash flow needs by having maturities that coincide with the timing of those needs. For example, if you will need $50,000 for travel in 20 years, you could buy bonds with a face value of $50,000 and a maturity of 20 years. If you hold the bonds to maturity, their face value provides the amount of cash flow you need, and you don't have to worry about interest rate or reinvestment risk. You can plan on having $50,000 in 20 years, barring any default.

If you had the $50,000 now, you could just stuff it under your mattress or save it in a savings account. But buying a bond has two advantages: (1) you may be able to buy the bond for less than $50,000 now, requiring less upfront investment and (2) over the next 20 years, the bond will also pay coupons at a higher rate than you could earn with a savings account or under your mattress.

bond laddering

A strategy of cash flow matching to create a series of regular cash flows from bond investments.

If you will need different cash flows at different times, you can use cash flow matching for each one. When cash flow matching is used to create a steady stream of regular cash flows, it is called **bond laddering**. You invest in bonds of different maturities, such that you would have one bond maturing and providing cash flow in each period (like the CD laddering discussed in Chapter 7).

Strategies such as immunization and cash flow matching are designed to manage interest rate and reinvestment risk to minimize their effects on your portfolio's goals. Since you are pursuing an active strategy by selecting individual bonds, you must also consider transaction costs and the tax consequences of your gain (or loss) at maturity and their effects on your target cash flows.

Life Cycle Investing

Bonds most commonly are used to reduce portfolio risk. Typically, as your risk tolerance decreases with age, you will include more bonds in your portfolio, shifting its weight from stocks—with more growth potential—to bonds, with more income and less risk. This change in the weighting of portfolio assets usually begins as you get closer to retirement.

For years, the conventional wisdom was that you should have the same percentage of your portfolio invested in bonds as your age, so when you are 30, you have 30% of your portfolio in bonds; when you are 50, you have 50% of your portfolio in bonds; and so on. That wisdom is being questioned now, however, because while bonds are lower risk, they also lower growth potential. Today, as more people can expect to live much longer past retirement age, they run a real risk of outliving their funds if they invest as conservatively as the conventional wisdom suggests.

It is still true nevertheless that for most people, risk tolerance changes with age, and your investment in bonds should reflect that change.

Key Takeaways

- One strategic use of bonds in a portfolio is to increase diversification.
- Diversification can be achieved:
  - by an active strategy, using individual bond selection; or
  - by a passive strategy, using indexing.
- Spreads indicate the "price" or the yield on default risk.

- Matching strategies to minimize interest rate and reinvestment risks can include:
  - immunization,
  - cash flow matching, and
  - bond laddering.
- Life cycle investing considers the relationship of age and risk tolerance to the strategic use of bonds in a portfolio.

Exercises

1. In My Notes or your personal finance journal, record your bond strategy. What will be your purpose in including bonds in your portfolio? What types of bonds will you include and why? Will you take an active or passive approach and why? How will spreads inform your investment decisions? Which bond strategies described in this section will you plan to use and why? How will your bond strategies reflect your needs to diversify, reduce risk, and maximize liquidity at the right times? How will your bond strategies reflect your age and risk tolerance?
2. For a different perspective on bond investing, read, "Do you really need to invest in bonds", at http://money.cnn.com/2017/03/01/retirement/bonds-retirement/index.html. Discuss with classmates how this perspective changes your views of bonds as an investment. Brainstorm additional questions about bond investing to ask the expert.

Endnotes

1. Isadore Barmash, *The Self-Made Man* (Washington, DC: Beard Books, 2003), 55.
2. George Burton Adams, *The Constitutional History of England* (London: H. Holt, 1921), 93.
3. TreasuryDirect, http://www.treasurydirect.gov/ (accessed June 2, 2018).
4. John L. Maginn, Donald L. Tuttle, Jerald E. Pinto, and Dennis W. McLeavey, eds., *Managing Investment Portfolios: A Dynamic Process*, 3rd ed. (Hoboken, NJ: John Wiley & Sons, Inc., 2007).

CHAPTER 17
Investing in Mutual Funds, Commodities, Real Estate, and Collectibles

17.1 Introduction

When people think of investing, they tend to think of stocks and bonds, investing in companies that create productivity, employment, and profit. Investments in stocks and bonds are ways of sharing in that profit and ultimately in economic growth.

While companies are the engines of economic growth, other assets such as real estate and commodities—natural resources or raw materials—fuel those engines. Increased market transparency and access, largely through the technologies of the Internet and global communications, have made it possible for more investors to invest in the "fuels" as well as the "engines" of commerce. Real estate and commodities investing have become increasingly popular as diversifiers for a sound investment portfolio.

Mutual funds are not another kind of asset but another way of investing in any kind of asset. The fund is a pool capable of much greater diversification than an individual's investment portfolio, given transaction costs. A mutual fund can also provide security selection, expertise, liquidity, and convenience. Some funds are even designed to perform the asset allocation task for the investor. Mutual funds are fast becoming the dominant investment vehicle for individual investors, changing the role of the broker and financial advisor.

17.2 Mutual Funds

Learning Objectives

1. Identify the general purposes of using mutual funds or ETFs in individual investment portfolios.
2. Analyze the advantages of an index fund or a fund of funds.
3. List and define the structures of mutual funds and ETFs.
4. Describe the strategic goals of lifestyle funds, leveraged funds, and inverse funds.
5. Identify the costs and differences in costs of mutual fund investing.
6. Calculate returns from mutual fund investing.
7. Summarize the information found in a mutual fund prospectus.

As defined in Chapter 12, a mutual fund is a portfolio of securities, consisting of one type of security or a combination of several different types. A fund serves as a convenient way for an investor to have a diversified portfolio of investments in just about any investable asset. The oldest mutual fund is believed to have been founded by Adriaan van Ketwich in 1774. Ketwich invited investors to contribute to a trust fund to spread the risk of investing in foreign bonds. The idea moved from the Netherlands to Scotland to the United States, where the Boston Personal Property Trust established the first mutual fund in 1893.[1]

FIGURE 17.1

© Shutterstock, Inc.

The mutual fund's popularity has grown in periods of economic expansion. At the height of the stock market boom in 1929, there were over 700 mutual funds in the United States. After 1934, mutual funds fell under the regulatory eye of the Securities and Exchange Commission (SEC), and it wasn't until the 1950s that there were once again over 100 mutual funds in the United States.

Mutual funds multiplied in the 1970s, spurred on by the creation of IRAs and 401(k) retirement plans, and again in the 1980s and 1990s, inspired by economic growth and the tech stock boom. By the beginning end of 2017, U.S. mutual funds—which account for just over half of the global market—had more than $18.7 trillion in assets under management in over 7,900 mutual funds. More than half of all individual retirement assets (i.e., 401ks and IRAs) in the United States are invested in mutual funds.[2] Mutual funds play a significant role in individual investment decisions.

A mutual fund provides an investor with cheaper and simpler diversification and security selection, requiring only one transaction to own a diversified portfolio (the mutual fund). By buying shares in the fund rather than individual securities, you achieve extensive diversification for a much lower transaction cost than by investing in individual securities and making individual transactions. You also receive the benefit of professional security selection, which theoretically minimizes the opportunity costs of lesser choices. So by using a mutual fund, you get more and better security selection and diversification.

A mutual fund also provides stock and bond issuers with a mass market. Rather than selling shares to investors individually (and incurring the costs of doing so), issuers can more easily find a market for their shares in mutual funds.

Structures and Types of Mutual Funds

index funds

A mutual fund designed to track the performance of an index for investors who seek diversification without having to select securities.

Like stocks and bonds, mutual funds may be actively or passively managed. As you read in Chapter 15 and Chapter 16, active management provides investors with professional management and the expected research, analysis, and watchfulness that goes with it. Passively managed **index funds**, on the other hand, are designed to mirror the performance of a specific index constructed to be representative of an asset class. Recall, for example, that the Standard & Poor's (S&P) 500 Index is designed to mirror the performance of the 500 largest large-cap stocks in the United States.

Mutual funds are structured in three ways:

1. Closed-end funds
2. Open-end funds
3. Exchange-traded funds

closed-end fund

A mutual fund that issues a limited number of shares, so that existing shares must be sold to new investors.

Closed-end funds are funds for which a limited number of shares are issued. Once all shares have been issued, the fund is "closed" so a new investor can only buy shares from an existing investor. Since the shares are traded on an exchange, the limited supply of shares and the demand for them in that market directly determine the value of the shares for a closed-end fund.

Most mutual funds are **open-end funds** in which investors buy shares directly from the fund and redeem or sell shares back to the fund. The price of a share is its **net asset value (NAV)**, or the market value of each share as determined by the fund's assets and liabilities and the number of shares that exist. Here is the basic formula for calculating NAV:

$$\text{NAV} = \frac{\textbf{Market value of fund securities} - \textbf{Fund liabilities}}{\textbf{Number of fund shares outstanding}}$$

Demand for shares is reflected in the number of shares outstanding because the fund can create new shares for new investors. NAV calculations are usually done once per day at the close of trading, when mutual fund transactions are recorded.

The NAV is the price that the fund will pay you when you redeem your shares, so it is a gauge of the shares' value. It will increase if the market value of the securities in the fund increases faster than the number of new shares.

Exchange-traded funds (ETFs) are structured like closed-end funds but are traded like stocks. Shares are traded and priced continuously throughout the day's trading session, rather than once per day at the end of trading. ETFs trade more like individual securities; that is, if you are trying to time a market, they are a more nimble asset to trade than open-end or closed-end funds.

Originally designed as index funds, exchange-traded funds now target just about every asset, sector, and economic region imaginable. Because of this, ETFs have become quite popular, with over $3.345 trillion invested in over 1,700 funds (as of the end of 2017).[3] Table 17.1 compares the features of closed-end funds, open-end funds, and ETFs.

open-end fund

A mutual fund in which shares are bought from and sold to the fund management; the number of shares is not limited.

net asset value (NAV)

When used regarding open-end mutual funds, NAV refers to the redeemable value of each fund share at that time, given the market value of the fund's assets and the number of shares outstanding.

exchange-traded funds (ETFs)

A mutual fund that is structured as a closed-end fund and actively traded on an exchange.

TABLE 17.1 Fund Features

	Closed-End	Open-End	ETF
Number of Shares	Limited	Unlimited	Limited
Trades	End of the trading day	End of the trading day	Continuously
Traded with	Other shareholders (after the fund closes)	Fund sponsor	Other shareholders

Shares of closed-end funds and exchange-traded funds are bought and sold on exchanges, much like shares of stock. You would go through a broker to make those transactions. Shares of open-end funds may be bought and sold directly from the fund sponsor, a mutual fund company or investment manager such as Fidelity, Vanguard, Janus, T. Rowe Price, or Teachers Insurance and Annuity Association-College Retirement Equities Fund (TIAA-CREF). You can make those transactions at any of the company's offices, by telephone, or online. About 40% of all mutual fund transactions are done directly (without a broker) through a retirement plan contribution or a mutual fund company.[4]

Some other types of mutual funds are shown in Table 17.2. Research companies, such as Morningstar, track dozens of different categories of mutual funds.

TABLE 17.2 Other Types of Mutual Funds

Funds of Funds	Mutual funds that own shares in other mutual funds rather than in specific securities. If you decide to use mutual funds rather than select securities, a fund of funds will provide expertise in choosing funds.
Lifestyle Funds	Funds of stocks and bonds that manage portfolio risk based on age or the time horizon for liquidity needs. Lifestyle funds perform both security selection and asset allocation for investors, determined by the target date. For example, if you were now 30 years old, you might choose a lifestyle fund with a target date of 35 years from now for your retirement savings. As the fund approaches its target date, its allocation of investments in stocks and bonds will shift to carry less risk as the target nears. Lifestyle funds are used primarily in saving for retirement; many are created as funds of funds.
Leveraged Funds	Funds that invest both investors' money and money that the fund borrows to augment the investable assets and thus potential returns. Because they use borrowing, leveraged funds are riskier than funds that do not use leverage.
Inverse Funds	Funds that aim to increase in value when the market declines, to be countercyclical to index funds, which aim to increase in value when the market rises. Inverse funds, also called bear funds, are set up to perform contrary to the index. As most economies become more productive over time, however, you can expect indexes to rise over time, so an inverse fund would make sense only as a very short-term investment.

Mutual Fund Fees and Returns

load fund

A mutual fund that charges a sales commission or fee upon investment or purchase of shares; the load is stated as a percentage of invested funds.

front-end load

The sales charge for mutual fund shares, quoted as a percentage of the funds invested; it cannot be more than 8.5 percent of investment.

no-load fund

A mutual fund that does not charge a sales commission or fee upon investment or purchase of shares.

back-end load

A deferred sales charge or sales fee charged when shares are redeemed.

All funds must disclose their fees to potential investors: sales fees, management fees, and expenses. A **load fund** charges a sales commission on each share purchase. That sales charge (also called a **front-end load**) is a percentage of the purchase price. A **no-load fund**, in contrast, does not charge a sales commission, because shares may be purchased directly from the fund or through a discount broker. The front-end load can be as much as 8.5%, so if you plan to invest often or in large amounts, that can be a substantial charge. For example, a $5,000 investment may cost you $425, reducing the amount you have to invest and earn a return.

A fund may charge a **back-end load**, actually a deferred sales charge, paid when you sell your shares instead of when you buy them. The charge may be phased out if you own the shares for a specified length of time, however, usually five to seven years.

A fund may charge a management fee on an annual basis. The management fee is stated as a fixed percentage of the fund's asset value per share. Management fees can range from 0.1% to 2.0% annually. Typically, a more actively managed fund can be expected to charge a higher management fee, while a passively managed fund such as an index fund should charge a minimal management fee.

A fund may charge an annual **12b-1 fee** or distribution fee, also calculated as not more than 1.0% per year of the fund's asset value. Some mutual funds charge other extra fees as well, passing on fund expenses to shareholders. You should consider fee structure and rate when choosing mutual funds, and this can be done through calculations of the expense ratio.

12b-1 fee

An annual management fee charged to mutual fund shareholders and calculated as a percentage of the assets under management.

Taken together, the annual management, distribution, and expense fees are measured by the **expense ratio**—the total annual fees expressed as a percentage of your total investment. In 2017, the expense ratio averaged around 0.59% for all mutual funds, but it may be more than 2% of your investment's value.[5] That may not sound like much, but it means that if the fund earns a 5% return, your net return may be less than 3% (and after taxes, it's even less). When choosing a fund, you should be aware of all charges—especially annual or ongoing charges—that can affect your investment return.

expense ratio

The total expenses of a mutual fund investment as a percentage of share value.

Say you invest in a load fund with a 5% front-end load and an expense ratio of 2.25% and suppose the fund earns a 5% return. Table 17.3 shows how your $5,000 investment would look after one year.

TABLE 17.3 Mutual Fund Example

Original investment	5,000.00
Load (5%)	- 250.00
Net investment	4,750.00
Return (5%)	+ 237.50
End-of-year assets	4,987.50
Less expenses (2.25%)	- 112.22
Ending investment	4,875.28
Net return (ending investment value – net investment)	125.28
Net percentage return	2.64%

Expenses can be a significant determinant of your net return, and since expenses vary by fund, fund strategy (active or passive), and fund sponsor, you should shop around and understand what your costs of investing will be.

Owning shares of a mutual fund means owning shares in a pool of assets. The returns of the fund are the returns of those assets: interest, dividends, or gains (losses). Income may come from **interest distributions** if the fund invests in bonds or interest-producing assets or as **dividend distributions** if the fund invests in stocks.

interest distributions

Mutual fund returns from any interest payments on the mutual fund holdings, such as bonds.

dividend distributions

Mutual fund returns from any dividends distributed by mutual fund equity holdings.

Mutual funds buy and sell or "turn over" the fund assets. Even passively managed funds need to rebalance to keep pace with their benchmarks as market values change. The **turnover ratio** is the percentage of fund assets that have been turned over or replaced in the past year, a measure of the fund's trading activity.

turnover ratio

A measure of how much annual trading activity there is within a mutual fund's holdings.

capital gains distributions

The shareholder's share of capital gains (losses) created by mutual fund turnover.

Turnover can create capital gains or losses. Periodically, usually once per year, the fund's net capital gains (or losses) are distributed on a per share basis as a **capital gains distribution**. You would expect turnover to produce more gains than losses. The more turnover, or the higher the turnover ratio, the greater the capital gains distributions you may expect.

Unless you have invested in a tax-exempt savings plan such as an individual retirement account (IRA) or a 401(k), interest and dividend distributions are taxable as personal income, as are capital gains, including capital gains distributions. A higher turnover ratio may mean a higher tax expense for capital gains distributions. Most open-end mutual funds allow you the option of having your income and gains distributions automatically reinvested rather than paid out, which means that you may be paying taxes on earnings without ever "seeing" the money.

Mutual Fund Information and Strategies

prospectus

A written statement of a mutual fund's structure, management, investment objectives, holdings, and historic and current performance; funds are required to make the prospectus available to all potential investors.

All mutual fund companies must offer a **prospectus**, a published statement detailing the fund's assets, liabilities, management personnel, and performance record. You should always take the time to read it and to take a closer look at the fund's investments to make sure that the fund will be compatible and appropriate to your investment goals.

FIGURE 17.2

For example, suppose you have an investment in an S&P 500 Index fund and now are looking for a global stock fund to complement and diversify your holdings in domestic (U.S.) equities. You go to the website of a large mutual fund company offering hundreds of funds. You find a stock fund called "Global Stock Fund"—sounds like it's just what you are looking for. Looking more closely, however, you can see that this fund is invested in the stocks of companies in Germany, Japan, and the United Kingdom. While they are not U.S. stocks, those economies are similar to the U.S. economy, perhaps too similar to provide the diversity you want.

Or suppose you are looking for a bond fund to create income and security. You find a fund called the "Investment Grade Fixed Income Fund." On closer inspection, however, you find that the fund does not invest only in investment grade bonds but that the *average* rating of its bonds is investment grade. This means that the fund invests in many investment grade bonds but also in some speculative grade bonds to achieve higher income. While this fund may suit your need for income, it may not be appropriate for your risk tolerance.

Mutual fund companies make this information readily available on websites and in prospectuses. You should always make the extra effort to be sure you know what's in your fund. In addition, mutual funds are widely followed by many performance analysts. Ratings agencies such as Morningstar and investment publications such as *Barron's* and *Forbes* track, analyze, and report the performance of mutual funds. That information is available online or in print and provides comparisons of mutual funds that you may find helpful in choosing your fund.

In print and online newspapers, mutual fund performance is reported daily in the form of tables that compare the average returns of funds from week to week. Reported average returns are based on the net asset value per share (NAVPS). Investors can use this information to choose or compare funds and track the performance of funds they own.

In conclusion, since a mutual fund may be made up of any kind or many kinds of securities (e.g., stocks, bonds, real estate, and commodities), it is not really another kind of investment. Rather, it is a way to invest without specifically selecting securities, a way of achieving a desired asset allocation without choosing individual assets.

The advantages of investing in a mutual fund are the diversification available with minimal transaction costs and the professional management or security selection that you get when you buy into the fund.

Compared to actively managed funds, passively managed or index funds offer similar diversification but with lower management fees and expense ratios because you aren't paying for market timing or security selection skills. The turnover ratio shows how passive or active the fund management is. About half of all equity mutual funds have a turnover ratio of less than 50%.[6]

Performance history has shown that actively managed funds, on average, do not necessarily outperform passively managed funds.[7] Since they usually have higher fees, any advantage created by active management is usually canceled out by their higher costs. Still, there are investors who believe that some mutual funds and mutual fund managers can, on average, outperform the markets or the indexes that provide the benchmarks for passively managed funds.

Key Takeaways

- Mutual funds provide investors with:
  - diversification,
  - security selection, and
  - asset allocation.
- Funds may be actively or passively managed.
- Index funds mirror an index of securities, providing diversification without security selection.
- Funds of funds provide the investor with preselected funds.
- Mutual funds may be structured as:
  - closed-end funds,
  - open-end funds, or
  - exchange-traded funds.

- Some funds are structured to achieve specific investment goals:
  - Lifestyle funds with target dates to minimize liquidity risk through asset allocation
  - Leveraged funds to increase return by using debt
  - Inverse funds to increase return through active management with the expectation of a down market
- Mutual fund costs may include:
  - a sales charge when shares are purchased, or front-end load,
  - a sales charge when shares are sold, or back-end load,
  - a management fee while shares are owned, or
  - a 12b-1 (distribution) fee while shares are owned.
- The management expense ratio is the total mutual fund cost expressed as a percentage of the funds invested.
- Fees vary by
  - fund sponsor,
  - fund strategy (active or passive), and
  - fund sales (direct or through a broker).
- Returns from a mutual fund include returns on the securities it owns, including:
  - interest distributions,
  - dividend distributions, and
  - capital gains distributions.
- A fund prospectus details the fund's investment holdings, historic returns, and costs. Mutual fund ratings in the financial media are another source of information.

Exercises

1. Survey the articles and tools at http://finance.yahoo.com/funds. Use the "Fund Screener" to find four mutual funds that you would use to create a diversified portfolio. How do the fund ratings influence your choices? Estimate the funds' returns and costs (as percentage rates) if you hold them for five years.
2. Securities regulations require complete and continuous disclosure, also referred to as transparency, so that investors will know what they are getting into when they invest. This requirement is partly satisfied through a fund prospectus. Read the SEC's advice on how to read a prospectus and what to look for at http://www.sec.gov/answers/mfprospectustips.htm. Then compare that information with the advice offered at http://www.getrichslowly.org/blog/2009/04/23/how-to-read-a-mutual-fund-prospectus/. On the same page, browse the "Best of Get Rich Slowly" links, too. How does this information reinforce the idea that you should thoroughly read and understand a prospectus before investing in a fund?
3. View Morningstar's performance data chart for various categories of mutual funds at http://news.morningstar.com/fundReturns/CategoryReturns.html. What general categories of funds are included in the chart? Over what time periods are average returns compared? Which fund sectors have performed best over the past five years?
4. Read Investopedia's article on the costs of investing in mutual funds at http://www.investopedia.com/university/mutualfunds/mutualfunds2.asp. What is your management expense ratio (MER)? Do mutual funds with higher expenses generally earn higher returns?
5. Take Investopedia's tutorial on how to read a mutual fund table in the financial news at http://www.investopedia.com/university/mutualfunds/mutualfunds4.asp. What do the columns mean? What is being compared? What can you learn from mutual fund tables that may help you choose funds or track the performance of funds you own? Share your ideas with classmates.

6. In My Notes or your personal finance journal, record your study of a fund you choose to track (perhaps one of the funds from exercise 1). Read the prospectus, check its ratings, and compare its week-to-week performance with that of similar funds in the mutual funds table in the financial section of a newspaper. Record your observations, questions, and commentary as you go about deciding hypothetically whether or not to invest in that fund.

17.3 Real Estate Investments

Learning Objectives

1. Distinguish between direct and indirect investments in real estate.
2. Identify the four main ways to invest in real estate indirectly.
3. Explain the role and the different kinds of REITs.
4. Discuss the role and uses of mortgage-backed securities.

When you buy a home, even with a mortgage, you are making a **direct investment**, because you are both the investor and the owner who holds legal title to the property. For most people, a home is the single largest investment they ever make.

As an investor, you may want to include other real estate holdings in your portfolio, most likely as an **indirect investment** in which you invest in an entity that owns and manages real estate. Studies have shown that real estate can be a good diversifier for financial investments such as stocks and bonds.[8]

direct investment

A real estate investment in which you are the owner and manager of property.

indirect investment

A real estate investment in which you buy shares of an entity that owns and manages property.

Direct Investments

Sonia is looking to buy her first home. After graduating from college, she decided to stay on because she liked the town and found a job as an elementary school teacher. She loves her job, but her income is limited. She finds a nice, two-family house in a neighborhood close to the college. It needs some work, but she figures she can use the summer months to fix it up—she's pretty handy—and renting to students won't be a problem. The tenants will pay their own utilities. Sonia figures that the rental income will help pay her mortgage, insurance, and taxes, and that after the mortgage is paid off, it will provide a nice extra income.

FIGURE 17.3

© Shutterstock, Inc.

Many real estate investors begin like Sonia, buying a rental property that helps them to afford their own home. If you actively manage the rental property, there are tax benefits as well. Of course, you have to provide maintenance services and arrange for repairs, and, in Sonia's case, perhaps give up a bit of privacy. A second home or vacation home can be used as a rental property as well, although the tax benefits are less assured. In both cases, the investor is making a direct investment in the property.

FIGURE 17.4

© Shutterstock, Inc.

commercial property

Property used exclusively to create rental income.

The advantages to a direct investment are the additional rental income and tax benefits. The disadvantages are that real estate is relatively illiquid, and the investment concentrates your portfolio in one asset class—residential real estate. Conventional wisdom was that real estate was a good hedge against inflation, but the 2007 burst of the housing bubble—not only in the United States but also worldwide—has cast a shadow on that thinking. Also, to realize the tax benefits, you must actively manage the rental property, and being a landlord is not for everyone.

Other direct real estate investments include **commercial property**, or property exclusively for rent, and undeveloped land. Developers buy property or land and seek to profit from quickly improving and reselling it. Both are more speculative investments, especially if purchased with debt financing. They may also prove to be illiquid and to concentrate assets, making them inappropriate investments for investors without a large and diversified portfolio.

Indirect Investments

Investors who want to add a real estate investment to their portfolio more often make an indirect investment. That is, they buy shares in an entity or group that owns and manages property. For example, they may become limited partners in a real estate syndicate.

A **syndicate** is a group created to buy and manage commercial property such as an apartment, office building, or shopping mall. The syndicate may be structured as a corporation or, more commonly, as a limited partnership.

In a **limited partnership**, there is a general partner and limited partners. The general partner manages the entity, while the limited partners invest in partnership shares. The limited partners are only liable for the amount of their investment; that is, they can lose only as much as they have put in. Limiting liability is particularly important in real estate, which relies on leverage or debt financing. Investors find syndicates valuable in limiting liability and in providing management for the property.

Another form of indirect investing is a **real estate investment trust (REIT)**—a mutual fund of real estate holdings. You buy shares in the REIT, which may be privately held or publicly traded on an exchange. The REIT is a fund invested in various commercial properties. Some REITs specialize, concentrating investments in specific kinds of property, such as shopping malls, apartments, or vacation properties.

To qualify as a REIT in the United States (for the allowable tax benefits), a fund must:

- be managed by directors as a corporation or trust,
- offer transferrable shares,
- not be a financial institution,
- have at least 100 shareholders,
- have at least 95% of income from interest, dividends, and property,
- pay dividends that are at least 90% of the REITs taxable income,
- have at least 75% of its assets invested in real estate,
- get at least 75% of gross revenue from real estate.

An equity REIT invests in property, while a mortgage REIT provides real estate financing. A hybrid REIT does both. REITs do for real estate what mutual funds do for other assets. They provide investors with a way to invest with more liquidity and diversity and with comparatively lower transaction costs.

Another way to invest in the real estate market is to invest in the real estate financing rather than the actual real estate. **Mortgage-backed securities (MBS)** are bonds secured by pools of mortgages owned by large financial institutions or agencies of the federal government.

It is difficult to price mortgage-backed securities—to gauge their present and future value and their risk. Like any bond, mortgage-backed securities are vulnerable to interest rate, reinvestment, and inflation risk, but they are also particularly vulnerable to economic cycles and to default risk. If the economy is in a recession and unemployment rises, mortgage defaults will likely rise. When mortgage defaults rise, and the value of mortgage-backed securities falls.

Because they are complicated and risky, mortgage-backed securities are appropriate only for investors with a large enough asset base and risk tolerance to support the investment. MBS investors are usually institutional investors or very wealthy individuals.

syndicate

A group of individuals formed to own property. The syndicate acts as a vehicle for indirect investment, hiring professional management for the properties it owns.

limited partnership

A partnership in which there are both general and limited partners (at least one of each). The limited partners have limited liability, and, much like corporate shareholders, cannot be liable for the partnership beyond their original investment.

real estate investment trust (REIT)

A corporation investing in real estate that, practically, behaves much like a mutual fund for real estate investors.

mortgage-backed securities (MBS)

A security such as a bond whose return is secured by the income (mortgage payments) from a pool of mortgages.

Key Takeaways

- Direct investments in real estate involve controlling ownership and management of the property.
- Indirect investment involves owning a share of a company that owns and manages the real estate.

- Indirect investments may be structured as:
  - a syndicate,
  - a limited partnership, or
  - a real estate investment trust (REIT).
- A REIT is designed as a mutual fund of real estate holdings.
  - An equity REIT invests in property.
  - A mortgage REIT invests in real estate financing.
  - A hybrid REIT does both.
- Mortgage-backed securities are another way to invest in a real estate market by investing in its financing, but they are considered too risky for individual investors.

Exercises

1. Read the article, "11 Biggest Real Estate Mistakes and What to Learn from Them" at https://www.forbes.com/sites/forbesrealestatecouncil/2018/01/02/11-biggest-real-estate-mistakes-and-what-to-learn-from-them/#5f0e7f5b2463. Based on these common mistakes that real estate investors make, what 11 things should you do to succeed?
2. What have been your experiences as a landlord or as a tenant? Collaborate with classmates to develop two lists: advantages and disadvantages of direct investing in rental property and of being a tenant in a residential or commercial space.
3. Are you already invested in real estate? Record in My Notes or your personal finance journal information about your investment and/or your strategy for including real estate in your investment portfolio. Will you invest directly, indirectly, or both? What is your plan and timetable for executing your strategy?
4. Read about REITs at https://www.reit.com/investing/why-invest-reits. What might be some advantages and risks of investing in REITs as part of your investing strategy?

17.4 Commodities and Collectibles

Learning Objectives

1. Define and describe the characteristics and uses of derivative contracts.
2. Explain the roles of precious metals in an investment portfolio.
3. Describe the methods available to individual investors in making commodities investments.
4. Compare and contrast the advantages and disadvantages of using collectibles in an individual investment portfolio.

Some investors prefer to invest directly in the materials that are critical to an industry or market, rather than investing in the companies that use them. For example, if you think that the price of oil is going to rise, one way to profit from the higher price would be to buy shares of oil companies that profit by refining oil and selling gasoline, fuels, and other petroleum products. Another way is to buy the oil itself as a commodity.

Commodities are raw materials—agricultural products, metals, energy sources, currencies, and so on—that go into producing goods and services. Investing in commodities is a way to profit directly from the raw material rather than from its products. As discussed in Chapter 12, commodities trading is not new—the first commodities exchange in the United States was established in 1848.

Because they are or rely on natural resources, commodities have a largely unpredictable supply. They have inherent risk because they are exposed to changes in weather or geology or global politics. Commodities trading began as a way for commodity producers and consumers to manage their risks. These traders are managing risks going forward; that is, they hedge by buying and selling commodities that they expect to exist in the future. This trading is done using future and forward contracts—types of derivatives, discussed in the Chapter 12.

Investing in commodities involves transaction costs and a time limit on realizing your gains (or losses) because derivatives are time-sensitive contracts created with an expiration date.

Commodity investing is risky business because it is done through derivatives—assets whose value depends on the value of another asset. For instance, the value of a contract to buy or sell soybeans at some time in the future depends on the value of the soybeans. When you invest in a derivative, you are taking on the risk of both the contract and the asset that it depends on. One strategy to manage this risk is to invest in both, creating a situation in which one investment can act as a hedge for the other. The way this works is if the underlying asset (the soybeans) gains value, you'll lose on the derivative (the futures contract on soybeans); but if the asset loses value, you can gain on the derivative.

One example of this is the "prebuy" offer common in regions where homes are heated by oil. When you heat your home with oil, you are exposed to the risk of volatility in the price of oil. This volatility can upset your household budget and, since heat is a necessity, can take away from your other spending needs. You could guarantee your winter's cost of oil by buying it all in the summer, but you would need a huge oil tank to store all that oil until winter. As an alternative and to attract customers, some heating oil suppliers offer a prebuy deal. During the summer, customers can buy their winter's supply of oil at a set price, and the oil company will then deliver it as needed over the winter months.

FIGURE 17.5

If the price of oil goes up, the customer is protected and gains by not having to pay the higher price. The oil dealer loses the extra profit it could have had. On the other hand, if the price of oil goes down, the dealer is assured its profit, while the customer pays more than necessary without the prebuy deal.

In the language of commodities trading, the customer is "short" oil—that is, he or she needs it and seeks to lock in a price through the prebuy deal. The oil dealer is "long" oil—that is, he or she has a supply and wants to sell it and so seeks to lock in the sale of a certain quantity at a certain price. The customer wants to lock in a low price, while the dealer wants to lock in a high price. Each is betting on what will be "low" and "high" relative to what the real price of oil turns out to be in the future. The hedge of the prebuy deal relieves both the customer and the dealer of the uncertainty or risk. The deal creates its own risks, but if those are smaller than the risk of oil's price volatility, then the dealer will offer the prebuy, and the customer will take it.

When you trade commodities, you are also exposed to the risks of trading in the commodities markets. Another reason that commodities investing is risky for individual investors is because professional commodity investors often take speculative positions, betting on the future price of derivatives without holding investments in the underlying assets. Speculators can influence that future price, which after all is just the market's consensus of what that price "should" be. For individual investors, the risks of commodities trading often outweigh the advantage of whatever diversification they bring to the portfolio.

Gold, Silver, and Precious Metals

Historically, gold and silver have been popular investments of individual investors. For thousands of years, gold and silver have been used as a basis for currency value, either minted into coins or used to back currency value. When a currency is backed by gold, for example, or is "on the gold standard," there should be a direct relationship between the value of the currency and the value of the gold.

In times of inflation or deflation, investors worry that the value or purchasing power of currency will change. They may invest in gold or silver as a more stable store of wealth than the currency that is supposed to represent the metal. In other words, if investors lose faith in the currency that represents the gold, they may trade their money for the gold.

Most currencies used today are not backed by a precious metal but by the productivity and soundness of the economy that issues them. For example, the value of the U.S. dollar is not related to the value of an ounce of gold, but to the value of the U.S. economy.

FIGURE 17.6

© Shutterstock, Inc.

When economic or political turmoil seems to threaten the health of an economy and hence the value of its currency, some investors choose to invest in the gold or silver that seems to retain its value. For that reason, gold or silver has historically been regarded as a hedge against inflation.

How exactly do you buy gold? Gold bullion is sold as bars or wafers in units of one kilogram or 32.15 troy ounces. Metal dealers and some banks will sell bars or wafers ranging from 5 grams (or 0.16075 troy ounces) to 500 ounces or more. Transaction costs are relatively high, between 5% and 8%, and there is the cost of storing and securing the gold bars or wafers.

A more popular way to buy gold is as coins, which are more easily stored and secured. Gold coins are minted by several countries, including the United States, and may be bought from banks, brokers, and dealers for a fee of about 2%.

Commodity Indexes and Exchange-Traded Funds

As with stocks, bonds, and real estate, the most popular way for individual investors to invest in any commodities—including precious metals—is through open-end mutual funds or exchange-traded funds (ETFs). The fund may invest in a variety of contracts, diversifying its holdings of the commodity. It has professional managers who understand the pricing of such contracts and can research the market volatility and the global economy. Using a fund as a way of investing in commodities thus provides both diversification and expertise. It can also give you more liquidity as fund shares can be quickly traded into the market.

For example, if you expect inflation and want to buy gold, instead of trying to buy gold bars, you could invest in an exchange-traded fund or mutual fund. Investing through a fund allows you to "own" gold but also to get diversification, expertise, and liquidity, reducing your risk.

There are mutual funds or exchange-traded funds for nearly every commodity that is traded. There are also passively managed commodity index funds, similar to stock or bond index funds. Investing in commodities can be a way to achieve asset diversification in your portfolio because often a commodity such as gold is countercyclical to the economy, and therefore is countercyclical to your stock and bond holdings as well. Commodities may also add significant risk to a portfolio, however, so the advantage of adding them as a diversification strategy may be canceled out by the additional risk.

Collectibles and Unique Investments

Any asset that is tradable may become an investment; that is, it may be purchased and held with the expectation that it can be sold when its value increases. So long as there is a market for it—a buyer—it potentially may be sold at a gain.

Collectibles and unique investments include the following:

- Antique furniture
- Stamps
- Coins
- Rare books
- Sports trading cards
- Vintage cars
- Vintage clothes
- Vintage wines
- Vintage vinyl
- Fine art
- Musical instruments
- Jewelry
- Historical curios
- Other ephemera

As investments, collectibles cannot be standardized in the way that stocks, bonds, or even real estate and used cars can be. Each asset has attributes that make it more or less valuable, even among similar assets. Its value is hard to judge, and therefore it is harder for buyer and seller to agree on a price.

Professional appraisers are knowledgeable about both the item and the market and are trained to evaluate such assets. Theirs is a better-educated guess, but it is still just an estimate of value. Individual investors also consult books on collectibles and may purchase professional market research, pricing indexes, and auction records.

Sometimes one person's trash is another person's treasure. It is fun to think that you may unearth a rare "find" at a garage sale or flea market or that some family heirloom has more than sentimental value. Usually, however, your ability to cash in on your luck is limited by your ability to convince someone else of its worth and to sell when its market is trendy.

Collectibles, including "ephemera" such as antique letters and photographs, are usually sold by dealers or collectors or through a private sale arranged between buyer and seller. The dealers may establish a gallery to showcase items for sale. Auction houses such as Christie's or Sotheby's organize auctions of many items or "lots" to attract buyers and provide catalogues with details on the items for sale, such as their "provenance" or ownership history.

The advantage of unique assets as investments is that you may enjoy collecting and having the items as well as watching their value appreciate. If you are a guitarist, for example, having and being able to play a vintage guitar may mean more to you than the fact that it may be a good investment. For some, collecting becomes a hobby.

The disadvantages of investing in collectibles are:

- high probability of mispricing, as markets are inefficient;
- lack of liquidity;
- lack of earnings, as there are no dividends or interest; and
- holding costs of the investment.

Unless you are knowledgeable about your item and its markets—and even if you are—it is common to suffer from mispricing. Collectibles' markets are relatively inefficient because trading partners vary widely in their knowledge about pricing. Both buyers and sellers try to persuade each other of an asset's rarity and value. It is easy to be misled and to make mistakes in this market. Online sales and auctions of collectibles at sites such as eBay may be fun for hobbyists, but they typically are not good venues for investors.

If you are trading through a dealer, you can check the dealer's reputation through professional organizations, local business bureaus, and Internet blogs and websites, especially where customers can provide a rating or critique. You should also always try to find comparable items to compare prices. If feasible, get a second opinion from an independent appraiser. Knowledge is an important bargaining chip. The more you know, the more likely you are to be satisfied with your investment decision, even if you ultimately walk away from the deal.

FIGURE 17.7

Unique investments may not be readily saleable, or their markets may be subject to trends and fashions that cause price volatility. This means that your investment may ultimately be a source of gain but that you cannot count on it as a source of liquidity. If you have foreseeable liquidity needs, it may not be appropriate to tie up your wealth in a Chinese vase, autographed baseballs, vintage action figures, or Navajo rugs.

There are no dividends or interest paid while you hold collectibles, so if you have income needs you should choose a more useful investment. There are also other costs, such as storage, security, maintenance, and insurance. Your investment actually returns a negative net cash flow—costs you more than it brings in—until you realize its potential gain by selling it.

Collectibles can be a source of joy and a store of wealth, and you may realize a healthy return on your investment. In the meantime, however, they create costs so that your eventual return will have to be large enough to compensate for those costs to make them a really worthwhile investment.

Key Takeaways

- Commodities are raw materials and agricultural products.
- Commodities are used to produce other goods and so are traded forward using derivative contracts.
- Derivative contracts can be used to hedge an investment in an asset, or to speculate on the price volatility of the commodity.
- Because of their volatility, commodities markets are riskier than asset markets.
- Precious metals, especially gold, are often used to lower portfolio risk by providing a hedge against inflation.
- Individual investors can invest in commodities using index funds and exchange-traded funds.
- Collectibles and unique assets may appreciate in value, acting as a store of wealth, but the disadvantages of using them as investments are:
  - high probability of mispricing,
  - illiquid markets,
  - illiquid returns or no returns until the asset is sold, and
  - holding period maintenance costs.

Exercises

1. View Bloomberg's commodities and futures charts at http://www.bloomberg.com/markets/commodities/cfutures.html. Choose one or two commodities to track and find out all you can about investing in those commodities. Read the article, "How to Read Commodity Charts", at https://www.commonsensecommodities.com/how-to-read-commodity-charts/. Create an annotated drawing to apply the information about reading a commodities chart to an example of a chart taken from the Bloomberg's website. Write an interpretation of the chart in My Notes or your personal finance journal.
2. Read Investopedia's article on investing in gold and silver at http://www.investopedia.com/articles/optioninvestor/06/goldsilverfutures.asp. According to this source, who should consider investing in gold and silver and for what reason? What are examples of other precious metals in the futures market? How do investors offset futures contracts before their delivery dates?
3. Sample the collectibles listed on eBay at https://www.ebay.com/b/Collectibles-Art/bn_7000259855. Find one that interests you and that you would consider investing in. Research this collectible to determine current pricing, locate markets, and identify dealers and experts. How long would you hold this collectible and what is your estimated return on the investment? Calculate your average annual return on this investment and compare it to the returns on an investment in a U.S. Treasury bond or an S&P 500 mutual fund over the same period of time.
4. What has been your experience with buying and selling collectibles? In what circumstances might you consider adding investments in a collectible to your portfolio? What would you collect?

Endnotes

1. James E. McWhinney, "A Brief History of the Mutual Fund," Investopedia, http://www.investopedia.com/articles/mutualfund/05/mfhistory.asp (accessed June 2, 2018).
2. The Investment Company Institute, *2018 Investment Company Fact Book, 58th ed., 2018*, https://www.ici.org/pdf/2018_factbook.pdf (accessed June 2, 2018).
3. The Investment Company Institute, *Investment Company Fact Book, 58th edition, 2018*, http://www.ici.org/ (accessed June 10, 2018).
4. The Investment Company Institute, *Investment Company Fact Book, 58th edition, 2018*, http://www.ici.org/ (accessed June 10, 2018).
5. The Investment Company Institute, *Investment Company Fact Book, 58th edition, 2018*, http://www.ici.org/ (accessed June 10, 2018).
6. The Investment Company Institute, Investment Company Fact Book, 58th edition, 2018, http://www.ici.org/ (accessed June 10, 2018).
7. Burton G. Malkiel, *A Random Walk Down Wall Street* 10th ed. (New York: W. W. Norton & Company, Inc., 2007), 360.
8. Jack Clark Francis and Roger G. Ibbotson, *Contrasting Real Estate with Comparable Investments, 1978–2004* (New York: Ibbotson Associates, 2007).

CHAPTER 18

Career Planning

18.1 Introduction

Bryon always knew he wanted to be a firefighter. Even when he was a small child, he was thrilled by the fire trucks as they screamed past on their way to helping people. He has always been sure that a career in protection services is the right choice for him. Given that people will always need those services, Bryon figures he'll have job security, will be able to raise a family, and will have many chances for advancement along with plenty of thrills on the job.

Although she is starting out as a lab technician, Tomika is not clear about her career ambitions. She wants to do something fun and interesting, where she won't hate going to work every day—but mostly she wants a career that will afford her the opportunity for professional advancement, increasing pay, and the chance to raise a family. She has enjoyed her science courses at school. She figures that since health care is a growth industry, with technological advancements and the aging population, she will choose a career in health.

FIGURE 18.1

Some people know what they want to do at an early age. For most people, however, the path is just not that clear. Career planning and development can be a process of trial and error as you learn your abilities and preferences by trying them out. Sometimes a job is not what you thought it would be; sometimes you are not who you thought you would be. The better your decision-making process—the more objective and methodical it is—the less trial and error you may have to endure.

Your financial sustainability depends on having income to support your spending, saving, and investing. A primary component of your income—especially earlier in your adult life—is income from your wages or salary, that is, from working, selling your labor. Your ability to maximize the price that your labor can bring depends on the labor market you choose and your ability to sell yourself. Those abilities will be called on throughout your working life. You will make job and career choices for many different reasons. This chapter looks only at the financial context of those choices.

18.2 Choosing a Job

Learning Objectives

1. Describe the macroeconomic factors that affect job markets.
2. Describe the microeconomic factors that influence job and career decisions.
3. Relate life stages to both microeconomic factors and income needs.
4. Describe how relationships between life stages, income needs, and microeconomic factors may affect job and career choices.

A person starting out in the world of work today can expect to change "jobs" many times before retiring. One study from the U.S. Bureau of Labor Statistics shows that people born between 1957-1964 held an average of 11.9 jobs between the ages of 18 and 50.[1] Those job changes may reflect the process of gaining knowledge and skills as you work or changes in industry and economic conditions over several decades of your working life. Knowing this, you cannot base career decisions solely on the circumstances of the moment. However, you also cannot ignore the economics of the job market.

career path

A planned progression of jobs or steps to advance in a profession or career.

You may have a career in mind but have no idea how to get started, or you may have a job in mind but have no idea where it may lead. If you have a career in mind, you should research its **career path**, or sequence of steps that will enable you to advance. Some careers have a well-established path, for example, careers in law, medicine, teaching, or civil engineering. In other occupations and professions, career paths may not be well defined.

Before you can even focus on a career or a job, however, you need to identify the factors that will affect your decision-making process.

Macro Factors of the Job Market

The job market is the market where buyers (employers) and sellers (employees) of labor trade, but it usually refers to the possibilities for employment and its rewards. These will differ by field of employment, types of jobs, and geographic region. The opportunities offered in a job market depend on the supply and demand for jobs, which in turn depend on the need for labor in the broader economy and in a specific industry or geographic area.

The economic cycle can affect the aggregate job market or employment rate. If the economy is in a recession, the economy is producing less, and there is less need for labor, so fewer jobs are available. If the economy is expanding, production and its need for labor are growing.

Typically, a recession or expansion affects different industries in different ways. Some industries are cyclical and some are countercyclical. For example, in a recession, consumer spending is often down, so retail shops and consumer goods manufacturers—in cyclical industries—may be cutting jobs. Meanwhile, more people are continuing their education to improve their skills and the chances of getting a job, which is harder to do in a recession, so jobs in higher education—a countercyclical industry—may be increasing.

Spring 2009 would have been a bad time to think about a career in auto manufacturing in the United States. Ford, General Motors, and Chrysler all announcing massive layoffs and plant closings and facing bankruptcy. The industry did survive, but many jobs were lost for good.

Global events such as an outbreak of war, the nationalization of a scarce natural resource, the price of a critical commodity such as crude oil, the collapse of a vital industry, and so on, may also cause changes in the global economy that affect job markets.

Another macroeconomic factor is change in technology, which can open up new fields of employment and make others obsolete. With the advent of digital cameras, for example, even single-use conventional cameras are no longer being manufactured in great quantity, and film developers are not needed as much as they once were. However, there are more jobs for developers of digital applications for creating images and using digital images in communications channels, such as mobile phones.

A demographic shift also can change entire industries and job opportunities. A historical example, repeated in many developing countries, is the mass migration of rural families to urban centers and factory towns during an industrial revolution. Changes in the composition of a society, such as the average age of the population, also affect job supply and demand. Baby booms create demand for more educators and pediatricians, for example, while aging populations create more demand for goods and services relating to elder care.

FIGURE 18.2 Workers in the Vacuum Cleaner Factory at Reedsville, West Virginia

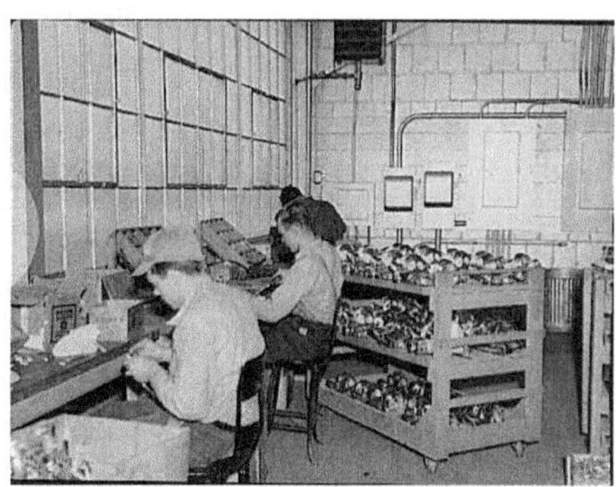

Library of Congress, February 1937

Social and cultural factors affect consumer behavior, and consumer preferences can change a job market. Demand for certain kinds of products and services, for example, such as organic foods, hybrid cars, clean energy, and "green" buildings, can increase job opportunities in businesses that address those preferences.

Changes in demand for a product or service will change the need for labor to produce it. On a larger scale, economies typically shift their focus over time as different industries become "growth" industries—that is, the drivers of growth in the economy. In the mid-20th century, the United States was a manufacturing economy, driven by the production of durable and consumer goods, especially automobiles. In the 1990s, the computer/internet/tech sector had a larger role in driving growth in the U.S. economy due to technological breakthroughs. Currently, health care is the fastest growing sector of the economy for employment, due to demographic and political changes and needs.[2]

If you are entrepreneurial and intend to be self-employed, your job opportunities may be affected by the ease with which you can start and maintain a business. Ease of entry, in turn, may be affected by macro factors such as the laws and regulations in the state where you intend to do business and the existing competition in the market you are entering.

In the last decade, technology has created new ways of having a "job" by supplying services to many "clients" instead of having one "employer." Also known as the "gig economy" model, the worker is cast as a self-employed entrepreneur, as a contractor to clients. Some workers find it advantageous to be able to diversify revenues from different clients, but others prefer the constancy of being an employee. As an industry's labor model shifts from using employees to using contractors, the level of competition in the labor market increases, typically affecting wage levels and earnings potential. When looking to be employed in a specific industry, you should think about whether that industry is likely to shift to using contractors instead of employees. That different kind of work structure may appeal to you, or not.

The labor market is very competitive, not just at an individual level but on a global, industry-wide scale. As transportation and, especially, communication technologies have improved, many steps in a manufacturing or even a service process may be outsourced, done by foreign labor. That competition affects the U.S. job market as jobs are moved overseas, but it also opens new markets in developing economies. You may be interested in an overseas job, as American companies open offices in Asian, South American, African, and other countries. Globalization affects job markets everywhere.

Micro Factors of Your Job Market

Whether you are employed or self-employed, whether you look forward to going to work every day or dread it, employment determines how you spend most of your waking hours during most of your days. Employment determines your income and thus your lifestyle, your physical well-being, and to a large extent your satisfaction or emotional well-being. Everyone has a different idea about what a "good job" is. That idea may change over a lifetime as circumstances change, but some specific micro factors will weigh on your decisions, including your

- abilities,
- skills,
- knowledge, and
- lifestyle choices.

Abilities are innate talents or aptitudes: what you are capable of or good at. Circumstances may inhibit your use of your abilities or may even cause disabilities. However, you often can develop your abilities—and compensate for disabilities—through training or practice. Sometimes you don't even know what abilities you have until some experience brings them out.

When Tomika says she is "good with people" or when Bryon says that he is a "natural athlete," they are referring to abilities that will make them better at some jobs than others. Abilities can be developed and may require upkeep; athletic ability, for example, requires regular fitness workouts to really be maintained. You also may find that you lack some abilities, or think you do because you've never tried using them.

Usually, by the time you graduate from high school, you are aware of some of your abilities, although you may not be aware of how they may help or hinder you in different jobs. Also, your idea of your abilities relative to the abilities of others may be skewed by your context. For example, you may be the best writer in your high school, but not compared to a larger pool of more competitive students. Your high school or college career office may be able to help you identify your abilities and skills and apply that knowledge to your career decisions.

Your job choices are not predetermined by your abilities or apparent lack of them. An ability can be developed or used in a way you have not yet imagined. A lack of ability can sometimes be overcome by using other talents to compensate. Thus, ability is a factor in your job decisions, but certainly not the only one. Your knowledge and skills are equally—if not more—important.

Skills and knowledge are learned attributes. A skill is a process that you learn to apply, such as programming a computer, welding a pipe, or making a customer feel comfortable making a purchase. Knowledge refers to your education and experience and your understanding of the contexts in which your skills may be applied.

Education is one way to develop skills and knowledge. In secondary education, a vocational program prepares you to enter the job market directly after high school and focuses on technical skills such as baking, bookkeeping, automotive repair, or building trades. A college preparatory program focuses on developing general skills that you will need to further your formal education, such as reading, writing, research, and quantitative reasoning.

Past high school or a year or two of community college, it is natural to question the value of more education. Tuition is real money and must be earned or borrowed, both of which have costs. There is also the opportunity cost of the wages you could be earning instead.

Education adds to your earning power significantly, however, by raising the price of your labor. The more education you have, the more knowledge and skills you have. The smaller the supply of labor with your particular knowledge and skills, the higher the price your labor can command. This relationship is the rationale for becoming specialized within a career. However, both specialization and versatility may have value in certain job markets, raising the price of your labor.

More education also confers more job mobility—the ability to change jobs when opportunities arise because your knowledge and skills make you more useful, and thus valuable, in more ways. Your value as a worker or employee enables you to command higher pay for your labor.

Statistics show a consistent relationship between education and earnings. Over a lifetime of work, say about 40 to 45 years, in the United States a person with a college degree will earn more than $1,000,000 more than someone with a high school diploma. According to a recent study,

> *"The evidence still strongly supports the conclusion that the long-term benefits of investing in postsecondary education exceed the costs, not just for society but also for the individual students who are bearing an increasing portion of the cost of their own education. The long-term upward trend in the earnings premium for college graduates has led to a focus on that growth. But the premium does not have to keep growing for the investment to be a good one.... According to Greenstone and Looney (2011) of the Brookings Institution's Hamilton Project, 'On average, the benefits of a four-year college degree are equivalent to an investment that returns 15.2 percent per year. This is more than double the average return to stock market investments since 1950, and more than five times the returns to corporate bonds, gold, long-term government bonds, or home ownership. From any investment perspective, college is a great deal.'"*[3]

Not only are you likely to earn more if you are better educated, but you are also more likely to have a job with a pension plan, health insurance, and paid vacations—benefits that add to your total compensation. Although it may seem quite expensive to you now, your college education is definitely worth it: worth the opportunity cost and worth the direct costs of tuition, fees, and books.[4]

Your choices will depend on the characteristics and demands of a job and how they fit your unique constellation of knowledge, skills, personality, characteristics, and aptitudes. For example, your knowledge of finance, ability to manage stress and tolerate risk, aptitude for numerical reasoning, enjoyment of competition, and preference to work independently may suit you for employment as a stockbroker or futures trader. Your manual speed and accuracy, verbal comprehension skills, enjoyment of detail work, strong sense of responsibility, desire to work regular hours in a small group setting, and preference for public service may suit you for training as a court stenographer. Your word fluency, social skills, communication skills, organizational skills, preference to work with people, and desire to lead others may suit you for jobs in education or sales. And so on.

Lifestyle choices affect the amount of income you will need to achieve and maintain your lifestyle and the amount of time you will spend earning income. Lifestyle choices thus affect your career path and job choices in key ways. Typically, when you are beginning a career and have few, if any, dependents, you are more willing to sacrifice time and even pay for a job that will enhance your skills and help you to progress along your career path. As a journalist, for example, you may volunteer for an overseas post; or as a nurse you may volunteer for extra rotations. As a computer programmer, you may assist in the development of open source software.

FIGURE 18.3

© Shutterstock, Inc.

As you advance in your career and perhaps become more settled in your life—maybe starting a family—you are typically less willing to sacrifice your personal life to your career, and you may seek out a job that allows you to earn the income that supports your dependents while not taking away too much of your time.

Your income needs typically increase as you have dependents and are trying to save and accumulate wealth, and then decrease when your dependents are on their own and you have accumulated some wealth. Your sources of income shift as well, from relying on income from labor earlier in your life to relying on income from investments later.

When your family has grown and you once again have fewer dependents, you may really enjoy fulfilling your ambitions, as you have decades of skills and knowledge to apply and the time to apply them. Increasingly, as more people retain their health into older age, they are working in retirement—earning a wage to improve their quality of life or eliminate debt, turning a hobby into a business, or trying something they have always wanted to do. Your life cycle of career development may follow the pattern shown in Table 18.1.

TABLE 18.1 Life-Cycle Career Development

Life Stage	Career Concerns
Exploration and Establishment	Develop your skills, acquire knowledge, explore jobs, start earning income, gain experience
Growth	Advance your career, leverage knowledge and skills, increase earnings
Accomplishment	Achieve your goals, maximize earnings, build on success and reputation
Late career	Redirect knowledge and skills, contribute, mentor successors

Regardless of age, your lifestyle choices will affect your job opportunities and career choices. For example, you may choose to live in a specific geographic region based on its:

- rural or urban location,
- proximity to your family or friends,
- differences or similarities to where you grew up,
- cultural or recreational offerings,
- political characteristics,
- climate, or
- cost of living.

Sometimes you may choose to sacrifice your lifestyle preferences for your ambitions, and sometimes you may sacrifice your ambitions for your preferences. It's really a matter of figuring out what matters at the time, while keeping in mind the effects of this decision on the next one.

Key Takeaways

- Macroeconomic factors affect job markets, including:
  - economic cycles,
  - new technology or obsolescence,
  - demographic changes,
  - changes in the global economy,
  - changes in consumer preferences, and
  - changes in laws and regulations.
- Job markets are globally competitive.
- Microeconomic factors influence job and career decisions, including:
  - abilities or aptitudes,
  - skills and knowledge, and
  - lifestyle choices.
- Microeconomic factors and income needs change over a lifetime and typically correlate with age and stage of life.
- Job and career choices should realistically reflect income needs.

Exercises

1. Record in My Notes or your personal finance journal your work history and current thoughts about your future work life. What jobs have you held? In each job, what experience, knowledge, or skills did you acquire or develop? What are your future job preferences, and why do you prefer them? Do you have a planned career path? What potential advantages and opportunities do your preferences or plans offer? What potential disadvantages and costs may your preferences or plans entail?
2. Go online to find out the differences in definition between an occupation and a vocation, profession, trade, career, and career path. Which combination of concepts best describes the approach you plan to take to satisfy your needs for income from future employment?
3. Take a free online career development aptitude test, such as the one at http://www.careertest.us/Career_Aptitude_Survey.htm. (Note that sites offering free aptitude, personality, or job preference tests often require online registration. You should evaluate the reliability, credibility, and security of any site you use to explore your career preferences.) What personality attributes and personal aptitudes are micro factors that may affect your career choices or your chances of success in a particular job?

4. Search online and view the kinds of behavioral assessments you may be asked to take as a job applicant or employee. Then read the article, "How to pass a personality test...", at https://www.predictiveindex.com/blog/how-to-pass-a-personality-test-and-common-questions-on-faking-assessments. Discuss with classmates how might an employer use the test results in evaluating a prospective employee, and how might a prospective employee use the test in evaluating the job.
5. In My Notes or your personal finance journal, list your most important job skills, aptitudes, and preferences on which you plan to expand or build a career. Then list the specific job skills you feel you need to develop further through additional education or experience. How and where will you get those skills and at what cost? Next, describe the lifestyle you hope to support through income from future employment. What aspects of that lifestyle would be easiest for you to modify or sacrifice for your career or income goals?

18.3 Finding a Job

Learning Objectives

1. List and describe venues for finding job opportunities.
2. Explain the value of networking.
3. Trace the steps in pursuing a job opportunity, specifically your cover letter, résumé, and interview.
4. Identify the critical kinds of information that should be provided in a job offer.

A job search is a part of everyone's life, sooner or later. It may be repeated numerous times throughout your career. You may initiate a job search in hopes of improving your position and career or changing careers, or you may be forced into the job market after losing your job. Whatever the circumstances, when you look for a job you are seeking a buyer for your labor. The process of having to "sell" yourself (your time, energy, knowledge, and skills) is always revealing and valuable.

Finding a Job Market

Before you can look for a job, you need to have an idea of the job market. The same macro factors you consider in your choice of career may make your job search easier or harder. Ultimately, they may influence your methods of searching or even your job choice itself. For example, as unemployment increased in the wake of the most recent financial crisis, the labor market became much more competitive for employees. As the economy recovered and unemployment rates fell to historic lows, it was employers who had to compete to fill jobs. To understand these kinds of macro factor shifts, a good place to start is the U.S. Department of Labor's "Occupational Outlook Handbook."[5]

Knowing the job classification and industry name will focus your search process and make it more efficient. Once you understand your job market, look at the macro and micro factors that affect it along with your personal choices. For example, knowing that you are interested in working in business, transportation, or the leisure and hospitality industry, you are ready to research that field more and plan your job search.

You are looking for a buyer of your labor, so you need to find the markets where buyers shop. One of the first things to do is find out where jobs in your field are advertised. Jobs may be advertised in:

- trade magazines,
- professional organizations or their journals,
- career fairs,
- employment agencies,
- employment websites,
- government websites,
- company websites, and
- your school's career development office.

Table 18.2 describes these venues in more detail.

TABLE 18.2 Sources of Information about Jobs

Trade Magazines	Publications that have classified ads listing jobs in your field or area of interest.
Professional Organizations	Associations that run ads or postings for jobs via their journals, websites, and discussion lists.
Career Fairs	Employers gather to recruit job applicants, often in a particular industry or region.
Employment Agencies	Businesses that work as "headhunters" for employers, who pay the agency a fee for finding and screening a good recruit.
Employment Websites	Places where employers and job seekers post and respond to information about job opportunities and work availability. You will find evaluations of employment websites at http://www.employmentwebsites.org (the International Association of Employment Web Sites).
Government Websites	Career information and current listings for state and federal government jobs. Listings for federal jobs are at http://federaljobs.net/federal.htm and http://www.usajobs.gov. State government jobs may be found at http://www.statelocalgov.net/50states-jobs.cfm.
Company Websites	Current job listings posted by a company's human resource personnel on the company's website.
College Career Development Office	Job placement services on campus for graduates and alumni, run by career counselors.

Consider Sandy, for example, who is graduating with a bachelor's degree in hospitality management. Her dream job is to work at an inn or bed and breakfast in a resort location. The Professional Association of Innkeepers International (PAII) offers a website and journal—good places to start reading and learning about the industry. It also lists upcoming trade conferences that may be a good opportunity for Sandy to meet some people in the industry.[6]

FIGURE 18.4

© Shutterstock, Inc.

Browsing online, Sandy learns about a big job fair coming to her region, sponsored by the PAII in association with a chamber of commerce and an economic development agency. This is her chance to meet recruiters in her industry and find out about actual opportunities. Each prospective employer will have a display, and Sandy will go from table to table, getting information, dropping off her résumé, and possibly setting up interviews.

She also plans to register with an employment agency that specializes in hotel management for smaller hotels and inns. The agency will screen her application and try to match her with appropriate jobs in its listings. For a specified time it will keep her résumé on file for future opportunities.

Sandy's strategy includes posting her résumé on employment websites, such as Monster.com, indeed.com, and Careerbuilder.com. Browsing jobs online, Sandy discovers there is a strong seasonal demand for hospitality workers on cruise ships, and this gives her an idea. If the right choice doesn't come up right away, maybe a summer job working for a cruise line would be a good way to develop her knowledge and skills further while looking for her dream job in management.

Sandy needs to research destinations as well as businesses and wants to talk with people directly. She knows that cold calling—contacting potential employers on the phone as a complete unknown—is the hardest way to sell herself. In any industry, cold calling has a much lower success rate than calling with a referral or some connection—otherwise known as networking.

networking

A process of using personal contacts to get information and find job opportunities.

social capital

Connections within and between social networks that may be useful, as an asset, in a market.

Networking is one of the most successful ways of finding a job. It can take many forms, but the idea is to use whatever professional, academic, or social connections you have to enlist as many volunteers as possible to help in your job search. According to popular theory, your social networks can be seen as assets that potentially help you build wealth. That is, the number and positions of people you can network with and the economically viable connections you can have with them are a form of capital, **social capital**.[7]

Word of mouth is a powerful tool, and the more people know about your job search, the more likely it is that they or someone they know will learn of opportunities. Sandy's strategy also includes joining online career networking sites, such as LinkedIn, and discussion lists for people in the hospitality industry. Sandy finds a helpful Yahoo! group called The Innkeeper Club and posts a query about what employers look for in a manager.

While Sandy was in college getting her degree in hospitality management, her best friend from high school was happily styling hair in a local salon. Sandy never thought to network through her friend, but it turns out that one of her friend's clients has a sister who owns a country inn with her husband, and they are thinking about hiring someone to manage their enterprise. After driving several hours to meet them, Sandy learns they have changed their minds and are not hiring now. However, they know of two other innkeepers who may be looking for help. Since they are impressed with Sandy, they are happy to pass along her name and résumé.

FIGURE 18.5

© Shutterstock, Inc.

That's how networking works—you just never know who may be helpful to you. The obvious people to start with are all the people that you know: former professors, former employers, friends, family, friends of family, friends of friends, family of friends, and so on. The more people you can talk with or send your résumé to (i.e., impress), the greater the chances that someone will make an offer.

Another good networking strategy is to call or e-mail people working in the industry, individuals who are currently in or just above the position you'd like to have, and ask to talk with them about their work. If you make it clear that you are not asking for or expecting a job offer from them, many people will be happy to discuss their jobs with you. They may have valuable tips or leads for you or be willing to pass along your name to someone else who does.

Selling Yourself: Your Cover Letter and Résumé

To get a job you will have to convince someone who does not know you that you are worth paying for. You have an opportunity to prove that in your cover letter and résumé and again in your interview.

The cover letter, whether mailed or e-mailed, is your introduction to your prospective employer. You have three paragraphs on one page to briefly introduce yourself and show how you can make a profitable contribution to the company. The objective of the cover letter is to get the reader to look at your résumé with a favorable impression of you, created by the letter.

Your first paragraph should establish your purpose in making contact, the reason for the letter. You should make it clear what job you are applying for and why you are making this particular contact. If someone referred you, mention him or her by name. If you met the addressee previously, remind him or her where and when that was, for example, "It was great to chat with you at the Jobs Fair in Cleveland last week." The more specifically you can identify yourself and separate yourself from the pool of other job seekers, the better.

The second paragraph of your cover letter should summarize your background, education, and experience. All this information is on your résumé in more detail, so this is not the place to expound at length. You want to show briefly that you are qualified for the position and have the potential to make a contribution.

Your third paragraph is your opportunity to leave the door open for further communication. Make it clear where and how you can be reached and how much you appreciate the opportunity to be considered for the position.

résumé

A document that summarizes job experience, education, and civic activities. It is commonly used in the job application process.

The **résumé**, the summary list of your skills and knowledge, is what will really sell you to an employer, once you have made a good enough impression with the cover letter to get him or her to turn the page. A good résumé provides enough information to show that you are willing and able to contribute to your employer's success—that it is worth it to hire you or at least to talk to you in an interview.

List the pertinent facts of where and how you can be reached: address, phone number, e-mail address. Your qualifications will be mainly education and experience. List any degrees, certificates, or training you have completed after high school. Be sure to include anything that distinguishes your academic career, such as honors, prizes, or scholarships.

List any employment experience, including summer jobs, even if they don't seem pertinent to the position you are applying for. You may think that being a camp counselor has nothing to do with being a radiology technician, but it shows that you have experience working with children and parents, have held a position where you are responsible for others, and that you are willing to work during your school breaks, thus showing ambition. If you are starting out and can't be expected to have lots of employment experience, employers looks for hints about your character—things like ambition, initiative, responsibility—that may indicate your success working for them.

Internships that you did in college or high school are also impressive, showing your willingness to go beyond the standard curriculum and learn by working—something an employer will expect you to continue to do on the job, too. While you are in school, you should recognize the value added by experiential learning and the positive impression that it will make. An internship can also give you a head start in networking if your supervisor will be a good reference or source of contacts for you. The internship may even result in a job offer; you may not necessarily want to accept, but at the very least, having an offer to fall back on takes some of the pressure off your search.

For each job, be clear about the position you held and the two most important duties or roles you performed. Don't go into too much detail, however. The time to expand on your story is in the interview.

If you have done internships or volunteer work or if you are a member of civic or volunteer organizations, be sure to list those as well. They are hints about you as a person and may help you to stand out in the pool of applicants.

A common mistake is to list too much extra information on your résumé and to focus too much on what you want—for example, stating an objective such as, "to obtain a great position in hotel management." Your employer cares about what you can do for the company, not for yourself. The following are some tips for developing your résumé:

- Avoid adjectives or adverbs when describing your past performance. If you were an achiever in school, that will be reflected in your grades, degrees, honors, and awards. "Hype" can sound boastful; besides, you can discuss your performance in detail at the interview.
- Be honest and state your case without exaggeration. It is easier than ever for employers to check on your history, and they will. Falsification of information on your résumé may become grounds for dismissal, if you are hired.

- Don't include personal details unless they are strongly relevant to the job you are seeking. Employers typically do not care that you love dogs, were raised in Seattle, or are a single mother.
- Be correct. Proofread your résumé and have someone else proof it as well. This is your opportunity to make a good impression. Any error indicates not just that you made an error, but that you are sloppy, lazy, or willing to let your work go public with errors.
- Keep it to one page, if possible. Employers typically are looking at many résumés to fill one position, so make it easy and quick for the reader to see how qualified you are.

Many sample résumés and sample cover letters may be found online, but be wary of templates that may not fit you or your prospective job. Employers in your field may have particular expectations for what should be on your résumé or how it should be structured. Maybe you should list your skills or perhaps your education first. Perhaps it would be preferable to list your past employment experiences in reverse chronology (with your most recent job first). Advice is plentiful about how to write a résumé, but there is no one right way or best way. Choose an appropriate style and format for your job category that will present you in the best possible light as a prospective employee.

Many employers want you to fill out an application form independently of or instead of a résumé. They may also ask for references, especially from former employers who are willing to recommend you. Be aware that hiring and human resources department personnel routinely follow up on references and letters of recommendation. Find out more about filling out employment applications at About.com at http://jobsearch.about.com/cs/jobapplications/a/jobapplication.htm and other sites.

There are many resources available in print and online to help you write a good résumé. In addition, résumé writing workshops and short courses are often held at community colleges or adult education centers.[8]

Selling Yourself: Your Interview

The interview—a face-to-face conversation with a prospective employer—is your chance to get an offer. You want to make a good personal impression: dress professionally but in clothes that fit well and comfortably. Be polite and cordial but also careful not to assume too familiar a tone.

You may be asked a series of predetermined questions, or your interviewer may let the conversation develop through open-ended questions. The interviewer may let you establish the interview's direction in order to learn more about how you think. However the conversation is guided, you want to be able to showcase your suitability for the job and what you bring to it. Table 18.3 identifies some questions employers commonly ask in job interviews.

TABLE 18.3 Questions Prospective Employers Commonly Ask

Questions
• Tell us a little about yourself and what brings you here today. • Why did you leave your last job?
• Why do you want this job? • What do you know about us? • Why do you want to work for us?
• How does your education/background/experience make you a good fit for this job? • Why do you think you're the best person for the job? • What qualities and skills can you bring to the job?

• Do you feel you have strong communication skills/technology skills/writing skills (etc., as relevant)?
• What can you do for our company? • How will you be an asset to us? • How can you help us improve our efficiency/productivity/products/services/bottom line (etc., as relevant)?
• What are your career goals? • Where do you see yourself in five years' time?
• Are you a team player? • Have you had much experience working as part of a team? • What was your contribution to the team? • What were the results of the team effort?
• What are your strengths and weaknesses? • What successes and failures have you experienced in your career so far?
• How would you handle a situation in which...? • What would you do if...? • Have you ever had a problem with...?
• What is your ideal job? • What qualities do you look for ideally in a position/company/boss/coworker?

behavioral interviews

A common type of job interview in which the candidate is asked about past behavior in a specific set of circumstances.

STAR Method

A popular method of preparing narratives for behavioral interviews by referring to job situations, tasks, actions, and results.

Be prepared for interviewers who prefer to focus on general behavioral questions rather than on job-specific questions. **Behavioral interviews** emphasize your past actions as indicators of how you might perform in the future. The so-called **STAR Method** is a good approach to answering behavioral questions, as it helps you to be systematic and specific in making your past work experiences relevant to your present job quest. The STAR Method is a process of conveying specific situations, actions, and outcomes in response to an interviewer's question about something you did.

- **S**ituation: Give specific details about the situation and its context.
- **T**ask: Describe the task or goal that arose in response to the situation.
- **A**ction: Describe what you did and who was involved.
- **R**esult: Describe the (positive) outcome.

For example:

Question: We are looking for someone who is willing to take initiative in keeping our office systems working efficiently and who can work without a lot of direct supervision. Does that describe you?

Answer: Absolutely. For example, in my last job I noticed that the office supply system was not working well. People were running out of what they needed before letting me know what to order (**S**ituation). I thought there needed to be a better way to anticipate and fill those needs based on people's actual patterns of use (**T**ask). So, I conducted a poll on office supply use and used that information to develop a schedule for the automatic resupply of key items on a regular basis (**A**ction). The system worked much more smoothly after that. I mentioned it in my next performance review, and my boss was so impressed that she put me in for a raise (**R**esults).

There are some questions employers should *not* ask you, however. Unless the information is a legal requirement for the job you are interviewing for, antidiscrimination laws make it illegal for an employer to ask you your age; your height or weight; personal information such as your racial identity, sexual orientation, or health; or questions about your marital status and family situation, such as the number of children you have, whether you are single, or if you are pregnant or planning to start a family.

It is also important for you to have questions to ask in an interview, so you should prepare a few questions for your interviewer. Questions could be about the company's products or services, the company's mission or goals, the work you would be doing, who you would be reporting to, where you would be located, and the opportunities for advancement. You want your question to be specific enough to show that you have already done some research on the company, its products, and markets. This is a chance to demonstrate your knowledge of the job, company, or industry—that you have done your homework—as well as your interest and ambition.

FIGURE 18.6

Unless your interviewer mentions compensation, don't bring it up. Once you have the job offer, then you can discuss compensation, but in the interview you want to focus on what you can do for the company, not what the company can do for you.

You can also use the interview to learn more about the company. Try to pick up clues about the company's mission, corporate culture, and work environment. Are people wearing business attire or "business casual"? Are there cubicles and private offices or a more open workspace? Are people working in teams, or is it more of a conventional hierarchy? You want to be in a workplace where you can be comfortable and productive. Be open-minded—you may be able to work quite well in an environment you have never worked in before—but think about how you can do your best work in that environment.

After your interview, send a thank-you note and follow up with a phone call if you don't hear back. You may ask your interviewer for feedback—so that you can learn for future interviews—but don't be surprised and be gracious if you don't get it. Always leave the door open. You never know.

Accepting an Offer

A job offer should include details about the work you will be performing, the compensation, and the opportunity to advance from there. If any of that information is missing, you should ask about it.

In many jobs, you may be asked to do many things, especially in entry-level jobs, so the job description may be fairly vague. Your willingness to do whatever is asked of you (within the law and according to ethical standards) should be compensated by what you stand to gain from the job—in pay or in new knowledge and experience or in positioning yourself for your next job. Some jobs are better looked at as a kind of graduate education.

compensation

Payment for labor, including wages, salaries, commissions, stock options, and fringe benefits such as health, disability, and life insurance.

Your **compensation** includes not only your wages or salary but also any benefits that the employer provides. As you read in previous chapters, benefits may include health and dental insurance, disability insurance, life insurance, and a retirement plan. Compensation also includes time off, sick days, and vacation days. You should understand the company's policies and flexibility in applying them.

Know what your total compensation will be and whether it is reasonable for the job, industry, and current job market. Asking around may help, especially on online discussion groups with relative anonymity. People often are reluctant to disclose their compensation, and companies discourage sharing this information because it typically reveals discrepancies. For example, people hired in the past may be receiving less (or more) pay than people hired recently for the same position. In addition, a gender gap—in which men receive higher pay than women in the same position—is often a problem.

To gauge how reasonable a job offer is, you can research professional associations about pay scales or find statistical averages by profession or region. Online resources include simple salary comparison calculators, such as the one at http://monster.salary.com, or even actual salaries posted by employees in reviewing the company, as at https://www.glassdoor.com/Salaries/index.htm. You also will find data and related articles linking salaries to specific job titles, area codes, states, educational levels, and years of work experience, for example, at http://www.payscale.com/research/US/Country=United_States/Salary.

Realistically compare the job offer to your needs. Different geographic areas have different costs of living, for example, so the same salary may afford you a very different lifestyle in Omaha than in New York City. Your employment compensation is most likely an important source—perhaps your only source—of income. That income finances your plan for spending, saving, and investing. A budget can help you to see if that income will be sufficient to meet your financial goals.

If you already have financial responsibilities—student loans, car loans, or dependents, for example—you may find that you can't afford the job.

You can negotiate your compensation offer; many employers expect you to try, but some will just stand by their offer—take it or leave it. Your ability to negotiate depends in part on the number of candidates for that particular job and how quickly the employer needs to fill it. You will find guidelines online for evaluating job offers and negotiating your compensation, for example, the "Job Offer Checklist" at http://www.collegegrad.com/offer.

In some cases, your employer may offer you a contract, a legal agreement that details your responsibilities and compensation and your employer's responsibilities and expectations. As with any contract, you should thoroughly understand it before signing. If you will be employed as a member of a trade union or labor union under a **collective bargaining** agreement, the terms of the contract may be applicable to all union members and therefore not negotiable by individual employees.

collective bargaining

The practice of union and employer representatives negotiating an employment contract to determine wages, hours, work rules, and working conditions.

It is exciting to get a job offer, but don't let the excitement overwhelm your good sense. Before you accept a job, feel positive that you can live with it. You never really know what a job is like until you do it, but it is better to go into it optimistically. When you are just starting a career or trying one out, it is most important to be able to learn and grow in your job, and you may have a period of "paying your dues." But if you are really miserable in a job, you won't be able to learn and grow, no matter how "golden" the opportunity is supposed to be.

Key Takeaways

- Venues for finding jobs include:
  - trade magazines,
  - professional organizations or their journals,
  - career fairs,
  - employment agencies or "headhunters,"
  - employment websites,
  - company websites,
  - government websites, and
  - your school's career development office.
- Networking is a valuable way to expand your job search.
- Selling your labor to a prospective employer usually involves sending a cover letter and résumé, filling out an application form, and/or having an interview.
  - The cover letter should get a prospective employer to read your résumé.
  - The résumé should get the employer to offer you an interview.
  - The interview should get the employer to offer you the job.
- A job offer includes information on the
  - job and its responsibilities;
  - compensation, including benefits;
  - opportunities for advancement.
- Accepting a job offer may involve:
  - evaluating the offer in relation to your needs,
  - examining a job contract, or
  - negotiating the compensation.

Exercises

1. Read "Most New Jobs" at the Bureau of Labor Statistics website at http://www.bls.gov/ooh/most-new-jobs.htm. What job categories are showing the greatest growth? Which job categories show negative growth? In what sector of the economy or in what industry will you seek a job or develop your career? Record or chart your thoughts in My Notes or your personal finance journal. What are the reasons for your choices? What education, knowledge, skills, aptitudes, preferences, and experiences do you bring to them?
2. In My Notes or your personal finance journal, list all the individuals and groups you can think of to tell about your job search or career development quest. Include their contact information. Write a message you could adapt, as needed, for each audience to send when you are ready. Then go online to research other individuals and groups you could include in your networking. Make a fact-finding appointment with a contact you find through networking and record your thoughts on the outcomes. Were you able to practice key networking skills? What did you learn?
3. Write or revise your résumé and draft a general cover letter you could adapt for different job openings. Network with classmates to get critiques and ideas for clarifying or improving these tools to attract a prospective employer. What other supporting documents could you include in your job application?
4. How will you prepare for a job interview? Read the Forbes article, "Ten Things I Look for in a Job Candidate" by Liz Ryan (https://www.forbes.com/sites/lizryan/2017/10/07/ten-things-i-look-for-in-a-job-candidate/#157b497e1730).

   What qualities of new recruits to corporate management does this manager look for?
5. Anticipate the questions you may be asked in an interview. For example, what could you say in a behavioral interview? Prepare your answers using the examples found at https://careers.uiowa.edu/types-interviews, and then look at Behavioral Based Interview Questions. For edification and fun, collaborate with classmates to do role-plays of job interviews. Record your interviews. View the video at the Vault.com at http://www.youtube.com/watch?v=S1ucmfPOBV8. As an employer, would you hire yourself? What interviewing preparations and skills do you think you need to work on?

18.4 Leaving a Job

Learning Objectives

1. Describe the processes of voluntary job loss.
2. Describe the processes of involuntary job loss.
3. Identify the financial impacts of an involuntary job loss.
4. Identify major federal legislation that addresses employment issues and describe its importance in labor markets.

Statistically, it is almost impossible for you to expect to have one job or career for your entire working life. At least once and possibly many times, you will change jobs or even careers. You will have to leave your current or former job and find another. Handling that transition can be difficult, especially if the transition is not what you would have preferred. How you handle that transition may affect your success or satisfaction with your next position.

You may leave your job voluntarily or involuntarily. When you leave voluntarily, presumably you have had a chance to make a reasoned decision and have decided that the net benefits of moving on are more than the net benefits of staying.

Leaving Voluntarily

You may decide to leave a job and move to another in order to:

- move to a position with more responsibility, opportunity to advance, or compensation.
- be in a more compatible work environment or corporate culture.
- learn a new skill.
- become self-employed by beginning an entrepreneurial venture.
- make a transition from a military to a civilian job or vice versa.

In other cases, you may leave employment permanently or temporarily because you want to:

- further your education.
- assume family care, for example of a child or parent.
- take time off for recreation.
- retire.

Whatever your motivation for leaving your job, your decision should make sense; that is, it should be based on a reasoned analysis of how it will affect your life. If you have dependents, you will have to consider how your decision may affect their lives too.

Since your job is a source of income, leaving your job means a loss of that income. You need to consider how you can maintain or change your current use of income (i.e., spending and saving levels) with that loss.

If you are changing jobs, your new job will replace that income with new income that is more than, equal to, or less than your old paycheck. If it is equal to or more than your former income, you may maintain or even expand your spending, saving, and investing activities. Extra income will provide you with more choices of how to consume or save. If it is less than your former income, you will have to decrease your spending or saving to fit your current needs. Your budget can help you foresee the effects of your new income on your spending and saving.

If you are leaving employment, then there will be no replacement income, so your spending and saving activities should reflect that loss, unless you have an alternative source of income to replace it. If you are going on to graduate school, perhaps you have a fellowship or scholarship. If you are assuming family care responsibilities, perhaps another family member has offered financial support. If you are retiring, you should have income from invested capital (e.g., your retirement savings) that can be used to replace your wages or salary.

If you are initiating the job change, be sure you try to cause the least disruption and cost to your employer. Let your employer know of your decision as soon as is practical, and certainly before anyone else in the company knows. "Two weeks' notice" is the convention, but the more notice you can give, the less inconvenience you may cause. Offer to help train your successor or be available to provide information or assist in the transition. The more cordially you leave your job, the better your relationship with your former employer will be, which may reflect well on you in future networking.

If you participated in a defined contribution retirement plan you own those funds to the extent that you are vested in your employer's contributions and have contributed your own funds. You can leave those funds as they are invested, or you can transfer them to your new job's plan and invest them differently. There may be some time limits to doing so, and there may be tax considerations as well, so be sure you consult with your former employer and understand the tax rules before moving any funds.

The decision to leave a job and perhaps to leave employment means leaving nonincome benefits that can create opportunity costs, including:

- intellectual or emotional gratifications of the work,

- enjoyment of your colleagues, or
- opportunities to learn.

If you have had a negative work experience, leaving may allow you to reduce boredom, eliminate job dissatisfaction, end conflict, avoid unwanted overtime, or reduce stress, but these are reasons for leaving a job that you probably should not share with a new or prospective employer.

According to a survey done by the Society for Human Resource Management (SHRM), overall job satisfaction in the United States rose from 2012 to 2016, with about 89% of employees mostly satisfied with their jobs. The most important factors for overall satisfaction are respectful treatment of all employees at all levels, compensation, trust, job security, and the ability to use skills. Other factors that concern more than half of all employees include the following:

- Relationship with a supervisor
- Benefits offered
- Employer's financial stability
- The work itself
- Communication
- Employee recognition[9]

FIGURE 18.7

© Shutterstock, Inc.

As you can see, many micro and macro factors may enter into a decision to leave a job. You spend many of your waking hours working, and deciding to change jobs is about much more than just income. It is still a decision about income, however, so you should carefully weigh the effects of that decision on your personal financial well-being.

Leaving Involuntarily

If you leave your job involuntarily, you will have to make adjustments for a loss of income that you were not planning to make. That may be difficult, but not so much as you think.

Involuntary job loss may be due to your employer's decision, an accident or disability, or unexpected circumstances, such as the acquisition, merger, downsizing, or closing of the company. Your employer also may decide to lay you off or fire you. A layoff implies a temporary job loss due to a circumstance when your employer needs or can afford less labor.

If the layoff is due to an economic recession when there is less demand for the product you create, then it may be affecting your entire industry. That would mean you would have a harder time finding a similar job. If layoffs are widespread enough, however, there may be federal, state, or local government programs aimed at helping the many people in your situation, such as a retraining program or temporary income assistance.

You may get laid off because your employer is no longer as competitive or profitable and so has to cut costs or because the company has lost financing. If the layoffs are specific to your employer, you may be able to find a similar position with another company or you may be able to establish your own competitive business in the same industry.

When you are fired, the employer permanently terminates your employment based on your performance. Involuntary **termination**, or getting fired, will cause a sudden loss of income that usually requires sudden adjustments to spending and saving. You may have to use your accumulated savings to finance your expenditures until that income can be replaced by a new job.

termination

The ending of an employment relationship; termination may be initiated by the employee (voluntary), the employer (involuntary), or mutually agreed upon by both.

An injury or illness—to you or a dependent—may create a temporary or permanent involuntary job loss. It usually also means a period of unemployment. Depending on the circumstances, your employer may be willing to help ease the transition, perhaps by offering you a more flexible schedule, adjusting your responsibilities, or providing specialized equipment to enable you to do a job.

By law, employers may not discriminate against people with disabilities so long as they are able to do a job. A **job accommodation** is any reasonable adjustment to a job or work environment that makes it possible for an individual with a disability to perform or continue to perform job duties.

job accommodation

A provision of the Americans with Disabilities Act of 1990 that employers make "reasonable accommodations" for employees with defined disabilities so as not to discriminate against them.

If you become disabled and unable to work, you may be able to replace some or all of your wage income with insurance coverage, if you have disability insurance that covers the specific circumstances (as discussed in Chapter 10). If your disability is permanent, you may qualify for federal assistance through Social Security. If someone else is liable for your disability, in the case of an accident or through negligence, his or her insurance coverage may provide some benefit, or you may have a legal claim that could provide a financial settlement.

If your employer initiates your job change, be sure to discuss his or her obligations to you before you leave. Some employer responsibilities are prescribed by law, as shown in Table 18.4. Other responsibilities are prescribed by union contract, if applicable, and some are conventions or courtesies that your employer may—or may not—choose to extend.

Severance is compensation and benefits offered by your employer when you are fired. Your employer is not obligated to offer any severance, but "two weeks' pay" is the convention for wages. Your employer is also not required to "pay" for your remaining sick days or vacation days or to extend your benefits, including retirement contributions or life insurance, unless specified in a contract. In most cases, your employer is required under federal law to offer you the opportunity to remain covered under your employee health insurance plan if you assume the cost. This continuation of health coverage is provided by COBRA, the Consolidated Omnibus Budget Reconciliation Act of 1986 (discussed in Chapter 10). Employers must also provide proof of "insurability," which enables unemployed workers to purchase private health insurance, if they wish, without having to undergo medical exams.

severance

Compensation upon dismissal from employment.

Employment Protection

Federal and state laws govern relationships between employers and employees. A large part of employment law addresses hiring and firing issues as well as working conditions. You should be familiar with the laws that apply where you work (as they differ by state and sometimes by county) so that you understand your responsibilities to your employer and your employer's obligations to you.

Major federal legislation that addresses these issues is outlined in Table 18.4.

TABLE 18.4 Major U.S. Employment Legislation

Legislation	Regulation	Applies to
National Labor Relations Act, 1935	Prevents employees who engage in union activity from being fired	Employers whose business is engaged in interstate commerce
Fair Labor Standards Act, 1938	Established minimum wage and overtime	All private employees, amended in 1974 to include state and local employees
Title VII, The Civil Rights Act, 1964	Prohibits discrimination on the basis of race, color, religion, sex, or national origin	Employers with at least 15 employees
Age Discrimination in Employment Act, 1967	Prevents discrimination on the basis of age against employees who are over 40 years old	Employers having at least 20 employees
Occupational Safety and Health Act, 1970	Established safety standards and employees' right to refuse to work in unsafe conditions	All employers
Employee Retirement Income Security Act, 1974	Prevents employees from being discharged solely to prevent them from vesting or qualifying for benefits under qualified pension plans	Employers who maintain qualified pension plans for their employees' benefit
Immigration Reform and Control Act, 1986	Prevents discrimination against employees on the basis of national origin or citizenship status	Employers having at least 4 employees
Consolidated Omnibus Budget Reconciliation Act (COBRA), 1986	Guarantees extension but not funding of health insurance coverage after termination for employees and dependents	Employers having at least 20 employees
Americans with Disabilities Act, 1990	Prevents discrimination against disabled employees	Employers having at least 15 employees
Family and Medical Leave Act, 1993	Guarantees a 12-week unpaid leave for illness, childbirth, or to care for an ill relative	Employers having at least 50 employees
Health Insurance Portability and Accountability Act, 1996	Limits exclusion from employer- sponsored coverage because of preexisting condition or medical history	All employers that offer employer-sponsored health insurance

U.S. Department of Labor, "Summary of the Major Laws of the Department of Labor," https://www.dol.gov/general/aboutdol/majorlaws (accessed July 20, 2018).

These laws cover all aspects of employment: hiring, negotiation, working conditions, compensation, benefits, and termination. Workers can sue a company for **wrongful discharge;** for being fired for any reason barred by an employment law. Employers often seek to protect themselves from suits by requiring terminated employees to sign a form releasing the company from liability.

Companies have ethical standards for dealing with the hiring and firing of employees, but they also may have informal practices for encouraging unwanted employees in good standing to leave. Employment laws cannot protect workers against some unethical practices, but they have clauses that prohibit **retaliation** against employees who invoke those laws or enlist government assistance to enforce them. The laws also protect **whistleblowers** who report employer infractions to government authorities.

The federal government provides unemployment compensation insurance through the Federal-State Unemployment Insurance Program to employees who "lose their jobs through no fault of their own."[10]

Your job and eventually your career will play many roles in your life. It will determine how you spend your time, who you spend your time with, where you live, and how you live. It will probably be a primary determinant of income and therefore of how much you can spend, save, and invest. How you chose to spend, save, and invest is up to you, and your financial decisions can have far-reaching consequences. The more you know and the more you understand, the more you can make decisions that can satisfy your dreams.

wrongful discharge

A legal term to describe a termination by the employer that violates the employment contract or the law.

retaliation

Actions by an employer to punish an employee who has complained of employer misconduct to authorities.

whistleblower

An employee who alerts authorities to possible employer misconduct.

Key Takeaways

- You can expect to leave a job several times in your career.
- You can leave a job voluntarily or involuntarily.
- You may leave voluntarily to change jobs or to leave employment, temporarily or permanently.
- You may leave a job involuntarily through a
  - layoff,
  - disabling accident or injury, or
  - firing.
- Leaving a job involuntarily means a sudden loss of income.
- Involuntary job loss may be compensated with
  - severance,
  - employment insurance, or
  - continuation of health and other benefits.
- Federal, state, and local laws address employment issues, including hiring, working conditions, compensation, and dismissal. Laws exist to protect workers.

Exercises

1. What do you look for in a job? Record in My Notes or your personal finance journal the characteristics of a job that you value most when seeking a job and the characteristics that bother you the most or would cause you to consider leaving a job voluntarily. Take an online job satisfaction survey or collaborate with classmates to develop questions for a job satisfaction survey that you can administer to other students. What do you find are the top 10 characteristics of a great job offering a lot of satisfaction?

2. View the list of acceptable reasons for leaving a job at https://careersidekick.com/why-did-you-leave-your-last-job-answers/. Have you ever cited one of those "wrong" reasons as the reason you left your job? What does the item say about you as a worker or as an employee?
3. Record in My Notes or your personal finance journal the outcome of every job you have held. For each job, have a column for listing your reason(s) for taking it and another column listing your reason(s) for leaving it. Also, note what you liked most and least about each job. Do you notice any patterns emerging in the data about your job history? Is there anything about those patterns that you would like to change?

Endnotes

1. U.S. Department of Labor, Bureau of Labor Statistics, "Number of Jobs, Labor Market Experience, and Earnings Growth Among Americans at 50: Results from a Longitudinal Survey," https://www.bls.gov/news.release/pdf/nlsoy.pdf (accessed July 18, 2018).
2. U.S. Department of Labor, Bureau of Labor Statistics, "Industries with the fastest growing and most rapidly declining wage and salary employment, 2016-2026," https://www.bls.gov/emp/tables/industries-fast-grow-decline-employment.htm (accessed July 24, 2018).
3. Sandy Baum, Jennifer Ma, and Kathleen Payea, *Education Pays: The Benefits of Higher Education for Individuals and Society* (Princeton, NJ: The College Board, 2013).
4. Sandy Baum, Jennifer Ma, and Kathleen Payea, *Education Pays: The Benefits of Higher Education for Individuals and Society* (Princeton, NJ: The College Board, 2013).
5. See, for example, U.S. Department of Labor, Bureau of Labor Statistics, "Occupational Outlook Handbook," http://www.bls.gov/ooh (accessed July 20, 2018).
6. The Professional Association of Innkeepers International, http://www.paii.org (accessed July 20, 2018).
7. Robert Putnam, *Bowling Alone: The Collapse and Revival of American Community* (New York: Simon & Schuster, 2000).
8. Ellen Gordon Reeves, *Can I Wear My Nose Ring to the Interview?* (New York: Workman Publishing, 2009).
9. Society for Human Resource Management, "Employee Job Satisfaction and Engagement 2017," https://www.shrm.org/hr-today/trends-and-forecasting/research-and-surveys/Documents/2017-Employee-Job-Satisfaction-and-Engagement-Executive-Summary.pdf (accessed July 20, 2018.)
10. U.S. Department of Labor, "Unemployment Insurance," http://www.dol.gov/dol/topic/unemployment-insurance/index.htm (accessed July 21, 2009).

APPENDIX A

Present Value and Future Value Tables

TABLE A.1 Present value of $1 discounted at discount rate *r* for *t* number of years.

	Discount Rate (r)									
Years (t)	**0.01**	**0.02**	**0.03**	**0.04**	**0.05**	**0.06**	**0.07**	**0.08**	**0.09**	**0.1**
1	0.990099	0.980392	0.970874	0.961538	0.952381	0.943396	0.934579	0.925926	0.917431	0.909091
2	0.980296	0.961169	0.942596	0.924556	0.907029	0.889996	0.873439	0.857339	0.841680	0.826446
3	0.970590	0.942322	0.915142	0.888996	0.863838	0.839619	0.816298	0.793832	0.772183	0.751315
4	0.960980	0.923845	0.888487	0.854804	0.822702	0.792094	0.762895	0.735030	0.708425	0.683013
5	0.951466	0.905731	0.862609	0.821927	0.783526	0.747258	0.712986	0.680583	0.649931	0.620921
6	0.942045	0.887971	0.837484	0.790315	0.746215	0.704961	0.666342	0.630170	0.596267	0.564474
7	0.932718	0.870560	0.813092	0.759918	0.710681	0.665057	0.622750	0.583490	0.547034	0.513158
8	0.923483	0.853490	0.789409	0.730690	0.676839	0.627412	0.582009	0.540269	0.501866	0.466507
9	0.914340	0.836755	0.766417	0.702587	0.644609	0.591898	0.543934	0.500249	0.460428	0.424098
10	0.905287	0.820348	0.744094	0.675564	0.613913	0.558395	0.508349	0.463193	0.422411	0.385543
11	0.896324	0.804263	0.722421	0.649581	0.584679	0.526788	0.475093	0.428883	0.387533	0.350494
12	0.887449	0.788493	0.701380	0.624597	0.556837	0.496969	0.444012	0.397114	0.355535	0.318631
13	0.878663	0.773033	0.680951	0.600574	0.530321	0.468839	0.414964	0.367698	0.326179	0.289664
14	0.869963	0.757875	0.661118	0.577475	0.505068	0.442301	0.387817	0.340461	0.299246	0.263331
15	0.861349	0.743015	0.641862	0.555265	0.481017	0.417265	0.362446	0.315242	0.274538	0.239392
16	0.852821	0.728446	0.623167	0.533908	0.458112	0.393646	0.338735	0.291890	0.251870	0.217629
17	0.844377	0.714163	0.605016	0.513373	0.436297	0.371364	0.316574	0.270269	0.231073	0.197845
18	0.836017	0.700159	0.587395	0.493628	0.415521	0.350344	0.295864	0.250249	0.211994	0.179859
19	0.827740	0.686431	0.570286	0.474642	0.395734	0.330513	0.276508	0.231712	0.194490	0.163508
20	0.819544	0.672971	0.553676	0.456387	0.376889	0.311805	0.258419	0.214548	0.178431	0.148644
30	0.741923	0.552071	0.411987	0.308319	0.231377	0.174110	0.131367	0.099377	0.075371	0.057309
40	0.671653	0.452890	0.306557	0.208289	0.142046	0.097222	0.066780	0.046031	0.031838	0.022095
50	0.608039	0.371528	0.228107	0.140713	0.087204	0.054288	0.033948	0.021321	0.013449	0.008519
100	0.369711	0.138033	0.052033	0.019800	0.007604	0.002947	0.001152	0.000455	0.000181	0.000073

TABLE A.2 Present value of an ordinary annuity that pays $1 every year for *t* years, discounted by discount rate *r*.

	Discount Rate (r)									
Years (t)	0.01	0.02	0.03	0.04	0.05	0.06	0.07	0.08	0.09	0.1
1	0.990099	0.980392	0.970874	0.961538	0.952381	0.943396	0.934579	0.925926	0.917431	0.909091
2	1.970395	1.941561	1.913470	1.886095	1.859410	1.833393	1.808018	1.783265	1.759111	1.735537
3	2.940985	2.883883	2.828611	2.775091	2.723248	2.673012	2.624316	2.577097	2.531295	2.486852
4	3.901966	3.807729	3.717098	3.629895	3.545951	3.465106	3.387211	3.312127	3.239720	3.169865
5	4.853431	4.713460	4.579707	4.451822	4.329477	4.212364	4.100197	3.992710	3.889651	3.790787
6	5.795476	5.601431	5.417191	5.242137	5.075692	4.917324	4.766540	4.622880	4.485919	4.355261
7	6.728195	6.471991	6.230283	6.002055	5.786373	5.582381	5.389289	5.206370	5.032953	4.868419
8	7.651678	7.325481	7.019692	6.732745	6.463213	6.209794	5.971299	5.746639	5.534819	5.334926
9	8.566018	8.162237	7.786109	7.435332	7.107822	6.801692	6.515232	6.246888	5.995247	5.759024
10	9.471305	8.982585	8.530203	8.110896	7.721735	7.360087	7.023582	6.710081	6.417658	6.144567
11	10.367628	9.786848	9.252624	8.760477	8.306414	7.886875	7.498674	7.138964	6.805191	6.495061
12	11.255077	10.575341	9.954004	9.385074	8.863252	8.383844	7.942686	7.536078	7.160725	6.813692
13	12.133740	11.348374	10.634955	9.985648	9.393573	8.852683	8.357651	7.903776	7.486904	7.103356
14	13.003703	12.106249	11.296073	10.563123	9.898641	9.294984	8.745468	8.244237	7.786150	7.366687
15	13.865053	12.849264	11.937935	11.118387	10.379658	9.712249	9.107914	8.559479	8.060688	7.606080
16	14.717874	13.577709	12.561102	11.652296	10.837770	10.105895	9.446649	8.851369	8.312558	7.823709
17	15.562251	14.291872	13.166118	12.165669	11.274066	10.477260	9.763223	9.121638	8.543631	8.021553
18	16.398269	14.992031	13.753513	12.659297	11.689587	10.827603	10.059087	9.371887	8.755625	8.201412
19	17.226008	15.678462	14.323799	13.133939	12.085321	11.158116	10.335595	9.603599	8.950115	8.364920
20	18.045553	16.351433	14.877475	13.590326	12.462210	11.469921	10.594014	9.818147	9.128546	8.513564
30	25.807708	22.396456	19.600441	17.292033	15.372451	13.764831	12.409041	11.257783	10.273654	9.426914
40	32.834686	27.355479	23.114772	19.792774	17.159086	15.046297	13.331709	11.924613	10.757360	9.779051
50	39.196118	31.423606	25.729764	21.482185	18.255925	15.761861	13.800746	12.233485	10.961683	9.914814
100	63.028879	43.098352	31.598905	24.504999	19.847910	16.617546	14.269251	12.494318	11.109102	9.999274

TABLE A.3 Future value of $1 compounded at discount rate *r* for *t* number of years.

	Discount Rate (r)									
Years (t)	0.01	0.02	0.03	0.04	0.05	0.06	0.07	0.08	0.09	0.1
1	1.010000	1.020000	1.030000	1.040000	1.050000	1.060000	1.070000	1.080000	1.090000	1.100000
2	1.020100	1.040400	1.060900	1.081600	1.102500	1.123600	1.144900	1.166400	1.188100	1.210000
3	1.030301	1.061208	1.092727	1.124864	1.157625	1.191016	1.225043	1.259712	1.295029	1.331000
4	1.040604	1.082432	1.125509	1.169859	1.215506	1.262477	1.310796	1.360489	1.411582	1.464100
5	1.051010	1.104081	1.159274	1.216653	1.276282	1.338226	1.402552	1.469328	1.538624	1.610510
6	1.061520	1.126162	1.194052	1.265319	1.340096	1.418519	1.500730	1.586874	1.677100	1.771561
7	1.072135	1.148686	1.229874	1.315932	1.407100	1.503630	1.605781	1.713824	1.828039	1.948717
8	1.082857	1.171659	1.266770	1.368569	1.477455	1.593848	1.718186	1.850930	1.992563	2.143589
9	1.093685	1.195093	1.304773	1.423312	1.551328	1.689479	1.838459	1.999005	2.171893	2.357948
10	1.104622	1.218994	1.343916	1.480244	1.628895	1.790848	1.967151	2.158925	2.367364	2.593742
11	1.115668	1.243374	1.384234	1.539454	1.710339	1.898299	2.104852	2.331639	2.580426	2.853117
12	1.126825	1.268242	1.425761	1.601032	1.795856	2.012196	2.252192	2.518170	2.812665	3.138428
13	1.138093	1.293607	1.468534	1.665074	1.885649	2.132928	2.409845	2.719624	3.065805	3.452271
14	1.149474	1.319479	1.512590	1.731676	1.979932	2.260904	2.578534	2.937194	3.341727	3.797498
15	1.160969	1.345868	1.557967	1.800944	2.078928	2.396558	2.759032	3.172169	3.642482	4.177248
16	1.172579	1.372786	1.604706	1.872981	2.182875	2.540352	2.952164	3.425943	3.970306	4.594973
17	1.184304	1.400241	1.652848	1.947900	2.292018	2.692773	3.158815	3.700018	4.327633	5.054470
18	1.196147	1.428246	1.702433	2.025817	2.406619	2.854339	3.379932	3.996019	4.717120	5.559917
19	1.208109	1.456811	1.753506	2.106849	2.526950	3.025600	3.616528	4.315701	5.141661	6.115909
20	1.220190	1.485947	1.806111	2.191123	2.653298	3.207135	3.869684	4.660957	5.604411	6.727500
30	1.347849	1.811362	2.427262	3.243398	4.321942	5.743491	7.612255	10.062657	13.267678	17.449402
40	1.488864	2.208040	3.262038	4.801021	7.039989	10.285718	14.974458	21.724521	31.409420	45.259256
50	1.644632	2.691588	4.383906	7.106683	11.467400	18.420154	29.457025	46.901613	74.357520	117.390853
100	2.704814	7.244646	19.218632	50.504948	131.501258	339.302084	867.716326	2199.761256	5529.040792	13780.612340

TABLE A.4 Future value of an ordinary annuity that pays $1 every year for *t* years, compounded by discount rate *r*.

	Discount Rate (r)									
Years (t)	0.01	0.02	0.03	0.04	0.05	0.06	0.07	0.08	0.09	0.1
1	1.000000	1.000000	1.000000	1.000000	1.000000	1.000000	1.000000	1.000000	1.000000	1.000000
2	2.010000	2.020000	2.030000	2.040000	2.050000	2.060000	2.070000	2.080000	2.090000	2.100000
3	3.030100	3.060400	3.090900	3.121600	3.152500	3.183600	3.214900	3.246400	3.278100	3.310000
4	4.060401	4.121608	4.183627	4.246464	4.310125	4.374616	4.439943	4.506112	4.573129	4.641000
5	5.101005	5.204040	5.309136	5.416323	5.525631	5.637093	5.750739	5.866601	5.984711	6.105100
6	6.152015	6.308121	6.468410	6.632975	6.801913	6.975319	7.153291	7.335929	7.523335	7.715610
7	7.213535	7.434283	7.662462	7.898294	8.142008	8.393838	8.654021	8.922803	9.200435	9.487171
8	8.285671	8.582969	8.892336	9.214226	9.549109	9.897468	10.259803	10.636628	11.028474	11.435888
9	9.368527	9.754628	10.159106	10.582795	11.026564	11.491316	11.977989	12.487558	13.021036	13.579477
10	10.462213	10.949721	11.463879	12.006107	12.577893	13.180795	13.816448	14.486562	15.192930	15.937425
11	11.566835	12.168715	12.807796	13.486351	14.206787	14.971643	15.783599	16.645487	17.560293	18.531167
12	12.682503	13.412090	14.192030	15.025805	15.917127	16.869941	17.888451	18.977126	20.140720	21.384284
13	13.809328	14.680332	15.617790	16.626838	17.712983	18.882138	20.140643	21.495297	22.953385	24.522712
14	14.947421	15.973938	17.086324	18.291911	19.598632	21.015066	22.550488	24.214920	26.019189	27.974983
15	16.096896	17.293417	18.598914	20.023588	21.578564	23.275970	25.129022	27.152114	29.360916	31.772482
16	17.257864	18.639285	20.156881	21.824531	23.657492	25.672528	27.888054	30.324283	33.003399	35.949730
17	18.430443	20.012071	21.761588	23.697512	25.840366	28.212880	30.840217	33.750226	36.973705	40.544703
18	19.614748	21.412312	23.414435	25.645413	28.132385	30.905653	33.999033	37.450244	41.301338	45.599173
19	20.810895	22.840559	25.116868	27.671229	30.539004	33.759992	37.378965	41.446263	46.018458	51.159090
20	22.019004	24.297370	26.870374	29.778079	33.065954	36.785591	40.995492	45.761964	51.160120	57.274999
30	34.784892	40.568079	47.575416	56.084938	66.438848	79.058186	94.460786	113.283211	136.307539	164.494023
40	48.886373	60.401983	75.401260	95.025516	120.799774	154.761966	199.635112	259.056519	337.882445	442.592556
50	64.463182	84.579401	112.796867	152.667084	209.347996	290.335905	406.528929	573.770156	815.083556	1163.908529
100	170.481383	312.232306	607.287733	1237.623705	2610.025157	5638.368059	12381.661794	27484.515704	61422.675465	137796.123398

Index